Crime and Culture

Essays in Honor of Thorsten Sellin

Edited by MARVIN E. WOLFGANG, *Department of Sociology, University of Pennsylvania.*

This book consists of a systematic collection of original essays written by some of the world's leading authorities on criminology, social deviance, and correction. The book is organized around a number of the major themes in the professional life and writings of Thorsten Sellin, former President of the International Society of Criminology.

CRIME AND CULTURE contains sections dealing with criminological theory, new empirical research, historical criminology and penology, and contemporary corrections. Contributions from psychology, psychiatry, and history are included despite a strong emphasis on the socio-cultural interpretation of crime and corrections. The book's worldwide intellectual and empirical scope permits a look beyond the parochialism of the sociology of deviance and criminology in the United States and explains what is going on in international cross-cultural work. It is up to date, with descriptions of such practices as the prison furlough system in Sweden, and including for the first time new research data on World War II collaborators.

This book can serve as an instructional companion to textbooks for courses in criminology, juvenile delinquency, and corrections. It is more than a reference book, although it serves that purpose as well, for it covers the theory and data behind the entire range of major issues in contemporary criminology and penology.

G received a
ollege, and an
he University
now Professor
University of
author or co-
cluding PAT-
. HOMICIDE
1, 1964) and
OF DELIN-
sten Sellin

Criminology
Criminal Law,
cience, Past
ican Society
ltant to the
n on Law En-
istration of
of the Advis-
ational Com-
the Federal

CRIME AND CULTURE

Essays in Honor of Thorsten Sellin

MARVIN E. WOLFGANG, EDITOR

Department of Sociology
University of Pennsylvania

John Wiley & Sons, Inc.

NEW YORK · LONDON · SYDNEY · TORONTO

LIBRARY OF CONGRESS CATALOG CARD NUMBER: 68-30925
SBN 471 95958 8
PRINTED IN THE UNITED STATES OF AMERICA

List of Contributors

Ancel, Marc
Andenaes, Johannes
Beattie, Ronald H.
Christiansen, Karl O.
Conrad, John P.
Cornil, Paul
Cressey, Donald R.
Drapkin, Israel
Eriksson, Torsten
Ferracuti, Franco
Gibbens, T.C.N.
Mannheim, Hermann
Nagel, Willem H.
Pinatel, Jean
Radzinowicz, Leon
Schafer, Stephen
Shoham, Shlomo
Szabo, Denis
Van Bemmelen, J. M.
Vold, George B.
Wilkins, Leslie T.

Preface

Crime and Culture is a collection of essays whose coherency stems from the life and writings of Thorsten Sellin. The volume is, therefore, both a tribute to this scholar and a compendium of some of the most current and provocative writings concerned with crime and corrections.

Many of the world's leading authorities are represented here. Authors were selected because they have been Professor Sellin's colleagues and friends—some for years that cover most of his professional career. An effort was made to provide a wide international distribution. There are many omissions of leading figures and of colleagues who have known Professor Sellin for a long time. For these omissions I am regretful, but the restrictions of space and time are common foes to most enterprises of this sort. I take full responsibility for the selections, translations, and editing. Not until all of the work was completed and submitted for publication was the knowledge of this volume made known to Professor Sellin.

The life of this great scholar is now only in a transitional state. As Professor Emeritus at the University of Pennsylvania, he has completed 46 years of teaching. His seminal mind and devotion to the intellectual interests that have absorbed his attention throughout his career continue to benefit the Center for Studies in Criminology and Criminal Law where he is engaged in research. Young scholars at the University will know his theoretical and empirical influence for many years to come, and his colleagues will seek his counsel.

On every level of his professional ambience, Thorsten Sellin has been an influential, admired, and effective leader. The Department of Sociology at the University of Pennsylvania developed a strong and lasting tradition of excellence in criminology because of his scholarship from the 1920's to the present, and he served as the Department's Chairman for 15 years. In Philadelphia he has been Chairman of the Board of Prisons for 13 years, guiding and advancing corrections on the local level. He has been on numerous state and national commissions, committees, and boards that covered activities from criminal statistics to the death penalty. As President of the International Society of Criminology he reflected the respect of scholars and administrators all over the world. For two generations his international reputation has been proclaimed every time his name has been mentioned. The status he enjoys in his field is shared by no one.

His book, *Culture Conflict and Crime*, published in 1938, has been for 30 years a major source of theoretical insights. No work in the field, prior or subsequent to that volume, has quite matched it for brilliance and parsimony of theory and logic. The title of this present volume is meant to convey the sociological import of his contributions, which *Culture Conflict and Crime* represented and generated. He drew attention to culture conflicts in terms of conflicting norms "when these codes clash on the border of contiguous culture areas." He spoke of "conflicts between the norms of culture systems or areas," and in this phrasing itself helped to transform research interests to the current focus. The current emphasis on subcultures has its antecedence in his own work, for he wrote: "Conflicts of cultures are inevitable when the norms of one cultural or subcultural area migrate to or come in contact with those of another. . . ."

His editorship of *The Annals of the American Academy of Political and Social Science* since 1929 is well known to thousands of scholars throughout the world. Performed with a quiet diligence and efficiency, this work alone could have crowned the career of any man. The many topics he chose over these years and the high caliber of these publications with articles from scientists, lawyers, administrators, government leaders, and others from many professional fields again speak clearly as encomia to his spirit and scholarship.

These few points of reference in his biography are meant only as illustrative. The outline of his career through publications appears as an Appendix to this book. A fuller personal tribute deserves a more appropriate setting and will surely be made. But as editor of this collection, I must take advantage of this opportunity to mark my own indebtedness to this man whose life has become so inextricably interwoven with my own. As a young graduate student directly after the Second World War, I first was exposed to his instruction, and since then the encounter with his world scholarship has never ceased to impress me. There is usually one great teacher in each of our lives, but few of us have the opportunity to live professionally with him. My gratitude for the years since 1947 is unbounded. Our research and teaching activities have intertwined and our writings are now joined. For over 20 years I have known his integrity, his scientific perspective, his humor, and the satisfaction he derives from fellowship or from a completed manuscript. We have had innumerable stimulating intellectual discussions with occasional fascinating differences of positions that generally produced accord or synthesis. Harsh argument never passed our way. His pursuit of scholarship never wanes, and his judgments of issues and of people have always been for me lessons in wisdom. Our lives, like the generations each of us represents, have been linked like the words we sometimes join into a single sentence in a manuscript. The dignity he attributes to all men has made my own transition in his years approaching retirement extraordinarily smooth. No one could plan for a more enduring, satisfying, and beloved partnership. Not even Odysseus could have been more content than I with the mentor whose counsel I shall continue to cherish.

The essays contained here were solicited; they are new and original writings, not published elsewhere at the time they were submitted. Each represents the author's understanding of the character of the volume and his desire to contribute. Each chapter is a discrete piece, yet major themes in the writings of Professor Sellin are clearly evident. The meaning of criminology as an area of disciplined attention, training, and knowledge is a topic to which Sellin addressed hmself in major ways throughout his writings. Jean Pinatel from France and Wilhelm Nagel from the Netherlands examine the issues in Section I, "The Field of Criminology," from a variety of perspectives and add the ingredient of Sellin's own impact on the field. Their perspectives are among the most comprehensive in the literature.

The eight chapters in Section II, "Theory," expand upon Sellin's proposition of culture conflict. The essay by the late George Vold may be his last published writing and constitutes the culmination of a carefully drawn statement by a sociological criminologist. Donald Cressey has drawn Edwin Sutherland and Thorsten Sellin, peers in the progress of criminological theory, together through a provocative chapter on the issues of normative conflict. By using data from Israel, Shlomo Shoham has refined and tested the culture conflict theory more elaborately, perhaps, than anyone and has shown its relevance to the broader arena of social deviance as well as to crime and delinquency. By linking culture conflict to anomie, Stephen Schafer makes a further valuable contribution to criminological theory. Denis Szabo, from his current concern and research in Montreal with moral values, represents an interdisciplinary perspective by combining psychological and sociological theory in an examination of the youth culture. This blending is enhanced by the psychiatric approach found in clinical criminology, an area well described by Trevor Gibbens from England, Professor Sellin's successor as President of the International Society of Criminology.

Probably no topic has been of such abiding concern to Professor Sellin throughout his professional career as has that of criminal statistics. In Section III, "Measurement and Criminal Statistics," Leslie Wilkins builds upon this interest in his uncommonly provocative essay on the measurement of morals and value judgments. John Conrad carefully outlines what yet remains to be accomplished to meet the criteria of adequate data collection, and Ronald Beattie describes the work being done and planned in California as a model for the future.

Although long acclaimed for his treatise on criminological theory, Thorsten Sellin has always been an ardent advocate of empirical testing of theory. Without data, our ideas have an unsteady and unsure posture. The three chapters in Section IV, "Empirical Research," provide new and carefully collected data on three topics often found in Professor Sellin's writings and in current literature. From Italy, Franco Ferracuti summarized, simultaneously for this volume and the Council of Europe, all of the best available research data on the present status of migration and crime in Europe. From Norway, Johannes Andenaes has applied his broad analysis of criminal law to the data on negligent homicide in several European countries and provides a cross-national view of wide dimensions over long stretches of time. The review of recidivism among collaborators from the Second World War, by Karl Christiansen, is an empirical study in depth in Denmark and a unique contribution to the sociology of crisis situations in a social system.

Few persons are so well equipped as Thorsten Sellin to write about the history of crime and punishment. It is especially appropriate, therefore, that Section V, "Historical Penology," appears in this volume. From his monumental work on the history of English criminal law, Leon Radzinowicz has contributed an amazing account of impressment into the army and navy as an instrument of preventive police and criminal justice in England, especially during the eighteenth and early nineteenth centuries. The relationship between the policy of impressment and the political and social structure is clearly described and provides the student of comparative social history with a fascinating insight into an earlier system of criminal justice. In a style similar to that which Professor Sellin used to bring the life and work of Dom Jean Mabillon and of Filippo Franci to the attention of contemporary scholars, Israel Drapkin makes a major contribution by his description of the penal innovations of Manuel Montesinos y Molina of Spain.

In the last section, "Contemporary Corrections," five European authorities offer what must be characterized as their latest thinking on the topics covered. These chapters, in congealed form, represent many years of experience in criminal law, research, and administration, and provide some of the most advanced theory in corrections. Basing his analysis on an earlier statement, Hermann Mannheim reviews the rationale and latest research on sentencing. The community of scholars know well the breadth and depth of Professor Mannheim's many treatises in criminology and will find here the insightful commentary they have come to expect from him. Marc Ancel, whose many important writings include the excellent review of the death penalty for the United Nations, offers his most current thinking on the problems of analyzing deterrence. Paul Cornil traces the trends of penal methods and suggests where we are heading by focusing on the major and often neglected area of prison labor. Professor van Bemmelen provides a critique of past and current modes of correction and makes innovative suggestions that could be implemented in the future without administrative difficulty. Finally, Torsten Eriksson, long identified with the progressive correctional system in Sweden, gives a full description of the developments in the rise of prisoner furloughs in that country and provides a working model for adoption elsewhere.

While this volume is a small vehicle for offering some tribute to Thorsten Sellin, the collection of essays covers a wide range of major themes in criminology and could, therefore, be viewed as a useful instructional accompaniment to standard texts. Because of the coverage of the field and the international representation of the contributors, this volume is not a parochial compendium. We hope, therefore, that the efforts involved in the production of this collection are a contribution to the dissemination of broad perspectives on crime and society's response to it.

Marvin E. Wolfgang

University of Pennsyvania 1968

Acknowledgments

I wish to convey my appreciation to my wife, Lenora Wolfgang, for her careful proof reading and sustained interest in the production of this volume from its inception.

Jean Wilmot and Elaine Silverman, administrative assistants of the Center for Studies in Criminology and Criminal Law, University of Pennsylvania, were responsible for typing portions of the manuscript and carrying on much correspondence with the contributors.

William Gum, in his role as Social Science Editor at John Wiley & Sons, has been a major source of support and encouragement. His help to an author far exceeds that required and attests to his many talents.

Marvin E. Wolfgang

Contents

I THE FIELD OF CRIMINOLOGY   1

   1 Thorsten Sellin and the Principal Trends in Modern
      Criminology
      JEAN PINATEL   3

   2 On Criminologists
      WILLEM H. NAGEL   11

II THEORY   31

   3 Social-Cultural Conflict and Criminality
      GEORGE B. VOLD   33

   4 Culture Conflict, Differential Association, and Normative
      Conflict
      DONALD R. CRESSEY   43

   5 Culture Conflict as a Frame of Reference for Research in
      Criminology and Social Deviation
      SHLOMO SHOHAM   55

   6 Anomie, Culture Conflict, and Crime in Disorganized and
      Overorganized Societies
      STEPHEN SCHAFER   83

   7 Psychocultural Basis of Contemporary Juvenile
      Inadaptation
      DENIS SZABO   93

   8 Problems of Clinical Criminology
      T.C.N. GIBBENS   111

III MEASUREMENT AND CRIMINAL
STATISTICS   131

9   Values v. Variates—An Essay on the Relevance of
    Measurement to Morals and Value Judgments
    LESLIE T. WILKINS   133

10 The Unfinished Business of Criminal Statistics
    JOHN P. CONRAD   157

11 A State Bureau of Criminal Statistics
    RONALD H. BEATTIE   169

IV EMPIRICAL RESEARCH   187

12 European Migration and Crime
    FRANCO FERRACUTI   189

13 Negligent Homicide in Some European Countries—A
    Comparative Study
    JOHANNES ANDENAES   221

14 Recidivism among Collaborators—A Follow-Up Study of
    2946 Danish Men Convicted of Collaboration with the
    Germans During World War II
    KARL O. CHRISTIANSEN   245

V HISTORICAL PENOLOGY   285

15 Impressment into the Army and the Navy—A Rough and
    Ready Instrument of Preventive Police and Criminal
    Justice
    LEON RADZINOWICZ   287

16 Manuel Montesinos y Molina—An Almost Forgotten Pre-
    cursor of Penal Reform in Spain
    ISRAEL DRAPKIN   315

VI CONTEMPORARY CORRECTIONS   347

17 Sentencing Re-visited
    HERMANN MANNHEIM   349

18 Some Thoughts on the Problem of Deterrence
    MARC ANCEL   375

19 Trends in Penal Methods—with Special Reference to
    Prison Labor
    P. CORNIL   387

20 New Ways of Punishment
    J. M. VAN BEMMELEN   405

21 The Swedish Furlough System for Prisons
    TORSTEN ERIKSSON   417

APPENDIX   429
Bibliography of the Writings of Thorsten Sellin   429

Biographies   443

Name Index   451

Subject Index   459

CRIME AND CULTURE

I
THE FIELD OF
CRIMINOLOGY

Thorsten Sellin and the Principal Trends in Modern Criminology

JEAN PINATEL

Criminology today is emerging from the somewhat scattered shape originally formed by its special branches. Verifiable facts derived from the several branches of criminology are being assembled into a harmonious whole, and criminological theory is beginning to take shape and to serve as a link between the different specialized branches of criminology.

When one looks at the principal trends in modern criminology, a striking fact is without doubt the deep and irresistible movement toward unity in the field. It is expressed by the social and cultural explorations that have developed, the experiments on criminal therapy carried out in various places, and the imperialism of mathematics that has become apparent in all forms of research.

The unity of criminology does not exclude the necessary division of work that accompanies scientific progress. It only enables specialists working on criminological research to be conscious of belonging to a team, of forming part of the same family, and of pursuing similar goals. After a basic training common to all, criminologists will increasingly find it more and more necessary to choose among the fields of social, cultural, clinical, statistical, and mathematical investigations.

What is true today was not quite true when Thorsten Sellin, a sociologist, first turned towards criminology. For him it was possible to take an interest in many different approaches, to feel at ease with each one of them; in short, to be to criminology what encyclopaedists or philosophers of the eighteenth century were, in their time, to the sciences in general.

I

American sociological criminology, which, under the influence of the theory of behaviorism following J. B. Watson, investigates the behavior of man as a number of reflexes and habits, does not substantially differ from Soviet criminology. Its difference, however, is that it tends to minimize the importance of the economy and to emphasize the broader culture. The first American sociologists who became interested in criminology took quite naturally the sociocultural direction. Thorsten Sellin's merit was in creating the theory of culture conflict.[1] The theory is based on the notion that a penal code is, to a large extent, an expression of the moral ideals and customs of a civilization. However, the moral and social values expressed at one time by the penal code may clash with new values resulting from historical development, or they may not have been assimilated or understood by a number of citizens. Culture conflicts can, therefore, be created in different ways. For instance, conflict can arise between two moral attitudes based on different values. This is the case in colonization when legislative assimilation is much too fast in political matters and when a class ideology is established legally. The conflict can also arise between laws that are arbitrary or favorable to corruption and individuals who obey healthy moral concepts. The conflict can also arise between laws that conform to socially accepted values and particular groups who possess their own codes of conduct (gypsies, immigrants). It can thus be seen that the theory of culture conflict is of a general nature, on the level of world society, and that it offers a major explanation of criminality.

This very far-reaching property of the theory of culture conflict explains the fact that it could be adapted to the other major concepts of American sociological criminology. Thus, in his theory of differential association, Sutherland,[2] for instance, who insists on the fact that antisocial behavior is acquired and clearly shows the all-powerful influence of culture and training, does not fail to leave some room for culture conflict. He underlines the fact that in certain societies the individual is surrounded by persons who invariably establish the codes as rules that must be observed. In other societies, on the contrary, he is surrounded by persons whose definitions of the codes are favorable to their violation, and there is a conflict of culture in respect to the codes.

[1] Thorsten Sellin, *Culture Conflict and Crime*, New York: Social Science Research Council, 1938, p. 116.
[2] E. H. Sutherland, *Principles of Criminology*, Philadelphia: Lippencot, 1947 edition, pp. 69–81.

The ecological studies of Clifford Shaw and of his students in Chicago have clearly led, via the concept of "delinquency area," to the description of criminal subcultures.[3] It can be said that the existence of subcultures of a criminal nature form a vivid illustration of the theory of culture conflict. Thus, as a consequence of its general nature, the theory of culture conflict has permeated many modern developments in American sociological criminology.

The observer, who sees things from afar and thus can discern only the large doctrinal variations, may question the exact scope of certain present trends and ask himself if in the end the predominance of culture over economy is not beginning to decline in the United States. Seen from the outside, this trend seems to stem from the studies of Sutherland on white collar crime. Based on this work, it is certainly possible to indict the culture of the business class, it morals, and traditions. It can be said that there exists a culture conflict between the legal principles and those typical of this class. But the question also arises whether the principles pertaining to the business circles do not, in fact, extend over a much broader basis and whether, in short, they do not actually touch the majority of social classes.

From this aspect, the work of Merton[4] throws some light on the difference that can exist between goals and means. By using and elaborating on the old concept of anomie by Durkheim, Merton has shown through present generalizations how deviation is of social origin. The absence of standards of conduct that are clearly defined leaves free scope to criminal influence. But it may be that these concepts are mostly or particularly applicable to the American economic system.

Using the concept of subcultures and expressing in detail what was hinted by Merton, Cloward and Ohlin[5] have logically contended that juvenile delinquency is the result of a lack of legitimate opportunities. This approach has become an integral part of crime-prevention programs. The *Chicago Area Project* endeavored to bring about changes in attitude, feelings, ideals, and respect of the law in order to create a common life that was more acceptable in the poorer districts; the *Mobilization for Youth* movement has established an overall program for improving the economic conditions in the delinquency areas.

[3] See especially A. Cohen, *Delinquent Boys* (The Culture of the Gang), Glencoe: The Free Press, 1955, p. 179.
[4] R. K. Merton, *Social Theory and Social Structure*, London: Collier MacMillan Ltd., 1964, 645 pp.
[5] R. A. Cloward and L. E. Ohlin, *Delinquency and Opportunity*, Glencoe, Ill.: The Free Press, 1960, 220 pp.

That the element of economy conditions culture to a certain extent has been clearly shown in American criminology, particularly in the field of crime prevention. This same kind of sociocultural conceptualization is by no means less important in the treatment of delinquents.

II

The link that unites American sociocultural criminology and modern criminal therapy can best be seen through the concept of personality. Even within the sociocultural framework we find, in fact, that biology and psychoanalysis can clarify matters only in terms of personality development. The latter is essentially represented by the cultural elements that constitute the state of the moral concepts of the subject. These moral concepts are acquired during a slow process of education and result from contacts with other persons; they include ideas, customs, beliefs, and attitudes about the type of behavior to be adopted in special or general situations. In criminology, the concept of criminal maturation defined by Sutherland assumes a general attitude towards criminal activity resulting from the subject's considering himself as having entered into a criminal career. Criminality becomes part of his mentality and morality. He turns to a system of behavior that has often been described as the criminal code. He thus opposes, on the value level, the code of honest people. He rationalizes this attitude and possesses a system of reference that is clearly deviant and exclusive. He justifies his behavior, shows it off, and tries to convince others of his perspectives.

Therefore, what is true for the criminal who has reached criminal maturity is in varying degrees also true for criminals subjected to other processes, starting from those whose behavior stems from an impulsive character to those whose behavior appears to have been premeditated for a long time. There exists, in fact, a very general mechanism of self-legitimation based on an egocentric morality that characterizes anti-social behavior.

Treatment aims at remodelling the attitudes and beliefs of the delinquent, to change his system of reference in such a manner that he conforms to commonly accepted values. What is here called "treatment" does not differ from what the old penitentiary practitioners called "amendment." Certain clinical experts too often embark upon experimental therapy without paying sufficient attention to the lessons of the past. It is suggested that they read the various works of Thorsten Sellin on the history of the treatment of offenders, especially his *Pioneering in*

Penology.[6] Beyond the intrinsic value of this work from the man whom the Penal and Penitentiary Foundation has elected President, the volume helps to form a link between scientific criminology and practical penology. Because of it, we can better understand the generous efforts of men who believed in penitentiary reforms and who tried to change prisons into institutions for improvement.

III

In the evolutionary process of criminology, Thorsten Sellin has been a sociologist with a broad outlook on theory and on history. But he is more than that. He is perhaps, above all, a criminologist who is familiar with all of the problems concerned with criminal statistics.

Criminal statistics were, for a long time, a tool for describing criminality. But a new development is beginning to take shape at present. This is not a phenomenon concerned with criminology exclusively, since it can be found in all the human sciences. Broadly speaking, it can be said that mathematics are playing an ever-increasing part in human sciences.

This development is based on the assumption that there exists only one type of science whose object is to satisfy conditions of positivity, objectivity, generality, analysis, determinism, and measurement. These conditions of scientific knowledge are found when the object to be investigated involves physics and chemistry. However, they cannot easily be combined when the object to be studied is man himself, unless at the price of omitting the inner life, or what may be called the subjective personality. This is actually what behaviorism creates: it makes an abstraction of psychological conscience and does not investigate the relations existing between the stimulus and the reaction expressed by a certain type of behavior.

Under these conditions, it was quite normal that Thorsten Sellin, whose work is dominated by the concept of behaviorism, followed the movement that tended to apply mathematics to criminology. This development already had become apparent in the application of probability theory to statistics concerning criminals, and it was amplified by improvement in prediction and evaluation techniques. It then reached criminal statistics where efforts are now being made to take data past the stage of description to the stage of measurement theory. This attempt is by no means of a purely theoretical nature. It has been stimulated by

[6] *Pioneering in Penology*, Philadelphia: University of Pennsylvania Press, 1944, 125 pp.

the necessity for a thorough evaluation of the results from prevention programs and by the measurement of juvenile delinquency before and after carrying them through. This bold effort by Thorsten Sellin and his colleague, Marvin Wolfgang, appears in their latest work entitled *The Measurement of Delinquency*.[7]

It would be out of the question at this point to try to describe the contents of this important work in a few words; hence I refer to an article dealing with this work in the *Revue des Sciences Criminelles*.[8] It will suffice to say here that this research is a remarkable effort from all points of view, especially in its technical aspects, to produce an authentic "Index of Delinquency."

What becomes strongly apparent in this effort is the necessity which the authors felt to take a definite stand and to invent new concepts such as those of "reportability" and "offensiveness" which, in our opinion, are new and more precise versions of the old concepts of the threshold of criminality and natural delinquency. Thus, main concepts in criminology, as in all sciences of man, are being subjected to measurement, despite the fact that measurements in the human sciences cannot be as precise as in physics or chemistry.

Our attempt to place the work of Thorsten Sellin in relation to the important trends in modern criminology would be incomplete if, in concluding, his own concept of criminology were not mentioned. We already know enough from his work to understand why and how he at first adopted a negative view of criminology as an autonomous and unitary science. His famous phrase, "Criminologists are kings without a kingdom," is well known. By this he suggested that although he understood that biologists, psychologists, and sociologists are capable of studying the phenomenon of criminality on the basis of their own respective principles and techniques, he did not see how criminal phenomena in their entirety could be dealt with by any one discipline. Criminologists had to be content to collect material discovered by others and had no proper field of their own, no kingdom belonging to themselves.

Nonetheless, by one of the customary quirks of fate, Thorsten Sellin, as President of the International Society of Criminology, took an active part in the expansion toward an autonomous and unitary criminology, concerning which he had shown such reserve initially. Today it seems that criminology covers a special field, namely, all scientific research concerning criminal phenomena. Whether he wanted it or not, Thorsten

[7] Thorsten Sellin and Marvin E. Wolfgang, *The Measurement of Delinquency*, New York: Wiley, 1964, 423 pp.
[8] Jean Pinatel, "La Mesure de la Délinquance Juvenile," *Revue des Sciences Criminelles*, 1965, pp. 689–695.

Sellin was projected into the center of this development and contributed to it. We who follow him are pleased to acknowledge the quality of method and the caliber of erudition displayed by this scientist whose work coincides with the transition of criminology from its infancy to its increasing maturity.

2

On Criminologists

WILLEM H. NAGEL

An excellent introduction to the problem I am about to discuss is to be found in the first chapter of Thorsten Sellin's *Culture Conflict and Crime* (1938), and if we did not have that, there would be Marvin E. Wolfgang's paper entitled *Criminology and the criminologist*.[1] But the problems presented by this subject have not yet been exhausted, and can at least be approached from other directions. We would like to come closer to the criminologist himself.

"THINKERS" AND "CALCULATORS"

A German proverb says: *Wo das Rechnen beginnt, hört das Denken auf.* If this adage were true, anyone seeking a classification for criminologists could easily divide them, for instance, according to the bad (that is, the calculating) and the good (the thinking) criminologists—or vice versa. But Thorsten Sellin has proven that the adage is not valid because he has shown himself capable of both thought and calculation, and thus the adage is a jest and not to be taken seriously. But the matter with which the jest is concerned is well worth closer examination.

In the sciences—under which I include Criminology—we have shifting hierarchies. The Houses of the seers, talkers, and fantasts change places with the Houses of the calculators. The inevitable failure of the one temporarily brings the other to supremacy. The futile calculations, for example, of many nineteenth-century statisticians did little to advance criminology and, when they did, it was often only apparently, which led to an enthusiastically received school of modern anthropological (or phenomenological or existentialistic) criminology, sweeping all before it, in the present century. (If the signs are not deceptive, the great

[1] *The Journal of Criminal Law, Criminology and Political Science*, 1963, pp. 155–162.

majority of the workers in this field—the field of correction, probation and rehabilitation—are again wondering what the experts really think they can actually *do* with these new ideas.)

Bonger[2] and Van Kan[3] both made copious collections of precriminological commentary by great thinkers and writers—Homer, Plato, Aristotle, Jesus, Thomas More—which are well worth reading. But the basis for a scientific criminology was first established by the meteorologist, physicist, and statistician, Quetelet. After him came doctors, philanthropists of all kinds, psychiatrists, numerous sociologists and psychologists and, except in Europe, jurists, and here and there (via criminalistics), a pharmacist. At present, if we ask a criminologist about his educational background, we can never predict the answer.

All these criminologists, whether they are calculators or speculators, have their own disciplines and (which is something else again) their own attitudes toward the subject of criminology. That subject is the social behavior of man, and man and his behavior are qualified in one way by some and in other ways by others.

Let us begin by subjecting the material of criminology to an analysis.

THE SUBJECT MATTER OF CRIMINOLOGY

I disagree fundamentally with those who hold that too much is said about the subject matter of criminology.[4] On the contrary, I believe that it has been too little considered, and that this neglect has impeded the development of the field itself.

To start with a definition susceptible to refinement: the subject matter of criminology consists of a segment from the following scale.

1. Normal behavior.
2. Deviant but not disturbing behavior.
3. Deranging but not juridically relevant behavior.

2 W. A. Bonger, *Criminalité et conditions économiques* (1905).
3 J. Van Kan, *Les causes économiques de la criminalité* (1903).
4 I.e. Leon Radzinowicz on the Second United Nations Congress on the Prevention of Crime and the Treatment of Offenders, London (1960) in his general lecture: ". . . that criminological research requires a clear perception of the scope of criminology and this still seems to be somewhat blurred and confused. What is criminology about? What is its subject matter? Already, on this preliminary point, I shall have to make a critical comment. Too much time is still being spent, especially on the continent of Europe, in trying to construct an elaborate and exhaustive definition of criminology. . . ." It would not be difficult to prove out of the discussions of this very congress how wrong Radzinowicz was.

4. Deranging and juridically relevant but not criminal behavior.
5. Crime.

It might be asked whether we really need a scale, and why we do not simply state that crime is the subject matter of criminology. The question can be answered visually for which, for the sake of simplicity, we may limit ourselves to three levels, as shown in Figure 1.

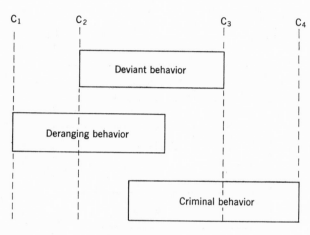

FIGURE 1

Once so represented, it is clear that:

1. Deviant, deranging, and criminal behavior do not always coincide.
2. Deranging behavior need not, for instance, always be deviant or criminal—rather, disturbing behavior of children is not yet very deviant and is not to be regarded as delinquency.
3. Not all criminal behavior is necessarily also deranging or even deviant—sometimes such behavior is stamped as criminal in the time in which the law is made because it is seen as deranging, but the law tends to lag behind and consequently includes measures against forms of behavior that sociologists would not find to be deviant.

Lines C (1–4) determine the location of the bars with respect to each other; they represent the tolerance of the society and the law in question; the distances separating them are variable.

The meaning of this figure will perhaps emerge most clearly if we draw it once again for totalitarian orders of law as shown in Figure 2.

Here, deviant behavior is considered deranging, which is more or less automatically considered criminal.

To say that the subject matter of the criminologist is crime would be a rather serviceable definition in totalitarian countries, but outside such countries the problem is not so easily solved.

There is actually a simple dodge by which to determine the subject matter of criminology, starting from crime. This is to see crime as the core of a wider field and use comparison of law to add a margin to that core.

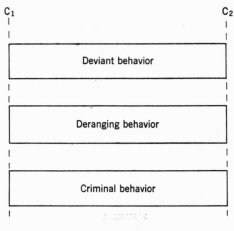

C_1 C_2

Deviant behavior

Deranging behavior

Criminal behavior

FIGURE 2

I distinguish two forms of comparison of law: the horizontal and the vertical. In horizontal comparison of law we see what is at present considered crime in other states and countries. For example, prostitution or suicide are not considered crimes in my country, but this is not the case in some other countries, so I add suicide and prostitution to my list of the subject matter of criminology. Vertical comparison of crime adds those kinds of behavior formerly but no longer considered criminal. Vertical comparison of crime can be used wherever our personal historical interests lead us; I prefer not to extend the use of this device further back than, let us say, the last century. We shall discover that the use of either device will roughly extend the subject matter of criminology by the same margin around the nucleus provided by the actual penal law. Suicide, for instance, we add via vertical, as well as horizontal, comparison of law. If we start from this notion of a core of criminality in every country and enlarge the core by this device of horizontal and vertical comparison of crime, we arrive, roughly speaking, at the same subject matter, the same field.

THE STAGE ON WHICH THE CRIMINOLOGIST
PERFORMS AND THE ROLE HE PLAYS

Horringa has said that the man trained in the social sciences can in practice present himself in three different roles: (1) the role of the investigator, (2) the role of the adviser, and (3) the role of the therapist.[5] This statement also holds true for the criminologist. But where is the stage on which he plays these roles? We can distinguish the law, the field of prevention, scientific investigation, the application of the law, the punishment of the responsible, and the treatment of irresponsible lawbreakers. To be more concrete, we can distinguish these factors:

1. The formulation and application of laws.
2. Mental hygiene and extramural education.
3. Extramural punishment and treatment.
4. Correction.
5. Mental hospitals.
6. (University) research centers.

The criminologist can shift from one stage to another. And he can have more than one role on a single stage. A rotation of roles need not mean a mixing of roles.

What is there against role rotation, multifunctionality? Of this, it is said in our profession that the man who carries the keys cannot treat, and the man in the white coat cannot at the same time help to maintain discipline. It is a question of whether this is properly defined. Man always lives multifunctionally. He eats to maintain his body because he enjoys eating, and (quite another matter) because he does not want to feel hunger. He marries to have children, but also because marriage can be enjoyable.

In the therapeutic situation, a mixture of roles will often be disastrous—but not always necessarily. It is when the investigator and the man who carries out policy duplicate each other's roles that the danger of the mixture indeed becomes great.

EXCHANGE OF ROLES AND DELINQUENCY

In a discussion of penal offenses, a detour to mention the criminologist would be acceptable. At this point in my discussion of the criminologist,

[5] D. Horringa, *Over rolrotatie en rolvermenging in het sociaal-wetenschappelijk onderzoek,* V.S.W.O.-Mededelingen, April 1962, No. 17.

a detour concerning the penal offense seems indicated. If we have called attention to the fact that criminologists have their stages and that they can play diverse roles on them, it must also be pointed out that the question of stage and role is, to a considerable extent, relevant with respect to the delinquent.

In *Culture Conflict and Crime*, Sellin laid the foundation for an investigation of this point. "The culture" is usually a composite of several, overlapping cultures. Each individual belongs to a number of social groups with cultural characteristics of which the norms are one example. The more complicated a culture is, the more probable that the number of normative groups to which one individual belongs is large. The greater is, then, the chance that the systems of norms of these groups conflict with each other, even though in reality they often, at least to a great extent, limit or overlap each other.

When more or less mutually divergent norms of conduct simultaneously dominate the special situation in which an individual finds himself, there is a conflict of norms (Sellin, p. 29). The American literature speaks in this context of subcultures, but I think it necessary that we distinguish between subcultures and the parallel (or collateral) cultures.

Under subculture I understand a divergent (possibly regional) culture within a national pattern. If a conflict of norms arises, the national pattern of norms will dominate. In this sense, in The Netherlands not long ago the culture of, for example Zwaagwesteinde, Ruinerwold, and Oss each formed a subculture. The subculture then submits to the culture anchored in the law.

But there are differences other than those between the cultures affirmed by the law and those which are not. There need be no correlation with the law for the difference in cultural norms to be important. Within one community, two or even more juridically dissimilar culture patterns can be observed to exist separately or intermingled; such cases can better be termed a parallel or collateral culture. Although it must be admitted that the difference between collateral cultures and subcultures is not always equally evident, it must be maintained for theoretical reasons.

The term subculture is more properly applied if the individual is faced with the choice between lawful and unlawful behavior, but the situation in which an individual finds himself can also be determined by the mutual divergence of juridically dissimilar collateral cultures. The following example seems to me to carry a rather European, perhaps even typically Dutch coloration.

A student who comes, for instance, from a rather strict Protestant home, in which the moral and cultural values of the milieu are maintained with a certain rigidity, may nevertheless find himself in a more or less different cultural group—for instance, a libertine student club or an artists' club. He may, without laying himself open to being called a hypocrite, be able to mix with two or three such culturally different groups without attracting special notice or giving offense. Difficulties will only develop when the two cultures encounter each other, because such an encounter often becomes a collision. The student would get into difficulties in the artists' club if a group of other students suddenly appeared, at least if they wished to play the role of a group of students there. In the reverse situation the same thing would occur. The conflict situation would probably become even more serious if, in addition, the sphere of the parental home were suddenly to be exposed to that of either kind of club.

In the Diagnostic Center in Topeka I observed the case of a young delinquent who had become entangled in this kind of multiplicity of roles. On the street, with his friends, he used a language to turn one cold and was the ringleader in making passes at girls. In this cultural community of the street, which in this case had a very low social level, his relationship to the adult world was quite different from when he was playing the role of the promising student in a senior high school in a distant neighborhood. And within the sphere of his home, for instance, during the walk to church on Sunday, he convincingly played the role of a sensitive, dependent boy. When this multiple-role player was unmasked, there was a merciless confrontation of the different worlds in which he had made himself at home.

In such an "unmasking" situation, the young person is forced to make a choice, with the self-fulfilling force that this choice can carry. By this I mean that the choice is almost unavoidably accompanied by an affective repudiation of one or more of the roles; this is often followed by a definitive conversion to one of the roles and the rejection of the other role or roles. In some cases the parental pattern wins. The individual then turns his back on the other spheres in a way that almost amounts to treachery. The change that one of the other roles will win is far from negligible. There is a very good chance that at this point the boy will become really delinquent. A choice of this kind has, as I have indicated, almost always something of the "self-fulfilling prophecy."

The great difficulty is that in this cultural clash the boy often does not make the choice among multiple roles, but that the choice is made for him by another or by The Others. This may occur, for instance, if, because of his behavior, his father seems to reject him, with the result that for the future one role is, as it were, denied him; it can also happen if the forces of law and order are somewhat too ready to treat him as a criminal and seem to fix him in a role. The confirmation, after the event, of an unfavorable choice is therefore relatively simple, for self-respect normally requires that the individual retain the illusion that he has made the choice himself. And because that choice must appear to be genuine, he will wish to demonstrate and defend it. Here we are on the terrain of hypostasization, a concept introduced into criminology by J. Ter Heide.[6] What it comes to is that if we are too quick to treat the boy as a scoundrel, we are choosing this role for him as the most fitting of his diverse roles and so, as I have said, we might fix him in this role. This is indeed the danger concealed in every punishment.

Despite the risk of disturbing the equilibrium of the structure of this argumentation, I would like to say the following. The child notices very early that his parents live in an assortment of roles. If, for instance, having awakened in fright late in the evening, he enters the adult circle— unexpectedly for the adults—he may observe how they attempt to adapt themselves to him. (The most unfamiliar visitors among them will, in all likelihood, do this most conscientiously.) The child feels whether the change in tone is achieved easily or is forced. Through such experiences he soon learns to see through the roles played by the adults who bring him up, and the main question is whether he has the impression that this occurs with some dignity, with embarrassment, or with crude falsity.

It may be that the ability to shift from one cultural milieu to another, with an immediate exchange of roles, is also a cultural product. Now, it is a fact that many young delinquents lack this shifting ability and are unhappy about it.

THE DISCIPLINES

We may now return to the working definition of the subject matter of criminology: crime is a segment of the scale formed by:

   I. Normal behavior.
  II. Deviant but not disturbing behavior.
 III. Deranging but not juridically relevant behavior.
  IV. Juridically relevant deranging behavior.
   V. Crime.

Now it might be asked: where does the criminologist come in? The answer, in principle, is at the horizontal line shown in Figure 3. And now we can construct a model of the "five-point scale,"[7] in Part A of Figure 3.

[6] J. Ter Heide, Vrijheid; over de zin van de straf (diss. Leiden, 1965).
[7] Here, of course, the word scale may only be used if it is consistently kept in mind that it is a sliding scale.

	I	II	III	IV	V
A	Normal behavior	Deviant not deranging behavior	Deranging not juridically relevant behavior	Juridically relevant deranging behavior	Crime
					Penal law
B				Law	
			Psychiatry		
	Psychology and sociology				

FIGURE 3

Apparatus B in Figure 3 shows us the disciplines related to the five kinds of behavior on the scale. Sociology and psychology encompass the entire scale, psychiatry only divisions III, IV, V. The lawyer has to interfere with certain kinds of behavior even though it cannot be said to constitute crime, for instance nonpayment of rent.

This difference between the civil attorney and the penal lawyer brings us to the next stepping-stone, although it is one that does not lie entirely in our main direction.

RESPONSIBILITY AND ACCOUNTABILITY

Consideration of this point is useful for the differentiation between the fields of psychiatry and law, that is, with respect to divisions III, IV, and V on the scale in Figure 3.

In civil law the guilt of the perpetrator interests us in a much more indirect way than it does in penal law; his accountability is what is involved rather than his responsibility. In penal law the emphasis is different. I would err here if I failed to draw attention to the accountability of the perpetrator of a crime, for it represents the reverse side of the victimological aspect of a criminal act and must therefore not be ignored. In penal law the accent falls on responsibility, in civil law on accountability, but where crime is involved we must consider both.

I cannot agree with Slovenko's notion of responsibility.[8] "A motorist has a heart attack and hits a pedestrian." Slovenko states that he is responsible for his act. "Who else, if he is not?" I doubt very much

[8] Ralph Slovenko, "Psychiatry, Criminal Law and the Role of the Psychiatrist," *Duke Law Journal,* Vol. 1963, no. 3, p. 404.

whether this event can be called an "act." I also doubt whether the motorist can be regarded as being "responsible" for his act in terms of civil law, but a certain degree of "accountability" may be involved, and accountability alone can never imply punishment. One thing seems to be certain: what should be spoken of in criminal cases is criminal responsibility and, in this case, there is no such thing. Since there is no crime, there can be no punishment.

We are now closer to our earlier problem of the subject matter of criminology. What is a crime? A crime is a segment, as we have said (made by the penal code), of conduct such that it disturbs society. Now we can see additional conditions[9]: (1) the act must be unlawful, and (2) the offender must be responsible.

To deal with point 2, we can examine several sets of points.

1. A. The offender is responsible.
   B. The offender is not responsible.
   C. The offender is partly responsible.

2. A. That the offender is responsible should be proved.
   B. That the offender is not responsible should be proved.

3. A. The jury should be asked whether or not the offender is responsible.
   B. The jury should not decide whether the offender is responsible.

4. A. The expert on this responsibility question is either a psychologist or a psychiatrist.
   B. The expert on this responsibility question is an objective panel of psychologists, psychiatrists, sociologists, and lawyers.[10]

5. A. The expert concludes about whether or not responsibility exists.
   B. The expert evaluates the offender's personality and leaves it to the judge to draw conclusions.

THE COLLABORATION BETWEEN THE PSYCHIATRIST AND THE LAWYER

Both the lawyer's and the physician's conclusions are diagnostic. The situation with which the lawyer deals is comparable to that of an in-

[9] It must be said that a psychological criterion, although scarcely regarded as such, also enters in here: it must be determined whether the criminal act has been committed with criminal intent or fault.
[10] See Gerhard J. Falk, "Criminal Responsibility in Socio-psychological Perspective," *Criminologica*, Vol. 2, No. 1 (1964), p. 19.

stantaneous photograph. As soon as or as far as his diagnostic conclusion is upheld by the judge, it is evident what will be done. The law speaks; the case is dismissed.

The lawyer always thinks about crime and delinquency in terms of the conflict between the individual and the legal order. He sees both parties as subjects and objects of rights. Such a conflict will be satisfied, to give an example, with the acquittal of a guilty person whenever the rules of the game demand an acquittal. On the other hand, for the medical man interested in crime, the acquittal of a guilty man will certainy not necessarily mean the end of his interest in the case. This may even be the point at which this case becomes very urgent: what should be done now? As soon as the criminologist sees the patient in the criminal (which a physician will tend to do soon enough), the judicial aspect of the conflict situation at once becomes less important.

The physician may consider "the patient's right to be ill."[11] The lawyer will absolutely not do the same.

It is obvious that both attitudes can render collaboration unproductive. I shall give here a practical example of the discrepancy. For the jurist, exhibition is not a serious offense. Thus, no preventive detention can be applied (in The Netherlands). But the psychiatrist considers exhibitionism as one of the most severe contact disturbances; he is convinced that the exhibitionist clearly requires treatment. In Amsterdam, in 1961, the girl Engelina Feenstra was murdered by a voyeur, an exhibitionist who was known to the police as such, but whom they had always let off with a warning or a light penalty. This man should have been treated many years before he became a murderer.

But just as the jurist wonders according to what law the (probably) dangerous voyeur can be subjected to a prolonged treatment against his own will, he also wonders whether the duration of a penal treatment may be reduced as a result of the incontrovertible recovery of the convicted man.

The conflict between different views on this problem reached rather distinct expression in a meeting of the Belgian and Dutch criminologists held in Leiden in 1962. At this meeting a discussion arose, in connection with introductory talks by Dupreel and Rijksen, about the question of conditional release. There proved to be a difference of opinion as to whether this release should be permitted after the convicted man had served two-thirds or one-third of his sentence. During the discussion, the psychiatrist Roosenburg remarked that a definite basis was difficult

---

[11] S. T. Hayward, "The Doctor's Place in the Patient's Hospital," *Lancet*, 1 (1961), pp. 387–389.

to prescribe. "If a man has tuberculosis," she said, "is it not also impossible to say in advance whether he will have recovered after five months of treatment?"

Now, the difficulty is that in some cases the delinquent is completely a patient, and in that case he belongs neither in court nor in prison. It may be that he is additionally a patient, but in that case he is something besides a patient, namely a delinquent. This means someone who chooses or, in a less severe case, risks being regarded as a delinquent, that is someone who willingly enters into an open conflict, or who will risk getting into a conflict situation. If such an individual sees that a conflict situation is about to happen against his will because he cannot control his behavior—and in cases in which the delinquent is not conscious of the conflict—there is room for an exclusively therapeutic attitude; in all other cases, for a penal attitude, at least partially. And in a penal consideration, the conflict is the proper subject matter. The legally-trained criminologist regards deviant behavior in the light of the norm. He is confronted by both the perpetrator and the victim and stands between them.

In the Bulletin of the Menninger Clinic,[12] in connection with an article by a jurist on the insanity defense, Dr. Karl Menninger said: "This is a phenomenon which we have not adequately studied—the intelligent, educated and obviously conscientious man of law who is apparently incapable of grasping the meaning of psychiatry." However, the same thing, but then the other way around, is said by jurists about psychiatrists.

Physicians will be in heartfelt agreement with what Erasmus had to say about jurists (which in English reads): "Among men of learned professions, the lawyers may claim first place for themselves, nor is there any other class quite so self-satisfied: for while they industriously roll up the stone of Sisyphus by dint of weaving together six hundred laws in the same breath, no matter how little to the purpose, and by dint of piling glosses upon glosses and opinions upon opinions, they contrive to make their profession seem the most difficult of all. What is really tedious commends itself as brilliant."[13]

The jurists, on the other hand, are convinced that the psychiatrists, by considering virtually every delinquent a patient, lose sight of the function of the legal norms and of the rights of the community and of the individual victim. The awkwardness in their collaboration, which is actually so essential to both, is an international and very grave phenomenon.

[12] Volume 25, Number 5, September 1961, pp. 266–267.
[13] Erasmus, In *The Praise of Folly*, translated by Hoyt Hopewell Hudson, ed., Princeton University Press, Princeton, N.J., 1945, p. 76.

THE PSYCHOLOGIST MAKES HIS APPEARANCE

The evaluation of responsibility is based on a study of the delinquent person. In some cases the psychologist can provide just as good information about the personality of the delinquent as the psychiatrist. Sometimes perhaps even better. Often, too, the psychiatrist will be unable to do his work without the assistance of the psychologist. On the other hand, there remain cases in which the specialized medical knowledge of the psychiatrist is required.

In addition to this clinical psychology of delinquency, a general criminology of deviant behavior is of importance to criminology. Clinical studies yield hypotheses; first, concerning the etiology of deviant behavior in some of those who are called criminals and, second, concerning those who designate as deviant and consider punishable certain kinds of behavior, that is, those who are under the impression that they form the legal order.

Criminologists often state that crimes are always harmful and at the same time to a certain extent immoral acts.[14] Now, if the democratic legislator makes behavior *a* punishable and not behavior *b*, it may be assumed that the community considers behavior *a* much more harmful than behavior *b*. Why? This is one of those questions to be called "fodder for psychologists."

Wolfgang[15] cites Sellin and Sutherland in support of Gillin's broad definition of crime: "an act that has been shown to be actually harmful to society, or that is *believed* to be socially harmful by a group of people that has the power to enforce its beliefs and that places such act under the ban of positive penalties." This provides not only a (broader) definition of crime but also indicates a point in a program for . . . what must I say, sociopsychologists or criminologists? I would say, for criminologists—new style.

It is here perhaps relevant to add some remarks about the "stimulus error." Linschoten[16] says, "the stimulus error occurs when the experimental subject describes the object that stimulates him and not the perception that the object provokes. . . . He remains naive and does what

[14] This definition is given by Van Bemmelen. I myself do not believe that the concepts immoral and harmful-to-the-community are strictly separable. Harmful acts can, by definition, be called immoral. Private "immoral" behavior which harms (offends or shocks) no one is "immoral" at a private level, hardly to be called immoral, and should not be punishable.

[15] *Op. cit.*, p. 158.

[16] J. Linschoten, *Idolen van de psycholoog* (1964), p. 42.

we always do in daily life: we go beyond the sensory data to what they signify for us. Titchener[17] calls this a mistake, but it is not; it only becomes a mistake when it deceives the psychologist; when the psychologist, in looking for characteristics of perception, speaks of characteristics of things."

A blindfolded subject is directed to run his finger over sandpaper and is then asked: "What do you feel?" He will then, because of the stimulus error, not state what he has perceived but, taking a shortcut to the meaning of the thing itself, say: "Sandpaper." This is exactly the kind of stimulus error we encounter when, having asked for an evaluation of certain behavior, we hear the jurist cite an article of the penal code or the physician a particular clinical picture. Who can see through this error better than the psychologist?

THE SOCIOLOGIST MAKES HIS APPEARANCE

I do not wish to detract from the classic role of the sociologist. When a delict has been committed, an attempt must also be made to determine the importance of the exogenous factors in the etiology of the violation.

But there is far more than just this. Granting the fact that crime is only a relatively random, mainly culturally-determined (which means man-made) cut of a series of normal acts of behavior, not quite normal but also not very deranging behavior, and so on, it is essential that the sociologist inform us about the backgrounds of such cuttings. He must warn us when, and in what direction, lines C in Figure 1 have shifted— the fact that they do not do this in time is responsible for the phenomenon of the lagging behind of the law.

Concerning the clinical importance of the sociologist, the following must also be said. In a series of difficult but valuable papers, M. P. Vrij,[18] Professor of Penal Law in Groningen, laid the basis for a concept of the subsocial as (third) element of the criminal act. To indicate what he meant by this, I shall give a simple illustration: a housemaid, in a hurry to write to her boyfriend, takes a postage stamp valued at 5 cents belonging to the woman by whom she is employed. Is her act unlawful? Yes. Is she responsible? Again, yes. Nonetheless, a sensible housewife will not go straight to the police and, if it came to that, a still more sensible policeman would see to it that it did not come to court. That the law takes action in every criminal act is thus not the same as the laws of the Medes and the Persians. There is, therefore, a margin of

---

[17] E. B. Titchener, *Experimental Psychology*, Vol. II, 1 (1905).
[18] Deceased in 1953.

otherwise punishable behavior with respect to which we think that the sword of Justice would be turned against herself if it were applied in such cases.

If we carry this thought even further, this margin is not determined solely by the objective seriousness of the delict. It is not a matter of the five cents. If the maid had been stealing regularly, this could have been the straw that broke the camel's back. Thus the margin is also determined by the subjective dangerousness of the perpetrator. The seriousness of the concrete disturbance of the legal order, added to the danger implied by the perpetrator's behavior, form the subsocial aspect of the delict, according to Vrij.

We have defined a crime as seen by the criminologist as follows: (1) The act is unlawful, and (2) the offender is responsible. We come now to a new formulation: (1) The act is unlawful, (2) the offender is responsible, and (3) the subsociality is considerable.

This last concept alone is sufficient to make the inclusion of the sociologist (or at least the social psychologist) desirable, but there still remains his role in classical criminology: the determination of the "social factors" of concrete criminality. And still we have not satisfied all our requirements. Connected with what has been discussed in the foregoing, there are also less clinical aspects. We also ask the sociologist to give advice more generally about what behavior can be accepted without putting the community in danger.

Both a general and a clinical importance of the sociologist will coincide in the investigation of the significance of the subcultural and collateral cultures I have already referred to. And it goes without saying that all this will broaden the role of the sociologist even further: he will help to locate the cutting that constitutes crime, that is, to determine where the line should be drawn between disturbing but not criminal behavior and deranging behavior that we then qualify as criminal . . . and treat.

BASIC TRAINING

Because criminology transects the disciplines of law, sociology, psychology, and psychiatry, and because it would hardly be practical for one person to take degrees in all these disciplines, there will always be a deficiency.[19] This deficiency is most acute when it becomes necessary for nonphysicians to work together with psychiatrists and their notions and concepts. "Experience shows that psychiatrists and jurists often

[19] Cf. S. H. Jameson, "Some Contradictions in Criminological Training," *Crime in America*, 1961, pp. 32–44.

misunderstand the basic assumptions of the other in protecting the rights of individuals and of groups."[20] As far as sociology, for example, is concerned, the psychologist and the lawyer can make up for their shortcomings by study, but they will never be able to talk with a psychiatrist on his level so long as they are not doctors of medicine. Now, there actually are some individuals who are both lawyers and psychiatrists, one being my colleague, Dr. P. H. A. Baan, of the World Health Organization in Geneva. However, I do not really believe that a combination of the study of law and medicine, plus a specialty in psychiatry, would be advisable for the education of a criminologist. First, it would demand far too much of most individuals and, second, society hardly would be able to reward the investment these studies would require.

So the question remains open. Let us start from the principle that a criminologist can only be a master of one trade and must be a jack of all the other disciplines. Then, which trade should he choose to begin with? Which discipline would be the most profitable as a basis? And what sequence would be the best?

We have need of some criteria. Here is one I can put forward: the first learned discipline should not form a way of thinking or an attitude that cannot easily be remolded. I think this criterion does not hold so much for psychology and sociology as it does for legal or medical training. The two latter disciplines tend to form a lasting attitude toward the individual and society.

If the training of the lawyer was good, he is ready to fight in the actual interests of a client who has come into conflict with another or others. (His client may be either a private person or the country—this makes no essential difference.) He will reduce the conflict to a legal contest. It is my opinion that his training makes this attitude rather deeply rooted for the lawyer.

Even more deeply rooted is the physician's attitude of the psychiatrist: the criminal is his "patient."

It is, in my opinion, not at all surprising that the conflicts between criminologists are most frequent and most intense when psychiatrists and lawyers confront each other. We do not find these deep-rooted attitudes, which hinder collaboration, in sociologists and psychologists.

The second criterion is self-evident. Some disciplines require that training take place at the earliest possible age and can only be taught in a teacher-student relationship in institutions such as hospitals and laboratories. Others can, if necessary, be acquired at home, in evening courses or by independent reading and training.

[20] L. Z. Freedman and H. D. Lasswell, "Cooperation for Research in Psychiatry and Law," *Amer. J. Psychiat.*, 1961 (692–694), cited from *Excerpta Criminologica*, 1961, no. 789.

If we restate our problem of which training should be preferred as the primary one for the future criminologist, we shall find that there are three questions to be answered:

I. Which primary training gives the most one-sided attitude with respect to the conflict between society and delinquent?

II. Which primary training takes root most deeply?

III. Which training is least susceptible to adaptation as a secondary, postgraduate, extramural training?

I do not pretend to be able to support my hypothesis with the results of research, but I think that our professions can be listed as follows in relation to these questions:

I	II	III
1 Law	1 Psychiatry	1 Psychiatry
2 Psychiatry	2 Law	2 Psychology
3 Psychology	3 Psychology	3 Sociology
4 Sociology	4 Sociology	4 Law

Summa summarum the sequence, starting with the least suitable, could be put:

Psychiatry	4
Law	7
Psychology	8
Sociology	11

but this is not to be taken seriously because in this way it is assumed that dimensions I, II, and III have the same weight and that the distance between 1, 2, 3, and 4 are similar, but the admissibility of these assumptions has not been demonstrated.

I would put it, however, that studies in sociology and psychology seem to be the most worthy of consideration as the basic training for the criminologist. We could also merge the two disciplines and say that the criminologist should begin as social psychologist. But with this we realize that social psychology is almost everywhere a specialization of one or another basic subject, and then we seem to be no closer to our objective.

But the solution lies elsewhere. "Criminology is not a matter for sociologists, jurists, psychologists, psychiatrists, etc., but for criminologists," according to a proposition put by the youngest Dutch professor of criminology (by training, social psychologist), W. Buikhuisen (of Groningen). He is right, and what he says may be extended to the education of the criminologist.[21] There is no objection to having prospective jurists

[21] Cf. L. Bavcon, *Excerpta Criminologica*, 1961, no. 750.

(and others) learn something of criminology from elective subjects, but a special training for criminologists should be instituted. It must be possible to form, from the medical background required by the psychiatrist, a fundamental nucleus to serve as an element in the education of a criminologist (who certainly does not have to become a physician). The same holds for law, psychology, and sociology, although for the last two the "nucleus" would have to be of a rather appreciable size.

For some time to come, the new academic department of criminology will to an appreciable extent, and even finally to some extent, also be the place in which people trained in another discipline can obtain a postgraduate education in this field.

SCIENTIFIC METHODS

I endorse what Wolfgang has to say at the end of his article: ". . . it should be clear and unmistakable that criminology means the use of scientific methods in the study and analysis of regularities, uniformities, patterns, and causal relationships concerned with crime, criminals, or criminal behavior" (*op. cit.*, p. 62). But what are "scientific methods?" There are those who seem to know exactly what they are. Karl Menninger, for instance, thinks that sooner or later the scientific attitude (of the medical profession) will replace the methods of the jurists.[22] But the methods used by the jurist are scientific, too, when they are good. However, there are different kinds of science. We find ourselves, with the question we have just put, back at the start of this essay. I said there that the Houses of speculators and those of calculators were alternately in the ascendant. But is it actually "scientific" to make a fundamental distinction between the natural sciences and the normative (or cultural) sciences? I at least am not certain of the necessity for criminology to make a choice between the two kinds of science.

It is true that the exact sciences are validly taken as the ideally typical form of all science. To do so implies "that the reduction to measures and numbers is accepted as the most exact way to describe."[23] I may quote further from Linschoten: "The condition for quantification is that it is possible to characterize phenomena by numerical values." He cites: "Quantification alone is not an objective of science. What is sought is that quantification which makes it possible to let a phenomenon pass through a series of numerical values to see whether the terms of that series (the series itself) form a function of another series (the other series itself)."

[22] Karl A. Menninger, *The Human Mind* (3rd ed., 1964).
[23] J. Linschoten, *op. cit.*, p. 26.

Nevertheless, it seems to me, at least for the present state of criminology, not yet justified to say that it can only be practiced scientifically if the phenomena can be described and explained by means of reduction models.

Another problem of importance is that criminological research works up only a small section of the deviant behavior in the scale first posed in the previous section on the subject matter of criminology: the segment "crime." But the limitation goes further. Only an exceedingly small proportion of those who commit a crime become the subject of criminological research. If the subject of study were to be the psychology of the trout, there would be little objection to concentrating the investigation on a certain number of captured trout. If, however, it had to be taken into account that because of special psychological characteristics certain trouts let themselves be caught more easily than others, this method would be unreliable. In considering criminology, it is essential that this special factor be kept in mind.

The great pitfall of classical criminology is concealed in the fact that the so-called *delitto naturale* (Garofalo) has been taken as the starting point. "Crime" is a man-made category, an artifact. Nineteenth-century criminology could not progress because, on the basis of this artifact—a totally unscientific starting point—it professed to practice "pure science." Classical criminology has interest for the offender only; we need more interest for the offense, which might lead us along a more intelligent route back to the offender.

Still another point is that the adage "spectator huius scena none actor" may never hold entirely, but for criminological investigations it does not hold in any sense whatever. To arrive at his reduced models the criminologist would have to have done a study in which he has included himself as one of the objects of the study, if only by the choice of his variables. The fact that such variables always differ somewhat from one investigator to another is caused by the difference in what these investigators have read. This brings us back to earlier authors, who in their time also included themselves in their research, authors from among whom present-day criminology makes a choice and furthermore, in choosing from that work, accepts some hypotheses and rejects others.

One gets the impression that criminology has not escaped the self-excepting fallacy, the delusion that he is not included in the object of his own investigation.[24]

The difficulty in which criminologists find themselves was recently made clearly evident when, at the Third United Nations Congress on the Prevention of Crime and the Treatment of Offenders (1965, Stockholm),

[24] M. Mandelbaum, "Some Instances of the Self-excepting Fallacy," *Psychol. Beitr.* 1962/1966, pp. 383–386.

no less a person that Julia Henderson raised the question of whether, with our present criminology, we "are not paying for our acquired freedom." This question gave many people food for thought. We are in need of such bold hypotheses. There is, of course, no denying that we can only contribute scientifically when we can test these hypotheses, and we cannot do that until we can reduce and quantify. I do not mean that, in the end, and also in the matter of Julia Henderson's question, that will not be possible. It must be possible. It is possible.

To conclude this section and with it this essay, I would refer to a book I have written about the prediction of criminal behavior,[25] in which I reviewed about a hundred prediction studies, most of them essentially scientific in nature. But they do not include a single *reductum*[26] that, in my opinion, has as much scientific criminological importance as the book—which was never meant in any sense as a criminological treatise— by J. P. Sartre, *Jean Genet, saint et martyr*, in which Genet's criminality is elucidated.

The future work of the criminologist will be to reduce the gap between the two ways of practicing criminology (the method of the natural sciences and that of the cultural sciences). He can only do that by standing now on one side of the gap, now on the other, alternately. Or, to put it another way, it is, as though a tunnel were being dug through a mountain from both ends; there is always a chance that the two sets of diggers have long since passed each other and could dig until eternity without ever meeting or without ever achieving one tunnel for both to use. It must be possible for both parties to keep in touch with each other, so that they can both work towards each other and make certain that they will eventually reach each other.

And when they have reached each other, the science of criminology will have returned, via purely factual material, to a theory that will make criminology part of a doctrine of human behavior.[27]

25 W. H. Nagel, *Het voorspellen van krimineel gedrag* (1965).
26 Linschoten uses the term *reductum* for the result of the reduction procedure.
27 Cf. Max Grünhut, "Moderne Arbeitsmethoden in der Kriminologie," *Z. ges. Strafrechtswiss.*, 1960, p. 276.

II
THEORY

3

Social-Cultural Conflict and Criminality

GEORGE B. VOLD

Numerous books and articles dealing with aspects of the relation between social-cultural conflicts and criminality have been published during the last quarter century or so. The pioneer study by Thrasher[1] set some kind of pattern or standard in that it was in large part the report of findings from the empirical study of actual gangs as found operating in the Chicago of post-World War I times. The relatively recent one by Yablonsky[2] is similarly based on experience with and observation of actual gang violence where the killing (murder?) of a member of an "enemy" gang is merely an incident in a continuing and deep-seated problem of cultural conflicts in the hodge-podge population of the New York City of today.

It is evident from the numerous specific studies already published that no single theory or type of explanation is adequate for the wide variety of behavior variously called "crime." In an earlier publication the present writer examined in some detail the factual data and the logic involved in the principal contemporary explanations of criminal behavior.[3] A good deal of attention was given to the facts and consequences of social-cultural conflict as a basic orientation for criminological theory. Conflict theory was shown to be especially applicable to the areas of mass behavior criminality such as traffic law violation, "black marketing" activity, violation of legal regulations in the use of alcohol and drugs, white collar criminality, organized crime, and similar types of criminal activity devoted to economic gain.

The present discussion will review some aspects of the general conflict approach and point to some applications in connection with a few

[1] Frederic Thrasher, *The Gang*, Chicago: University of Chicago Press, 1927; 2nd ed., 1936.
[2] Lewis Yablonsky, *The Violent Gang*, New York: Macmillan, 1962.
[3] George B. Vold, *Theoretical Criminology*, New York: Oxford Univ. Press, 1958.

well-known types of nonconforming behavior (criminality?) in relation
to law enforcement in the perspective of contemporary American life.

SOCIALIZATION

Any consideration of group antagonisms and criminality must come
to grips with some of the fundamentals in the relationship between the
individual and his group. A good point to begin with is the basic consideration that man is a group-oriented being, that always and everywhere
he stands in various vital relationships to a surrounding milieu of other
human beings.

The human infant generally starts life with a cry of protest against
the change from the pleasant security of the womb to the unpleasant
uncertainty of the outside world. His behavior patterns all need to be
acquired or developed. Some behavior will win the approval of his
family and surrounding group of human beings; other behavior will
be disapproved of and lead to unpleasant consequences.

Acquiring approved behavior patterns, learning what behavior is
proper and what is not, is a process usually called socialization. It is
always group centered—that is, proper behavior is understood and defined by some particular group, usually and especially at first by those
most directly in contact with the individual. It is only later, as the child
grows older or as the sheltered or provincial adult learns more of the
ways of the world, that awareness of differences in group behavior
patterns is encountered.

Socialization is a learning process. The "laws of learning" (or the
"curve" of learning or of forgetting, as developed in many an educational
psychology textbook)[4] provide a good deal of information about the
conditions of the learning process, but give no real explanation of *why*
learning takes place in one instance but not in another. There is always,
apparently, an uncertain question of whether the individual "tries" to
learn, whether he is "interested," or whether he is merely going through
the motions of learning without acquiring any new knowledge or behavior.

An internal, subjective "mental set" or "attitude" favorable to the
task will apparently greatly facilitate learning. Given such a "functional
state of readiness,"[5] learning will take place rapidly insofar as ability
permits but, without the favorable attitude, repetitive behavior may go
on endlessly without any learning taking place.

[4] See Edward L. Thorndike, *Educational Psychology: Briefer Course*, New York:
Columbia Univ. Press, 1914; or E. R. Hilgard, *Theories of Learning*, New York:
Appleton-Century, 1948.
[5] Muzafer Sherif, *An Outline of Social Psychology*, New York: Harper, 1948, p. 202.

As part of this same problem, there is no clear answer as to the *why* of particular "attitudes" or "mental sets" necessary for learning. As encountered in group behavior situations, they are presumably the product of innate characteristics and capacities molded by the ever-present surrounding milieu. Intimacy groups of primary contacts become especially important here in defining for the individual the basic patterns of attitude regarding what is, or should be, approved or disapproved in behavior situations.

If intimacy group contacts are important to the criminal way of life, it follows that the acquiring of attitudes favorable to crime, as well as the learning of necessary behavior patterns for specific criminality comes about through the normal psychological process of learning in the same way that the law-abiding members of society come by their attitudes and behavior.

A further aspect of the "socialization" of the individual is the development of loyalty to and identification with a particular group. Both loyalty and identification are words used to describe a subjective condition or characteristic involving deep-seated emotional, irrational, and often unconscious elements. Loyalty is peculiarly the basic quality of the relationship involved when it is appropriate to say that the individual and the group "belong" to one another. Likewise it is fundamental to and gives meaning to the terms "in-group" and "out-group," "we-group," and "others group." As often noted by social psychologists,[6] this feeling of belonging to and of being part of an ongoing group of fellow human beings is an important "anchorage" in the personality development of the individual.

ETHNOCENTRISM

A singularly important aspect of this development of the individual in relation to his group is the phenomenon called "ethnocentrism" by William Graham Sumner in his *Folkways*,[7] namely the tendency to evaluate or judge one's own group as possessing superior or somehow better qualities than other groups. Ethnocentrism is not the same as egotism in the individual; it is rather a group quality, a sort of collective self-appreciation transmitted by the group to the individual as part of the socialization process. It appears to be a normal quality of collective life— all groups apparently are ethnocentric. Certain individual members may not subscribe to this favorable view of their own group, but this would seem to be primarily a matter of ineffective socialization.

[6] Muzafer Sherif and Carolyn W. Sherif, *An Outline of Social Psychology*, New York: Harper, revised edition, 1956, pp. 62–66.
[7] William Graham Sumner, *Folkways*, New York: Ginn & Co., 1906, p. 13.

The pervasive nature of ethnocentrism in all kinds of groupings needs to be emphasized. It is clearly to be seen in the approved sentiment of patriotism in the area of national and linguistic groupings, but it is equally significant in the confrontation of one group by another in more informal areas of contact. Thus, for example, as between religious denominations, political parties, academic specialties or "sciences," labor unions, college fraternities, boys gangs, and so on, the group with which the individual identifies himself becomes the center or standard whereby all others are judged.

COMPETITION AND CONFLICT

The truism, "The first task of life is to live. . . .", is as applicable now as when it appeared in the first paragraph of Sumner's *Folkways*. The attainment of life objectives is always complicated by the fact that things are not equally desirable or valuable, nor are they equally available to everyone. Competition and striving for place and position become a necessary part of life where others are seeking the same ends or objectives. The outcome of this endless striving—that is, the actual position or place that one is able to achieve or hold—is the essential substance of what is usually called "status."

It is not a static or fixed condition; one may gain status, or lose status, depending on how the continuing struggle goes. Groups as well as individuals face up to this situation. The individual must find his place in a group or in various subgroups of a larger general group, and any particular group must similarly find its place in the community of other groups. But any position sought will also be the objective of others, and in the resulting contest only one can be in top place. That is the special characteristic of status—it cannot be divided or shared. There is only one top place; other positions are secondary, of lesser significance.

Groups come into existence and continue to exist so long as they serve the common interests and needs of their members. When they no longer serve that function they soon disappear. Thus new groups come into being as new needs or interests appear, and some old groups become enfeebled and ultimately disappear when the reasons for their existence no longer prevail.

In this continuous process of changing groups in the social structure, any particular group must protect itself against being taken over or replaced by another group operating in the same area of interests and needs. When groups are not operating in the same area or sphere, their interests do not collide, and no group needs to fear that another will replace it or take over its functions. Collision and conflict occur when they become competitive for members or for power and influence. Actions taken in defense of group self-interest to protect place, position, and influence constitute the background for the violent behavior that not infrequently defies lawful authority and tends to become criminal.[8]

PROTEST AND THE CONTROL OF CONFLICT

In the troubled America of the 1960's there are numerous incidents that vividly illustrate the profound and deep-seated differences between differing groups of Americans in their interpretation of what constitutes the expected or required obligations of American citizenship. "Protest" marches in support of this or that cause are the familiar subject matter of a considerable portion of the news of the day.

The "moral right" to civil disobedience for the purpose of promoting the ends or objectives of some particular group or movement is loudly proclaimed by those who join such movements. Much of this activity inevitably goes counter to the requirements of local law and authority, thus becoming illegal and tending to negate efforts at law enforcement. Hence, reports of direct clashes of various groups of objectors or demonstrators with the police are frequent.

The essential realities of "pressure politics" must be kept in mind. Groups without sufficient political power to get favorable consideration from the state, as a matter of course, must undertake activity designed to influence state action in their favor.

This activity, variously designated (depending on the allegiance of the one using the term) as "educational programs," "lobbying," "petitioning for redress of grievances," or "demonstrations to call attention to the seriousness of the problem," has the common purpose of influencing the state to more favorable action on behalf of those supporting the activity. The object of the activity is to "put pressure" on those in a position to promote or otherwise bring about favorable action.

But action programs, designed to bring about certain objectives favored by one group, quite automatically call up counteraction programs by those in opposition, designed to prevent such accomplishment. The resulting conflict often includes various kinds of behavior more generally considered as criminal.

Under the American scheme of government the control of crime

[8] George B. Vold, *op. cit.*, Chapter 11, "Group Conflict Theory as Explanation of Crime," pp. 203–219; Chapter 12, "Organized Crime and Conflict Theory," pp. 220–242.

becomes the business of the local community. Police forces are normally under the control of municipal or county units of government. The general theory is simply that the police are of the people, and that they are the servants of the people of the community. This is democracy in action. It is the local community conception of what is right and proper that determines the formal legal definitions of behavior and that sets the standards for law enforcement.

The local community, however, is not a unity but rather a hodge-podge of various groups and subgroups with different ideas about what should be permitted and what should be prohibited in manners, morals, and behavior. Control of political power lies in the hands of the dominant group, or coalition of groups within the community. Because the police are the products of the local community and are employed by the local community, it follows that the groups that dominate the community will be the ones that set the standards for police activity and provide the principal guide for law enforcement.

Some of the ticklish problems of law enforcement stand out much more clearly when examined from the standpoint of the group and culture conflicts involved. In labor disputes the crisis known as a "strike" often involves behavior that poses a number of problems in law enforcement clearly related to community backgrounds and the delicate question of who, or what group, controls political power. Thus, may strike pickets block a street, a highway, or other public thoroughfare in their efforts to prevent access to a plant and thereby enforce their union's demands? Of course not, in theory and in law, but in many strike situations the answer will depend largely on which group, or groups, dominate the community and control police power.

Typically, in past industrial conflicts the dominant groups have been "the owners" and police action has been directed to the protection of property and to keeping the streets and highways open, thus permitting free access to the plant and a clear entrance by "scab" labor. As labor union power increased, both in union membership and in the development of a politically potent "labor vote," both behavior on the picket line and police response to picketing have changed.

The most obvious result of this increase in labor union strength has been the change in attitude and public sentiment about labor unions and their proper place in production. Moreover, there has been a considerable change on the part of most companies as employers of labor in that usually no effort is now made to "break" a strike by attempting to keep operations going with the use of nonunion labor. Instead, a plant is closed down and there is usually little or no physical violence or disorder; there is only the economic damage represented by loss of production and of payrolls. When plants are kept open and the police offer their protection to competitive nonunion labor to cross picket lines, violence usually results, and in the course of this fighting all manner of ordinary criminal law offenses may occur. Typical of such offenses are assault and battery, assault with a dangerous weapon, and sometimes even manslaughter or murder, not to mention a wide variety of property damage offenses.

The relative absence of violence and criminality in connection with most modern labor disputes, in comparison with the situation forty or fifty years ago, is due not to any great change in police action—the police are committed to the task of enforcing the law, now as then—but rather to deep-seated social and political changes in the community at large. The interests of capital and labor are still in conflict, but the battle is now more likely to be carried on as discussion around the bargaining table, or before a mediator, or in the courtroom rather than by direct physical violence on the picket line. The real change has been in the balance of power in the adjustment to one another of the several different conflicting groups within the larger community.

The mass activity of "marches" and "demonstrations" connected with the so-called civil rights movement has presented many problems in law enforcement and have generated considerable criticism of certain local police practices with charges of "brutality" and "discrimination." It was police attention to a problem of everyday law enforcement, the apprehension of a culprit observed to have violated traffic regulations, that triggered the riots in Watts, Newark, Detroit, and many other cities throughout the United States.

Reactions of various groups, pro and con, to the practical, common-sense recommendations of the Special Commission appointed by the governor to report on the riot in Watts points up the sharp disagreements and deep-seated conflicts within the community.[9] Enforcement of law cannot be a smoothly performing operation in this area so long as wide divergences and antagonisms exist within the community.

Two aspects of the activity growing out of the civil rights movement need to be distinguished. One aspect accepts the principle of gradualism in social change and gives its energy to problems of political organization, legislation, and educational programs directed at a future somewhat beyond the present. The other aspect demands "change now" and is the activist approach. It is the latter type that has created various crises and set up direct challenges to established law and practice.

The activist approach may easily lead to quite open defiance of local

[9] For details of the Watts riots, see the Associated Press dispatches for the critical days in August 1965; for a brief review of the suggestions and recommendations of the Special Committee, headed by John McCone, formerly of the Central Intelligence Agency, see *Time Magazine*, December 17, 1965, p. 21.

authority in the attempt to dramatize the plight of a self-conscious "minority" seeking what it considers to be "justice" and the end of what it calls "discrimination." The locally dominant majority does not accept this formulation of the situation at all. It finds the activity offensive, due to "trouble makers," and often in violation of law. Police action, arrests, and court convictions often follow in their effort to maintain "law and order," that is, the status quo. The conflict of interests between community groups is not the same thing as the criminality involved in day-to-day contacts, but it gives the best clues as to why the criminality takes place.

Divergence of views relating to American foreign policy, especially the handling of the Viet Nam situation, has brought out various "protest marches," "peace demonstrations," and the like, to dramatize opposition to official action. Violence and criminality have not been a characteristic part of this activity, but the whole situation reflects deep-seated differences in the political and ideological orientation of various groups and individuals in the population. The passionate vehemence with which government policy has been attacked or defended testifies to the depth of the cleavage between pro and con. The discussion taking place suggests the social psychological characteristics of "in-group" versus "out-group" attitudes. It is perhaps best described by the Arab aphorism: "In the dialogue of the deaf, both sides talk but neither side listens."

The dramatic episodes of "draft card burning" appear as an off-shoot or by-product of the furor over policy in Viet Nam. Professional pacifists have joined in the demonstrations. Their position is usually justified in the name of the moral and ethical principle of "freedom of conscience." Any criminality involved in refusing to obey government instructions or in resisting government action is brushed off as of no great significance because compliance would have involved behavior contrary to the dictates of conscience. The high moral tone of this position is perhaps somewhat clouded by the persistent and insidious suspicion of group and individual self-interest. Life in an American prison is quite obviously less upsetting and far less dangerous than the battles in the jungles of Viet Nam.

CONCLUSION

No inferences should be drawn from this discussion concerning what ends or objectives should be favored in any particular instance or episode of group conflict mentioned. The object has been rather to emphasize again the fact that many kinds of criminal activity are the by-product of action taken in defense of group positions ethnocentrically defined and held by individuals loyal and faithful to their group.

The central significance of the conflict approach was carefully spelled out and clearly demonstrated by Thorsten Sellin nearly thirty years ago in *Culture Conflict and Crime*.[10] In this work, he demonstrated effectively the basic cultural setting for the crucial definitions concerning the appropriateness of specific behavior as to whether it should be considered as crime or viewed as compatible with customary conduct.

Customary behavior within a minority culture group may be regarded as illegal and criminal by the dominant majority in control of the state. The problem, then, is no longer a behavioral one but becomes one of political organization, of what group or what elements within a population are dominant and give direction to the formal machinery of crime control. This aspect of the crime problem suggests the desirability of a shift in emphasis in criminology from concern with the sciences of individual human behavior to a greater awareness of the scientific study of political organization and the control of power in the state. Judging by the contents of contemporary textbooks in the field, that is still some time in the future.

[10] Thorsten Sellin, *Culture Conflict and Crime*, New York: Social Science Research Council, Bulletin Number 41, 1938.

4

Culture Conflict, Differential Association, and Normative Conflict

DONALD R. CRESSEY

In 1935 the Social Science Research Council appointed Professor Thorsten Sellin and Professor Edwin H. Sutherland to constitute a Subcommittee on Delinquency of the Council's Committee on Personality and Culture. The appointment was based on the view that criminological research and theory is a subsystem or subset within more general anthropological, social psychological, and sociological frameworks. This view had a powerful impact on the criminology of the time, and it has been influential in criminology, especially American criminology, ever since. The Subcommittee on Delinquency decided to explore some of the basic concepts underlying criminological research and to uncover research questions which might, when answered, expand our knowledge of etiological processes. Both tasks were finally undertaken by Professor Sellin, the Chairman of the Subcommittee, and one outcome was his now-famous monograph on culture conflict and crime.[1]

In this monograph, Sellin reaffirmed the notion that the criminal law is a body of norms that are binding on all who live within the political boundaries of a state and are enforced through the coercive power of that state, and he then went on to indicate that the specific character of these legal rules depends upon the character and interests of those groups in the population that influence legislation.[2] He stressed the idea that such groups are not necessarily in the majority, a notion that was becoming popular at the time.[3] His emphasis was on lack of con-

[1] Thorsten Sellin, *Culture Conflict and Crime*, New York: Social Science Research Council Bulletin No. 41, 1938.
[2] *Ibid.*, p. 21.
[3] Sellin cites the following two works: Joseph A. Leighton, *Social Philosophies in Conflict*, New York: Appleton-Century, 1937; Manuel Gamio, *Hacia un Mexico Nuevo*, Mexico City: Author, 1935.

gruence between criminal laws promulgated by a dominant majority or minority and the moral ideas of different social groups subjected to the laws of the state. Because the norms embodied in the criminal law change as the values of the dominant groups change, what is "crime" varies from time to time and place to place.

This kind of observation, coupled with observations on the difficulties of identifying the relationships between "culture" and "personality" (an exciting theoretical problem in 1938, as now) led Sellin to formulate the "conduct norms" concept. Conduct norms are rules based on the social attitudes of groups toward the various ways in which a person might act under certain circumstances. When a human acts or reacts, his activity is called "behavior," but when these actions or reactions are governed by rules or norms, they constitute a subtype of this general category and are classed as "conduct." Accordingly, conduct, by definition, can "occur only in situations which are defined by some social group and governed by a rule of some sort."[4]

In his next logical step, Sellin combined two ideas: the notion that the members of a society are not equally committed to the norms contained in the criminal law, and the notion that members of a society are not equally committed to other conduct norms. The result of these variations in degree of commitments, he observed, is conflict:

Every person is identified with a number of social groups, each meeting some biologically conditioned or socially created need. Each of these groups is normative in the sense that within it there grow up norms of conduct applicable to situations created by that group's specific activities. As a member of a given group, a person is not only supposed to conform to the rules which it shares with other groups, but also to those which are peculiarly its own.[5] A person who as a member of a family group—in turn the transmitting agency for norms which governed the groups from which the parents came—possesses all its norms pertaining to conduct in routine life situations, may also as a member of a play group, a work group, a political group, a religious group, etc., acquire norms which regulate specialized life situations and which sustain, weaken or even contradict the norms earlier incorporated in his personality. The more complex a culture becomes, the more likely it is that the number of normative groups which affect a person will be large, and the greater is the chance that the norms of these groups will fail to agree, no matter how much they may overlap as a result of a common acceptance of certain norms. A conflict of norms is said to exist when more or less divergent rules of conduct govern the specific life situation in which a person may find himself. The conduct norm of one group of which he is a part may permit one response

[4] *Op. cit.,* p. 28.

to this situation, the norm of another group may permit perhaps the very opposite response.[5]

After making these observations on conflicts of norms, Sellin went on to examine the concept of "culture conflict," pointing out that "in recent years a number of studies have been made on 'culture conflict' and delinquency, studies which assume the existence of legal and non-legal conduct norms in conflict with each other."[6] He reported that the concept had been used in two senses—sometimes culture conflict was regarded as the result of the migration of conduct norms from one culture complex to another, sometimes as a by-product of a cultural growth process.[7]

We shall discuss, below, Sellin's refinements of both uses of the term, and then we shall elaborate on the second meaning, which we call "normative conflict." Here, we merely wish to state our belief that, despite Sellin's detailed discussion of the two meanings, the early use of "culture conflict" in two different senses has meant that the impact of the concept on criminological theory and research has not been as great as it might have been had two different terms been used. We believe, in other words, that use of "culture conflict" to refer to *both* kinds of conflicts of norms has meant that the processes associated with immigration and diffusion of norms have been overemphasized, while the processes by which conflicts develop as by-products of increasing societal complexity have been underemphasized.[8] Because American sociologists customarily showed great concern for "the immigrant problem," it was easy to conclude that "culture conflict" was to be used in this context, and it also has been easy to conclude, erroneously, that the concept has lost its usefulness now that assimilation of vast numbers of immigrants is no longer a major social problem.

[5] *Ibid.*, pp. 29–30.
[6] *Ibid.*, p. 57.
[7] *Ibid.*, p. 58.
[8] Three volumes appearing shortly after Sellin's volume was published show the emphasis on migration of norms from one culture complex to another. In 1940, the Gluecks cited three pages of *Juvenile Delinquents Grow Up* (New York: Common-wealth Fund) under "culture conflict" in their index; all three references are to discussions of nativity, birthplace, and religion. Similarly, in the third edition of Gillin's *Criminology and Penology* (New York: Appleton-Century, 1945), Sellin's monograph is cited, but the discussion of "culture conflict" is devoted exclusively to consideration of the idea that alien cultures have been brought into contact with each other through development of easy and rapid means of communication. Consistently, the six references to "culture conflict" in the revised edition of Barnes' and Teeters' *New Horizons in Criminology* (New York: Prentice-Hall, 1945) all refer to immigrant problems.

MIGRATION OF NORMS

Sellin demonstrated that "culture conflict" can arise because of the interpenetration of conduct norms. "Conflicts of cultures are inevitable when the norms of one cultural or subcultural area migrate or come in contact with those of another, and it is interesting to note that most of the specific researches on culture conflict and delinquency have been concerned with this aspect of conflict rather than [with the one stemming from the cultural growth process]."[9] Interpenetration of norms can occur in three different ways.[10]

First, the codes may clash on the border of contiguous culture areas. Behavior which is not defined as crime in one area may be crime in an adjoining area, resulting in serious problems of identifying the legal ways of behaving in border areas. With the growth of communication processes, the borders between such conflicting culture areas has become extremely broad, since knowledge concerning divergent codes no longer arises out of limited direct personal contacts.

Second, in colonization the criminal laws of one group may be extended to the territory of another, with the result that traditional ways of behaving suddenly become illegal. When Soviet law was extended to Siberian tribes, for example, women were forbidden to wear the traditional veils. But those who obeyed the law and laid aside their veils were killed by their relatives for violating the codes of the tribe.

Third, when the members of one cultural group migrate to another culture, they may take with them values which condone ways of behaving that clash with the codes of the receiving culture and are, therefore, illegal. This process is the reverse of the one just mentioned, and it occurs when the migrant group is politically weaker than the group whose territory is invaded. If the Siberians in the above illustration had moved to Russian cities, they would have introduced divergent norms there.

COMPLEX SOCIAL SYSTEMS AND
DIFFERENTIAL ASSOCIATION

Sellin also demonstrated that as a modern industrial and mercantile society has arisen, the process of social differentiation has, by itself,

[9] *Ibid.*, p. 63.
[10] *Ibid.*, pp. 63–67. The following summary is a revision of the discussion appearing in Donald R. Cressey, "Crime and Delinquency," Chapter 14 in Leonard Broom and Philip Selznick, *Sociology: A Text with Adapted Readings*, 3rd ed., New York: Harper and Row, 1963, pp. 549–550.

produced a conflict of conduct norms, and there has been a vast exten-sion of impersonal control agencies, "designed to enforce rules which increasingly lack the moral force which rules receive only when they grow out of emotionally felt community needs."[11] One by-product of the development of complex civilization, then, is certain life situations "governed by such conflicting norms that no matter what the response of the person in such a situation will be, it will violate the norms of some social group concerned."[12]

It was "culture conflict" of this second kind that Sutherland considered basic to the explanation of crime, and the concept in this sense later became the principle of differential association. Accordingly, the history of the "culture conflict" concept is tightly entwined with the history of the "differential association" concept. In discussing the history of his theory, Sutherland reported that he rather inadvertently stated the fundamentals of differential association before he realized that he had a theory.[13] Significantly, this statement, made in 1934, included the concept "conflict of cultures."

The general hypotheses of this book are as follows: First, any person can be trained to adopt and follow any pattern of behavior which he is able to execute. This pattern may cause him to suffer death, physical injury, economic loss, sacrifice of friendship, and any other type of loss or sacrifice, but be followed nevertheless even with joy, provided it is accepted as the thing for him to do. Second, failure to follow a prescribed pattern of behavior is due to the inconsistency and lack of harmony in the influences which direct the individual. *Third, the conflict of cultures is therefore the fundamental principle in the explanation of crime.* Fourth, the more the cultural patterns conflict, the more unpredictable is the behavior of a particular individual. It was possible to predict with almost certainty how a person reared in a Chinese village fifty years ago would behave because there was only one way for him to behave. The attempts to explain the behavior of a particular person in a modern city have been rather unproductive because the influences are in conflict and any particular influence may be extremely evanescent.[14]

It probably also is significant to the history of both the culture-conflict concept and the differential association theory that the 1939 edition of *Principles of Criminology* uses "culture conflict" in a discussion of what crime *is*: "Crime may be considered, in the light of the discus-sion in the preceding sections, to involve three elements: a value which

[11] *Ibid.*, pp. 59–60.
[12] *Ibid.*, p. 60.
[13] Edwin H. Sutherland, "Development of the Theory," in Albert Cohen, Alfred Lindesmith and Karl Schuessler, eds., *The Sutherland Papers*, Bloomington: Indiana University Press, 1956, pp. 15–16.
[14] Edwin H. Sutherland, *Principles of Criminology*, Second Edition, Philadelphia: Lippincott, 1934, pp. 51–52.

is appreciated by a group or a part of a group which is politically important; *isolation of or cultural conflict in another part of the group so that its members do not appreciate the value or appreciate it less highly and consequently tend to endanger it*; and a pugnacious resort to coercion decently applied by those who appreciate the value to those who disregard the value."[15] It is possible to derive the theory of differential association from this statement.

In the first formal statement of his theory, Sutherland made seven assertions, in contrast to the nine assertions contained in the revised, and still current, statement. The sixth assertion in the early version went as follows: *"Cultural conflict is the underlying cause of differential association and therefore of systematic criminal behavior."*[16] In elaborating on this assertion, Sutherland pointed out that differential association is possible because society is composed of groups with varied cultures containing norms supporting conduct which is generally regarded as desirable and also containing norms supporting conduct which is generally regarded as undesirable. "The criminal culture is as real as lawful culture and is much more prevalent than is usually believed." "The more the cultural patterns conflict, the more unpredictable is the behavior of a particular person." The seventh assertion in this early version of the differential association theory was: *"Social disorganization is the basic cause of systematic criminal behavior."* In elaborating on this assertion, Sutherland tried, in a brief and fleeting way, to account for "the origin and the persistence of culture conflicts relating to the values expressed in the law and of differential association which is based on the cultural conflicts." He found them in "social disorganization," and then went on to say: "Cultural conflict is a specific aspect of social disorganization and in that sense the two concepts are names for smaller and larger aspects of the same thing."[17] This primitive statement of the theory was summarized as follows: "Systematic criminal behavior is due immediately to differential association in a situation in which cultural conflicts exist, and ultimately to the social disorganization in that situation."[18]

Although these statements seem to take the "by-product of cultural growth" position with reference to culture conflict, Sellin pointed out

---

[15] Edwin H. Sutherland, *Principles of Criminology*, 3rd ed., Philadelphia: Lippincott, 1939, p. 19. Italics added. Only the phrase "or culture conflict in" was added in the 1939 edition. The remainder of the statement appeared on p. 11 of the 1934 edition. It also appeared in Edwin H. Sutherland, *Criminology*, Philadelphia: Lippincott, 1924, p. 21.

[16] Third edition (1939), p. 7.

[17] *Ibid.*, p. 8.

[18] *Ibid.*, p. 9.

that Sutherland's early statements really do not argue that culture conflicts arise *solely* within a culture. While such development is theoretically possible, in practice as cultures expand there is an introduction of disharmonious norms from other culture areas or systems.[19] Nevertheless, Sellin argued, a clash between the norms of Negroes and whites in the United States is indigenous in origin, and other clashes of norms in our country could have developed without the influx of national and racial groups who brought with them the legal norms of other cultural or subcultural areas of the world. In time, this idea that "culture conflict" involves more than a clash between the legal norms of immigrant cultures and host cultures became the foundation of the theory of differential association. Sellin pointed out that Shaw's studies of delinquency areas, for example, showed that while the areas were largely inhabited by European immigrants, the fact that the inhabitants were immigrants was of minor importance, compared with the conditions of "disorganization" in the areas.[20] Sellin concluded, "It is likely that in large European cities with homogeneous populations, the same conditions breed high delinquency."[21]

Despite this conclusion, Sellin placed great emphasis on the migration of legal norms, rather than on the conflict of norms developing as a consequence of the rise of complex social systems. This emphasis may be seen in his view that culture conflict growing out of social differentiation is "secondary":

> If the immigrant's conduct norms are different from those of the American community and if these differences are not due to his economic status, but to his *cultural origin* then we can speak of a conflict of norms drawn from different cultural systems or areas. Such conflicts may be regarded as *primary* culture conflicts. They may in turn aggravate the disorganizing factors in the social environment by forcing an immigrant into lower-paid occupations, bad neighborhoods, etc., which in turn may have etiological importance in abnormal conduct, regardless of the nativity or the cultural origin of those subjected to them. The conflicts of norms which grow out of the process of social differentiation which characterize the evolution of our own culture may be referred to as *secondary* culture conflicts.[22]

---

[19] *Op. cit.*, pp. 61–62. Sutherland's uncertainty can be observed in his explicit use of "conflict of cultures" to refer to the migration of norms: "Conflict of cultures' has to some extent been studied from the statistical point of view, although these statistics, also, are extremely inadequate as a measure of conflict." He then cites data on cultural marginality, including data on crime rates of immigrants and their sons. Second edition (1934), p. 73; and third edition (1939), pp. 79–80.

[20] Clifford R. Shaw, *Delinquency Areas,* Chicago: University of Chicago Press, 1929.

[21] *Op. cit.*, pp. 62–63.

[22] *Ibid.*, pp. 104–105.

As indicated, the social science culture of the 1930's demanded an emphasis on problems of immigration and on the study of the relationship between "personality" and "culture," rather than on problems of social structure and differentiation. Sociologists, psychologists, and psychiatrists were using the term "culture conflict," but in criminology the theoretical controversy about it centered on the problem of whether culture conflict is relevant to crime and delinquency only if it is experienced by individuals as psychological conflict.[23] Sellin settled this controversy by citing the case of a Sicilian father in New Jersey who had killed the seducer of his daughter and who was surprised at his arrest, since he had merely defended his family honor in a traditional Sicilian way. The crime occurred because the acculturation process was so incomplete that there could be no mental conflict at all about the killing. Perhaps it was this controversy and the theoretical efficacy of the case cited that led Sellin to devote most of the last half of his monograph to a discussion of differences between the norms of immigrants and the norms included in American criminal laws.[24]

NORMATIVE CONFLICT

In order to distinguish between the two kinds of "culture conflict," we have found it convenient to use the term "normative conflict" to refer to conflicts between legal and other norms that arise through the societal growth process and to restrict the term "culture conflict" to conflicts arising through the migration of cultural codes. I began using this terminology in 1960, when I found that even my sociologist friends were interpreting "cultural conflict," as used in differential association theory, to mean conflict between American legal norms and the legal norms of immigrant groups.[25] I began calling Sutherland's statement a "principle of normative conflict," and the words "normative conflict" were substituted for the words "culture conflict" in a quotation from Sutherland because colleagues could not understand the quotation in its original form:

The second concept, differential association, is a statement of [normative] conflict from the point of view of the person who commits the crime. The

23 Louis Wirth, "Culture Conflict and Misconduct," *Social Forces*, 9:484–492, June, 1931.
24 *Op. cit.*, p. 68.
25 Donald R. Cressey, "Epidemiology and Individual Conduct: A Case From Criminology," *Pacific Sociological Review*, 3:47–58, Fall, 1960.

two kinds of culture impinge on him or he has association with the two kinds of cultures and this is differential association.[26]

Perhaps the most important theoretical problem regarding the epidemiology of crime is one of establishing the relationship between normative conflict on the one hand and high crime rates on the other. This problem was attacked by both Sellin and Sutherland but, as we have seen, the attack was blunted by the popularity of the "migration of norms" meaning of culture conflict. Associated with this theoretical problem is the problem of identifying the processes by which normative conflict develops. This is the problem that Cloward and Ohlin *say* they are going to attack when they ask, "Why do delinquent 'norms' or rules of conduct develop?"[27] However, the book in which they raise this question is devoted principally to examination of the relationship between high rates of gang delinquency and high degrees of normative conflict.[28] The question of how the social structure generates conflicts between legal and illegal norms remains unsettled.

Sorokin, among others, has pointed out that the penal law consists of "law norms" which defined the rights and duties of actors in definite social relationships.[29] Law norms are "universal" rules which ought to be followed by everyone except the very young and the insane. They differ from moral norms, which recommend but do not require certain courses of conduct. Every society has several sets of moral norms which are both based on and give support to the ordering of people. These moral norms, thus, make up the dimensions of the social structure. Some common dimensions of social structure of interest to criminologists, for example, are class status, sex status, age status, health status, ethnic status, and family status. The norms surrounding these statuses distinguish persons in terms of rights, privileges, duties, and prestige, which means, simply, that they define expectations for conduct. While the normative expectations of the society as a whole vary with the structural conditions of class, sex, age, ethnicity, etc., the expectations and requirements of the law norms do not allow for this variability.[30] If variations

[26] "Development of the Theory," *op. cit.*, pp. 20–21.
[27] Richard A. Cloward and Lloyd E. Ohlin, *Delinquency and Opportunity: A Theory of Delinquent Gangs*, Glencoe: The Free Press, 1960, p. ix.
[28] Donald R. Cressey, "Differential Association and Delinquent Subcultures," paper read at *Det Åttende Nordisk Forskningsseminar for Kriminologi*, Helsinki, June, 1966. To appear in the *Proceedings* (in press).
[29] Pitirim A. Sorokin, *Society, Culture and Personality*, New York: Harper, 1947, pp. 69–91.
[30] Dennis McElrath, "Normative Conflict and Crime Rates," *Unpublished Manuscript*, January, 1955, p. 8.

in normative conflict are related to the epidemiology of crime, then crime rates should be high at those points in the system where the laws are incompatible with the moral norms based upon differentiation.

McElrath has suggested that among the characteristics of the legal process that seem relevant to normative conflict are the discrepancies between the moral norms of the lawmakers and the norms of the persons to whom the law norms are to apply; the peculiar characteristics of law norms, as compared to moral norms, in such aspects as specificity, harm, intent, and punishment; the slowness of the process of change in penal law norms (the lagging of law behind morality); and the processes by which judges, juries, prosecutors, and public defenders are selected.[31] For example, if class status is viewed as a set of "positional" moral norms, it becomes obvious that these norms permit differences in power, prestige, and other behavior. Significantly, as Sellin suggested, among the behavior items on which differences are expected is the behavior relevant to establishing law norms. In simple terms, law norms are likely to reflect the more general behavior of the powerful classes. If the moral norms of the powerful classes are incompatible with the moral norms of other classes and, if the norms of the powerful classes become law norms, then variations in crime rates can readily be predicted from a study of the conflicts between the norms of this class and the norms of other classes. Miller has, in a sense, made such predictions on the basis of his studies of the relationships between delinquency and lower class norms.[32]

It should be noted, however, that while the norms of class position allow for implementation in the penal law of the norms of the powerful, the locus of power shifts from time to time. Accordingly, at various times different positional moral norms get incorporated into the law norms. Because the penal law is slow to shed the older norms, normative conflict comes to reside within the legal structure itself. Sellin made this point by saying, "The criminal norms, i.e. the conduct norms embodied in the criminal law, change as the values of the dominant groups are modified or as the vicissitudes of social growth cause a reconstitution of these groups themselves and shifts in the focus of power."[33]

Further, it probably cannot be rightfully assumed that the content of any set of positional moral norms is itself unitary and harmonious. Even within a socioeconomic class, one norm may recommend something con-

[31] *Ibid.*, pp. 4–5.
[32] Walter B. Miller, "Lower Class Culture as a Generating Milieu of Gang Delinquency," *Journal of Social Issues*, 14:5–19, 1958. See also the quotation of Sutherland at note 15, *supra.*
[33] *Op. cit.*, p. 22.

trary to what is recommended by another. Thus, while individuals may be similar in terms of class position, they differ in terms of other differentiating criteria, such as age, sex, family status, and ethnicity. One is middle class or upper class, but he also is old or young, urban or rural, male or female, sick or well, Negro or white. The moral norms relevant to one of these systems of status differentiation may be inappropriate to the moral norms defining another of the positions.[34] Such conflicts of norms get "resolved" in the legislative process, but such "resolution" does not mean that the ensuing law norms are subscribed to uniformly or universally.

Normative conflict, then, is inherent in social structure. The conflicts of relevance to crime are those in which choices available to a person, because of one or more of his positions in the social structure, are inappropriate to the choices that the law norms demand that he make. Rates of violation of criminal law norms are a function of the system-related norms as well as of the law norms themselves. To take a simple example, it is apparent that young persons do not have the access to the lawmaking process that is available to middle-aged persons. Accordingly, in many respects juvenile crime is an expression of a condition of conflict between the norms of youth and those of adult lawmakers whose norms become the law norms that direct youth to behave in certain ways. However, older persons, who have low crime rates, do not have access to the lawmaking process either, so differential access to the lawmaking process cannot be the only relevant variable.

Yet another problem arises: given incompatible normative expectations at different positions in the social system, why are the criminal law norms, rather than other norms, violated? In any action situation, positional moral norms are subject to broad tolerance limits and, as indicated, they stand as general recommendations regarding desirable but not necessarily compulsory conduct. But law norms are applied universally and, moreover, they *direct* action. In a situation of normative conflict, the tolerance of violations of positional norms may be generalized, even among the lawmakers, to law norms. Williams indicates that this situation is handled by the following process: "(a) Public affirmation of the norm; (b) covert acceptance of widespread violation or evasion; (c) periodic token or 'ritualistic' punishment and/or punishment of those whose arrears unavoidably become public."[35] By making compulsory that which is ideal and by making specific that which is general, the law imposes demands for common modes of adaptation; this

[34] Compare the quotations of Sellin at notes 5 and 12, *supra*.
[35] Robin M. Williams, *American Society: A Sociological Interpretation*, New York: Knopf, 1951, p. 356.

process, by definition, introduces both a condition of normative conflict and a high rate of violation of law norms.

Another source of normative conflict and, consequently, of law violation is mobility. As Sellin showed, mobility sometimes creates a conflict of law norms. But mobility also involves changes in status positions and, hence, in positional moral norms. If one is to conform to either law norms or positional norms, McElrath suggests, he must (1) know what the norms are, (2) identify with them, and (3) receive support and reinforcement from others.[36] Some statuses might not provide for these processes. More important, some statuses might interfere with these processes as they apply to *law* norms. Just as some immigrants experience "cultural conflict," so a young man experiences "normative conflict" as he reaches the age of responsibility, for the legal norms applying to him do not change regularly and systematically as he grows older.

[36] *Op. cit.*, p. 9.

5

Culture Conflict as a Frame of Reference for Research in Criminology and Social Deviation

SHLOMO SHOHAM

Culture conflicts are sometimes regarded as by-products of a cultural growth process—the growth of civilization—sometimes as the result of the migration of conduct norms from one culture complex or area to another. However produced, they are sometimes studied as mental conflicts and sometimes as the clash of cultural codes.

Thorsten Sellin[1]

Culture conflict has mainly been associated in criminological research with social change and especially with immigration. The latter is indeed a natural, conspicuous and, methodologically, the most convenient choice.[2] The clash of conduct norms due to external and internal migration and its link with crime and deviation is more readily researchable than almost any other form of social change. One recent example from one of the author's current projects is the extreme clarity and focus of the norm conflict experienced by Arab villagers, who migrated to Israeli towns after the June 1967 war, as compared to the rather amorphic and relatively slow norm conflict resulting from the secularization of the traditional structures in the Arab village itself. It is evident from our opening citation and Sellin's subsequent work that

[1] *Culture Conflict and Crime*, New York: Social Science Research Council, 1938, p. 58.
[2] Mannheim comments on the expediency of immigration as a medium of culture-conflict research as follows: "The concept of culture conflict covers a field much wider than the conflicts likely to arise through migration from one country to another with possibly very different language, mores and laws. In fact, however, it has been studied, mainly in relation to the foreign immigrant where it provided a welcome ready made opportunity to blame the immigrant for the increasing American crime rate," *Comparative Criminology*, Vol. II, London: Routledge and Kegan Paul, 1965, p. 539.

he conceived the culture-conflict premises as having a rather wide theoretical scope, transcending the area of social change towards the dynamics of normative systems on the social level and norm conflicts as personality processes on the individual level.[3]

Wolfgang predicted recently a shift of interest of the sociologically orientated criminologist from theorizing and research on the socio-cultural level to the deeper microanalysis of deviant personalities. He said: "Having mapped out the intellectual past and present of criminology as shifting from the personality to the social to the cultural system, we may now look ahead. It is not belief in cyclical change that leads me to suggest that the next shift will be back to the personality system. But the return to an emphasis on personality will be different from the early experience. The social and cultural systems will be taken for granted as operative, and major manipulations of man's environment will be made in monumental proportions. . . . Social control will be less by law and more by manipulation of social forces that will function from command rather than from fortuity. But within this milieu some deviance will still occur. Criminal deviance will be viewed once again, however, as more idiosyncratic or biological, and biologically and psychologically controllable."[4]

It is our purpose, therefore, in the present paper to delineate the possible directions in which the theoretical premises of culture conflict may be expanded both on the relatively well-cultivated social level and the meagrely explored personal one. It would be rather fruitful to guide our analysis by the following trichotomy:

(1) Culture conflict as mental conflict. These normative conflict situations would take place, presumably, within the arena of the personality of the potential criminal or deviant prior to his first criminal acts or his initial "recruiting" to a deviant subculture. These internal conflicts and their subsequent first overt manifestations are crucial in the differentiation process of defining a person to himself and to his relevant others as delinquent and deviant. This is the rather abrupt transfer from the "right" side of the legal and social barricade to the "wrong" one.

(2) The gradual deeper integration of an individual within the criminal or deviant group and his corresponding rejection of the "legitimate" or "square" normative systems involves rather elaborate conflict processes: the narrowing of socioeconomic opportunities, the rupture

---

[3] T. Sellin: *Culture Conflict and Crime, op. cit.*, Chapter IV: "The Conflict of Conduct Norms," pp. 57–107.

[4] M. E. Wolfgang: "The Viable Future of Criminology," an address delivered at the XVIth International Course in Criminology, August 1967, Montréal, Canada.

or jeopardizing of marriage and other domestic affiliations, the stigmatizing rejection and counterrejection of friends, community, voluntary
associations, and most of the former membership and reference groups.
The last step in this process is full-fledged membership in the criminal
or deviant group. The resolution of the internal conflicts with the "right"
side of the barricade at this advanced stage of deviance is by severing
most relevant normative ties with it. The normative clashes of social
control as a vestige of external conflict between the deviant's own group
and the organs enforcing the laws of the "legitimate" groups.

(3) The third level of analysis is the perennial favorite of culture-
conflict theorists: the fluctuations of crime rates in a given community
for a given time, the genesis and volume of special types of crime and
deviance, urbanization, industrialization, internal and external migration,
disintegration and secularization of traditional and tribal structures,
and the *ex-definitione* link among most of the other forms of social
change and the conflict of conduct norms. However, before delving
into the actual application of culture conflict to these three levels of
etiological research we shall have to make some unavoidable methodological notes and conceptual clarifications.

A FRAME OF REFERENCE

Sellin evaded the pitfalls of a generalized "nothing-but" monistic
theory. He did not impute to his culture conflict premises an explanatory
range covering the whole phenomena of crime and deviation. It seems
to us that culture conflict may quite adequately be regarded as a frame
of reference. This term "denotes the larger contextual system with
respect to which an object (or a process) is viewed or judged."[5] In
other words, a frame of reference is a common boundary of phenomena
that has an empirical common denominator. The common denominator
may not necessarily characterize the *whole* phenomenon under consideration; it would be sufficient that a part of its factual manifestation
would fit into the common boundary of the frame of reference. By exclu-

[5] This definition is taken from D. Krech, R. Crutchfield, and E. Ballachey: *Individual
in Society*, New York: McGraw-Hill, 1962, p. 32. The classic definition by E. W.
Hobson is incorporated in the following passage by H. Becker: "Scientific sociology
regards human beings as pieces on the giant chess-board of life; with each succeeding move (social occurrence) they draw closer together, separate or converge
in certain respects and diverge in others. . . . Such approach and avoidance constitute the basis of the sociological frame of reference." H. Becker: *Systematic
Sociology on the Basis of the Beziehungslehre and Gebildelehre of Leopold von
Wiese*, New York: Wiley, 1932, p. 39.

sion we may note that the culture conflict premise is not a theoretical system in the engulfing Parsonian sense; nor is it of similar scope to the conflict theory of society, which society (according to the expounders of Simmel's thought) is held together in dynamic equilibrium by diverging normative discord. We hold, moreover, that culture conflict is also not a "middle range theory" by which Merton denoted the relatively limited theories applied to rather narrow and well-defined areas of study. Culture conflict is both wider and deeper and at the same time less systematic than a middle range theory. The latter operates on one level of analysis whereas culture conflict may include in its premises phenomena that occur on different planes of a space which need not have clear-cut delineations.

We may refer for comparison to Sutherland's differential association theory, which we may regard for our present purposes as a middle-range theory. Sutherland would have objected violently to our label because he imputed, at least to his first formulations of his theory, the widest scope of applicability to the whole area of crime causation. However, the differential association theory may indeed be regarded as a middle-range theory because it applies to the crime-as-business, as a way of life group-type of criminals, and not to the deranged, compulsive, sexually perverted, and other abnormal offenders. The main reason for regarding differential association as a middle-range theory is its holding constant its level of analysis. Sutherland did not concern himself with differences of personality structure and their possible bearing on crime causation. He also disregarded any somatic attributes and their hypothetical link to crime and deviation. The culture conflict premise does not confine itself to clearly cut levels of analysis; it is, therefore, not a middle-range theory but a more loosely defined and rather flexible frame of reference. Precisely, this flexibility makes it, we believe, more useful from the methodological point of view. Sutherland's disregard of, for instance, personality factors stemmed from his assumption, which was crucial to his theory, that there would not be any significant differences between the prevalence of structural personality defects or conspicuities between the criminal population and the population at large; also, there would be similar distributions of introversion and extraversion, high and low frustration, levels among Bugs Moran's mob, the British Horticultural Association, the Rotary Club of Tel Aviv and the inmates of Leavenworth Prison. This assumption has landed differential association in violent disputes which are easily avoided by culture conflict as a theoretical frame of reference.

Personality elements are, inter alia, internalized patterns of culture. We may assume that many norms, when deeply internalized and thus incorporated into the personality structure, would be linked to neutral or even commendable behavior in one sociocultural set and reprehensible or illegal behavior in another cultural context. In some types of crime and deviation these *personality elements, being subjectivized culture, would be crucial in explaining the conflict of norms and the ensuing criminal or deviant acts.* On the other hand, in other "life situations" no conflict would occur between the norms incorporated within the personality and the relevant norms at large. Only in the latter instance could the personality factors be disregarded.

Another asset of culture conflict as a frame of reference is its heterogeneous applicability to various levels of abstraction. We may illustrate this attribute of culture conflict by referring to a model we have constructed for social factors of juvenile delinquency in Israel.[6] This model synchronizes two levels of causal analysis; the first is a configuration of predisposing factors, a remote descendent of the multiple-factor approach. It is, however, selective and expressed in clusters of probabilities. It has, therefore, no resemblance to the non-theory and amorphic-mass-eclecticism aspect of the multiple-factor approach. The second causal level of the model is a chain of dynamic pressures which lead a given individual to associate with criminal groups and absorb their patterns of behavior. The predisposing factors include some anomalies in the structure of the family unit, ecological and economic factors, social change by industrialization, urbanization, migration, social disorganization, and anomie. Culture conflict may apply to all or to some of these predisposing factors and at various stages of their genesis. The disintegration of most immigrant family units by divorce, for instance, cannot be directly linked to the families' adjustment pains in their absorbing countries. Some families' disintegration may, however, be clearly linked to the accumulation of hardships due to the clashes with the normative system of the absorbing country. Culture conflict, here, besides being an independent variable to delinquency in its own right as inherent in the social change aspect of migration, is also linked to the disintegration of the family unit which, in turn, is a classic factor of delinquency. Ecological factors may be related to the culture conflict frame of reference in the case of two or more different cultural areas that are situated in tangential proximity. An appropriate example for the present context was the high-rate delinquency areas at the contact zones between the Jewish and Arab quarters in the Jaffa-Tel Aviv area.

---

[6] This model is incorporated in the author's paper: "Stigma and Subculture" (in press), the *International Journal of Social Psychiatry*, London.

Economic hardship or affluence as *subjectively defined by* an individual are linked to the culture conflict frame of reference and ultimately to crime and deviation if an individual's traditional self-image of economic sufficiency is being shattered by the normative mandates of conspicuous consumption to which he is or becomes exposed. The last two groups of predisposing factors, i.e., social change and disorganization are linked almost by definition to the culture conflict frame of reference. The second dynamic causal chain includes the processes of differential identification with criminal and deviant images, access to the illegitimate structure of the differential opportunity structure, differential association with criminal groups, learning their patterns of behavior, and being branded by the social stigma of criminal and deviance as a final tag of identification of those who are hard-core members of the criminal and deviant group. At the basis of this jargonized description of a causal chain lies a continuous normative struggle: the gradual rejection of the norms and values of the "legitimate" group and the absorption of the normative system of the deviant group. This pushing of an individual over to the "other" side of the legal and socionormative barricade may, therefore, be interpreted by the culture conflict frame of reference.

We may proceed, then, to study in detail our three stages of the etiology of crime as related to culture conflict. Most of our empirical illustrations are from criminological research projects carried out in Israel.

CULTURE CONFLICT AS MENTAL CONFLICTS

Norm Conflict in Socialization as an Etiological Link to Delinquency

The culture conflict thesis, when applied to normative conflicts within the personality, might reveal some clues as to why one individual commits delinquent and deviant acts and another does not, although both are exposed to similar predisposing factors. It may also provide the missing etiological link between these predisposing factors and the dynamic process of association with the criminal or deviant patterns of behavior. This link, as we have stated elsewhere,[7] relates to the attitude of the individual toward the restraining norm, to the degree that the individual internalized the restraining norm as a personality element,

[7] S. Shoham, "Conflict Situations and Delinquent Solutions," *The Journal of Social Psychology*, 1964, Vol. 64, pp. 185–215.

and to what process is necessary to overcome or "neutralize"[8] the restraining force of the norm or norms (in case these have been internalized) on the personality level. Without this link, any causal schema of criminal or deviant behavior is bound to remain incomplete.

The starving Hindu has all the reasons (and all the pressures) in the world to slay one of the holy cows that roam the streets and to fry himself a steak, but would not dream of doing so because of the deeply internalized religious norm forbidding it.[9] The same inhibition is even more apparent with the masses of religious dissenters, "freedom fighters," and rebels throughout the ages who suffered extreme torture and death but did not act contrary to a deeply internalized set of norms.

The process by which an individual is indoctrinated to comply with a given set of norms may be presented by the following model: the norm-sending by the group requires a *statement as to the desired behavior,* the maintenance of *surveillance* by the group to ensure compliance to the norm and to apply *sanctions* for infringement of the norm. The individual receiving the norm may conform to it for fear of negative sanction (*sanction orientation*), be lured to conform by rewarding sanction (identification), or internalize it very deeply within his personality structure so that conformity becomes "the right thing to do" (*moral orientation*). At this deep level of internalization where the norm becomes a personality element, surveillance or sanctions are superfluous.[10] The norm conflict frame of reference would apply to the present premise when the norm-sending process is plagued by conflict situations, that is, two or more inconsistent rules governing the same factual situation (as defined by the individual). These conflict situations may appear in all three stages of the norm-sending process. The extent and the severity of these conflict situations (which could be eventually expressed quantitatively) may determine the weakness or strength of a certain norm to regulate the relevant behavior of an individual and indicate thus the extent to which this individual is ready and ripe for the differential association and differential identification processes that may lead him to crime or deviation as a way of life. This might also help to clarify the crucial question in criminological theory, that is, that even in the worst of slums plagued by poverty, bad living conditions, criminal gangs,

[8] This is totally different from the "Techniques of Neutralization" of Sykes and Matza. The latter are more techniques of rationalization or defense mechanisms in the psychoanalytic sense. See "Techniques of Neutralization: A Theory of Delinquency," *Amer. Sociol. Rev.,* 1957–1958, Vol. 22, pp. 664–670.

[9] This example is cited in E. H. Sutherland and D. R. Cressey, *Principles in Criminology* (6th ed.), Chicago: Lippincott, 1960, p. 195.

[10] See J. W. Thibaut and H. M. Kelley: *The Social Psychology of Groups,* New York: Wiley, 1959.

prostitutes, and dope peddlers, only some boys become delinquent, whereas a far greater number remain law-abiding.

The effect of this norm conflict might proceed along two channels: *first*, the injury of the conflict situations might make the whole process of norm-sending ineffective so that the norm is internalized by the individual at a very shallow level or even not at all. *Secondly*, the continuing conflicts in the norm-sending process might injure a set of norms that has already been previously internalized by the individual. The higher the intensity and extent of conflict situations in the socialization process, the greater the shift on the continuum from moral orientation to sanction orientation, the final product being that the normative barrier against a given crime is completely shattered, and the crime then is in being caught and not in committing the offense.

Incidentally, our present analysis of culture conflict as mental conflict might provide a methodological tool to measure the "resistance potential" of a norm not only by the group (as originally proposed by Sellin) but also as a function of the depth to which a norm has been internalized by the individual.

Norm Conflict Resulting from Role Conflict and a Stigmatizing Rejection and Counterrejection of the Socializing Agency

Another application of the culture conflict frame of reference to the etiology of crime and deviation, which operates on an even deeper level of the personality, relates to normative conflict at early childhood within the child's family or immediate community. In this case we may also illustrate how the norm conflict frame of reference which is rather factual and operates on a lower level of abstraction may be drawn and incorporated into the social stigma theory of crime and deviation,[11] which is a typical "middle-range" theory. The culture conflict frame of reference may therefore be likened to a reservoir of some basic mechanical components that are vital for the construction of different machines that may perform widely divergent functions. We may dichotomize our present analysis into norm conflict in a child's formative years, which might result in compulsive deviance and normative conflict in early socialization that terminates in a rejection and counterrejection relationship with the socializing agency. Both these types of normative conflicts and deviant solutions are portrayed by the initiation into prostitution of girls from North African authoritarian families in Israel.

It would be outside the scope of the present paper to describe at

---

[11] The author has recently formulated this theory in a volume entitled *The Mark of Cain*.

length the stigma theory as applied to prostitution.[12] We may, however, visualize the domestic background that served, presumably, as fertile ground for the genesis of the relevant role and norm conflicts. The authoritarian family is characterized, inter alia, by a clear-cut definition of roles in terms of one-sided expectations for the child. The interaction framework in the family is based more on duties than affection, and there is a normative stress on stereotyped behavior and rigid roles. Also, the normative structure of the Jewish North African families prohibits or proscribes for girls the choice of role models outside the family. The members of the family would tend, therefore, to restrict the roles to be internalized for the construction of their ego-identity to the members of the family and especially to parents. This presupposes that a girl in a North African family would tend to absorb the norms and roles imposed on her within the family without much partiality as to whether her roles and norms are commendable or derogatory (stigma). The deterioration of the families' social position as a result of immigration might even increase this normative tendency of the North African Jewish family "to arrange matters within the family." That means that the parents' control over the child in the family would tend to be stricter as a result of anxiety and fear that their traditional authority is seeping through their hands. We might rely on the dissonance theorists in this matter that the father's status anxiety would make his control over his family even more authoritarian.

The girl would tend to be intolerant of ambiguity in her formative years and after, while still being in a state of ego-diffusion. The first characteristic of the family that breeds intolerance of ambiguity was held by Frenkel-Brunswick to be the social marginality of the parents.[13] Saenger adds his observation that the parents of the family would experience as a rule status anxiety.[14] This ties up with our characterization of the North African family experiencing status and role deprivation due to their immigration to Israel. The status anxiety in the present context could also be linked to the physical incapacitation or other personal deprivation of the father, which we have hypothesized as underlying his pressures to stigmatize. The authoritarianism of the family and especially the father is by itself a potent breeder of intolerance of

[12] An unpublished research report by the author and Mr. G. Rahav entitled "Social Stigma and Prostitution," deals with the empirical application of the stigma premises to the etiology of prostitution.
[13] E. Frenkel-Brunswick, "Intolerance of Ambiguity as an Emotional and Perceptual Variable" *Journal of Personality*, 1949, 18; "A Study of Prejudice in Children," *Human Relations*, 1948, 1.
[14] Saenger, *The Social Psychology of Prejudice*, p. 124.

ambiguity. Normative mandates and values tend to converge around the two extreme poles of "positiveness" and "negativeness" with very little in between. Things are either very good or very evil, pitch dark or radiating with light, utterly polluted or divinely pure. The girl would show quite distinct compartmentalization of her ego. This would be linked presumably to the extreme polarization of attitudes inherent in intolerance of ambiguity as a personality trait. We may skip over, at this stage, all the processes which predisposed the father to stigmatize his daughter and the latter to serve as a receptacle of these derogatory attributes. These were relevant for the actual study of the etiology of prostitution and not for our present purposes. We may, however, proceed from the stage when the girl has already started to internalize the derogatory roles assigned to her by the stigmatizing members of the family. This would take place presumably at the formative years, pre-adolescence, and adolescence in a state which is denoted by Erikson as ego-diffusion.[15] This would make the stigma of badness, pollution, inadequacy, "source of trouble," and all the other derogatory tags hurled at her in these relevant periods the most readily accessible "raw material" which the girl would internalize as the framework and anchor of her ego-identity.

We may hypothesize at this stage that at least a part of her self-concept has been built and reinforced by the internalized evil, pollution, and projected vileness cast on her by the stigmatizing others. If we follow, which indeed we do, the Meadean hypotheses of self-formation and the other symbolic interactionists, we may see the girl as building her ego-identity only and insofar as it is a role-complementarity of the expectations of the generalized or relevant others. In the tightly knit North African family, internally cohesive, and relatively isolated, normatively, the role expectations in the family from the girl, in this case the stigma, would have optimal force and efficacy. We may even go so far as to hypothesize that the stigma projected towards her would be the most relevant component with which the girl constructs her ego identity in a "symbolic interaction" frame of reference. After the internalization of the stigma and partial achievement of ego-identity thereby we may avail ourselves of the norm conflict frame of reference and hypothesize a dichotomous divergence of the effects of stigmatization as related to Rosenzweig's conceptualization and tracing of an individual's reaction to frustration.[16] We may exclude the possibility of the girl reacting in an

[15] Erik H. Erikson, *Childhood and Society*, Norton & Co., 1950; "The Problem of Identity," *Journal of American Psychiatric Association*, 1956, 1.
[16] Saul Rosenzweig, "Types of Reaction to Frustration" and "Study of Repression," in Murray's *Explorations in Personality*, New York: Oxford University Press, 1938.

impunitive passive manner as quite remote. This is so because the extreme stimuli she is exposed to, as hypothesized by us in relation to both the parent's and the girl's predisposition to stigma, would generate, presumably, an extreme or at least active reaction and not a passive one. The remaining relevant reactions would be either the intrapunitive, that is, relating the causes of failure to herself, or the extrapunitive one, that is, relating the causes of failure to the outside world, in this case her parents and her family.

In the intrapunitive reaction the normative conflict would develop in the following manner: the girl would internalize the projected derogatory image as a compliance with the expectations of her socializers, in this case the stigmatizing member of the family. She would then expect a reinforcement of her conduct by the relevant adults. We have hypothesized the complementarity of roles inherent in the stigmatizer-stigmatized relationship; the compliance of the girl with the stigma induces her to expect acceptance, approval, and a sanction of accomplishment from her parents. After all, she has complied with their overt and covert expectations from her. She expects, in a way, her parents to fulfil their part of this "dyadic bargain." Naturally it fails to materialize and here is where the norm conflict frame of reference steps in, because no parents would approve cognitively of the "evil" behavior of their daughter, although they prescribed this behavior subconsciously by transmitting stigmata on her. This is the initial normative conflict to which the girl has to react. Being intrapunitive she would impute the causes of this conflict between the expectations of her parents and their actual reaction to her behavior to herself. She would tend to blame herself for not complying properly enough to the stigmatizing expectations of her parents. She would therefore carry on compulsively and ever more extremely the derogatory behavior prescribed by her parents. Expecting thereby a complementary acceptance by them. She is geared of course to receiving subconsciously their transmissions of stigma as inherent in their behavior towards her. This is to her the actual behavioral mandate to which she imputes legitimacy. The overt vociferous rejection of the parents, which she experiences subsequent to her behavioral compliance with the stigma, is of course perceived by her as a dissonance. However, she would again tend to blame herself for this normative conflict resulting in the positive feedback cycle of extreme negativistic behavior, which might result in almost ritualistic performance of the various deviations connected with sexual promiscuity and other breaches of accepted norms. Characteristically, it would not be coupled with the rejection of the stigmatizing parents, however harsh they would be in their treatment of her both verbally and physically.

The other channel of normative-conflict linked with an extrapunitive type of reaction would be as follows. After complying with the derogatory image cast on her and behaving accordingly, for example, sexual promiscuity, petty larceny, truancy, etc., the girl will also expect an initial reinforcement sanction from the parents. Failing this, a sharp normative conflict would ensue, and the girl would accuse her parents of bringing upon her this cognitive dissonance. She will react to her parents' rejection of her by her counterrejection of them. The positive feedback cycle in this case would result in a complete separation of the girl from her family with an ultimate severance of all ties between them.

These two instances of role and norm conflict as mental conflicts may seem to be rather extreme "pure" theoretical cases that rarely exist in real "life situations." The various possibilities short of the extreme dichotomous reaction to the norm conflicts are also feasible as well as a combination of the two. However in the present case of girls from North African authoritarian families, the rather extreme polar reaction to norm conflict would be more probable. This is so because the very traits which predispose the girl to be a recipient of stigma, for example, conspicuity, "other-directedness," intolerance of ambiguity, with her resultant compulsive overconformity to or rejection of the stigmatized roles and norms projected on her tend to make her marginal and estranged within the family. We have evidence that marginal individuals would tend to be of higher ego-involvement towards roles and norms.[17] The girl would therefore be more predisposed to alternate extremely in her roles and to be more vulnerable to normative conflicts. The choice of either the intrapunitive compulsive conformity to stigma and the extrapunitive rejection and counterrejection of family cycle would be presumably more imminent in her case.

Norm Conflict and Value Deviation

In the two previous sections we have dealt with the application of the norm conflict frame of reference to the etiology on the personality level of delinquency and overt deviant behavior. In the present section we shall try to link norm conflict as mental conflict with value deviation that is not necessarily accompanied by overt deviant behavior. We have shown elsewhere that the generic syndrome of social deviation, taken as the dependent variable, would have social stigma, deviant behavior, and value deviation as the independent variables.[18] Indeed norm con-

[17] M. Sherif and H. Cantril, *The Psychology of Ego-Involvement*, New York: Science Editions, 1967, pp. 21 and 61.
[18] See S. Shoham. *Crime and Social Deviation*, Chicago: Henry Regnery Co., 1966, Chapter 14.

flicts as mental conflict are almost *ex definitione* a condition precedent to value deviation.

Albert Camus sees the absurd, which is the epitome of value deviation, as the confrontation of the irrational world and "the wild longing for clarity whose call echoes in the human heart."[19] In crude epistemology this would mean that value deviation is a disjuncture between one's own ideal image of what things should be and what they are now. We may reformulate Camus' statement as meaning that value deviation is a state of mind following an unsuccessful attempt to bridge over a normative disjunction between previously internalized norms and novel normative transmissions at a given time.

Our conception of value deviation is therefore a dynamic one, a final link in a trichotomous chain. First, there is the initial normative gap between the norms already internalized by a person and the diverging or contradicting norms that are subsequently sent over toward him by the group. Second, there are the efforts of the individual to resolve this normative conflict, and, finally, in case of failure, there is a breakdown of values, a stultification of involvement.

This dynamic conception of value deviation as a process differs from the exposition of anomie, deviation, and alienation by Merton, Parsons, and Seeman. Theirs is more of a static description, a taxonomized typology. In a sense, our conception of an individual's final failure to resolve his internal normative conflicts is of the ultimate in despair, value-wise, whereas many instances of anomie as described by, inter alia, Merton and Parsons, are faulty coordination of goals and means with the former and a disjuncture between the congruity motive and the activity-passivity continuum with the latter. This, to be sure, is *the initial normative gap* only prior to ego's involvement to bridge it. Moreover, Merton's and Parson's modes of anomic or alienative "adaptations" may be regarded paradoxically as "success stories." Ritualism, for instance, is one of the most coveted "adaptations" or "adjustments" by employers the world over. The ritualist employee at the assembly line or near a desk in the Kafkaesque halls of the mammoth bureaucratic impersonal structures is an asset. His ability to raise means to the level of ends in themselves make him an "ideal worker," a "perfectly adjusted individual" and "an integrated teamworker" in the jargon of the industrial psychologist.

We may examine now the application of the norm conflict frame of reference to the three stages of the process which lead to value deviation. We may start from the basic epistemological premise that a normative

[19] Albert Camus, *The Myth of Sisyphus*, New York: Vintage Books, 1961, p. 61.

disjuncture may occur between the already internalized norms relating to others, self image and objects (the apperceptive configuration) by an individual up to a given time, and the subsequent normative transmissions directed toward him (the transmission configuration). An initial normative gap is thus formed which is subject to two complementary pressures, which have been empirically observed, to close or narrow this normative rift. The first is that ego tends to perceive the new normative transmissions as being more similar, closer, or less contradictory to the previously internalized norms than they are in reality.[20] In other words, ego's subjectivistic bias twists, so to speak, his perception of the new normative transmission to be more in line with his previously internalized ones.[21] This subjective bias serves to adjust or bring the normative transmissions of the group closer to ego's own stance. However, we also have ample empirical evidence on a norm rapprochement initiated from the other direction. Mohammed's tendency is to go over to the normative mountain if the latter fails to comply with the Prophet's perceptual wish that it move over to him. Ego's tendency to conform to the normative transmissions of the group as recorded, inter alia, by Sherif, Asch, Crutchfield, and Stoner indicate also the basic need of the individual homo sapiens for value and norm congruity. Whatever the sources or theoretical explanations of this need, which are far from being clear, we may take it as axiomatic that human beings abhor a normative disjunction. The individual's tendency to conform to the normative transmissions of the group is complementary to his tendency to subjectivize his novel perceptions so that they concord more to his previously internalized norms. As far as congruity is concerned, these two have the same effect of closing or narrowing the initial normative disjuncture.

It should be stressed that these two complementary factors, which are linked with the narrowing of a normative gap as perceived by an individual, are *measurable personality traits* that determine the perceived normative conflict as being wide or narrow. The subsequent stage would be ego's congruity motivated involvement to bridge this initial normative rift. Another relevant variable is the *scope* as distinguished from the *depth* of norm internalization. The former is related to ego's levels of knowledge. The crudest level would be mere perception, generated by whatever the distal object "out there" may be, as stimulus and absorbed by ego's senses. This is hardly knowledge. Here physical perception is

[20] This presupposes that we know what the norms really are in the epistemological sense, which, of course, we do not. We have chosen, however, the easy refuge of disregarding the intricacies of the ontology of norms altogether.
[21] S. F. Myamoto and S. Dornbush: "A Test of the Symbolic Interactionist Hypothesis of Self-Conception," *Am. J. Soc.*, 617:399–403 (March 1956).

rather meaningless. It does not define for ego his rights and duties in relation to the perceived stimuli. Meaningful knowledge is normative knowledge, and normative knowledge may be further dichotomized into intellectual normative cognition and affective knowledge of normative feeling. Naturally the ability of the previously internalized norms to hold their own against the assailing new norms would depend on the former operating with full affective normativeness, so that ego *feels* and is attached *emotionally* to them or they may be related to ego by rational cognition only.[22] As an interim summary of our present efforts to relate norm conflict as mental conflicts to the genesis of value deviation, we may specify two contrasting probability profiles at the two extremes of a continuum. The high conflict profile would have a deep previously internalized set of norms coupled with its affective cognition by ego. The inconsistent new normative transmission would be effective and a wide initial gap (relative to content) would exist between the two sets of norms. The low conflict profile would be related to ineffective normative transmission, to the narrow gap between the transmitted and internalized sets of norms, and to a shallow previous internalization of norms and their cognitive knowledge. The high conflict profiles would be the arena of ego's involvement to resolve and bridge over the normative disjuncture constituting his mental conflict. He would be urged and pressed to accomplish it by his mysterious need for coherence, unity, and harmony, which has been known to motivate the *homini sapienti* from the times of Parmenides to the modern exponents of the principle of consistency in social psychology. This has been established both theoretically and empirically. The so-called "principle of consistency" has been studied extensively. "The human mind" says Roger Brown, "has a strong need for consistency and attitudes are generally changed in order to eliminate some inconsistency. This principle derives in part from the many experimental studies that antedate its systematic formulation."[23]

Why there should be a human tendency to look for the consistent, for the comprehensive unity and harmony, is a matter of conjecture. It is, however, evident that most innovators in the study of human behavior from Freud to Lewin have taken this principle of consistency as one of their basic axioms. Brown's own hypothesis seems sound enough to be theoretically attractive. He says: "A situation of inconsistency is one that calls for mutually incompatible actions. Inconsistency in the mind threatens to paralyze action."[24] Indeed, whoever propels us

[22] Sellin also stresses the emotional significance of a norm as a barrier against its infringement. *Culture Conflict and Crime, op. cit.*, p. 44.
[23] Roger Brown, *Social Psychology*, New York: Free Press, 1965, p. 549.
[24] *Ibid.*, p. 606.

to move, to act, to perceive, to cogitate, and react affectively installed built-in defenses against paralyzing norm conflicts. Normative dissonance might amount to inertia and lead to the mythical fate of Burridan's Ass.

NORM CONFLICT AND THE CRIMINAL
OR DEVIANT GROUP

Wolfgang and Ferracuti have based their recent analysis of the subculture of violence on the axiomatic premise that criminal groups are *part of and not apart* from the value systems of the prevailing culture.[25] Some of the values of the subculture may be tolerated by and concordant to the values of the prevailing culture and some intolerant by the latter and discordant to them.[26] This approach would be quite in line with the norm conflict frame of reference. It is an entirely different level of analysis than the group conflict conception of Simmel, Park, Burgess, and Coser stemming out of the conflict theory of society. By applying the culture conflict premises to the dynamic normative conflicts between the criminal group and the prevailing culture, we are operating on a rather pragmatic level, and we need not take sides in the mainly ideological deliberations of the conflict theorists, whether the groups (criminal subcultures inclusive) that are in conflict with the prevailing society are functional or dysfunctional to it.[27]

We may, therefore, hypothesize two norm and value continua, one for the criminal group and the other for the individuals who are associated with it. These continua would have at one extreme the ideal-type conformist individual (or the group as measured by its total score on appropriate attitude scales) whose discordant values and conflicting norms with the prevailing normative system would be minimal. On the other extreme would be the individuals or groups in total war with the "legitimate" normative system. These complete normative negations would occur with the "contracultures" as described by Yinger:[28] a subculture which is in antithetical normative opposition to the prevailing culture. An individual or group may be placed at a given time on a point on the continua or move along it depending on the amount and severity of their normative conflicts with the predominant normative system.

[25] M. E. Wolfgang and F. Ferracuti, *The Subculture of Violence*, London: Tavistock, 1967, p. 111.
[26] *Ibid.*
[27] The "off the record" view of the author is that the criminal group is indeed functional in many ways to the society at large.
[28] Milton Yinger, "Contraculture and Subculture," *Am. Soc. Rev.*, 25:625–635 (October 1960).

Sellin and Wolfgang have devised a ratio scale to measure the concord or discord of the values and norms of a given subculture vis-à-vis the predominant culture.[29] The author and a research team are presently engaged in the construction of some interval scales to measure norm conflict among delinquent youth in Israel as auxiliary tools to an action research on street-corner youth in some slum areas in Tel Aviv.[30]

Norm Conflict and Juvenile Subcultures in Israel

The project was planned for boys and girls between 14 and 18 and organized into some thirty informal "street-corner" groups. Coming from slum areas these boys and girls stem by definition from families of lower socioeconomic status. They are mostly of oriental origin (Middle Eastern basin and North Africa) and have a significantly high proportion of first generation children of immigrant parents. The groups ranged *prima facie* from slight deviancy to overt delinquency with heavy police records. We assumed also[31] a significant homogeneity of the groups as far as ethnicity, socioeconomic status, and length of stay in the country was concerned.

Our first task was to devise an instrument by which to measure the value and norm discord of the groups so that they may be placed on the conformity-deviation continuum in relation to the prevailing normative system. In order to quantify the range between discord and concord we have taken the inmates of Tel Mond Prison to represent extreme deviance. Tel Mond would be the last stage of the punitive measures taken against a young-adult offender after probation, binding over to keep-the-peace, juvenile institutions, and suspended sentences of imprisonment have proved to be of no avail.[32] The extremity of deviance for girls would be represented by the inmates of Zofia, an institution for young prostitutes and girls "in need of care protection," most of whom were already associated with the pimp-prostitute-gambling and drug subcultures.[33]

The conformity pole would be represented by a youth club in southern Tel Aviv. The distribution of ethnicity, socioeconomic status and length

[29] T. Sellin and M. E. Wolfgang: *The Measurement of Delinquency*, New York: Wiley, 1964, Chapters 15–20.

[30] The project is carried out under the joint sponsorship of The Ministry of Education and Culture, Jerusalem, Israel, and the Department of Psychology, Tel Aviv University. The educational supervision is carried out by Mr. A. Kreisler of The Ministry of Education, and the planning and execution of the research is carried out by the author.

[31] This assumption was endorsed initially by a pilot study.

[32] S. Shoham, Y. Kaufmann, M. Menaker, "The Tel-Mond Follow-Up Research Project," Part I (in press), *The Houston Law Rev.*

[33] As for the nature of these subcultures in Israel, see S. Shoham, R. Keren, and G. Shavit, "Pimps and Prostitutes: A Criminal Dyad," *Revue Abolitionniste*, 1965.

of stay in the country of the boys and girls in this club are not significantly different than the corresponding distributions among the lads of
Tel Mond and girls at Zofia. The former, however, are attending secondary
school, which by itself is considered a symbol of achievement,[34] and
are pursuing sports, as well as artistic and other leisure-time activities,
approved by the prevailing normative system. In order to identify the
items that discriminate between the concordant and discordant extremes,
we constructed two questionnaires: the first comprised the predisposing
factors to delinquency and deviation that have been found to apply to
Israel. These factors were: broken or conflict-ridden families, more
criminals or deviants in the family, postadolescent maladjustment, mal-
cohesion of family unit, slackening of parental control, urban areas, high
rate of delinquency areas, and relative economic need as defined by the
individual.

This questionnaire posed no special problems of substance or method.
Difficulties were concentrated in the second questionnaire which was
supposed to indicate the extent of discord or alienation from the prevailing values and norms and the adoption of the values and norms of
the delinquent or deviant group. We have tried to utilize some inventories that have been used in the United States to differentiate between
criminal or deviant and noncriminal or conformist individuals. We have
hypothesized that these inventories would be suitable for our purposes
because of the considerable similarity in some relevant aspects between
the United States and Israeli processes of social change. Both societies
have been the site of mass immigration and accelerated urbanization.
Although there is a time-span difference of at least half a century between
the initiation of these processes of social change in the United States
and Israel they have, no doubt, similarly influenced the shaping of both
societies. Moreover, the discord and ethnic conflict experienced by
Negroes and more recently by Puerto Ricans in the United States are
not dissimilar in content, although infinitely smaller in magnitude and
narrower in scope, to the pains of integration of the Oriental Jews in
Israel.

Eight of the inventories that we have intended to use were *prima facie*,
adequate for our purposes because they were supposed to measure
norm and value discord of a subculture vis-à-vis the dominant culture
and the processes of an individual's alienation from the normative system
of his group. These eight scales were: Rothstein's Self-Concept Scale,[35]

[34] Not unlike Whytes' "college boys" in his Street Corner Society. *The Social Structure of an Italian Slum*, Chicago: The University of Chicago Press, 1955, pp. 95 et seq.
[35] Edward Rothstein, "An Analysis of Status Images as Perception Variables Between
Delinquent and Non-delinquent Boys," unpublished Ph.D. dissertation, New York
University, 1961.

the Pd Scale of MMPI,[36] the Crissman Moral Judgments Scale,[37] the Neal and Rettig scales for powerlessness and normlessness,[38] the Srole scale of anomie,[39] and the Landis and Scarpitti instruments to measure value orientation and awareness of limited opportunity.[40]

Of these eight instruments the first six did not discriminate properly between the delinquents and nondelinquents in Israel.[41] This quite unusual result might perhaps be explained by the intrinsic difference between the processes of cultural integration and change in the United States and Israel. The Jews of the Diaspora belonged invariably to a minority that cherished a value and norm system quite distinct from the dominant culture. They were more or less a subculture within the prevailing wider culture. When he immigrates to Israel, the Diaspora Jew realizes that the norm and value system of his Jewish minority subculture in his country of origin loses its meaning and he is confronted with the normative system of the wider Israeli society to which he is supposed to adjust. This would apply particularly to the youth of Oriental immigrant parentage. As a result of the slackening of parental control after immigration, the weakening of the authoritarian structure of the family and the influence of his peers, he would be oriented toward the wider Israeli culture to which he is constantly exposed through school, youth movements, and the army. This process might be rather different from the culture conflict generated by immigration to the United States or other immigration countries. The Puerto Rican immigrant, for instance, is transformed from a member in a dominant culture to a member in an ethnic minority to which he may retreat and look for solace from the plights of his confrontation with the prevailing American culture. This aspect of culture conflict, which has not been explored as yet in sociological literature might account for the inapplicability of the six inventories to the Israeli youth. A further support for this hypothesis stems from the replication to Israel of the two Likert-type scales de-

[36] Starke H. Hathaway and Elio D. Monachesi, "The Minnesota Multiphasic Personality Inventory in the Study of Juvenile Delinquents," *American Sociological Review*, 17:704–710, 1952.

[37] Paul Crissman, "Temporal Changes and Sexual Differences in Moral Judgments," *Journal of Social Psychology*, 16:29–38, 1942.

[38] Arthur G. Neal and Salomon Rettig, "Dimensions of Alienation Among Manual and Non-manual Workers," *American Sociological Review*, 28:599–608, 1963.

[39] Leo Srole, "Social Integration and Certain Corollaries," *American Sociological Review*, 21:709–716, 1956.

[40] J. R. Landis, S. Dinitz, and W. C. Reckless, "Implementing Two Theories of Delinquency: Value Orientation and Awareness of Limited Opportunity," *Sociology and Social Research* (1963), Vol. 47, No. 4.

[41] S. Shoham and E. Shaskolsky, "A Cross-Cultural Analysis of Delinquents and Non-delinquents in Israel," a paper delivered at the annual meeting of the A.S.A. at San Francisco, August 1967.

veloped by Landis and Scarpitti to measure the applicability of the Albert Cohen and the Cloward and Ohlin theories on the subcultures of delinquency. These have proved to be of a greater significance to the etiology of delinquent gang formation in Israel than in the United States.[42] It might tentatively be explained, at least as far as Cohen's theory is concerned, that a mass immigration country like Israel, the Jewish population of which has quadrupled in the last two decades, could be more fruitfully studied for the purposes of determining the pressures towards juvenile subculture formation within the culture conflict frame of reference, as an arena of norm conflict between the conduct norms of the various ethnic groups and the new immigrants holding (mutatis mutandis) the underprivileged position that the lower classes held in Cohen's causal scheme.[43] We have then constructed four additional scales of our own to measure norm conflict within the family and with other socializing agencies, awareness of access to *illegitimate* structures, awareness of social stigma as a pressure to delinquency and deviation, and the value affinity to the delinquent or deviant group.

After the two extremes of the value and norm discord-concord continuum are determined and the items that discriminate significantly between the delinquent or deviant and the nondelinquent or conforming youth are chosen, the various groups through their individuals would be placed on this interval scale. The latter would be readministered to the groups every two months to measure their movement along the scale towards or away from conformity. The field workers assigned to the groups would have a dual task: the educational and preventive task which has to be carried out through acceptance by the group. In order to have any effect at all the workers have to penetrate the groups and seek the voluntary collaboration of their individuals *on the latter's own terms.* This is no mean task and its success or failure, which would be more determined by the workers' personality than by any ready-made recipe, would be a condition precedent to the subsequent correctional and research activities of the field worker. The preventive efforts would evidently not be directed towards the predisposing crimogenic factors. These are inherent in the social structure and cultures of societies.

The Extreme Pole of Normative Negation

A case that may portray, mainly for didactic reasons, the extremity of normative discord of a criminal and his group with "legitimate society"

[42] S. Shoham, R. Erez and W. C. Reckless, "Value Orientation and Awareness of Differential Opportunity of Delinquent and Non-delinquent Boys in Israel," *British Journal of Criminology*, July 1965.
[43] *Ibid.*, p. 331.

is Jean Genet the thief-playwright-philosopher. Genet has succeeded in conveying in a devastatingly sincere manner his self-image as a criminal and the ideology of the criminal group. He records with minute details his self-image as a criminal and describes in a greater-than-life grandeur the underworld, along with its norms and values. He also raises to antimatter absolutes his diametric negativity towards the legitimate world and its institutions. Genet's self-image is, no doubt, one of a thief, an ex-con, and a member of the criminal subculture. His writings are very personal. Although fact and fiction intermingle, most of the episodes happened in one way or the other with Genet as participant. The result is a melange of personal experience, feelings, and reminiscences. Genet describes the structure of the criminal group as a loosely organized band. The leaders, the "directors," chose the location of the "job," drew the plans, supervised the performance, and sold the stolen property for a considerable commission, of course.[44]

The value and norm-separation of the stigmatized criminal and deviant from the rest of "your (legitimate "square") world" creates a caste of outcasts who have to unite for sheer survival and create a normative system of their own. This system is based on the common denominator of apartedness but it needs also a common value system and an *apologia pro esse suam*. Criminals and deviants must find, therefore, a justification for being what they are "otherwise how could one live"?[45] Like everyone else they must create a coherent self-image and determine for themselves the essence of their reference and membership groups. The criminals and deviants envelop themselves in a woven garment of rationalizations, of explanations and explained-away *resentiment* to build and define one's image as a member of a criminal and deviant group and, what is more, to protect themselves from the corroding attacks of "your world."

The novice criminal looks for value rationalizations to account for his criminal deeds; not so the hardened professional one—he has no illusions, his ambivalence towards the legitimate norms is a thing of the past, and he knows that the immediate aim of his crime is purely lucrative. The trinity of moral vigor, freedom, and fulfillment imputed by Genet to his own crimes is inevitably related to the criminal and deviant existence of the group as a whole. With them, moral vigor is also inherent in the acceptance of their destiny.[46] They have finally become what they have been tagged as being. "Your world" defined and isolated the group and allocated for them some space outside the borders of the legitimized

[44] *Our Lady of The Flowers,* New York: Bantam Books, 1964, p. 103.
[45] *The Thief's Journal,* New York: Grove Press, 1964, p. 12.
[46] *Ibid.,* p. 101.

norms. By accepting the roles of criminals or outsiders in a special group, they have been, so to speak, institutionalized within the social structure, although the "wrong" part of it. Being a criminal clarifies any ambiguity we may have as to our identity. Doubts are subsided by every subsequent criminal act, which reinforces the resolution of inner conflicts. The thief in the group defines himself by his crime. Each consecutive theft delimits his social contours, and he liberates himself thereby from norm and value confusion. Murder is considered to be the most noble of crimes because, inter alia, it has (more than any other crime) the ritualistic finality of severing its perpetrator from "your world," the society of legitimized fakes. The murderer holding the knife, the gun, or the phial has the superhuman and extralucid state of mind of the damned.[47] He has started thereby the descent (or ascent) to the precipice.

CULTURE CONFLICT, CRIME, AND DEVIATION ON THE SOCIAL LEVEL OF ANALYSIS

Fluctuations in crime rates and special types of delinquency and deviation in a given society and their significant links to some socio-cultural factors have been a perennial prime area for culture conflict research. Most of the frequently quoted research findings in the field, which have been associated with the culture conflict frame of reference, have dealt with the rates and volume of crime in a specific culture as a unit of analysis. To be included here are the classic studies summarized by Sellin[48]—Thomas and Znaniecki, Pauline Young, Hayner, Lind, Ross and Stofflet—as well as the later studies by Van Vechten,[49] Savitz,[50] Wood in Ceylon,[51] Garavaglia & Ponti in Italy,[52] and Shoham in Israel.[53]

Israel is a natural laboratory for studying the hypotheses related

[47] *Our Lady of The Flowers*, p. 120.
[48] *Culture Conflict and Crime*, Chapter IV.
[49] "Criminality of the Foreign Born," *J. Crim. L. and Criminol.* July-August 1941, Vol. 32, pp. 139–147.
[50] "Delinquency and Migration," in Wolfgang et al., *The Sociology of Crime and Delinquency*, pp. 199–205.
[51] A. L. Wood, "Crime and Aggression in Changing Ceylon," *Transactions of the American Philosophical Society*, Vol. 51 (1961).
[52] "Immigrazione e Criminalità," *Quaderni di Criminolgia Clinica*, July-Sept. 1963, pp. 347–58.
[53] "The Application of the 'Culture-Conflict' Hypothesis to the Criminality of Immigrants in Israel," *J. Crim. L., Criminol. and Police Sci.*, June 1962, pp. 207–214; with N. Shoham and A. Abd-El-Razek: "Immigration, Ethnicity and Ecology as Related to Juvenile Delinquency in Israel," *The Brit. J. of Criminology*, October 1966, pp. 391–409.

to the culture conflict frame of reference on the social level.[54] This is mainly for the following reasons:

1. Israel has more than 70 ethnic groups, which display a wide cultural divergence among its nearly 2.5 million Jews.

2. The flow of Jewish immigration into the country was almost continuous from the end of last century to the present. The most conspicuous fact about this immigration is that it quadrupled the Jewish population of the country. The population census from the beginning of 1948 (toward the end of the British Mandate) showed 649,700 Jews whereas, at the end of 1964, there were in Israel 2,155,600 Jews.

3. A quarter of a million Arabs have lived for the last 20 years in Israel and were exposed to Jewish value systems. After the war in June 1967, another million Arabs are being exposed to a sudden culture conflict which, no doubt, engulfs its whole normative system.

4. The rural-urban distribution is varied, ranging from the communal Kibbutzim to highly urbanized centers. This affords an adequate application of the culture conflict thesis to the ecological dimension.

5. Marked fluctuations from social anomie to extreme eunomie have been observed through the periodic wars, that is, from 1949 to 1956 to 1967.

6. The country is relatively small (7992 sq. miles) and all the discordant cultural heterogeneities inherent in the demographic structure of its population are contained within a rather compact arena.

Indeed some meaningful findings have been gleaned from recent research on culture conflict, crime, and delinquency in Israel. These dealt, inter alia, with the following: the crime rates of immigrants compared with the rates of native-born and those who immigrated to Israel before the establishment of the State (May 1948); the divergence of types and severity of crimes committed by immigrants from different countries of origin and different ethnic groups; the delinquency of native youth (or those who immigrated very young) of foreign-born parents;[55] the rates of crime and delinquency as related to the cultural gap between the immigrants and the absorbing community; the rural-urban variable, homogeneity of ethnicity or the lack of it in a settlement or a community, and high or low normative cohesion as related to juvenile delinquency; horizontal and vertical mobility of immigrants and the barriers against the latter related to the delinquency and crime rates in some ethnic groups.[56]

[54] S. Shoham, "Criminology in Israel," *The Juridical Review*, 1966, Part 1, p. 30.
[55] S. Shoham, "The Application of the 'Culture-Conflict' Hypothesis etc.," *op. cit.*
[56] S. Shoham, N. Shoham, and A. Abd-El-Razek, "Immigration, Ethnicity etc. . . .," *op. cit.*

However, no full-scale exhaustive research on social change, crime, and deviation in Israel has, as yet, been undertaken. The next decade would be, presumably, ideal for this comprehensive research because the processes of cultural integration in the receiving community of the immigration waves of the early fifties would be in full force. These could be related by themselves to delinquency and deviation as well as compared with cultural conflicts and norm discord, which would still be rife.

Some Criminal and Deviant "Life Situations"

Sellin has advocated research into delineated relatively narrow "life situations."[57] These are some distinct types of criminal or deviant acts which have not only a common legal or other socionormative basis but also a behavioral common denominator. The application of the culture conflict thesis to the study of these criminal "life situations" might open up new vistas of insight when carried out in countries of mass immigration and rapid social change, such as Israel. Even a superficial survey of the homicide cases investigated last year by the Israeli police reveals the following motivations: "blood-revenge" among Bedouins and vendettas among Jewish communities of Oriental origin; daughters becoming pregnant out of wedlock; an argument on different styles of prayer in a synagogue in a rural settlement in the Negev; an Arab wife who insisted on wearing "modern" occidental dresses instead of the customary ones worn by the wives of the *Fellahin* in the village; patricide ensuing out of the Oriental Jewish father's insistence on his traditional right to marry a second wife against the will of his grown up sons; and, finally, a ritualistic sacrifice of the best-looking five-year-old girl in a family of six daughters as a traditional "sure-magic" guarantee for the birth of a son and heir.

A recent explorative study of drug addiction in Israel describes the smoking habits of Jews who immigrated to Israel from North Africa and the Middle East. The use of hashish was formally forbidden in their countries of origin but was deeply ingrained in the cultural systems of some regions or at least tolerated by them. This is explained by the Moslem proscription of alcohol but not of other narcotics or intoxicants. In Israel they found no difficulty in providing themselves with enough hashish to satisfy their habit. Israel is on the traffic line between Syria and Lebanon, which are the major producers and exporters of the drug, and Egypt, Sudan, and the countries of the Maghreb, which are the main consumers of hashish in the area.

The group in the research population used to purchase the hashish

[57] *Culture Conflict and Crime*, pp. 44–45.

"soles," weighing approximately 300 grams from a Bedouin smuggler in Be'ersheba. There were various brand names, but they usually purchased the best which bore, incidentally, the name of Gamal Abdel Nasser. The group convened every Thursday evening in a room that was equipped with cushioned Oriental sofas, water pipes, and a television set tuned to Cairo. The smoking would start with the program by the Egyptian singer Um-Khaltoum, which lasts from four to five hours. The members of the group getting "high" from a combination of hashish and the smoky voice of the singer. At these sessions the group which consisted of around fifteen persons would consume a whole "sole" of hashish averaging two "fingers" (approximately 20 grams) per person.[58]

As for the prostitution study and its relation to the culture conflict thesis as a sui generis "life situation," we may note the preponderance of the North African prostitutes in the country and the specific cultural attributes inherent in the etiology of prostitution as related to the authoritarian structure of the North African Jewish family. Forty-two percent of the prostitutes in our research sample were from North African origin.[59] The latter comprised 50 percent of the foreign-born of our research sample, compared with 13 percent in the total population of Israel. The data as to the age distribution of the sample reveals a middle-age group of 18–20. That means that the majority of North African prostitutes have entered the country with their parents while being less than ten years old in the great influx of Jewish immigration to the country in the years 1956–1958. These findings would be supported by the fact that 40 percent of the immigrants from North Africa in the relevant years (1957–1958) were children of less than 14 years of age. This by itself may indicate two complementary avenues of research based on both culture and stigma premises. The first one is related presumably to the culture patterns of some families of North African origin that are presumably more predisposed towards the phenomenon under consideration. One fruitful source of investigation would be a deep anthropological study of Jewish life in the Melah and the other Jewish quarters in the major towns in North Africa. This type of research has not been explored to our knowledge; however, some relevant studies have been carried out on North African immigrants after their immigration to this country. Some findings of these studies, which are closely linked to the culture conflict thesis may be briefly mentioned.

The Jewish North African immigrants to Israel had some well-focused

[58] Irit Friedman and Ilana Peer, "Drug Addiction among Pimps and Prostitutes in Israel." An unpublished report, submitted to the Department of Psychology, The University of Tel Aviv, 1967.
[59] S. Shoham and G. Rahav, "Social Stigma and Prostitution," op. cit., p. 40.

adjustment problems in their countries of origin. The latter underwent a rapid process of modernization in the last decades. In this process, the Jews suffered special strains because they were both a minority group and the local middle class, so that they had experienced high barriers against upper vertical mobility.[60] To these stresses we may add the secularization of the communities, the disintegration of the patrilineal units, and the political struggle, which made it clear that the Jews were a marginal group outside or between the combatant "imperialists" and the "patriots." Most postimmigration problems stemmed from the fact that largely the lower and middle classes immigrated to Israel, while the upper classes and the intellectual elite immigrated to other countries, mainly France.[61] The new immigrants, who came to Israel full of expectations to ameliorate their socioeconomic status, suffered deep frustration and a feeling of discrimination when their lower educational and technical levels forced them to remain largely in the lower classes of this country.[62]

Worse still, the "Moroccan" became a stereotype for scapegoating, for symbolizing all the "negative" qualities of the Oriental Jews, as perceived by the Europeans. This collective stigmatization caused the North Africans in many instances to accept the stereotype and, having no internal leadership,[63] they experienced self-hatred and community disorganization with marked symptoms of group and individual anomie. The social status of the family subsequent to immigration to Israel has been described in half of the cases of our research sample as lower than in the countries of origin. The overall picture that emerges is a family controlled by a rigid and authoritarian father. Twenty-five percent of the parents, either father, mother, or both, have been physically or mentally ill. More than 30 percent of the fathers were found to be drug addicts and alcoholics. The families were riddled with inadequacies and physical sickness, and their socioeconomic status had deteriorated because of immigration to Israel. These findings support initially a hypothesis based on culture conflict premises as to the predisposition of the father toward stigmatizing his daughters with deviant roles due to his incapacitation, personal deprivation, and relative deprivation as a result of the change in his social position following immigration.

[60] A. Weingrod, Moroccan Jewry in Transition, "Megamot," Jerusalem, January 1960. H. H. Tahon, Subgroups in Israel, Jerusalem, 1957. R. Bar-Josef, The Moroccans, "Molad," Jerusalem, July 1959.
[61] R. Zamir, Beer-Sheva, 1958-1959, The Hebrew University, 1964.
[62] J. Matras, Social Change in Israel, Chicago, 1965.
[63] R. Bar-Josef, ibid. J. Shuval, "Social Problems in Development Towns," The Institute of Applied Social Research, Jerusalem, 1959, pp. 43, 56-57, 67.

Culture Conflict, Delinquency, and Deviation
Among Arab Youth in Israel

Our last area of study in the present context is loaded with some violent processes of norm conflict. It is related to social change and deviance among both the Arab minority in Israel, which has been exposed to Jewish culture for the last twenty years, and the Arab population in the new areas, which became exposed to Israeli culture after the war in June 1967. The striking fact here is that only 15 percent of the 17–19 year-olds in Israel were Arabs,[64] and yet they committed 31 percent of all delinquent acts for this age group. Thus, their delinquency rate is twice that of their Jewish peers. The background for this seems quite fruitfully to be related to culture conflict.

There has been a marked internal migration of Arab rural youth to Jewish urban centers. Many Arab youth leave their villages for the city where the opportunities for employment are considerably greater. In the city they are immediately confronted with insurmountable problems. They are unable to obtain decent housing for a complex of reasons, ranging from general unavailability of good low-rental housing to the reluctance of some Jewish families to rent to Arabs. As a result, the Arabs are forced to move into slums where they must pay relatively high rents in order to live in crowded substandard quarters. The marginality of the Arab youth is augmented by lack of almost any integration with their Jewish peers. They are also unable to meet girls with whom they can live socially acceptable lives. They are forced to consort with prostitutes because Arab girls do not migrate to the city, and intermarriage is considered undesirable by both Jews and Arabs.

The Arab village itself is also undergoing a rapid process of secularization. Traditionally, the village was divided into 2–6 groups (Hamolah), each Hamolah being an independent economic unit. The Hamolah was composed of the old father, his wives, his married sons, their wives and children, and his unmarried sons. All the males worked on the farm while the women, guided by the husband's eldest wife, worked in the home and engaged in light agricultural tasks. When the father died, his land was divided equally among his sons. With the establishment of the State of Israel, more jobs became available both within and outside the village. This weakened the father's authority and the family cohesion. The Arab village is also being urbanized at such a rapid rate that it is predicted that within the next decade it will closely resemble the city so far as its normative structure is concerned. However, a twofold point should be stressed: (1) despite changes in village life,

[64] This is before June 1967.

its structure and demands on the youth are in sharp contrast to those of city life; (2) because of changes in village life itself, a certain amount of value conflict exists even before the youth leaves the village. The culture conflict thesis applied to the present context would postulate that the shock of urban society, coupled with a changing traditional society, generates strain, a condition congenial to delinquency. Judging from research on the American Negro, individuals who experience the strain engendered by this kind of conflict and, particularly, those who experience these structural barriers often turn to deviant behavior, develop *lower aspirations* and motivations, and may even be incapable of taking advantage of opportunities that may become available later.

As a possible model for research we may focus on the following independent variables as linked to the dependent variable of delinquency and deviation among the Arab youth in Israel: (1) the urbanization of the Arab village and the disintegration of its rural-agricultural structures; (2) the secularization of its traditional structures. The weakening of family ties and religious authorities; (3) norm conflict due to migration of the youth to Jewish centers and exposure to Jewish conduct norms that are brought over to the Arab areas. These three groups of variables are not truly independent of each other; internal migration, for instance, would, no doubt, enhance the urbanization and secularization processes and vice versa. The control aspect is inherent in the almost perfect isolation of norm conflict due to migration, from the other variables of social change. The Arab population in Israel was subject to the former as a result of its contact with the Jewish population for the last nineteen years. In the new areas, however, the urbanization and secularization processes indeed took place but the exposure to Israeli patterns of behavior and mutual normative contact started only with the opening of the borders after the Six Days War in June 1967. Thus, there exists a rare opportunity to study some major forms of social change, highly focused and differentiated from the other independent variables, and relate them to norm conflict, delinquency, and deviation.

6

Anomie, Culture Conflict and Crime in Disorganized and Overorganized Societies*

STEPHEN SCHAFER

The term "anomie" first appeared in 1893 in Emile Durkheim's *Division of Labor in Society*,[1] but almost a half a century passed before it had been revived and applied to the understanding of crime,[2] and another two decades before it became one of the most popular explanations in present-day criminology. Although the pattern and quality of crimes have changed since Durkheim observed anomic situations—and they are likely to change even more as society witnesses new power structures and culture conflicts—there is a continuing interest to foster the use of anomie as a conceptual medium for understanding criminal man and delinquent youth.

The discrepancy between culturally prescribed aspirations and social opportunities, in other words the "anomie" situation, is most frequently shown as the fundamental cause of high probabilities of crime in society. Undoubtedly, in recent times the concept of anomie proved to be the most stimulating and provocative contribution in the search for answers to the crime and delinquency problem. However, despite the widespread acceptance of anomie as an explanation of crime, there is surprisingly little reference to its strong relationship to culture conflict, and an even less systematic and operational answer to the problem of finding solutions that an explanation based on anomie would demand.

* It is the author's great personal and professional privilege to offer this paper in honor of Thorsten Sellin: the man, the teacher, and the thinker. It would be difficult to tell the most important issue among the many that Thorsten Sellin has explored and promoted to the lasting enrichment of criminology. This paper has been inspired by one of them: Sellin's theory on culture conflict and crime.
[1] Emile Durkheim, *The Division of Labor in Society*, Glencoe: Free Press, 1950.
[2] Robert K. Merton, "Social Structure and Anomie," *American Sociological Review*, October 1938, Vol. 3, pp. 672–682.

The restriction of most discussions and analyses of anomic situations to the allegedly disorganized American culture, as if anomie were the main explanation for *American* crime or the major characteristic of *American* delinquent subcultures, is an assumption that may lead to some misinterpretation of criminal and delinquent behavior. Authors in some studies apparently try to avoid overt admission of the use of the Mertonian variation of Durkheim's explanation of suicide as their point of departure; at the same time, however, they continue to talk in terms of striving for goals, blocked aspirations, and choices of illegitimate means for achieving these goals. They think in terms of structural imperfection, rather than in terms of conflict. They seem to feel that American crime and delinquency can be explained by the fact that not all of our success values and aspirations are attainable, being blocked in large part by such handicaps as class barriers. This understanding has been advanced as if success goals, aspirations, and barriers to their achievement for a considerable part of the population were exclusively American phenomena. It is as though, in one form or another, they were looking for some *American* but undefined explanation of crime, rather than trying to translate these so-called American symptoms of social structure into the language of culture conflict and to apply them to the universal crime problem. For these studies the "dissociation between culturally defined aspirations and socially structured means"[3] is an exclusive or typical feature of the American society and is necessarily characteristic of its disorganization.

However, the opportunities or lack of opportunities for achieving goals have always been present in all societies, regardless of how they structured themselves. Wealth, income, job, status, prestige, and the like, are goals sought not only by Americans and not only in our affluent if disorganized society, but by other peoples, both now and in other ages. If this were not true the comparative picture of crime as a world problem would appear quite different, and we would see radical differences in the nature of crime throughout the world. If, for instance, the major fact in the explanation of gang behavior is that a significant number of lower-class members "aspire beyond their means,"[4] this same situation could be demonstrated for other groups in other societies. It would seem, therefore, that the concept of illegitimate means for achieving blocked goals is an oversimplified generalization or characteristic and is not the real or only cause of crime or delinquency; at least, it does not provide the answer for these problems. Because all human beings have goals, not all of which

[3] *Ibid.*, p. 679.
[4] Richard A. Cloward and Lloyd E. Ohlin, *Delinquency and Opportunity: A Theory of Delinquent Gangs*, Glencoe: Free Press, 1960, p. 88.

can be achieved by any one person, why have not all people, rather than only a fractional proportion of them, turned to illegitimate alternatives?

From this perspective it seems that anomie might serve as *one* way (and only a generalizing way) of explaining *all* crimes at *all* times rather than just *American* crime and delinquency. Because, as far as we know, crime has been found since the beginning of human history, from the point of view of this approach all crimes have always been committed because of blocked aspirations, whatever their nature: economic, intellectual, communal, sexual, or otherwise. Moreover, it could be said that the whole course of human personality development, from infancy and early childhood to later life, has always been based primarily on learning to strive for certain goals and to live with the attendant frustrations if the goals are, for certain reasons, unattainable. This learning process and their accompanying frustrations have always been a necessary part of group membership. Even in the so-called primitive era of private vengeance and blood revenge the "offender" did not attack his victim only because of some innate drive toward violence, but rather because the victim had some things he wanted and could not achieve them as easily in another way. Perhaps it was food, the skin of an animal, a special stone, or it might even be the status to be gained by power and success. The criminal and delinquent, in a certain sense, have always been goal-oriented; the criminal of today is not basically different from the offender of any other period. Only his aspirations have changed from time to time and from place to place, according to the cultural definitions of that era and society and according to the degree of conflict between his and the law-making culture. It was Sellin who called attention to social groups with "complexes of conduct norms" that "appear to set them apart from other groups in many or most respects."[5]

For example, contrasted with the allegedly disorganized America, the Soviet Union can be regarded as an overorganized society. However, aspirations, goals, barriers, and illegitimate alternatives are far from unknown there. The emphasis on achievement, the upward striving, the encouragement for competition, and the declaration of equal rights for all are not only part of the Soviet culture, as they are of the American society, but are officially stressed and very much encouraged. After all, it was Lenin who said that "only socialism . . . opens the way for competition on a really mass scale,"[6] and Khrushchev who confirmed four decades later that "every person who lives in a communist society must

[5] Thorsten Sellin, *Culture Conflict and Crime*, New York: Social Science Research Council, 1938, p. 63.
[6] Vladimir Iljits Lenin, *The Immediate Tasks of the Soviet Government, Selected Works*, New York: International Publishers, 1943, Vol. VII, p. 333.

make a contribution by his or her labor toward the building and further development of that society."[7] The "Stakhanovite movement"[8] encouraged individuals to produce more than their quotas and so to reap both financial rewards and greater status and prestige. In addition, the network of various "socialist competitions," both in physical and intellectual work, emphasized achievement and made substantial awards of money and decorations. Even the entire range of Communist Party positions, from top to bottom, have always been open to fierce competition, at least partially, because of the higher status and better living conditions that come with them. As Rostow noted, the Soviet regime has developed the incentive for competition by a "rising scale of real income for those who work harder or who are prepared to accept more responsible tasks," as well as an "elaborate graduation of awards and prizes to supplement material incentives with the almost universal desire of men for communal approval. In general the regime does not frustrate those ambitions to acquire prestige."[9] Some of the status symbols, for which people in the Soviet Union do not aspire any less than Americans do for their status symbols, are permission to use an automobile for private purposes, occasional passports for foreign travel, accommodation during paid vacations at a domestic resort, bigger apartments, better clothing, and other symbols.

This is not to say that opportunities are not also limited in the Soviet-type society. Although positive propaganda and more highly organized and pervasive social control than Americans are generally aware of try to develop the necessary restraints so that people in general will accept the available rewards, dissatisfaction cannot be avoided in those cases where individuals or social groups cannot achieve the desired goals. Culture conflicts are not absent from the socialistic type societies. For example, the proletariat or working class, composed predominantly of old and new industrial workers, in alliance with the peasants, serves as the basic source of the new "middle class," blocking the aspirations of the old middle class even more sharply than the aspirations of the American lower class are blocked. In addition, "it appears to be the case that important conflicts exist between the aspirations and expectations which are generated by life in Soviet Russia and the realities which are

[7] Nikita Khrushchev, Speech to the 13th Komsomol Congress, as recorded in a Moscow radio broadcast, April 18, 1958, in *Soviet World Outlook*, Department of State Publication, Washington, D.C.: U. S. Government Printing Office, 1959.
[8] Alexei Stakhanov in 1935 cut a record amount of coal and in a few hours earned more than the coal miners' average monthly wage.
[9] W. W. Rostow, *The Dynamics of Soviet Society*, New York: The New American Library, 1960, pp. 164–165.

confronted."[10] Not only is the old middle class with its traditional culture, destined to permanent lower-class status, but other groups also have to face disappointments. To eliminate culture conflicts through education is one of the major goals of the Soviet-type society. If in America the encouragement to compete is not balanced with the offer of unlimited opportunities to succeed, this is even more so in Soviet territories, and the extreme American emphasis on success models and role models is also found in the Soviet Union where the goals are apparently equally uncoordinated with opportunities. In this respect the basic distinctions between the two societies seem to consist of a greater amount of state compulsion under the Soviet system, the different cultural definitions of aspirations, and the composition of the privileged and underprivileged groups; but problems arising from social stratification and conflicts between subcultural groups seem to be ever-present once societies have evolved beyond the simplest level.

The explanation of crime and delinquency in terms of blocked aspirations may resemble the "conflicts on the conduct of specific persons," as Sellin referred to the studies of "some scholars,"[11] or the individual's drive for "power and superiority" in Alfred Adler's works. In his individual psychology, the delinquent's freedom of action is apparently severely inhibited by his style of life. He becomes obsessed with himself and loses his ability to relate properly to other people.[12] From this point of view, the status-seeking strivings of immature individuals, learned from and supported by their respective subcultures, can be understood only as an individual rejection of socially approved ways of achieving one's ambitions. Similarly, most modern gang studies too frequently assume that the adolescent gang delinquent, as an individual, wants upward mobility in the normal middle-class fashion. This rather metaphysical approach to an allegedly class-conscious gang delinquent (a viewpoint with which the public generally concurs) tries in vain to measure delinquency and adolescence in terms of what some researchers think should be, as opposed to what actually is. As suggested, this imaginary working-class boy "standing alone to face humiliation at the hands of middle-class agents is difficult to comprehend."[13] This whole approach stands up only if the criminal's or delinquent's ambition to challenge the middle-class system can be seen and interpreted as some substitute social gratification for

[10] *Ibid.*, p. 189.
[11] Sellin, *op. cit.*, p. 65.
[12] Alfred Adler, *Understanding Human Nature: A Key to Self-Knowledge*, transl. W. Beran Wolfe, New York: Fawcett Publications, 1961, p. 155.
[13] John I. Kitsuse and Daird C. Dietrick, "Delinquent Boys: A Critique," *American Sociological Review*, April 1959, Vol. 24, p. 211.

his lack of constructive ambitions. However, this would presume that he has an accurate picture of himself, his social environment, the society's class system, and its culture conflicts. To make this assumption is to contradict what we already know about criminals and mainly about these adolescents. The ability to perceive, learn, think, and reason in a mature fashion cannot be taught effectively if one lives and functions exclusively in some isolated subculture.

Under these circumstances it seems likely that for individuals such as criminals or delinquent gang adolescents, inadequate socialization results in a lack of constructive ambitions or positive values. It seems to be as a conflict of their culture with the lawmaking culture, rather than their nonacceptance of values. The only alternatives available must be destructive in nature. In other words, "rolelessness" may develop instead of "roleness"; because of his inadequate socialization, the criminal or the delinquent youth cannot determine what are his rights and duties, and so cannot identify those constructive rules he would otherwise play.

Daniel Glaser suggests[14] that the members of a delinquent gang have specialized roles to which they are socialized and which provide them with aspirations that are positive from the viewpoint of the subculture in which they are socialized, even if they appear negative and destructive to us. Glaser thinks of "role-taking" as having reference to the adaptation of persons to the expectations of other persons in any situation where people interact, rather than conformity merely to roles approved by the dominant members of a society. He tends to use "socialization" in a somewhat universal fashion, much like Simmel's "Vergesellschaftung." No possible objection can be raised against the logic and right of his usage; after all, "delinquency," "socialization," "subculture," "role," and other terms cover highly relative concepts, and their treatment is open to the user's interpretation. Even the Simmelian "Vergesellschaftung" can be translated or understood as socialization as well as only "companization" or "associationalization," which reduce the larger society to smaller groups, companies, or associations. However, the division of the larger society to smaller groups, and the culture to subcultures, is openended and, taking it *ad absurdum*, may lead to such an atomization where the individual emerges as the unit, and society and social control (as we understand them now) finally disappear. A society, if its members want to preserve this mode of life, can tolerate multidirectional socialization, conflicting role-takings, and differential expectations and adaptations only to a certain limit, namely so long as these varieties do not endanger the peaceful living together of the group members. An operational social

14 At this point the author is grateful for Daniel Glaser's counsel: he contributed considerably to the classification of the author's thoughts.

system necessarily entails the highest possible degree of regular under-standing and acceptance of the existing dominant system, since, without this, anarchy or confusion may develop rather than the reign of such values that secure the minimum cohesion to remain united in one society. Certainly this is not proposed by Glaser, yet an overly liberal and multi-directional understanding and usage of the terms "socialization," "role-taking," and others, may lead to the misconceived function and validity of social control. Thus it is necessary here to avoid misunderstandings by referring to socialization, role-taking, aspirations, etc., in terms of posi-tive values as approved by the dominant members of the society.

Given the roleless state, the criminal's or delinquent's lack of recog-nition of positive values prohibits the formation of positive aspirations. If the criminal or the delinquent youth turns to destructive ambitions, this action then is not a matter of value nonacceptance or value-refusal, but represents a conflict of cultures. It is not so much a matter of choice among alternatives as it is the only option available to him in the absence of a positive value system as approved by the dominant part of the society. It is naturally conceivable that there are some criminals or delinquents who, even though they have been adequately socialized and thus have positive and constructive aspirations, find that their opportuni-ties for acquiring higher status and upward mobility are blocked and so engage in delinquent behavior. Generally speaking, however, most crim-inals and delinquents are not recruited from this latter group, but rather from the former inadequately socialized persons for whom the lack of understanding of socially positive values means a lack of self-guidance in their activities. This hypothesis of rolelessness seems to go a long way in explaining the utterly destructive and nonutilitarian character of many criminal or delinquent acts, even though some delinquents are on occasion used by criminals for their own interests. In the same way, their role-lessness may eliminate their "need to be loved" while their search for belonging may explain why they form groups or join gangs where the lack of constructive ambitions is accepted or even welcomed, and where rolelessness no longer operates as a frustration.

Given the sort of personality development of these persons, crime and delinquency are difficult to understand in terms of class struggle or status seeking within a middle-class system; rather it appears as an expression of inadequate socialization and of immature personality de-velopment. Cloward's and Ohlin's question of how society "persuades the poor man to accept his station in life as just"[15] may be on the wrong track, dealing with the problem as if it were the problem of the distri-

---

[15] Cloward and Ohlin, *op. cit.*, p. 79.

bution of wealth. Instead, if we wish to answer the general question of the relationship of poverty to crime or delinquency, the concept of adequate socialization may provide a better clue. Any explanation of crime and delinquency must realize that most crimes and delinquencies are ascribed rather than achieved, ascribed by inadequate socialization.

In addition, the concept of the lower class versus the middle class, and the predominant identification of the lower class with crime or delinquency makes sense only if the middle class can be identified with the norm-forming social power. In no known human society or organized group are the privileges and prohibitions evenly distributed, and the question of "whose ox is gored" depends for the most part on the ruling social power; that is, the law. The individuals and groups who are disadvantaged feel frustrated, while the privileged ones enjoy their own position and find the incumbrances placed upon the others completely justified. For the privileged ones, the prevailing value system set by the ruling social power—in other words, set by themselves—is internalized; for the disadvantaged persons it appears as some external phenomenon. It appears for the latter as a quite different culture. But if the barriers could be internalized, then they would more easily be accepted, for they would lose many of their frustrating characteristics. In any case, societies for the foreseeable future will continue to be limited so far as opportunities are available to their members. The hopes and goals of many individuals will continue to remain unsatisfied, regardless of their living in a capitalistic-democratic or a Soviet-type social system.

It is impossible to judge whether the barriers in American society against the lower class or those in Soviet society against the old middle class are "right" or "wrong"; the values of the norm-forming social power are neither good nor bad in an absolute sense. Rather, these values have to be accepted. A close understanding of the law-breaking processes can be approached first of all through the understanding of the lawmaking process.

It should also be kept in mind that the existence and operation of any power structure may well lead to the development of an opposing structure which may be capable ultimately of taking over the existing one and of changing the value system in part or in whole. The dynamics of such a change depend largely on the amount of discomfort caused by the disagreement in values. Where such an upheaval is successful, a new value system may be formed and new norms created with the previously accepted values being rejected and reversed or somewhat modified. However, so long as the existing social power prevails, aspirations and goals are available or blocked, roles are accepted or rejected, and socialization takes place according to the values of this existing power. In this sense, socialization does not teach what the individual needs to know or learn, but what he has to know in order to participate in his given group. Aspirations and goals are seen as constructive and legitimate, barriers to them justifiable, and socialization is adequate only if we are conditioned to acknowledge and accept these basic values as our own. These circumstances may lead to a disapproval of the values; however, it vitiates the culture conflict.

The criminal or the delinquent has destructive ambitions, he is role-less, and he violates the legal norms because he has not been socialized to accept the value system of the ruling social power. His culture is in a conflict with the law-making culture. In other words, he has not been socialized to accept the commonly acknowledged values of "constructive" aspirations; the proper roles and legal norms have not "come through" to him. His crime or delinquency is thus not an act of opposition against this norm-forming power because he does not know and hence cannot judge these values. Rather, the culture and its law, in their deepest sense, appear to him as alien and external phenomena with which he is totally unfamiliar and whose rationale is incomprehensible to him. Wolfgang and Ferracuti suggest that anomie as culture conflict means "that there is one segment (the prevailing middle class value system) of a given culture whose value system is the antithesis of, or in conflict with, another, smaller, segment of the same culture."[16] As these authors also appear to assert, crime or delinquency seen in terms of revolt against, and not in conflict with, the social power—in other words, against the middle class— makes sense only if the criminal or the delinquent understands the values on which the norms are based. In most instances he knows the formal norms and is aware of what can and cannot be done but, because of his lack of adequate socialization of dominant culture values, he is not and cannot be acquainted with the values underlying the norms. The criminal or the delinquent knows that murder, rape, or shoplifting is prohibited, but in a deeper or real sense he does not understand why. He does not understand the law-making culture; he only notes that some conduct prohibited by the law-making culture are permitted by his own. He only notes the conflict of cultures, without understanding this con-flict. He knows that for other people, more opportunities for advancement and improvement are available while many of his aspirations are blocked, but he does not understand the values used to justify the distribution of opportunities and blockades. Yet, without this understanding, the criminal or delinquent can form only a phenomenalistic judgment where the world appears to operate without rhyme or reason and in an arbitrary manner,

[16] Marvin E. Wolfgang and Franco Ferracuti, *The Subculture of Violence*, London: Tavistock Publications, 1967, p. 151.

which leaves him at its mercy. The fact that he understands and accepts the norm only as a regulation reveals his inadequate socialization: his anomic situation means that he is in a culture conflict.

It is the powerful thrust of Sellin's propositions of twenty years ago that provides the most universally applicable explanation of crime and delinquency today.

7

Psychocultural Basis of Contemporary

Juvenile Inadaptation*

DENIS SZABO

INTRODUCTION

From writers and philosophers to specialists in the human sciences, students of the social scene have focused attention on the succession of generations. The world of youth at the apex of its biopsychological development is impetuous, whereas the world of adults is already subjugated to the conformism imposed by the burden of traditions embodied in social institutions. The clash of these two worlds is of interest to the criminologist because he thinks that therein lie the roots of many individual and collective maladjustments.

Complex problems are contained in the analysis of adolescent life. Its spleen, its anarchism, its vandalism, and its alienation are some manifestations of the obstacles to be one's self and to obtain identity. Such an analysis well becomes talented writers such as Gide or Moravia in "Les Caves du Vatican" or "Les Indifférents." Their portraits are psychologically so sound and morally so authentic as to be rarely equalled by those who use the often grim conceptual framework of the social sciences.

The phenomenon is not peculiar to our era. Adolescents were always opposed to the older generation, and innovators have always had to fight conformists. What gives it nowadays a dramatic and urgent call? Perhaps the scale of the problem has radically changed. The affluent society, subjected to continuous technological progress, has generalized a phenomenon which used to be a characteristic only of a minority. The middle class—which is middle only by a geometric witticism because it spreads over the vast majority of our society—no longer falls under the constraints of the industrial society that Marx had rightly called

* Translated from French by André Normandeau.

93

brazen laws. Our civilization of leisure is similar, *grosso modo*, to the one lived by the nobility of the *ancien régime*: free from socioeconomic constraints, it frees itself cheerfully of moral constraints. In this perspective, the renewal of interest for the work of Sade is symbolic. The royal civilization, where nothing was supposed to limit the instinctual aspirations—be it pride, vanity, or the will of power—is within almost everyone's range. This new civilization is a real *bouillon de culture* of moralities of all kinds. Men, young or old, have more and more difficulty selecting firm criteria for their choices and coherent rationales for their actions. The psychosocial moratorium described by Erickson[1] can be taken as the general framework of our analysis. The lengthening of compulsory education delays the access of adolescents to the responsibility associated with adult status. Learning and socialization alone do not provide young people with adequate moral preparation or maturity.

If the name of Erickson refers to a precise psychocultural tradition of analysis, the contribution of Thorsten Sellin represents an equally important source of inspiration. In effect, at a time when sociology was still young and had to affirm its scientific character by refining and increasingly using quantitative methods of analysis, Sellin did not hesitate to show his interest for the cultural and qualitative aspects of the scientific study of society. The theory of culture conflict was already pregnant with contemporary developments in the explanation of deviant behavior. The thinking of the present author has been profoundly influenced by it. This essay tries to sketch certain "culturalist" interpretations in a macrosociological tradition and in the perspective of the interaction between "culture" and "personality."

THE MACRO-SOCIOLOGICAL HYPOTHESIS

Neoteny and Misoneism: Elements of a Definition

We shall try to define two seldom utilized concepts in order to pinpoint a reality that constitutes the macrosociological framework of our analysis: neoteny and misoneism. The first refers to the innovating role of youth in the social dynamic; the second, to the stabilizing role of the social structure.

Neoteny is an interpretation of man's evolution. It considers the adult not as a terminal stage but as a point of departure. In the classical evolutionary perspective, the child prepares the adult. To become a man

---

[1] E. H. Erickson, "Youth: Fidelity and Diversity," in E. H. Erickson (ed.), *Youth: Change and Challenge*, New York: Basic Books, 1963.

is to "actualize the perfectibility characterizing the species."[2] This concept designs at the same time a fact, for example the existence of batrachians, which keep their larval shape and are perpetuated as such, and an idea, Darwin's idea: juvenile shapes, fixed through evolution, would have chronologically followed an ancestral adult shape. If the neotenist is an adolescent who has replaced the adult, the child can succeed the adult rather than precede him. This hypothesis leads us to conclude that progress does not occur through improvements of adult shapes, but can thus inscribe itself, as noted by Lapassade, in stabilized embryonic shapes.

To say that a man is a neotenist is to indicate that he has maintained the plasticity of embryonic and juvenile life as well as its brittleness. The human species is thus characterized by an open indetermination, branded forever by the original incompleteness. The neotenist man, concludes Lapassade, is not only immature, he is also premature. Human life, in this perspective, considers the adult state as forever removed from human condition. "The permanent incompleteness of the individual resembles the permanent incompleteness of the species."[3] Incompleteness means the preservation of juvenile shapes, of the plasticity of the juvenile stages in opposition to the adult stability. Progress asks for plasticity characterizing the embryonic shapes of life and becomes its very principle.

Now contemporary mass society has accelerated this progress. This is the fundamental condition of its functioning: "deviant" is everything that does not adapt itself to it. Lapassade's hypothesis seems to us particularly interesting because it gives us an explanation of the increasing role of youth in contemporary society. It is necessary, however, to examine its consequences in the moral order and in the transmission of cultural values. Such a study shows us that a profound stability and continuity as well as a certain break between generations mark our civilization. We can assume that the crisis manifests itself during precise periods of socialization and that it is amplified by circumstantial sociocultural factors. Neoteny thus seems a valid hypothesis to explain youth crisis and the major role of youth in the transformations of mass society, a society apparently devoted to "progress," to a state of unbounded mutations. If so, how can we become aware of the fundamental stability of social organizations, structures, or institutions? Many labels could be attached to this collective conscience, characterized by Durkheim as exterior and constraining in regard to individual consciences. However, we must admit that it thrusts power breaks upon the neotenic movement.

[2] G. Lapassade, L'Entrée dans la vie, Paris: Minuit, 1963, p. 24.
[3] Ibid., p. 30.

We shall call "misoneism" this resistance to change, this fundamental stability of the institutional and organizational social relations. All sociological analyses that tried to explain social organizations have reasoned in terms of equilibrium, change, and adaptation, rather than in terms of progress and transformation.

Scholars have often denounced the conservative character of such a sociology associated most of the time with the contemporary functionalist school. For us, misoneism is a corollary concept of neoteny, and we must use them simultaneously because they pinpoint different but coexistent realities. The following table summarizes our viewpoint on the action of misoneistic and neoteinic forces:

Transmission of the values of the work environment: *Misoneistic Forces*	20–30 years
Transmission of the values of peer groups: *Neoteinic Forces*	10–20 years
Transmission of the values of parents: *Misoneistic Forces*	0–10 years

The general hypothesis maintains that neoteny and misoneism are two macrosociological concepts that shed light on the mechanisms concerned with the transmission of moral values. These values are successively functions of the experiences bound to the action of neoteinic and misoneistic forces. They explain the sociological, anthropological, or philosophical paradox that seeks a total explanation of the human condition: the propensity to change as well as the stability.

Neoteny, Misoneism, and Morality

The neoteny that characterizes our society is a consequence of the demands created by the continuous and accelerated progress of techniques that give rise to an increasing consumption of qualities peculiar to youth. This neoteny has important repercussions in the moral order. Compulsory rejuvenescence of leadership cadres seems to establish, as the dominant and sole virtues leading to success, plasticity of character, convenient adaptation of personality to new and diversified tasks, dynamism and swiftness of judgment and decision-making. But what are the moral consequences of neoteny?

If experience becomes a synonym of routine, if firmness of character is associated with rigidity, we may derive certain moral corollaries of this new situation. Ambiguity in regard to values, uncertainty in moral judgment, indecision about fundamental options implicit in any compliance to rules of conduct—here are some traits that we have associated with the unsettled structure of the moral conscience in full evolution and with the maturation of adolescents, and that are thus found in adult society. We can now see why Durkheim's[4] concept of *anomie*, initially designed to explain the etiology of one of the variants of suicide in industrial society, has become, via Merton,[5] one of the keystones of modern sociological thought. Normlessness, value ambiguity, and instability of human relations not only lead to suicide, delinquency, and miscellaneous neurotic manifestations in the modern megalopolis, they pervade our entire civilization. There are two main reasons: first, the generalization of the urban mode of life which implies *anomie* and, second, the neoteny bred by the dynamism of our economic system.

Youth morality becomes, in this perspective, the adult morality. The uncertainties of the future and the ill-controlled frustrations verging on aggressivity without a cause are self-generating in the "neotenized" society. The birth and success of moralities used to diagnose this situation—such as Sartre's, Genet's, Camus', Vian's, to mention only some French thinkers—have a symbolic value in this respect. Alienation, non-commitment, vandalism, and sadistic manifestations that touched only a few economically privileged or marginal beings are now spread over more and more population strata and among "youth" whose age is closer to thirty than to twenty. Adolescence is lengthened and the gerontocracy of ancient and modern times is succeeded by a juvenocracy, a phenomenon whose economic, sociocultural, and moral consequences are not yet fully measurable.

The incentives for action reflect this general erosion of the behavioral norms and this moral pluralism. Youth socialization takes place under very precarious psychosociological conditions. The educational methods, based on transmitted experience from generation to generation, and the carrying on of a certain continuity across time, are called into question. Nobody can systematize the present experience in order to constitute a solid foundation for the education of future generations. The "neotenized" adults no longer convey coherent behavioral models, and the representation they have of these models, for identification purposes by young people, are ambiguous.

Many aspects of neoteny deserve study in depth. Let us simply assert here that the study of the moral conscience, of its training, and of its orientations are the foci of those concerned with the relation between

[4] E. Durkheim, *Sociologie et Philosophie*, Paris: Presses Universitaires de France, 1951.
[5] R. K. Merton, *Social Theory and Social Structure*, Glencoe: Free Press, 1957.

social and moral progress. Our methods are still imperfect for measuring the interaction of the variables that are of interest to us. The writer of essays is still ahead of the researcher in dealing with these problems. However, we can attempt to list the questions while preparing the base lines for observation.

Through universal suffrage and the vote of youth, each citizen has an impact on the orientation and the collective destiny of the community. Mass media diffuse values and ideologies and stir up expectations; choice is difficult because the moral sentiment of the population is deadened. Any adventure is possible, any cause has its advocates. Adults lack conviction and are insufficiently motivated by the presentation of values and moral norms; a character of ungenuineness thus becomes attached to them as seen by young people in search of their identity.

Sociocultural neoteny is allied to evolutionary theories that have suggested some parallelisms between genetic evolution, technological progress, and socioeconomic transformations. This theory is at the root of liberal thinking (Condorcet, Rousseau) and socialist thought (Marx). It looks forward to a society that will guarantee a moral progress parallel to material progress. This intellectual tradition sees man's nature as greatly flexible and almost absolutely plastic *vis-à-vis* the requirements of socioeconomic structures. These structures follow unavoidable natural laws, and man conforms to them and integrates them through his instincts and his morality. Because this social transformation is teleological, oriented to an increased improvement of the collectivity as well as of the individual, the latter morally develops by ameliorating his conditions of existence. Modern behavioral sciences tell us that socialization shapes the individual in a considerable fashion. We are what society demands us to be, which is congenial to the functionalist credo.

It is difficult to explain the contemporary moral crisis in an evolutionary perspective. Some writers tend to consider all these problems as vague epiphenomena, derived from dialectic contradictions of gestatory structures that carry a superior order of civilization, which will eventually resolve all these problems by absorbing them. However, we are forced to acknowledge the permanence of the problems that rise between psychological traits, norms and cultural values, on one side, and the requirements and conditions of socioeconomic existence, on the other.

Another intellectual tradition, more pessimistic this time, calls upon the relative rigidity of human nature, whose variations and reactions to certain situations take place only within precise boundaries. Man's propensity to progress is largely counterbalanced by his propensity to tradition. This notion is allied with profound instincts of conservatism and security. Conformism, mistrust of the new, fear of alteration, and the flat refusal of innovation are the backbones of this spirit. The Christian tradition, Hobbes' philosophy and the thinking of Sorel, Pareto, or Sorokin belong to this framework. History and evolution do not follow a continuous and teleological ascent that would accomplish a moral ideal through technological and socioeconomic transformations. Contrariwise, changes are cyclical; progress and regressions in the history of civilizations reflect man's natural contradictions that can be limited by education and socialization without being eliminated. This second tradition calls upon misoneism and a resistance to change, which can be explained by a more pessimistic evaluation of human nature's resources and orientations.

What are the relations between neoteny and misoneism in the interpretation of the contemporary moral crisis, in particular the crisis that confronts adolescents in a mass society? Our general hypothesis states that misoneism explains the consequences of neoteny. Let us be more explicit. It appears plausible that neoteny, as a corollary of rapid and permanent technological transformations, overestimates the capacity of individual adaptation—at the level of values and norms—to new socioeconomic structures. Misoneism is different and can be reduced to the following question: what is the quality and quantity of the transmitted values in socialization from one generation to another? If we reason in the Freudian perspective of the development of the ego, we know that the role of parents and of peer groups are operative only within a precise spatiotemporal framework. The instinctual structure of personality imposes certain orientations as well as certain boundaries to the normal exogenous influences. The values and norms that are derived from the parents' new sociocultural experience and that they are willing or able to transmit to their children seem very limited. This is particularly true because marriage takes place at an earlier age, and "neotenized" parents lack both motivation and adequate methods for the transmission of some of these values and norms.

In regard to the hypothesis of misoneism, the plasticity of human nature is not confirmed, thus explaining the stability of the sociocultural structures and of the personality in a mass society, in spite of spectacular but superficial changes. The outbursts of violence and moral nihilism are more powerful among adolescents in our societies because of the effects of neoteny. However, it calms down as soon as adolescents enter upon the ordinary channels that lead to positions of responsibility. One commonsense observation sheds light on what we want to say: if the value system and world view of an adolescent tend to be diametrically opposite to those of his parents, these differences will gradually grow smaller as his accession to adult responsibilities grows larger. It would

be very interesting, in this perspective, to undertake a comparative research of the world view of generations between 15 and 65 years of
age. We would expect the effects of neoteny to predominate during the
first stages, then later the effects of misoneism.

Morality and Ethics

On what is the crisis focused? On adult beliefs fabricated through
experiences sanctioned by a series of successes or failures? Or on
perceived moral ideals and duties by the young who are unable to
experience them as authentic?

Nietzsche noted that our conscience is made of precepts that result
from repeated and unjustified demands by persons to whom we are devoted during infancy, a veneration mingled with awe. And Freud
specified that moral anxiety, resulting from the fear of losing parental
love, was the major resource of the moral conscience. An important
source of confusion is related to the ambiguity of the term "morality,"
which is always contingent, only partially communicable, and represents
the end result of the compromises that an individual has realized in the
complete life cycle. Loring[6] is right when she says that there is no universal language and standard by which to evaluate ethics. One principle
remains universal: each must act in conformity to his own sense of
duty. Diversity of experiences, temperaments, tastes, and existential
sociocultural frameworks explain and justify the diversity of moralities.
The homo sapiens' condition explains and justifies this ethical principle
implicit in the human conscience. The absence of this ethical sense,
whatever the real content may be, characterizes precisely the criminal
psychopath, an extreme variant of homo sapiens.[7]

Mass society and culture, however, unify the experience of individuals in our technological societies. Would it be possible, then, to
talk about a progressive backing of the moralities tinted with ideologies
—i.e., of autojustifications, of speeches for the defense of men, of
classes, of races—on behalf of a universal ethic? The collapse of traditional moralities under the impact of rapid socioeconomic transformations reinforces the effects of neoteny. How then are the continuity of
culture and the stability of the social structure maintained through
what Erickson[8] calls the demands for youth loyalty to a profound
identity between aspirations and ways of being? This loyalty asks for
a disciplined self-devotion and for a commitment to current experiences.

[6] L. M. Loring, *Two Kinds of Values*, London: Routledge and Kegan Paul, 1966.
[7] G. M. Stephenson, *The Development of Conscience*, London: Routledge and Kegan
Paul, 1966.
[8] Erickson, *op. cit.*

Adolescents thus assume its traditions, utilize and renew its technology, rebel against antiquated moralities, and reformulate its ethical claims. This process follows the effects of misoneism.

These brief remarks do not warrant any precise conclusion or hypothesis. Erickson is right, perhaps, when he hopes for the progressive coming of this common ethic as a result of a common work of adolescents who are not prey to myths and ideologies and of the people less young who are not prisoners of the morality of their experiences. We can only formulate the wish that philosophers and moralists join with the social scientists in their common understanding of the human condition.

PSYCHOCULTURAL STUDY OF THE OBLIGATION: THEORETICAL AND METHODOLOGICAL CONVERGENCES

The Obligation: Prime Basis of Morality

Psychocultural analysis has full meaning when we tackle the study of morality or moral fact. In effect, the obligation to accomplish this or that act constitutes the principal energy of interaction in a social system. As Durkheim said, moral rules are invested with a special authority by virtue of which we obey them because they command. On this issue, he is following Kant for whom duty imposed itself by its own virtues and was the chief basis of human action. He adds desirability as a second criterion. We cannot set aside the content of the act that is called for; if we want to comply, it must summon our sensibility, it must interest us intimately. What Durkheim calls general morality and Mead calls "the generalized other" embodies the behavioral anticipations that become possible for all those who are part of its reference system.

Let us recall the main ideas of Durkheim. (a) His aim was to demonstrate the social character of the moral obligation and its value, both relative and absolute, as the pillar of collective life. (b) A certain parallelism exists between this point of view and the observations made above about culture and personality. Moral reality, for Durkheim, has a double aspect: objective and subjective. The first aspect appears under the general configuration of public opinion that prevails in a given time, in the name of which people judge, evaluate, and sanction. The moral conscience of each individual, however, expresses in its own way the common conscience. Under the influence of the educational milieu and of heredity, it looks at the moral rules in a particular way. The variations of individual morality exist below and above the general morality's average.

The specificity of the moral rule, in comparison with all the other rules that regulate the social life, lies in the reaction that it creates. The violation of a hygienic rule, for example, leads to pernicious consequences, where the causal relation between act and consequence is obvious. However, it is impossible to arrive analytically at such a consequence in regard to a moral rule. There is nothing in the intrinsic nature of homicide or rape, for example, that leads us to expect a sanction. The sanction does not proceed from the act as such, but from the fact that the act is not congenial to the rule which proscribes it. The sanction is the end result of a rebellion to this preestablished rule. The obligatory character of the moral rule is due to the interdiction attached to the rule.

To maintain that the origin of the moral obligation is linked to experience means for the researcher: (a) that these characteristics must be explained in relation to the sociocultural reality; (b) that the individual chooses his moral option between diverse norms and within boundaries that vary from one civilization to another and from one time to another.

A study of the interaction between culture and personality must constitute a matrix analysis of the psychocultural bases of morality.

Bergson,[9] in his "Two Sources of Morality and Religion," also denounces the rationalist conception of the obligation. He maintains that if rationality leads us to the obligation, it does not mean that the obligation is rational. What he calls the "totality of the obligation," referred to by Durkheim as the objective aspect of morality, is a "concentrated extraction, the quintessence of thousands of particular demands made by social life." This is what we mean when we say "we must because we must." We can analyze rationally the relationship between a rule and a given social function or a given value. But this rule is not justified by virtue of a rational principle.

In these conditions, we must look at the obligation as a weight that lays stress on the will somewhat like a habit exercising its influence. Each obligation carries the accumulated stock of others and thus utilizes the expression of the entire stock. This is what Bergson calls elementary morality and Durkhein refers to as common morality.

The other aspect of the obligation, the subjective one, deals with desirability. We aim at an end because the end seems good and desirable. Here again, Durkheim distinguishes the quality of desirability of the moral act from the other desirable objects. To aim at it is not without difficulty, effort, or sacrifice. The duty or the obligation implies

[9] H. Bergson, *Les deux sources de la morale et de la religion*, Paris: Presses Universitaires de France, 12e ed., 1962.

a desirability accompanied by a tension that is due to the fulfilment of the moral act in what Durkheim calls another part of self.

Freudians would designate this "other part of self" by an id and an ego rather poorly socialized. The habit to catch habits, to use Bergson's words, conditions society's existence and its function. The sociocultural evolution is similar to the regulative effects of the instincts in the biological order. Bergson is right when he talks of a "virtual instinct" as a process of conditioning that feeds us with obligations of all kinds. As Bergson states it, "a human being feels constrained only if he is free, and each obligation in itself involves freedom" (p. 24). What gives pleasure and makes desirable the fulfilment of the moral act is the exercise of this freedom, which is oriented towards the accomplishment of duty as indicated by the rewards and sanctions of culture.

This subjective aspect of the moral reality asks for the existence of a sensibility by which we become receptive to certain objectives and to certain objects to the exclusion of others. All values can be justified with a more or less logical demonstration, and they can also be contested with other arguments. The sentiment of authenticity, which they promote in the minds of their partisans, is not altered by these rationalizations.

Enthusiasm is the element that unlatches the motor of the obligation. It is promoted by a given value and is rooted in psychocultural experience of solidarity.

Sensitiveness rises as a response to an amalgam of values. The individual temperament of each of us devises infinite variations out of this amalgam. This sensitiveness develops by the enculturation of the newborn baby in a particular milieu. Virtual instincts of an equal power superimpose themselves upon the inherited instincts of the biological order. They are the end results of a behavioral and normative learning, constituted of obligations that involve constraints, sanctions, and rewards. The cultural order is a set of norms whose functions, according to Lorenz,[10] are analogous to the philogenetic ritualism. It will be perceived and felt differently by persons socialized in different cultures. The error of perspective of the philosophers who analyze this very phenomenon is understandable. The core of this process is happening beyond the conscience and thus escapes the main method for a long time utilized in philosophy, that is, auto-observation.

The moral fact, in its objective and subjective dimensions, constitutes the central problem: How to explain the radical and universal calling in question of the bases of the moral order? If we want to answer this

[10] K. Lorenz, *On Aggression*, London: Methuen, 1966.

question we must grant a privilege to the analysis of the mechanisms and processes that preside over the interiorization of moral values in different cultures. What kind of enthusiasm lies in a particular man, in a particular category of men, an enthusiasm that will show the way of his future, often in an irreversible fashion? Enthusiasm means, in Greek, possessed by God; in German, *Begeisterung*, possessed by a spirit. This militant enthusiasm, as Lorenz[11] calls it so aptly, is thrust upon men of each generation during their pubertal period and thereafter becomes the compass and motor of their existence. The sociologist well knows that beyond individual variations, we find the regularities and the tendencies imposed on enthusiasm by the sociocultural system. This enthusiasm, however, constitutes the dynamic principle of social change.

We then ask the following questions. (a) Who are the gods who inhabit the present generation of youth? (b) What is the relation between their aspirations and those of past generations? (c) Are they distributed in the same way in the different strata of society, thus giving rise to cultures, subcultures, or even diversified contracultures? (d) How are they shaped in the course of culturation and learning?

Paradigm for a Study of Morality

(a) *How to state the problem.* If morality is acquired in the course of socialization and represents, in its objective and subjective aspects, the claims of a particular culture aiming at harmonious functioning, the following question is important: how can we analyze the totality of norms, attitudes, and sensitiveness whose interaction and entanglement constitute the basic materials of moral conscience and morality?

The growth of the ego during infancy and the internalization of the claims of a culture within the superego are the basis and point of departure for investigation. Mass society, and its corollary mass culture, create conditions particularly complex in regard to the acquisition of morality's objective and subjective elements. We have evoked these problems in the first part of our essay. The hypotheses of neoteny and misoneism explain the specificity of the crisis and of the confusion that distinguishes the moral crisis in our civilization in comparison with those known to other civilizations.

The acquisition of an autonomous morality from an heteronomous morality, as described in the works of Piaget,[12] is of great interest. However, instead of individual psychology, we shall endeavor to link the elements which make up the morality and the moral conscience to the culture associated with diverse social systems.

[11] K. Lorenz, "Ecce Homo," *Encounter*, September 1966, pp. 25–39.
[12] J. Piaget, *Le Jugement moral chez l'enfant*, Paris: Alcan, 1932.

This choice is closer to Kohlberg's research on morality than to the conceptions of Freud or Piaget. In effect, according to Freud, the institution of the framework of moral reference is achieved, practically speaking, around five years of age; all the later experiences are sorted out and organized in relationship to criteria already incorporated in the moral conscience. Piaget, who gives more importance to cognitive and intellectual factors, pushes this boundary up to ages eight to ten; Kohlberg[13] finds that the crystallization is operative near the end of adolescence, around seventeen years of age.[14] We think that the objective aspect of morality, the crystallization of the obligations as rules and norms, is transmitted primarily by the most important agents of socialization such as the family, school, mass media, peer-groups, etc. It is interiorized in relation to the subjective aspect of the adolescent's conscience. The latter is profoundly altered and disturbed by the contradictory character of the messages which are transmitted by the agents of socialization. These agents find it difficult to sort out coherent and significant behavioral models among the array offered by the objective morality in a mass society.

Without taking a stand on the problem of the priority of the objective or subjective morality in individual conscience, let us say that sensitiveness to values (subjective aspect) is linked to knowledge and acts. The latter will vary in relation to sociocultural criteria because the individual subjective reality is patterned and suited to the objective reality of the world culture.

We are in accord with Brown who deplores the fact that these three dimensions of morality are not studied simultaneously. The behavior and the rules which govern it have been analyzed most of all by Bandura,[15] Sears,[16] and McCord;[17] the sensitiveness to values already was studied by Freud. It seems that the two aspects of morality, as stated by Durkheim and Bergson, take into account this interdependence. In any event, research must be focused on the study of the interaction of the diverse aspects and of their relative consistency. We are aware of the great methodological difficulties encountered in such a joint analysis of the different aspects of morality with the underlying hypothesis of a certain

[13] L. Kohlberg, *The Development of Modes of Moral Thinking and Choice in the Years From Ten to Sixteen,* Chicago: thesis not published, 1958.

[14] See R. Brown, *Social Psychology,* New York: Free Press, 1965.

[15] A. Bandura and R. H. Walters, *Adolescent Aggression,* New York: The Ronald Press Company, 1959.

[16] R. R. Sears, E. E. Maccoby, and H. Levin, *Patterns of Child Rearing,* New York: Row Paterson, 1957.

[17] W. and J. McCord, "A Tentative Theory of the Structure of Conscience," in D. Willner (ed.), *Decisions, Values and Groups,* New York: Pergamon Press, 1960.

coexistence between theory (cognitive aspect) and sensitiveness (subjective aspect) at the level of moral behavior.

The balance sheet of these studies is not very promising. Moral conduct does not seem to derive directly from knowledge, and sensitiveness does not always create sentiments of guilt when confronted with acts that the learned moral theory disapproves. Brown summarizes well the researcher's perplexity before the contradictory and meagre results of contemporary research when he says: "It may just happen that there is no morality which is shared by all the members of society; the morality proposed by parents may represent learning problems of a great diversity; children, maybe, learned at a different tempo the norms pertinent to certain values; the processes of learning, itself, may be different for certain norms, the latter being linked only to certain values; and at last, instead of constituting the dimensions of a unique phenomenon, localized in the super-ego, the morality is constituted, maybe, of many different systems which entertain one with another much more complex relations than we believed".[18]

(b) *Macrosociological paradigms.* We shall examine successively three dependent variables: knowledge, sensitiveness, and behavior. We shall then link them to a series of independent variables.

Knowledge and morality are acquired through learning and enculturation in the midst of the family, school, and peer groups, and by immersion in the mass culture. The influence of these factors is not the same according to age, social and cultural milieu, and the quality of contacts between children and their agents of socialization. The factors must be carefully weighted on the basis of representative samples taken in the global culture and society. The more innovating elements of morality, without doubt, come from the peer groups who are strongly influenced by the mass culture; the family and the school, with more or less coherence, transmit a more traditional morality. Tensions and conflicts arise and the relative impact of knowledge may be measured by some scales of attitudes or objective testing.

Sensitiveness takes shape out of two elements, that is, knowledge, as mediated by the culture, and character. The latter prints in the moral conscience an idiosyncratic quality and the more specific nuances. The relation between the biological instincts and the virtual instincts of culture are here more direct and intimate. Individual temperament differently colors moral knowledge, whereas affectivity will intervene in the selection and training of reactionary elements. The role of people who symbolize the moral norms and values is of great importance inasmuch

---

[18] Brown, *op. cit.*, pp. 410–411.

as it facilitates or hinders the identification of youth. An examination of empathy, which leads to the acquisition of moral values, and the process of acquisition itself, by means of certain disciplinary methods, should be analyzed in depth. Small groups of adolescents can be selected in regard to pertinent sociocultural criteria, and objective and projective tests administered to them.

Moral behavior involves knowledge and sensitiveness. The first implies the situation of a person and of his group in the cultural and subcultural societal stratification; the latter deals with the structure and character of personality. Attention should be focused on the degree of coherence of moral behavior in regard to knowledge and sensitiveness. This coherence will depend upon the convergence or confusion of the values and norms that are in conflict in the midst of the different poles of socialization (family, peer groups, school, etc.).

Adolescents may interiorize, in varying degrees, contradictory values and norms. According to their character, they may suppress, sublimate or exteriorize aggressively their reaction when confronted with these contradictions. The severity or efficacy of the sanction, and the effective connotation of a certain value may be considered as many factors that influence moral behavior. The type of discipline to which a child is subjected also plays an important role. The application of attitude scaling and of objective or projective testing to the same sample could permit us to collect the data necessary for such a study.

Conclusion: Morality and Civilization

Two ideals call upon the aspirations of men: security in the midst of powerlessness and power in the midst of uneasiness. Cazeneuve, who thus defines the poles toward which men strive in their quest for happiness, states: "Most of the important social conflicts can be explained by the tension between the conditioned and the unconditioned, by the situation of man who organizes reality but is not satisfied with it, a man who wants to seclude himself and then to go beyond himself, and, at last, a man who is moved by an instinct for rule and order, but also, at the same time, feels a mysterious penchant towards that which threatens and goes beyond rule and order."[19] Ethics and moralities, innovations and tradition, are based on this quasi-instinctual structure of social man. Using a scale for civilizations, in order to establish a typology, the line of cleavage would be one of calm and movement, being and existence, attraction for the unknown and adhesion to the well-known. This line of demarcation, which Cazeneuve suggests between types of happiness,

[19] J. Cazeneuve, Les Rites et la condition humaine, Paris: Presses Universitaires de France, 1958, p. 185.

brings us back to the one that exists between youth and maturity, adolescents and adults. The antinomy between neoteny and misoneism, as sketched earlier, embraces other antinomies of a psychological and sociocultural order. Man and collectivities are caught between two temptations: faithfulness to the ancestral conditions of existence, confined within the walls of what is given and conditioned by the thousands of traditional ties, or a rushing into the unknown, asserting oneself by the risk-taking that is hidden in the uncreated.

In reality, the collective structures of a civilization favor by turns the incarnation of one or the other tendencies. Two orientations can be extricated: civilizations with an opportunist bent and those civilizations that aim at the absolute. What is the morality sanctioned by each? As we noted earlier, moral behavior may be evaluated by its consequences (teleological morality) and by its instrinsic intentions (deontological morality). A civilization oriented towards the absolute would favor the former, whereas an opportunist civilization would deliver the latter. Anthropologists, in particular Ruth Benedict, have christened these two archetypes "Apollonian" and "Dionysian." The former favors an ideal of peace and calm in a man who is seen as an harmonious being and who expands himself in a stable and equilibrated present. The deontological morality guarantees a good conformism and the firm traditional basis of the social institutions. It also justifies resistance to radical change and to any upsetting of the established order. In such a civilization, strongly determined by the effects of misoneism, the adult world sets the pace for the younger generations.

In a Dionysian civilization, passions and movements are dominant and push man towards questioning permanently his existence. Innovation is the rule, and there is a law for everybody; adaptation or inadaptation is measured by comparison with the rod of progress. Neoteny is king because the adolescents have priority, biologically and psychologically. The teleological morality is the indispensable dynamic energy because the moralities of past generations are set aside due to their fruitless scruples and the fact that they impede the coming-of-age of important changes.

These two types are extrapolations, ideal and extreme arrangements, and it is obvious that the moralities of progress and the moralities of order are entangled in each civilization. This is so because two moralities as well as neoteny and misoneism, specific adaptations made by men and particular groups, seem to be based on the nature of man.

The man who is well surrounded by the rules of a republic of wise men, when the Apollonian ideal is established in every conscience, seems to be attracted by the tempting prestige of adventure, whereas the citizen of a Dionysian libertine society is attracted by conformism. Both are caught up in the antinomies that mark the history of thinking about the human condition and that we call (according to disciplines, schools, or eras) objective or subjective, transcendent or imminent, neoteinic or misoneistic.

This is probably the essence of man who is refracted in diverse prisma and is scattered in many categories. It reflects his enigmatic metaphysics.[20] For the sociologist who probes man's conscience with inadequate instruments in order to investigate the reflected lights of civilization, this venture is bound to be a lesson in Promethean endeavor and in modesty.

[20] *Ibid.*

8

Problems of Clinical Criminology

T . C . N . G I B B E N S

The clinical criminologist must operate along the interface between the sociological and psychiatric aspects of crime. Criminals have to be dealt with as individuals, yet in the analysis of the individual situation these two sciences have shown little progress in learning to collaborate with one another. Thorsten Sellin and the school that he founded have always seemed to the author to be in the forefront of progress in recognizing that some sort of collaboration or "bipartisan policy" is needed if essential problems in the treatment of offenders are to be solved.[1] In 1938[2] he wrote that man

. . . absorbs and adapts ideas which are transmitted to him formally or informally by instruction and precept . . . these ideas may be regarded as *cultural elements* . . . which tend to become fixed into integrated systems of meaning. Embodied in the mind they become *personality elements,* and the sum total of all such elements may be commonly called *personality,* as distinguished from the person's biological individuality or his inherent or acquired morphological and physiological traits. Personality then rests upon a biological foundation, which is of the greatest importance in the formation of personality. The biological make-up of an individual fixes limits to personality development, determines the character of the receptive and adaptive processes and transforms cultural elements into personality elements, and influences the latter's expressions in social activity.

Sellin quite rightly takes issue with the complaint of Allport, a psychologist, that "personality is more than the 'subjective side of culture,'" pointing out that the sociologists cannot be criticized for "placing upon their enquiries the limitations imposed by their science. This does

[1] M. E. Wolfgang and F. Ferracuti, *The Subculture of Violence,* London: Tavistock Publications, 1967.
[2] T. Sellin, "Culture Conflict and Crime," *Social Science Research Council Bulletin,* 1938, 41:17–32.

not mean that the sociologist is not interested in 'the dynamic organization within the individual of those psychophysical systems which determine his unique adjustment to his environment' and that these
'psychophysical systems' can be left out of consideration in the study of
social phenomena. It does mean, however, that sociologists are not
prepared to investigate these 'systems' since they are not psychologists or
biologists."

No doubt most social scientists and physicians would subscribe to
these views, if pressed; but in the last twenty years this broad concept
of scientific role playing has often been forgotten in favor of scientific
role conflict. It is obviously necessary that each discipline should clarify
its subject matter and pursue its own interests, but many psychiatrists
and some schools of sociology have adopted a policy of being the
repository of all truth. Each hunts its own hares and loses all interest
when the hares cross the boundaries into that of another discipline.

The cause of this scientifically asocial or delinquent behavior on
the part of psychiatrists and sociologists has always seemed to me susceptible to explanation in terms of the theory of "delinquency and opportunity." The psychiatrists' delinquent opportunity lies in maintaining
that he can treat his patients successfully, that he knows so much about
them that he cannot begin to put it down in writing, and that his cases
are too few to allow of any statistical proof of success. Maintaining this
claim brings him more patients, which represents his criterion of success.
The sociologist, however, owing to the structure of university life, is
obliged to establish himself by pronouncing some new sociological
theory; the pressure is so great he can rarely nowadays afford the time
to collect the empirical evidence to support it, but tends to argue it
prematurely as an intellectual exercise in advance of the facts.

Nowhere is this tendency to theorization more noticeable than in
the vigorous attempts made to evolve a universal theory of crime
causation. This is, in my view, inherently unlikely to achieve any useful
purpose, when one considers the whole range of criminal behavior. One
of the most acceptable of these theories is that of "differential association," mostly because it is sufficiently vague to allow a place for all other
scientific theories. It seems to amount to the statement that delinquency
is learned behavior. Each discipline can read something into it. The
psychiatrist can subscribe to this quite comfortably, since he maintains
that a young child can "learn" such lessons from differential association
with an abnormal mother, that his capacity to "learn" normally later on
is seriously handicapped.

The alternative, the theory of multifactorial causation, has been criticized, especially by Wilkins,[3] for being no theory at all. But if we compare this with a variety of behavior about which a great deal more is known, namely sick behavior, we see that it may be wise to have no theory. The only universal theory about the cause of disease would have to take such a form as "a failure of homeostasis in the body's reaction to internal or external environmental changes." Such a theory, like "differential association," has very little value in generating useful hypotheses except in opposition to some other universal theory as, for example, one that might claim that crime and disease are caused by demons or genetic predisposition.

The conclusion to be drawn from this argument, if it has any validity, is that sociologists should produce more empirical evidence and more subsidiary theories, while forensic psychiatrists should concentrate more on theory and large-scale observations than on the minute empirical observations to which they are at present confined. In the following pages I should like to refer to some recent studies—many of them unpublished—of the relation of mental abnormality to crime and, especially, to recidivism.*

World War II made it necessary to survey the mental resources of the combatant nations. This development and the establishment in Great Britain of the National Health Service have initiated the epidemiological or public health phase of psychiatric and other medical research. We want to know about the size, scope, and distribution of a problem as a corrective to the view from the clinic or consulting room. We know a great deal about crimes but little about the origin, development, and distribution of criminals as individuals. The early studies, for example, of Sir Norwood East in a London Remand Prison reveal that 15 percent of exhibitionists were schizophrenic, but when the national survey of sex offenders by the Cambridge Institute of Criminology showed that 80 percent of exhibitionists were not reconvicted after being fined for the first time, the situation looked different. Much of the literature refers to highly selected samples. In 1927, Bromberg[4] reported on the psychiatric examination of 10,000 consecutive cases of felony but, since then, there have been, so far as I know, no studies of unselected offenders appearing before the courts. Nearly all studies refer to inmates of particular institutions, those serving particular sentences, or those referred from some form of special examination.

---

[3] L. T. Wilkins, *Social Deviance*, London: Tavistock, 1964.
[4] W. Bromberg and C. B. Thompson, "Relation of Psychoses, Mental Defect and Personality Types to Crime," *Journal of Criminal Law and Criminology*, 1937, **28**:70.
* Much of this paper was delivered at the Annual Address to the Mental Health Research Fund of Great Britain.

Now that forensic psychiatrists are no longer limited to the diagnosis of the grosser forms of abnormality—psychosis and subnormality—but take part in the treatment of lesser forms of psychopathy or neurosis, we have encountered what seems to me the most serious problems in research: the lack of an acceptable nosology or diagnostic classification of mentally disturbed offenders. Professor Marc Ancel has said that it is only when a work ceases to have any technical or specific meaning that it enters the definitive criminal law, and this seems to have been happening to the work "psychopath," which has recently entered at least into English legislation in relation to mental health. Certainly, attempts to study the part which psychiatric treatment does or could play in the treatment of offenders is handicapped by these difficulties about terminology. The long-term follow-up of childhood behavior disorders by Robins and O'Neal,[5,6] though of great value, was forced to use very broad categories. In a current study of the subsequent criminality of boys seen at the Institute for the Study and Treatment of Delinquency twenty years ago, Mitcheson has found that similar conditions tend to be called "behavior disorders" in children under 10, "character disorders" in 10 to 14, and "psychopaths" at 15 or 16. Warren[7] is completing a study of treatment in the Adolescent Unit at Bethlem Hospital. He found that "neurotic" boys did better in terms of both subsequent ill health or antisocial behavior than those who were mixed neurotic and conduct disorders or pure conduct disorders. The pure conduct disorder (the less seriously disturbed delinquents), admitted to hospital to test the usefulness of inpatient psychiatric treatment for this type of case, were helped in about half of the cases but were much more often involved in further crime than the others. Each category seemed to remain fairly consistent in any later disturbance that they showed.

In 1948, Stafford-Clark, Pond, and Lovett Doust[8] made psychiatric and E.E.G. examinations of 104 of the most seriously psychopathic offenders to be found in London prisons compared with 61 controls. Because they were selected with the agreement of the Prison Medical Officers, who from their great experience are unlikely to use the diagnosis of "psychopath" lightly, they can be assumed to be serious cases. The author has been following their subsequent convictions ever

[5] L. N. Robins and P. O'Neal, "Mortality, Mobility and Crime: Problem Children 30 Years Later," *American Sociological Review*, April 1958, 23:162–171.
[6] L. N. Robins, *Deviant Children Grown Up*, Edinburgh: Livingstone, 1966.
[7] W. J. Warren, "A Study of Adolescent Psychiatric In-Patients and the Outcome Six or More Years Later," *Journal of Child Psychology and Psychiatry*, 1965, 6:1–17.
[8] Desmond Pond, J. W. Lovett Doust, and D. Stafford-Clark, "The Psychopath in Prison: A Preliminary Report of a Co-operative Research," *British Journal of Delinquency*, 1951, 2:117–129.

since.[9,10] As expected, the great majority have become or remained serious recidivists, in many cases serving long sentences of preventive detention; but the most interesting finding was that 24 percent were never reconvicted in five years and ever since, in most cases, and we checked that they were not in mental hospitals and not dead. They were mainly young psychopaths with few previous convictions. As many studies have suggested, the length of the criminal career is a better predictor of future crime than the psychiatric state. There are many indications that young but seriously psychopathic offenders can grow out of this condition even if one assumes that they did not receive enough treatment to have much effect. The psychopaths also showed, as expected, a great excess of abnormal E.E.G.'s (usually a nonspecific maturation defect). It was interesting to find that in those aged 25 or over, an abnormal E.E.G. was a rather *favorable* prognostic sign, for they were reconvicted less often. Presumably when there is "something wrong" which has a chance of correcting itself by maturation, the outlook is more favorable.

Psychopaths who are diagnosed in a prison or criminal setting are apt to be very different from those presenting themselves in other ways. We have recently been studying the reverse process—the criminal behavior of psychopaths or neurotics admitted to a large mental hospital. Briscoe, Dell, and I have obtained the criminal records of all inpatients, between 1948 and 1958, who were admitted with a diagnosis of psychopathic personality or of neurosis and who admitted having a previous criminal record. Then we obtained the criminal records, if any, of twice that number of patients of the same age and diagnosis with no admitted history of crime. Each has a very detailed item sheet of information about history, symptoms, personality etc., already coded. Anyone with a hitherto unknown criminal record (there were very few) or any with only subsequent offenses after leaving hospital were put in the offender group, and the controls were then matched very carefully with them for age (which is so crucial in crime) and subsidiary type of psychopathy or neurosis. (It would clearly be useless to compare a number of sex deviants with nondeviants or obsessional neurotics with hysterical neurotics.) The international terminology recognizes schizoid, paranoid, cyclothymic, inadequate, antisocial, asocial, sexually deviant, and other types of pathological personality, as well as five types of immature personality and seven types of neurosis. These types had to be balanced as far as possible with the controls for both age and subsidiary

[9] T. C. N. Gibbens, D. Pond, and D. Stafford-Clark, "A Follow-up Study of Criminal Psychopaths," *British Journal of Delinquency*, 1955, 6:126.
[10] T. C. N. Gibbens, D. Pond, and D. Stafford-Clark, "A Follow-up Study of Criminal Psychopaths," *Journal of Mental Science*, 1959, 105:108.

type of diagnosis. In the end we were left with 89 psychopathic offenders and 107 nonoffending psychopaths; 72 neurotic offenders (these were all we could find) and 91 controls with the same primary and secondary diagnosis.

It is as true of the hospital population as of the general population that offenders and nonoffenders are mainly distinguished by the circumstances of their early environment—early lack of maternal or paternal care, disrupted homes, poor family relationships, poor physical environment, both before and after the age of ten. Illegitimacy, for example, was three times more common among the offender group. Psychopathic offenders and nonoffenders were not distinguished in these respects. The history was equally bad in both, but the psychopathic offenders had a much worse educational and work record, a more frequent history of suicide attempts, and such personality features as being impulsive, suspicious, without ambition, and unmoved by religious, moral or ethical considerations. Psychopathic and neurotic offenders, though similar in having a poor early history, education, and work record, were fairly sharply distinguished in the expected direction, the neurotics being more anxious, agitated, depressed, and sleepless; the psychopaths more impulsive, explosive, overtly aggressive, and casual about money or morals. Psychopaths had a much more frequent history of rivalry with siblings, and their condition was considered to be lifelong, constitutional in origin, and treatment was thought to have been ineffective on discharge. The neurotic offenders were distinguished from neurotic nonoffenders not only by poor education, falling work position, and frequent unemployment, but their breakdown was less often precipitated by physical or sexual causes than was the case with nonoffenders. The neurotic offenders were more often overdependent and weighed down by feelings of inferiority.

Neurotic and especially psychopathic patients, who are not popular in mental hospitals, would not be admitted to hospitals as inpatients unless they were quite seriously disturbed, but few were admitted in direct relation to a suicidal attempt. From the criminal point of view, which is our present concern, nearly half had committed fairly minor offenses for which they had not been sent to prison, but 40 percent had over four previous convictions, and these included some very serious offenses. Most of them were property or mixed offenders; 28 percent of the psychopaths had committed aggressive offenses at some time but only 16 percent of the neurotics. Only 14 percent of the psychopaths and 16 percent of the neurotics had sex offenses at any time, and only one-third or half of these were only convicted of sex offenses: that is, about 5 percent of the whole, or about the usual proportion of sex offenders among any mixed group of offenders. It is rather surprising to find that the age of onset of crime was rather younger in neurotics, especially in the middle adolescent period, 14–20 years old. About 40 percent of the psychopaths were first convicted between 20 and 30 as opposed to only 25 percent of neurotics. The neurotics tended to come into hospital at the end of a fairly long criminal career. There is much to suggest that when offenders give up crime they are often liable to depression.

The main interest for our present purposes is in the criminal career. The follow-up was fairly long; in over half it was for more than five years. Only one-third of the psychopaths and a quarter of the neurotics had under three years of follow-up since their last recorded offense. The main fact that emerges is that 40 percent of the psychopaths and 70 percent of the neurotics were not reconvicted after leaving the hospital. Fifty-five percent of psychopaths had convictions before and after hospital and 20 percent of neurotics; while five percent of psychopaths and 10 percent of neurotics had no offenses before hospital but only after discharge, a fact that may partly have influenced the diagnosis.

In general, psychopaths were very frequently reconvicted, but usually only once. The neurotics were further on in their criminal careers with more previous convictions; they were much less often reconvicted after hospital treatment but, when they were, it was relatively more frequently. The psychopaths were sporadic and more dangerous offenders; the neurotics were repetitive, property offenders. The only feature that emerged clearly in relation to the type of subdiagnosis was that hysterical neurotics were noticeably more incorrigible than others, especially hysterical swindlers.

These mentally disturbed offenders, then, have not turned out very differently from any group of mixed offenders that one might come in contact with in prisons or in the courts, although the psychopaths were not often thought to have benefited in any way from treatment. The degree of mental disorder, in fact, is not necessarily relevant to the continuation of crime. Grünhut,[11] in his study of psychiatric treatment as a condition of probation in England and Wales, found that when doctors said that the patients had benefited and that prognosis was good, they were usually right; but when they said that prognosis was bad and the patient was unaffected by treatment, half of the cases nevertheless did not break their probation and were not reconvicted in the following year. It seems that the prognosis disorder given by psychiatrists may well have been correct of the personality, but the relationship of this to continuation of crime is something much less certain than they supposed.

[11] M. Grünhut, *Probation and Mental Treatment*, London: Tavistock, 1963

A second study concerned 200 boys, aged 17 to 21, whom I saw twelve years ago on sentence to Borstal training and who have been followed ever since.[12] In those days boys sentenced to Borstal were subject to a report on their suitability that excluded all cases of psychosis, serious subnormality, or those with serious physical defects, epilepsy, etc. In the 200 there was only one clear psychotic, one epileptic, and a few borderline subnormals. Nevertheless, 27 percent were regarded as mentally abnormal or psychiatric cases in the sense that a psychiatrist would regard them as coming within his province at least with regard to treatment, advice, and guidance; about 12 percent among these were regarded as suitable for individual or group psychotherapy; and about five percent were severely psychopathic youths who might have been dealt with by the provisions for psychopaths in the English Mental Health Act. About 60 percent were regarded as being mentally normal or showing, at most, personality problems that would not be regarded as within the province of the psychiatrist, and there was an intermediate group of 14 percent who could only be regarded as "problem" cases in the sense that they could not be fitted into either of the other groups.

The prognosis of further crime, so far as one could judge, was very variable both for the abnormal and more normal groups. Events have shown that it is quite easy to pick out the extremes: the definitely neurotic boys with little criminal potential who, as expected, have never been reconvicted, although there have been recurrences of psychiatric symptoms; at the other end of the scale were about 10 percent who were severely psychopathic, although without any acute disturbance that called for mental hospital treatment. As expected, 80 percent of this small group have become persistent offenders. However, in the middle range of criminal potential—the severely unstable, conflict-ridden youths who may alternate between suicidal attempts and criminal offenses—the possibilities seemed quite open. They are, perhaps, older versions of what Warren calls "mixed neurotic and conduct disorders." In some the mental disturbance has cleared up and criminality has cleared up with it; others have been repeatedly convicted. Very few, as far as we know, have entered mental hospitals, although two or three have developed schizophrenia (one just before committing a murder) and one has been removed to a hospital for the criminally insane as a psychopath. The extremely variable outcome for the middle range of mentally disturbed boys is shown by the fact that the only boy who had his parole cancelled because his good conduct and stability clearly made it unnecessary was within this group. It has to be appreciated that a sound system of training

[12] T. C. N. Gibbens, et al., *Psychiatric Studies of Borstal Lads*, Oxford: University Press, 1963.

such as that provided in Borstal can be very successful with many quite unstable boys, partly perhaps because it lasts longer than many forms of psychiatric treatment in hospitals. Most of this abnormal group, of course, would ideally receive a combined form of psychiatric treatment and training of a type that is now provided in the Boys' Section of Grendon Psychopathic Prison.

After twelve years they have separated into six career types, which show the difficulties of defining the success or failure of penal treatment.[13] Forty-five percent have not been reconvicted, and most of them are known to be working well; but 20 percent have become seriously persistent offenders; five percent have become very petty persistent offenders, with repeated fines for drunkenness and minor assaults, and are probably on their way to becoming alcoholics but, not in a serious way, criminals. Two interesting groups have changed position in the course of time: 15 percent were reconvicted at first and were early "failures," according to the criteria used in most prediction studies, but have now been free of convictions for five or six years. Another 10 percent have done the reverse and are now starting a new criminal career after several years, often on parole or in the Army, when they were crime-free. One explanation is that these two groups correspond, respectively, to independent (resentful of parole) and dependent (responding to parole) types. The remaining five percent are sporadic offenders, convicted of minor thefts every year or two, but working, as we know, quite well throughout this time. The original "success rate" of 47 percent has gradually risen to 65 percent.

The 20 percent of serious recidivists demonstrate my point about the uncertainty of the significance of psychiatric diagnosis. Half of them were certainly severely psychopathic when seen twelve years ago, but the other half were *not* originally regarded as presenting serious psychiatric problems. The "cultural" or "social" delinquent appears even among seriously persistent offenders. It appears to be true, as the Gluecks[14] found in their first long-term follow-up, that the chances of further crime in the more mentally abnormal group were distinctly worse: about 30 percent of the mentally abnormal group were seriously reconvicted, compared with only 10 percent of the socalled normal group. Nevertheless, both in relation to minor reconvictions and also in relation to serious persistence in crime, the mentally abnormal features do not serve to distinguish with any accuracy those who are going to get into trouble in the future.

[13] T. C. N. Gibbens and J. E. Prince, "Results of Borstal Training," *Sociological Review*, 1965, Mono., 9:227–236.
[14] S. Glueck and E. Glueck, *Five Hundred Criminal Careers*, New York: Knopf, 1930.

Mental abnormality, of course, means many different things and it is only possible to give some clinical indication of the varieties found. There were first five cases of relatively minor or even incidental neurosis of a sort that would have been accepted for treatment on probation but might well respond to Borstal training without any specific treatment. There were three excessively timid neurotics, whose whole attitude to life was as if they had been cast into a den of lions. They shrank from everything and produced somatic symptoms extremely easily. They were, I think, very difficult cases because they aroused little sympathy and very easily became surly, resentful, and self-pitying. This sort of personality is well represented among preventive detainees. The problem is whether they are going to be frightened out of crime or frightened into it.

Five were what might be called serious concealed neurotics who are often accepted as good training prospects. They are quiet, intelligent, very cooperative overtly, and from fairly good background; but detailed examination—which is the only way they can be detected—shows them to have severe conflict, or to have an abnormal motivation for their offenses (for example, fetishism). Some have concealed homosexual problems. They are extremely reserved and especially likely to escape attention. The follow-up has revealed that this type especially, although given a good prognosis by the institution, is likely to become seriously recidivist unless specific treatment is provided.

Four were florid hysterical cases of the sort that would often be called "hysterical psychopaths," or personalities showing periodic psychopathic reactions, moving from one dramatic crisis to another. Again, they are often intelligent and overtly cooperative, almost too ready to admit that they are grossly unstable, committing pointlessly impulsive thefts or frauds that are bound to be detected, punctuated by suicidal attempts when things go wrong. There were also five very unstable, overt homosexuals.

These groups, who represent the abnormals with a better prognosis, and whom I have called neurotic, although there is naturally a high degree of acting-out behavior, seemed in many cases to be suitable for the recognized forms of individual or group psychotherapy, possibly within an institutional setting. The difficulty is that many of them, as follow-up has shown, make a very good response to Borstal training alone. It may be clear that their essential problems have not been touched, but nevertheless they show a great overall improvement in adjustment.

The remaining abnormals present a much darker picture of increasing degrees of psychopathy. They are, of course, much more difficult to classify briefly. There were seven cases of severe personality damage from early deprivation, which seem to have led to disintegration rather than distortion of personality, with a completely ambivalent or disorganized attitude to their families and with sometimes a vivid fantasy life that gave rise to quite unpredictable behavior. Perhaps their main characteristic is that there is more anxiety about the future development of a psychosis than about future crime, although the lads were socially quite incompetent in the brief time they were at liberty. They correspond closely to Jenkins'[15] group of emotionally disturbed asocial boys, who are likely to become inadequate psychopaths unless they receive intensive treatment.

Then there were six crude and primitive psychopaths from a background of extreme family violence and the lowest standards, who showed much latent aggression and perhaps casual sexual perversion; six borderline defectives with added complications; four cases of persistent wandering and escaping since the earliest years, which present so many insoluble problems; and some others. Lastly, there were four compulsive thieves who must be included, I think, among the psychopaths. They tend to assume an almost standard syndrome; they are highly intelligent, intensely deprived, very friendly and cooperative, and quite unable to prevent themselves from stealing from anyone who helps them or establishes some sort of relationship with them. They have no friends of their own age and certainly no delinquent associations of any kind; their ambitions are to be architects, doctors, commercial artists, etc. They often have been recognized as abnormal from an early age and in these actual cases have had psychiartic treatment on and off all of their lives, until they were eighteen or nineteen, without avail except that it had kept them detached from delinquent groups. They can still view their stealing as a symptom. This social aspect of psychiatric treatment is often overlooked. There comes a time in the career of such boys when they say to themselves "I am a thief," and then throw in their lot with organized crime and become skilled professionals. Even if the psychiatric treatment is not successful, it may still preserve the image to them of an abnormal symptom. They continue to make the attempt to find a regular job and if, by happy accident, they find some more suitable situation in life, the prospect of their abandoning crime is probably much easier.

When the normal and abnormal groups were contrasted in the objective factors of their social history there were two satistically significant associations with abnormality that were very clearly marked. First, the abnormal youths had often committed their offenses alone and were free from association with groups or other criminal friends; very often, like children, they stole from home or broke into their own gas meters, and

[15] R. L. Jenkins, *The Psychopathic Delinquent*, National Conference of Social Work, 1949, June 12–17.

so on. Second, at least one-third of them were torn by obvious sexual conflicts, very often centering around problems of sexual identification and homosexuality. Crime is in the main a masculine activity, although there is no reason to suppose that girls are less often subject to severe deprivation or are less often psychopathic, and, as Adelaide Johnson has said, girls seem to steal from home in early years as often as boys. But much crime represents the pursuit of an image of excessive masculinity, and it is perhaps logical that disturbed boys should have conflicts about sexual identification.

These subdivisions may be compared with the categories described by Jenkins[16] in his study of a similar institution in the United States. He described 17 percent as "situational" cases who were not in need of institutional treatment; 14 percent as "pseudosocial," those with strong gang and cultural associations; a large group of 64 percent were in the "personality" category—those boys who had personality problems of a distinctly more serious type that would require institutional treatment for their solution; and the final 5 percent were "asocial," boys who were either likely to become aggressive or inadequate psychopaths unless some efficient form of treatment could be devised.

The prognosis of further crime, so far as one could judge, was very variable both for the abnormal and the more normal group, although it must be emphasized that the dimension of future criminality is not the same as the dimension of mental abnormality, according to the criteria that psychiatrists adopt.

Devising a system of classification that will bear a close relation not only to treatment but, especially, to the chances of further crime (which is what the courts want to know) is, therefore, an urgent need. P. Scott[17] has made an important contribution with his fourfold typology based upon social learning: (1) those well-trained to antisocial standards; (2) the ill-trained with poor ego formation and little directional control; (3) the "reparative" offenders who have deep conflicts, which crime helps for a time to resolve, and (4) "maladaptive" delinquents who commit pointless, stereotyped offenses, perhaps because normal learning processes have broken down early in life. Several others—the Gluecks,[18] Kinch,[19] Gibbons and Garritty,[20] Jenkins[16]—have tried to extract what is common

[16] R. L. Jenkins, "Adaptive and Maladaptive Delinquency," *Nervous Child*, 1955, 11:9.

[17] P. D. Scott, "Assessing Offenders for the Courts," *British Journal of Criminology*, 1960, 1:116–129.

[18] S. Glueck and E. Glueck, "Varieties of Delinquent Types," *British Journal of Criminology*, 1965, 8:236–249.

[19] J. W. Kinch, "Continuities in the Study of Delinquent Types," *Journal of Criminal Law, Criminology and Police Science*, 1962, 53:323–328.

[20] Gibbons, *Social Enquiry*, 1962, 1:235–244.

among numerous classifications. Perhaps the most successful devised by Marguerite Grant based upon the psychology of which divides delinquents according to levels of maturity in interpersonal relations. When we try to decide about the criminal prognosis, it is certainly to the type of relationships that a boy is capable of, how he sees the world, and what he expects from it that we look in order to make an assessment. Psychiatric disturbance may, in a sense, lie on the surface of such a level of personality development and may be less important in determining social behavior.

Social and psychological forces enter, of course, into the development of all these types. Nothing is to be gained by trying to exclude from social consideration a group of pathological offenders, as some sociologists do. Because an offender is an epileptic, for example, this does not absolve him from social pressures; in fact, there is increasing evidence that the unavoidable psychological effects of epilepsy are usually minimal. The undesirable effects are mostly due to changes in the attitudes of others to the epileptic and alterations in his self-image. The mentally abnormal offender is as much influenced by social forces as anyone, although the effect may be quite unusual and the fact of his mental abnormality clearly has to be taken into account.

Nevertheless, it is in relation to the "pseudosocial" or "well-trained to antisocial standards" types that the psychiatrist is apt to say that there is no abnormality of mental functioning, even if behavior is highly deviant, that the interaction of social and psychological is most in need of analysis. And allied to this is the extremely important question of "professionalization." Here, too, the psychologists and sociologists understand the type in different ways. The sociologist thinks in terms of delinquent subculture in the area, to which the delinquent makes a perfectly normal adjustment, of gang or group participation, etc. The psychiatrist tends to concentrate upon the individual's need to naturalize his instabilities and conflict-driven behavior, and to find a deviant group in which it seems justified and natural.

One alternative to attempts at psychiatric or psychological classification is to study the environment. This is the method often employed by criminologists, since environmental differences can be classified reasonably objectively and are fairly clearly anomalous in many cases of delinquency—the broken homes, separations from parents, parental discord, types of discipline, supervision, or affection. I doubt whether this form of attack will ever be successful in predicting the long-term prognosis of offenders, although it may be useful in defining a broad class of juveniles who are likely to come before the courts at some time.

We have tried hard to extract meaningful information from the environment of the Borstal boys, studied fifteen years ago in relation to their subsequent crime. At the time they were carefully assessed, after home visits in most cases, for affection and discipline, separation, relationship between parents, and so on. Assessing one parent without the other has little value because so many compensatory attitudes can be adopted. The largest single group were those boys who had two parents who were affectionate or even warmly affectionate, whatever their other shortcomings were. Their children were no less persistently criminal than others. The second largest group were those with parents who had both rejected and abandoned them; these did not do significantly worse than the others. Separation from mother or father at different ages or for different periods was not significantly related to the final outcome, even when the question of effective substitutes was taken into account. All one could say was that, where parents had very poor relations with one another *and* had both abandoned the boy, then these boys were more persistently criminal than boys whose parents had had a good relationship and had both accepted the boy! This was hardly a very surprising finding! It certainly seems that the relationship *between* the parents was the most important feature to look at, perhaps because it can be fairly accurately assessed. Their individual attitudes to the boy tend to be a derivation from this; the quality of discipline was also in practice related to this. If they had good relations with one another, discipline tended to be rated as lax or normal. If they did not get on with one another, one of them was likely to be rated as erratic or even harsh. Even if the parent was dead or divorced, the attitude of the surviving parent tended to derive from the quality of the marriage. The only close association with persistent crime was that eleven out of twelve boys who had overstrict parents were reconvicted at least for a period of time.

There is no doubt nothing new in this, but so often life experiences are assumed to have equal and inevitable consequences. In a recent book, *Family Environment and Delinquency*, Sheldon and Eleanor Glueck[21] have shown how untrue this is. Environmental difficulties may reveal those who are likely to become delinquents, but this is not a question of much importance. What one needs to know is who will persist or be difficult to treat, and for this one needs to have some measure of the response tendency. Within limits, the greater the disruption the more natural the delinquency, and the better the response to a better environment. Those who have been seriously affected by adverse environments must be measured in a different way. We found that normal and abnormal boys, in general, recovered equally well if home stress was minimal. The normal boys, however, recovered much better, even if the home

21 S. Glueck and E. Glueck, *Family Environment and Delinquency*, London: Routledge, 1962.

stress were severe, than those with psychiatric problems in a similar environment.

One of the perennial problems of the psychiatrist who moves away from the central field of medicine toward that of crime is whether he can really limit himself to this sort of deviance. Criminologists keep firmly to the view that they are only concerned with the treatment and prevention of crime, but a psychiatrist cannot help comparing alternative deviations. A hundred years ago Henry Maudsley spoke of those who would become insane if they were not criminals. Some years ago, the Mental Health Research Fund gave a grant to Martin Silberman and me to study the clients of prostitutes and other sexually promiscuous men in a venereal disease clinic.[22] These subjects have recently been compared with a representative group of prisoners seen in three London prisons. The striking thing at the time was that many of the clinic cases came from very disturbed backgrounds and in the poor quality of most of their human relationships they were just as deviant as persistent offenders; yet the number of those with a criminal record was apparently no higher than any general sample of the population, namely, about 11 percent. Why were they not offenders? Some would say that they were just as deviant or delinquent even if they did not break the letter of the law. However that may be, compared with offenders, they came from much smaller families and had on the whole a better education. But the outstanding feature was that they accepted the need to work and seemed to get some satisfaction from it. Compared with them, the work record of the Borstal boys, for example, who have been followed up for fifteen years, presents a curious picture. You will remember that 45 percent of them had not been convicted since, and most of these worked quite steadily; but even including them, the 200 Borstal boys have been unproductive for an average of four out of the ten years of their initial follow-up. This is not merely an indication of the amount of time they have spent in prison. Their work record is not entirely related to reconviction. The 5 percent who were persistent petty offenders were repeatedly fined for drunkenness or minor assaults and have worked very rarely. The 20 percent who were persistent serious offenders, however, often worked very well when they were out of prison and may be almost as productive as the unconvicted but work-shy. The late failures or late successes showed a close relation to improvement or deterioration in work pattern. The 5 percent labeled sporadic offenders, convicted of some minor offenses only every two or three years, have been quite industrious if apparently rather light-fingered.

Research has often shown that the experienced staff of penal institu-

[22] T. C. N. Gibbens and M. Silberman, "Clients of Prostitutes," *British Journal of Venereal Diseases*, 1960, 36:113–117.

tions find it no easier than the rest of us to pick out those who will or will not be reconvicted. Indeed, we cannot help doubting whether the prediction of further *crime* can ever be very accurate; it is like the outbreak of fire in an overheated pile of brushwood; we can measure the temperature and the general risk, but the actual site of the fire may be very largely due to chance factors. However, when the subsequent work record was compared with reports from the institutions about application, industriousness, and competence, whether the boy had worked well or erratically or with steady improvements or hopelessly, there was a much closer and more constant relationship with the events of the next ten years. Energy and industry appear to be rather basic qualities of personality.

The psychiatry and psychology of unemployment and inactivity is, I think, exceptionally difficult and rather neglected. It is true that Freud defined mental health as the ability to love and work; but, on the whole, psychiatrists have concentrated until recently on the loving part and have regarded work capacity as entirely subsidiary. Of course, work capacity is seriously affected by emotional problems—attitude to authority, lack of interest due to anxiety, considerations of status, and so on. But if I understand the work of some of our recent reeducators, they tend to support the view that interest and intellectual growth, the cultivation of enthusiasm for anything, can in fact resolve emotional problems just as often, and the solution of the emotional problems may free the energy and interest of the individual. In the penal field the problems of work and training have always been regarded as central; it is the psychiatrists who have always insisted that habit of industry and regular work may not alone achieve what is needed. Psychiatrists in the Health Service have done much recently to study the mental health relationships of work. Perhaps in the delinquency field we should change roles with the prison workers, that is, invite them to consider group therapy and counselling and ourselves make some detailed investigations of the psychiatry of the work bench and trade training. There are many complications, however, for we found that those boys who were not good enough for trade training or who failed in their exams were very often *not* reconvicted, whereas some of the excellent workers who passed all their exams were too efficient later on as criminals.

Among the comparative forms of social deviance we must include the criminality of girls and women. As is well known, thefts tend to be quite transitory for girls and women, but the girls who come before the juvenile courts in increasing numbers at fifteen or sixteen are in need of care or protection or in moral danger. One of the problems is to what extent these areas of behavior can be usefully treated, and how many of these disturbed girls become adult offenders. Mrs. Way, at the Institute for the Study and Treatment of Delinquency, is completing a study of the adult convictions of nearly 800 juvenile girls who were before the juvenile courts about twelve years ago; 300 were a consecutive group of cases whom I saw in the remand home, nearly all aged fifteen and sixteen and in need of care and protection or beyond control, and on whom I made a report to the courts. On these there is extensive social and psychological information. There is also a group of approximately 500 girls, about whom information was collected by Mr. Marriage, which consisted of every girl of any age who was brought before the London juvenile courts within the course of six months from September 1951 to March 1952. The contribution to adult crime of these two groups has been very moderate indeed, although the remand home girls were a very disturbed group. Only 25 percent have been convicted as adults, usually only once and for a minor theft or shoplifting; 10 percent, mostly in the same group, have been convicted of prostitution. There is a marked tendency among women for theft, drunkenness, and prostitution to be combined if there are several convictions. Only 6 percent were ever sent to prison, and only two cases were sentenced to more than six months.

The total sample of 500 from the courts presents a rather different picture and shows how selective one's experience tends to be. There were twice as many cases of minor shoplifting and other theft as there were of care and protection cases. The largest group was formed by 75 girls who were convicted for not paying for a railway ticket, none of whom has been convicted since. Adult crime was even lower, for only 13 percent were convicted of any crime, and 2 percent were convicted of prostitution. However, considering that they were such trivial cases and that the group included very many young children, the actual number convicted from this six-month total sample was not much less than the group seen in the course of eighteen months for a psychiatric report, which included much more severely disturbed girls.

Cockburn and Maclay[23] have recently studied the difference in background of boy and girl delinquents, and Ruth Morris has shown in a most interesting way that girls in their social setting are much further removed than boys from influences that condone delinquency. One might suppose that the antisocial trends in girls, which appear to pass off so quickly, would give place to neurotic or mental health problems later on. Women are no less often mentally ill than men, and from data in general practice they seem even more often ill in the middle-aged

23 J. J. Cockburn and I. Maclay, "Sex Differentials in Juvenile Delinquency," *British Journal of Criminology*, 1965, 5:289–309.

period. Women in prison certainly seem to have a much higher incidence of psychiatric disturbance. But Warren[7] found in his adolescent unit that the girls recovered better than the boys in conduct disorders *and* in neurotic disorders.

The long-term outlook for delinquent boys is of course much less favorable, although not so bad as many people seem to believe. At the Institute for the Study and Treatment of Delinquency, Mrs. Rose and Dr. Mitcheson have been looking into the criminal careers of boys treated at the Portman Clinic over twenty years ago. Follow-up of this length gives a real picture of criminal careers, for they are now in their late thirties and early forties. All had committed offenses at the time of their attendance, but about a quarter had not been brought before a court and, in the outcome, about 20 percent were never convicted. The contribution to adult crime has not been great; 79 percent have no convictions over the age of 21, although many were in difficulties before that. About 10 percent have become fairly persistent offenders with four or more sentences in prison. Yet from the records of the time they seem to have been very seriously disturbed in many cases. As before, we found that those few who were diagnosed as psychopaths—a diagnosis not lightly made at the clinic—had hardly turned out worse than other diagnostic groups. One of the striking findings is how early their disturbed behavior began: some 30 percent were showing difficulties in behavior before the age of 7, yet the majority of these were not referred to the clinic until the age of 15 or 16.

A follow-up of such juvenile cases may be compared with the results of examining a group of adult offenders in prison, most of whom were multi-recidivists. Among such adult offenders, 45 percent with relatively few convictions had juvenile convictions, compared to about 50 percent of the persistent offenders. Over the whole group, only 30 percent had been in institutions for juveniles or in Borstals. These data may indicate that the mass of juvenile delinquency is being effectively treated even if it is not being prevented; but it does suggest that there are psychological and psychiatric problems to be examined in relation to adult offenders. In the whole group, for example, 15 percent had been in mental institutions of some kind and about one third were exceptionally heavy drinkers. What are the factors behind this criminality of late onset?

In the course of the Borstal study, extensive intercorrelations were made from the many factors in the history and personalities of the boys. One component emerged which was fairly strongly related to reconvictions. It consisted of the following features. The boy was rated as having a generally inadequate response to life, to be hopeless, unrealistic, lacking in energy, solitary, submissive, with weak sex interest, with marked conflicts, and in the mentally abnormal group. By contrast, those rated as "aggressive, overassertive, realistic, extravert, and dynamic" had a neutral or slightly favorable outlook. These energetic, inspiring qualities have often been shown by the Gluecks and others to predict that a boy will come before the juvenile court. But at the Borstal age, when he can leave home, they may be qualities which enable a normal boy to make his way in the world, to marry, and to settle down. But there may be many unhappy and passive children of the first type who would never come before the juvenile court, who cause no trouble in the care of the local authority when they are abandoned, or at school, but who fail to support themselves when they become adult or when their parents can no longer care for them. Once they arrive in prison, they may settle to the life all too readily. The indication is that the child-care services will need to pay attention to the negative patterns of maladjustment as well as to the positive ones that draw attention to themselves.

The studies I have been describing are largely criminological and only partly psychiatric. I do not wish to suggest for a moment that there is not a great need for the detailed intensive study of the particular syndromes and treatment procedures, such as behavior therapy for transvestists and fetishists, of morbid jealousy as a motive for murder or murder followed by suicide and so on. These are, in Wilkins' words "attacks in depth on a narrow front" and will always be essential, especially in psychiatry. I am only suggesting that we also need to obtain a correct perspective over a broad front as they are doing at present in the health services.

The greatest need, perhaps, is to evaluate the different methods of treatment of offenders. Banks[24] has been doing this with the Borstal age group (17–21), as has Craft,[25] in his studies of alternate regimes for psychopaths at Balderton Hospital. But there is little to compare with the large researches in California. Most of the results, like those of Craft, show that there is no best method of treating delinquents, that some juveniles benefit from permissive, self-governing regimes with group therapy, while others may actually be confused by this and do better with a directive, authoritarian, paternalistic approach. Craft's psychopaths benefited more from the authoritarian regime when the two methods were compared. Similarly, there are now detailed Californian studies of types of probation officers and types of probationers, suggesting which types of combination lead to the most effective treatment, the dependent youths preferring the more authoritarian officers, and so on.

[24] C. Banks, *Boys in Detention Centres, Studies in Psychology*, London: University Press, 1965.

[25] M. Craft, *The Studies into Psychopathic Personality*, Bristol: Wright, 1965.

Such evaluation studies are needed not only in the penal field but also in the psychiatric institutions to which juvenile delinquents come, for at present there is little to indicate that that sort of delinquent would benefit most from penal or psychiatric treatment, or any combination of methods. We must avoid the assumption that many laymen make, namely, that cases may be merely graded as simple, more difficult, and psychiatric. It is probable that psychiatric treatment, though very helpful, is suited for only a certain range of cases throughout the whole dimension of criminal behavior. Rollin's[26,27] very interesting studies of psychotic offenders and the difficulty of dealing with them in conventional open mental hospitals underlines the fact that there are problems in the penal and health-service fields in dealing with such cases. These problems, I believe, must be studied both inside and outside the prisons, with a foot in both camps. As the coordination of health services inside and outside prisons increases, so, I hope, will the coordination of research.

[26] H. R. Rollin, "Social and Legal Repercussions of the Mental Health Act 1/59," *British Medical Journal*, 1963, 1:786–788.
[27] H. R. Rollin, "Mental Hospitals Without Bars," *Proceedings of the Royal Society of Medicine*, 1966, 701–704.

III

MEASUREMENT AND CRIMINAL STATISTICS

9

Values v. Variates—An Essay on the Relevance of Measurement to Morals and Value Judgments

LESLIE T. WILKINS

Lord Kelvin has been credited with saying that "when you can measure what you are speaking about and express it in numbers you know something about it, but when you cannot measure it, when you cannot express it in numbers your knowledge is of a meagre and unsatisfactory kind."[1] There seems to be some doubt that this remark was ever made by Kelvin, and recent editions of Pearson's Tables (a usual reference for this phrase) omit the quotation. Many would dispute the general claim, whether made by Kelvin or not. But few would disagree with the proposition that Professor Sellin's work in criminal statistics and the measurement of crime has represented a major contribution to knowledge in this field. Statistical methods have many critics in the legal, criminological and social action field. Some of the criticism has been extended to include specifically some of the work of Sellin. It might not be inappropriate, therefore, in this collection of essays, for some defense to be made of the use of statistical methods in general and of the work of Sellin in this sector in particular. I am aware that this may seem presumptuous—like some small-town lawyer rushing to the defense of Perry Mason in respect of an "open and shut" case! Perhaps it may be pleaded that although Sellin is more than capable of defending his own methods for himself, this takes up valuable time, which may be better spared by a lesser authority.

[1] Karl Pearson, *Tables for Statisticians and Biometricians*, Griffin: London.

COUNTING AND CONFUSION

The layman is inclined to regard the statistician as a kind of number accountant, dealing in a rather crude fashion with large quantities of numbers, adding together items that he, the layman, from his experience knows to be different things. A large part of this misunderstanding is transferred to those in other disciplines who make use of the statistical method in any overt form. Yet the layman uses numbers, frequencies, similarities, differences, equalities, and inequalities to assist him in his own thinking. It seems that the objection to the use of the statistical method does not spring from the rejection of the logic of the methods so much as from a rejection of their formality and rigour. With this must be coupled, in most cases, a misunderstanding of what is involved in the nature of the concept of valid inference. The layman, who is in every way an amateur in the fields of both statistics and the disciplines in which they are applied, is not the only critic of the statistical method and approach, but he attacks from a viewpoint different from that of the clinician, lawyer, judge, or other person having other skills in the field concerned. Basic to the layman's criticism is an unsophisticated approach to the concept of probability. The layman wants to be certain and feels that certainty is within his reach; he wants to be told for a "fact"—after all, does not the statistician deal with facts? Then what is all this about uncertainty and probability? The lawyer, on the other hand, has concepts of "reasonable doubt" and "beyond reasonable doubt" that imply some concept of probability with respect to a body of available information, and the available knowledge is usually acknowledged to be partial. Yet decisions have to be made on the basis of partial knowledge. Underlying this concept is often the other thought that if only enough were known, then there would be no doubt, and the exact role of probability is still not fully appreciated. In such cases, criticisms of statistical methods usually focus upon the feature of quantification of probabilities. Some critics even go as far as to say that, while they can accept logical analysis, the statistical approach is unacceptable to them.[2]

Few critics seem to be familiar with the philosophy of Hans Vaihinger —the philosophy of AS IF,[3] and its implications in decision-making systems. It is rational to operate with AS IF situations and avoid all reference to concepts of exactly what IS. This arises particularly in the

[2] A. E. Fink and others (1962), "Current Thinking on Parole-Prediction Tables," *Crime and Delinquency* **8** (3), 227.

[3] H. Vaihinger (1924), *The Philosophy of AS IF*, Kegan Paul: London.

discussion of rational decision processes. For example, the statistician will not claim that from his observations he can deduce a true probability but only estimates; and he will then go on to show how these estimates may be used with certain (specified) degrees of confidence in any decision problem. The probability for a class group is not the "true" probability for any individual in that group. This kind of situation occurs in all forms of statistical analysis, which have been inappropriately called "prediction methods." However, it is claimed that decisions made AS IF the probability applied to members of the group can be a class of rational decisions and even rational decisions regarding individuals within the group. Again, the limitation of information relevant to the decision is a critical consideration. Whether a "better" decision can be arrived at by other means depends, of course, on exactly what is meant by "better" and, once this is determined, the question of which approach is preferable can be tested empirically. The test is not to be made with reference to the *means* whereby decisions are made, but in terms of the objectives. It is not how a thing is done, but how well it is done, and what it was intended should be done. Comparative empirical studies, such as that of Meehl,[4] show that the statistical basis for prognosis is, in general, more accurate than assessments by other means. Nevertheless, Meehl uses as examples of the statistical approach a number of cases that would not be regarded as very powerful or efficient in terms of present-day knowledge in this field.

ACTION, REACTION, AND RESEARCH

It seems that the main underlying problem regarding statistical methods that worries most intelligent professional persons is not specific to the statistical approach. It is often easier to see a problem when someone else is seen to have it! There is a general dilemma of our age shared alike by those who prefer subjective, clinical, or other methods of analysis and those who prefer the methods of the model builders and statisticians. Both statisticians and clinicians (if these two terms may be taken as opposites for the sake of brevity) are equally reluctant to acknowledge the dilemma. Not long ago the implicit philosophy underlying the social research worker's methodology and particularly the early social surveyors like Booth was that "if only people knew what was happening, they would do something about it." Thus Booth was interested to measure poverty, and Cadbury and Beveredge used social survey data to press for forms of social security through legislation. To

[4] Paul Meehl, *Clinical v Statistical Prediction*.

them the relationship between facts and action was a fairly simple and direct matter. Today, no matter how we assess the facts or even the interpretations of facts, we are not so sure about what action is desirable. This is particularly the case regarding crime and criminals, whether we believe we know something about the size of the crime problem or not. Whatever our reaction to information of any kind, we are not very certain as to what might or ought to be done about it—or even frequently what "it" is.

THE PROBLEM OF CRITERIA

The outstanding problems today are not those mainly concerned with methods of solving problems; our doubts and difficulties are related to the questions regarding what problems should be selected for attack and with what objectives. It is possible to use statistical and other systems to obtain reasonable measurements, predictions, and prognoses, but the problem is what to predict or what to measure and for what purposes. The concept of the operational definition opens up many means for research and analysis. But there are serious difficulties in stating operational definitions that meet with any degree of support. If an operational definition is derived by the research worker in order to enable him to make any progress, his basic definitions are attacked when he presents his findings by those who might be concerned with the implementation of his results.

Sellin and Wolfgang have recently sought an operational definition of the concept of "seriousness" in relation to the implicit continuum of crime—from the trivial to the most heinous. Basically, they relied on a further concept of democracy that again was operationalized by using different groups of persons as assessors. This work has had its critics, and some further consideration of other points will be given later in this essay. Most of the criticism seems to come from those who feel that the concept of "seriousness," which they had and were happy to utilize without exact specification, was changed in the process of "operationalizing." Such criticisms may be dismissed fairly lightly, since the critics are not willing or able to operationalize their definitions, preferring instead broad generalizations that may be interpreted in many ways. Thus, interpretations may be chosen according to the situation that seems most rewarding or that happens most to fit with their views of "what ought to be done."

However, given any operational definition of "seriousness," the action regarding "serious" and "nonserious" crimes is not defined. It may be assumed only that *different* degrees of "seriousness" require *different* actions and decisions. *What* actions and *what* decisions present another and difficult issue of quite a different order.

It was simpler when evil was perceived as clearly differentiated from good, when right was separated from wrong, and truth was divided from falsehood by a void; when rightness and wrongness were determined authoritatively by an elite; when communication was restricted and cultural variants were unknown except to a minority. Now we cannot ignore cultural variants because some have become powerful and knowledge of their existence is widespread. Nevertheless, as in the past, they can still be condemned as "evil." The connection between "evil" and the unknown and between "evil" and falsehood is a most interesting one, both in history and today. Our philosophy of knowledge has undergone great changes, but it seems that the relationship with "truth," "evil," and similar value concepts has not changed accordingly. It is, however, not appropriate to explore this interesting topic here, except perhaps to note one point that is closely related to the philosophy underlying the statistical approach.

In a social system that is functioning according to clear rules and laws and with which we are familiar, we may predict the behavior of individuals to a considerable degree of accuracy. In such circumstances we are not threatened by uncertainty. (Merton notes this feature with particular reference to bureaucracies.) In a system that we do not know and for which we are unaware of the rules, or in a system that is characterized by considerable deviance from the rules, we are presented with problems of adjustment to persons and situations. If we know the dangerous areas of a city, if we can recognize clues to the probability of injury or loss, and we have freedom of movement, we may avoid the threatening situation. We are utilizing a subjective prediction system as a guide to our decisions. When, however, our implicit internal subjective prediction system breaks down, for whatever reason, we are inclined to regard the situation as dangerous and hence "evil." Not that all that is unknown is perceived as evil, nor all that is perceived as evil necessarily unknown. There is a positive correlation between these concepts even today, though of less significance than to primitive man. What is important for purposes of the argument at this point is that in the past what was "known" was as clearly divided from what was "unknown" as was "right" from "wrong." In simple arithmetic, if you "know" how to do a sum, then you can get it "right." But the calculus of probabilities brings in a different concept, the concept of measurable uncertainty, to which is closely related the concept of degree of belief. A little knowledge (information) is not, as the old proverb suggests, a dangerous thing, since all information (if it is information and not "noise") possesses a potential utility. A large quantity of information can be equally as misapplied as a little, and no knowledge is complete. Instead of knowing or not knowing, instead of right and wrong, belief and disbelief, good and evil, we have a world of continuities with which we must contend. Our moral values and our scientific models must reflect this quality if an adequate system of social control is to be maintained. *A relationship that the culture can accommodate must exist between the value systems and the system of knowledge.*

It seems that at the present stage of our social development we have one language (a new one) for the field of knowledge and another language (an older one) for the field of values. There exists as yet no system for the translation of the one language into the other, and our thought processes are inhibited by our lack of semantic tools. To some the resolution is found in ignoring one or the other of the two systems— the scientist rejects religion and tries to avoid value concepts, while the religious wish they could ignore the field of science. Others try to settle for two distinct worlds that can be considered as totally independent, and this approach is not very different from the old dichotomous model of the universe of primitive man. Neither of these solutions can commend themselves to criminologists, lawyers, and others concerned with justice and social deviance. The law, for example, cannot help being associated with concepts of moral questions and with value judgments.

THE SIMPLE DICHOTOMOUS MODEL

It must be acknowledged that many people are trying to use the limited perceptual models of the past when they consider values and moral issues. For them we can only discover ourselves by a return to the simple structure of dichotomies. We must find again the beliefs in absolute values that guided our forefathers, they claim. The present age is out of joint! But is a belief in the absolute values of the past likely to be functioned today, even if it were possible? It may be questioned whether, in fact, our forefathers were guided by absolute values. Perhaps some were persuaded to act as they did because value systems were suggested to them by others who found them functional for preserving their power and self-interest? Were some fooled by a primitive public relations technique, while others operated the system? Whatever any individual may answer to these questions it is significant that the present generation is capable of asking them.

Perhaps our problems do not lie in the "wrong" values, but in an inadequate value conceptualization. There is a danger of incorrect inference; indeed it is almost certain that incorrect inferences will be derived if the models of the situation we use are deficient. This condition will apply whether the models are mathematical, structural, or linguistic. Let us consider this possibility: the world of politics is divided conceptually into a dichotomy—communist and noncommunist. Which is "right" and which is "wrong" depends upon geography. In the same way and by the same type of thought processes (linguistic models), we used to divide the world into Christian and heathen if, that is, we were living in a "Christian country" (whatever that might be!). But does the simple dichotomy provide an adequate model of the world or the means to make logical inferences regarding anything in it? Perhaps, for some purposes, there exist dichotomies that are useful as classifications, but where this may be it may be so only because we lack information. For some purposes, even perhaps the most obvious of dichotomies of male and female may be challenged. When we consider value statements and complex concepts of abstract principles, the dichotomy becomes even less adequate than when we are classifying phenomena and observed data.

There is considerable confusion today because at some levels of thinking it is convenient for most people to use concepts of simple order. It is convenient, for example, to think of offenders as either "responsible" or "not responsible" for their actions and, of course, to leave somewhat obscure what is meant by "responsibility." The drafting of laws allowing of the plea of diminished responsibility for certain offenses has presented many problems because it breaks away from the simple all-or-none, black-or-white patterning of the usual ethical systems. The substitution of the simple dichotomy of the past by the idea of a graduation raises implicitly the problem of measurement. It is no longer satisfactory merely to know whether we are on land or on sea; we have to find ways to chart our position, and we cannot do this by any system of absolute measurement.

Few are skilled in the use of the language of measurement. For many the absence of black and white produces only an undifferentiated grey. Therefore they are lost. They have only regrets that the simple perceptual model of the world (their model lacking any informational power) is no longer possible for them. A recent blues song by Oscar Brown, Jr., plaintively puts the dilemma of these persons:

> When I was a lad simple notions I had
>   There was wrong, here was right
> It was plain black and white
>   Ah, but now that I'm grown in a world on my own
> The scenes I survey show nothing but grey.

At night in my sleep I hear voices,
    I'm never quite certain what's said,
They offer me too many choices,
    There's no black, there's no white
Where is wrong, where is right
    I'm confused and unable to say
How does a man find his way
    In a world full of grey?[5]

There may be fundamental divisions of opinion in reaction to the theme of this song. Some will see the problem as related to those who are out of step, like Oscar Brown. It is only because they have not seen the light that they see the world as full of grey—there is wrong, there is right—but the tragedy is that people have lost faith in the guiding light. But that "light" is conceived quite differently even within countries as well as between them. Some of the youth of the USSR have lost sight of the guiding principles of Marxist-Leninism; some have lost faith in Buddha's way, others see the light as certain dogmatic fundamental beliefs—for all such there is no doubt that the others are wrong. There can be no compromise in values. Truth exists; it is only that observers (other observers!) cannot see it. Truth to some is dogma to others, but both are equally dogmatic. If, on the other hand, we reject dogma, if we cease to be certain, we are left without solid value systems or, at least, the classical value systems that rely upon dichotomous classification. These were concordant with a philosophy of knowledge that is now no longer tenable. Some belief system may be necessary, but does it have to be related to a philosophy that is out of date? Can there be no belief system that can underpin values without reliance upon an all-or-none model of the universe?

The statistical concepts of variance, probability, and uncertainty are concepts that often provide reasonable tools for description and analysis of human as well as natural phenomena. There are other methods of even more recent origin and all of them are developing rapidly. But while tools exist, and while they are used in many fields of human endeavour without emotional involvement, in other areas there remains a conflict both with regard to the model and the language.

In statistical methodology, dichotomous classifications of observations are sometimes used, and frequently it is helpful to have them. It is also normally obvious that a simplification of the situation is involved in the use of these procedures. Simplification for purposes of classification and inference has a utility, but we should not simplify our thought processes in the same operation. The "model" must be under control.

[5] Oscar Brown, Jr., *Between Heaven and Hell* (record jacket), C.B.S., BPG 62016.

We may simplify, knowing that we simplify as a facilitating system, but our basic thinking must still to be in control of the simplification. Belief in simple dichotomies is a different matter altogether from the utilization of dichotomies.

DICHOTOMIES AND THE LAW

The nearer we get to a concern with issues that are related to concepts of ethics or values, the more pressing seems to become the tendency to invoke dichotomous models of man and the universe. This seems to be particularly true in regard to law. If we cannot think of "justice" as being directly opposed by "injustice," if right and wrong are not separated by a gulf of nothingness, if the basis of moral absolutes is gone, how can we proceed? Can we no longer divide the "guilty" from the "not guilty?" Are there degrees of guilt? If so, then "guilt" may be capable of measurement in relative terms. But relative to what? There are difficulties unless, at some point, it is possible to describe or refer to some concept of an absolute. If all things are variable, what scales can be used to ascertain our position? Indeed, at present, we do behave AS IF there were some fixed point, but the basis of the relationship of other factors to it and its nature remain determined only by individual subjective values of our justices and arbitrators.

There can be no doubt that, in practice, guilt is assessed in relative terms. The variations in the patterns of sentencing by the courts would seem to imply varying value reference points or varying systems of values. Moreover, pleas in mitigation are admitted in many juisdictions, and this implies a quantitative aspect of guilt. Yet these considerations are like an appendage to a system that, in the main, clings to the language and philosophy of dichotomies. First, find the offender "guilty" or "not guilty," then proceed to bring in the modern concepts of graduation—diminished responsibility or mitigating circumstances; and then, even these considerations are, in turn, dealt with in the dichotomous framework: there is a case for diminished responsibility or there is not; there were or were not mitigating circumstances. How often is the question asked in court "Is that 'true' or 'false?'", and how often is the witness forced to "answer 'yes' or 'no?'"

It is, of course, not only in the court proceedings that difficulties arise from the new concepts of probability and uncertainty. Similar problems arise in all cases of concepts where the theory of knowledge is out of step with other theories. In the past, little difficulty had been thought to exist because value concepts were related to ideas of absolute values, and these were not inconsistent with concepts in other sectors; we could be "sure" and many things could be "proved." The language of science has no difficulty in accommodating change. Why should the language of ethics?

Is there any meaning in the language we used in the past? What can be the meaning of history if the total system of reference has changed? Can there be found any clues in the past to assist with the present dilemma?

Reference has already been made to the dichotomous value systems used in political language. It is interesting, however, that in one sector of international affairs, sufficient consensus has been reached to enable activities to function smoothly and resolution by arbitration of differences to be generally accepted. The area concerned is of course that of international trade. In other fields of international activity, the slogan-logic of black/white, of red/other color continues unabated. There may be many reasons contributing to this feature of international law, but perhaps one factor might be that, in trade, the values are not dichotomous and a recognized system of relationships is provided by what we call "money." The logic of number and of continuities supplements the logic of verbal discussion.

The relationship between statistical concepts and moral value systems, which is considered to be important in any consideration of the conflict of views between clinicians and jurists on the one hand and the statisticians and model builders on the other may now be clear, if not established. Concepts of graduation, variation, relative comparisons, and uncertainty are the stock-in-trade of the statistician. There would seem to be no doubt that much of the criticism of statistics, as the "cult of measurement," reflects only or mainly the uncertainty of larger issues and also reflects the attempt to reject the "world full of grey" as an unsatisfactory world. But measurement is a means of grading greyness. It might seem that the answer to Oscar Brown's question regarding how a man may find his way in a world of grey is that the greyness is not homogeneous. It is necessary to increase our perceptual acuity, to find ways to differentiate the greyness.

THE NECESSITY FOR THE DEVELOPMENT
OF MEASUREMENT

Measurement is achieved by the use of instruments and by agreed standards of reference to which deviations may be related. It is not, however, possible to develop general purpose instruments. We do not use the same instruments for widely different purposes. We use the same eyes to look at stars and at insects, but no sooner are we required to increase the power of our vision than we must decide to differentiate the insects from the stars. This process is, of course, self-evident. We select the reflector or radio telescope, the magnifying glass or the electron microscope according to our specific purpose. There is always a reference to purpose in these choices. Yet, in the human field, it is the reference to purpose, which is the most difficult to make and, without it, valid instrument construction is not possible. It is as useless asking the human scientist for general purpose instruments as it is to ask the natural scientist for an instrument without stating the purpose for which it is required. It is necessary to say what it is that we want to do about offenders, about psychopaths, about all the other problems in our field before instruments can be made. We are now at a critical stage. We have the necessary knowledge of how to make instruments to increase our ability to describe social behaviour and "crime," but what kind of instruments should we be making?

It is this difficulty that gives rise to another type of criticism of the statistical approach in criminology. The rational man seeks information on which to base his decisions, and the information he can now obtain is often deficient in those qualities that might indicate the nature of an effective action. The critic may, to some extent, be justified therefore, in his criticism of the type of data produced by these methods, but only to a very limited extent. It may be that people want to be told what to do— so they often say. Statistical methods and similar types of analysis, they claim, do not give the necessary information. This criticism may be based on a misunderstanding and may be asking for the cart to be placed before the horse. The language of *IS* differs from the language of *SHOULD*. Statistical methodology and the scientific method, generally, has nothing to say about questions of *SHOULD*. It is possible, as has been noted, to use the concept of AS IF—but not SHOULD. The roles of these languages must be distinguished. It will be necessary to return to this point in more detail later, but first there is another type of criticism that should be discussed.

THE REACTION CRITICISM

Those who say that statistics are not satisfactory because they do not say what should be done might be termed the ACTION Critics.

They should be distinguished from those whose criticism is based on a different foundation and who might be termed the REACTION Critics.

Our society has developed in such a way that many persons and organizations have an investment in particular forms of action. Careers and status depend upon the acceptance by the people (or at least the people in power positions) of lines of action already highly structured and formalized. It is thus essential for those involved in these processes to believe in them. As the writer noted[6] regarding Borstal governors who made poor assessors of the future of their inmates, a good governor with therapeutic ability doubtless *has* to believe in the effects of the treatment programme. This belief, perhaps highly functional in the human relationship situation, was not functional for valid assessment of the prognosis. Thus we have a further distinction: irrational beliefs may be functional in certain settings. The society in which we live has many highly structured settings—institutions, organizations, professions, and the like— each and all of which have aims and objectives that may present areas of conflict of interest. A developed skill is a personal asset that involves the individual very closely with the organization that utilizes it. And not only this but the skill itself becomes the central feature of further organizations like trade unions and professional bodies and, it might be added, even learned societies. Much is heard of the "restrictive practices" of trade unions in their defense of the welfare of their members, but little is heard of "restrictive thinking" or bounded reasoning that may be a function of any institutional involvement.

In addition to the formal structures of institutions and professional bodies, the mere development of a terminology presents somewhat similar problems. Even technical terms come to be the focus for schools of thought (or sometimes schools of nonthought). Jargon can attract adherents. Consider, for example, two terms chosen for no particular reason except that they have been coined to describe areas in our field of concern—"criminology" and "social defense." If and when these terms are challenged, are there not many persons who will exhibit a trace of institutional defensiveness? If the structures of content usually suggested by these terms are called into question, even more involvements may be threatened and the thought processes will tend to be restricted. Yet, perhaps these terms might now be challenged with some advantage together with others like them. Of course, the challenge is not merely to be directed to the terms, since any word may be defined in other words, but should extend to the institutionalized content of the concepts. Superstructures of great complexity have been built around these terms, but

[6] Hermann Mannheim and Leslie T. Wilkins (1955), *Prediction Methods in Relation to Borstal Training* (H.M.S.O., London).

only in relation to *sets of beliefs*. The initial sets of beliefs have become institutionalized in the terminology, and the terminology has reinforced the beliefs. The actions which have been derived from these beliefs now involve many career structures and, with them, the individual motivation and group defensiveness. Yet the basic beliefs must be challenged and continuously reexamined if we seek advance. Not that it is possible to remain stationery; we must accommodate to other changes in other situations with which our field is related. It is possible that rationality has limits, but we should not behave as though these limits were exactly coterminous with our institutional boundary conditions.

Revision of content and challenge to institutionalized meanings of terms may often be achieved by a modification of the terms themselves. Words are the means by which our thought processes are mainly operated and the means by which we manipulate concepts. But at the same time a terminology may restrict our thinking and even enslave us. Numbers possess the same positive and negative elements. Perhaps the only presently known safeguard against the deification of terminologies and the related ossification of our thought, is the interdisciplinary team. Perhaps the future will be characterized, not so much by the great individual social scientists as by the great collaborators. Thorsten Sellin is, without doubt, both.

THE LANGUAGE OF IS AND SHOULD

The language of number is limited by the logic of inference. In addition it possesses limitations not common to ordinary verbal communication. It does not attempt to embrace the concept of "should" or "ought," concepts that feature frequently in criminological writings. The language of "what is" and "what ought to be" can appear confusingly similar, and the essential distinction is frequently not made or inadequately considered. It is, as the last sentence shows, extremely difficult to communicate in words without direct or implicit use of the language of "should." Yet in the sentence the term "inadequate" might, given certain further considerations, be reduced from an "ought" language (the implicit assumption is that the procedure should be "adequate") to the language of inequalities.

Statistical language can cope with inequalities but, in order to transform certain questions, further dimensions have to be stated or left to be filled in by the reader. Consider, for example, the question, "What ought to be done about the death penalty?" In this connection it may be appropriate to refer to Sellin's classical analysis of murder rates and the use of the death penalty.[7] The implicit administrative question might have been phrased, "Is it safe to remove the death penalty?" This question has still some element of the language of "should"—it should not be removed if it is not "safe" to do so. The question, then, is to be transformed into a question or questions in the language of IS and use made of established inequalities for purposes of further inferences. The questions as examined by Sellin were "Is there any evidence that the death penalty deters, in that murder rates are lower where it applies than where it does not?" and "Does the presence of the death penalty relate to police safety?" By careful comparisons between states having and not having the death penalty and to some states that changed their policies, Sellin was able to show that the answer to both questions was "No." But does this answer the administrative question? Not directly. The answers provided by Sellin were to two arguments usually used to support the retention of the death penalty, and these arguments were not supported by the data. There may be advanced further arguments for the retention, and these too might be capable of further examination by similar means.

The answers do not indicate what should be done. Nor do they deal with such ethical questions as whether death is more humane than alternative penalties that might be used, as, for example, incarceration for life. Nor is there any other indication of what action authority might or might not take in dealing with murderers. This is, in the particular and simple example, very obvious. In other cases it is not so obvious and it may not be surprising how often, in more complex cases, arguments are made against the scientific approach on the grounds that the "essential"(!) elements in the situation have been ignored in the analysis. On the other hand, the mirror image error is also frequently noted, namely, that analogous with suggesting that in the light of the answers to the derived questions, the initial (administrative) question has also been directly answered.

This error is made very frequently in relation to parole prediction systems—whether subjective or obtained from the use of tables. When the parole applicant is assessed as having a high chance of recidivism, it is often assumed that the action directly indicated by the prognosis is to retain him longer in the prison. Similarly, if an offender, after having been found guilty is said to have a poor chance of reform, his sentence is made more severe (longer "treatment"). As though the only way to modify treatment is in terms of time! The questions of prognosis (estimates of probability) may be answered with some precision, but this

[7] Thorsten Sellin in *The Sociology of Punishment and Correction*, edited by Johnson/ Savitz/Wolfgang (Wiley, New York).

answer does not indicate the appropriate action. The action implies an objective. The estimates of probability of recidivism are "information," but only information. Rational action demands a basis in the logical relationship *between* information (only one component) and the objective desired in terms of the room for maneuver (decision variety). Thus in the concept of rational decisions there are three components: (1) information, (2) objective, (3) decision.[8]

To some degree it is possible to infer the objective of a decision that has been made by reference to the information and the decision variety, assuming rationality. It is possible to state that the decision maker behaved AS IF he were trying to maximize an objective that may be assumed to follow from the processes of rational thought in terms of what it was possible for him to do. For example, parole prediction tables (so miscalled) have been produced in some states, but parole boards have been known to object that these tables do not provide guidance of use in parole decisions. This may indeed be so, but not usually for the reasons given. If the board states that its decisions are based on the likelihood of reconviction, then the tables provide information of the kind said to be sought. But parole boards do not behave as though this were the information most useful to them. A case that has attracted considerable public outcry will be treated with much more caution than another of similar probability of recidivism. This caution may not be unreasonable, but it is irrational to claim that the objective sought is to minimize recidivism. Rather, it might more rationally be claimed that the objective is to minimize adverse publicity of the decisions of the board. A different criterion requires a different solution of the problem of relationships between information and decision. It would be possible to construct parole experience tables which, instead of or in addition to reconviction of the failures, the degree of failure was assessed by the quantity of adverse publicity. A weighted decision guide could be provided.

Perhaps parole boards would find such tables more useful and more in accord with the objectives that are in fact sought in their decisions. Then why should they not request the scientist to construct such tables? It may be supposed that some ethical difficulties are seen in the explicit adoption of such a criterion. But why? The press is an organ of democratic social systems outside the control of the parole board and provides one way of assessing public concern regarding decisions that the public sees as unacceptable. The press is not the most satisfactory indicator of social concern and may, at times, create public opinion rather than reflect it. Nonetheless, if boards are in fact mainly influenced in their decisions by

[8] Leslie T. Wilkins (1965), *Social Deviance*, Prentice-Hall and Tavistock.

the press, then systematic objective analysis of the press comment can provide better guidance for their decisions than the objective assessment of other criteria. If this issue raises further questions, they too can be the subject of rigorous methods of analysis and study. The inappropriate stating of objectives provides only inappropriate answers. If the objectives that the boards consider they *ought* to seek are unrealistic, and these objectives are used as the basis for scientific work, then the scientific work will be unrealistic.

The exploration of the nature of systems enables hypotheses to be stated in such a way that they may be tested, but the criterion or objective that the system is designed to maximize or attain may not be the same as those concerned with it would wish it to be seeking. Displacement of goals can take place in very subtle ways. Thus, sometimes, rigorous methods of study may reveal issues of ethical importance previously not suspected to exist in the situation.

Sellin, in his previously quoted study of murder and police safety reveals a most interesting feature as a side issue of the data analysis. He noted that in states where the death penalty *was* in force, 90 percent of reporting police officers subscribed to the view that it helped with police safety, whereas in states where there was no death penalty 74 percent believed that it did *not*. It may be assumed that there was no major selection factor in the police recruitment policy in the different states that could give rise to this crossover of the bulk of opinion. It would have been interesting to know the nature of the process of the suspected change of police opinion on abolition. Was the change of opinion simultaneous with the change in the law? Did the swing in opinion begin then and increase with experience? If so, what characterized the change from 10 percent to 74 percent? How did the rate of change vary in relation to incidents of effect upon police as against incidents of murder not having such an impact? Perhaps, rather, in all states, police officers feel reasonably safe (if not, they might no longer be police officers—a self-selection factor may apply). This subjective feeling of reasonable safety (experience) may then be related to the question roughly as follows: "I feel safe; there is a death penalty," or "I feel safe; there is no death penalty." On the other hand, it might be thought that the law was itself a norm-*giving* system as well as a norm-defining system, and that the norm of attitude was itself modulated by the change of law. Promulgation of laws is a means of informing the public generally and particularly the sectors of the public most concerned (for example, the police) of the definitions of the norms that the legislature has accepted according to the particular theory and practice of government of the country or state. The press also informs regarding norms, mainly by means of negative definitions, by information about deviations from norms and the consequences of such deviation. The system of social control is essentially one of information. The situation as it may be *in fact* provides *no control*, but beliefs regarding the situation, which may or may not be closely related to fact, may be the control mechanism.

Of course, there are some areas of behavior covered by the law where consensus may be assumed, especially in regard to prohibitions regarding events termed "serious crimes." Indeed the concept of "seriousness" may be defined in terms of the degree of consensus. If everybody in a country regards an act as an offense, then it is likely to be regarded as a "serious" offense. General consensus is expected in the Western world in regard to the concept of murder as a "serious crime"—everybody thinks it *is* wrong; therefore, everybody individually tends to regard it as wrong to a considerable degree. Frequency of a response to an opinion in a group and intensity of belief in the individual are certainly different dimensions, but they would appear to be generally positively correlated in terms of social control systems. A minority who rejected with great intensity the majority view would not be expected to conform to the encoded majority opinion as represented in the law or other forms of social control. If a matter is not seen as a serious issue and if intense opinions are not held regarding it, then the norm-making effect of the law may be expected to be of little significance. These questions may be of importance in any consideration of the importance of the general preventive aspects of the law but, as has been shown many times, they do not apply in the specific case of murder in Western countries.

As Sellin has shown, there is no evidence that the death penalty is any deterrent for murder in the United States. How far it may be possible to generalize to other countries or even within the United States to other crimes is a matter for investigation. Perhaps as Wootton[9] has suggested, the deterrent effect of law diminishes as the "seriousness" of crime increases. Nonetheless, the concept of seriousness (an intensity measure) and the concept of consensus are not exactly similar. Indeed the disparity between these two dimensions may offer a useful tool of analysis of relevant issues.

THE SERIOUSNESS OF CRIME

The concept of "serious" or "not serious" crime is, perhaps, the basis for the historical division of some legal codes into indictable and

[9] Barbara Wootton (1959), *Social Science and Social Pathology*, Allen and Unwin (London).

nonindictable offenses. In other codes, misdemeanours are separated from offenses. Again we see the simple dichotomy. Although seriousness has long been considered a continuous factor, the system of justice has had to proceed by adjustment after the basic dichotomy had been made. Perhaps until we can measure "seriousness," our knowledge is of a meagre and unsatisfactory kind.

Those who agree with this proposition will give much credit to the work of Sellin and Wolfgang in their recent book *The Measurement of Delinquency*[10]. Here they attempted to find some basis for the assessment of the "seriousness" of different offenses. Their method was closely related to the methods of the psychophysicists. I was privileged to be associated in a small way with this work.

Subsequent to the publication of this work, some criticisms have been noted. Some of these have attacked the utility, others have attacked the theoretical basis for the approach.

Previous attempts to assess the seriousness of crime have relied on the legal descriptions of the criminal event. For example, where the law lays down minimum and maximum penalties or both for offense categories, it may be assumed that the intention of the legislature was to indicate the seriousness of the category of the events so described. Hence, it may be argued that offenses may be ranked by the legal categories in terms of the range of penalties available to the court in disposing of proved offenses under the appropriate categories. There are, of course, two weaknesses to this method: first, that the range of behaviour *within* any legal category is often very great; and, second, that statutes often reflect historical features in that penalty limits may have been fixed at different times and in regard to different situations than those now prevailing. It is possible that the division into indictable and nonindictable offenses was at one time related to some simple concept of seriousness through the range of available penalties and, hence, the level of the court that might dispose of the case.

Another approach due to Silvey[11] uses the basic idea of contemporary democratic assessment, but again with reference to legal categories. Some critics of Sellin and Wolfgang's work have relied heavily on these types of prior analyses. In particular, the degree of consensus found in Sellin and Wolfgang's study between the ratings by different groups has been doubted because some prior studies have failed to show any real consensus. Silvey's study does certainly show a wide range of variation of

[10] Thorsten Sellin and Marvin E. Wolfgang (1964), *The Measurement of Delinquency* (Wiley, New York).
[11] J. Silvey (1961), "The Criminal Law and Public Opinion," *Criminal Law Review*, pp. 345–432.

opinions regarding the seriousness of criminal acts by the method which he used. A sample of 907 persons answered questions that asked them to select the most serious ("the worst") crime from a list of 15 offenses. The frequency analysis for those attaining any real proportion of the vote (the first eight with a population frequency of 5 percent or more) are noted below:

Offense Selected as "Worst Crime"	Population Sample Percent
Indecent assault	25
Cruelty to children	21
Planned murder for money	20
Killing a policeman to escape arrest	9
Robbery with violence	6
Causing death by dangerous driving	6
Rape	6
Drunk in charge of car	6

Silvey, commenting on these results, says that the "lack of agreement is perhaps the most surprising feature. . . ." Not more than one in four persons agreed in the selection of the "worst crime." But what was the nature of the disagreement. Can it really be inferred that the interviewees disagreed regarding the seriousness of any criminal event? It seems certain that, at least in part, it was disagreement regarding what sort of event *might* be described by the terms used, or what event might have been included within the definition of the legal phrase. It should also be noted that frequency and intensity are confounded in Silvey's study. The proportion of persons (frequency) is interpreted as a measure of seriousness (intensity). In any event, the public can only respond in terms of information in their possession.

It must be acknowledged that the main source of information regarding crime for the layman is the press report. These reports do not cover a representative sample of crimes, but they cover a most selective one. The events that are reported have a quality of "newsworthiness." What is reported of offenses, selected from categories that are for the most part trivial, will not be trivial cases. There may be few murders in a community and perhaps the majority will be reported in some detail in the press. (This is certainly the case in the United Kingdom where the sample of public opinion was taken.) There may be many cases of indecent assault, and the sample selected as "newsworthy" will, therefore, possess special characteristics. The amount of space allocated to a murder story in which the offender commits suicide will be much less than to one that leads to a manhunt. If a female hunt is involved, perhaps even more space still! There is a relationship between the degree of "unusualness" of an event and the amount of attention it receives in the press. Such background information is not a very adequate basis for the public to form very reasonable opinions regarding either the general pattern of crime or the seriousness of types of legal categories; nor, it might be added, of making sound inferences from criminal statistics. Even if it were possible to overcome this difficulty, there are difficulties that arise directly from the nature of the legal descriptions. The famous train robbers in England who were sentenced to the longest terms of imprisonment ever used in recent times were guilty of robbery with violence, and many small children are also found guilty of robbery with violence—the same legal category. In the former case the haul was over $10 million, but when one small boy hits another and takes his pocket money, the sum involved may be only ten cents. Both acts, however, consist of the same legal elements—removal of property with use of violence or threat of violence. Few persons, and certainly not the courts today, would regard the two offenses as in any way similar in degree of seriousness. Thus the legal category does not provide any longer (if it ever did) a basis for assessment of seriousness.

But this was the basis of the public opinion sample in Silvey's study. What specimen of the offense category might the average citizen have had in mind when asked to assess the seriousness of, say, robbery with violence? Did he think of the small boy or the train robbers? There is no way of knowing because this question was not asked in Silvey's study, as it was in the study by Sellin and Wolfgang. It is meaningless to consider an average seriousness for any category of offense so wide, but this has been done. Relating of offense category to the courts' decision as to disposal is implicitly utilizing an average seriousness index for a total category. Criticism of Sellin and Wolfgang's work, which relies on evidence of the kind discussed above, is clearly unsound.

Other writers have referred back to Professor Sellin's comments on criminal statistics made in 1931[12] and see the recent work as inconsistent with his previous views. In general, such critics prefer the earlier view. If there is any "inconsistency," it is not necessarily a bad thing. Surely no intelligent person should be denied the right to change his views without being called "inconsistent." If a change of view is indicated, then the new concept is the more worthy of our attention. But, rather, it seems that interpretation of the reading of the original statement is to blame for the apparent difference. The relevant passage reads:

[12] Thorsten Sellin (1931), "The Basis of a Crime Index," *J. Crim. Law and Criminol.*, **22**, 333–356.

Due to a number of variable elements represented by changes in administrative policies and efficiency, the value of a crime rate for index purposes decreases as the distance from the crime itself in terms of procedure increases. In other words, police statistics particularly those of "crimes known to the police" are most likely to furnish a good basis for a crime index.

Thus, if we wish to discuss crimes, we are concerned with "events," certainly not with "persons." Persons arrested, persons found guilty, persons detained, and any other persons-based measures are measures related to *decisions*, not to *events*. Unless somebody *decides* to arrest, detain, or imprison a person, the person does not become a statistic in any system based on these concepts and definitions. In such cases it is the decisions that are counted. There is no inconsistency in the major point here, for in the recent work, Sellin and Wolfgang insist upon the "event" as the unit and not the decisions made about it. Of course, when we are concerned with "juvenile delinquency," the person concerned with the event is confounded with the conception of the "event" and, clearly, there can be no index of juvenile delinquency as such, for there is no way whereby the acts due to juveniles are identified prior to the clearance of the incident.

Sellin suggested in 1931 that changes in the administrative policy would influence administrative decisions. Decisions regarding "crimes" (whatever the decision might be) provide no index of "crimes" (whatever crimes might be defined to be). Nevertheless, data regarding the decision process has a potential utility. It is not necessarily the statistician who is at fault if incorrect inferences are made. In general, the counting operation is done with reasonable precision, and the classification systems used are usually interpreted and applied with care. But the problems arise in the stage of utilization of the data. Figures that are not, in fact, measures of "what we are talking about" are quoted as though they were.

In most fields of social research and measurement it is necessary to utilize several measurements rather than to attempt simplification of the data-collection process. The problems are complex and cannot be enlightened by excessively simplified data systems. Simplification may be possible if the inferences with which the policy maker will be concerned can be stated *first*. We are, here again, back at the problem of criteria.

It is clear that one of the concepts of significance in the decisions regarding criminal policy is that of the "seriousness" of offenses, and to this must be added and eventually related the concepts of social cost and social benefits. These concepts enable us to think of criteria other than the moral absolutes, as a means for evaluation of our social control systems.

A NOTE ON SOCIAL COST

It is generally believed and almost universally shown in criminal statistics throughout the Western world that crime (mainly offenses against property) has increased rapidly in recent years and that the trend is continuing. Ignoring possible doubts and without even exercising reasonable scepticism regarding the basis for this, it may be remarked that the gross national product of the countries concerned with the rise in "crime" has also increased very considerably. Perhaps the number of illegal transactions has not increased more sharply than the number of legal transactions. If we look at crime, not in terms of moral absolutes, but in relative terms, our strategy for social action could, perhaps, be patterned in a different and more effective way.

Implicitly, the murder rate uses as its base number the population at risk to being murdered. The base for property crimes is not property at risk to being stolen, but again, persons. A change of base would certainly show a different pattern in the trends of "crime." Which base should be used and for what purposes raises again issues of morals and value systems. It must be conceded that the point at which moral issues come most closely into touch with the scientific attitude is in the fields of law, jurisprudence, criminology, and corrections, particularly with regard to the criteria of evaluation and social action research analyses.

The social scientist cannot claim that he is totally unconcerned with moral issues, but he is not the acknowledged expert in this area. There are operations that the scientist carries out that are value-free: measurement is possible, systematic study of decision processes can be made, and analyses of situational data can be effected that provide information directly relevant to decisions. But problems of moral issues enter immediately when we consider what to measure, for example, what situations should receive priority for study. In particular, when we are concerned with equations that will indicate which lines of action will maximize the probability of a certain payoff, the particular criterion or objective to be inserted in the equations is not a value-free problem. Procedures that examine the critical path to maximum payoff are known but, while the methods of solution themselves involve no value systems of choices, the setting up of the matrices is a matter involving judgment. These are problems that cannot be dealt with by the social scientist alone.

A means of collaboration between the user and producer of social research data must be found. This means that a link must be developed between moral questions and the scientific method. User and producer cannot go on ignoring each other's existence. If communication is to take place, a suitable language must be found. The language of moral absolutes will not translate into scientific models. Some new conceptualization of value systems in terms of a modern language must be devised.

The Unfinished Business of Criminal Statistics

JOHN P. CONRAD

One of the more amiable disputes in an acrimonious age concerns the nature of criminology. Is it an independent discipline with a conceptual life of its own, as some would contend?[1] Will a worldwide quest discover a consensus on its objectives and boundaries?[2] Is it a chimera subsisting on the exchange of ideas and findings among the basic behavioral disciplines concerned with understanding the criminal and his aberrations? So long have such controversies flourished in journals and common rooms, and so sorely would they be missed if they were ever settled that it would be presumptuous to venture a resolution in these pages.

But much can be discovered about a country and its culture from a scrutiny of its most admired inhabitants. In the domain of American criminology, the first citizen is Thorsten Sellin. If a cartographer of the social sciences would understand criminology in the United States today, he must begin with a review of Sellin's career. I shall leave this felicitous task to more competent hands. For me it is enough that whatever criminology is, Sellin is a criminologist. For his colleagues, however eminent or humble, this conclusion is of surpassing significance. Sellin has set the style and pace that determine our standards of performance. We may fall short of his excellence, but he has pointed the way to new uses for an old discipline.

To be specific, Sellin's prodigious labors over a half century in this vineyard have mightily contributed to the transformation of criminology from a speculative occupation to an empirical study. From the first, he has insisted that propositions about the prevention and control of crime must proceed from the analysis of relevant facts scrupulously collected. To be sure, this is an insistence that conforms to the *Zeitgeist* of the age. Sooner or later someone would have had to distract criminology from the metaphysical debates of the nineteenth century to the application of

[1] Marvin E. Wolfgang and Franco Ferracuti, *The Subculture of Violence: Towards an Integrated Theory in Criminology*, London: Tavistock Publications, 1967.
[2] Leon L. Radzinowicz, *In Search of Criminology*, London: Heinemann, 1961.

scientific method to its substance. The point is that Sellin has always been in the forefront of the movement to build a criminology grounded on evidence. Because he thought and wrote as he did, it is no longer quite so easy for jurists and moralists to invoke the rhetoric of tradition in support of their pronouncements about crime and their exhortations about its remedy. Those with a predilection for the fustian of old dogmas can still find forums in which they can extol the wisdom of our ancestors in controlling human behavior and maintaining righteousness. They will seldom be asked by the pious to prove that these ancestors were especially effective in coping with the crime of their day or that their methods could be successfully applied to ours.

But the public is learning to listen to a new theme in the incessant debate over measures for reducing crime and our anxieties about it. It is learning to assume that, as to the solution of the crime problem, knowledge will produce understanding and understanding will lead to control, much the same way as in other human activities. The evidence that this new and hopeful approach is gaining adherents is to be found wherever crime is seen as a problem to be solved with reason and goodwill rather than as a monster to be viewed with delicious alarm. The most recent testimony to the acceptance of a heuristic criminology is the report of the President's Commission on Law Enforcement and the Administration of Justice,[3] in which a conservative group of establishmentarians attacked the hydra-headed beast with the weapons of science and statistics rather than with rhetoric and invective. When recommendations could be supported with data, the data were joyously exploited for all they were worth. Where no data were to be found, which was far too often the case, the Commission was loud in the expression of its disappointment. One of its most vigorous recommendations would create a National Criminal Justice Statistics Center that would prevent the stultification of future studies of the crime problem by the absence of information on its elementary dimensions.

This is the climate that Sellin did so much to create. For him and for those who have worked with him, the beginning of knowledge is measurement. Central to his career is his insistence on the collection of comprehensive, reliable, and relevant statistics. So many are the pitfalls in achieving this objective, and so essential is it that these pitfalls should be seen and avoided that Sellin devoted great thought to the principles and the structure of data collection that would assure the integrity of the statistical systems on which scholars and administrators must depend. In like vein, he strove for comparability from city to city,

[3] *The Challenge of Crime in a Free Society*, A Report by the President's Commission on Law Enforcement and the Administration of Justice, Washington: United States Government Printing Office, 1967.

from state to state, and from nation to nation. Finally, knowing that new tools of analysis would be needed if the data amassed were to provide new insights, he worked at the creation of methods of measurement whereby the significance of crime could be assessed in terms of the damage done. The methodology presented in the culminating achievement of his partnership with Professor Wolfgang offers criminology a means to make comparisons of the social damage caused by crime under varying community conditions. Measurements of this kind can give us a notion of the effectiveness of the various means adopted in different communities to combat delinquency.[4,5]

The achievement of Sellin's minimum requirements is far from complete. When viewed over the perspective of the decades, the gap between achievement and clearly defined goals, prescribed by the highest kind of authority, is immense and discouraging. In 1931, another Commission, the National Commission on Law Observance and Enforcement, reviewed the issues confronting the nation in the achievement of a comprehensive system of criminal statistics. It considered the feasibility of solving these problems and stated the importance of setting about it at once. The Wickersham Commission urged, among other things, that:

1. Compilation and publication of criminal statistics should be centralized . . . in some one place in each jurisdiction, and that should be one in which experts on statistical methods are available.

2. There should be a correlation of State statistics and of State and Federal statistics in one Federal bureau. . . . (which) should gather or receive and then correlate and put upon a comparable basis the whole body of criminal statistics. . . . so as to make the resulting information available for general purposes.

3. Local officials ought not to be expected to do more than turn in to the appropriate central office exactly what their records disclose. Putting the collected data into a general plan for country-wide purposes should be the work of statistical experts. . . .

4. For the purposes of a check upon the different agencies of criminal justice it is important that the compiling . . . of statistics should not be confided to any bureau or agency which is engaged in administering the criminal law. . . .

5. There should be a comprehensive plan for an ultimate complete body of statistics, covering crime, criminals, criminal justice, and penal treatment. . . ."[6]

[4] Thorsten Sellin and Marvin E. Wolfgang, The Measurement of Delinquency, New York: John Wiley, 1964.
[5] Thorsten Sellin, "International Criminal Statistics," Criminologica, 5:2:2–11, August 1967.
[6] National Commission on Law Observance and Enforcement: Report on Criminal Statistics, Washington: United States Government Printing Office, 1931, pp. 5–6.

I have exhumed these incontrovertible principles from the volume in which they have languished as a sober reminder that the most laudable plan must be not merely well-laid but also pushed with administrative and legislative vigor. Although there was no organized opposition to these recommendations at the time, nor has any become manifest since, we are about as far from the achievement of these goals as we ever were. In 1950, Sellin urged the enactment of the Uniform Criminal Statistics Act by each state and territory; to date, only California has managed to take this obviously needed step.

In 1955, Ronald Beattie, one of the country's most experienced and distinguished managers of criminal statistics, prescribed the elements of an optimal state criminal statistics system.[7] Although he was hardly propounding a set of novel demands, no state has yet achieved compliance—not even California where Beattie himself has labored diligently and long to meet his own requirements. The methodical accounting for crime and criminals from arrest through prosecution to correction and final discharge from the system, allowing for all the options available at each step of the way, is an objective as desirable in 1968 as it was in 1931, in 1950, in 1955, and even more feasible. It is an objective which is still unrealized.

A complete inventory of the gaps in our crime statistics would be long, tedious to compose or review, and a wearisome belaboring of the obvious. It must be left to those who will administer the system that will eventually come. What is less obvious and much less frequently remarked upon in scholarly forums is the solid progress that has been made in the quality of criminal statistics, in spite of our completely unorganized effort to deal with the problem as a whole. Not only is the progress significant but there is much promise of more progress to come.

Most important is the increasingly impressive series of *Uniform Crime Reports* published by the Federal Bureau of Investigation. Critiques of these reports have been searching, to say the least, but the FBI has also shown their value by adjusting statistical practice to meet professional objections.[8,9,10] New studies have been added to increase the value of the series to the professional fields concerned as well as to the public. The new enterprise, in following the criminal careers of a cohort

[7] Ronald H. Beattie, "Problems of Criminal Statistics in the United States," *Journal of Criminal Law, Criminology and Police Science*: 46:178–186. July-August 1955.

[8] Marvin E. Wolfgang: "Uniform Crime Reports: A Critical Appraisal." *University of Pennsylvania Law Review*: 111:708–738 (1963).

[9] Raymond E. Bauer, Editor: *Social Indicators*. Cambridge: The M.I.T. Press, 1966. Pp. 113–129.

[10] Albert J. Reiss: "Measurement of the Nature and Amount of Crime." Unpublished MS. submitted to the Office of Law Enforcement Assistance. April 1967.

of Federal offenders, is welcome to students of correctional effectiveness and will eventually produce invaluable base lines for studies of the capabilities of correctional agencies to reduce recidivism. It is a statistical venture that deserves emulation by state correctional research bureaus. We can only expect such proliferation if administrators as well as scholars learn to make use of this kind of study for action and planning.

Continued experience with new data-processing capabilities will augment the versatility of *Uniform Crime Reports*. It is neither a complete system, nor is it perfected so far as it goes. The important and heartening augury is that it is improving annually both in its structure and in its reliability.

Parallel to the improvement of the *Uniform Crime Reports* is the computerization of the large state systems, most notably those of California and New York. This is a process that is far from complete, even in these states, but plans are so well advanced and resources so wisely committed that we can expect that the end results will be major additions to the capacity of criminal statistics. In both California and New York, advantage is to be taken of the computer's resourcefulness to create information systems on crimes committed and the criminals who commit them.[11,12] Systems of these kinds are not solely intended for statistical purposes, but they are capable of the comprehensiveness urged by the Wickersham Commission nearly forty years ago.

NEED, TECHNOLOGY, AND SYSTEM

The prospects for accelerating improvements in criminal statistics are brighter than ever before. The reasons that burnish the prospects will also determine the scope of the system. Unless we consider carefully the implications of the forces making for a comprehensive statistical system, we may well end up with an excellent accounting system, but with little more understanding than we have in the present state of our ignorance.

The first stimulus to statistical improvement is administrative need. The *Uniform Crime Reports* do not emanate from a selfless concern by the FBI for information for information's sake. The series conveys many messages, but there is one insistently overriding theme. This *leitmotif*

[11] "The California Correctional Information System: Preliminary Information Requirements," Sacramento, The Institute for the Study of Crime and Delinquency, April 1967.
[12] "New York State Identification and Intelligence System: System Development Plan," Albany, April 1967.

tells us that there is an ominous and indubitable rise in the volume and commission of crime. Every year the volume leaps with the population. Every year the rates increase; in 1966 this increase was about 10 percent. These themes support and document our concern with the predicament of the police. Their workload is increasing; if their job is to be done at even the present level of effectiveness, their numbers must increase or their quality must improve, or both. Whatever the policy decision inferred by legislators from the FBI's somber accounting, it is clear that action is needed. Without the statistics so impressively marshalled by FBI statisticians, those who plan and determine organizational and budgetary changes would be at the mercy of rhetoric and anecdote. Criticisms of the technique and style of the FBI in fairness should take into account the purposes for which its statistics are compiled and published. On the other hand, continued collaboration by scholars and professional users of the system should find ways of exploiting the enormous capabilities of the FBI's data-collection system for the advantage of criminology as well as that of police administration. A first step in this necessary direction is the appointment of an Advisory Group to the Committee on Uniform Crime Records of the International Association of Chiefs of Police, announced in the 1966 issue of the *Uniform Crime Reports*. This group should become a channel between the professional criminologist and the FBI; this channel should be a frequently traveled thoroughfare.

However, *Uniform Crime Reports*, as presently constituted, cannot now meet some readily foreseeable demands. At every level of government today, there is an awareness that advanced fiscal practice requires that agencies formulate their objectives in measurable terms. Administrators should present for legislative decision an array of options for achieving objectives, each option being costed in advance. This is the essence of performance budgeting. It is far from a perfected art, especially in those fields of government where the output of the system is not measurable in money. Not all legislators are convinced of its worth, even though the system will place in legislative hands a leverage which they have never had before over policy and the level of expenditure. In the administration of criminal justice, the methods by which objectives can be quantified have yet to be conceptualized. Whatever the methodology turns out to be, it is certain that it will depend on the measurement of many kinds of variables, some of which are not even counted now. Police departments will have to study the consequences of the deployment of personnel in accordance with varying enforcement requirements. Courts will have to compare the consequences of differing sentencing policies in terms of the achievement of a wide variety of judicial objectives. Correctional agencies will have the same kinds of problems, to which they must add the study of management decisions required of any organization which must dispose of the daily routines of large numbers of staff and clients.

Any thoughtful person concerned with economy and efficiency in government must welcome performance budgeting. For the statistician of crime the pleasure is greatly enhanced; he can plainly look ahead to the compilation of masses of statistics that would have been fanciful to request less than a decade ago. That these data are not to be compiled for scientific use should not deter the criminologist from looking over the budget analyst's shoulder. Most of the data will need the analysis and explication of the criminologist to be of use to an administrator. The thoroughfare has two sides, and the criminologist must expect that his expertise will be needed for purposes of which he did not dream in the academia of the past.

The need for criminal statistics will vastly increase production. So, too, will the new technology available to the statistician. As everyone knows from the gloating accounts of cybernetic triumphs, the computer has made possible methods of information storage, retrieval, and transmission that have transformed the very nature of information. What this process has meant to the meaning of knowledge is beyond my scope in this essay. What it has already done to the administration of justice is discernible in such projects as the FBI's National Crime Information Center and the New York Identification and Intelligence System. It takes no soaring leap of the imagination to extrapolate from such achievements as these to the creation of a nationwide information system, one of whose outputs would be a periodic statistical accounting for all criminal activity and the reciprocal actions of police, courts, and correctional agencies. All that is needed is an array of concepts and an administrative appartatus to match the technology on hand.

Finally, as needs are defined and technology is elaborated to meet administrative requirements, new systems come into being that have needs of their own. For many years the orderly mind of Thorsten Sellin has seen the need for a Uniform Criminal Statistics Act. Other priorities have supervened in the legislative maelstrom; except for California, we cannot yet point to much success for a movement that would contribute so much understanding at so little cost. But the computer is a harder taskmaster than the professor, especially when the computer has taught the administrator to depend on the information it processes to make the decisions and the policies for which he is responsible. It is not unreasonable to foresee that the computer will at last make possible the aspiration of the Wickersham Commission for an "ultimate, complete body of statistics."

Here is a rosy future indeed! The United States, so long the leader of the civilized world in the volume and rate of crime, will at last have a statistical system capable of accounting for it in all of its variety and all of its consequences. There can hardly be an objection to this entirely probable outcome of the combination of innovations in fiscal practice, technological capabilities, and systems development. Rational management controls of the administration of justice will at last become realities, replacing the hoary rules of thumb which have prevailed for so long. With these controls there will also become available great quantities of data never before accumulated, which can surely be manipulated to great criminological advantage.

NEW QUESTIONS FOR NEW UNDERSTANDING

While we rub our hands in anticipation of the statistical feast in store for criminologists, we still have time to consider carefully the implications of the prospects ahead. Criminologists are not administrators. The demands we make on a system of criminal statistics must differ, even if in meeting administrative requirements the system can produce much information of scientific value. We must not allow ourselves to become too easily satisfied with the abundance that is about to flow in our direction. We can assure ourselves that our dissatisfaction will be academically becoming if we keep in mind the objectives of criminology.

I shall persist in my evasion of a definition of the status of criminology as a discipline clearly separable from the basic behavioral sciences. But surely the object of criminology is the informed understanding of crime and the criminal. Although some may claim that this is enough, as a criminologist in the market place I must assert that the understanding we achieve should culminate in the effective prevention of crime and the safe restoration of the offender to the community. Now that we have at long last an integrated accounting system in sight—even though it is still not in hand—what more can we ask of the statistician to help us understand the phenomena of crime to the end that it will be better prevented and controlled?

Let us begin with establishing the true volume of crime. For generations, criminologists have worried about the dark side of criminal statistics. What we really know about crime and the criminal is derived from cleared crime reports and caught criminals. What we know about uncleared crime reports, unreported crime, and uncaught criminals is speculative, and there have been few credible indices to the volume of any of these categories.

One of the happiest inspirations of the recent President's Commission on Law Enforcement and the Administration of Justice was the creation of a Task Force on the Assessment of Crime. An outstanding achievement of this Task Force was the initiation of a study of the victims of crime, based on a large sample of the whole population. The extent of unreported crime varied from offense to offense. Except for homicide and auto theft, unreported crime exceeded the rates reported in *Uniform Crime Reports* by wide margins. The principal reasons cited for failure to report were unwillingness to harm the offender and lack of confidence in the police.[13] Clearly there are many questions that must arise about the methodology of victim research surveys. The comments of the Task Force stressed some of the potential uses to which studies of this kind could be put. Programs to increase police effectiveness could be studied in terms of victim survey research; so also could delinquency-prevention projects. Data from such surveys would provide an excellent check of the validity of official statistics.[14] The Task Force did not think it necessary to conduct annual victim surveys on a national basis.

Assuming that the methodology can be further refined to an accepted level of confidence, it is hard to see why the advantages of a regular series of victim research surveys would not be obvious and of sufficient value to justify the great expense of conducting them. Unreported crime represents damage of a specially insidious kind. Its damage to the victim is no less because it is unreported. The assurance it gives to the offender of the odds in his favor is no less menacing because it may be spurious. As a social indicator of the confidence of the people in the police, a regular survey of this kind, which offered regional and local details, would provide urban planners with an instrument for assessing the worth of available options in law enforcement.

For the criminologist preoccupied with the longer range, a victim research survey, conducted in a regular series, offers the best hope of understanding the uncaught criminal. In most kinds of unsolved crime, only the victim, if anybody at all, has any information about the perpetrator. Through watching his shadow over time, we may find some ways of assessing his numbers. Perhaps we may also find ways of catching him or of inducing his victims to report him.

The truism that crime does not occur in a vacuum has inspired remarkably little interdisciplinary action. The connections between economic, political, and social conditions have received speculative attention, but they have not been illuminated by data or correlations. The

[13] *Task Force Report: Crime and Its Impact—An Assessment,* Washington: United States Government Printing Office, 1967, pp. 17–18.
[14] *Ibid.,* p. 132.

relationship between unemployment and delinquency has been studied by Glaser, but using far less comprehensive data than are now in sight.[15] To establish that the connection exists is far from exploiting the finding so that it can be used. Statisticians should seek procedures whereby crime and social indicators can be correlated so that intervention programs can be planned, implemented, and tested through trend analysis.

Other correlations are obvious enough, awaiting the data and the imagination to use them. Measures of the effectiveness of educational systems could be tied to the data of crime. So also could the rates of suicide and mental illness, geographical mobility, income levels, and many other variables. Many of these connections were made in Chicago thirty or forty years ago. They should be reexamined periodically to study the interactions of social movement and change.

Criminologists have subsisted for so long on starvation rations that they will find it hard to adjust to conditions of statistical abundance. The coming age of statistically grounded administration and legislation will offer many answers to long-oustanding questions. The answers will be most usable when criminologists and the administrators who produce the data have collaborated in asking the questions, in preparing tables in advance, and in considering the needed continuities. These are urgent needs; there is time to meet them, but the time will run out.

A first consideration is an organized scientific support for the development of a national system. We have seen how the recommendations of the Wickersham Commission for an integrated criminal statistics system languished in ignominious obscurity for nearly four decades. In the final report of the President's Commission on Law Enforcement and the Administration of Justice, substantially the same recommendation appears[16] in somewhat broader language. The Commission recommends the establishment of a National Criminal Justice Statistics Center that would collect, analyze, and disseminate data on criminal careers and data on crime and the system's response to it, as reported by criminal justice agencies at all levels.

Such a center is not the only conceivable solution to the problem of maintaining adequate national intelligence about crime and criminals. Its structure is not specified in detail by the Commission and many administrative issues have yet to be addressed. The Commission rightly points out that the creation of such a center will not in itself bring about a precipitous drop in the incidence of crime. But social problems do not reach solution in the presence of myths and ignorance. As to

[15] Daniel Glaser, *The Effectiveness of a Prison and Parole System,* Indianapolis: The Bobbs-Merrill Company, 1964, pp. 9–10.
[16] *The Challenge of Crime in a Free Society, op. cit.,* p. 269.

crime and the problems surrounding its reduction, the United States is in far worse condition than any of the undeveloped countries. The reasons for its backwardness have to do more than anything else with ignorance and myths, which resist new ideas and new instruments. Among our domestic problems, only the growing division between the races exceeds crime in the damage done to the social fabric or in national anxiety about the stability of our institutions. Indeed, there is plenty of evidence that there is a steady interaction between the crime problem and the race problem, confusing the solution of both. Such confusions can only respond to the uncovering of the relevant facts. The National Criminal Justice Statistics Center presents the best hope of unraveling the strands of hysteria that paralyse the nation into inaction. Without the early establishment of such a center, the country cannot plan to fight crime intelligently, nor can the impact of the plans be reliably assessed.

The history of science abounds in leaps ahead, which have resulted from the happy conjunction of new technology with imaginative conceptual thought. The most recent example is the field of economic theory in which advances in statistical theory made possible the analyses of Keynes and Schumpeter. These analyses, in turn, led to social controls of the economic cycle, which have virtually eliminated the crises that, in the past, have produce so heavy a load of human misery in the industrial nations.

Surely it is not idle to hope that a conjunction of the spacious ideas of Thorsten Sellin with the technology of a National Criminal Justice Statistics Center will result in an empirically based criminal justice by which crime can be humanely controlled and imaginatively prevented. Ideas emerge from the informed review of facts. Sellin has taught us how such a review should be conducted. The unfinished business of criminal statistics is to assemble the facts comprehensively enough so that we can go beyond control to action. It is a business that, by its nature, is likely to remain unfinished, thereby calling the criminologist to a struggle that is no less exciting in spite of its essentially Sisyphean nature.

A State Bureau of Criminal Statistics

RONALD H. BEATTIE

It seems most fitting, in a volume that is to recognize and honor Thorsten Sellin, to describe a major achievement in criminal statistics in the United States; the development of a central state bureau in California, the only such central bureau in the United States to date.

Sellin has contributed a great deal to the development of the California Bureau of Criminal Statistics, probably far more than even he realizes. He served as a valued counselor and guide during the late 1930's when I first became involved in the problems of collecting and interpreting national criminal statistics for the United States Bureau of the Census. Since then, Sellin has been a constant source for knowledge and encouragement in almost every phase of the writer's professional experience.

Because of his outstanding leadership, Sellin was requested to author a uniform act that would provide the states with a model for the collection and standardization of criminal statistics. This model act was promulgated by the Commissioners on Uniform State Laws in 1946. When the present Bureau of Criminal Statistics was created by executive order in 1945, the proposed organization was modeled on the general structure that Sellin was then formulating for the model uniform act. I, who became the first chief of the California bureau, cannot adequately express my appreciation for the encouragement and direction that I have continuously received from this great scholar and leader in the field of criminology.

THE NEED FOR CRIMINAL STATISTICS
IN THE UNITED STATES

The need for basic data on criminal justice in the United States has been cited repeatedly during the last four or five decades. Before World War I the only information to be found, except for scattered state and local court or correctional reports, was in the highly limited data collected by the Bureau of the Census describing persons incarcerated in correctional institutions.[1] There simply was no public accountability of crime, let alone of the processes of criminal justice administration. Following World War I, a surge of interest in the need for better information developed among sociologists specializing in criminology, which stimulated and effected a series of valuable surveys developing factual data on the amount and degree of crime and society's effort to control it.

These studies are still pointed to as models of the kind of information that should be continuously available; subsequent years have not diminished their value, rather their worth has been reaffirmed. The earliest of these studies was the Cleveland Survey undertaken about 1919 and followed by surveys in Missouri, Illinois, and New York.[2] I carried out another such study in Oregon from 1929 to 1932 together with Wayne L. Morse, then professor and subsequently Dean at the University of Oregon Law School.[3]

These surveys proved it was feasible and desirable for states to account statistically for the processes used to handle criminal offenders. Further, they outlined for the first time the quantitative facts relating to arrest, prosecution, and conviction of persons accused of crime including the processes of correctional treatment.

In 1929, President Hoover established a commission titled, "The National Commission on Law Observance and Enforcement." It was headed by Mr. George Wickersham and thereafter was usually referred to as the Wickersham Commission. Many aspects of the crime problem and the administrative and judicial procedures used to deal with them were reviewed by the Commission, and at least a dozen reports were published. In the report on criminal statistics, the Commission pointed out that the surveys of the 1920's had demonstrated the possibility of organizing a reporting system to show what happens to persons arrested and prosecuted and that such information could be made available regularly to those responsible for administering the various justice-type agencies and to all concerned with improving the processes of criminal justice. The Commission stressed that because criminal justice was primarily a state matter, each state should undertake to set up and

[1] Special counts of prisoners were made and published by the Census Bureau in 1904, 1910, and 1923.
[2] Roscoe Pound and Felix Frankfurter, *Criminal Justice in Cleveland*, Cleveland: Cleveland Foundation, 1922. Missouri Association for Criminal Justice Survey Committee, *The Missouri Crime Survey*, New York: Macmillan, 1926. New York (State) Crime Commission, Subcommittee on Statistics, Report, February 28, 1928, Albany, 1928; Report, February 28, 1929; Report, December 28, 1929, Albany, 1930. Illinois Crime Survey, Illinois Association for Criminal Justice, Chicago, 1929.
[3] Wayne L. Morse and Ronald H. Beattie, *Survey of the Administration of Criminal Justice in Oregon*, Eugene: University of Oregon Press, 1932.

develop a system of statistical reporting that would supply accurate uniform data on crime, the administrative processes of handling offenders, together with detailed information about the offenders themselves.[4]

During the same period of time other related events occurred. The Census Bureau, after a comprehensive census survey of persons in prisons during 1923, had undertaken an annual reporting scheme that would permit describing all persons committed and released from state and federal prisons and reformatories. Annual summaries on prisoners were published by the bureau for the years 1926 through 1946. Only a brief summary was issued in 1947. Subsequently, the United States Bureau of Prisons assumed responsibility for this series. A brief annual summary, entitled National Prisoner Statistics, has been issued for each year since 1948, giving the number of prisoners received in the institutions of each state and the federal government, and the number and type of releases.

During the ferment of this decade, the International Association of Chiefs of Police became concerned with the need for uniform data describing criminal justice at the police level. Through a grant, the Rockefeller Foundation sponsored a study that resulted in a proposed uniform crime-reporting system for police agencies.[5] This new system was commenced in 1930. Before the end of that year, by action of Congress, it became the responsibility of the Federal Bureau of Investigation, which has carried this series ever since. The data collected are regularly published by that bureau under the title, Crime in the United States—Uniform Crime Reports.

To supply the need for information on the prosecution and conviction of offenders, the Census Bureau agreed to undertake a new reporting series and to obtain from courts of general jurisdiction annual tally sheets recording the number of defendants prosecuted and disposed of in the courts by certain offense groups and the kinds of sentences they received. The basic pattern for this development came from studies made at Johns Hopkins University under the leadership of Leon Marshall.[6] The first reports were collected for the year 1932; by 1937, approximately 1500 courts of general jurisdiction in some 30 states were sending in such reports. The writer served as the first statistical technician in the Census Bureau, exclusively responsible for both the court and prison data between 1937 and 1940.

[4] National Commission on Law Observance and Enforcement, Report on Criminal Statistics, No. 3, Washington, D.C.: U.S. Government Printing Office, 1931.
[5] International Association of Chiefs of Police, Uniform Crime Reporting, New York: J. J. Little and Ives, 1929.
[6] California Department of Justice, Bureau of Criminal Statistics, Crime in California, Sacramento: Annual, 1952-1958.

In all of these developments, Thorsten Sellin had a primary role serving on nearly every committee in the formative stages of these national collections and continuing as a special consultant to the Census Bureau in its prison and court statistics.

Among criminologists, administrators, and others concerned with the problem of crime these new reporting series were acclaimed with enthusiasm. Little attention was given to the recommendation in the Wickersham Commission report that the states undertake the development of basic criminal statistics within their own borders. Somehow it was assumed that the new national reporting systems would automatically supply the type of information desired without the states assuming any responsibility.

The inherent weakness of this approach was most vividly demonstrated in the collection of court disposition information. In each state reporting in this series, arrangements were made to designate a Special Agent of the Census Bureau, often a person in the State Attorney General's Office. This made possible the use of the government postage frank in sending forms and returning reports. This agent's responsibility presumably was to insure completeness of reporting from all counties within the state, although he was not assigned responsibility for the accuracy of the information or its interpretation. As might be anticipated, the result was a great lack of uniformity in the way data were completed. There was no possibility of the Census Bureau's office in Washington exercising any effective control over more than 1500 separate reporting agencies in 30 states. The problems of variability among the state court systems, particularly with respect to jurisdictional coverage of criminal cases, became increasingly complex and could not be resolved satisfactorily. The last annual publication in this series was for the year 1946. The series was then abandoned because of its incompleteness and the tremendous difficulty in obtaining uniform and comparable data from local counties without state responsibility for collecting, checking, and editing the information summarized at the end of each year.

Today, at the close of 1967, there exists only the two national series of statistical reports on crime: Uniform Crime Reports, which covers primarily data on the offenses in seven major groups reported to the police, and National Prisoner Statistics covering admissions to and releases from state and federal prisons and reformatories. There is also a recent pilot experiment in uniform parole reporting being carried on in cooperation with a number of states under the auspices of the National Council on Crime and Delinquency.[7] This effort may well develop a

[7] "Uniform Parole Reports—A Feasible Study," National Parole Institutions, administered by the National Council on Crime and Delinquency, December 1965.

standardized method of reporting on parole that could eventually be incorporated in the National Prisoner Statistics series.

LIMITATIONS OF PRESENT CRIMINAL STATISTICS

The 1967 report of the President's Crime Commission has again called attention to the deficiencies found in criminal statistics in the United States. It has pointed out that there is still a dearth of reliable information that describes the criminal justice system and systematic ways of reporting criminal events, offenders, and processes of criminal justice and recommends the establishment of a National Criminal Statistics program.[8]

It is somewhat startling to find in this report a questioning of the recommendations made in the Wickersham Report of 1931 for the development of state responsibility for criminal statistics as the only basis on which to build a national system.[9] Apparently, the fact that, aside from California, there has been no serious attempt to establish a state central system is the basis of an assumption that state responsibility is not a practical way to approach a system of national uniform statistics on crime. It is the writer's contention, based on years of experience in local, state, and national levels and, more particularly, with the development of the one-state system that exists, that it will not be possible to produce the kind of factual information needed for a national picture unless and until each of the states undertakes the development of its own statistics.

There is, however, a strong need for the creation of a national center to be a focus for stimulation and coordination and to promulgate and develop uniform classifications and standards of accountability among the states. It is completely impossible for a national center in Washington to undertake the direct collection and compilation of data from all of the local agencies involved in crime control that exist in the municipalities, counties, and states of this nation. On the other hand a national center would aid and assist states to develop procedures to undertake this responsibility. There are six or eight states with well-established reporting procedures in certain portions of the crime picture that could readily begin to build up a state bureau with support and encouragement.

The administration of criminal justice in the United States is char-

[8] "The Challenge of Crime in a Free Society," Report of President's Commission on Law Enforcement and Administration of Justice. *Task Force Report, Crime and its Impact—An Assessment*, Chapter 10; *Criminal Statistics—An Urgently Needed Resource*, Government Printing Office, 1967.
[9] *Ibid*, pp. 124–125.

acterized by its divided responsibility among the thousands of independent agencies involved. There are, for example, over 8000 municipalities, each with its own independent police departments; there are well over 3000 counties, each with its own set of courts, procedures, and correctional agencies. Probation departments, for the most part, are organized either on a municipal or county basis, although there are a few states that provide central probation services. Each of the 50 states is a sovereign in the field of crime control. Each state enacts its own criminal laws and sets up its own structure for the administration of justice, the only common requirement being that laws and procedures must conform to the general provisions of the federal constitution. Definitions of criminal offenses vary from state to state; procedures followed in the handling of offenders vary. The organizational structure of agencies involved in the control of crime also differs widely from state to state. However, within each state there is a basic uniformity to be found in the constitutional provisions; the laws, the procedures, and the administrative setup of criminal justice. Therefore, it is possible to organize a uniform reporting of information to a central bureau within and under the authority of the state, which would be the proper agency to report to a national center. Further, it would permit each state to progress beyond the more general standards of information required for national reporting to supply more specific data needed by the state agencies.

Sellin has been a chief proponent of the development of responsible and uniform criminal statistics in the United States for more than 40 years.[10] As mentioned earlier, he authored the Uniform Criminal Statistics Act promulgated in 1946 by the commissioners for Uniform State Laws and recommended for passage by the sovereign states. This Uniform Law provided for a Bureau of Criminal Statistics to be placed in an appropriate department of state government and to be staffed by competent knowledgeable people in the field. The bureau was charged with the development and collection of all significant information in the field of crime and delinquency within the state from all persons and agencies who officially had responsibility in this area. The whole purpose of this effort was to provide a means of building what the Wickersham Report had already advocated—state responsibility for collecting, analyzing, and publishing the specific data on crime and delinquency on offenders and on all the processes of criminal justice. In 1955, the California Legislature adopted the Uniform Act which provided the bureau with full statutory authority for its work that had been carried on for a 10-year period by agreement and executive order.

[10] See Culver and Tompkins bibliographies on Crime and Criminal Justice and other bibliographies for numerous articles and publication in this field by Sellin from 1926 through 1967.

One of the main purposes of a central statistics system is to provide data and analyses of the administrative processes of justice in specific areas. The county is a basic unit in our governmental structure on which the operations of criminal justice should be gauged. In most of the United States prosecution in courts of general jurisdiction is carried on by a county prosecutor or district attorney having countywide jurisdiction. Local correctional facilities are usually found in county jails or in the operations of the county probation departments. The county prosecutor bridges the gap between police and courts and, more than any other figure in justice, coordinates general law enforcement policies that may exist within the county. For example, California has 58 counties but over 400 primary law enforcement agencies at local levels. Consequently, to determine the patterns of arrest, prosecution, and disposition of convicted offenders, information needs to be developed, not only on a statewide basis but also on a county basis.

Obviously, only a state bureau having full reporting within the state would be in a position to develop and analyze data in these county terms. It would be utterly impossible for a single national bureau to provide analytical detail for even a part of the 3000 counties found in the United States.

THE CALIFORNIA DEVELOPMENT

California has for many years been a state in which there was widespread interest in the better administration of criminal justice. Because it has grown rapidly, state, local, and county officials for the most part have been somewhat more progressive and interested in the accomplishment of effective law enforcement than has been the case in some of the more established and comparatively unchanging states saddled with strong political traditions in the operations of justice controls.

California has also been fortunate in much of its early leadership in criminal justice. August Vollmer, Chief of Police in Berkeley and, later, a renowned teacher at Northwestern University and the University of California, was a strong proponent of professional competence in the administration of law enforcement. He was highly influential in the creation of California's pattern for well-trained, carefully selected police personnel and acceptance by the local agencies of goals and objectives necessary for efficient and effective police operations.

The state, under the influence of such governors as Hiram Johnson and Young, around the early 1920's had set a tone of nonpartisan service to be rendered in government circles. Men of influence in California's universities helped to advance the concept and acceptance of trained and effective public administrators. Samuel C. May at the University of California at Berkeley, John C. Pfiffner at the University of Southern California, among others, had a profound influence in raising performance standards in all phases of criminal justice administration.

California started a central Bureau of Identification, which was formally reorganized in 1930, that served as the early-day center for gathering statewide police data. The position of statistician was filled by Fred A. Knoles, who had been the first Los Angeles Police Department statistician when August Vollmer reorganized that department in 1923. In 1930, Mr. Knoles became the new state statistician accounting for police-type events until the Bureau of Criminal Statistics came into being in 1945. He served as assistant chief of the bureau from 1945 until 1961 when he became chief until his retirement in 1965.

Earl Warren, now Chief Justice of the United States Supreme Court, had been an outstanding prosecutor in Alameda County. About 1930 he was characterized by Raymond Moley as the most effective prosecutor in the United States.[11] After he became Governor of California he promoted the expansion of the limited crime statistics then available into a state center of information on crime and the administration of criminal justice.

New departments of state government were created in 1943 and 1944: a Youth Authority, headed by Karl Holton, former chief probation officer of Los Angeles County and a Department of Corrections headed by Richard A. McGee, one of the outstanding correctional leaders in the United States. In 1945, the interest and combined efforts of these leaders, together with Attorney General Robert C. Kenny's support, led to the organizing of the Bureau of Criminal Statistics in the Department of Justice.

In its first years of existence the bureau's major efforts were devoted to developing a system of statistical controls for the two new state departments—Youth Authority and Corrections. By 1950, the systematic procedural accounting for these two departments had been well established and efforts were then turned to the developing of reporting from all agencies in California cities and counties that dealt with primary criminal activity.

A reporting system was designed and experimented with in 1951 and begun in 1952 that systematically accounted for major offenses reported to the police. This somewhat paralleled reporting to the Federal Bureau of Investigation in Uniform Crime Reports, but gave emphasis to state Penal Code provisions. In addition, a full monthly accounting was made of all arrests, both adult and juvenile. This gave the California agencies

[11] Raymond Moley, *Politics and Criminal Prosecution,* New York: Minton, 1929.

details required for their operations plus data for comparative analyses not available under the national system.

Experimentation was undertaken with an individual defendant reporting system for persons prosecuted in the trial courts (superior courts) of the state. This reporting was through the district attorneys of each county in California since they have responsibility for all superior court prosecutions. After a demonstration period with six counties, this collection proved so administratively useful that by 1952 all of the state's 58 counties were reporting. These individual defendant disposition reports had been expanded in 1966 so that each defendant's prior criminal history was included, permitting an analysis of the processes in superior courts as related to the types of persons handled. Also, the defendants prosecuted were identified as to their current status as parolees or probationers.

Probation in California is administered at a county level. While the promotion of probation standards, both with regard to personnel and to supervision practices, was the California Youth Authority's task, the collecting of statistical information was assigned to the Bureau of Criminal Statistics. To accomplish this, an individual-type reporting system was begun that gave information on each juvenile referred to the probation departments, which are the administrative arm of the juvenile courts in California. In the case of adults, an individual report was supplied on each defendant receiving a presentence investigation in the superior courts and a further accounting was made for each person placed on probation by the superior courts. In more recent years, because the probation departments also serve municipal courts, reporting has been enlarged to cover misdemeanor probation cases for about one-half the counties of the state.

Since 1954, the bureau has had almost complete coverage on major crimes reported, arrests, prosecutions, and subsequent procedural events from some 400 local police departments plus 58 county sheriffs and from 58 district attorneys on all persons prosecuted in the superior courts. In addition, for the last ten years, there has been reports on each offender whose felony charges were dismissed by the district attorney, on all persons referred to juvenile probation, and on all persons referred for presentence investigation or placed on probation by the superior courts of the state.

In 1958, as a result of legislation, the Departments of the Youth Authority and Corrections were each given a research staff. The administrative statistics for these two departments, which from 1945 had been the responsibility of the Bureau of Criminal Statistics, were turned over to those respective departments. However, by law and mutual agreement, the bureau still obtains all information needed from these departments to present the total picture of the administration of criminal justice in California. These summary data showing commitments and releases are published in the bureau's annual report, *Crime and Delinquency in California*.

RECENT DEVELOPMENTS

In 1958, there was a great deal of concern in California over what appeared to be a growing narcotic problem. Because drug abuse involved a unique offense category, the kind of information from the bureau's regular statistical processes failed to reveal the kinds of offenders and the specific narcotics involved. Therefore, the bureau was authorized to undertake a special project to collect from law enforcement and other sources all possible information on persons arrested for narcotic involvement and to build a file on narcotic offenders. This study began July 1, 1959 and has been continued over the past eight years. Special annual publications have been issued showing the characteristics of offenders, the kind of narcotics involved, and the disposition made of the arrests. Although the original concern was over heroin and other addictive narcotics, the facts established show quite clearly that over this eight-year period there has been relatively little growth in the number of persons involved in hard narcotics; there has been a phenomenal increase in the number of persons arrested on marijuana and dangerous drug charges. The accounting for all narcotic arrests will be continued; however, it is now felt that the amount of detail and effort expended can be reduced by using sampling procedures to analyze the basic characteristics of the offenders.

Other special studies carried out by the bureau recently involve two cohort studies of homicidal events and persons arrested for such offenses: an initial cohort study of all homicides reported in California in 1960 and a three-year study of homicides for 1963, 1964, and 1965. Because of public concern over the alleged growth of bank robberies, a report was issued that not only analyzed the California bank robbery data for 1965 but, in addition, covered national information gathered through the American Bankers Association beginning with the depression years of the 1930's to the affluent 1960's.

Very little statistical information has been developed that describes county jail operations even though they are prime agencies in criminal justice administration. The most complete jail reporting in past years has been the data collected in Pennsylvania. In 1965, through the interest and support of certain sheriffs, the bureau started such a jail-reporting project. County sheriffs in California are responsible for operating the county jails. Data on every sentenced prisoner in 5 of the 57 county jails of the state were received at the time of release. This provided new and informative administrative data. However, such pronounced differences between counties were shown that additional provision was made for expanding this system. In 1966, eight county jails supplied information for the year; in 1967 there will be a report covering 18 county jails; probably in another year the study will be expanded to cover 75 percent of the jails in the state. These reports record information on persons committed from both superior and lower courts by offense; the sentences imposed; the actual time served; the method or reason for release; and such characteristics as sex, age, and race of sentenced prisoners released. The variety of correctional practices and types of sentences in the various jails inevitably leads to the conclusion that criminal justice is a county-dominated operation.

Another development commenced in 1967 with legislative budget support was an experimentation with individual reporting of arrests. Arrest data since 1952 have been supplied the bureau through monthly summary reports. However, it has always been recognized that, unless individuals arrested are identified and traced through the various stages of criminal justice, only limited understanding of the prosecution and correctional processes would be possible. Three smaller counties in the state, encompassing 20 law enforcement agencies, have joined with the bureau in this project of developing an individual standard arrest report. It is anticipated, if this procedure proves feasible and from all appearances it does, that future reporting will be made on an individual basis for all felony arrests and the more serious misdemeanors. For the first time this will give the desired type of accountability called for in the surveys of the 1920's.

California's Bureau of Criminal Statistics has developed a refined and detailed reporting on persons involved in the administration of criminal justice based on fingerprint identification reports. The fact that the Bureau of Criminal Identification and Investigation, a sister bureau, receives fingerprint information from the great majority of arrests made in the State of California makes it possible to identify or account for individuals sentenced to various forms of correctional treatment. Thus, it is possible to follow them in their criminal careers after their graduation from the correctional treatment given them. This permits the bureau to begin to build a factual basis for evaluating the results of treatment by identifying persons who have avoided further criminality and those who have not. The bureau now has a criminal careers unit that has begun such studies. The first project is an evaluative review of a substantial sample of all persons arrested for narcotics in 1960 that follows and analyzes the narcotic and other criminal history during the

subsequent five-year period. It will be published early in 1968. Another
cohort study being launched is of persons placed on probation in 1966.
These will be analyzed as to their subsequent criminal experience after
one, two, and three years. A similar study will be made of persons
who have been given jail sentences and those released after the Youth
Authority and Corrections institutional experience.

To obtain a complete picture of California's crime problem, it was
also necessary to develop statistical reporting from the more specialized
treatment agencies. In California many offenders are committed to the
Department of Mental Hygiene for an indeterminate period as mentally
disordered sex offenders (formally called sex psychopaths). Also, California has established a Rehabilitation Center as a special treatment
facility for drug addicts who, after criminal conviction, receive civil
commitment for treatment. These two offender types are being accounted
for by the bureau. In addition, a study is being undertaken of offenders
who appeal their convictions. This study will answer such questions as
what proportion of each type of defendants appeal and what ultimately
happens to those whose convictions are reversed on appeal.

Other special presentations of California data are being made of
particular phases of the crime field including studies of law enforcement officers killed in line of duty since 1960 and of persons charged
with kidnapping. The analysis of information reported on juveniles and
youths has been fairly limited in the past but the bureau has the essential data to examine in much greater detail these areas of delinquency
control as related to the general crime problem within the State of
California.

Today, the Bureau of Criminal Statistics is receiving enough solid
information to outline a fairly realistic accounting of the amount of
crime, the offenders involved, and the activity carried out by the
agencies administering criminal justice in California. An annual report,
Crime and Delinquency in California, presents the essential data for all
of these areas. Also, there is a special annual publication, *Drug Arrests
and Dispositions in California*, that accounts for persons arrested in the
state's drug traffic. The data that the bureau has developed and issued
in special reports give a solid research base for further exploration of
particular phases of criminal problems.

FUTURE PROGRAMS

The statistical data on criminal offenses reported by law enforcement
to both the Federal Bureau of Investigation and Bureau of Criminal

Statistics have severe limitations. The information gathered is presented in such gross terms, without any refinement, that it is impossible to determine, even roughly, the relative seriousness of offenses. Those classified as burglary range from serious offenses such as organized safe burglaries or other break-ins, where goods of great value are taken, to offenses negligible in the terms of value of the property taken (which at best are petty thefts), cloaked by technicality as burglary.

The fallacy of statistically lumping together nuisance crime and serious crime is obvious. The California burglary statutes are so broad that a mere entering of an area closed by a roof (three walls with a semblance of a fourth) without reason for being there can be interpreted as entry with intent to commit a theft and be counted as burglary. Likewise, some robberies are of the most vicious type, while others fall into the more passive class of rolling drunks or a school boy forcibly taking a coin away from another. When these varied offense types are lumped together it makes it impossible to determine whether an increase in the number of crimes reported actually reflects a growth in the more serious types of crime. Few attempts have been made to classify crime in any order of seriousness. A pioneer study made by Thorsten Sellin and Marvin Wolfgang analyzed offenses reported to the Philadelphia Juvenile Bureau and developed a uniform weighting scheme, taking into account elements of value and elements of injury that could be applied to the offenses reported.[12] There is a great need to develop these distinctions for crimes reported even though it may have to be in relatively crude terms. Some acceptable method is needed to distinguish at least between the more serious crimes, the run-of-the-mill offenses, and those that are obviously of a minor nature. With availability of large numbers of well-prepared crime reports from police agencies in California it is hoped that some progress can be made in this area and that statistics of offenses can be broken down into more refined and descriptive classes.

A second needed development is an accountability of what happens to persons prosecuted in municipal and justice-type courts. Where a state has a center for criminal information that has almost complete identification and statistical data on offenders, it would seem that one way to gather accurate information on prosecutions would be through reports from the clerks of courts on the disposition of each criminal defendant. These would identify the defendants prosecuted, the charges, courts, dates of filing, dates and types of disposition, and the sentence imposed for defendants convicted. In California, oddly enough, there is a statutory

[12] Thorsten Sellin and Marvin Wolfgang, *The Measurement of Delinquency*, New York: Wiley, 1964.

requirement for the courts to report the disposition of traffic violations to the State Department of Motor Vehicles, but not the disposition of criminal defendants. It would seem that there ought to be as close an accounting for taking away an individual's freedom of movement by incarceration as there presently is for accounting for traffic fines.

A third critical area, which is very much the concern of crime commissions and all agencies involved in criminal justice, is the problem of integrating into one information system, through the use of computers, all data needed or desired in the administration of criminal justice. There is no question that some integration of the various information reported from different sources, all relating to the same offender, should be accomplished. Today, the basic information on offenders is found in the rap sheet of offenders arrested and reported to a central agency. The FBI with its massive fingerprint files puts together a criminal record or rap sheet recording every fingerprint received on an offender that carries the information as to the date of arrest, the arresting agency, the charge and, hopefully, the disposition. Similar information is compiled in the California identification system.

These criminal record histories are the best available, but they are far from satisfactory. Not all arrested offenders are fingerprinted, nor does every agency fingerprint in the same terms. This means that we are never sure whether the rap sheet is a complete history of criminal arrest activity. Dispositions for the most part are sent in as a follow-up after the fingerprint is received reporting the arrest. In many instances a disposition report is never received by the identification bureaus. In other instances when it is received, it is not clear as to the specific offense for which the defendant was finally convicted or it may show most incomplete and inadequate sentence information.

Criminal career studies of any set of offenders are dependent on the development of a reliable consistent record of the offender's appearances in arrest, prosecution, and correctional records as a result of his criminal activity.

Modern computers have been proposed as the basic means by which a complete information system relating to crime and criminal justice can be developed. Theoretically, the capacity of these great machines is such that almost any kind of information, if properly classified and indexed, can be recorded and stored in memory and be retrieved on a moment's notice. Thus, the proposal—why not store every possible item of information about every offender in the computer and obtain almost instantaneously anything anyone wants to know about the offender. There are many studies being undertaken to create some sort of system of this nature. There have been at least three such programs undertaken in California. The New York (NYSIIS) system has these specific objectives as its aim. A less comprehensive approach, yet one aimed in the same direction, is found in the establishment of a national information system under the auspices of the FBI (NCIC) in which data related to auto thefts, gun registrations, stolen property, and wanted persons is stored in central or national computers.

There is no question that these sophisticated tools can be of tremendous aid in many aspects of our efforts to control crime. Centralized data files relating to stolen property and gun registration are most practical and can save the expense in having these files duplicated to some extent in each law enforcement agency. Unfortunately, the idea that all kinds and types of information can be placed in one central computer generally ignores the practical problems that must be faced in obtaining input data from literally hundreds of different types of independent agencies that are engaged at the many levels of criminal justice administration throughout the country. When such difficulties have been brought to the attention of those who are developing information systems, these difficulties have been brushed aside apparently on the ground that, somehow, after the model is put together someone else will find a way to make it work.

A well-developed computer record of an offender's history in relatively complete terms is a most desirable and feasible goal for a computerized information system. Each additional step in the history of a person could be immediately added to the existing record and a current print-out made at any time. Such a source of information on an offender would supply a much improved history over what is now available on ordinary rap sheets. Such information is needed by each agency or official handling an offender. It also makes possible ready access to the continuing criminal history of an offender, which is the basis on which follow-up or criminal career studies can be made.

The input process cannot be handled entirely on a mechanical basis. The data reported on an offender to a state central agency through fingerprints, crime reports, arrest reports, disposition reports, reports from the courts on prosecution and outcome, reports from the probation officers on investigations for treatment, reports from the various correctional facilities as to persons committed to them, the time they stay, their method of release, etc., will be supplied for a long time to come on different formats.

This means that there must be a process at the central agency for interchecking, editing, and reviewing to organize the information reported on a single individual into the standard uniform terms that will be put into the computer. There has been very little effort given to this problem. One of the most critical deficiencies is the lack of a common identification on the various reports concerning the person received. Names frequently change, offenses charged are reported in different terms, accounts of court dispositions vary, and even the sentences imposed will be reported differently from two sources recording the same event. Usually, the differences can be resolved and organized into a uniform history record. It requires, however, technical know-how by persons thoroughly acquainted with the vagaries of procedures, terminologies, and records among the agencies involved.

Those who are working out plans for an overall general information system indicate that all agencies and personnel who file reports will have to submit the data in exact uniform terms and language, although how this is to be achieved is generally not discussed. It is hard to conceive of what kind of policing operations or penalties can possibly be used to bring hundreds of autonomous agencies into line in this respect.

A review of the lack of progress in achieving uniform criminal statistics since the 1920's might suggest to a thoughtful person that the practical difficulties involved in uniform records and uniform crime reporting from highly independent and uncoordinated agencies have as yet not been resolved. There is no way by which computers of the present day can suddenly overcome in this respect the problems that have hindered progress over the past 40 years.

It does seem that California is in a favorable position to undertake the beginnings of a criminal justice data system. It is the only state with an identification bureau in which a pattern of reporting offense descriptions and arrest fingerprints has existed over a long period and in which the more than 400 law enforcement agencies in the state fully participate; it has the only central Bureau of Criminal Statistics which is receiving specific information on every person prosecuted in the felony field in reasonably uniform terms.

The major problem to be faced is how to organize and integrate the data into a complete individual information record. It is suggested that a practical approach to building an information system would be to start with the records of persons prosecuted on felony charges during a given year. Thus, over a period of five years, an information file would be established in this state that, at the rate of 40,000 records a year, would total about 200,000 records and would undoubtedly include the bulk of the individuals currently involved in serious felony-level crime. A similar file for the serious felony-related misdemeanors would about double this. If all this were accomplished, probably better than 95 percent of California's serious offenders would be readily identifiable through automatic data processing.

The reporting of information from the various sets of agencies would have to continue for such data must be put together and analyzed to show the procedures and outcomes of the administrative processes for each particular group of agencies each year. There has to be an accounting of crimes reported by law enforcement, of arrests made, and of their disposition at police level; of persons prosecuted in the courts and of their disposition; and of persons committed to each type of correctional facility such as county jails, probation, youth institutions, and adult institutions. Also an accounting should be kept on defendants handled in specialized treatment facilities used for sex offenders and narcotic addicts.

All of these sets of information theoretically could be placed in the massive storage banks of a computer, but how practically could all the different and varied inquiries from each agency, administrator, or worker be answered has never been demonstrated. The programming problems would be tremendous. Many organizations have already found that converting from punch cards handled by ordinary electronic accounting machines (EAM), which are most flexible, to ADP computers, which in reality are quite inflexible, has created problems necessitating many and additional costly programs. Once a computer program has been evolved there is a dogged resistance to making changes. Yet, experimentation and change in the analysis of data are the very essence of its appropriate use.

SUMMARY

The main argument of this paper is that the development of statistics describing crime and criminal justice is based on the collection of information from thousands of official agencies engaged in efforts to control crime in the United States; that each state is a primary unit; that the organization of the collection, compilation, and analysis of these data should be centered within a single bureau in each state. This was the concept recognized and fostered by Sellin in authoring the Uniform Criminal Statistics Act. The need is as great now as it was then.

California, up to 1968, is the only state that has established such a central bureau. In its 22 years of existence, California has developed reporting that at least approaches the goal of accounting for the totality of the criminal picture within the state. For the first time since the special studies of the 1920's, it is possible to discern the dimensions, outcomes, and results of the processes of criminal justice within a state and its individual counties.

While there is an urgent need for a national center of criminal information that will function as a coordinating and unifying agency in the development and collection of criminal statistics, there is no practical way in which such a center can assume responsibility for the direct collection of information from all the local agencies in all the cities and counties of the United States or produce the kind of information that is needed by those in the cities, counties, and states that administer criminal law. Furthermore, even within a state where it is feasible to develop information needed for a criminal record history on individual offenders, this cannot be done on an automatic input basis. The state's center for statistics and identification should receive the essential reports, but there must be a process of review and editing to insure standardization and completeness of record information before computer storage. When such information is built into a standard record, it would then be available for a national center of information on individual offenders.

Historically, almost every effort that has advanced the cause of improving and expanding criminal statistics through such achievements as Uniform Crime Reports, the Census Bureau efforts, the Uniform Criminal Statistics Act, and the California developments has been nurtured by the contributions of Thorsten Sellin.

IV

EMPIRICAL RESEARCH

European Migration and Crime*

FRANCO FERRACUTI

INTRODUCTION

The large number of European migrant workers, especially from Mediterranean to Central and Northern European countries, is one of the major problems of the European continent and deserves close attention by interested governmental officers and scientists.[1] The adjustment of migrants has been for a long time a primary object of interest in criminology, particularly in the United States but also in other parts of the world. Psychological problems of the migrants' adjustment and the resulting sociopathological phenomena have been the object of extensive research efforts. Parallel to the problem of foreign migrants, the development of large-scale internal migrations and the urbanization of large numbers of rural workers in many countries have also been studied. After World War II a wave of migratory movements took place in the resettlement of large numbers of persons displaced by the resulting political changes.

More recently, European economic development, integration, and other recent political changes have caused the temporary or permanent displacement of several millions of persons who face the problem of working and living in a foreign country. The governments of the countries affected by postwar migration quickly manifested their interest in the problem[2] and, from the viewpoint of the criminal behavior of the

---

* This chapter was written not only for the present volume but was commissioned by the Council of Europe for the Fifth European Conference of Directors of Criminological Research Institutes.

[1] Crime Problems Division, Directorate of Legal Affairs, *Delinquency and Other Forms of Anti-Social Behaviour Among Migrant Workers,* Council of Europe, Strasbourg, 1966, DPC (66), 2, revised.

[2] Many international meetings have been convened on the subject and official agencies have been established in several countries, generally under the administrative structures of the Ministries of Labor and Foreign Affairs, or of their equivalents.

migrants, a few research papers have appeared. Several research projects are now in progress on this topic in some countries.[3] In other countries the problem of the returning migrant and his readjustment to his country of origin is now emerging. The present paper represents a preliminary discussion of the antisocial behavior of European migrants. Although data on crime are concentrated primarily on countries that are members of the Council of Europe, occasional references will be made to migration in other countries or areas.[*]

THE GENERAL PROBLEM OF MIGRATION AND CRIME

The criminality of migrants was a major area of study for criminologists during the first half of this century. Particularly in the United States, the high rates of crime that occurred in the large urban areas directed interest towards an analysis of the criminality of the immigrants who tended to concentrate in the same areas. Popular opinion often expressed the view that migrants were responsible for a large fraction of the crime rate. However, objective studies of crime rates quickly showed that migrants were not the major contributors to the growing rates of urban crime. Restrictive legislation, however, had already been enacted, particularly in the United States, to keep out "undesirable foreigners."[4]

The pioneer work of Thorsten Sellin,[5] based on the careful analysis of

Several treaties and agreements have been signed to regulate many aspects of the workers' migrations. The Council of Europe has taken a great interest in the problem, both in its social and criminological aspects and its work program includes several areas related to it.

[3] A complete list of projects is not available, but studies are in progress in France, in Switzerland, in Sweden, and in the United Kingdom. To our knowledge no large-scale, international project is being planned.

[4] An analysis of past and present American immigration legislation is available in the September 1966 issue of The Annals of the American Academy of Political and Social Science, dedicated to the problem of "The New Immigration."

[5] Thorsten Sellin, Culture Conflict and Crime, Social Science Research Council, New York, 1938.

[*] The help of the Division of Crime Problems of the Council of Europe, of the Criminological Section of the Centro Nazionale di Prevenzione e Difesa Sociale of Milan, and of the Italian Ministry of Foreign Affairs is gratefully acknowledged. Several colleagues in Europe and America, too many to be listed individually, have generously contributed important information incorporated in the report. No complete coverage of the literature was possible in view of the limited time and resources available. However, it is hoped that the report may constitute a starting point for an enlarged discussion of the problem.

existing data, demonstrated how untenable was the proposition that migrants were responsible for the increase in crime. As Sellin pointed out, the crime rates of migrants had to be interpreted in terms of their adjustment to the new norms and laws to which they were exposed and in terms of the resulting culture conflicts. Any racial interpretation of crime had to be discarded in favor of more dynamic etiological explanations. Sellin also pointed out that the process of migration involved a change from a rural or semirural environment to an urban ambiance. Culture conflicts could explain the criminality of the second generation migrants and also the changes in the criminal phenomenology that occurred in the process of Americanization of the descendants of the foreign born.

Sellin differentiated between primary culture conflict, when the conflict norms consisted of the attrition between different cultural systems or areas and secondary cultural conflicts that were due to a process of social differentiation caused by the evolution of a single culture. The role of culture conflicts in the genesis of crime was easily accepted as an important etiological fact by many authors.[6] However, the objective study of such conflicts was, admittedly, very difficult because of the limitations of available statistical data and of the several biases that operated in the migrant's group. Even in the second-generation migrants, as Sutherland[7] states, a linear relationship with crime is not demonstrated. Crime rates vary widely among different immigrant groups and the types of crimes committed also vary according to the national origin of the migrants. According to Sutherland,[8] account must be taken also of the point in the process of acculturation in which the criminal statistics are taken because crime increases when, after the first steps of integration in the community are overcome, the contacts with the same community multiply. A more recent analysis of the variations of criminal phenomenology in the process of the assimilation of immigrant groups has been made by Cloward and Ohlin.[9]

[6] See, for example, the following: I. G. Brown, *Immigration Cultural Conflicts and Social Adjustment*, Longmans, New York, 1933; S. N. Eisenstadt, "Delinquent Group-Formation Among Immigrant Youth," *Brit. J. Delinquency*, 1951, 2, 34–45; S. Shoham, "The Application of the Culture-Conflict Hypothesis to the Criminality of Immigrants in Israel," *J. Crim. Law, Criminology and Police Science*, 1962, 53(2), 207–214.

[7] E. H. Sutherland, *Principles of Criminology* (revised by D. R. Cressy), fifth edition, Lippincott, Chicago, 1955.

[8] *Ibid.*, p. 147.

[9] R. A. Cloward and L. E. Ohlin, *Delinquency and Opportunity*, Routledge and Kegan Paul, London, 1961.

A detailed summary of the literature on mobility, migration, and crime has recently been published by Mannheim.[10] After a careful analysis of classical and more recent studies, Mannheim concludes that, with the exception of certain groups and of certain types of crime, the subject has nowadays lost most of its practical interest. Mannheim states, however, that "it is one of the lasting merits of modern American criminologists to have destroyed the old antiimigrant myth, although full success was achieved only after the flood of immigrants had already been brought to a halt by legislation." Of course, in some countries such as, for example, Israel, Australia, and Canada,[11] the problem is still very important; and more recently in Europe, the workers' migration has revived interest in the topic.

Migration will remain a general phenomenon in the search for better opportunities or for more acceptable conditions of life. Its positive effect in economic and other terms cannot be denied, although the results are not easy to evaluate.[12] However, those who migrate will often present, except in the case of political displacement, some selective traits associated with greater aggressiveness, dominance, instability, and intolerance.

[10] H. Mannheim, *Comparative Criminology*, Vol. 2, Routledge and Kegan Paul, London, 1965, pp. 536–544. For an earlier statement by the same author, see: H. Mannheim, *Group Problems in Crime and Punishment*, Routledge and Kegan Paul, London, 1955, pp. 194–205. Most of the earlier relevant literature is reviewed in these two sources. Another useful review of classic literature on migration and crime is available in L. D. Savitz, *Delinquency and Migration*, Ph.D. Thesis, University of Pennsylvania, 1960.

[11] See footnote 6 above for studies in Israel. An important study on immigrants' assimilation in western Australia has recently been published: R. Taft, *From Stranger to Citizen*, Tavistock Publications, London, 1966. Several Canadian studies exist or are in progress.

[12] The economic and social balance of migration is a very difficult evaluative problem in planning and assessment. Although migration follows, in general, economic rules, sociopsychological forces enter into the decision to migrate. The effects of migration on the original and on the host country can be beneficial in some areas and negative in others. One problem that often is overlooked is the drain in manpower, both at the skilled and at the unskilled levels. For a discussion of several aspects of migration, see the following publications: Ministero degli Affari Esteri, Direzione Generale dell-Emigrazione, *Problemi del lavoro italiano all' estero. Relazione per il 1964*, Rome, 1965. Lucrezio-Perotti-Falchi, *L'emigrazione italiana negli Anni '70*, Morcelliana, Rome, 1966. J. Doublet, "Les Movements Migratoires en Europe," *Revue Internationale de Sciences Sociales*, 1965, 17(2), 304–317. Department of Economics and Social Affairs *1965 Report on the World Social Situation*, United Nations, New York, 1966. Conseil de l'Europe *Dixième rapport d'activité du représentant spécial du Conseil de l'Europe pour les réfugiés nationaux et les excédents de population*, Strasbourg, 1965. Conseil de l'Europe, Conférence demographique européenne, *Documents officiels de la Conférence*, Vol. II, Strasbourg, September 1966; T. Brinley, *International Migration and Economic Development*, UNESCO, Paris, 1961.

On the other hand, as Clinard states,[13] the mere fact of urbanization is associated with many negative elements, and yet it provides so many positive factors that the "pull" of the city remains an undeniable moving force. Still according to Clinard,[14] mobility weakens attachment to the local community and increases secondary group ties and the number of contacts with a divergent value system. Mobility also reduces social control by decreasing the value placed on "reputation."

The process of migration inevitably exposes the subject to several types of frustration. According to Dalla Volta,[15] some antisocial behavior may result from the increase of criminal activities in the areas where migrants congregate, while other more primitive and more culturally bound types of crime may lead to a "restriction" of the criminal phenomenology. However, according to the same author, part of the criminal behavior of the migrant results from defense mechanisms against frustrations due to the migration situation itself.

Another theoretical approach to the problem of the migrant adjustment focuses around the concept of anomie. Following the original formulations of Durkheim and Merton,[16] anomie, either as culture conflict or as a conflict of norms, suggests a useful theoretical frame of reference for the analysis of the psychosociological events in the life of the immigrant, which may lead to antisocial behavior. As has been stated elsewhere[17] the very broadness of the concept of anomie is in a way self-defeating from the point of view of the differentiation and of operationalization of relevant variables. The parsimony of nomenclature, which is offered by the concept of anomie, does not necessarily produce fruitful research

[13] M. B. Clinard, *Sociology of Deviant Behavior*, Holt, Rinehart and Winston, New York, 1964.
[14] *Ibid.*
[15] A. Dalla Volta, "Revisione del concetto di frustrazione in psichiatria sociale," *Annali di Neurologie e Psichiatria e Annali Ospedale Psichiatrico di Perugia*, 1965, LIX, 1. *Frustrazioni costruttive e frustrazioni negative nei comportamenti migratori*, XIX Congresso Nazionale della Società Italiana di Med. Leg. e delle Assicur., Cagliari-Sassari, pp. 15–19, ottobre 1965. *Migrazioni e condotte anti antisociali*, Ralazione al I convegno Nazionale di Antropologia Criminale, Alghero 19 ott. 1965, Medicina Legale e della Assicurazioni, 1966, XIV, 4.
[16] E. Durkheim, *Suicide*, Glencoe, Ill., The Free Press, 1951; R. K. Merton, "Social Structure and Anomie," Chapter 4, in *Social Theory and Social Structure*, Glencoe, Ill., The Free Press, 1967. See also: H. L. Ansbacher, "Anomie, The Sociologist's Conception of Lack of Social Interest," *Journal of Individual Psychology*, 1959, 15(2), 212–214. S. H. Davol and G. Reimanis, "The Role of Anomie as a Psychological Concept," *Journal of Individual Psychology*, 1959, 15(2), 215–225.
[17] Marvin E. Wolfgang and Franco Ferracuti, *The Subculture of Violence*, Tavistock Publications, London, 1967, pp. 268–269.

efforts. In a recent survey of studies on anomie, Clinard[18] does not list any specific research on migration. In a study of internal migrants, Alberoni[19] analyzed the anomic effects of migration with specific examples. A UNESCO conference on migration was held in Havana in 1956, and in the proceedings of the conference, edited by W. D. Borrie,[20] several aspects of the migrants' adjustment are analyzed but, unfortunately, the criminal behavior of migrants did not constitute a major topic in the agenda of the conference.

Generalizations about the high level of criminality of foreigners are often a cover for the expression of xenophobic feelings, along the same lines as the more frequent statements about the danger of economic damage to local workers or as other biased expressions of hostility.[21] As we shall see later, the fears of increased criminality, which have been expressed occasionally, did not materialize to any large extent in the present European workers' migration. It is the task of criminologists to assess the situation and to provide an objective view of the status of the problem, of its real level of danger, and of the possible preventive or remedial measures. The problem of the workers' temporary or permanent migration is surely not limited to Europe, since other countries are experiencing similar social phenomena with varying levels of resulting maladjustment.[22] The European situation is one of the most comforting from the point of view of the degree of social disorganization resulting from migration, and analysis of this situation may be informative for other areas.

THE PSYCHOLOGICAL ADJUSTMENT
OF MIGRANTS

The problem of the psychological adjustment of migrants is the object of a very extensive body of literature. No attempt will be made to summarize it, since most of its content is only indirectly and marginally related

[18] Clinard, M. B., (ed.), *Anomie and Deviant Behaviour*, The Free Press, Glencoe, Ill., 1964.

[19] Alberoni, F., *Contributo allo studio dell'integrazione dell'immigrato*, Vita e Pensiero, Milano, 1960.

[20] Borrie, W. D., *The Cultural Integration of Immigrants*, UNESCO, Paris, 1959.

[21] Many xenophobic statements have appeared in European newspapers concerning migrant workers. Another recent example of this trend is a report for the Puerto Rico Bar Association on the danger of economic competition by Cuban refugees, using questionable labor extrapolations (Colegio de Abogados de Puerto Rico, San Juan, P.R. *Estudio sobre el impacto de la immigraciòn en Puerto Rico, 1967.*)

[22] A number of case studies are reported in the book by Borrie (see footnote 20). The general bibliography presented in the appendix to this report lists many examples from different countries.

to crime. From the viewpoint of the mental health of the migrant, voluntary migration must be differentiated from involuntary displacement. The latter's finality, brutality, and unplanned character make it a much more damaging phenomenon. Much of the literature on refugees has little relevance for the problems of voluntary migrants. Moreover, modern workers' migration in Europe has distinctive characteristics that nullify the validity of older studies. The present migrant worker in Europe often leaves with the definite goal of returning to his country of origin. In many cases, immigration is planned and assisted. Planned occupational placement is, in general, consistent with the migrant's abilities, and often his family accompanies him or joins him quickly. The final and tragic cut of ties with the country of origin, which was a feature of previous migration across the Atlantic, is largely absent. In the case of illness the immigrant is protected, treated and, if necessary, repatriated with a minimum of psychological damage.

Information available to the migrant on the country that he is about to enter is abundant and objective, and the country itself constitutes a physical reality. These facts decrease the psychological imaginative tension that is part of the migration shock. In most cases, the expectations of the migrant have a more realistic correspondence to the objective possibilities and opportunities of the new working environment. Yet, the process of migration continues to be a major stress that sometimes exceeds the adjustment possibilities of the individual. Classical studies on the mental health of the migrant, such as those of Ødegaard,[23] Malzberg,[24] Tyhurst,[25] Listwan,[26] Eisenstadt,[27] Weinberg[28] and Ginzberg,[29] provide

[23] Oe. Ødegaard, "Emigration and Insanity," *Acta Psychiatrica et Neurologica*, Suppl. IV, Levin and Munksgaard Publishers, Copenhagen, 1932.

[24] B. Malzberg, "A Statistical Study of First Admissions with Psychoneuroses in New York State 1949–51," *Amer. J. Psychiatrist*, 1959, **116**, 152–157; B. Malzberg, "Migration and Mental Disease Among the White Population of New York State 1949–1951," *Hum. Biol.*, 1962 34(2), 89–98.

[25] L. Tyhurst, "Displacement and Migration—A Study in Social Psychiatry," *Am. Journal of Psychiatry*, 1951, 107, 561–568.

[26] I. A. Listwan, *Paranoid States: Social and Cultural Aspects*, World Mental Health, 1959, **II**, 171–177.

[27] S. N. Eisenstadt, "The Place of the Elite and Primary Groups in the Absorption of New Immigrants in Israel," *American Journal of Sociology*, 1951, **57**, 222–231; *The Absorption of Immigrants*, Glencoe, Ill., The Free Press, 1955.

[28] A. A. Weinberg, "Psychosomatic Factors in the Adjustment of New Immigrants," *Acta Med. Orient.*, *Jerusalem*, 1949, **8**, 13–19; A. A. Weinberg, "Mental Health Aspects of Voluntary Migration," *Mental Hygiene*, N.Y., 1955, 39, 450–464; A. A. Weinberg, *Migration and Belonging*, The Hague, Netherlands, Martinus Nijhoff, 1961, **XXII**, 402.

[29] A. Ginzberg, *Un estudio psicologico de imigrantes y migrantes*, 1961; *Alguns problemas de adaptacao de immigrantes, estrangeiros ao nove meie*, Rio de Janeiro, 1959.

interesting data on the incidence and prevalence of serious mental illness among migrants. It is a widely accepted fact that the decision to migrate appeals selectively to persons with unstable, aggressive, and dominating traits. It is also known that paranoid reactions and, more generally, schizophrenic syndromes appear to have a high incidence among migrants. However, some of the early, more pessimistic studies, such as those of Malzberg and Lee,[30] have to be revised if a more careful analysis of the available data is conducted. For example, a study of Judith Lazarus, B. Z. Locke, and Dorothy Swaine Thomas[31] indicates that the color variable of the subjects is more important than the migration status.

In internal migration, many studies have indicated a high level of incidence of mental illness. Of particular interest are recent Sardinian researches.[32] Some of the paranoid reactions of migrants appear to be purely environmental, due mostly to the social factors of migration stresses and, according to Listwan,[33] they have, in general, a good prognosis. Other frequent psychopathological manifestations are depressive reactions with occasional suicides. From the point of view of the assessment of the psychopathological syndromes, one important element is the need for psychiatrists and social workers, dealing with maladjusted cases, to be fully aware of and conversant with the cultural and subcultural characteristics of the migrant's background. Occasionally the cultural distance between the cases and the mental health worker may result in incorrect diagnoses, often of a serious nature, with highly damaging consequences for the proper handling of the patients.

In addition to the older studies that have analyzed the incidence of specific psychiatric syndromes among immigrants, several more recent researchers may be mentioned. In 1953, Alliez and Jaur,[34] in a study

[30] B. Malzberg and E. S. Lee, *Migration and Mental Disease*, New York, Social Science Research Council, 1956.

[31] J. Lazarus, B. Z. Locke, and D. S. Thomas, "Migration Differentials in Mental Disease," *The Milbank Memorial Fund Quarterly*, January, 1963, XLI(1), 25–42.

[32] R. Camba and N. Rudas, "Emigrazione e patologia mentale: Il problema etiopato-genetico," *Rivista sarda di criminologia*, 1965, I(3), 223–272; "Emigrazione e patologia mentale: risultanze epidemiologiche, aspetti clinici e patodinamici," *Rivista sarda di criminologia*, 1965, I(3), 273–335; "Emigrazione sarda e integrazione sociale: aspetti dello stereotipo verbale," *Rivista sarda di criminologia*, 1965, I(4), 445–472; "Emigrazione e patologia mentale: Primi rilievi statistici relativi all'emigrazione sarda," *Rivista sarda di criminologia*, 1965, I(4), 473–506.

[33] J. A. Listwan, *op. cit.*; see also J. Triseliotis, "Casework with Immigrants: The Implications of Cultural Factors," *British Journal of Psychiatric Social Work*, 1965, 8(1), 15–25, for the need to take into account specific cultural and subcultural factors in the diagnosis.

[34] J. Alliez, and J. M. Jaur, "Etude de l'adaptation des immigrants de seconde génération dans les milieux du travail," *Revue Psychologique Appl.*, 1953, 3, 295–297.

conducted in Marseilles on the adaptation of immigrants from different nationalities, underlined the importance of the original social set in the process of overcoming the original living habits and social inhibitions. Of paramount importance in the process of adjustment is, of course, the attitude of the receiving country and its integrative and levelling requisites. The tolerant capacity of the receiving country to accept the foreigner's values and ways of life, without requesting or expecting a quick total integration and assimilation and without xenophobic "singling out" of foreigners' traits, is a crucial element of adjustment. Taft[35] has discussed the "monistic" and "pluralistic" handling of immigrants. In the former, elimination of old values and ways of behavior is the criterion of assimilation; in the latter no such loss is required, and only acceptance of differences and acquisition of the tools that facilitate interaction is necessary. Clearly favoring the latter approach, Taft introduces in the process of assimilation the sociopsychological concept of the "shared frame of reference" as a useful tool for the analysis of the process.

In a detailed survey, based in part on direct experience with the work of the Intergovernmental Committee for European Migration, Durante[36] underlines the need for "total" study of the emigrant, conducted in all his human itinerary, from the decision to migrate to the adjustment in the new environment and, finally, to the terminal integration in the new country. This author discusses several types of adjustment and analyzes Menges' "emigrant potential,"[37] defined as the potentialities of the immigrant to reach gradually and quickly his internal equilibrium and, at the same time, to integrate into the new environment in such a way as to avoid being a disturbing element. Durante[38] proposes a detailed scheme of analysis and emphasizes the need for deep personality studies, not limited to questionnaires (as many researches are) and including an assessment of the intelligence level of the subjects. In his work with European migrants to South America, Durante has found that only 38 percent of the subjects could be considered fully "normal." The dynamic elements of the motivation to migrate and a full understanding of the existential experience of migration and of the personality pattern of the migrant should be objectively assessed to enable the researcher to "predict" the success or failure of the migrant's adjustment.

[35] R. Taft, "The Shared Frame of Reference Concept Applied to the Assimilation of Immigrants," Human Relations, 1953, 6, 45–55.
[36] A. Durante, "Problemi psicologici dell'emigrazione. Contributo alla conoscenza psicologica del fenomeno migratorio," Clinica Psichiatrica, 1966, II(1), 31–65.
[37] A. Durante, op. cit.
[38] A. Durante, op. cit.

Villa[39] has discussed the problems of migrant adjustment based on experience in Switzerland, particularly with Italian and Polish subjects. He underlines the "feeling of being exploited" as a maladjustive factor, and the difficulty of adapting to an alien cooking. He presents a number of practical suggestions, such as the publication of special newspapers for immigrants, to facilitate the adjustment process.

A more general document on the psychological behavior of migrant workers and on their adaptation to the social environment of the receiving country was published in 1963 by the *Comité des Conseilleurs du Représentant Spécial du Conseil de l'Europe pour les Réfugiés nationaux et les Excédents de Population en Europe.*[40] This general report analyzes several aspects of the adjustment process, both from the perspective of the migrants (or refugees) and from the perspective of the host country. The report underlines the differences between the migrants of the early 1950's (more qualified and engaged in a type of work more similar to the one held at home), and the migrants after 1957 (less qualified and changing not only country but also type of work). The report maintains that there is no common pattern in the migrant's adaptation but only different degrees that lead him gradually from the total isolation of the first day of work to a degree of identification with the environment. The actual experiences lived by the migrant and his "temperament" are of paramount importance in the process. The value of the feeling of "responsibility" of the migrant is stressed.

In a paper on psychopathological data from 709 psychiatric clinical records of Italian migrant workers in Switzerland, Risso[41] stated again the importance of the personality patterns preceding the actual illness and of the actual social situation and referred to the preventive value of the presence of the family and of acquaintances and friends.

A recent book by Ex[42] deals with the adjustment of emigrants to the Netherlands from the Dutch East Indies. The author makes a detailed analysis of the methodology that can be followed for researches of this type. He differentiates between singular and genetic studies. Among the latter, a further distinction is made between intercomparative and intracomparative studies. The former analyzes the process of adjustment by

[39] J. L. Villa, *Le comportement psychique des travailleurs migrants et leur adaptation au milieu social du pays d'accueil,* Council of Europe, Strasbourg, July 1962, RS 27 (1962).

[40] *Introduction à l'étude du comportement psychique des travailleurs migrants et leur adaptation au milieu social du pays d'acceuil,* Council of Europe, Strasbourg, mai 1963, RS 43 (1963).

[41] M. Risso, *Primi risultati di un' indagine sociologica e psicopatologica sugli emigrati italiani nella Svizzera tedesca.* Il lavoro neuropsichiatrico, Atti del XXVIII Congresso della S.I.P., Naples, 6–10 June 1963.

[42] Jacques Ex, *Adjustment after Migration,* The Hague, Martinus Nijhoff, 1966.

mutual comparison of immigrants of a similar origin, but with a dissimilar duration of stay in the new environment. The latter is focussed on one group of immigrants examined at successive intervals in the new country. Ex reports an interesting study of the genetic-intracomparative type involving 40 families from Indonesia, followed through four systematic interviews conducted after three months, then one, two, and three years after the arrival in the Netherlands. Through a careful statistical analysis of the variations of opinions expressed by the immigrants on several crucial areas, the author studied the process of change in values and manners of life in the adoption of the autochthonous ways of conduct, through what he calls the "hetero-social identity experience."

Although this work has no relevance to the problem of the criminality of migrants, some of its methodological aspects are of obvious interest and could be utilized in a research on the antisocial behavior of the migrant workers. Ex[43] distinguishes among three components of the adjustment process: habituation, assimilation, and acculturation. Other distinctions on similar lines had been made before.

Borrie[44] provided a theoretical analysis of the adjustment process in terms of the differences between assimilation into a monocultural system and integration into a system allowing for plurality of cultures. The latter implies flexibility, both in the emigrant group and in the host country. Integration based on cultural pluralism is considered as just a step on the way to eventual assimilation, absorption, and total identification with the culture of the receiving society. The reciprocal adjustment between the immigrant and the culture of his adopted country is a continuing process. However, it should be remembered that present workers' migration in Europe frequently does not require any of the processes listed above because the migrant maintains his contacts with the original country and lives, with other conationals or with migrants from other countries, a kind of encapsuled life in the new culture. The contacts with the host community are often minimal. Permanent absorption is often neither sought nor desired.

THE PROBLEM OF INTERNAL MIGRATION

Internal migrations are taking place in several European countries and have been the object of many detailed studies. As has been stated, the study of internal migration overlaps with the study of the problem of urbanization and industrialization.

[43] Jacques Ex, *op. cit.*
[44] W. D. Borrie, *op. cit.*

A research conducted by Introna[45] points out the important changes in criminal phenomenology and rates taking place in Italy as a consequence of the huge migratory movement from the rural south to the industrial north. The exodus from the country to the city is, however, a much more general phenomenon, and we should only limit ourselves to recall the fact that often the rural-urban changes complicate the adjustment process of the worker who migrates abroad. Migration from some areas of southern Italy to the "industrial triangle" involves processes not dissimilar from those that take place in the course of a transfer to a foreign country. The separation and difference between the original and the host cultures are not dissimilar. In Italy, internal migration has changed and increased the amount of crime in the northern part of the country.[46] In a superficial inspection, it appears as if the Italian internal migrant is more prone to antisocial behavior than the Italian migrant worker abroad. The problem certainly warrants further study. Of particular interest would be the analysis of criminal migrants abroad who have first migrated internally and then, after a failure in adjustment, decided to expatriate. This two-step migration compounds the frustrating and new maladjustive factors.

A large-scale study of internal migration has recently been conducted in America by Shannon and collaborators[47] on Mexican Americans, Anglo-Saxons, and Negroes who migrated to Racine, Wisconsin. Although the study is not relevant to our theme because of the cultural and economic differences of the subjects, methodologically it presents an adequate model. The essential hypothesis is that certain sociological variables, as mediated by sociopsychological and other sociological variables, are the determinants of the values that will be assimilated by a group of persons or of the extent to which the group will be integrated into the culture. Integration into the culture will almost always be followed by behavioral changes. The authors use the frame of reference of Sutherland's differential association theory.[48] They suggest for further study the use of the concept of differential identification[49] and make reference to the possibility of utilizing the research approach, for the

[45] F. Introna, "Aspetti degenerativi e criminologici delle migrazioni interne," *La Scuola Positiva*, 1963, V(4), 668–692.

[46] See, for example, the analysis of the juvenile delinquency statistics conducted in A. Franchini and F. Introna, *Delinquenza Minorile*, Cedam, Padova, 1961.

[47] L. W. Shannon, E. Krass, E. Meeks, and P. Morgan, *The Economic Absorption and Cultural Integration of Immigrant Workers*, Department of Sociology and Anthropology, The University of Iowa, Iowa City, 1966.

[48] E. H. Sutherland, *op. cit.*

[49] D. Glaser, "Criminality Theories and Behavioral Images," *American Journal of Sociology*, March 1956, 61, 433–444.

analysis of differential association theory, proposed by De Fleur and Quinney.[50] Any failure in the process of acculturation may, of course, be conducive of maladjustment and antisocial behavior.

In September 1967 the United Nations conducted in Budapest and Tihany, Hungary, a meeting of an expert group on "Social and Related Aspects of Rural-Urban Migration in Europe."[51] The documents of the meeting provide an interesting picture and a valuable bibliographical source on rural-urban movements in Europe. No reference was made, in the documents available to us, to the criminality resulting from this migration.

THE EUROPEAN WORKERS' MIGRATION

It will not be possible, in the context of the present report, to present a detailed analysis of the history and extent of migrant workers in Europe. The picture changes quickly in relation to variations of the manpower market and to the economic development of the different countries. In general, the movement is from southern or Mediterranean countries to northern countries. Accurate figures are very difficult to obtain because not all migrants are registered. For Italy, during 1946–1964, emigration to other European countries amounted to 3,502,700 persons, while repatriation was 2,075,700, leaving an out-migration balance of 1,427,000. The migratory flux increased from an average of 72,800 in 1946–1951 to 83,900 in 1958–1964. During this latter period, the migratory movement of Italians in Europe constituted about 70 percent of the total Italian migration.[52] Western Germany, Switzerland, Belgium, and France re-

[50] M. L. De Fleur and R. Quinney, "A Reformulation of Sutherland's Differential Association Theory and a Strategy for Empirical Verification," *Journal of Research on Crime and Delinquency*, January 1966, 3(1), 1–22.

[51] Several papers prepared for this Expert Group meeting have been consulted: E. W. Hofstee, *Recent Trends and Characteristics of Rural-Urban Migrations*, UN/SOA/ SEM/25/WP.3; J. Gorynsky, *Problems and Consequences in the Rural Environment* (Eastern Europe), UN/SOA/SEM/25/WP.4; G. Barbichon, *Adaptation industrielle*, UN/SOA/SEM/25/WP.5; C. Barberis, *Problems and Consequences in the Rural Environment*, UN/SOA/SEM/25/WP.8; E. Dimitros, *Effets démographiques, économiques et sociaux des migrations dans les ensembles urbains*, UN/SOA/SEM/25/ WP.6; S. Barkin, *Measures to Influence Reorient or Assist Rural Migrants Moving to Urban Areas*, UN/SOA/SEM/25/WP.10. The final documents of the meeting were not available at the time this report was written.

[52] See the report by the Direzione Generale dell'Emigrazione, Ministero Affari Esteri, 1965, and the study by Lucrezio, Perotti, and Falchi (footnote 12, above) for data on the Italian migration.

ceive the largest number of migrant workers. Immigration into England comes mostly from Ireland and the Commonwealth. Migrant workers are, however, present in all countries, in varying numbers (for example, Finnish migrants go to Sweden, etc.). In recent years a large migratory movement has begun from Greece, Turkey, Yugoslavia, and Spain toward northern Europe.

At a recent meeting of the European Population Conference held by the Council of Europe in 1966, there was collected important and recent data on the size, trends, and economic effects of European migration.[53] The data are incomplete, and they "age" quickly in view of the rapid economic changes of the European continent. Nevertheless, it is clear that migration directly involves several millions of workers, from different nationalities, and other millions of family members of migrants indirectly through the temporary or prolonged absence of the migrants. Consequently, the European countries have developed a complex system of treaties to protect the legal rights of the workers,[54] and the United Nations convened an expert group in 1962[55] and held a seminar in Spain in 1964 to discuss social welfare programs for migrant workers.[56] Many private organizations have taken an active role in the assistance of the migrants and of their families.[57]

Although it is not possible to predict the future evolution of the migrant workers phenomenon, it is unlikely that it will terminate quickly. Eventual European integration, in the future, may reduce its size, but this will take a long period of time. In view of the temporary character of the migration and of the efforts to facilitate the transfer of manpower

[53] See: Conseil de l'Europe, Conférence démographique européenne, *Documents officiels de la Conférence Vol. II*, Strasbourg, September, 1966 (quoted already in footnote 12 above).

[54] The references listed in an Appendix to the report presented to the Council of Europe include several important sources for the legal aspects of European migration.

[55] Social welfare programmes for migrant workers, *Report of the Expert Group*, Mont-Pelerin, 7-13 October 1962, United Nations, Geneva, 1963, SOA/ESWP/EG/Rep.2.

[56] European seminar on social welfare programmes for migrant workers, *Report*, Madrid, Spain, 2-10 April 1964, United Nations, SOA/ESWP/1964/2.

[57] A listing of all organizations is not possible here. The problem is of such size and presents so many different aspects that very different sectors of the social and welfare structures in most countries have been involved. (See Orlando, F., *Guerra alla povertà*, Sansoni, Firenze, 1966, for an analysis of some of the resulting social problems.) The World Council of Churches, Division of Inter-Church Aid, Reference and World Service, Secretariat for Migration, publishes a journal, *Migration Today*, which is an excellent source of data and of bibliographic information. The U.I.M.P. has, in October 1967, convened an International Meeting in Rome, where the moral situation of the migrants and of their families was discussed.

from country to country, there is a tendency to discuss the phenomenon in terms of the "free circulation of manpower in Europe."

Revisions in American immigration laws should not have much effect on the migratory trend in Europe.[58] A migration of intellectuals is also in progress, but it does not reach a very high level and is primarily directed outside Europe.[59]

Welfare activities directed toward remedial or preventive action on migrant workers and on their families are too numerous to be recorded here. In most host and originating countries, special groups or committees are at work with varying degrees of success. Special legislation has been proposed or enacted in many cases, with focus on the efforts related to the families of migrants and to their adjustment in the host country. The Ministries of Foreign Affairs and of Labor (or their equivalents) in many countries have set up special committees or offices.[60] A better coordination of the spontaneous welfare activities with official organized efforts is viewed as desirable.

THE CRIMINALITY OF EUROPEAN MIGRANT WORKERS

We are now approaching the central subject of this paper. Unfortunately, as we shall see, the number of available studies is small and no systematic research effort embracing the full picture of the European scene is available. We shall analyze the recent research papers that are available in chronological order. Although we shall focus on workers' migration and on the member countries of the Council of Europe, occasional references will be made to other types of migrants and to non-

[58] However, migration towards Canada, Australia and other non-European areas should remain high or increase. New migratory currents open for skilled workers in many developing nations. For an analysis of the new American legislation, see E. M. Kennedy, "The Immigration Act of 1965," *The Annals of the American Academy of Political and Social Science*, September 1966, 367, 137–149.

[59] The migration of intellectuals, although numerically not very relevant, can be highly damaging to the home country. Several of the sources consulted in the preparation of this report discuss the negative effects of the so-called "brain drain" (see, for example, the references in footnote 12). Some sections of this migration will tend to increase in the future. Training abroad is often the first irreversible step to a change of values that eventually uproots the intellectual from his home country.

[60] The size and level of governmental interest and intervention in present migration in Europe and outside of the European continent is probably one of the decisive preventive factors of major sociopathological manifestation. In this sense, migration in Europe seems to have benefited from a high level of informed preventive social planning.

member countries. A useful research report, which presents data on the criminality of migrants is the study by McClintock and Gibson on robbery in London.[61] According to these data, robberies committed by Irish immigrants are increasing in London. Irishmen in London are single and appear to be heavy drinkers. In Ireland itself the crime rate is generally very low. Social factors other than migration, such as unemployment, social rank, and type of residence, should be taken into account before any direct relationship is established, as Bottoms[62] states in a careful and detailed recent paper. Gibbens and Ahrenfeldt[63] present an interesting hypothesis to explain the high criminality level of Irish immigrants. They maintain that the strong external controls of the Irish society (church dominance and overprotective mothers) are internalized by the Irishmen as external controls. Migration removes these controls upon contact with a more flexible and fluid society, and delinquency develops. The maintenance of the internal controls causes conflicts, which are acted out in drinking and in other types of maladapted behavior. The hypothesis does not explain why internal controls alone do not possess enough containment value, and it has not been tested through an objective study.

The migrants' crime picture in England is atypical because of the large number of permanent and non-European migrants. Other aspects of this specific situation will be discussed later on. Another British study, by Gibbens and Prince,[64] deals with the specific type of crime of shoplifting. These authors in a sample of 532 female shoplifters, collected in 1959 from three adult courts of London, located 150 foreign shoplifters (29 percent) out of a total of 537. Eighty-eight cases were under 30 years of age and, in this group, the "au pair" girls prevailed. Seventy percent of the foreign shoplifters were Europeans, 16.1 Asians, and 4.6, each, of American white dominions and colored dominions. The "au pair" girls are those whose working situation most closely resembles the psychological and sociological patterns of the migrant workers. The factors that appeared to be involved in the dynamics of shoplifting by foreign girls were the following: relative poverty and lack of experience with the profusion of unguarded goods in shops; resentment about the conditions of employment in England; isolation and lack of identification with cultural standards; social detachment and irresponsibility; and identification with "friends" who also were shoplifters.

61 F. H. McClintock and E. Gibson, *Robbery in London*, MacMillan, London, 1961.
62 A. E. Bottoms, *Delinquency Amongst Immigrants*, Race, 1967, **VIII**(4), 357–383.
63 T. C. N. Gibbens and R. H. Ahrenfeldt, (eds.), *Cultural Factors in Delinquency*, Tavistock Publications, London, 1966.
64 T. C. N. Gibbens and J. Prince, *Shoplifting*, The Institute for the Study and Treatment of Delinquency, London, 1962.

It is interesting to note that multiple arrests (shoplifters who work in couples) are present in 29 percent of the foreigners and in only 19 percent of the British-born, suggesting some element of cultural support and reinforcement. Sexual promiscuity seems to be inversely related to shoplifting. The nationalities for which the percentage of shoplifters exceeds the percentage of the subjects present in the country are Italian, Spanish, Austrian, Yugoslav, Portuguese, Indian, and Persian. Colored immigrants are not heavily represented in the shoplifters group.

The first large-scale study of the criminality of migrant workers was published by Neumann in 1963 on the criminality of Italian workers in the Zürich "Kanton."[65] This very systematic and detailed study deals with Italian nonresident (seasonal or short term) workers guilty of one or more offenses according to the Swiss law, on the basis of judicial statistics (court and police files). There were 200 police and 650 court records located, of which 650 concerned Italian workers. Additional information was obtained from the press. The study covers the years 1949, 1954, 1955, and 1960. The social acceptance of foreign workers in the Zürich Kanton is not high and they are mostly tolerated because of their contribution to the economy. Discovery and prosecution are more likely for foreign workers than for Swiss nationals. Police supervision is closer. In the administration of justice, in the case of foreign workers, there is a tendency not to request a psychiatric evaluation. High reporting of criminal behavior is also typical, contrary to expectations, within the migrants' group.

Sexual misbehavior is more promptly reported when an Italian migrant worker is involved. The general crime rate for Italian workers, although increasing, is lower than the rate for the Swiss nationals. Moreover, the seriousness of Italian criminality, in spite of the tendency of the courts to impose prison sentences instead of fines in cases involving foreign workers, is less serious than that of the indigenous population. Neumann analyzes these surprising (in view of the general belief that the level of criminality of Italian foreign workers is high) results. Although in the years prior to 1955 female workers exceeded males, after 1955 this ratio was reversed, and therefore sex differences cannot explain the low criminal rates. The age composition of the migrant group is relatively young, a fact that gives an even more surprising value to the low criminal rates, which should ordinarily be higher for this age group. The work status, both in terms of the low level of employment and in terms of types of occupations, such as hotel or house servants who often have high crime rates, are also more unfavorable to immigrants than to Swiss nationals. Homesickness and maladjustment should also cause much more

[65] Neumann, K., *Die Kriminalität der italianischen Arbeitskräfte im Kanton Zürich*, Juris Verlag, Zürich, 1963.

crime than the available statistics indicate. All these conditions give an added weight to the low crime rates of the Italian migrants.

The increase in crime in recent years appears due in part to the increase of potential victims, because of the larger number of migrants, as most crimes (particularly of the nonproperty types) occur within the group. Violent crimes are not infrequent (although when occurring within the immigrant group they are frequently not reported). Theft is frequent and often committed just prior to departure. Some cases are aimed at correcting a mistake, such as adulteration of milk, or at showing diligence. Threats and offenses against morality are often due to cultural misunderstanding, and age and sex distributions should be taken into account. Sexual misbehavior often results from misunderstanding of legal norms. For example, Italian workers are astonished to discover that, if they get sexually involved with a girl under 16, their willingness to marry her or the fact that she was already "depraved," do not absolve them from guilt as is the case according to Italian law. Other types of crimes are irrelevant in the migrant group. One exception is male prostitution, which appears to be relatively high. No case of rape was found in the available files.

In a paper on young adult (16 to 25 years of age) Italian migrants in the area of Liège, Liben analyzes many sociological variables. Although no control data are presented, the conclusion is that the migrant group does not commit more crimes than the comparable group of the host country. There may be more violent behavior, but this is due to original cultural traits and not to the migration process. The point is made that possibly the large number of Italian migrants helps to minimize their cultural conflicts. The strength of the Italian family ties and the strong paternal authority seem also to have a preventive value.[66]

In a paper by Wenzky[67] in 1965, a superficial analysis is reported on the criminality of foreigners in the most industrialized county of Western Germany, Nordrheim-Westfalen. According to police statistics, 1.4 percent of foreigners in 1962 and 1.6 percent of foreigners in 1963 committed offenses. Of particular interest is the participation of foreigners in crimes of violence, especially murders, 20 percent of which are committed by foreigners. Violent crimes, he points out, are committed mostly by foreigners from Mediterranean countries and Africa. But the author gives no indication about the victims (which would be of particular

---

[66] Liben, G., "Un reflet de la criminalité italienne dans la région de Liège," Revue de Droit Pénal et de Criminologie, December 1963, 44(3), 205–245. Another study of the Liège region has been conducted by Wathar and Bastin: "Aperçu général de la criminalité des étrangers de la région liégeoise," Revue de la gendarmerie belge, April 1965.

[67] O. Wenzky, "Analyse zur Ausländer Kriminalität", Kriminalistik 19, 1965, I, 1–5.

interest, in view of the international character of violent crimes among migrants, indicated by other studies) and presents no control data. Wenzky indicates, as causes of the migrants' crimes, alcohol, sex, linguistic misunderstanding, and feelings of isolation. Of particular interest to the prosecuting authorities was the fact that many foreigners had already been prosecuted in their home country for similar offenses.

Kurz[68] theoretically analyzes the group structure and adaptation processes and dispositions in an Italian guest workers' camp. The anomic situation of the workers results from conflicts between the strong loyalty demands of the Italian homeland environment, focused on expectations of return, and the loyalty demands of the living-working group in relation to the German host community, focused on economic goals. When the group structure is less firm, the economic goals are smaller, and this prevents cultural and normative conflicts. Individual motivation becomes, in this case, a special form of social regulation, which differs from Durkheim's conceptualization of anomie as the absence of solidarity in the working community. The reference group of Italian guests of the work camps is the Italian family on whose expectations they chiefly orient their behavior. This has a protective and preventive effect, in view of the relatively loose regulations of the camp, which permits a high degree of fulfilment of the individual role expectations and motivations of return. Group coherence is therefore stabilized in relation to the German host community. At the same time, the total integration of the individual into his southern family may facilitate disintegration from larger social relationships and lack of internalized guiding images, which might regulate conduct in nonfamilial groups. Thus, the "enclave" system of the camp may act as a protective element. This hypothesis corresponds to the opinion of some American studies,[69] which claim that the probability of antisocial behavior increases when the contacts with the host community increase (and resulting value change is initiated). (Other papers published in 1965 include a British study by Bulmer[70] and a study conducted in Limburg by Torfs.[71])

Of marginal interest to the problem of crime among migrants is a paper by Willcox,[72] published in 1965, which states that about half of the cases of gonorrhea and four out of ten cases of syphilis in males

[68] U. Kurz, "Partielle Anpassung und Kulturkonflikt. Gruppenstruktur und Anpassungsdispositionen in einem italienischen Gastarbeiter-Lager." Kölner Z. Soziol., Sozial Psychol., 1965, 17/4 (814–832).

[69] E. H. Sutherland, op. cit.

[70] J. H. Bulmer, "Birds of Passage," The Police Journal, July 1965.

[71] Torfs, "Vreemdelingen in Limburg," Revue van de Rijkswacht, April 1965, 18, 23–35, July 1965, 19, 21–30.

[72] R. R. Willcox, "Venereal Diseases and Immigrants," Practitioner, 1965, 195(1196), 628–638.

attending clinics in England and Wales are due to immigrants. West Indian groups particularly appear affected by venereal diseases. The social conditions of the immigrants and the lack of female immigrants are considered responsible for the situation. A more recent paper on the same subject[73] shows a somewhat more optimistic picture, with a decline in the proportion of new immigrant cases.

An important study on the criminality of foreign workers has been published by Graven in 1965,[74] who makes reference to a "Colloque sur les migrations de travailleurs en Europe," which took place in Geneva in October 1965 at the International Institute of Social Studies of the Organisation Intérnationale du Travail, and summarizes several other studies and data relevant to the problem. In 1964, foreign workers in Switzerland reached the high figure of 720,901, of which 68.1 percent were Italians. Public concern about the criminality of this large group grew, and several xenophobic statements appeared in the daily press, particularly against Mediterranean workers, claiming that there was imminent danger from the high level of criminality of foreigners. An examination of the available data, however, shows that proportionally the level of criminality is higher among Austrians, followed by Germans, Italians, Arabs, Turks, and French. This last group is largely composed of people living near the border who are therefore more adjusted to migration. Most of the criminals, predictably, belong to the younger age groups. The overall ratio for crimes is slightly higher for foreign workers than for the general Swiss population: 441 per 100,000 v. 315 per 100,000 in 1963. These data should of course be corrected for sex and age. Graven analyzes the social causes of the problem and the possible legal corrective measures, and sees no cause for alarm.

In 1966, several papers appeared in Europe, all consistently presenting a rather optimistic picture of the criminal situation of migrants. An article by Wehner[75] on data collected in Düsseldorf shows that the number of offenses committed by non-Germans increased slightly, but this increase is misleading, according to the author, because many are illegal immigrants. The ratio, corrected by the author, is less than half that of the criminality of the local population. In a paper by Händel,[76] an analysis is made of the defense pleadings of the Italian immigrant workers, who often use as an excuse the legal differences between Italy and Germany,

[73] British Co-operative Clinical Group, "Gonorrhoea Study, 1965," *British Journal Venereal Diseases*, 1967, 43/1 (25–31).

[74] J. Graven, "Le problème des travailleurs étrangers délinquants en Suisse," *Revue Internationale de Criminologie et de Police Technique*, 1965, **XIX**(4), 265–290.

[75] B. Wehner, "Gastarbeiter Kriminität—auch ein Schlagwort?" *Kriminalistik*, April 1966, 175–176.

[76] K. Händel, "Verteidigungsvorbringen italienischer Gastarbeiter," *Kriminalistik*, July 1966, 360–362.

particularly concerning sexual offenses and offenses committed while under the influence of alcoholic beverages. Several practical suggestions are given for the examining magistrates.

An interesting and careful research paper by Pradervand and Cardia[77] examines the criminality of Italians in Geneva, taking into account several sociological variables, including age differentials. The different experimental and control groups studied rank in criminality, from the highest to the lowest, in the following way: Fribourgeois, Valaisons, Genevois, and Italians. The low crime rate of the Italians, compared to the other groups, sharply contradicts the prejudices often held against the migrant workers. The study does not include seasonal workers, but their inclusion would lower still more the ratio of criminal behavior among the migrant workers.

In another methodologically sound paper, Zimmermann[78] corrects criminal data for age and sex (only males aged 18 to 50, with appropriate controls are included) and studies four migrant national groups, Italians, Greeks, Spaniards, and Turks, making adequate corrections for tourists, members of foreign armed forces, and international criminals. By equating the crimes committed by Germans to 100, and calculating the proportional ratio of crimes committed by foreign workers, the author obtains, for the most common crimes, the figures shown in Table 1 for 1965.

TABLE 1

Crime	Germans	Italians	Greeks	Spaniards	Turks
All crimes	100	50	72	32	88
Murder	100	133	66	66	366
Attempted murder	100	133	183	83	517
Serious personal lesions	100	250	150	50	100
Lesions	100	112	139	75	287
Rape	100	123	150	63	323
Crimes against the morality of children	100	163	115	63	160
Robbery	100	69	77	46	163
Thefts	100	69	86	54	59
Qualified thefts	100	31	28	23	18
Fraud	100	23	38	11	50

[77] P. Pradervand, and L. Cardia, "Quelques aspects de la délinquance italienne à Genève," *Revue internationale de Criminologie et Police Technique*, 1966, XX(I), 43–58.
[78] H. G. Zimmermann, "Die Kriminalität der ausländischern Arbeiter," *Kriminalistik*, December 1966, 623–625.

In this study, crime among foreign workers is, in general, lower than that in the population of the host country. Spaniards and Italians appear to be the least criminal groups, and the Turks and Greeks the most criminal. Crimes against the person are higher in the migrant workers, but it should be remembered that these crimes are mostly committed among the workers themselves and only infrequently involve the population of the host country. An intragroup or intracultural characteristic of violent crimes is here noted, not dissimilar from that found by Wolfgang[79] for Negroes in his Philadelphia study of homicide, which would tend to indicate the subcultural (or cultural) character of these violent, antisocial manifestations.[80]

In Finland, a study of the criminality of Finnish migrants in Sweden is in progress and has been reported as a project by the Council of Europe.[81] In Sweden, several studies have been made and are in progress. Schmidt[82] published an analysis of the convictions of aliens in Stockholm in 1965. Out of a total of 415 convictions, 255 were Finns. The next largest group were Norwegians (27 convictions). No rates were calculated. In another research published by Klemming,[83] 32 Greeks and 20 Yugoslavs were convicted in Stockholm in 1965. The Yugoslav group had 65 percent of offenses against the person (only 12 percent were intoxicated at the time of the crime); the Greeks, instead, had only 25 percent convictions for crimes against the person, almost all committed while intoxicated. These data confirm an hypothesis of Sveri about the cultural differences among the two groups. Sveri[84] has published a more comprehensive study of migrants' crime, following a "culture-conflict" theoretical model. The nature of the conflict and its possible outcome, either in terms of dissolution and assimilation of the group or formation of new groups, or in terms of adaptation to the new culture, when the conflict is not on vital areas

[79] Marvin E. Wolfgang, *Patterns in Criminal Homicide*, University of Pennsylvania Press, Philadelphia, 1958.
[80] For a discussion of the subcultural aspects of violent crimes, see M. E. Wolfgang and F. Ferracuti, *The Subculture of Violence*, Tavistock Publications, London, 1967.
[81] V. A. Kaironen, *A Study of the Criminality of Finnish Immigrants in Sweden*, Council of Europe, International Exchange of Information on current criminological research projects in member states. Strasbourg, 1966, DPC/PRC (66) 2, 202.
[82] K. Schmidt, *Utlänningars brottslighet i Stockholm*, 1965, Inst. for Criminal Science, Stockholm, 1966.
[83] L. G. Klemming, *Grekers och Jugoslavers Kriminalitet*, Institute for Criminal Science, Stockholm, 1967.
[84] Information on this and the two preceding projects is due to the courtesy of Professor Knut Sveri of the Institute for Criminal Science, of the University of Stockholm. See K. Sveri, "Culture Conflict and Crime," in David Schwarz (ed.), *Svenska minoriteter*, Aldus, Stockholm, 1966, 107–119.

or values, can most easily be studied in the migration situation, according to the author. By using criminal data from 1962 and corrected data from the 1960 census, the following criminal rates per 1000 persons were calculated for different nationality groups: Hungarians and Yugoslavs, 10–12; Poles, 7; Finns, 6; Swedes, 6; Norwegians, 6; Danes, 6; Italians, 4; and Austrians, 2.

Hungarians and Yugoslavs have a high rate of crimes against the person. Their conflicts are culture conflicts, of the simplest kind, with Swedish laws, and they are accustomed to solve them through the use of force. Different cultural solutions are open to the adaptation problem and a role of paramount importance is played by the behavior and attitudes of the Swedes themselves towards the foreigners. At present, a large-scale triennial study is beginning in Sweden on this topic.[85]

In a study published in 1967 by Nann,[86] an analysis was made of 110 Italian workers' offenses, compared with 173 German workers from the court districts of Stuttgart, Stuttgart-Bad Cannstatt, and Esslingen in the southwest area of Western Germany. The convictions had taken place in the years 1960–1962. Germans had more offenses against property. (These offenses had been committed by the Italians mostly in dormitories and outside houses.) The Italians had four to five times more offenses against the person, and they came mostly from southern Italy. Their criminality appeared to be primarily socially motivated.

The British migration picture, as noted in the studies quoted at the beginning of this section, is less optimistic than that of the rest of Europe. It has been noted also that migration into England has very peculiar characteristics. The problem of a colored minority complicates the adjustment of migrants. Moreover, the migrants are mostly permanent and concentrated in slum areas not dissimilar in ecology and in social pathology from those areas in the United States where riots make summer headlines with consistent and disturbing regularity.

A recent paper by Wallis and Maliphant[87] presents an important methodological point, which should be kept in mind in future studies of urban immigrant criminality. In a very detailed study of delinquent areas of the county of London, the authors found that the important element in the relationship between immigrants and crime is not the ratio of immigrants to the population but the speed of the immigrant influx.

[85] This study is financed by the Tri-Centennial Fund of the Bank of Sweden.
[86] E. Nann, *Die Kriminalität der italienischen Gastarbeiter im Spiegel der Ausländer Kriminalität*, Kriminologische Schriftenreine aus dei Deutschen Kriminologischen Gesellschaft, Vol. 28, *Kriminalistik*, Verlag, Hamburg, 1967.
[87] C. P. Wallis and R. Maliphant, "Delinquent Areas in the County of London: Ecological Factors," *The British Journal of Criminology*, July 1967, 7(3), 250–284.

If the static immigrant population and delinquency rates are compared with the nonimmigrant population, no significant association is found; but if the comparison is made in terms of the influx immigration and delinquency, a significant association appears (at the 5 percent level).

Bottoms, in a paper already mentioned,[88] also analyzes the Commonwealth immigration into England and finds the delinquency rates to be generally low (except for violent crimes) where, however, domestic disputes play an important role. Bottoms remarks that, according to American studies, crime is higher among those immigrant groups who are not bound together and isolated from the host culture in tightly-knit groups (a fact that might explain the differences between the British and the continental European aspects of this phenomenon), and that rates for the second generation immigrants are higher. Again, in the case of European migration, it is too early to assess the impact of crime among the children of immigrants, and very often they are left behind in the home country.

Gillioz,[89] in a paper published in 1967, discusses the difficulties of estimating objectively realistic crime rates for foreigners in Switzerland. If the data are corrected for the different types of foreigners and for age and sex, the crime rate of foreigners is not high. As in the other studies previously analyzed, it is lower than that of the host country. Similar to previous studies, however, violent crimes show a relatively high rate for foreigners.

A personal communication from Interpol[90] points out the scarcity of available data, the frequency of intragroup criminality, which often escapes the attention of police authorities, and the importance of criminal behavior connected with traffic of narcotic drugs, particularly by some national groups, such as Turks, Commonwealth migrants, and North Africans.

The Italian Ministry of Foreign Affairs[91] has requested data on the criminality of Italian migrant workers from Italian consulates and embassies in Europe. Data have been made available from France, Denmark, and Germany. Although the data are too incomplete for detailed presentation, they consistently indicate a low crime rate.

[88] A. E. Bottoms, op. cit.
[89] E. Gillioz, "La criminalité des étrangers en Suisse," Revue pénale suisse, 1967, 2(83), 178–191.
[90] Personal communication to the Council of Europe from Interpol Secretary-General, J. Nepote, November 1966.
[91] These data, on convictions, have been made available through the cooperation of the Directorate for Emigration of the Italian Ministry of Foreign Affairs. An expression of gratitude is due to the several staff members from the Ministry and from Embassies and Consulates who have generously contributed their time and efforts to the preparation of the report.

In France, a large-scale study of the criminality of foreigners has been in progress since 1966, under the direction of Mr. Pinatel and Mr. Epoud.[92] Upon its completion, it will undoubtedly provide interesting data. The French situation is particularly interesting in view of the older migratory movements, particularly from Italy, and of the French government's policy of attempting to assimilate foreign workers.

A few police and prison reports from European countries have been examined for data on crime and migration. The French report for 1966[93] states that on 1 January 1967, the number of foreign inmates in the French system was 5250 or 16.8 percent of the total, with an 8 percent decrease from 1965 and a 19 percent decrease from 1964. The decrease is attributed to the strict enforcement of expulsion orders. Yet, according to the report, the number of foreign inmates is disproportionately high: there is one inmate for every 1800 Frenchmen, one for every 550 foreigners, and one for every 190 Algerians. These figures, of course, are of little significance for they are not corrected for age and sex of the groups under examination. The Swiss criminal statistics for 1965,[94] published by the police, were analyzed by Gillioz, in a paper mentioned earlier.

Swedish correctional statistics for 1966[95] show an increase from 888 to 1186, from 1965 to 1966; 60 percent of the foreign inmates were Finnish, while 11 percent were Norwegians. The remainder represented 25 different nationalities. Again, the figures are not corrected for age and sex. German police statistics for 1965 also show an increase in the criminality of foreigners. Again, no correction is made for age, sex, or number of foreigners present in Germany. A similar increase is reported for 1966.[96] In general, official statistics, uncorrected and limited to gross

[92] Personal communication from Professor J. Pinatel, May 1967. For the criminality of North Africans in France, see C. A. Hirsch, "La criminalité nord-africaine," *Revue internationale de criminologie et de police technique*, 1953 (October-December), 298–302; C. A. Hirsch, "La criminalité nord-africaine en France est-elle ume criminalité par défaut d'adaptation?" *Revue internationale de criminologie et de police technique*.

[93] R. Morice, *Rapport présenté à Monsieur le Garde des Sceaux, Ministre de la Justice*, 1966, Conseil Supérieur de l'Administration pénitentiaire.

[94] *Statistique de la Criminalité en Suisse*, 1965. Bureau central suisse de police, Bureau fédéral de statistique, Berne, 1966.

[95] Sveriges Officielle Statistik Rättsväsen, *Kriminalvärden, 1966*, Kriminalvardsstyrelsen, Stockholm, 1967.

[96] For 1965, see *Die im Jahre 1965 in der Bundesrepublik Deutschland einschlieplich Berlin (West) Bekanntgewordene Kriminalität*. Bulletin de Press und informationsamtes der Bundesregierung, I, 83/6, 660–664, 23 June 1966; II, 84/5, 668–671, 24 June 1966; III, 85/6, 678–680, 28 June 1966. For 1966, see Holle, R., "Kriminalität 1966 in der Bundesrepublik Deutschland," *Kriminalistik*, August 1967, 410–414.

figures and percentages, are of little use in a scientific study of the phenomenon.

As it can be seen from the above review of available studies, crime among Eupopean migrant workers is, with the possible exception of Britain, not such as to cause alarm. The criminal phenomenology of migrants differs from that of the host countries and, although isolated areas of concern exist, the "dangers" claimed by some sections of the public have not materialized. Yet, many areas remain unexplored, and several crime-migration hypotheses need to be tested for a full comprehension of the phenomenon. The fact that present crime rates appear to be low does not mean that efforts should not be made to reduce them even more. A comprehensive, long-term study is sorely missing.

THE RETURN MIGRANT

Much current European migration is seasonal and involves only temporary displacement for short-term employment. Even in the case of longer work contracts and assignments, in the majority of cases, migration is not seen as a permanent and definitive transfer. The worker keeps his ties with the home country, minimizes his integration with the host community, and eventually returns to his country of origin (although, often, not to the same residence or occupation). This fact, on one side has compensated for some of the more traumatic and maladjustive aspects of migration but, on the other, has opened a relatively new chapter of social pathology, of which very few examples existed before: the problems of the return migrant. The attrition with the host culture, changes in values and aspirations, the problems of reinsertion into a community that no longer constitutes the only life experience of the subject, frequent conjugal problems, difficulties of occupational placement, a broader vision, and an enlarged level of aspirations often not corresponding to the static or slowly changing reality in the home country—all of these are problems that threaten the social adjustment of the returning migrant. The idealization of the home country, which takes place in the permanence abroad, changes the terms of reference of the migrant and occasionally builds unfulfilled expectations. Sometimes, the psychological displacement and social distance of returning amount to a second migration. Also, in the original country, the migrant is sometimes perceived as an alien, with foreign tastes, manners, and values. The number of return migrants has been rapidly increasing, and it is impossible at this stage to predict the future evolution of the problem. In other cases, economic recessions and changes in the host country may cause large-scale variations in the employment level of migrant workers, with resultant damaging effects in occupational or geographical areas of the original countries where unemployment may suddenly increase.

Although the problem of the return migrant is new, some attention has already been directed to it and to possible remedial action. In 1963, the Council of Europe[97] initiated an analysis of the policies of different member countries vis-à-vis the return migrants. Catalano[98] published a paper on the topic and discussed the relationship between migratory trends and economic conditions and developmental steps both in the host and in the home countries. The original countries, in some cases (Greece and Turkey are two examples), do not wish to lose permanently the migrant manpower and stress the importance of the vocational training that the migrant receives in the host country. Yet, sometimes this training is illusory, because it takes place in working areas and with industrial tools that do not exist in the home country. Occasionally, the vocational training received in the host country contributes to the displacement of the worker upon his return, uprooting him from a rural or low-level employment.[99] Psychological aspects of the migration and of the return decision are of paramount importance.

An important study of the return migrants' problems has been published by Sjollema.[100] This author discusses the different types of returnees and the economic problems caused by migration, including damage to the original countries where economic and social structures are often seriously affected by the exodus of large groups of their more productive population. Political-opinion changes in the migrant workers are analyzed (on the basis of Spanish and Italian examples), and the need for cooperation between the home and host countries is stressed by Sjollema.

Some of the problems of the return migrants were examined by the *Comité des Conseilleurs du Représentant Spécial* of the Council of Europe in 1966.[101] No mention, however, is made in the available documents of the sociopsychological adjustment problems caused by the

[97] Comité des Conseilleurs du Représentant spécial, Problèmes posés par les Retours des Travailleurs migrants dans leur pays. Council of Europe, 1965 (RS 78–1965).
[98] R. Catalano, "I problemi posti dal ritorno dei lavoratori migranti," *Italiani nel mondo*, 25 July 1965, N. 14, 7–12.
[99] The uprooted rural worker very rarely goes back to the country. Urbanization is a one-way process, and several economic and psychological factors make impossible a voluntary return to a low level of social stratification.
[100] B. Ch. Sjollema, "Return migration and developmental aid," *Migration Today*, 1965, 5, 14–22.
[101] Several documents have been issued by the Comité des Conseilleurs du Représentant spécial of the Council of Europe in 1965 and 1966. The topic is included in the work programme for 1968.

return, although some economic problems are discussed. Recently, attention was given in Italy to the question of the loss of residence of the migrant workers, which could cause problems upon their return.[102] The current recession in England, West Germany, and the Netherlands may increase, in the immediate future, the size of the return migration.[103]

A Council of Europe paper, prepared in 1967 by Uner for the Committee on Population and Refugees, deals with Turkish migrant workers and their return. In the period 1961–1966, 195,000 workers were sent abroad by the Turkish Employment Bureau (87 percent went to Germany). The Turkish return migrants are generally people who first migrated from the country to the city. They often change work and appear very mobile. Rural return migrants appeared to readjust better to the home country.[104]

A serious problem of adjustment of the return migrants is being experienced by other non-European countries. In Puerto Rico[105] the large size of the returnee group has brought new criminal phenomenologies (such as drug addiction and juvenile gang delinquency), which previously were minimal or nonexistent. Of particular difficulty is the adjustment of the children born abroad and often unable to speak the mother language. The probability that sociopathological manifestations due to the phenomenon of the return migrants will increase in the future is high, and appropriate prevention steps need to be taken.

CONCLUSIONS AND RECOMMENDATIONS FOR FUTURE RESEARCH AND ACTION

The preceding summary of the main relevant points of the problem of European migration and crime should enable us to reach tentative

---

[102] See, for example, "La posizione anagrafica dei lavoratori emigrati," *Il Messaggero,* 16 May 1967, p. 12.

[103] See, as an example of the general concern for the problem, the following: R. C. Doty, "Flow of Workers from Southern Europe to the North is Halted," *The New York Times,* Int. Ed., 27 February 1967, P.L. Also, *Perdieron el sol....y el trabaio,* Vision, 23 de Junio de 1967, p. 73.

[104] Uner, S., *The Problem of Turkish Workers Abroad and of Their Return Home.* Committee on Population and Refugees, Council of Europe, Strasbourg, 18 August 1967, AS/PR (19), 8.

[105] See, for preliminary studies of the problem in this country, J. Hernandez Alvarez, *Return Migration to Puerto Rico,* Institute of International Studies, University of California, Berkeley, 1967. Also, Ferracuti, F., *Juvenile Delinquency and Social Change in Puerto Rico,* International Mental Health Research Newsletter, Summer 1967, 9(2), 8–10.

conclusions and recommendations, although relevant and valid data presently available are scarce.

1. The general literature on the problem of migration and crime is only of marginal relevance to the present European workers migration. The social and economic differences and the psychological characteristics of European migrants make it difficult or meaningless to transfer hypotheses and results from earlier studies to the present. The same applies to the data on displaced persons.

2. The crime rate of European migrants in the host countries, in spite of their greater visibility and greater probability of being reported, appears to be about equal to or lower than the crime rate of the host population. The high criminality of foreign migrant workers is an xenophobic myth. Yet migration to the United Kingdom and some African migration to France is linked with a high rate of crime. Crime rates of migrant workers, in gross figures at least, seem to be increasing. The specific phenomenology of some of the criminality of migrants, particularly for violent crimes and sex crimes, indicates the exportation to northern countries of cultural and subcultural elements, which would be wise to prevent. A detailed, large-scale study of the global picture of the European workers migration and crime should be undertaken in order to maximize the effects of preventive, remedial, concerted, and coordinated action by the member countries.

3. Such a study should include all the major hypotheses based on existing criminological literature. None of the theoretical formulations presented so far—cultural conflict, anomie, differential association or identification, subcultural identification, differential opportunity structure, frustration and aggression—will explain all the antisocial behavior of all migrants. In different subjects, different mechanisms, or patterns of mechanisms, will enter into the criminogenetic and criminodynamic processes leading to the criminal act. These mechanisms and the differential personality pattern and typological traits of delinquent or potentially delinquent migrants must be studied at a clinical, individual level[106]

[106] The clinical approach, as presented by Di Tullio (B. Di Tullio, *Principi di Criminologia Clinica e Psichiatria Forense*, Instituto di Medicina Sociale, Rome, 1963) does not conflict with a general study of the problem. Several cases of criminal behavior linked to internal or external migration are included in the case studies published in the *Quaderni di Criminologia Clinica* (see *Caso P*, 1962, pages 333–366, *Caso V*, 1964, pages 201–227, *Caso Z*, 1964, pages 351–358, and *Caso A/1*, 1964, pages 441–473). The possibility of integration between the clinical approach and the sociological search for general theories has been the object of several writings. See, for example, F. Ferracuti and M. E. Wolfgang, "Clinical v. Sociological Criminology: Separation or Integration," *Excerpta Criminologica*, 1964, p. 4.

without losing sight of the need for broad, encompassing generalizations that might enable legislators and social operators to take appropriate corrective steps. In the study, the previous and concomitant phenomenology of internal migration should be included. The "natural history" of the individual migration process, including eventual return migration, should be analyzed in representative groups in a variety of cultural host settings. The possible alternation and equivalence of antisocial acts and psychopathological behavior should be included in the matrix, together with the industrialization and urbanization components of the migratory process.

4. Such a study should move, in its theoretical formulations, from an adequate migration theory. Since Ravenstein's first attempts to formulate a law of migration,[107] little has been added to the theoretical aspects of the field. Demographers and economists have not contributed substantially to conceptualizations about the migratory process, and the psychological and psychopathological formulations have never claimed nor obtained the general level of a "law" or theory. Sellin's culture conflict, in the fields of social pathology and sociology, is the only exception. Only recently, Lee[108] has presented a theory that accounts for the several variables included in the process. The theory should be enlarged to embrace the sociopathological aspects of migration and be subjected to objective study and testing.

5. The low crime rates of current migrant workers in Europe is undoubtedly due to several causes. The efforts of national and international public and private organizations have certainly been contributions. A better coordination of the various efforts should be achieved, possibly through a centralized agency. The Council of Europe could probably, through one of its already existing bodies or through a newly established one, assume leadership in this coordinating activity, as well as in promoting the large-scale research discussed above.

6. The theory proposed by Lee[109] embraces the following hypothesis: "The characteristics of migrants tend to be intermediate between the characteristics of the population at destination." This statement implies that a new type of person is emerging from the migration process. In all probability, the "European man" that we are striving to generate will in large part result from the migration and reflect its vicissitudes. His birth should receive careful attention.

[107] E. G. Ravenstein, "The Laws of Migration," *Journal of the Royal Statistical Society,* June 1885, **XLVIII** (Part 2), 167–227, and E. G. Ravenstein, "The Laws of Migration," *Journal of the Royal Statistical Society,* **LII**, June 1889, 241–301, quoted by Lee (see following footnote).

[108] E. S. Lee, "A Theory of Migration," *Demography,* 1966, 3(1), 47–57.

[109] *Ibid,* p. 57.

In a book on migration written in preparation for his proposal for new immigration legislation in the United States, the late President John Kennedy[110] quoted Walt Whitman:

> "These States are the amplest poem,
> Here is not merely a nation but
> A teeming Nation of nations."

The migrant is the spearhead of the process which will permit us to extend Whitman's image of the United States to Europe. He deserves our interest, our informed respect, and understanding in his odyssey to build a European "poem."

[110] J. F. Kennedy, *A Nation of Immigrants*, Popular Library, New York, 1964.

13

Negligent Homicide in Some European Countries—A Comparative Study

JOHANNES ANDENAES

THE LEGAL PROVISIONS

Negligent homicide is an offense which in most European countries is defined in substantially the same way. The essential elements of the offense are two: negligent behaviour and the death of another as a result of the negligence. The German Penal Code, Section 222 could be taken as a prototype: "Anybody who negligently causes the death of a human being shall be punished. . . ."[1] The provisions of the Scandinavian penal codes are with slight variations framed on the same pattern.[2] The French Penal Code, Article 319, has a more elaborate definition: "Any person who by lack of skill, imprudence, carelessness, negligence or failure to observe regulations, involuntarily commits or brings about a homicide, shall be punished. . . ."[3]

In English Law, there is no statutory offense of negligent homicide. The nearest approach is the Common Law crime of involuntary manslaughter.[4] The definition of the subjective element in this crime is however far from clear. Certainly, ordinary negligence is not enough; the debatable point is whether the requirement of *mens rea* should be

[1] The translation is from The American Series of Foreign Penal Codes, No. 4 (1964).
[2] See the Danish Penal Code of 1930, Section 241, the Finnish Penal Code of 1889, Chapter 21, Section 10, the Norwegian Penal Code of 1902, Section 239, the Swedish Penal Code of 1962, Chapter 14, Section 9.
[3] The translation is from The American Series of Foreign Penal Codes, No. 1 (1960).
[4] Manslaughter falls into two main categories: voluntary manslaughter, which comprises intentional killing not amounting to murder (for example, due to provocation or diminished responsibility), and involuntary manslaughter, which comprises all other categories. See *Russell on Crime*, 2nd ed., by J. W. C. Turner (1958), Vol. 1, p. 622.

defined as recklessness or as gross negligence.[5] A special rule in a practically important area is the penal provision in the Road Traffic Act on causing death by reckless or dangerous driving.

This article deals primarily with negligent homicide in the Scandinavian countries,[6] but some comparisons will be made with other countries, especially Germany, France, and England. The study does not aim at analyzing the legal concept of negligence in each country, although legal problems will occasionally be considered. The object is rather to examine the relationship between the conviction frequency and the social conditions and systems of procedure. The starting point of the study was a feeling of surprise at the great discrepancy between the figures for Norway and those for other countries with which Norway may naturally be compared.

TRENDS IN THE RATE OF CONVICTIONS

Figure 1 shows the development of the rate of convictions for homicide in the Scandinavian countries from 1925 to 1960.[7] The diagram gives the absolute figures. The population of Sweden is nearly twice as large as that of Denmark and Finland and slightly more than twice as large as the population of Norway.[8] It should also be mentioned that the Danish criminal statistics prior to 1960 did not include persons who were sentenced to pay fines. If the ratio of fines to prison sentences was the same before 1960 as after that year, the figures for Denmark should be increased by about 60 percent to provide a correct comparison.

Figure 1 reveals considerable differences among the countries despite their close similarity in economic and cultural development. Norway in particular stands in a class by itself, with a very low and surprisingly stable figure for convictions for negligent homicide. This stability goes far back in time. Since the conviction figures are so small, relatively considerable variations are bound to occur from one year to

[5] See *Russell on Crime, op. cit.*, pp. 644–660, *Kenny's Outlines of Criminal Law*, 18th ed., by J. W. C. Turner (1962), pp. 178–185; Glanville Williams, *Criminal Law. The General Part*, 2nd ed. (1961), pp. 100–115, T. C. Willett, *Criminal on the Road* (1964), pp. 79–89.

[6] For a more detailed study, see J. Andenæs and R. Hauge, *Uaktsomt drap i de nordiske land* (Negligent homicide in the Scandinavian countries) (stencilled in Norwegian, 1965).

[7] The figures quoted here and on the following pages have been taken from the respective countries' official criminal statistics.

[8] The figures for 1960 are the following: Denmark, 4.6 million; Finland, 4.4; Norway, 3.6; and Sweden, 7.5 million.

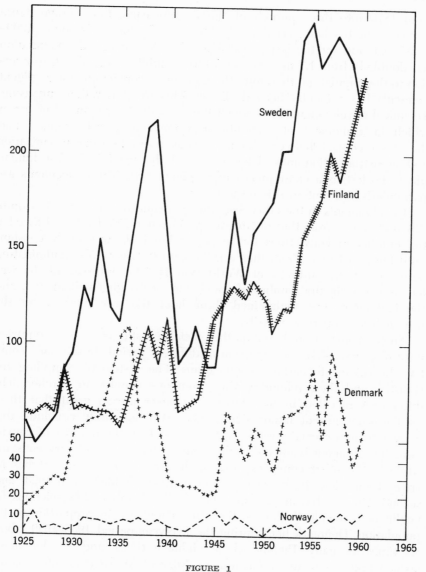

FIGURE 1

Persons convicted for negligent homicide in Denmark, Finland, Norway, and Sweden —1925 to 1960.

another. The figures for the last 100 years have varied between 0 and 13 (0 in 1950 and 13 in 1908 and 1926). If, however, we divide these 100 years into five-year periods, we find a high degree of stability and an even higher degree if we use longer periods. If we divide the time from 1870 into three periods of thirty years each, the average figure per year for the first period (1870–1899) is 5.1, for the second (1900–1929) 5.9, and for the last (1930–1959) 5.8. Meanwhile the population has doubled (from 1.7 million in 1870 to 3.6 million in 1960). In proportion to the population, therefore, the number of convictions for negligent homicide has evidently been declining. This trend is rather surprising. Technical developments have given the individual a command of forces which in a moment of inattentiveness may cause catastrophes, and the closer contact between human beings resulting from urbanization and industrialization must have increased the possibilities for human life to be lost as a consequence of negligent acts. Traffic accidents are particularly relevant in this respect.

Developments in the other Scandinavian countries have taken a quite different course from that in Norway. In Denmark, Finland, and Sweden the number of convictions for negligent homicide was fairly constant until the mid-1920's. From then on, the figures rose rapidly, culminating before or at the outbreak of World War II. The outbreak of the war led to a drop in the number of convictions for negligent homicide, and the low figure was maintained throughout the war years. After the war, it has again risen rapidly.

Such a comparison, based on the official statistics of various countries, must of course—like a comparison of different periods in the same country—be subject to certain qualifications. The system of compiling the statistics and their reliability vary from one country to another. The differences revealed in the statistics however are so great that these qualifications are of minor significance. We can safely conclude that Norway is in a special position in two ways: first, the number of convictions for negligent homicide in this country has remained very constant, while in the other countries—except during the war years—it has increased considerably, being now several times as high as in 1920; and, second, Norway has at present a far smaller number of convictions for negligent homicide than have the other countries. In proportion to the population, Denmark had, during the five-year period 1955–1959, about six times as many, Finland about eighteen times, and Sweden about sixteen times as many convictions as Norway. If we take into account the fact that the Danish statistics for that period do not comprise persons who were fined, Norway's position becomes even more unique, the ratio of the Danish to the Norwegian figures being in that case ten to one.

The same trend as in Denmark, Finland, and Sweden is found in France and Germany too: a steady increase up to the outbreak of World War II, a rapid decline during the war, followed by a very steep rise during the postwar years. This trend will be seen from Figure 2, which shows the average number of convictions for negligent homicide from 1925 through 1963. (The figures for the prewar years apply to the whole of Germany, the postwar figures to the German Federal Republic only. If East Germany had been included, the increase over the prewar figures would have been considerably greater.) As for the number of convictions from 1940 to 1949, no figures are available for Germany, but the figures for the years before and after that period make it very likely that the number of convictions during the war years declined radically.

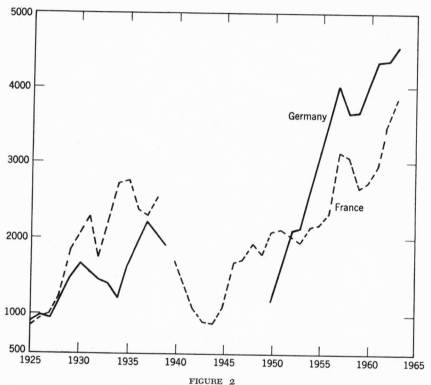

FIGURE 2

Persons convicted for negligent homicide in France and Germany— 1925 to 1963.

Compared to the population, the figures for France and Germany are higher than for the Scandinavian countries. During the five-year period, 1955–1959, the conviction frequency in Germany was about twice as high as in Finland and Sweden and fully thirty-three times as high as in Norway. The conviction frequency in France was slightly less than in Germany; in Italy it was a little more than half (in 1959, 2336 convictions in a population of about 50 million). In Switzerland, the conviction rate was even higher than in Germany; in 1959 there were 442 convictions in a population of 5.2 million.[9]

TRAFFIC ACCIDENTS AND NEGLIGENT HOMICIDE

Unlike the statistics for the Scandinavian countries, the German statistics from and including 1954 also specify the number of convictions for negligent homicide due to road traffic accidents and other accidents, respectively. These figures are found in Table 1.

TABLE 1

Convictions for Negligent Homicide in the German Federal
Republic from 1954 to 1963

	Traffic Accidents	Other Accidents	Total
1954	2012	543	2554
1955	2516	613	3129
1956	3029	624	3653
1957	3463	597	4060
1958	3057	615	3672
1959	3101	612	3713
1960	3468	552	4020
1961	3822	552	4374
1962	3884	515	4399
1963	4036	520	4556

The table shows that the increase in the number of convictions for negligent homicide during the postwar period is due exclusively to negligent homicide occurring in traffic accidents. The number of convictions for other kinds of negligent homicide has remained surprisingly constant.

Going further back, we find an even more remarkable constancy. During the five-year period, 1910–1914, the average number of annual convictions for negligent homicide in Germany was 728—the highest figure being 807 in 1913 and the lowest 673 in 1910. This was before

[9] See Erwin Frey in *Die Rechtsordnung im technischen Zeitalter. Festschrift der rechts—und staatswissenschaftlichen Fakultät der Universität Zürich* (1961), p. 271. In Belgium the criminal statistics do not comprise negligent offenses, for these offenses do not imply in the actor "la perversité morale qui au sens de la présente étude, constitue le critère de la criminalité" (Statistique Criminelle de la Belgique, 1963, p. 9).

motor vehicle traffic became an important factor, and we might think therefore that these convictions would be approximately comparable to the convictions pronounced in 1954 and later for negligent homicide occurring otherwise than in motor vehicle accidents.[10] The absolute figures from the 1950's and 1960's are somewhat lower than the figures from before the World War I, but it should be remembered that the postwar figures apply only to the German Federal Republic.[11] Altogether it seems justifiable to say that the number of convictions in Germany for kinds of negligent homicide other than motor vehicle accidents has remained exceedingly stable.

In order to ascertain whether this was the case also in the Scandinavian countries, we examined all the convictions for negligent homicide during one year (1959) in Denmark, Finland, and Sweden. Although it is, of course, conceivable that a single year is not fully representative, we feel that it does provide grounds for certain conclusions. For Norway, where the annual figure is small, we studied the four-year period 1958–1961. In all four countries, the motor vehicle accidents dominated, although in a varying degree. Of the convictions for negligent homicide, negligent motor drivers accounted in Denmark for 87 percent, in Finland 84 percent, in Norway 77 percent, and in Sweden 91 percent.

The trend of the conviction frequency for negligent homicide occurring other than in motor vehicle accidents seems on the whole to be the same in Denmark, Finland, and Sweden as in Germany. In Denmark, during the years 1915–1924, an average of 8 persons per year were convicted of negligent homicide, whereas 9 persons were convicted in 1959 of negligent homicide occurring other than in motor vehicle accidents. In Sweden, during the years 1915–1924, an average of 27 persons were convicted of negligent homicide, whereas the 1959 figure was 22 when motor vehicle accidents are excluded. For Finland, statistics for such an early period are not available, but if we consider the period 1920–1924, when the motor vehicle traffic still had not become very widespread, we find that an average of 50 persons per year were convicted of negligent homicide, whereas the 1959 figure excluding motor vehicle accidents was 34. These figures indicate that the increase in the number of convictions for negligent homicide, which has taken place during this century is due nearly exclusively to an increase in the number of con-

---

[10] The figures of negligent homicide in connection with road traffic accidents also comprise other categories of offenders than motorists, for example pedestrians or cyclists, but such cases are comparatively so rare that they could be ignored in this context.

[11] Germany's population in 1910 was about 65 million; the population of West Germany (excluding Berlin) in 1957 was about 52 million.

victions for negligent homicide occurring in motor vehicle accidents. Nor can there be reason to doubt that the rapid decline in the figures for negligent homicide during the war was due to the extensive restrictions imposed on motor vehicle traffic by the war.

In Norway the situation is different. As we have seen, the annual number of convictions has remained approximately constant over the last 100 years. But because a new kind of negligent homicide—the kind occurring in motor traffic accidents—has emerged and accounts today for the great majority of the convictions for negligent homicide, this constancy means that the number of convictions for the "traditional" forms of negligent homicide in Norway has in reality declined radically. Whereas previously (that is, before the motor vehicles became a factor) an average of 6 persons were convicted each year of these forms of negligent homicide, the average annual number during the period 1958–1961 was only 2.

We shall look a little closer at the incidence of negligent homicide occurring in motor vehicle accidents. The most obvious explanation of Norway's unique position in this area is that the standard of negligence itself is different from that which applies in the other Scandinavian countries. But we cannot rely on this hypothesis until other possible explanations have been examined. We might, for example, imagine that the difference is due to the fact that Norway is less motorized than the other Scandinavian countries. A study of the statistics of the growth in the number of motor vehicles reveals however that this explanation must be rejected.[12] If we consider the number of inhabitants in each country in 1959 viewed in relation to the number of registered motor vehicles in the same year, we find that Norway had 8 inhabitants for each motor vehicle, Denmark 6, and Sweden 5. Finland had 11 inhabitants for each motor vehicle. We hasten to add that the figures should be accepted with certain reservations, for the Scandinavian countries may conceivably differ in their definitions of motor vehicles that are liable for registration and that are thus included in the official statistics. On the whole, however, the figures should be comparable.

Not only the concentration of cars but the frequency of traffic accidents varies from one country to another. Instead of comparing the number of motor vehicles in the various countries, it might therefore be reasonable to compare the number of fatalities due to traffic accidents. We find that the situation in Norway to some extent differs from that of the other Scandinavian countries. Norway is the country having the lowest rate of traffic accident mortality. This is so both in absolute

[12] *Sources:* The Statistical Yearbook for each country.

terms and in proportion to the number of motor vehicles. If we compare the number of motor vehicles with the number of lives lost in traffic accidents in 1959, we find that one fatality occurred in Denmark for 900 vehicles, one in Finland for 600 vehicles, one in Norway for 1500 vehicles, and one in Sweden for 1400 vehicles. Also, in regard to the definition of traffic accidents, differences may exist from country to country, but it is hardly conceivable that such differences could affect the pronounced tendencies we have found.

We cannot account for these differences in the mortality rate. They may be due to such things as speed limits and other traffic rules, the condition of the roads, etc. We have not penetrated far enough into the field of traffic research to hazard any opinion on this point. But if the mortality rate differs from one country to another, these differences are small as compared with differences in the frequency of convictions for negligent homicide. We can illustrate this by examining how many traffic fatalities, out of the total number, led to convictions for negligent homicide.[13] In making this calculation we have relied on the above-mentioned grouping of negligent homicide into motor vehicle and other accidents, and with regard to Denmark we have compensated for the fact that the criminal statistics prior to 1960 did not include negligent homicide punished by fines. For the five-year period, 1955–1959, we find then that each seventh traffic accident death in Denmark led to conviction for negligent homicide. In Finland and Sweden the proportion during the same period was 1:4. In Norway it was 1:46, a quite different order of magnitude.

The proportionate figure for Finland and Sweden is close to the corresponding figures for France and Germany. In Germany, 13,536 persons were killed in 1959 in traffic accidents, while 3101 persons were convicted of negligent homicide in traffic accidents, a proportion of about 1:4. No corresponding calculation can be made for France, for we do not know how many of the acts of negligent homicide occurred in traffic accidents. Assuming that negligent homicide was represented by traffic accidents and other accidents in approximately the same proportion as in Germany, we shall find for France too a proportional figure of about the same size.[14] The same holds true for Italy[15] and Switzerland.[16]

[13] Because a considerable part of the involved drivers are killed in the accident, the ratio between killed persons of other categories and surviving drivers would perhaps have been more interesting. However, we did not have figures for such a comparison.
[14] According to the criminal statistics for 1959, 2671 persons were convicted of negligent homicide, while 7298 were killed in "accidents d'automobiles." Assuming

In England, on the other hand, the situation is entirely different. Only a quite insignificant number of persons are convicted of manslaughter in connection with traffic accidents. During the years 1954–1956, the figures were, respectively, 9, 3, and 4.[17] In 1956 a statutory amendment made it a special crime to cause death by reckless or dangerous driving.[18] As a result, convictions for manslaughter in connection with the driving of motor vehicles have practically disappeared. But the number of convictions for causing death by dangerous driving is also fairly small. While in 1959, 3101 persons were convicted in Germany of negligent homicide in connection with traffic accidents, only 228 were convicted in England of causing death by dangerous driving.[19] In proportion to the number of traffic accident fatalities (6026), this is about 1:26. Since then, there has been some increase in the number of convictions for causing death by dangerous driving. The average figures for the five-year period, 1959–1963, was 273.

If we look at the development that has taken place in the various Scandinavian countries, we might say that the graph for motor vehicle accidents and the graph for negligent homicide run fairly parallel in the other Scandinavian countries, but not in Norway. Both in Norway and in Sweden the number of traffic accident fatalities is approximately quadrupled from the period 1925–1929 to the period 1955–1959. In Sweden the frequency of negligent homicide quadrupled during the same period, while in Norway it was practically unchanged. These developments are illustrated by Figure 3 where we have compared the number of convictions for negligent homicide, the number of motor vehicle fatalities, and the number of motor vehicles during the period, 1925–1960, in Norway and Sweden, respectively.

---

that about 400 of the convictions were for negligent homicide not connected with automobile accidents, the proportion will be closer to 1:3. The "Annuaire Statistique de la France," 1961, p. 320, has a somewhat larger total accident figure, at the same time specifying that only victims who die in the course of 3 days are included under fatalities. In Germany and the Scandinavian countries the limit is 30 days.

[15] According to the criminal statistics for 1959, 2336 persons were convicted of negligent homicide, while the Statistical Yearbook gives a figure of 7160 persons killed in traffic accidents.

[16] See the figures by Frey, *op. cit.*, pp. 271 and 282.

[17] Willett, *op. cit.*, p. 159. The number of prosecuted persons was far higher. The conviction percentage during the three years was 25.7, 10.3, and 10.0 percent, respectively.

[18] Road Traffic Act 1956 (4 and 5, Eliz. 2), Section 8, now superseded by the Road Traffic Act 1960 (8 and 9, Eliz. 2), Section 1.

[19] Willett, T. C., which is based on the Home Office returns of *Offenses relating to motor vehicles*. The criminal statistics show a somewhat lower figure, which might be caused by the omission of offenses dealt with in conjunction with another offense, so that no separate punishment is statistically recorded.

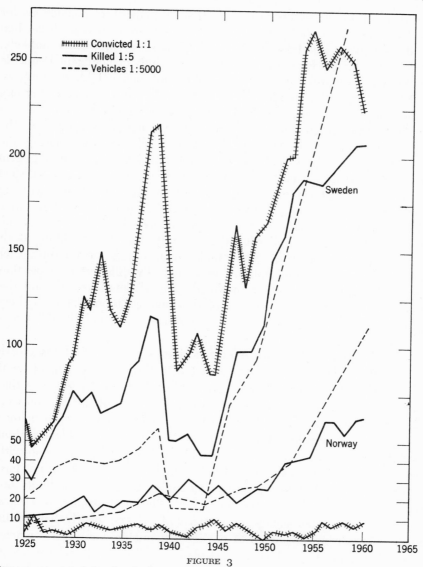

FIGURE 3

Persons convicted for homicide, persons killed by road accidents, and number of motor vehicles in Norway and Sweden—1925 to 1960.

THE CRITERION OF NEGLIGENCE IN THE VARIOUS SCANDINAVIAN COUNTRIES

Until we know something definite about the reasons for Norway's favorable position in regard to the number of traffic accidents, we can-

not theoretically reject the possibility that the paucity of convictions for
negligent homicide in Norway is due to more careful driving here than
in the neighbor countries. Still, this hypothesis seems rather unlikely.
In fact, the figures for convictions for other kinds of negligent homicide
in Norway are also far lower than those of our neighbor countries,
and the figure is far smaller than it was before. We find here a strong
indication that it is the standard of negligence itself that differs.

To clarify this matter, we decided to examine specific cases in the
various countries. For Norway, we studied all the trials during the
four-year period, 1958–1961, which had led to conviction for negligent
homicide. For the other Scandinavian countries, we had to be satisfied
with letting assistants in each country study the records of negligent
homicide trials in 1959 and, from these records, give a brief description
of the acts and circumstances involved in each accident. Although attempts were made to standardize these descriptions, they could obviously
give only the outlines of the actual circumstances surrounding each
fatality. Because the descriptions were made by different persons, they
may differ from one another in the degree of detail and the relative
emphasis on the various elements of the total situation. Yet we believe
that they provide some insight into differences and similarities between
the four countries in this area.

Considering, first, motor vehicle accidents, the descriptions clearly
show that the drivers who were convicted in Norway of negligent homicide had, on the whole, shown a far higher degree of negligence than
the drivers in the other Scandinavian countries. Five of the 24 who were
convicted during the years 1958–1961 of negligent homicide, in connection with traffic accidents, had fled from the site of the accident without
giving the victims any assistance, two had driven in the dark, one without any light and the other with hardly any light, and four did not have
driving licenses. Moreover, serious violations of the speed limits and
technical defects in the cars were typical. The most striking fact, however, is the high percentage of intoxicated drivers: nearly half of the
number of persons convicted of negligent homicide were also convicted
of driving under the influence of alcohol,[20] and of the 13 who were not
convicted of doing so, six were under a strong suspicion of having
actually been driving under the influence of alcohol. The high percentage of intoxicated drivers among the convicted persons is all the

[20] Under the Motor Vehicle Act of February 20, 1926, Section 17, second paragraph,
the driver shall always be considered as being under the influence of alcohol if he has
driven with an alcohol concentration in the blood larger than 0.05%. A similar rule
is found in the new Road Traffic Act of June 18, 1965, Section 22.

more odd because drunken driving is so rarely a cause of accidents in Norway.[21]

In a few of the cases, the negligence seems to have been fairly excusable, but these cases show a marked difference from the great majority of the cases. If we consider, on the other hand, the situation in the other Scandinavian countries, it becomes evident that what are exceptions in Norway are the rule in the other countries. In Finland and Sweden the negligence that has been shown is usually fairly slight, that is, most fatalities are caused by moderate speeding and other relatively modest violations of the traffic laws. It is far between the drunken drivers and the serious violations of traffic laws. Denmark seems to take an intermediate position. The negligent homicide drivers there seem on the whole to have shown a higher degree of negligence than is the case in Finland and Sweden, but the negligence is not so serious as it usually is in convictions in Norway.

This difference between Norway and the other Scandinavian countries is perhaps even more pronounced in cases of negligent homicide other than those that are caused by motor vehicle accidents. We have in Norway only 7 such cases in the course of the four-year period, and most of them border on intentional homicide. Four of these 7 persons had originally been charged with intentional homicide; only when the jury had found the defendant not guilty of this charge was the question of negligent homicide brought up. In the other countries this situation did not occur at all. The negligence that was shown there was in nearly all cases very far from intention and, as in the motor vehicle accidents, it was the relatively excusable negligence that dominated.

The foregoing statements may lead to two conclusions:

1. The courts in Norway require a far higher degree of negligence in order to pronounce a conviction for negligent homicide than do the courts of the other Scandinavian countries. Thus nearly identical definitions of offenses may in practice result in substantial differences, even in countries that culturally, economically, and socially are as closely related as the Scandinavian ones. The differences are of course due to the large discretionary element in the concept of negligence. One cannot conclude that definitions of other kinds of offenses will lead to equally disparate results.

[21] Our study of fatalities in 1960 showed that of 341 drivers involved in 274 fatalities, 10 were under the influence of alcohol within the terms of the Act. One cannot assume that the influence of alcohol was, in all these cases, the cause of the accident. Of these 10 drivers, 9 were killed in the accident. In 1951 the corresponding figures were 10 and 4, see *Schram*, Trafikkulykker og alkohol (Traffic Accidents and Alcohol), Motortidende 1954, p. 10.

2. There is reason to believe that the content of the concept of negligent homicide has undergone a change in Norwegian court practice during this century, so that the courts now require a higher degree of negligence than they did previously.

This conclusion is confirmed by a study of recorded trials chosen at random from the last century. On the whole, these cases involve negligence, which does not seem very serious, a fact that is also reflected in the choice of punishment.

We believe that the explanation of both circumstances can primarily be found in the jury system. Norway is the only Scandinavian country where trials for negligent homicide are decided by a jury. The jury system was introduced by the Criminal Procedure Code of 1887, which came into force on January 1, 1890. There is much evidence to show that a jury is reluctant to brand an otherwise good man as a criminal merely because of a moment's thoughtlessness or carelessness. The emotional overtones of the expression "negligent homicide" may also have some effect. The concept of negligence is so difficult to define in general terms, and the decision in each specific case is so discretionary that even after having heard the judge sum up the case, the jury will often answer "no" to the question of guilt without having any clear feeling of acting contrary to the law. And because the jury does not state its reasons for the decision, it is impossible for the Supreme Court to control proper application of the concept of negligence.

We find our hypothesis confirmed by the experience in England, which, besides Norway, is the sole country that we have studied where cases of this kind are decided by jury. As mentioned above, the crime of "causing death by dangerous driving" was introduced by the Road Traffic Act, 1956. The reason was the criticism of the jury's reluctance to convict for manslaughter, and it was hoped that juries might be more willing to convict when the charge was causing death by dangerous driving than when the "barbarous-sounding charge of manslaughter" was used (*The Times*, May 30, 1956).[22] This hope has to some degree been fulfilled.[23] Still, the figures for convictions for causing death by dangerous driving are also very small compared with the figures for negligent homicide convictions in France and Germany. The difference is no doubt partly due to the fact that under the Act, dangerous driving is a more serious offense than careless driving,[24] but it is probably also

[22] Quoted from Willett, *op. cit.*, p. 77.
[23] See the figures on p. 231 above.
[24] Road Traffic Act, 1960, Section 2, imposes punishment for driving recklessly, or at a speed or in a manner that is dangerous to the public. Section 3 imposes punishment for driving without due care and attention, or without reasonable consideration

of significance that trials for causing death by dangerous driving are decided by juries.[25]

Now it follows from the statistical figures that the number of convictions for negligent homicide did not undergo any rapid change in Norway when the jury system was introduced in 1890. Only gradually has Norway's special position become more pronounced. It seems therefore that the reluctance of juries to convict for negligent homicide has been increasing, especially from the time when the traffic fatalities became a serious factor.

There is one circumstance that apparently does not accord with the explanation we have given for Norway's special position. Also, as regards *bodily injury caused by negligence* (the Penal Code Sections 237 and 238), the figures in Norway are very low, although trials of this kind are not heard by a jury. During the five-year period, 1960–1964, the average annual number of convictions was six, that is, even less than for negligent homicide, although accidents involve far more injuries than deaths. The explanation must be that causing injury through negligence is in Norway subject to public prosecution only at the request of the victim, and for some reason such requests are rarely presented. This explanation follows also from the fact that the police statistics for investigated cases of injury caused by negligence are very small. The annual average during the same years was no more than 17 charges for causing injury by negligence, and only in 8 cases per year did the police conclude by proposing prosecution. One might reasonably think that the practice followed by the prosecutors may be affected by the standard of negligence that has become established in connection with negligent homicide, but the figures of the police statistics seem to show that this can only be a subordinate factor.[26]

---

for other persons using the road. There are about ten times as many convictions for careless driving as for reckless or dangerous driving. In 1963 the figures were 79,000 and 8000, respectively.

[25] Willett, *op. cit.*, pp. 132–133. Kalven and Zeisel, *The American Jury* (Little, Brown and Company, 1966) found in American juries the same reluctance towards convicting for negligent behaviour (see Ch. 24).

[26] Owing to differences in the rules of prosecution, in the degree of injury that is required and other circumstances, the figures for bodily injury caused through negligence vary even more from one country to another than do the figures for negligent homicide. In Sweden, where prosecution for injury caused by negligence could only be undertaken by the victim before the Criminal Code came into force on January 1, 1965 (Penal Code 15:45), the number of convictions was very low. In 1960, there were 15 convictions. In Finland, where public prosecution, as in Norway, is subject to request by the victim (Penal Code 21:14), there were in the same year 175 convictions. In Denmark, public prosecution takes place in the most serious cases of

THE PENALTY FOR NEGLIGENT HOMICIDE

The sanctions that are imposed for negligent homicide vary very considerably from one country to another. A study of the sentences pronounced in the Scandinavian countries during 1959 (for Norway the four-year period, 1958–1961) shows that Norway is in a quite special position in that all the convictions involved deprivation of liberty (imprisonment or labor school). In Sweden only 23 percent involved deprivation of liberty, the rest of the convicted persons were fined. In Denmark, 55 percent were deprived of liberty, in Finland 43 percent. The discrepancy is even more marked if one considers the duration of the imprisonment and whether it is suspended. In Norway, all convictions were for *90 days or more*. Convictions involving deprivation of liberty were for *less than 90 days* in 65 percent of the cases in Denmark, 27 percent in Finland, and 62 percent in Sweden. The country closest to Norway as regards the duration of terms of imprisonment is thus Finland but, on the other hand, 62 percent of the prison sentences there were suspended as compared with only 9 percent in Norway. In Denmark and Sweden the percentage of suspended sentences is 3 and 32, respectively. In sum, whereas the reaction in Norway consists in relatively long, nonsuspended terms of imprisonment, the situation in the other Scandinavian countries is marked by a predominance of fines and short suspended or nonsuspended prison sentences.

This special situation existing in Norway does not mean that the courts tend to give stiffer sentences than do the courts in the neighbor countries, but reflects the difference in the criterion of negligence. If we study the cases in the other Scandinavian countries in which the of-

---

injury caused by negligence; in other cases the offender will be prosecuted only at the demand of the victim or if the public prosecutor finds that the public interest so requires (Penal Code, Section 249). In 1960, 34 persons were sentenced to a severer penalty than fines; in addition there were a probably somewhat higher number of fines.

These figures from the Scandinavian countries pale to insignificance beside the German figures.

In 1960, Germany had 103,000 convictions for causing injury through negligence, a figure that is far higher than the combined figure for simple and aggravated forms of larceny! Prosecution there depends on a request by the victim, unless the Public Prosecutor for special policy reasons deems prosecution necessary (Penal Code, Section 232). It is obvious that prosecution for negligent bodily injury is used in Germany as a means of securing safety on the roads in a way totally different from the Scandinavian countries. France seems to be in an intermediate position.

fender's negligence is as gross as in the cases leading to conviction in Norway, the reaction there is quite as severe as in Norway.

A study of the sanctions for categories of negligent homicide other than motor vehicle accidents, reveals, on the whole, the same situation.

Fines are also the dominating penalty in France. In 1959 nearly two-thirds (64 percent) of the convictions for negligent homicide involved fines, the rest imprisonment. Of the prison sentences, more than four-fifths (82 percent) were for three months or less, and three quarters (76 percent) were suspended. In Germany the punishment was more severe. Excluding, for the sake of simplicity, all those who were convicted under the special rules applying to juveniles, we find that less than a quarter (23 percent) were fined, the rest received prison sentences.[27] Of the prison sentences, slightly less than half (48 percent) were for three months or less, while the percentage of suspended sentences was about the same as in France (73 percent). In Italy all receive prison sentences, most of them for more than three months, but more than three quarters of the sentences are suspended.[28]

In England, where convictions for involuntary manslaughter and for causing death by dangerous driving are comparatively rare, one might expect the punishment to be correspondingly more severe. This is indeed the case for manslaughter. All 16 convictions in 1954–1956 for manslaughter in connection with motor vehicle accidents involved loss of liberty.[29] Of those who during the five years, 1960–1964, were sentenced for causing death by dangerous driving, only 22 percent on the other hand were deprived of liberty, while 75 percent were fined. The punishment in such cases in England seems thus to be considerably milder than in the other countries included in our study.

APPLICATION OF OTHER PENAL PROVISIONS

The fact that the perpetrator of a fatal accident in Norway is very rarely punished for negligent homicide does not automatically mean that he escapes every kind of penal sanction. He may, for instance, be punished under the general prohibition against negligent driving in the

[27] Elmar Müller, *Das Strafmass bei Verurteilungen wegen fahrlässiger Tötung,* *Zeitschrift für Verkehrssicherheit* (1960), p. 291, points out that imprisonment for negligent homicide is used to a far greater extent than before, a fact that he explains by the introduction of suspended sentences (Strafaussetzung zur Bewährung). In his material from Saarland, 1955–1957, the average term of imprisonment was about six months.

[28] See *Annuario di Statistiche giudiziarie* (1961), pp. 277 and 285.

[29] Willett, *op. cit.,* pp. 132–133, 152.

Motor Vehicle Act, Section 17,[30] or under other provisions in the Motor Vehicle Act or the traffic rules.

To clarify this matter we have studied the records of investigation in all traffic fatalities in Norway from 1960, involving motor vehicles. The analysis comprises 274 fatalities involving 341 motor vehicles and the same number of drivers. That the number of drivers and vehicles involved was higher than the number of fatalities is of course due to instances of collision and other accidents between two or more motor vehicles. Of 341 drivers, 109 were killed. Thus, there were 232 surviving drivers who might be held liable.

Penal sanctions in one form or another were applied against 75 of them. Only two were convicted of negligent homicide. On the other hand, no less than 42 were found guilty under the negligence provision of the Motor Vehicle Act, Section 17. Other common violations were speeding (18 cases), no driver's licence (11), failure to grant right of way (8), unlawful parking (8), and unlawful loading (7). One was convicted of driving under the influence of alcohol (in addition to negligent homicide).

As for the sanction, most of them were fined (57). Eleven were given prison sentences, seven were suspended and four nonsuspended. Apart from the two who were convicted of negligent homicide, none of the sentences exceeded 90 days' imprisonment.

We have previously indicated the ratios of traffic fatalities to the consequent convictions for negligent homicide.[31] In Denmark the ratio was 1:7, in Finland and Sweden 1:4. If for Norway we add the convictions for negligent homicide to the convictions under the negligence provision of the Motor Vehicle Act, the ratio is 1:7. If we include all the 75 persons who were subject to sanctions, the ratio becomes 1:4.

These figures may indicate that most of those who, in the other Scandinavian countries are convicted of negligent homicide in traffic accidents, would also be punished in Norway, but only for violation of the motor vehicle legislation. Our study of the various trials, compared with the study of trials for negligent homicide in the neighbor countries, tends to support this assumption. On the other hand, most of those who are punished in Norway for violation of the Motor Vehicle Act or other penal provisions connected with fatalities would in the other Scandinavian countries have been convicted of negligent homicide.

There is, of course, no complete accordance. Plainly, the drivers

[30] This section requires the driver of a motor vehicle "always to drive with due care and pay every attention that he does not cause damage or inconvenience to others." A similar provision is found in the new Road Traffic Act, 1965, Section 3.
[31] See footnote 13.

APPLICATION OF OTHER PENAL PROVISIONS

sentenced in Norway include some who would not have been convicted of negligent homicide in the other countries, either because they were guilty of purely formal violations (for example, driving without a license or overloading trucks), or because, although they were guilty of negligence, there was no causal connection between the negligence and the fatality, as the latter would have occurred even if the driver had not committed any error. An examination of the trials indicates, however, that these cases do not make up any large share of the total.

On the other hand, fatalities occur also in our neighbor countries, which lead to punishment for other violations but not for negligent homicide. Information about the extent to which this occurs can be obtained only from scattered sources. Some material from Skåne for the years 1957–1961 has been studied by Magnus Carlquist.[32] Fifty fatalities there led to prosecution for negligent homicide in 15 cases, to conviction in 13 cases. Only in one of the cases that did not lead to conviction for negligent homicide was the defendant punished for another violation (no driving license). In Denmark the situation seems somewhat different. According to information we have received from the Danish Chief Public Prosecutor, 21 acquittals in trials for negligent homicide occurred in 1959. In 16 of the cases, the defendant was sentenced under provisions of the Traffic Act.

It would be tempting to compare the sanctions applied against the drivers who were sentenced in Norway for violations in connection with fatalities—for whatever violation they were sentenced—with the sanctions applied against the drivers convicted in Finland and Sweden of negligent homicide. Such a comparison involves, however, so many uncertainties that we have abstained from the attempt. We shall only mention that prison sentences account for a smaller share of the total in Norway than in the other countries, and that the fines here are also on the whole smaller. (For Finland we lack information about the amount of the fines.)

As a result of jury reluctance to return a verdict of negligent homicide, a meeting of judges presented in 1953 a request to the Ministry of Justice for an amendment to the Motor Vehicle Act introducing severer punishment when violation of the provision against negligence in the Motor Vehicle Act, Section 17, resulted in death. This would be a kind of parallel to the English provision on causing death by dangerous driving, but under the Norwegian rules of procedure the violation would not be tried by a jury. Hitherto, however, no formal proposal has been presented for an enactment in that sense.

[32] Magnus Carlquist, "Causing the death of another in connection with traffic accidents." (Applied studies of criminal law. Stencilled in Swedish. Year not indicated.)

LAW IN BOOKS AND LAW IN ACTION

The original purpose of this study has not been legal clarification of the concept of negligent homicide. While this study was in progress, however, the Norwegian Supreme Court pronounced an important decision relating to the concept of negligence in this context, the *Haug* case (1963).[33] Because it was quite conceivable that this decision might cause the lower courts to alter their practice, we considered it necessary to discuss the decision in some detail.

The Haug case concerned an appeal lodged by an accused who had been convicted of negligent homicide. In his directions to the jury, the judge had declared that, in his opinion, one could not require a higher degree of negligence to convict of negligent homicide under the Penal Code, Section 239, than to convict under the general provision regarding negligent driving in the Motor Vehicle Act, Section 17.[34] Counsel for the defense argued that the judge's opinion was contrary to the practice followed by the courts and the prosecuting authorities in Norway, a practice that had lasted so long and had become so firmly established that it should be considered as having acquired force of law. In the opinion of the defense, conviction for negligent homicide presupposed particularly serious misconduct on the part of the offender.

The Supreme Court unanimously rejected defense counsel's opinion and dismissed the appeal. In principle, one could not, in relation to the Penal Code, Section 239, concerning negligent homicide, impose other requirements to a driver's consideration and attentiveness than those imposed by the application of the Motor Vehicle Act, Section 17. The Court added, however, that conviction for negligent driving under the Motor Vehicle Act does not inevitably, if the driving causes a death, lead to conviction for negligent homicide. Conviction under Section 239 requires more than careless driving, it requires that the driver was negligent (grossly or less grossly) in not anticipating the possibility that the driving might result in a fatality. A similar requirement cannot be set up in relation to the said provision of the Motor Vehicle Act, for conviction under that provision does not require any injury to have been caused at all, far less a fatality.

This qualifying statement by the Supreme Court is hardly of much practical significance. There may no doubt be cases in which a fatality does not appear to be any realistic possibility, for instance, a case of

33 Norsk Retstidende (The Norwegian Law Reports), 1963, p. 744.
34 See above, p. 238, n. 30.

reckless movements in a parking area or in a slow-moving line of cars. The driving may in such cases be negligent, because of the danger, for example, of causing damage to other vehicles. But should unforeseeable circumstances lead to a fatality—a door of another car bursts open, for example, and a child falls out and under the wheels—the death would not have been caused by negligence. In most cases of negligent driving, however, it is not possible to predict the kind of damage that may occur. It is a matter of chance *whether* any damage occurs and *how serious* it may be. That is in general the situation in cases of customary errors such as inattentiveness in the traffic, speeding, dangerous overtaking, driving with defective brakes or other defective equipment. Our study of specific cases of negligent homicide indicates that traffic fatalities will very rarely provide grounds for declaring that negligence was shown in relation to the Motor Vehicle Act, Section 17, but not in relation to the fatality.

There is another difference between the descriptions of the offense in the Penal Code, Section 239, and in the Motor Vehicle Act, Section 17, which may sometimes motivate different results. Conviction for negligent homicide requires a *causal connection* between the negligence and the death. Let us consider the case of a car that is driving at dangerous speed. A small child runs suddenly out into the roadway, is run over, and is killed. The events are such that we must assume that the accident could not have been prevented even if the car had been driving at normal speed. In that case the driver can be convicted of negligent driving under the Motor Vehicle Act but not of negligent homicide. He has driven negligently, and he has caused the death of the child, but there is no causal connection between the negligence and the death.

This requirement of causality may create problems of a legal nature with regard to the evidence, but our study of fatalities in Norway does not indicate that it creates particular problems in many of the cases where the driver is convicted under the Motor Vehicle Act, Section 17, of negligent driving. The same conclusion may be drawn from Carlquist's information about his Swedish material where, in cases of fatal accidents, a charge was brought both for negligent homicide and for negligent driving or for neither.[35]

SUMMARY

In our study of the Norwegian motor vehicle accidents resulting in fatalities in 1960, we have seen that 42 drivers were sentenced under the

[35] *Carlquist, op. cit.,* p. 32.

general negligence provision of the Motor Vehicle Act, while only two were convicted of negligent homicide. Further, we have reason to conclude that most of the 42 should have been convicted of negligent homicide according to the principles of the Haug case. We are thus confronted with a marked discrepancy between "law in books" and "law in action."

That the Supreme Court refused to accept the argument that the existing practice had altered the content of the laws was not surprising. This practice has never been confirmed by the Supreme Court itself, nor has it been uniform. As mentioned in the decision, the courts have occasionally convicted of negligent homicide without finding gross negligence. The practice we have described reflects the average tendency of public prosecutors and juries, and although the tendencies are both strong and widespread, it was natural that the Supreme Court refused to accept them as making law. It was, however, conceivable that the decision in the Haug case had led to a change in the practice of the prosecutors and the courts, which had smoothed out the previous disagreement between the law and the realities. In order to clarify this, in May 1965 we sent an enquiry to all Norwegian public prosecutors and criminal court judges, soliciting their opinion in this matter. They all replied.

With one exception, all the public prosecutors declared that the Supreme Court decision had not had any effect on their choice of the charge to be brought in each case. Charges under the Penal Code, Section 239, are brought only in more serious cases. One public prosecutor says that it seems unduly officious to bring a charge under the Penal Code, Section 239, before a jury court, when exactly the same, or perhaps even a more severe, penalty is obtained by a trial under the Motor Vehicle Act, Section 17, before a lower court. (The lower court consists of a professional judge and two assessors who jointly decide both the question of guilt and the penalty.) Another public prosecutor says, however, that in some cases he has felt obliged to bring the charge under the Penal Code, Section 239, owing to the decision in the Haug case, but the result has been acquittal by the jury court.

A few public prosecutors believe that the decision in the Haug case is of importance in the cases that come before a court. The majority however are more sceptical. One of the latter says that "the fine distinctions made by the presiding judge and the Supreme Court in applying the law are quite beyond the jury, who understand nothing at all of this. What counts is defense counsel's argument that the jury will brand the defendant as a killer if he is convicted under the Penal Code, Section 239. Recently, it has been practically impossible to obtain any conviction for negligent homicide." Several public prosecutors say that according to their experience it is easier to obtain a conviction for negligent homicide when the offense has involved driving under the influence of alcohol.

All judges who have presided over trials for negligent homicide after the decision in the Haug case, were asked whether the principle for defining negligence, which the Supreme Court expressed in that case, corresponded to their previous opinion of the law on this point. Most of the judges replied that the decision conformed to their previous opinion; others said that they had previously thought that a higher degree of negligence was required for conviction under the Penal Code, Section 239, than under the Motor Vehicle Act, Section 17. It appears that most of them now use the decision in the Haug case as a model for their instructions to the jury.

Asked whether they had an impression that the decision had led to any change in the jury's attitude in these cases, most of the judges answered no, but some say that they do not have sufficient experience from which to form an opinion. Some of the judges mention that it is hard to obtain convictions for negligent homicide, and that it is difficult to achieve uniformity in the decisions.

We have also gone through all the judgments pronounced by jury courts in cases of negligent homicide during a two-year period after the decision in the Haug case (from July 1, 1963 to June 30, 1965). In the course of those two years, altogether 32 trials of negligent homicide were heard, including one with a charge for murder but in which the defendant was convicted of negligent homicide. Of the 32 cases, 28 concerned motor vehicle accidents; 15 cases resulted in conviction under the Penal Code, Section 239, and 11 of those concerned motor vehicle accidents.

These figures correspond closely to the tendencies we found when examining convictions for negligent homicide during the four-year period 1958–1961. Both the total number of convictions and the proportion of motor vehicle accidents are nearly the same as in the previous period. The large number of acquittals indicates that the public prosecutors bring a charge of negligent homicide when there are reasonable prospects of conviction.

If we consider, in particular, the motor vehicle accidents, no less than eight of the eleven sentenced persons were simultaneously convicted of driving under the influence of alcohol. Five of the cases involved wild driving in a state of intoxication. The correlation between intoxication and conviction for negligent homicide is thus even more pronounced than in the preceding period.

When a person is convicted of negligent homicide he is nearly always guilty of a serious breach of law, but the material contains two or three cases in which the court may perhaps be said to have applied a more severe standard than usual.

Seventeen motor vehicle drivers were charged with negligent homicide but were acquitted of that charge. In no less than 11 of these cases, the defendant was convicted of violating the negligence provision of the Motor Vehicle Act, Section 17.

In summary, one can say that the statements both by the public prosecutors and by the judges as well as the examination of the cases in 1963–1965 tend to show that the Supreme Court's decision in the Haug case has not significantly affected the practice of the prosecutors and courts. A charge of negligent homicide is rarely brought, even in cases in which the conditions for conviction are clearly satisfied according to the view expressed by the Supreme Court. And if such a charge is brought, the outcome will often be an acquittal, the defendant instead being convicted under the negligence clause of the Motor Vehicle Act, Section 17. Thus the discrepancy that we pointed out in the analysis of the Haug case, between the legally correct view and the actually practiced system, still persists.

14

Recidivism among Collaborators—A Follow-up Study of 2946 Danish Men Convicted of Collaboration with the Germans during World War II

KARL O. CHRISTIANSEN

INTRODUCTION

After the war some 14,000 Danes were prosecuted for collaboration with the Germans during the occupation: 13,521 persons, 12,877 men and 644 women, were convicted and sentenced to relatively long terms of imprisonment. Later most of the sentences were reduced and, by 1950, 90 percent of the collaborators had been released (paroled or pardoned).

At the beginning of the Danish purge in 1945 the present author, among others, expressed fear of the consequences of sending so many people into prison to serve long sentences. This procedure might very well create criminal dregs, which for a long number of years would impose a heavy burden upon the Danish society. A high rate of recidivism was to be expected when such a large proportion of the population, most of them previously unpunished, were treated as criminals and for a number of years were locked up in the ordinary prisons or in the camps that were about to be established. According to an amendment of June 1, 1945 to the penal code, parole was ruled out, the minimum sentence was four years, and no treatment of the collaborators was foreseen. A second amendment of June 29, 1946, introduced parole and fixed the minimum sentence at two years of imprisonment.

It has been said that it is difficult to predict the future. The statement, undoubtedly based on solid experience, has once more proved sound: the number of recidivists among the collaborators turned out to be far and significantly below what could be expected.

245

The present paper aims primarily at giving a survey of the main results of a follow-up investigation of about 3000 male collaborators. It may, however, be expedient to start by looking at a few of the characteristic traits of this specific type of criminality and its background, adding some general remarks about the purge, the sentences, and the practice of the courts.

THE AMENDMENTS TO THE PENAL CODE

The German occupation gave rise to the formation of several German or German-sponsored corps in which a number of Danish citizens initiated various types of collaboration with the occupying power. After the war such service was retroactively made criminal in spite of the fact that during the occupation its illegal nature was not, and could not be, established. The same was true of propagandist activities and of certain forms of industrial and economic cooperation. Less dubious was the guilt of the informers who endangered the lives, health, or freedom of their countrymen. On the other hand, some of the collaborators committed ordinary crimes, ranging from murder, assault, arson, blasting of buildings, railway attacks, etc., to property offenses, illegal possession of weapons, and some quite harmless petty offenses. The criminal character of these last-mentioned acts were beyond debate.

Section 2 of the amendments to the Penal Code states that it only applies to crimes committed by persons of Danish nationality, which implies that the German war criminals could not be punished according to this act. The main groups of offenses punishable by the amendments were:

1. Acts indictable by the clauses of the Criminal Code insofar as they were committed "in order to further German interests or with other aims injurious to the State in mind" (Section 8).

2. Most acts indictable in accordance with the Criminal Code "if the offender at the time of the acts was wearing German uniform or in other ways identified himself as a member of the occupying power or of bodies cooperating with the occupying power or in other grossly offensive ways exploited the emergency situation brought about by the occupation" (Section 9).

A large number of the offenders covered by these sections of the Act served in the German police forces, the Hipo Corps,[1] and the Schalburg Corps.[2]

[1] See p. 249 (6).
[2] See p. 249 (5).

3. German war service (Section 10, subsection 1).

4. "Service in a corps working in collaboration with the occupying power against the lawful organs of the Danish state or against the interests of Danish citizens, or who, in this country, in German service have carried out Police duties" (Section 10, subsection 2).

5. Performance of police duties in various corps after September 19, 1944[3] (Section 10, subsection 3).

The majority of the convicted collaborators fall into categories 3, 4, and 5.

6. Unsolicited help to the occupying power by Danish officials (Section 11).

7. Informing, defined as acts, the result of which "any person was arrested or exposed to arrest by German authorities or by any organization or person collaborating with the German authorities, or was arrested or punished in accordance with the provisional Danish emergency laws passed at the instigation of and in the interest of the German authorities" (Section 12).

8. Different forms of collaboration with the occupying power and/or the exploitation of the occupation of the country for economic or other gain (Sections 13–16).

Danish pro-German or pro-Nazi propagandists were among those convicted in accordance with these sections of the Act. Numerically they form only a small group. Flagrant cases of economic collaboration could be punished in accordance with Section 15. Most of these cases were, however, convicted under the sections of the Act of June 1, 1945, that criminalized various forms of unwarrantable collaboration with the occupying power. This category, comprising a little more than 1100 persons, falls outside the scope of the present survey.

THE COLLABORATING CORPS

The great majority of the male collaborators performed service in German or German-sponsored corps. Female collaborators are not dealt with in this article. According to the prevailing type of service, the convicted men can be classified into the following nine types:

1. *Watchmen in Denmark* performed their service within the country. The most important were naval watchmen, airfields watchmen, firemen, and corps whose service predominantly was of a civil character; they were organized in a number of different units. They were generally uniformed and armed, although there were a few exceptions to this rule.

[3] See p. 254.

The formation of these corps began in 1940. The rate of recruitment may be illustrated by the following estimated, monthly average of new recruited men within the periods[4] mentioned:

Apr. 9, 1940– Dec. 31, 1941	1942	Jan. 1, 1943– Aug. 29, 1943	Aug. 30, 1943– Dec. 31, 1943	Jan. 1, 1944– Sept. 20, 1944
7	21	77	78	141

Sept. 21, 1944– Dec. 31, 1944	Jan. 1, 1945– Mar. 31, 1945	Apr. 1, 1945– May 5, 1945
99	70	15

It will be seen that the influx did not culminate until 1944, and that as late as at the beginning of 1945 it was almost on the same level as in 1943.

2. *Watchmen abroad* served as watchmen in Germany, France, Italy, or Norway. Most of them belonged to Organization Todt (OT), which existed in Germany before the war. Danish collaborators were recruited as shown by the estimated, monthly averages:

Apr. 9, 1940– Dec. 31, 1941	1942	Jan. 1, 1943– Aug. 29, 1943	Aug. 30, 1943– Dec. 31, 1943	Jan. 1, 1944– Sept. 20, 1944
2	5	25	36	54

Sept. 21, 1944– Dec. 31, 1944	Jan. 1, 1945– Mar. 31, 1945	Apr. 1, 1945– May 5, 1945
39	40	0

The trend is not very dissimilar to what was found for watchmen in Denmark.

3. *Soldiers.* The main part of the soldiers belonged to "Frikorps Danmark," or the German Waffen SS, and served on the Eastern Front. SS-Standarte Nordland, originally a regiment of Waffen SS, was set up in 1940, and the Danish free corps, in 1941. The estimated, monthly intake shows the following distributions:

Apr. 9, 1940– Dec. 31, 1941	1942	Jan. 1, 1943– Aug. 29, 1943	Aug. 30, 1943– Dec. 31, 1943	Jan. 1, 1944– Sept. 20, 1944
62	66	79	36	35

Sept. 21, 1944– Dec. 31, 1944	Jan. 1, 1945– Mar. 31, 1945	Apr. 1, 1945– May 5, 1945
28	27	19

Contrary to the trends for watchmen the majority of the soldiers were recruited during the beginning of the war.

4. *Zeitfreiwillige* (part-time volunteers) were members of the German minority in South Jutland. They were supposed to take part in the defense in case of an allied invasion of the country. The Zeitfreiwillig

[4] On August 23, 1943, the Danish government broke with the Germans; on September 19, 1944 the police was seized by the Germans. The remaining time limits are chosen relatively arbitrarily.

Corps was formed in 1943 and most of its members recruited immediately thereafter.

5. Members of the *Schalburg-Corps* was named after the first chief of "Frikorps Danmark" who fell in Russia; later, after a formal abolition, it changed its name to "SS-Vagtbataillon Sjælland." Some of the members served as policemen toward the end of the occupation. The corps was established in February, 1943, and had its greatest influx of members towards the end of this year and the beginning of 1944 (monthly average, Aug. 29, 1943–Sept. 19, 1944, estimated at 35). It underwent a number of upheavals, but recruited new members up to the end of the war (monthly average in 1945 was over 10).

6. *Hipo members* (Hipo = Hilfspolizei = Auxiliary Police). The corps cooperated with the Gestapo. Several of the most criminal and dangerous gangs belonged to it. Hipo grew out of the ET (= Efterretningstjenesten = Secret Service) of the Schalburg Corps. It was established as a (relatively) independent corps at the end of 1944, but many of its members were former members of Schalburg or other corps at an earlier point of time. In 1945 the estimated monthly average of newcomers for the whole group was over 45. It is known that 1000 persons applied in vain for a job in the corps.

7. *The German police.* Most of its members belonged to the Gestapo, a minor part to the Sicherheitsdienst (Security Service) or the German (civil) police. The German police had its units in Denmark from the very beginning of the occupation, but the main influx of Danish collaborators to the corps fell at the beginning of 1945, with an estimated monthly average of more than 30.

8. *Propagandist, Nazi leaders, recruiters.* A number of active Nazis operated in the radio and the press, and some operated within the party as recruiters to some of the above-mentioned corps. They are recruited rather evenly during the years of the occupation.

9. *The informers* were not organized as such, although a minor part of them might also be classified as actual or previous members of one or more of the corps. Informers were especially frequent from September 1943; the estimated monthly average of new informers was almost the same for the rest of the war, close to 30.

THE INDIVIDUAL SOCIAL BACKGROUND
OF THE COLLABORATORS

In a general way, the background of the collaborators, classified according to dominating type of collaboration, may be described as follows:

1. *Watchmen in Denmark*, according to the sentences imposed and the relatively infrequent appearance of serious breaches of the civil penal code, belonged to the "minor," less dangerous collaborators. Typically they originated from the lower social classes, often from large families and, probably as a result of this, frequently had relatively poor schooling. Many of them had an occupational career characterized by unemployment, and a large number had during the war, but before their recruitment, worked in Germany. They belonged to lower social classes than the average of the collaborators. A large number of them were classified as politically immature and disinterested. Economic and occupational factors rank highest among the recorded individual conditions leading to collaboration activities.

2. *Watchmen abroad* were also a relatively harmless type of collaborators. Together with the informers they belonged to the socially most deviant types. This generalization applies to their childhood, as well as to their later economic and occupational careers and their general social status. They, too, could be described as politically immature and disinterested. Previous criminality is more widespread than in the other dominant groups, again apart from the informers, and their previous sentences were, on the whole, of relatively long duration. Here again, economic and occupational factors are the most frequently recorded, but escape from difficulties and "love of adventure" also played an essential part.

3. *Soldiers*. Generally speaking, military service could in most cases be classified as an equally harmless form of collaboration. Socially the soldiers stood very close to the average of the collaborators, occupationally they were even somewhat more stable. Among the individual circumstances that may be assumed to have been factors associated with their recruitment, Nazist and—less marked—national attitudes rank the highest; but escape from difficulties and "adventure-seeking" have also played an essential role. It spite of this, occupational and economic conditions in a number of cases undoubtedly have been of some significance.

4. *The Zeitfreiwillige (Part-Time Volunteers)* belonged with few exceptions to the German-minded South Jutlanders. Typically, the Zeitfreiwillige grew up under the best social circumstances, and, occupationally and economically, as well as in other respects, they managed better than any of the other dominant types. Physically and mentally they were healthier. Their national and, to some extent also, their political attitude, in connection with the general influence from the German culture in this part of the country, constitute the most important factors behind their collaboration.

5. Members of the *Schalburg Corps* belong to the most severely punished collaborators. This is due less to the fact that crimes of violence in connection with service in this corps were more widespread than to the fact that a large number of them were sentenced for having performed service as policemen. The group represents histories of a somewhat increased number of child welfare cases, of school problems, and of frequent school transfers, but beyond that, the group did not differ in any way from the average. Among the individual conditions, the economic and occupational factors again rank highest, most often in the form of unemployment. "Adventure-seeking" appears to have been of a certain importance. The same applies to nazist conviction. Only a few German-minded members were found within this corps, which emphasized Danish nationalism and in the last months of its existence was in opposition to Waffen-SS.

6. The members of the *Hipo Corps* were more dangerous and violent than collaborators belonging to the other dominant types. A somewhat larger number of unfortunate family conditions during childhood and of school problems characterizes the group but, from a sociological point of view, it appears in other respects to be close to the average of the entire material. The corps counted relatively many Nazis. In spite of this and in spite of the seriousness of the crimes they committed, the economic and occupational considerations still rank high. It should, however, be remembered that a relatively large number of the Hipos started their criminal careers in other corps. The Nazist attitude comes only second.

7. The members of the *German Police Corps*, together with the Hipo-members, belonged to the most dangerous type of all collaborators. Socially they do not differ much from the average, but the corps counted an increased number of previous convicts sentenced for crimes of violence. For the members of the German Police Corps, economic and occupational factors are again the most frequently recorded individual conditions of their collaboration, with nazist attitudes in second place.

8. *Propagandists, et al.,* were punished comparatively leniently; but their dangerousness appears clearly from a higher percentage of persons who were also convicted of unlawful coercion, threats, and informing. Apart from some overrepresentation of irregular family relations, the group was essentially more favorably situated than any of the other dominant groups, with the exception of the Zeitfreiwillige. Many Nazis were found, although the political conviction appeared less rooted than with the Zeitfreiwillige. Cases of previous light penalties for minor political offenses were rather frequent within this group. Political (Nazist) conviction, and often direct suggestions of other party members to

collaborate, rank highest among the recorded individual conditions; however, here as elsewhere, economic and occupational considerations have played a role.

9. The criminality of *the informers* can be briefly characterized as gross and dangerous. From a social point of view, the informers typically belonged to the most unfavorably placed of the collaborators. There were comparatively many Nazis of a political, rather unstable type. Mentally and physically they were the most poorly endowed of the collaborators. Previous criminality was widespread, and those informers with previous records had been convicted relatively often and given relatively long sentences. Psychological factors in a more restricted sense, most often activated by provocation or a specific state of agitation, appear together with Nazist and German national attitudes as the most frequently recorded individual background feature. Economic and occupational conditions played a minor role. Only a few of them committed their crimes for gain.

NATIONAL AND POLITICAL BACKGROUND

According to their national and political affiliations, the collaborators belong to one of three population groups: the German minority in South Jutland (I), the members of the Danish Nazi Party (II), and the Danish Non-Nazis, that is, the rest of the population (III).

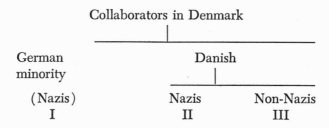

Collaborators in Denmark

German minority	Danish	
(Nazis)	Nazis	Non-Nazis
I	II	III

The members of the German minority were easily identified. The population in South Jutland described itself as Danish *or* German. The Germans were all members of the German Nazi Party, NSDAP, and were linked to the occupying power both by national and by ideological ties. To this group collaboration was a duty.

Members of the Danish Nazi Party, DNSAP, could be identified on the basis of their own archives which, after the war, were seized by the Danish police. They did not try to deny their political affiliations with the Germans but, in accordance with their political ideology, they also wanted to demonstrate their national loyalty to Denmark, and sometimes they actually did it in opposition to the occupying power.

The Non-Nazi population had no national or political affiliation with the Germans who were still "the hereditary enemy" of the country. They are defined negatively and, in the investigation, are identified as people for whom no evidence of membership of the two other groups could be found.

In terms of "group resistance[5] against collaboration with the occupying power," the three population groups might be described in the following way: in the German minority group resistance against collaboration did not exist. Collaboration was a national (and political) obligation. The Danish national norms were not incorporated as personality elements in the members of the minority. The German occupation created a number of situations that were, in advance, defined in a manner different from the conception in the rest of the population, including most of the Danish Nazis.

The Danish Nazis may be described as a group with a considerably reduced group resistance against collaboration, most of its numbers possessing the national Danish norms as personality elements, but, side by side with them, political norms that defined the critical situations during the occupation differently. This last set of norms of pro-Nazi content were by far the strongest.

Among the Non-Nazis the resistance against collaboration was much stronger but not complete. Although no national norms demanded the types of collaboration that were later made punishable, especially during the first years of the war, a number of governmental statements appealed for a positive and, in a way, cooperative attitude towards the occupying power. However, group resistance was much greater than among the Danish Nazis.

For a number of reasons the resistance against collaboration in population Group III increased considerably from 1940 to 1945. Until 1943 the official Danish policy was described by the word *adjustment*; cooperation, especially in financial and economic affairs, was recommended. The government asked people to preserve calm and order and expressed its confidence in a German victory. After 1942, sabotage was combated by legal measures, including the cooperation of the police and the courts. The government's break with the Germans (August 23, 1943) led to a complete change in the official attitude. The governmental requests of cooperation disappeared, and the belief in a German victory dwindled away. The propaganda against the Communists and against sabotage

[5] See Thorsten Sellin, *Culture Conflict and Crime*, Social Science Research Council, New York, 1938, especially pp. 33–34 and 42–43.

was left to the Germans assisted by the Danish Nazis. The police no longer played an active role in the fight against sabotage, and after September 19, 1944, when the police were seized by the Germans and deported (or, to avoid this, went under ground), cooperation came to an abrupt end. A number of other factors contributed to the change in group resistance: the growth of the resistance movement and the steadily increasing, more violent German infringements being two of the most important.

If group resistance is defined objectively as the disapproval of the breach of certain norms in a specific population group, the strength of group resistance depends upon at least three factors: (1) the number of disapproving members of the group, (2) the emotionally determined strength of the disapproval, and (3) the degree to which the disapproving members are organized. From this point of view, the author has elsewhere compared the resistance against collaboration within the three population groups and analyzed the development during the war. It seems impossible to invent any exact scale for an ex post facto measurement of the group resistance during the war. In spite of that, the general results of the comparison cannot be questioned.[6]

Summarizing the results of this analysis of the group resistance against collaboration with the Germans during the occupation of Denmark, the following propositions may therefore be advanced.

1. In the German minority in South Jutland no resistance against collaboration with the Germans can be found.

2. Resistance existed but was relatively weak among the Danish Nazis.

3. Group resistance was much greater although not complete in the major part of the Danish population, which had no national or political affinities with the Germans.

4. In population Group (III), resistance increased considerably from 1940 to 1945, with 1943 as the crucial year.

FREQUENCY OF COLLABORATORS WITHIN THE THREE POPULATION GROUPS

Group resistance influences the occurrence of norm violations within the group. If the frequency of violators were a simple function of group resistance, we would expect the highest rate of collaborators within the

[6] Cfr. Karl O. Christiansen, Landssvigerkriminaliteten i sociologisk belysning (Collaboration with the Germans. A Sociological Study), Copenhagen 1955, pp. 95–135, summary pp. 133–135.

German minority, a somewhat lower rate among the Danish Nazis and the lowest in the Non-Nazi group. *Opportunities*, which under the occupation meant among other things the relative intensities of the recruitment campaigns, do, however, play an important role as well. Sufficient quantitative data on the endeavors of the Germans and the Danish Nazis to enlist members of the collaborating corps do not exist, but most probably it varied inversely to the group resistance and so reinforced the effects of this factor.

TABLE 1

Frequency of male collaborators within population groups

	Males over 14 Years	Collaborators	
		Numbers	Percent
German minority	10,938	2,777	25.4
Danish Nazis	33,200	3,379	10.2
Danish Non-Nazis	1,390,000	5,607	0.4
Total	1,434,138	11,763	0.8

Table 1 includes the total number of male collaborators, with the exception of 1092 convicted of financial cooperation. As can be seen from Table 1, male collaborators appear with a frequency of approximately 25 percent in the German minority, 10 percent among the Danish Nazis, and 0.4 percent in the Danish Non-Nazi population. It is hardly necessary to mention that such great differences are highly significant.[7] Whether they resulted from variations in group resistance or in opportunities cannot be determined on the basis of this analysis. Probably both sets of factors were influential.

THE RELATIVE FREQUENCY OF DEVIANTS AMONG DIFFERENT GROUPS OF COLLABORATORS

In *Culture Conflict and Crime*, Thorsten Sellin recommends that research should "concentrate on persons who have violated norms (a) with high resistance potentials, (b) incorporated as personality elements, and (c) that possess strong emotional tone." Having defined personality as a sociological or a social-psychological concept, Sellin adds: "Offenders

[7] Even if those collaborators in South Jutland who were only convicted of service as part-time volunteers are excluded, the frequency in this population group would hardly fall below 20 percent.

who have overcome the greatest and most pervasive group resistance probably exhibit more clearly than others the personality types that have significance for our research purposes."[8]

Regarding Danish collaborators, the consequences of this hypothetical statement must be that those population groups and those periods that have shown the greatest group resistance should also contain the highest frequencies of deviants. This proposition is probably true, not only for psychological but for social deviations as well. Accordingly, the rate of deviant collaborators should be lowest within the German minority, higher among the Danish Nazis, and highest in the remaining part of the population (III); and within the last group, higher among the late recruits than among the early recruits.

Elsewhere the author has analyzed some of the social data on the collaborators and shown that these hypotheses are actually valid.[9] Table 2 illustrates some of the findings.

TABLE 2

Male Collaborators According to Frequency of Certain Social Factors
(Percent)

	German Minority	Danish Nazis	Danish Non-Nazis Dates Recruited	
			1940–1943	1944–1945
N =	361	859	670	1077
Illegal birth	4	11	15	18
Parents separated/divorced	2	8	13	12
Only elementary schooling	44	44	62	71
Unskilled workers	6	17	26	33
Unemployed when recruited	13	25	34	51
Considerable increase in income on turning collaborator[10]	22	24	20	43
Previous criminality	7	14	25	32
Lower class	10	25	38	47

It can be seen that collaborators among the Non-Nazis included significantly[11] more socially deviating persons than the Danish Nazi collaborators and the German collaborators. The differences between the Danish Nazis and the German minority are less outstanding and only

[8] *Op. cit.,* p. 44.
[9] See the above mentioned study by the author (note 6). Reference is especially made to Chapters 9, 10, 12, and 13.
[10] More than 70 kr. (during the war approximately 15 $) per week.
[11] Defined as $p \leq 0.05$.

significant with respect to unfavorable family conditions in childhood and lower-class attachment. The differences between early and late recruited collaborators within the rest of the population (III) are considerable and statistically significant.

THE PURGE

The application of a retroactive law is bound to create difficulties, with respect both to the definition of punishable acts (see above, pp. 246–247) and to the fixing of sentence. The reduction of the minimum sentence for collaboration from four to two years of imprisonment by the second amendment to the Criminal Code of June 29, 1946, merely constituted the legalization of a practice that the courts had already embarked on, adducing extenuating circumstances which, from a strictly legal point of view, sometimes were rather dubious. The development may be illustrated by Table 3 showing sentences passed from the beginning of July, 1945, to the end of June, 1946. In order to keep the definition of crime as consistent as possible, a single group, Watchmen in Denmark, was selected for this purpose.

TABLE 3

A total of 1093 Watchmen in Denmark, by Date of Final Conviction and Length of Sentence (Percent)

| Date of Conviction | N | Length of Sentence (in Years) | | | | | | | |
		−1½	−2½	−3½	−4½	−5½–7½	−8½–20	Life	Total
1945									
July	37	2.7	13.5	13.5	51.4	18.9	—	—	100.0
August	108	3.7	5.5	4.6	57.0	28.3	0.9	—	100.0
September	154	8.4	14.3	5.8	46.2	23.4	1.9	—	100.0
October	165	11.6	19.5	14.6	41.5	12.8	—	—	100.0
November	169	17.8	24.9	15.4	34.2	7.7	—	—	100.0
December	124	20.0	34.4	13.6	28.0	3.2	0.8	—	100.0
1946									
January-February	203	22.2	37.9	19.3	14.8	5.3	0.5	—	100.0
March-April	96	12.5	32.3	24.0	25.0	6.2	—	—	100.0
May-June	37	5.4	24.3	43.3	18.9	2.7	2.7	2.7	100.0

In the course of July and August, 1945, over half the Watchmen were sentenced to about four years of imprisonment. During the months of November and December, 1945, prison sentences of two and four years were more or less equally frequent, and from the beginning of 1946, sentences to two years were clearly predominant. The same tendency can be observed for other sentences. This development is even more remarkable, as it may be assumed that the first cases dealt with were far less serious than the subsequent ones.

The prison sentences of 11,554 male collaborators are distributed as shown in Table 4.

TABLE 4

A Total of 11,554 Male Collaborators According to Length of Sentence at Final Conviction

					Length of Sentence (in Years)				
	−½	+½ to −1	+1 to −2	+2 to −3	+3 to −4	+4 to −8	+8 to −12	+12 to −20	Life
Number	383	2179	4019	1774	1333	1055	499	246	66
Percent	3.3	18.9	34.8	15.3	11.5	9.1	4.3	2.1	0.6

In addition, 76 persons were sentenced to death, and 140 were sentenced to Youth Prison, preventive detention, institutions for the insane or feebleminded, or other special sanctions.

Table 4 shows that 78 percent were sentenced to more than one year imprisonment, 43 percent more than two years, and 16 percent more than four years. The comparative figures for ordinary crimes committed in 1946, that is, the year in which most of the collaborators were sentenced, were, 11, 3.5, and 1 percent respectively.

By means of commutation of the sentences, pardon, and (normal) release on parole, introduced by the amendment of 1946, the authorities sought to level out the discrepancies resulting from the above-mentioned changes in the penal policy and, more generally, sought to mitigate the very severe sentences. Close to 80 percent of the collaborators had some part of their sentences remitted. Owing to the long period of internment before they were brought to trial, many of the minor collaborators with prison sentences of up to 18 months actually spent longer time in prison than their sentence warranted. The reduction of the sentences were mainly to the advantage of collaborators with longer sentences.

Of the 76 persons sentenced to death, 30 were commuted to life imprisonment, while 46 were executed. The last two collaborators were released in 1960.

SPECIAL PROBLEMS REGARDING "RECIDIVISM" AMONG COLLABORATORS

It goes without saying that when the basic sample of offenders consists of persons who during a war period have collaborated (illegally) with an occupying power, it is only possible to speak about recidivism in the case of new offenses if the word is used in a very formal sense. Recidivism here, therefore, refers to the previous collaboration as well as to subsequent ordinary offenses, both of which are punishable acts. The question of homologous recidivism does not arise except in the relatively small group of previously punished collaborators for whom offenses committed after release may be considered homologous in relation to their prior noncollaborationist offenses. In the present study the subsequent career is as a rule considered in relation to the collaboration and, consequently, recidivism must be of a heterologous character. Thus far, one must expect types of correlation between punishment and recidivism other than would be the case if these prisoners had been released after having served sentences for ordinary crimes. The fundamental conditions of the collaborationist activities no longer exist, but factors of ordinary crime and ordinary recidivism are still effective. For such reasons, several questions could be raised:

1. Do the same factors of recidivism (leading to ordinary offenses) emerge after the offender serves a sentence for collaboration as when the original offense is an ordinary one? The following two questions may be of primary interest:

2. Is the rate of recidivism among the previously *unpunished* collaborators higher than what might be expected from what we know about the risk of crime in the corresponding population groups?

3. Is the rate of recidivism among the previously *punished* collaborators higher than was to be expected from what we know about the risk of recidivism in corresponding groups of ordinary prisoners?

In the debate around the purge it was stated that the collaborators were "so depraved" that it would be difficult or even impossible to bring them back to a normal life when they were released. Now, if this conception contains a grain of truth, participation in those activities that most resembled ordinary crimes—especially organized gang activities— would also imply the highest rates of recidivism. We, therefore, must ask the following questions:

4. Are there any significant differences between different types of collaborators? If so, is it higher within the Hipo Corps, the German

police, and the informers than in the other corps when age, previous criminality, and other relevant factors are controlled?

THE FOLLOW-UP MATERIAL

The follow-up investigation is based on a study of 2946 male collaborators, interviewed by the author and members of his staff at the special classification center for collaborators established after the war by the Danish prison service.[12] Of these, 46 died before or after release without having committed new offenses. There were 227 (7.7 percent) who were sentenced for minor offenses to fines or simple detention,[13] and 314 (10.7 percent) who were convicted of more serious offenses and sentenced to imprisonment or various special measures such as detention for criminal psychopaths, workhouse, preventive detention, etc.

THE METHOD

The length of the observation period, for the main part of the collaborators (90 percent), has been 7–8 years or more. In 1955, when the collection of data on recidivism was terminated, over 98 percent had been at liberty for five or more years.

The data on recidivism were collected in the Central Police Register (*Rigsregistraturen*) where cards for all the collaborators as well as for

[12] Established at the initiative of Mr. Hans Tetens, Director, and Mr. Hye-Knudsen, Vice-Director of the Danish Prison Service, supervised by Dr. Georg K. Stürup, and with the author as its daily leader. Under the auspices of the Danish Prison Service, the following works on the collaborators have been published: Karl O. Christiansen, Mandlige landssvigere i Danmark under besættelsen. En kriminografisk og sociologisk oversigt over 5.107 mænd dømt efter straffelovstillægget af 1.6.1945 og 29.6.1946 (Male Collaborators with the Germans in Denmark during the Occupation. A Criminographical and Sociological Survey concerning 5,107 Men, convicted according to the Supplements of 1.6.1945 and 29.6.1946 to the Civil Penal Law. With a Summary in English); Udgivet af Direktoratet for fængselsvæsenet (published by the prison administration), Copenhagen, 1950. Gunnar Mortensson, Psykiatrisk undersøgelse af mandlige landssvigere i Danmark (Psychiatric Investigation of Male Collaborators in Denmark). Nordisk Tidsskrift for Kriminalvidenskab (Nordic Journal of Criminal Science), 41(1953), pp. 2ff; and Thomas Sigsgård, Psykologisk undersøgelse af mandlige landssvigere i Danmark under besættesen (Psychological Investigation of Male Collaborators in Denmark during the German Occupation), Copenhagen, 1954.

[13] Simple detention is a type of "mild" imprisonment where the prisoner preserves his right to wear his own clothes, procure his work himself, etc. For this and the below-mentioned special measures, see The Danish Criminal Code, with an Introduction by Dr. Knud Waaben, Professor A.I., in the University of Copenhagen, 1958, Copenhagen 1958.

other offenders were filed. This card index, for the postwar period, may be considered complete. The data comprise all the existing information registered on the cards, that is, the type of subsequent crimes, type of sanction(s), number of sanctions with deprivation of liberty, and time of first offense after release.

RECIDIVISM WITHIN THE POPULATION GROUPS

According to Table 5, the frequency of recidivism was lowest in the German minority (6 percent), higher among the Nazis (10 percent), and highest in the third population group (25 percent).

TABLE 5

The Follow-Up Material According to Population Group and Incidence of Recidivism

		Total N	Recidivists N	Percent	Recidivists (Narrow Sense) N	Percent
I	German minority	361	20	5.5	6	1.7
II	Danish Nazis	851	87	10.2	35	4.1
III	Danish Non-Nazis	1734	454	26.2	273	15.7
	Total	2946	561	19.0	314	10.7

If recidivism is taken in the more narrow sense of the word (see above), the differences are even more striking, although the numbers are somewhat smaller—2, 4, and 16 percent in the three population groups, respectively. However, it may be more appropriate to underline the fact that these figures are considerably lower than would be expected if ordinary criminals were released from a Danish state prison. The rate of recidivism for this latter group during a similar period of observation would rise to about 50 percent. Even in the Non-Nazi group, for whom recidivism amounts to 16 percent, we are far below what could be expected for ordinary offenders. In the following paragraphs, recidivism includes only reconvictions in the narrow sense.

DOMINANT TYPES AND RECIDIVISM

Table 6 illustrates the frequency of recidivism among the various categories of collaborators defined by major type of collaboration. Because of great differences among the population groups, the material here and in the following tables is subdivided according to this criterion.

TABLE 6

The Follow-Up Material According to Population Group, Dominant Type, and the Incidence of Recidivism

	I German minority			II Danish Nazis			III Danish Non-Nazis			Total		
		Recidivists			Recidivists			Recidivists			Recidivists	
	N	N	Percent	N	N	Percent	N	N	Percent	N	N	Percent
Watchmen Denmark	122	2	1.6	330	7	2.1	672	75	11.2	1124	84	7.5
Watchmen Abroad	22	0	0.0	13	3	23.1	311	65	20.9	346	68	19.7
Soldiers	77	3	3.9	215	16	7.4	362	86	24.0	654	105	16.2
Part-time volunteers	118	0	0.0	0	—	—	0	—	—	118	0	0.0
Schalburg	0	—	—	87	0	0.0	144	19	13.2	231	19	8.2
Hipo	2	0	0.0	67	1	1.5	65	3	4.6	134	4	3.0
German Police	12	1	8.3	65	1	1.5	89	13	14.6	166	15	9.0
Propagandists	1	0	0.0	33	0	0.0	18	1	5.6	52	1	1.9
Informers	7	0	0.0	41	7	17.1	73	11	15.1	121	18	14.9
Total	361	6	1.7	851	35	4.1	1734	273	15.8	2946	314	10.7

Within the German minority the absolute numbers are so small that they do not justify any conclusion.

Among the Nazis (Group II) the overall rate of recidivism is 4 percent. Above this we find watchmen abroad (23 percent), informers (17 percent) and, somewhat lower, the soldiers (7 percent). The remaining dominant types show small rates of recidivism (0–2 percent).

In Group III the average rate of recidivism is 16 percent. Higher rates are found only in two of the dominant types, soldiers (24 percent) and watchmen abroad (21 percent). Close to the average come the informers (15 percent), the German police (15 percent), and members of the Schalburg Corps (13 percent). Below the average for the group are placed watchmen in Denmark (11 percent), members of the Hipo Corps (5 percent), and propagandists, et al. (6 percent).

Watchmen abroad, soldiers, and informers ostensibly show relatively high rates of recidivism, while Hipo members, propagandists, and watchmen in Denmark are placed below the average. It is also worth noting that the part-time volunteers (all belonging to the German minority) have no recidivists.

In the original investigation, the correlation between the type of dominating collaboration and the incidence of social deviations in the prior histories of the individuals was a very weak one. Apparently the dominant type plays a greater role with respect to recidivism. This question will be dealt with in more detail in a following paragraph.

AGE AND RECIDIVISM

Table 7 shows the material distributed according to population groups and age at the initiation of the collaborationist activities. The major part of the collaborators were on the average 5–6 years older at their release than at the time of their recruitment; at the end of the observation period or when reconvicted, all of them except the oldest belonged to age groups one or two "steps" above those referred to in the original investigation and utilized in this analysis. Table 7 demonstrates clearly what has been observed in a number of previous investigations,[14] namely, that the frequency of recidivism decreases by increasing age. It is considerably higher for the collaborators recruited before the age of 26 than for the 26–40 years age group ($p < 0.001$) and still lower for those over 40 years ($0.01 < p < 0.02$). These differences are most

[14] See, for instance, Thorsten Sellin, "Recidivism and Maturation," *National Probation and Parole Association Journal*, 1958, pp. 241–250.

TABLE 7

The Follow-Up Material According to Population Group, Age, and the Incidence of Recidivism

	I German minority			II Danish Nazis			III Danish Non-Nazis			Total		
		Recidivists			Recidivists			Recidivists			Recidivists	
	N	N	Percent	N	N	Percent	N	N	Percent	N	N	Percent
−20 years	60	2	3.3	160	14	8.8	566	111	19.6	786	127	16.2
21–25 years	43	1	2.3	156	14	9.0	481	96	19.8	680	111	16.3
26–30 years	40	1	2.5	146	3	2.1	269	26	9.7	455	30	6.6
31–40 years	97	2	2.1	197	2	1.0	264	36	13.6	558	40	7.2
41–50 years	79	0	0.0	134	2	1.5	109	4	3.7	322	6	1.9
51+ years	42	0	0.0	58	0	0.0	45	0	0.0	145	0	0.0
Total	361	6	1.7	851	35	4.1	1734	273	15.7	2946	314	10.7
−30 years	143	4	2.8	462	31	6.7	1316	233	17.8	1921	268	14.0
30+ years	218	2	0.9	389	4	1.0	418	40	9.6	1025	46	4.5
Total	361	6	1.7	851	35	4.1	1734	274	15.8	2946	314	10.7

TABLE 8

The Follow-Up Material According to Population Group, Geographical Milieu and Incidence of Recidivism

	I German minority			II Danish Nazis			III Danish Non-Nazis			Total		
	N	Recidivists N	Percent	N	Recidivists N	Percent	N	Recidivists N	Percent	N	Recidivists N	Percent
Capital	35	0	0.0	418	20	4.8	856	145	17.1	1309	165	12.8
Provincial towns	179	4	2.2	236	8	3.4	416	66	15.9	831	78	9.4
Rural districts	124	2	1.6	134	4	3.0	321	37	11.5	579	43	7.3
Abroad + Mobile	23	0	0.0	63	3	4.8	141	25	17.7	227	28	12.3
Total	361	6	1.7	851	35	4.1	1734	273	15.7	2946	314	10.7
Capital + Abroad/Mobile	58	0	0.0	481	23	4.8	997	170	17.2	1536	194	12.6
Provincial towns + Rural districts	303	6	2.0	370	12	3.2	737	103	14.0	1410	120	8.8
Total	361	6	1.7	851	35	4.1	1734	273	15.7	2946	314	10.7

pronounced among the Nazis and in the Non-Nazis group. The German minority only contains six recidivists. Transformed to age at the time of release, the observation may be formulated in the following way: collaborators released before the age of 30 show a significantly higher frequency of recidivism (among the Nazis, 9 percent and in the Non-Nazi group, 20 percent) than collaborators released when they were in the 30–45 years age group (among the Nazis, about 1–2 percent and in population Group III, about 12 percent).

GEOGRAPHICAL MILIEU AND RECIDIVISM

When the material is classified by population group and geographical milieu at the time of recruitment (see Table 8) it is seen that recidivism occurs with the highest rate in the capital (13 percent), a somewhat lower rate in the provincial towns (9 percent), and the lowest in the rural districts (7 percent). For collaborators who were recruited abroad or were so mobile that they could not be referred to any of the three above-mentioned milieux, the rate was 12 percent. The figures quoted are lower among the German minority and the Nazis, higher in the Non-Nazi group, but the trend is the same in all three groups. The difference is not statistically significant ($0.10 > p > 0.05$), but the tendency is clear enough and shall not be disregarded at this point of the analysis.

PREVIOUS CRIMINAL CAREER AND RECIDIVISM

In most, if not in all, follow-up studies, the importance of previous criminality as a factor of recidivism has been clearly demonstrated. It is reasonable to believe that this connection will manifest itself even if the basic material consists of collaborators, not least because both the previous and the later type of offenses belong to the same broad category of criminal acts defined in the civil penal code. Table 9 shows that this holds true. In all three population groups the rate of recidivism is higher for the previously punished collaborators than for the unpunished. The difference is statistically significant ($p < 0.001$). For all three groups as a whole it is 7 and 25 percent respectively. The lowest rate (0.9 percent) appears in the unpunished part of the German minority, and the highest (29 percent), among the previously punished collaborators in the Non-Nazi group.

This result will be discussed in more detail below.

TABLE 9

The Follow-Up Material According to Population Group, Previous Criminal Career, and Incidence of Recidivism

	I German minority			II Danish Nazis			III Danish Non-Nazis			Total		
	N	Recidivists		N	Recidivists		N	Recidivists		N	Recidivists	
		N	Percent		N	Percent		N	Percent		N	Percent
Previously unpunished	335	3	0.9	729	21	3.0	1227	122	9.9	2291	146	6.4
Previously punished	26	3	11.5	122	14	12.0	507	151	29.8	655	168	25.6
Total	361	6	1.7	851	35	4.1	1734	273	15.7	2946	314	10.7

SOCIAL STATUS AND RECIDIVISM

The material has been classified into the following four social classes: lower class, lower-middle class, upper-middle class and upper class, defined by occupation and income. This classification is, with some modifications, based on Geigers' classification of other Danish population groups.[15] In the lower class we find the unorganized laborers, messengers, hawkers, (rural) day laborers, and people subsisting on public relief. It accounts for 34 percent of the examined collaborators: 10 percent in the German minority, 25 percent among the Danish Nazis, and 43 percent in the Non-Nazi group. The lower-middle class included, among others, organized and skilled workers, seamen, small shopkeepers, the lowest grades of civil servants, office workers and small holders. This class makes up 63 percent of the follow-up material: 77 percent of the German minority, 74 percent among the Danish Nazis, and 56 percent of the

TABLE 10

The Follow-Up Material According to Population Group, Social Class, and the Incidence of Recidivism

	I German Minority	II Danish Nazis	III Danish Non-Nazis	Total
Lower classes				
N	32	213	754	999
Recidivists				
N	4	17	165	186
Percent	12.5	8.0	21.9	18.6
Higher classes				
N	329	638	980	1947
Recidivists				
N	2	18	108	128
Percent	0.6	2.8	11.0	6.6
Total:				
N	361	851	1734	2946
Recidivists				
N	6	35	273	314
Percent	1.7	4.1	15.7	10.7

[15] Theodor Geiger, "Den danske intelligens fra reformationstiden til nutiden" (The Danish Intelligentsia from the Age of the Reformation to the Present Time), *Acta Jutlandica*, **21**, Aarhus and Copenhagen, 1949.

third population group. The upper-middle and the upper class consist of the more well-to-do master artisans, larger shopkeepers, the higher grades in trade and industry, members of the liberal professions, farmers, estate owners, etc. They make up a total of only 3 percent in the German minority, and in the other two population groups, 1 percent each. In the analysis of recidivism, the important thing is to separate the lower class from the higher classes.

Table 10, in which the material is classified by population group and social class, demonstrates as expected that social class is a recidivism factor of great importance. In all three population groups the lower class has a considerable and significantly higher rate of recidivism than the three other (joint) classes. In the German minority the rates are 12.5 percent, in the lower class and 0.6 percent in the higher classes ($p < 0.001$); among the Danish Nazis they are 8 and 2.6 percent respectively, ($0.002 < p < 0.01$); and in the Non-Nazi group 22 and 11 percent respectively ($p < 0.001$).

SOME CROSS-TABULATIONS

Further subdivisions are not practicable for the German minority because they had only six recidivists, nor for the Danish Nazis, with 35 recidivists. In the third group, however, it is possible to carry the analysis of the influence of the above-mentioned factors one or two steps further.

In Table 11, the basic material of population Group III is classified according to age, previous criminal career, and recidivism. The table shows that the rate of recidivism is higher both among the previously punished and unpunished collaborators in the age-class below 25 than in the older classes, and higher in the middle-aged class than in the oldest class. Both differences are statistically significant ($p < 0.001$ and $0.002 < p < 0.01$, respectively).

The rates of recidivism in the two youngest age classes are considerably and significantly lower among the previously unpunished than among the previously punished collaborators (in both cases corresponding to $p < 0.001$). In the oldest age-class the trend is reversed, for there are 3.5 and 0 percent recidivists among the previously punished and unpunished collaborators, respectively. This negative difference is not significant ($0.05 < p < 0.10$), and the combined probability for all three classes is positive and high ($p < 0.001$). It seems safe to conclude that the previously punished collaborators have a significantly higher rate of recidivism than the previously unpunished in the age groups under 40.

Table 12 shows the same population group classified by age, geo-

TABLE 11

The Follow-Up Material in Group III According to Age, Previous Criminal Career, and Incidence of Recidivism

	Previously Unpunished			Previously Punished			Total		
	N	Recidivists		N	Recidivists		N	Recidivists	
		N	Percent		N	Percent		N	Percent
−25 years	757	97	12.8	290	110	37.9	1047	207	19.8
26–40 years	356	21	5.9	177	41	23.2	533	62	11.6
41+ years	114	4	3.5	40	0	0.0	154	4	2.6
Total	1227	122	9.9	507	151	29.8	1734	273	15.7

TABLE 12

The Follow-Up Material in Group III According to Age, Geographical Milieu, Previous Criminal Career, and Incidence of Recidivism

		Previously Unpunished			Previously Punished			Total		
		N	Recidivists N	Percent	N	Recidivists N	Percent	N	Recidivists N	Percent
Capital	−25 years	339	45	13.3	160	64	40.0	499	109	21.8
	26–40 years	189	14	7.4	89	20	22.5	278	34	12.2
	41+ years	56	2	3.6	23	0	0.0	79	2	2.5
Provincial towns	−25 years	190	28	14.7	61	23	37.7	251	51	20.3
	26–40 years	79	3	3.8	46	11	23.9	125	14	11.2
	41+ years	31	1	3.3	9	0	0.0	40	1	2.5
Rural districts	−25 years	163	13	8.0	49	14	28.6	212	27	12.7
	26–40 years	52	2	3.8	30	7	23.3	82	9	11.0
	41+ years	20	1	5.0	7	0	0.0	27	1	3.7
Abroad + Mobile	−25 years	65	11	16.9	20	9	45.0	85	20	23.5
	26–40 years	36	2	5.6	12	3	25.0	48	5	10.4
	41+ years	7	0	0.0	1	0	0.0	8	0	0.0
Total	−25 years	757	97	12.8	290	110	37.9	1047	207	19.8
	26–40 years	356	21	5.9	177	41	23.2	533	62	11.6
	41+ years	114	4	3.5	40	0	0.0	154	4	2.6

graphical milieu, previous criminality, and recidivism. The age differences
with respect to recidivism are most pronounced between the two youngest
age classes (significant at $0.02 < p < 0.05$). The comparison of the
two older age-classes is less obvious and not significant ($0.05 < p < 0.10$).
The importance of previous criminal career, however, is maintained after
the introduction of the criterion "geographical milieu." On the other hand,
no significant differences with respect to recidivism can be demonstrated
among the milieux.

In Table 13 the same material is classified according to age, previous
criminal career, dominating type of collaboration, and recidivism. The
absolute numbers are in some of the subgroups so small that it is difficult
to draw any conclusions. However, the following main trends seem to
be evident: The rate of recidivism is again higher in the youngest class
and lowest among the oldest. A comparison between the class below
age 26 and the following age-class demonstrates that the rate of recidivism in 13 out of 14 subcategories that contain recidivists is higher among
the youngest than among the older collaborators. This is sufficient to
conclude that the difference is significant ($p < 0.002$). A comparison of
the group aged 26–40 years and the oldest collaborators similarly shows
that recidivism is more frequent in the middle-age class than among
the oldest in 10 out of 11 categories containing recidivists ($p < 0.05$). It
is again demonstrated that the rate of recidivism decreases with increasing
age.

The importance of the previous criminal career can be shown in
the same way. In 21 out of 24 subcategories, the previously punished
collaborators contain more recidivists than the previously unpunished.
This difference is highly significant ($p < 0.002$).

The comparison of the different types of major collaboration with
respect to recidivism only shows that soldiers have a higher rate of
reconvictions than the other types, but nothing else. A simplified version
of the table comprising soldiers and a joint group of all the other collaborators is given in Table 14. The existing difference between the two
groups is most pronounced among the youngest and among the previously
punished collaborators, but the trend is the same for the older and for
the unpunished. The total of differences is statistically significant ($0.01
> p > 0.002$).

Table 15 shows recidivism among the members of Hipo, the German
police, and informers (combined), as against a joint group of propagandists and members of the various watchmen corps, in Denmark and
abroad, and the Schalburg Corps. It may be stated without further
proof that the differences between these two main groups are small and
insignificant.

TABLE 13

The Follow-Up Material in Group III According to Age, Dominant Type, Previous Criminal Career, and Incidence of Recidivism

	−25 Years			26–40 Years			41+ Years			Total		
		Recidivists			Recidivists			Recidivists			Recidivists	
	N	N	Percent	N	N	Percent	N	N	Percent	N	N	Percent
Watchmen Denmark												
Previously punished	77	20	26.0	70	16	22.9	23	0	0.0	170	36	21.2
Previously unpunished	263	24	9.1	173	12	6.9	66	3	4.5	502	39	7.8
Watchmen Abroad												
Previously punished	67	29	43.3	42	11	26.2	5	0	0.0	114	40	35.1
Previously unpunished	155	23	14.8	32	1	3.1	10	1	10.0	197	25	12.7
Soldiers												
Previously punished	81	42	51.9	30	8	26.7	2	0	0.0	113	50	44.2
Previously unpunished	176	31	17.6	64	5	7.8	9	0	0.0	249	36	14.4
Schalburg												
Previously punished	27	8	29.6	12	1	8.3	1	0	0.0	40	9	22.5
Previously unpunished	81	10	12.3	19	0	0.0	4	0	0.0	104	10	9.6
Hipo												
Previously punished	4	0	0.0	2	0	0.0	4	0	0.0	10	0	0.0
Previously unpunished	34	3	8.8	18	0	0.0	3	0	0.0	55	3	5.5
German Police												
Previously punished	16	6	37.5	8	1	12.5	2	0	0.0	26	7	26.9
Previously unpunished	27	4	14.8	30	2	6.7	6	0	0.0	63	6	9.5
Propagandists												
Previously punished	2	1	50.0	0	—	—	0	—	0.0	2	1	50.0
Previously unpunished	4	0	0.0	6	0	0.0	6	0	0.0	16	0	0.0
Informers												
Previously punished	16	4	25.0	13	4	30.8	3	0	0.0	32	8	25.0
Previously unpunished	17	2	11.8	4	1	7.1	10	0	0.0	41	3	7.3

TABLE 14

The Follow-Up Material in Group III According to Age, Previous Criminal Career, Dominant Type (Soldiers versus Others), and the Incidence of Recidivism

	25 Years and Younger			26 Years and Older			Total		
	N	Recidivists		N	Recidivists		N	Recidivists	
		N	Percent		N	Percent		N	Percent
Soldiers									
Previously punished	81	42	51.9	32	8	25.0	113	50	44.3
Previously unpunished	176	31	17.6	73	5	6.9	249	36	14.5
Total	257	73	28.4	105	13	12.4	362	86	23.8
Remaining types									
Previously punished	209	68	32.5	185	33	17.8	394	101	25.6
Previously unpunished	581	66	11.4	397	20	5.0	978	86	8.8
Total	790	134	17.0	582	53	9.1	1372	187	13.6

TABLE 15

The Follow-Up Material in Group III According to Age, Previous Criminal Career, Dominant Type (Watchmen, Schalburg Corps, and Propagandists versus Hipo, German Police, and Informers), and Incidence of Recidivism

	25 Years and Under			26–40 Years			41 Years and Above			Total		
	N	Recidivists		N	Recidivists		N	Recidivists		N	Recidivists	
		N	Percent		N	Percent		N	Percent		N	Percent
Watchmen, Schalburg, Propagandists												
Previously punished	173	58	33.5	124	28	22.6	29	0	—	326	86	26.4
Previously unpunished	503	57	11.3	230	13	5.7	86	4	4.7	819	74	9.0
Total	676	115	17.0	354	41	11.6	115	4	3.5	1145	160	14.0
Hipo, German Police, Informers												
Previously punished	36	10	27.8	23	5	21.7	9	0	—	68	15	22.1
Previously unpunished	78	9	11.5	62	3	4.8	19	0	—	159	12	7.6
Total	114	19	16.7	85	8	9.4	28	0	—	227	27	11.9

TABLE 16

The Follow-Up Material in Group III According to Age, Previous Criminal Career, Social Class, and Incidence of Recidivism

	Lower Class			Higher Class			Total		
		Recidivists			Recidivists			Recidivists	
	N	N	Percent	N	N	Percent	N	N	Percent
-20 years									
Previously punished	92	39	42.4	34	10	29.4	126	49	38.9
Previously unpunished	214	38	17.8	226	24	10.6	440	62	14.1
Total	306	77	25.2	260	34	13.1	566	111	19.6
21–30 years									
Previously punished	147	49	33.3	101	29	28.7	248	78	31.5
Previously unpunished	175	19	10.9	327	25	7.6	502	44	8.8
Total	322	68	21.1	428	54	12.6	750	122	16.3
31+ years									
Previously punished	60	15	25.0	73	9	12.3	133	24	18.1
Previously unpunished	66	5	7.6	219	11	5.0	285	16	5.6
Total	126	20	15.9	292	20	6.9	418	40	9.6
All-age group									
Previously punished	299	103	34.5	208	48	23.1	507	151	29.8
Previously unpunished	455	62	13.6	772	60	7.8	1227	122	9.9
Total	754	165	21.9	980	108	11.0	1734	273	15.7

The most important factors of recidivism apparently are age, previous criminal career, and social class. These three factors are cross-tabulated in Table 16, which illustrates that all three factors play a role in the incidence of reconvictions within population Group III. The rate of recidivism is significantly higher in the lowest age-group than in the group between 21 and 30 $(0.02 < p < 0.05)$, and higher in this group than in the oldest $(0.01 < p < 0.02)$, but apparently the age limit at 25 (see the previous tables where the material is subdivided in age-groups) is more relevant, so far as recidivism is concerned, than the limit of 20 years of age. More important is previous criminal career: there is a highly significant difference between the previously punished and the previously unpunished collaborators $(p < 0.001)$. Similarly, recidivism is significantly more frequent among collaborators of lower class status than among the higher classes $(p < 0.001)$. It is, however, evident, that previous career is a better discriminator with respect to recidivism than is social class, for the overall results of the comparisons show 28 percent recidivists among the previously punished as against 11 percent among the unpunished, while the difference between lower and higher class collaborators is 22 percent as against 11 percent. As will be seen from the table, this trend is the same in all the subgroups.

A mere detailed analysis based on the same population, classified as above, but further broken down by geographical district, has on the whole confirmed the above-mentioned impression and once again shown that the rates of recidivism are not significantly different in the four geographical districts.

DISCUSSIONS AND CONCLUSIONS

Let us now return to the questions we asked before analyzing the data.

1. The question about *the nature of the factors associated with recidivism* of the collaborators can only be answered in a very general way. We have analyzed the connection between recidivism and political and national affiliations with the Germans, dominating type of collaboration, age, geographical milieu, previous criminal career, and social class. We have further analyzed the relation of recidivism to family relations, schooling, unemployment, considerable increase in income on turning collaborator, and to the point of time of recruitment. It has not been possible to cross-tabulate the material into all the subcategories of these criteria at the same time without creating subcategories with only a very

limited number of elements. However, some of the results of the analysis may be mentioned.

All factors seem to be of some importance, but some of them are undoubtedly highly correlated. For instance, the difference between early and late recruited collaborators disappears when these two groups are subdivided by social class and previous criminal career. Geographical milieu apparently is of secondary importance; even taken by itself it discriminates less sharply among collaborators than among ordinary offenders.

Generally, however, it would appear safe to conclude that the factors of recidivism among released collaborators are the same as among ordinary offenders. This is not surprising, for recidivism in both cases relates to a relapse into ordinary (noncollaborationist) crime. On the other hand, we cannot exclude the possibility that other and unknown factors might be of greater importance than those selected for this study. The results concerning the influence of previous career suggest that the background for recidivism among collaborators is more complicated than in ordinary crime.

2. Table 17 shows the incidence of *recidivism among previously unpunished and punished collaborators* within the three population groups. Questions 2 and 3 refer to the actual and the expected rates in the same categories. It would be difficult, and dubious too, to attempt a further subdivision of the material and equally detailed estimates of the expected rates of crime and recidivism in the corresponding categories. Instead of using such a procedure, the expected rates have been estimated for the six subgroups of the table in the following way: (1) the six basic population categories are constructed as miniature populations that correspond to the collaborators in the same categories with respect to age, geographical milieu, and social class; (2) the number of first offenders through a seven-year period are computed on the basis of risk figures from 1951;[16] as no earlier figures are available, the number of recidivists among the previously punished are computed on the basis of figures from a follow-up investigation of 2180 male prisoners, released in 1956.[17]

[16] Karl O. Christiansen et al., "Kriminalitetsrisikoen i Danmark før og efter krigen" (The Risk of Being Registered for Crimes in Denmark Before and After the War), *Nordisk tidsskrift for kriminalvidenskab* (Nordic Journal of Criminal Science) 1960, pp. 300–313 and 1961, pp. 73–78.

[17] Beretning om fængselsvæsenet i Danmark 1961, Afgivet af Direktøren for fængselsvæsenet (Report about the Danish Prison Service 1961, by the Director of the Prison Service). Copenhagen 1961, pp. 88–120.

TABLE 17

The Follow-Up Material According to Population Group, Previous Criminal Career, and Incidence of Recidivism. (Expected Rates of Crime and of Recidivism in Population Groups Corresponding to the Previously Unpunished and the Previously Punished Collaborators, Respectively)

	Previously Unpunished			Previously Punished			
	N	Recidivists	Expected Recidivism Rates Percent	N	Recidivists		Expected Crime Rates Percent
		N	Percent		N	Percent	
German minority	335	3	0.9	0.8	26	3	11.5	35.0
Nazis	729	21	3.0	1.1	122	14	12.0	40.0
Non-Nazis	1227	122	9.9	1.5	507	51	29.8	50.0

For the previously unpunished collaborators the actual crime rates after release are higher than the expected, the difference being very small within the German minority but with a ratio of one to three among the Nazis and of one to seven in the Non-Nazi group. The basis of the estimated rates is the corresponding male population figures (which in the last-mentioned group is almost all male Danes above 15 years of age); it is evident that the difference between the actual and estimated rates are highly significant.

For the previously punished part of the collaborators the situation is the opposite. The actual rates of recidivism are only about one-half to one-third of what would have been expected if the released prisoners had been ordinary criminals. These differences are highly significant.

A number of explanations of these peculiar differences may be offered. The overall low rate of recidivism among the collaborators might perhaps be seen as a consequence of the severe punishments and considered as a general support of the well-known demand of applying longer and more deterrent sentences for ordinary criminals. Some observers would object to this conclusion by referring to the practice of mitigating the sentences through the various forms of revision of the sentences that were actually applied in most cases. These revisions, they would add, created some kind of gratitude, which was an important psychological factor in the process of resocialization after release.

From such general considerations, however, it seems difficult to explain why the influence of the purge on the previously unpunished collaborators was the opposite.

A third type of hypothesis comes closer to the relevant facts. A severe sentence breaks the criminal career for a long period of time. The connections with the old environment, with old friends and old fellow criminals, have been changed, perhaps torn apart. It is well known that ordinary criminals despised the collaborators. For the previously unpunished a similar break did not occur. On the contrary, they had, after all, been in prison, and some routes to future crime that did not exist before might have opened. Thus, generally, the difference perhaps may be explained by the theory of differential association. The second half of this explanation is the most problematic, although it should not be left completely out of consideration.

It appears fruitful to change the emphasis of this theory slightly by means of the concept "status change," that is, improvement or depreciation of the social status through punishment. Now, it is quite clear that a prison sentence of long duration, even for something which may be termed "a poltical offense," has a tendency to reduce the social status of a previously unpunished person, and the increased crime rate in this group may be seen as the consequence of social stigmatization through the conviction and the prison sentence. To push the idea one step further, we might consider the threefold to sevenfold increase in the ordinary crime rate of previously unpunished persons as some sort of a measure of the unfavorable consequences of conviction and imprisonment. Admittedly, this may be an oversimplification of the problem, since it is a fact that participation in collaborationist activities in itself had some degrading consequences. Still, it seems as if we are close to the point where we can observe the effects of sending a person who is not guilty of ordinary offenses to prison for a long period of time.

The status improvement of the previously punished collaborators is not less evident. From the rank of ordinary, petty, or maybe more successful thieves, embezzlers, swindlers, forgers, and so forth, they climbed the social ladder and reached the step of political criminals, undoubtedly below, but not far below the law-abiding citizens. It is a fact that they looked down upon the ordinary "pack of thieves"; *they* had never stolen anything belonging to others; they were social and honest people. We know from a few institutions where collaborators and ordinary prisoners were kept together that this depreciation was reciprocal (the ordinary criminals "had never betrayed their country"), and vivid enough to create problems in the daily life of the prison. However, by far the largest number of collaborators served their sentences in prison or camps without ordinary criminals as fellow prisoners. It appears most likely that this status improvement lasted beyond imprisonment and, as the years passed by, the general population probably adopted the view that collaboration was only some kind of a political type of offense. In any case, social stigmatization from the sentence must have been less perceptible than the stigmatization from sentences they served for their ordinary crimes. It was not without importance that a number of the previously punished collaborators, perhaps for the first time in their life, experienced a strong feeling of belonging to a group.

In this way the reduced recidivism of the previously punished and the increased crime rates of the previously unpunished collaborators are explained by the same hypothesis: the effects of a penal sanction per se depend upon its capacity for changing the social status of the offender. This capacity may depend upon the offender and his situation as well as upon the punishment. It is possible that other types of sanctions might have given more favorable results than exerted by the severe punishments actually applied. The need for the widest possible differentiation in the choice of legal sanctions and in the ways in which they are executed has thus once more been emphasized.

3. The hypothesis that certain types of collaboration had a more devastating influence on the personality than others has little support from the empirical facts. At least one must admit that it does not apply to the members of the Hipo Corps, the German Police Corps, or to the informers. The hypothesis is, however, confirmed regarding the soldiers who, in spite of generally better social conditions, manifest the highest rates of recidivism. This is especially applicable to soldiers from population Group III, and among them in particular to the previously punished persons. It might perhaps be said that the demoralizing effect of the front life was most predominant among the collaborators who joined the German army without any idealistic motive, in search of adventure, trying to escape from difficulties or maybe acting for economic reasons. That it is even more pronounced among the previously punished soldiers is probably a consequence of their marginal status as deviants in this specific respect.

Members of the Hipo Corps have an extremely low rate of recidivism, but it cannot be demonstrated that it is significantly lower than the rate in a combined group of the other collaborators, with the exception of the soldiers. A higher number of examined Hipo members might very well have shown that they had a significantly lower recidivism rate than both the soldiers and the remaining part of the collaborators. This result is, after all, not particularly amazing. The Hipo Corps established its headquarters at "Politigaarden" (the Danish Police Headquarters) in Copenhagen, and they had, as did the Germans, easy access to the criminal cardex. It is known that they did not accept applicants for employment, of which there were plenty),[18] who did not have a clean record. It is most probable that they also utilized other types of information to insure employing members of a certain standard, however their requirements may have been defined.

SUMMARY

1. After the German occupation the Danish parliament retroactively introduced laws according to which 12,877 men and 644 women were convicted of collaboration with the occupying power.

2. The most important types of collaboration were (a) committing acts which were indictable in accordance with the criminal code of 1930 if they were committed in the interest of the Germans, or if the offender wore a German uniform, or identified himself as belonging to the occupying power, (b) participating in German war service, (c) serving in German or pro-German corps, including police service, (d) informing, (e) engaging in pro-Nazi propaganda and similar acts, and (f) committing various forms of economic collaboration. The last category (1100 persons) and the women fall outside this survey.

3. Collaborators belonged to three population groups: (I) the German minority in South Jutland, (II) the Danish Nazi Party, and (III) the Danish Non-Nazis (the rest of the population).

(a) In the German minority in South Jutland, no resistance against collaboration with the Germans was found.

(b) Resistance existed but was relatively weak among the Danish Nazis.

(c) Group resistance against collaboration was much greater although not complete in the major part of the Danish population, which had no national or political affinities with the Germans (Group III).

(d) In this Group (III), resistance increased considerably from 1940 to 1945, with 1943 as the crucial year.

4. In the German minority, the frequency of male collaborators was 25 percent, among the Nazis it was 10 percent, and in population Group III 0.4 percent. The relative frequency of deviants among the collaborators was highest among the late recruited Non-Nazis (III), somewhat lower among the early recruited in the same population group, still lower among the Nazis, and lowest within the German minority.

18 See above, p. 249.

5. During the purge, 78 percent of the male collaborators were sentenced to more than one year of imprisonment, 43 percent to two years or more, and 16 percent to four years or more. In the same period the corresponding figures for offenses against the criminal code were 11, 3.5, and 1.0 percent, respectively. About 80 percent of the collaborators had some part of their sentence reduced. Seventy-six persons were sentenced to death, but for 30 the sentence was commuted to life.

6. The follow-up investigation is based on 2946 male collaborators interviewed before their conviction by the author and members of his staff. Data on recidivism were collected from the Central Police Register.

7. The rates of recidivism (not including sentences for minor offenses as fines or simple detention) are 2 percent in the German minority, 4 percent among the Nazis, and 16 percent among the Non-Nazis (Group III).

8. Recidivism decreases with growing age.

9. Recidivism does not vary significantly with geographical milieu.

10. Recidivism depends to a large degree on previous criminal career.

11. Recidivism increases with decreasing social status.

12. Recidivism is significantly higher among the soldiers and especially the previously punished from Group III and lower, but not significantly so, between members of the Hipo Corps, who during the occupation committed some of the most atrocious crimes of the war period.

13. Even if the rate of recidivism within the German minority is low, it may be stated: (a) that in all three population groups the actual rates of recidivism of the previously unpunished collaborators are considerably higher than the expected crime rates within the same groups; and (b) that in all three population groups the actual recidivism rates of the previously punished collaborators are considerably lower than the expected rates of recidivism within similar groups of ordinary prisoners. These two facts may be explained by a decrease in the social status of the previously unpunished and an increase in status of the previously punished collaborators, the first category being for the first time sent to prison and thereby stigmatized as criminals, the second category being pushed upward on the social ladder from "the ordinary pack of criminals" to what they themselves called "political offenders."

V

HISTORICAL
PENOLOGY

15

Impressment into the Army and the Navy—A Rough and Ready Instrument of Preventive Police and Criminal Justice

LEON RADZINOWICZ[*]

HAPHAZARD CONSCRIPTION

"To students of the history of law," observed Maitland, "the most interesting thing about the navy is impressment."[1] The primary object of impressment was to supply the forces necessary to safeguard British interests abroad and to defeat her foreign enemies. It had an important secondary function, however, as a weapon against those who were thought to threaten security at home. The internal enemy could thus be diverted to the defeat of the external, a striking example of penal economy.

It was stated in the House of Commons in the mid-eighteenth century that impressment was coeval with our monarchy and that press warrants were on record going back to the reign of Edward III.[2] The practice of impressing seamen was not systematically adopted, however, until the great naval wars. During the reign of Elizabeth, the Lords Lieutenant of the counties were given the duty of maintaining the strength of the navy, a duty which they, in turn, delegated to mayors and others, who were ordered to summon all seafaring men between the ages of eighteen and fifty to present themselves before the pressmasters.

---

[*] This paper has also become part of Volume 4 of the *History of English Criminal Law and Administration*, which has been written under auspices of the Rockefeller Foundation.
[1] F. W. Maitland, *Constitutional History of England* (1919), p. 461.
[2] Welbore Ellis, "Debate in the Commons on the Bill for the Encouragement of Seamen and Speedily Manning the Navy" (December, 1755), *Parl.History* (1753–1765), Vol. 15, cols. 544–616, at col. 559.

The latter were required to select the necessary recruits, who were given the imprest of a shilling and conduct money at the rate of a halfpenny a mile. The derivation of the word impressment has been traced to the French "emprestre," which implies a voluntary contract rather than compulsion, but the system could not, in practice, be applied without coercion.[3]

Impressment for the army was also resorted to from time to time up to the end of the eighteenth century.[4] It was necessitated in times of war by the British prejudice against the maintenance of a large standing army. Army conditions, like those of the navy, offered no inducement to volunteers: barracks were miserable, pay poor, punishments savage, and service abroad as bad as, if not worse than, the transportation reserved for criminals.[5] The statutes sanctioning impressment were designed not only to supply men directly for the armed forces but to induce them to enter voluntarily by offering better terms, such as shorter service and exemption thereafter, thus making pressing in the long run less necessary.[6]

The demand for men for the navy reached its height in the latter years of the Napoleonic Wars. Between 1792 and 1812 the total number trebled, and in 1809 a hundred and thirty thousand men were voted to it by Parliament.[7] Naval impressment became a large-scale business, de-

[3] Daines Barrington, *Observations on the more ancient Statutes, from Magna Carta to the Twenty-first of James I* (3rd ed., 1769), p. 300. Barrington adds "The first use, that I have happened to meet with, of the term *press*, as applied to mariners, is in a proclamation of the 29th of March, in the fourth year of Philip and Mary. . . .", *ibid.*, at p. 300. But see also F. W. Maitland's remarks on the origin of the word in his *Constitutional History of England* (1919), p. 461.

[4] See, for example, 17 Geo. 2, c. 15, An Act for the speedy and effectual recruiting of His Majesty's Land Forces and Marines for the Year One thousand seven hundred and forty-four (1744); 18 Geo. 2, c. 10, An Act for the speedy and effectual Recruiting of His Majesty's Regiments of Foot serving in Flanders, Minorca, Gibraltar and the Plantations, and the Regiments of Marines (1745); 29 Geo. 2, c. 4, An Act for the speedy and effectual Recruiting of His Majesty's Land Forces and Marines (1755); 30 Geo. 2, c. 8, similar title (1757).

[5] For many appalling details of army conditions, and for the size and distribution of the military establishment, 1773–1802, see The Hon. J. W. Fortescue, *A History of the British Army* Vol. 4 (1906), Part II, pp. 882–883, 897–900, 922–926, and Appendix C, pp. 938–939. See also Charles M. Clode, *The Military Forces of the Crown*, etc. (1869), Vol. 2, p. 14.

[6] "Debate in the Commons on the Bill for better Recruiting the Army" (January, 1779), *Parl.History* (1778–1780), Vol. 20, cols. 112–114, at col. 113.

[7] See Appendix No.12 (No.1) to the "Report of the Commissioners Appointed to Inquire into the Best Means of Manning the Navy" [2469], 1859, *Parl.Papers* (1859), Vol. 6, p. 1, at p. 347. See also P. Colquhoun, *A Treatise on the Wealth, Power and Resources of the British Empire*, etc. (2nd ed., 1815), p. 47.

manding extensive organization. "This most unpleasant and difficult, though indispensable, service," observed John Adolphus, "is reduced to regularity and method by the division of the United Kingdom into twenty-six stations, to the officers at which press warrants are directed. At each station is a captain, and generally two . . . lieutenants, who have under them bodies of seamen, called gangs, or generally press-gangs. . . . The officers and men on this duty have extraordinary pay. The lieutenants attend with the gangs, and place the men whom they impress on board a vessel prepared for the purpose, and called a tender, where they undergo an examination before the regulating captain, and unless they can show sufficient reason to obtain a release, they are consigned to such of the King's ships as are in want of hands, and compelled to serve during the residue of the war, or until discharged."[8]

The Impressment Establishment in full swing was a formidable force indeed. Attacking it in Parliament in 1824, Joseph Hume claimed that during the war with France, over three thousand men had been employed in press-gangs at a cost of between three and four hundred thousand pounds a year. A later opponent of the system put the port establishments alone at one thousand five hundred seamen, and the cost—calculated at its lowest but including wages, ships, provisions, and maintenance, at two hundred thousand pounds a year.[9] If they were to be effective at all, it was essential that the gangs should be large, swift, and ruthless, for their victims moved quickly: "it frequently happened, that when twenty thousand available seamen existed in the sea-port towns at the breaking out of a hot press, a few hundred were caught on the first day, and on the following morning, nineteen thousand out of the twenty would be scattered and dispersed towards every point of the compass inland, and were thus as completely lost to the service for which they were required as if an earthquake had ingulfed them all."[10]

Contemporary periodicals and parliamentary debates were full of

[8] John Adolphus, *The Political State of the British Empire*, etc. (1818), Vol. 2, p. 224.
[9] "Impressment of Seamen," H.C. (June 10, 1824), *Parl.Debates* (1824), n.s., Vol. 11, cols. 1171–1194, at col. 1185; "Impressment," H.C. (August 15, 1833), *Parl. Debates* (1833), 3rd s., Vol. 20, cols. 636–695, at cols. 653–654.
[10] "Impressment," H.C. (August 15th, 1833), *Parl.Debates* (1833), 3rd s., Vol. 20, at cols. 649–650. For a case in which *habeas corpus* was invoked by the victim of a press-gang, and subsequent alterations in the law, see: *Parl.History* (1753–1765), Vol. 15, "Proceedings in the Commons on the Bill to explain and amend the Habeas Corpus Act" (February 21, March 8, 1758), cols. 871–897; *ditto*, Lords (May 9, May 25, May 26, June 2, 1758), cols. 897–926, where the opinions of the judges are reproduced. See also Sir William S. Holdsworth, *History of the English Law* (1926), Vol. 9, p. 121 and 56 Geo.3, c.100, "An Act for more effectually securing the Liberty of the Subject" (1816).

horrifying accounts of the lengths to which the press-gangs would go. They were known to invade churches during marriages or other services, dragging out their victims at random, to break into houses at night, to collect spectators from around the pillory, and to carry off some of Wesley's preachers; even a peace officer was not safe.[11] Villages might be surrounded by regular soldiers, who stood by the doors with fixed bayonets to assist their naval colleagues. Whole towns and the country around them might be plunged into terror for several months. Merchant ships nearing home after long voyages might be boarded and almost stripped of their crews.[12]

The arrival of the press-gang could lead to tragedies. Mary Jones (nineteen years old and the mother of two children), left to fend for herself after her husband was impressed, stole from a shop and was hanged for it.[13] Masters wanting to escape the obligation to feed, clothe, and house apprentices for seven years, sometimes contrived to have them taken by the press-gang; watermen who had poor boys as apprentices found it profitable to do the same, especially in time of war, since all of the boy's wages and even his prize money, was legally the property of his master.[14] Voltaire tells of going out on the Thames with a waterman who seized the opportunity to extol English liberty, saying that he would rather be a modest boatman on the Thames than an archbishop in France. The next day the philosopher saw him in heavy

[11] See "Debate in the Commons on the Bill for speedily Manning the Navy," H.C. (June 25, 1779), Parl.History (1778–1780), Vol. 20, cols. 962–1008, at col. 966; "The London Packet, Nov. 8, 1770," quoted by William Connor Sydney, England and the English in the Eighteenth Century (2nd ed., 1892), Vol. 1, at p. 338; W. E. H. Lecky, A History of England in the Eighteenth Century Vol. 3, (1905), p. 74; Lord Kenyon, C. J., ex parte Fox (1793) 5 T.R. 276. It was held that exemptions must depend on positive provisions in statutes.

[12] "Debate in the Commons on the Bill for the Encouragement of Seamen and Speedily manning the Navy" (December 2, 1755), Parl.History (1753–1765), Vol. 15, cols. 544–616, at col. 549 and "Debate in the Commons on Mr. Temple Luttrell's Bill for the more easy and effectual Manning of the Navy," H.C. (March 11, 1777), Parl.History (1777–1780), Vol. 19, cols. 81–103, at cols. 82–83 and 86.

[13] See Vol. 1 of this History, Note 5, at p. 475.

[14] See M. D. George, London Life in the Eighteenth Century (1925), pp. 230, 234, and Appendix IV, "Apprenticeship Cases from the Middlesex Sessions Record," ibid., pp. 418–424, Nos. 1 and 27. Impressment produced its own folklore and ballads—the press-gang songs. One began:

> "Cruel was the winds, for they would't blow contrary;
> Cruel was the ship, for it took her love from Mary;
> Cruel was the cap'n and the bo'sun and the men
> For they didn't care a farden should us never meet again"

"Press Gang Songs," Notes and Queries (9th Ser., 1900), Vol. 6, pp. 28 and 96.

chains, bitterly complaining of the abominable government that took him by force from his wife and children to serve on the King's ship in Norway. The misfortune of this man and the flagrant injustice moved Voltaire deeply, but he could not resist adding "Un Français, qui était avec moi, m'avoua qu'il sentait une joie maligne de voir que les Anglais, qui nous reprochent si hautement notre servitude, étaient esclaves aussi bien que nous."[15]

Corrupt practices added to the injustice. Those in charge of press-gangs allowed some of their victims to buy themselves off, while others took the conduct money but failed to present themselves for service.[16] Not surprisingly there were instances of thieves posing as press-gangs so as to extort money.[17] Illegal impressment by the East India Company, partaking of the character of criminal kidnapping, called forth protests, although unavailing, from Clive.[18] The system could also be used as an instrument of private malice. In 1770, for example, the wedding of a colored man and a white woman was interrupted by a press-gang; a fight ensued and the clergyman conducting the ceremony was struck.[19] Fielding was not indulging in a flight of literary fancy when, in "Tom Jones," he made Lady Bellaston suggest that Lord Fellamor might employ a press-gang to dispose of his rival: " 'I am thinking, my Lord,' added she, '(for this Fellow is too mean for your personal Resentment) whether it would not be possible for your Lordship to contrive some Method of having him pressed and sent on board a Ship. Neither Law nor Conscience forbid this Project: for the Fellow, I promise you, however well drest, is but a Vagabond, and as proper as any Fellow in the Streets to be pressed into the Service.' "[20]

Violent measures provoked violent retaliation, often taking the form of serious riots, savage fights and reckless escapes, which sometimes ended in murder. In a cottage near Calne a member of a press-gang was

---

[15] Quoted by W.C. Sydney, *England and the English in the Eighteenth Century* (2nd ed., 1892), Vol. 1, p. 338.

[16] See on this and other interesting details of that early system, C. L'Estrange Ewen, "Impressment for the Navy," *Notes and Queries* (1937), Vol. 172, pp. 222–223.

[17] See John Cordy Jeaffreson, *Middlesex County Records*, Vol. 3 (1888), pp. 163 and 169; Vol. 4 (1892), pp. 2 and 35; "Debate in the Commons on the Bill for the Encouragement of Seamen and Speedily manning the Navy," H.C. (December 2, 1755), *Parl.History* (1753–1765), Vol. 15, cols. 544–616, at col. 578.

[18] See John George Phillimore, *History of England During the Reign of George the Third* (1863), Vol. 1, p. 60. See also *Annual Register* (1767), Vol. 10, p. 82; *ibid.* (1768), Vol. 11, p. 123; and Alexander Andrews, *The Eighteenth Century, or Illustrations of the Manners and Customs of our Grandfathers* (1856), pp. 209–213.

[19] See *Annual Register* (1770), Vol. 13, p. 161, Note of Nov. 5, 1770.

[20] Henry Fielding, *The History of Tom Jones* (ed. of 1749), Book XVI, Ch. 8, p. 218.

stabbed to death while trying to bind the householder. Men confined in a tender fought their way out, killed the captain, and escaped. Sailors were tried for the murder of a publican at whose house men were being impressed. The captain of a whaling ship was charged with murder after his crew had fought off a press-gang with harpoons, knives, and lances.[21]

Public sympathy was usually with the victims of the press-gangs, and there were many protests. In particular the power of a naval officer with a press warrant to call directly upon the military for help was resented as a threat to public security and individual freedom, bypassing the civil power: "to order our regular troops to assist or to protect our press-gangs, without the interposition of a civil magistrate, is a direct breach of our constitution, and of the most dangerous consequence to the lives as well as the liberties of the people."[22] In 1747 a "Seamen's Bill" authorizing impressment was attacked as reducing "multitudes of our fellow subjects to the miseries of slavery, to the malice of private, lurking informers, and the hateful insults of petty authority. . . . It condemns those who have dedicated their lives to the most useful employment, and wasted their strength in the most important service of their country, to be hunted like beasts of prey, or like murderers and felons, whom it is the common interest of mankind to search out and to destroy."[23]

There were exemptions, conferred by statute or by Admiralty orders, but they could be, and frequently were, revoked by the same means.[24] Often, too, they were violated once the press-gangs were set in motion. Some of them were a matter of priviliege: no press warrant could legally be executed in the City of London without the authority of the Lord Mayor and Aldermen, who were usually sufficiently powerful to maintain the City as "a sanctuary for their servants" against the "set of law-

[21] See *Annual Register* (1770), Vol. 13, p. 147; (1779), Vol. 22, pp. 215–216; G. Pyme, *Autobiographic Recollections* (1870), p. 27.

[22] "Debate in the Commons on the Bill for the Encouragement of Seamen and Speedily manning the Navy," H.C. (December 2, 1755), *Parl.History* (1753–1765), Vol. 15, cols. 544–616, at col. 602.

[23] "Debate in the Commons on The Seamen's Bill," H.C. (February 27, 1741), *Parl.History* (1741–1743), Vol. 12, cols. 26–143, Philip Gybborn, at col. 28. The debate was recorded by Dr. Johnson.

[24] See, for instance, the 38 Geo. 3, c. 46, An Act for the more speedy and effectual Manning of His Majesty's Navy (1798), passed during the wars with France. The second section of this Act was typical in overriding previous statutes granting exemptions with the provision "That no Person or Persons shall be sued or molested for taking and impressing, or causing to be taken and impressed, within the Time aforesaid, any Person or Persons, for His Majesty's Service at Sea." On the revocation of protection granted by the Admiralty, see John Adolphus, *The Political State of the British Empire*, etc. (1818), Vol. 2, at p. 225, where it is stated that protections were "revoked without notice to the Parties."

less ruffians" let loose as press-gangs.[25] Exemption might be granted as an inducement to accept important responsibilities. In 1798 protection from the press-gang was one of the privileges accorded to fishermen, sailors, and others who joined the Sea Fencibles, forerunners of the modern coastguards.[26] Fire insurance companies could get exemption for those serving in their regular brigades.[27] Seamen might be protected by age or length of service, masters of ships might buy security for a certain number of men on their vessels by paying a fee for the Admiralty.[28] Sometimes exemption was granted to a whole group of ships returning from abroad, as in 1729, when an order was issued "to forbear impressing Seamen from on Board the Homeward-bound Ships upon their Arrival from foreign Ports."[29]

But the exceptions were precarious and often illogical, the operation of the system arbitrary and oppressive. The call for something more rational, more certain, and more just was heard even before the end of the seventeenth century. It was suggested that parishes should be called upon to provide quotas of soldiers and seamen under the authority of the local justices; that an Act of Parliament should specify the classes of the population to be exempt from such conscription and those to whom it should be applied; and that precedence in recruitment should be given to criminal and antisocial elements.[30]

[25] See *Annual Register* (1770), Vol. 3, pp. 161–162, 169, and 170; (1771), Vol. 14, pp. 16, 68–70.

[26] Wm. Laird Clowes, *The Royal Navy. A History from the Earliest Times to the Present* (1899), Vol. 4, p. 186.

[27] 6 Ann, c. 58 (1706–7) and the consolidating Act of 14 Geo. 3, c. 78 (1774), An Act for the further and better Regulation of Buildings . . . and for the more effectually preventing Mischiefs by Fires, etc. in the London area, still very lengthy.

[28] See "Debate in the Commons on the Bill for Speedily Manning the Navy," H.C. (June 25, 1779), *Parl.History* (1778–1780), Vol. 20, cols. 962–1008, at cols. 1006 and 986. The privilege was sometimes extended to others not covered by statutory exemptions. See text of a Notice issued by the Commissioners for Executing the Office of Lord High Admiral of Great Britain and Ireland, published at South Shields on November 5, 1803, when impressment was about to be enforced, reproduced in "Certificate of Protection Against Press Gangs," *Notes and Queries* (1929), Vol. 149, p. 410. See also *ibid.*, p. 350, for a reproduction of a certificate by a Justice of the Peace in 1815 to the Master of a ship "employed in the Coal," in respect of James Dale, who was in charge of the vessel. The certificate was addressed to "All commanders, and officers of His Majesty's Ships, Press Masters, and others whom this may concern," and contained a description of James Dale, together with the substance of a sworn declaration by the Master that he was necessary to the business, did not belong to any of his Majesty's ships, and had not deserted from them.

[29] Extract from *The Universal Spectator and Weekly Journal*, August 16, 1729, quoted in "Two Hundred Years Ago," *Notes and Queries* (1929), Vol. 157, p. 110.

[30] See "A Discourse about raising Men; In which it is shewed, That it is more for the Interest of the Nation that the Parishes should be obligded by Law to provide

Those great oracles of law of the eighteenth century, Foster, Mansfield, Blackstone, all upheld the legality of impressment.[31] Foster, its leading exponent, while admitting that no statute directly authorized impressment for the navy, stated roundly that it was "a prerogative inherent in the Crown, *grounded upon common-law, and recognized by many acts of Parliament.*"[32] Lord Mansfield observed that "the practice was deduced from that trite maxim of the constitutional law of England, that private mischief had better be submitted to than that public detriment and inconvenience should ensue."[33] Blackstone, more cautious, admitted that the power of impressing seamen had been a matter of some dispute but, since it must reside somewhere, "it must, from the spirit of our constitution . . . reside in the crown alone." Nevertheless he held that it was "only defensible from public necessity, to which all private considerations must give way."[34]

On the other hand, even before prolonged peace and a sufficiency of volunteers had undermined the argument of public necessity, there had been jurists who contended that the methods of impressment, "the arbitrary and capricious seizure of individuals, from among the general body of citizens," were in conflict with the rules of law. "It differs from conscription," protested one of them, "as a particular confiscation differs

---

Men for the Service of the War, than to continue to rais 'em in the ordinary way: And all Objections are answer'd; and particularly that Popular one, viz. That this way of raising Men is a Violation of Liberty and Property," 1696, in *A Collection of State Tracts published during the Reign of King William III* (1706), Vol. 2, at pp. 539–550. For the details of this ingenious and drastic plan, see Vol. 2 of this *History,* pp. 23–25.

31 Foster, *Crown Cases* (3rd ed. by M. Dodson, 1792), pp. 178–179; Blackstone (17th ed. by E. Christian, 1830), 1 *Comm.* 420; Lord Mansfield in *R. v. Tubbs* (1776), Cowp. 11, 512; Buller J. in the *Goldswain Case* (1778) 2 Black W. 1207; Kenyon L.C.J. in *ex parte Fox* (1793), 5 T.R. 277. The point at issue in *Tubbs' Case* was that he was a certified waterman of the City of London who had been impressed for the navy: he claimed that his certificate exempted him from impressment. The essentials of Mansfield's view are reproduced in W. C. Costin and J. Steven Watson, *The Law and Working of the Constitution, Documents, 1660–1914* (1952), Vol. 1, p. 316. For similar pronouncements, see "The Case of Pressing Mariners, on the Trial of Alexander Broadfoot, for Murder, Bristol, Aug. 30, 1742," 18 St. Tr. 1323–1362, note at 1359–1361. Here the issue was that Broadfoot was charged with the murder of a member of a press-gang that boarded the ship on which he was serving: Foster directed the jury to find him guilty of manslaughter only, largely on the ground that the press warrant had not been properly executed, in that no commissioned officer accompanied the gang.

32 *Crown Cases* (3rd ed. by M. Dodson, 1792), p. 159; his italics.

33 *R. v. Tubbs* (1776), 11 Cowp. 512.

34 Blackstone (17th ed. by E. Christian, 1830), 1 *Comm.* 420.

from a general tax."[35] The argument was the same as that employed by
Benjamin Franklin: "when the personal service *of every man* is called
for, nere the burthen is equal. Not so, when the service of part is called
for, and others excused."[36] The claim that impressment was an exercise
of the royal prerogative by no means modified the opposition. On the
contrary, it encouraged charges of despotic tyranny. Sir Matthew Decker
wrote "The custom of impressment puts a freeborn *British* sailor on the
same footing as a *Turkish* Slave: the Grand Signior cannot do a more
absolute act, than to order a man to be dragged away from his family,
and against his will run his head before the mouth of a canon."[37] David
Hume complained that a continued violence was permitted in the Crown,
that liberty was left without defense in a country that prided itself on
liberty, that great violence and disorder were being committed with
impunity.[38] Emlyn later observed that Sir Matthew Hale "did not concur with the then prevailing practice, a practice which seems repugnant
to the liberties of an *Englishman,* and irreconcilable to the established
rules of law, viz. that a man without any offence by him committed, or
any law to authorise it, shall be hurried away like a criminal from his
friends and family, and carried by force into a remote and dangerous
service."[39]

Such objections died down, however, when it came to the impressment of criminals, vagabonds, or other socially dangerous individuals. A
story told in Parliament by Robert Dundas well reflects the general attitude. A man complained he had been wrongfully impressed. It turned
out that the whole of his village had wanted to be rid of him "because
he was a fellow so idle and profligate that he was more likely to ruin
than provide for his family." His wife, when privately questioned, con-

[35] Sir Thomas Erskine May (afterwards Lord Farnborough), *The Constitutional History of England* (11th ed., 1896), Vol. 3, p. 20.
[36] See Benjamin Franklin, "The Right of Impressing Seamen. Remarks on Judge Foster's Argument in Favour of the Right," in *Complete Works* (ed. by John Bigelow, 1887), Vol. 4, pp. 70–79, at pp. 70–71 and 79.
[37] See Sir Mathew Decker, *An Essay on the Causes of the Decline of Foreign Trade,* etc. (ed. of 1756), pp. 24–25.
[38] See David Hume, Essay X, "Of some Remarkable Customs," in *Essays Moral, Political and Literary* (ed. by T. H. Freen and T. H. Grose, 1907), Vol. 1, pp. 374–381, at pp. 380 and 381. D. Barrington, although not disputing the legality of impressment, agrees that it was "the greatest hardship an Englishman is still obliged to submit to, in this otherwise free country;" see *Observations on the more ancient Statutes, from Magna Charta to the Twenty-first of James I* (3rd ed., 1769), p. 301.
[39] For Hale's view see 1 *Pleas of the Crown* (S. Emlyn's ed., 1736), 678 and 679. For Emlyn's own view of impressment practices, see his "Preface to the Second Edition of the State Trials" (1730), reproduced in 1 St.Tr., pp. xxii–xli, at pp. xxvii–xxviii.

fessed that she had signed a petition for his release, only because she feared he would have murdered her if he got his freedom in some other way, that he often robbed her of money she herself earned, sold, or pawned the clothes of their six children for drink, and beat her cruelly lest she should dare to complain. "Let Gentlemen judge, Sir," exclaimed Dundas, "whether I could order such a fellow to be discharged: are not all such fellows liable to be pressed? . . . If we had in this country any such things as galleys, they ought to be made galley-slaves for life."[40] So enthusiastically was this policy adopted that it was claimed that only those "with something of the vagabond in their character" were likely to be impressed. A similar discrimination was urged in the seizure of seamen for the navy.[41]

This was "preventive police," the protection of society, often without judicial process and largely by administrative means. It could secure, with a minimum of effort and a high degree of permanency, the removal from the community of elements held to be dangerous. It was because press-gangs performed this function so conveniently that, in spite of abhorrence of their arbitrary proceedings, they were long regarded as a most valuable adjunct of criminal justice. They were, in their time, one of the few police instruments that could be used to strengthen the authority of the law and protect public order.

SEIZURE OF SOCIAL PARASITES

The Elizabethan Vagrancy Act of 1597 listed classes of disreputable characters liable to impressment for service in the fleet.[42] The provision was reaffirmed in the reign of Queen Anne, which laid down that, "as divers dissolute and idle Persons, Rogues, Vagbonds, and sturdy Beggars, notwithstanding the many good and wholesome Laws to the contrary, do continue to wander up and down, pilfering and begging throughout all parts of this Kingdom, to the great Disturbance of the Peace and Tranquility of the Realm," all such persons, whether boys or men, declared to be rogues or beggars under the Act of 39 Eliz., c.4, were to be taken up and conveyed into the Queen's service.[43]

[40] "Debate in the Commons on the Bill for the Encouragement of Seamen and Speedily manning the Navy" (December 2, 1755), Parl.History (1753–1765), Vol. 15, cols. 544–616, at col. 564. According to VI D.N.B. 195, only one of his speeches in Parliament is recorded, that on the Bill for speedily manning the Navy, from which the above extracts are quoted.
[41] George Haldane, Parl.History (1753–1765), Vol. 15, at col. 547.
[42] 39 Eliz., c. 4, An Act for Punishment of Rogues, Vagabonds and sturdy Beggars (1597).
[43] See 2 and 3 Ann., c. 6, An Act for the Increase of Seamen, and better Encouragement of Navigation, and Security of the Coal Trade (1703).

Justices were requested to raise and levy such able-bodied men as had no lawful calling or employment, or visible means for their maintenance and livelihood, and to hand them over to the officers of Her Majesty's forces. This was designed to give the proceedings a civil, as distinct from a military, character. The recruit, however, was to receive only twenty shillings (as compared with forty shillings paid to volunteers) and the constable who brought him in was also to receive ten shillings. The Mutiny Act and Articles of War were to be read over to him in the presence of the justice, under whose certificate he was then deemed to be an enlisted soldier.

By similar means the supply of vagrants was to be cut off at its very source. Two or more justices, and all mayors, aldermen, bailiffs, and overseers of the poor, with their consent, were enabled to bind as apprentices to the Sea Service any boys from the age of ten who were, or whose parents were, chargeable to the parish or who begged for alms. On reaching the age of eighteen such boys could be "compelled or impressed, or permitted" to enter the navy. The idea that naval service was a particularly appropriate occupation for pauper children recurred for many years. William Pulteney, afterwards the Earl of Bath, suggested that every charity school should allot a number of boys to the service of the sea, thus providing a steady flow of man power that would considerably reduce the need for impressment. In the charity schools, he argued, "the children of the poor receive an education disproportioned to their birth. This has often no other consequences than to make them unfit for their stations by placing them, in their own opinion, above the drudgery of daily labour, a notion which is too much indulged; as idleness co-operating with vanity, can hardly fail to gain the ascendance, and which sometimes prompts them to support themselves by practices not only useless but pernicious to society."[44] Much later Southey, in an article in the *Quarterly Review* in 1812, demanded "why should not government extend its military and naval seminaries, so that every body who needed an asylum should know where to find one? Would it not be better that the workhouses should empty themselves into our fleets and armies, than that they should pack off children by waggon-loads, to grow up in the stench and moral contagion of cotton mills while the trade flourishes, and to be thrown out of employ, and turned upon the public when it meets any sudden revulsion? Seminaries of this kind may be so conducted as to cost little more than well-regulated workhouses. Boys become useful at sea at a very early age."[45] Later still, W. H. Saunders

---

[44] "Debate in the Commons on The Seamen's Bill" (February 27, 1741), *Parl.History* (1741–1743), Vol. 12, cols. 26–143, at col. 66.
[45] "Inquiry into the Poor Laws," *The Quarterly Review* (September to December 1812), Vol. 8, pp. 319–356, at p. 353.

produced a scheme of "Home Colonies" for the unemployed, idlers and mendicants, in which such a course might be pursued in the education and amusements of the male children as to inspire them with an early desire to follow the profession of arms; they could then be enlisted, as soon as they were old enough, at half the expense of the recruiting system.[46] Looking back from the very end of the nineteenth century, a historian of the Poor Laws reflected that although there might be objections in principle to compulsory apprenticeship, it was a means of "attacking mendicancy at its source," the importance of which could "hardly be over-estimated on social grounds, independently of the political considerations involved in it."[47]

The Vagrancy Act of 1744, which remained in force until 1822, provided that male vagabonds over twelve years of age, after being punished for their offenses, could be sent to be employed in His Majesty's service by sea or land, a power frequently used under the authority of the Privy Council.[48] At the suggestion of George Grenville, afterwards the Marquis of Buckingham, a clause was introduced into the Impressment Act of 1779 under which persons convicted at Quarter Sessions of having deserted their wives and children, who were liable to transportation or hard labor as incorrigible rogues, were instead to be handed over to the recruiting officer and, if able-bodied, deemed to be enlisted. In such cases the recruiting officer was to pay forty shillings to the overseers of the poor of the parish towards the maintenance of the men's families.[49] Soon afterwards proposals were put to the Home Office for the use of impressment to clear the roads of the "present desperate banditti,"[50] and in 1783 Thomas Townsend, then responsible for the

[46] See William Herbert Saunders, *An Address to the Imperial Parliament, upon the Practical Means of gradually Abolishing the Poor Laws, and Educating the Poor Systematically* (1821), pp. 79–80. See also William Clarkson, *An Inquiry into the Cause of the Increase of Pauperism and Poor Rates; with a Remedy for the Same, and a Proposition for Equalizing the Rates throughout England and Wales* (1815), pp. 47–48.
[47] Sir George Nicholls, *History of the English Poor Law*, etc. (1898), Vol. 1, pp. 363–364.
[48] 17 Geo. 2, c. 5, An Act to amend and make more effectual the Laws relating to Rogues, Vagabonds, and other idle and disorderly Persons, and to Houses of Correction (1777).
[49] 19 Geo. 3, c. 10, An Act for repealing an Act, made in the last Session of Parliament, entitled, 'An Act for the more easy and better recruiting of His Majesty's Land Forces and Marines,' etc. (1779). See also "Debate in the Commons on the Bill for better Recruiting the Army" (January, 1779), *Parl.History* (1778–1780), Vol. 20, January 21, 1779 at cols. 112–114, January 25 at col. 114, January 26, cols. 114–124, at col. 114.
[50] Notes, unsigned, in H.O. 41/1 (Public Record Office).

Home Department, told the House of Commons that he had seriously considered the project of a "land-press," not primarily to provide men for the army but to get rid of the idle elements who, without any visible means of livelihood, assembled together up and down the country to plan depredations.[51]

Yet another statute, passed at the end of the eighteenth century when the threat of revolutionary France had increased both the need of sailors for defense and the fear of the "dangerous classes" at home, was of great importance in encouraging the impressment of vagrants, paupers, and actual or potential criminals. This was specifically entitled "An Act for enabling the Magistrates, in the several Counties in Great Britain, to raise and levy, under certain Regulations, such able-bodied and idle Persons as shall be found within the said Counties to serve in His Majesty's Navy." Originally designed to operate only for a year, it remained in force right up to the Statute Law Revision Act of 1871.[52] Its enforcement was again entrusted to the justices of the peace, who were to "use their utmost Care and Diligence that his Majesty's Service, in making such Levies, be not neglected or disappointed." Sessions were to issue warrants enabling general search to be made throughout each area for all "able-bodied, idle, and disorderly Persons, who cannot upon Examination prove themselves to exercise and industriously follow some lawful Trade or Employment, or have some Substance sufficient for their Support and Maintenance," as well as all deemed to be, under the Vagrant Act, idle and disorderly persons, rogues and vagabonds, or incorrigible rogues, and all smugglers, thieves, and embezzlers of His Majesty's naval stores. The measure was apparently considered peculiarly appropriate to smugglers; years later Sir James Graham referred to "the practice but too frequent in the last war, of sending smugglers on board His Majesty's ships as a punishment." The actual rounding up of these potential recruits was the duty of the high constables and parish officers, supported by other authorities, while the selection of men from among those taken by the civil power fell to officers appointed by the Admiralty. No time limit was prescribed for the service of men conscripted in this way: they could be retained for life. On the other hand, they were safe from being "taken out of his Majesty's Service by any Process, other than by some criminal Process, for some criminal Matter punishable by the known Laws of the Land."

This Act is an example of the detailed legal formulation of procedures

[51] See "Bill for preventing the receiving of Stolen Goods" (12 February 1783), H.C., Parl.History (1782–1783), Vol. 23, cols. 364–365.
[52] 35 Geo. 3, c. 34 (1795). The Act was originally to remain in force until March 25, 1796.

which had in fact been followed, with varying intensity, over a long period. It laid down that the men concerned should be brought before the Petty Sessions and, having been declared to be within the Act, handed over to the appointed officer. It bristled with incentives and rewards. Clerks could be employed to help the magistrates in its execution and were to be entitled to two shillings for every man entered; parish officers were allowed twenty shillings, high constables up to two shillings, anyone giving information leading to the discovery and enlistment of an able-bodied man, ten shillings. On the other hand, if any parish officers neglected to secure the men, they were liable to a fine not exceeding ten pounds, while anyone failing to assist in the enforcement of the Act could be fined up to twenty pounds, one half of which was to go to the Crown, the other being allocated "for the Use of the Informer or Informers."

Apart from this specific provision for the impressment of the less desirable sections of the community, the process was undoubtedly stimulated by two other Acts passed in 1795; these Acts placed an embargo on all British ships in the ports until they had contributed a quota of men for the armed forces and laid down quotas to be raised in each county of England and Wales, proportionate to their populations. Thus while Rutland had to find only a score of men, Yorkshire was expected to produce more than a thousand, Liverpool nearly two thousand, and London well over five thousand. The totals were to be nearly ten thousand from the counties and twenty thousand from the ports.[53] Although these statutes also made conditions of service more attractive than they had been, it was necessary to resort to impressment on a large scale to meet the quotas. Quite aside from statutory measures, a little local cooperation was all that was needed to ensure that it was the black sheep who were the first to go.

In coastal districts, where the best sailors lurked and where press-gangs were the most active, their officers would enter into agreements with captains of the merchant service or local authorities. In meeting their quotas under these arrangements, the owners and captains of merchant ships could seize the opportunity of ridding themselves of the worst elements in their crews. Similarly the authorities ashore would,

[53] See Wm. Laird Clowes, et al., The Royal Navy. A History from the Earliest Times to the Present (1899), Vol. 4, p. 156. The rapid expansions in demand for men for the navy can be seen from the statement made by the Earl of Sandwich in Parliament that in 1759 there were 86,700 men in the fleet, and in 1779 there would still be 81,000, in spite of the loss of 18,000 with the breakaway of the American colonies (Parl.History (1778–1780), Vol. 20, col. 974). Between 1792 and 1812, again, the number increased from 36,000 to 114,000.

whenever possible, send off the most undesirable members of their communities, thus minimizing opposition and even enlisting the co-operation of respectable local inhabitants.

Magistrates in other parts of the country, conscious of the numbers of vagrants in their areas, were not slow to use their powers. In 1803 the Buckinghamshire justices, for example, declared themselves satisfied that it was, "in the present situation of affairs, most necessary that a general search should take place throughout the County in order to take up all idle and disorderly persons, for the purpose of sending such as may be fit for service to serve His Majesty either in the army or navy." They ordered the Clerk of the Peace to write to all the acting magistrates in the county, advising them that a general and privy search should take place, the date to be kept secret and the search repeated once a month.[54] Similarly, the justices of Westminster and Middlesex were in the habit of issuing "general privy search warrants" for prearranged nights. Even the Lord Mayor of London, while standing upon his right to refuse to back press warrants in the City, had not scrupled on occasion to have public houses searched by his own officials and send "loose and disorderly men" found in them aboard a tender to serve the King. "By this judicious step," it was observed "many idle persons were obtained, and the more industrious escaped being illegally forced from their friends and families."[55]

Impressment was also held out as a way of escape for debtors unable to buy their way out of prison. This was sometimes portrayed as a gesture of mercy, as in an Act of Charles II for the "Relief and Release of poor distressed Prisoners for Debt."[56] A similarly named statute some years later, however, forbade any discharge of an insolvent male debtor under the age of fifty unless he enlisted in the army or navy.[57] Under Queen Anne the priorities were made quite clear in an Act designed to secure "the supply of her Majesty with Recruits both by sea and land

[54] For this and the preceding illustrations, see "Jackson's Oxford Journal" of March 6, 1756; March 13, 1756; M.S. Minutes, Petty Sessions, Marylebone (Middlesex), Nov. 18, 1776; M.S. Minutes, Quarter Sessions, Buckinghamshire, Midsummer, 1803, all quoted in Sidney and Beatrice Webb, English Local Government: English Poor Law History, Part I, "The Old Poor Law" (1927), pp. 368–369 and 366.

[55] See William Thornton (assisted by George Smith and the Rev. Alex Townsend), The New, Complete, and Universal History, Description, and Survey of the Cities of London and Westminster, the Borough of Southwark, and the Parts adjacent, etc. (1784), p. 380. See also "Middlesex Order Book, November 1776," quoted by M. D. George, London Life in the Eighteenth Century (1925), Note 94, at pp. 362–363.

[56] 22 and 23 Car. 2, c. 20, An Act for the Relief and Release of poor distressed Prisoners for Debt (1670).

[57] 7 and 8 Will. 3, c. 12, An Act for Relief of poor Prisoners for Debt or Damages (1696).

during the war, as well as to relieve the poor prisoners." Debtors owing
less than a hundred pounds could be released if either they enlisted
themselves or they could find a substitute to do so; enlistment, however,
was for the duration of the war rather than an indefinite period.[58] These
statutes were widely used. The last measure to sanction the policy,
passed in 1760, was more restricted, being concerned only with debtors
who had been mariners or had already served in army or navy and were
thus especially well qualified "to serve his Majesty by Sea or Land."[59]

In 1795 local authorities, attempting to find their quotas of recruits,
offered high bounties as inducements to debtors confined in prison. It
was said that "these desperate men were a very bad element in the
navy. In 1797 they combined with the United Irishmen, of whom large
numbers had been drafted into the fleet as vagabonds, to give a very
dangerous political character to the mutinies at the Nore and on the
south of Ireland."[60] The device of enlisting debtors, with all its dangers,
had its uses in providing soldiers and sailors in time of extreme need.
But it could offer no permanent solution to the general problem of the
debtor without means to pay.[61]

During the period of the wars with revolutionary France it was suggested that impressment might be used to dispose of men suspected of
stirring up unrest in industry or the merchant navy. Pitt was informed
by a correspondent who had been in the West of England of discontent
among certain men employed in the clothing business and told that
manufacturers were anxious to get rid of such "turbulent spirits," since
they were having to pay them nine shillings a week to keep out of their
workshops where they spoiled the work done by the hated machines.
The clothiers suggested that these men "might be made useful to their
Country in the Army and Navy. Their present Masters would provide for
their Families." If the government were sympathetic to the proposal, the
writer offered to make a list of between three and four thousand men
who had already repeatedly broken the peace in a very flagrant manner.
"I need not surmise to you, Sir," he concluded, "the great Caution necessary to be used should you think the Plan eligible, as should it be
known, and not put into effect, the consequences might be dreadful to
those who had embarked on it."[62]

[58] 2 and 3 Anne, c. 16, An Act for Discharge out of Prison such Insolvent Debtors
as shall serve or procure a Person to serve, in Her Majesty's Fleet or Army (1703).
[59] 1 Geo. 3, s. 17, An Act for Relief of Insolvent Debtors (1760).
[60] Encyclopaedia Britannica, etc. (11th ed., 1910), Vol. 14, article on impressment,
p. 346, at p. 347.
[61] For an example of both legal and illegal protests by debtors, see The Annual
Register (1770), Vol. 13, pp. 163–164.
[62] See letter of Thomas Phipps Howard, June 29, 1796, in Chatham MSS 146, 30/8,
146 (Public Record Office).

Although this ingenious proposal was not accepted, there is evidence that, at a later stage in the war, impressment was used against strikers, especially when the dispute involved crews of merchantmen in port. This came to light almost accidentally, as a result of a petition presented in 1814 by Lord Archibald Hamilton on behalf of the Clyde shipowners, praying that masters of ships of fifty tons and upwards might not be subject to impressment. He complained of lack of uniformity in the enforcement of impressment in the north, while another member of Parliament wanted to know whether it was still being practiced on the Thames. Dundas replied that impressment was necessary as long as hostilities against America continued, "but it was so reduced, that whereas it formerly used to produce from 70 to 100 men per month, in the last month only five men were pressed, three of whom the officer had been desired to impress as riotous persons."[63] This prompted Samuel Whitbread to ask for fuller particulars of the three men and of the circumstances. The reply was that the Admiralty did not designate those to be pressed, and that "when the impress was slack" officers did not visit the ships with particular diligence; instead, as a favor to the masters, they allowed them to choose which men they would retain, "and then, if sailors were idle or riotous, the master might inform the impress officers that they would do him no harm by taking such or such persons."[64]

But instances had in fact occurred when men demanding higher wages were impressed as riotous on orders given by the Admiralty. Thus, only two years earlier, the *Newcastle Chronicle* had reported that "near thirty riotous seamen were taken on the Tyne at Shields and lodged safe in His Majesty's ship *Transit*. The peace of this port has frequently been disturbed, under pretence of demanding more wages; but now positive orders were given by the Admiralty to the commanding officers here to impress such lawless hands and send them to the Nore."[65]

PRISONS AS RECRUITING DEPOTS

In the days when Pepys was at the Navy Office, criminals who were sent to man the ships of war were known as "Bridewell Birds";[66] in the eighteenth and nineteenth centuries they went under the more prosaic

---

[63] "Impressment of Seamen," *Parl.Debates* (1813–1814), Vol. 27, H.C., May 27, 1814, cols. 1030–1032 and June 1, 1814, cols. 1038–1039.
[64] "Impressment of Seamen," H.C. (May 27, 1814), *Parl.Debates* (1813–1814), Vol. 27, col. 1039.
[65] "Newcastle Chronicle," Feb. 20, 1812, quoted by Élie Halévy, *A History of the English People in 1815* (1924), Note 1, at p. 48.
[66] *Parl.Debates* (1833), 3rd s., Vol. 20, at col. 645.

title of "civil power men."[67] Indeed, it was largely because crews included so many convicts and social undesirables that many who were opposed to flogging in general were reluctant to support its abolition in the navy, because they felt discipline could not be maintained without it.

A regular statutory system for the enlistment of criminals sentenced to death, transportation or imprisonment, was initiated in the Mutiny Acts of 1701 and 1703.[68] To obviate the long delay that usually occurred between notification of the royal intention to grant a conditional pardon in a particular case and the issue of the next general pardon, which the offender could plead in court, judges were empowered, on receipt of a warrant for pardon on condition of enlistment, to require the sheriff or keeper of the gaol to hand over the prisoners immediately. This procedure was confirmed by a further statute in 1768.[69]

The Mutiny Act of 1765 included a curious variant. A court martial was empowered to sentence any deserter not deserving capital punishment to serve in foreign parts, either for life or for a limited period.[70] This provision was kept in full force between 1807 and 1812 and was not finally abolished until 1826. A deserter could either be transported as a felon or put "at the disposal of His Majesty for service as a soldier in any of His Majesty's forces, at home or abroad, for life or otherwise, as His Majesty shall think fit." Thus, even within the forces themselves, compulsory service became an alternative to transportation.[71]

It was in fact becoming an integral part of the penal system. Prison sentences could be interrupted if prisoners agreed to join the navy or army. "The gaols have also been occasionally drained," commented a contemporary, "in order to make up the deficiencies of the ordinary

---

[67] "Impressment of Seamen," H.C. (March 4, 1834), Parl.Debates (1834), 3rd s., Vol. 21, cols. 1063–1113, Buckingham, ibid., at col. 1097.

[68] 1 Anne, St. 2, c. 16, An Act for punishing Officers or Soldiers, who shall mutiny or desert her Majesty's Service in England or Ireland, etc. (1701) and 2 and 3 Anne, c. 20, An Act for punishing Mutiny, Desertion, and false Musters, and for better paying of the Army and Quarters, etc. (1703).

[69] 8 Geo. 3, c. 15, An Act for the more speedy and effectual Transportation of Offenders (1768).

[70] 6 Geo. 3, c. 8, s. 7, An Act for punishing Mutiny and Desertion; and for the better Payment of the Army and their Quarters (1765).

[71] See "Statement of the Number of Soldiers sentenced to General Service, and to Transportation, by General Courts Martial, in the years 1809, 1810 and 1811," Journals of the House of Commons (1812), Vol. 67, Appendix 5, at pp. 674–676. In this account, which includes the names of deserters and their regiments, some of the headings summarize the ways in which they were dealt with: "Desertion, being the 2d time General Service, and marked with D"; "Transportation as a felon for life, but remitted for General Service"; "Transportation for 3 years, but commuted for General Service."

supply."[72] Death sentences, then so frequently imposed, could be commuted on the same basis: "His Majesty has approved of the proposal contained in the letter from the Recorder of London, which is enclosed with a list of convicts in Newgate. Directs him, therefore, to order a proper person to examine which of the convicts may be fit for H.M.'s service, that warrants for pardon may be prepared accordingly."[73] Many similar letters are to be found in the Calendar of *Home Office Papers*. One, from the Earl of Rochford, emphasizes the punitive element, revealing that the King had ordered that the forces to be stationed on the unhealthy West Coast of Africa should be supplied rather "with such men as must look upon that duty as a mitigation of their sentences than with well-deserving volunteers."[74]

The outbreak of war with the American colonies drastically curtailed and eventually ended the possibility of transporting offenders to America. The problem of what to do with them at home thus became, in itself, as urgent as that of finding soldiers and sailors for service abroad. In 1776, Lord Harcourt, Lord Lieutenant of Ireland, wrote to the Secretary of State, Lord Weymouth, complaining that the Irish gaols were full of convicts under sentence of transportation. He proposed to pardon such of them as were fit and serviceable men "on condition of their entering into His Majesty's land and sea service, as I shall direct." Lord Weymouth replied that such a measure "has been of late in many instances pursued here, and Mis Majesty approved of your granting pardons to prisoners in the several gaols of Ireland under those circumstances." He added, however, that before pardon was granted the prisoners should be thoroughly examined as to their fitness for service, and that particular care should be taken that "this kind of recruit . . . be considered rather in a different light from those who enter voluntarily."[75]

In England there was great reluctance to face the task of setting up penitentiaries as an alternative to transportation, but it was some years before anywhere could be found for a new penal colony abroad, and convicts were accumulating in the prisons at an alarming rate. It was in an attempt to meet this dilemma, if only temporarily, that the Act of 16 Geo. 3 was passed in 1776, permitting hard labor in the galleys on the Thames to be substituted for transportation either as the original

[72] See "Observations on the Means of increasing the Regular Army," *The Edinburgh Review* (1807–1808), Vol. 11, pp. 171–182, at pp. 172–173.
[73] *Calendar of Home Office Papers of the Reign of George III, 1766–1769*, (1879), Vol. 2, No. 1190, p. 468.
[74] *Ibid.*, No. 1200, p. 470.
[75] Government correspondence in the Irish State Paper Office, quoted by W. E. H. Lecky, *A History of England in the Eighteenth Century*, Vol. 4 (1906), Note 3, at pp. 346–347.

sentence or as an alternative to capital punishment.[76] In the former case the period to be served was from three to ten years, in the latter it was left to the discretion of the Secretary of State. Meanwhile the existing prisons were becoming increasingly overcrowded and at the same time the very war that had hindered transportation accentuated the demand for manpower for the services. Thus the war gave a new impetus to the pardoning of criminals on condition of enlistment.

This convenient interchangeability between the penalties of death, transportation or imprisonment, and forcible enlistment in the army or navy became established by statutory authority and administrative precedent, with impressment emerging as a powerful measure of crime prevention and a *de facto* legal sanction. Like transportation, it provided protection and a sense of security by long-term elimination of offenders from society, as well as satisfying a national need. Together with transportation, it came to represent one of the major expedients of British penal policy.

Moreover, unlike the regular penalties, it was a convenient means of dealing with suspects, as well as with offenders who could actually be convicted. Robberies were daily compounded before the magistrates, on condition that the thief would be handed over to the tender. The press-gang could be brought into operation where an offense could not be legally proved but where there was strong reason to suspect particular persons, or where a raid on the headquarters of a gang of known criminals seemed desirable. In 1782 it was reported that "a press-gang, having received intelligence of a house near Poplar, where the Thieves skulk till the evening, when they commence their depredations, went very unexpectedly and surrounded the house, from which they took seventeen and carried them away to the tender at the Tower."[77] This operation, except in its conclusion, is hardly distinguishable from a raid by a reguarly constituted detachment of police. Even convicts who had served their sentence were not safe, but might be pounced upon by the press-gangs as soon as they stepped through the prison gates.

The extensive drafting of criminals into the army and navy could not fail to provoke a certain amount of protest from the services themselves. In 1773 the Lords of the Admiralty emphatically expressed "their wishes that no more convicts may be ordered on board H.M.'s ships, as such persons may not only bring distempers and immoralities among their companies, but may discourage men of irreproachable character from

[76] 16 Geo. 3, c. 43, An Act to authorize, for a limited Time, the Punishment by Hard Labour of Offenders who, for certain Crimes, are or shall become liable to be transported to any of his Majesty's Colonies and Plantations (1776), ss. 1 and 2.
[77] "Old British Spy," *The Public Advertiser*, September 21, 1782.

entering H.M.'s service, seeing they are to be ranked with common malefactors."[78] The army felt much the same. Viscount Barrington, directed to send a proper person to examine the fitness of a batch of convicts pardoned on condition they enlisted, took the opportunity to point out that "the commanding officers of the several corps abroad are very much averse to accept men under such circumstances." He added the warning that it would introduce "great uneasiness and confusion into the service if these convicts should be put into H.M.'s regiments for a limited time, when the honest volunteer engages to serve for life."[79]

In 1777 Temple Luttrell, putting forward a bill for the more effectual manning of the navy, was able to say in the Commons, without fear of contradiction, "When an alarm of war was sounded throughout Great Britain and Ireland in 1770, press warrants were issued and continued in execution five months: you then swept the refuse of the gaols, and the outcasts of almost every town and hamlet."[80] In similar vein, a historian of the navy has described an arrival in Portsmouth of the *Stirling Castle*, "with four hundred and eighty men, of whom two hundred and twenty-five were the pressed refuse of gaols and scum of streets. She was full of fever and other sickness, and when the diseased had been sent ashore, but one hundred and sixty men remained for duty." In the course of a major attack on the dying system of impressment in 1833, Buckingham alleged that "it arrived to such a pitch at last, that these men, the scourings of gaols, actually came on board in draughts of forty and fifty, with a mark against their names, as sent by the civil power . . . so that a ship of war, instead of being the home, as she ought to be, of a superior class of men, anxious to serve their country with honour, was converted into a receptacle of the violators of the law, where criminals of every shade and hue were to mingle in one common mass, till each contaminated the other down to the lowest degree of turpitude."[81] Sir Edward Codrington averred that when he had last been appointed to command, "seven-and-twenty men were sent on board who had just been taken out of irons . . . on looking to the hands of these men, he found they were as soft as those of young ladies, and fit for no purpose that he knew but

[78] *Calendar of Home Office Papers of the Reign of George III, 1770–1772* (1881), Vol. 3, No. 604, p. 228.

[79] *Calendar of Home Office Papers of the Reign of George III, 1766–1769* (1879), Vol. 2, No. 1193, p. 469.

[80] "Debate in the Commons on Mr. Temple Luttrell's Bill for the more easy and effectual Manning of the Navy," H.C. (March 11, 1777), *Parl.History* (1777–1778), Vol. 19, cols. 81–103, at col. 86.

[81] "Impressment," H.C. (August 15, 1833), *Parl.Debates* (1833), 3rd s., Vol. 20, cols. 636–695; Buckingham, *ibid.*, at col. 645. See also for similar instances of "compounding robberies before magistrates," *ibid.*, cols. 644 and 646.

picking pockets. He gave notice that it was impossible they could be useful to him, and they would demoralise his crew; but the answer was, that it was desirable, that they should leave London, and that the Lord Mayor wished it." He had equally resented the fact that poachers were often sent to the fleet, "a class not very agreeable on land, and who certainly did not improve either as company or in usefulness at sea." The system, he concluded with disgust, simply "gave an opportunity of sending all the rogues and vagabonds in the country that the Magistrates were anxious to get rid of on board the fleet."[82]

There was reluctance on the part of the authorities to divulge the full extent to which criminals were being enlisted in the army, a reluctance that, in itself, hinted that the practice was widespread. In 1812 a member moved in the Commons "that there be laid before this House, a return to the number of persons, who, since the 1st of January 1810, have been directed to be transported either having been capitally convicted or by original sentence, and who have been discharged on condition of entering into the army or navy, and also of those who, within the same period have received free pardons." The practice of enlisting convicts might be perfectly justifiable in certain cases and to a limited extent, but he suspected that it was being considerably extended, as was the number of free pardons, an "unwise and indefensible excess, and a total negligence in the exercise of the prerogative of the crown in this respect." He contended, further, that both pardons and enlistments had been arranged on the recommendation of Mr. Graham, Superintendent of the hulks, without any regular enquiry by the Home Secretary into the offences and characters of the criminals or the opinions of the judges who had tried them. It was a question of the administration of the penal law, as well as of the effects of such a system on the discipline and character of the army.[83]

The Secretary of State, Richard Ryder, refused thus to be put on the defensive and vigorously affirmed the virtues of the system as a means of reforming offenders. He made no attempt to deny that convicts had been drafted into the forces in considerable numbers, admitting that in the past more than five hundred such men had been dropped in a single batch into the army or navy. In particular, he referred to three regiments composed entirely of convicts, which had been highly praised by their comrades for their gallantry and irreproachable conduct. What might appear an undue severity, such as the granting of a pardon only on

82 *Ibid.*, col. 687.
83 "Motion respecting Convicts Discharged upon Entering the Army or Navy," H.C. (March 11, 1812), *Parl.Debates* (1812), Vol. 21, cols. 1253–1258, at cols. 1253 and 1254.

condition of enlistment for life, had been softened by giving the men the chance at some time to "revisit their native country again, and be returned to their families and friends." Enlistment under these conditions he regarded as a most valuable means both of encouraging good behavior and of countering the danger that criminals let loose on society, would return to their old habits.[84]

Sir Samuel Romilly could not accept these arguments, deprecating as he did the whole system of relying upon the royal prerogative of mercy to mitigate the barbaric severity of the capital laws. The need for recruits rather than the conduct of the offenders was, he objected, the determining factor in granting pardons.[85] Wilberforce, on the other hand, supported Ryder, although he suggested it would be better to mix these men with the older corps than to form them into special regiments. This brought the indignant retort from a General that the army did not want "gaol-birds" to lower the tone of the regular regiments now that their moral prestige had so much improved.[86] Nevertheless the motion was defeated and the administration was not called upon to give a fuller account of its use of impressment as a penal measure. After all, as Lecky later observed, "It is indeed a curious thing to notice how large a part of the reputation of England in the world rests upon the achievements of a force which was formed mainly out of the very dregs of her population, and to some considerable extent even out of her criminal classes."[87]

OUTGROWING IMPRESSMENT

Even during the reign of William III an Act had been passed to provide an alternative to impressment in the registration of thirty thousand seamen, with an annual retaining fee, ready to man the navy in time of need.[88] A similar scheme on a smaller scale was put forward in the middle of the eighteenth century.[89] Ironically, both attempts were defeated in the name of liberty. The Statute of William III was repealed in the following reign, on the ground that it introduced a system of legal

[84] *Ibid.*, cols. 1254–1256.
[85] *Ibid.*, cols. 1257–1258.
[86] *Ibid.*, col. 1258.
[87] W. E. H. Lecky, *A History of England in the Eighteenth Century*, Vol. 4 (1906), p. 347.
[88] 7 and 8 Will. 3, c. 21, An Act for the Increase and Encouragement of Seamen (1696).
[89] "Debate in the House of Commons on a Plan for speedily Manning the Navy" (April 14, 1749), *Parl.History* (1747–1753), Vol. 14, cols. 538–562; *ditto* (May 3, 1749), *ibid.*, cols. 562–563. See also William Coxe, *Memoirs of the Administration of the Right Honourable Henry Pelham*, etc. (1829), Vol. 2, pp. 66–70.

slavery.[90] The later proposal was opposed as a scheme for extending government patronage and buying the votes of such seamen as were registered.[91] Hostility proved obdurate: referring to the repeal of the seventeenth century statute, the economic historian, David Macpherson, commented in 1805, "though many schemes have since been laid before the public, yet so many objections have been stated, that no law has yet been framed for so important a matter as having a competent number of seamen continually in readiness for the navy, without having recourse to the barbarous and unconstitutional practice of pressing."[92] Apart from the imputation of bribery, the objections reflected a fundamental tenet of the eighteenth century Whigs, with their deep suspicion of bureaucracy and opposition to any extension of the influence of the central power. As Halévy has said, they preferred, "as more in harmony with the spirit of a free constitution, the irregular method of the press to be bureaucratic order, temporarily Introduced by William III."[93]

Others had justified impressment as the only practical means of supplying the armed forces in time of war. Chatham was convinced that "without impressing, it is impossible to equip a respectable fleet within the time, in which such armaments are usually wanted."[94] In war or danger such an argument inevitably had much weight. The system thus maintained its own momentum until the ending of the Napoleonic Wars. The peace that ensued, however, gave opponents of impressment an opportunity of which they were not slow to take advantage.[95] Southey caused a stir in 1816 by suggesting that the improved conditions of military and naval service would in time make impressment unnecessary.[96] Three years later a naval physician of considerable experience produced

[90] The argument that slavery was involved is similar to that advanced against early proposals to replace the death penalty by forced labour in the dockyards. The latter was opposed as being incompatible with the status and dignity of an Englishman; see this History, Vol. 1, p. 422.

[91] Speech by the Earl of Egmont, Parl.History (1747–1753), Vol. 4, at cols. 542 and 544.

[92] See David Macpherson, Annals of Commerce, Manufactures, Fisheries, and Navigation . . . Containing the Commercial Transactions of the British Empire and Other Countries, etc. (1805), Vol. 2, note at p. 683. On the suffering of the seamen, see Pepys, Diary (ed. by H. B. Wheatley, 1895), Vol. 5, p. 98 and Vol. 6, p. 220; also Vol. 6, p. 362 for an account of a meeting of the Committee of the Privy Council convened to discuss pressing.

[93] Élie Halévy, A History of the English People in 1815 (1924), p. 47.

[94] "Debate in the Lords on the Duke of Richmond's Motion respecting the Seizure of Falkland's Islands" (November 22, 1770), Parl.History (1765–1771), Vol. 16, cols. 1081–1119, at col. 1101.

[95] See, for instance, the forcible tract Remarks on Impressing Seamen (1810).

[96] See [R. Southey], "The Poor," The Quarterly Review (1816), Vol. 15, pp. 187–225, at p. 234.

a *Practical Plan for Manning the Royal Navy, and Preserving our Maritime Superiority, without Impressment.* Appeals were made to Wilberforce, so active in the campaign against slavery abroad, to lend his influence to the fight against something very like slavery at home.[97]

In 1824 Joseph Hume, an old campaigner against flogging in the army, launched a vigorous though unsuccessful attack in Parliament.[98] He affirmed that his aim was "not to cripple our navy . . . but to render it strong and irresistible; which, under the present system of coercive service, it never could be." He argued that "the cause of unwillingness to enter into the navy was the extensive power of arbitrary punishments," and it was this unwillingness that had made impressment necessary. He urged the House to accept a motion condemning the evils of impressment and to take advantage of the period of peace to find means of obviating them.[99] Although he failed to get sufficient support at that time, the view that the way to man the navy was to attract volunteers rather than to rely on pressed men was not allowed to drop. In 1825 a naval historian reiterated, "We have no right to say that we cannot raise men without impressment, until we have tried every means by which they might be induced to give their voluntary services." Apart from the cruelty of naval discipline, he pointed out, sailors could earn much more in the merchant service.[100]

In 1833, the parliamentary initiative was taken by Buckingham, who attacked impressment on grounds of public policy and social justice, outlining a combination of measures that he considered would make the use of impressment in future wholly unnecessary. His resolution

[97] See Thomas Urquhart, *Letter on the Evils of Impressment, With the Outline of a Plan for doing them away, on which Depend the Wealth, Prosperity, and Consequence of Great Britain* (1816), dedicated to the Prince Regent, originally written as a Letter to Lord Viscount Melville in 1815 under a different title but with emphasis on how "to do away with the evils of impressment." Ditto, *A Letter to Mr. Wilberforce, on the Subject of Impressment; Calling on him and the Philanthropists of this Country to prove those Feelings of Sensibility they have expressed in the Cause of Humanity on Negro Slavery, by acting with the same ardour and zeal in the cause of British Seamen* (1816). Ditto, *A Letter to Admiral C. Pole on his Answer to W. Smith,* etc. (1816).

[98] Hume spoke often on military matters. "His experience of field-service in India, added to abundant inborn shrewdness," writes Fortescue, "enabled him to speak with authority on diverse matters which were utterly hidden from the ordinary member of Parliament, and he was by no means ill-disposed towards the British soldier, nor disdainful of the military profession as a whole"; see The Hon. J. W. Fortescue, *A History of the British Army,* Vol. 11 (1923), pp. 84–85.

[99] "Impressment of Seamen," H.C. (June 10, 1824), *Parl.Debates* (1824), n.s., Vol. 11, cols. 1171–1197, at cols. 1172–1174; "Flogging in the Navy," in H.C. (June 9, 1825), *Parl.Debates* (1825), n.s., Vol. 13, cols. 1097–1110, at col. 1098.

[100] Edward Pelham Brenton, *The Naval History of Great Britain,* etc. (1825), Vol. 5, p. 258.

claimed "that the forcible Impressment of seamen for His Majesty's Navy is unjust, cruel, inefficient, and unnecessary; and that it is the duty of this House to avail itself of the present period of profound peace, to provide some means of manning the ships of his Majesty in time of war, without violation of the liberties of any class of His Majesty's subjects."[101]

The following year Sir James Graham, First Lord of the Admiralty, announced a change of policy.[102] At last "the practice of making his Majesty's ships serve as places of punishment and prisons for smugglers" was to be replaced by such inducements to voluntary enlistment as better pay and leave, limitation of the length of service, and rewards for faithful discharge of duty, all designed to improve the conditions of seamen and encourage voluntary enlistment. Normally nobody was to be kept in the service for more than five years without his consent, and after serving that period he was entitled to a certificate exempting him from further service for two years.[103] Although the legality of impressment was carefully maintained, in practice it became unnecessary. Only a year later the House was told that "the fishermen and boatmen who used formerly to run away from impressment now cheerfully and willingly came forward to enter."[104] Impressment might still be legal but it was also obsolescent.

Some twenty-five years later the completeness of the change was demonstrated by the evidence of almost all the witnesses before a Commission on the manning of the navy. There was general agreement that "the system of naval impressment, as practised in former wars, could not now be successfully enforced." This conclusion was reached not on grounds of humanity or justice, of political or popular opposition, but in severely practical terms: times had so far changed that impressment

101 "Impressment," H.C. (August 15, 1833), *Parl.Debates* (1833), 3rd s., Vol. 20, cols. 636–694, at col. 636. Buckingham's speech fills the first forty-five columns of the debate.

102 "Impressment of Seamen," H.C. (March 4, 1834), *Parl.Debates* (1834), 3rd s., Vol. 21, cols. 1063–1113, at cols. 1080–1090; "Impressment—Registration of Seamen," H.C. (March 17, 1835), *Parl.Debates* (1835), 3rd s., Vol. 26, cols. 1120–1132; "Enlistment of Seamen" (June 10, 1835), *Parl.Debates* (1835), 3rd s., Vol. 28, cols. 621–624; see also Lord John Russell, *ibid.*, cols. 622–623.

103 5 and 6 Will. 4, c. 24, An Act for the Encouragement of the voluntary Enlistment of Seamen, and to make Regulations for more effectually manning His Majesty's Navy (1835), and 5 and 6 Will. 4, c. 19, An Act to amend and consolidate the Laws relating to the Merchant Seamen of the United Kingdom and for forming and maintaining a Register of all the Men engaged in that Service (1835), known as the Merchant Seamen's Act.

104 "Enlistment of Sailors" (April 15, 1836), *Parl.Debates* (1836), 3rd s., Vol. 32, cols. 1107–1108. See also Arwel B. Erickson, *The Public Career of Sir James Graham* (1952), pp. 357–358.

was no longer feasible. The sailor who wished to avoid it could easily desert in foreign ports or escape after his return home; improvements in gunnery had revolutionized naval warfare, and "rendered it absolutely necessary that our vessels should in any future war be manned, not by a promiscuous collection of untrained men, such as impressment formerly provided, but by seamen who are practised gunners."[105]

As so often, however, a virtue was being made of necessity. "I have great doubts whether you could impress men as you did in the last war," a speaker in the Commons observed in 1850. "The opinion of the country would rise against you as one man, and compel you to a more constitutional course . . . I have arrived at the conclusion that the boldest and most frank way of dealing with the question is also the wisest, and that impressment by armed gangs should be abolished, as contrary to the spirit of the constitution, derogatory to the honour of the country, and injurious to the efficiency of the Navy."[106] There was, in fact, no formal abolition, but "the press-gang proved to be no more necessary than any other of the abuses to which men still clung because they were old; and though the Crown retained—as it still retains—the prerogative of pressing men into its service, the exercise of the prerogative was thenceforward condemned by what a great historian has called 'the unwritten law of the Constitution.'"[107]

Yet long after impressment for army or navy had ceased to serve the purposes for which it was designed, and long after its application to the ordinary citizen had become unthinkable, there lingered a nostalgic regret for so convenient and economical a method of eliminating those considered a social danger, combined with a genuine belief in its reformative value. Charles Clode, the military historian, compared it with the new system of tickets of leave for convicts released from prison under nominal police supervision, which he had seen established in his lifetime: "formerly the offenders were provided with the means of earning an honest living and a good name under the strict discipline of the Army, whereas in recent years they are turned loose upon the civil community, to get—what is next to impossible under the surveillance of the police— an honest living with a dishonest character."[108]

[105] See "Report of the Commissioners Appointed to Inquire into the Best Means of Manning the Navy" [2469], 1859, Parl.Papers (1859), Vol. 6, p. 1, point (32) at p. 11.
[106] "Supply—Impressment of Seamen," H.C. (May 23, 1850), Parl.Debates (1850), 3rd s., Vol. 111(3), cols. 279–285. The Hon. Captain E. A. J. Harris, ibid., at cols. 281 and 280.
[107] See Sir Spencer Walpole, A History of England from the Conclusion of the Great War in 1815 (1905), Vol. 4, pp. 432–433.
[108] Charles M. Clode, The Military Forces of the Crown, etc. (1869), Vol. 2, p. 14.

16

Manuel Montesinos y Molina—An Almost Forgotten Precursor of Penal Reform in Spain

ISRAEL DRAPKIN

La prision solo recibe al hombre.
El delito queda a la puerta.
(The prison only receives the man.
The offense remains at the gate.)

Montesinos

INTRODUCTION

It is a well-accepted fact that the origin of the deprivation of liberty, as a means of punishment for behavior considered criminal, is linked in Europe to the early Christian church. In the 6th century, especially in Italy, the Church had already established within monasteries the "carceri" (plural of "carcere"). These were special sections isolated by a closed gate in which the inmates were kept without care or vigilance, nourished with bread and vegetables. These "carceri" deteriorated to such an extent that during the 12th century the underground "carcere" at the monastery of San Martino del Campi was known as "vade in pace" (go in peace) to indicate that those who entered it were considered as good as dead.[1] This is perhaps one of the main reasons why, until today, deprivation of liberty, particularly for long periods, is considered by many to follow immediately after the death penalty in the scale of severity of punishments. Similar "carceri" were later established in other Italian cities, such as Como (1279), Lucca (1399), Padova (1399). Such a situation called for urgent and fundamental improvement, and awakened the idea of penal reform in some outstanding European personalities. However, in the meantime, the basic concepts and characteristics of these monastic "carceri" were soon transplanted to other European

[1] Ladislao Thot, *Ciencia Penitenciaria*, Biblioteca de la Revista de Identificación y Ciencias Penales, Universidad Nacional de La Plata, Argentina (240 pp., La Plata, 1937), p. 21.

countries and served as basis for the evolvement of their respective penal systems.

Apart from the few isolated attempts at penal reform in Europe during the 17th and 18th centuries and in the United States of America, especially due to the Quakers, it is actually during the first half of the 19th century that we find a persistent movement, both in theory and in practice, oriented toward the rehabilitation of offenders, based on humanitarian principles. Thus, long before the "parole" or the "conditional release" systems were legally sanctioned, their main principles—first, that good conduct should be rewarded by shortening the sentence; and second, that release should be under supervision and conditional on continued good conduct on the outside—were already being applied in the British Colony of New South Wales, in Australia, as early as 1790 "when Governor Phillips was given the power of conditional pardon over criminals transported there from England."[2] In New York, in 1817, a "good time" law was passed. Prison inspectors were given the power to release, after having served three-fourths of his sentence, "any convict sentenced to imprisonment for not less than five years, provided he could produce a certificate from the principal keeper, showing that his behavior had been good, and that from his net earnings there had been set aside and invested for his personal account not less than fifteen dollars per annum."[3] A similar system was established in 1825 in the Houses of Refuge in the United States.[4] In 1832, young delinquents of "La Petite Roquette" prison, in France, were granted conditional release. In 1835, in Spain, Montesinos started his own program in the prison at Valencia. Maconochie, in 1840, introduced his "mark system" at the Norfolk Island penal settlements. Obermaier, in 1842, developed his system of supervision in the prison of Munich, Germany. Bonneville de Marsangy proposed, in 1846, the system of "libération préparatoire."[5] Maconochie's basic ideas were taken up by Sir Walter Crofton who, in 1854, became Chairman of the Directors of Convict Prisons in Ireland, developing what is known as the Irish Penal System. There cannot be

[2] G. I. Giardini, "Parole," in Vernon C. Branham and Samuel B. Kutash, eds., Encyclopedia of Criminology (XXXVII, 527 pp., New York, Philosophical Library, 1949), p. 285.

[3] Fred E. Haynes, "Criminology" (2nd ed., XI, 497 pp. New York, McGraw-Hill, 1935), p. 392.

[4] Harry E. Barnes and Negley K. Teeters, "New Horizons in Criminology" (2nd ed., XVI, 887 pp., New York, Prentice-Hall, 1951), p. 778.

[5] André Normandeau, "Arnould Bonneville de Marsangy (1802–1894), Un Précurseur de la Criminologie Moderne," Revue de Science Criminelle et de Droit Pénal Comparé, Librairie Sirey, Paris, Nouvelle, Série, No. 2 (Avril-Juin, 1967, pp. 385–410), p. 389.

the slightest doubt that "the work of all of them resulted in something sufficiently permanent to give tangible proof that the principle of conditional release, combined with supervision and retention of legal control over the parolee for a period of time after release, is workable."[6]

Practically every author dealing with the problem of penal reform agrees that parole and conditional release did not appear as the outcome of the work of one person, but rather as the materialization of ideas floating in the penal atmosphere of that period. Even outstanding Spanish authors concur with this point of view.[7] And because "caution must at all times be used in making claims of specific credit in a historically evolving institution,"[8] we have not taken here a one-sided position, implying that Montesinos was the only or the most important precursor. What we do claim is that he certainly deserves a more important place than that given him until now in the history of the development of the penal reform movement. To prove this is the main purpose of this paper.

SPANISH PRISONS BEFORE MONTESINOS

To evaluate Montesinos' work it seems necessary to present a brief description of the prison situation in Spain before 1830. As elsewhere in Europe during the Middle Ages, deprivation of liberty as a means of punishment was practically unknown in Spain. There existed a number of what were known as "cárceles" (synonym of "carceri" or jails), where those suspected or accused of having committed an offense were held until they were brought before the judge and for the duration of their trial. In the famous "Las Siete Partidas," the Laws of Castile, compiled by order of King Alphonso X, known as the Wise, who reigned from 1252 until 1284 as successor of King Ferdinand III, it is stated (Law II, title II, paragraph VII) "Ca la carcel debe ser para guardar los presos, e non para facerlos enemiga, nin otro mal, nin darles pena en ella." (That the "carcel" should only be for keeping prisoners, neither to ill-treat them in any way, nor to punish them.) And later on, in Law IV, title XXXI, paragraph VII, "Ca la carcel non es dad para escarmentar los yerros, mas para guardar los presos tan solamente en elle fasta que sean judgados." (That the purpose of the "carcel" is not to correct faults, but

[6] G. I. Giardini, *op. cit.*, p. 286.

[7] Eugenio Cuello Calón, "Montesinos, Precursor de la Nueva Penologia," *Revista de Estudios Penitenciarios*, Dirección General de Prisiones, Madrid, España, Año XVIII, No. 159 (October-December 1962), pp. 43–66. (This particular issue of the Revista will be referred to from now on only as *Revista.*)

[8] Walter C. Reckless, "Criminal Behavior" (XI, 532 pp., New York, McGraw-Hill, 1940), p. 337.

to hold the prisoners until they be judged.)[9] In the Kingdoms of Castile and Aragon there were several kinds of "cárceles": public for commoners, feudal for Lords; monastic for monks, etc. Usually these "cárceles" were underground dungeons where the unfortunate inmates had to live under subhuman conditions. For many centuries they accomplished their task of receiving and keeping the human flesh of the miserable and the outcast. The walls and pavements were impregnated with their sweat, blood, and tears, while the echo of their vaults endlessly repeated their curses and lamentations. The inmates had to pay for their personal expenses, as well as for their release; food was terrible; hygienic conditions nonexistent; torture and corporal punishment an almost daily experience; and death, sooner or later, the most natural outcome. In the Spanish folklore there are many popular songs, known as "carceleras," short melancholic poems expressing how much better it is to be dead than to be in prison:

> "Mejor quisiera estar muerto
> que estar pasando la vida
> en este penal del Puerto,
> Puerto de Santa María."[10]

(I would prefer to be dead—than to carry on living—in this prison of the Port—the Port of Santa Maria.)

The earliest legal traces of these "cárceles" are found in the "Fuero Juzgo," the Spanish version of the "Forum judicum" of the Visigoths' compilation of Roman and Gothic Laws. It was first published by order of King Ferdinand III during the 13th century, and it is considered as one of the main sources for the study of the historical evolution of Spanish legislation. During the 14th century, Alphonso XI, King of Castile, introduced some legal improvements such as the abolition of torture, separation of sexes, and compulsory periodical visits to the "cárceles" by judges.[11] Unfortunately most of these measures were more an expression of royal goodwill than a step forward in the humanitarian treatment of offenders.

It is true that in England, France, Italy, the Netherlands, and other European countries, there were quite a number of penal reform precursors during the 17th and 18th centuries, but it is rather difficult to find any during the 16th century. In Spain, a country with a long tradition in this particular field, there are at least three writers well known for their important work. The first is Bernardino de Sandoval, a learned

[9] Constancio Bernaldo de Quiros, "Lecciones de Derecho Penitenciario" (296 pp., México, Imprenta Universitaria, 1953), pp. 43–44.
[10] Constancio Bernaldo de Quiros, ibid., p. 32.
[11] Ladislao Thot, op. cit., p. 24.

clergyman who, in 1564, published in Toledo his "Tractado del cuydado que se debe tener de los presos pobres" (Treatise on the care to be taken of poor inmates). In this work he considers the "cárceles" as a necessary evil, but demands good care of the inmates, better food, greater frequency of judges' visits, moral assistance, abrogation of payment during imprisonment and before release, as well as all the other physical and moral suffering imposed by the pitiless exploiters. The second is Thomás Cerdán de Tallada, a legal defender of prisoners, with his "Visita de la cárcel y de los presos" (Visiting jails and prisoners), dated Valencia 1574, where he makes a severe criticism of the prevailing conditions in the "cárceles" and, in a remarkable sketch of prison regulations, requests more hygienic and larger cells, with more light and ventilation; separation of sexes, still not implemented; and periodic visits to the "cárceles" by the judges so that they be in a position to evaluate not only the behavior of the inmates but also the care with which they were being dealt, control of their food, etc. The third of these writers is Cristobal de Chaves who, in Sevilla in 1591, in his "Relación de las cosas de la cárzel de Sevilla y su trato" (The state of affairs at the Prison of Sevilla and its treatment) stresses, almost two centuries before John Howard in his "The State of Prisons in England and Wales" (1777), the chaotic state of a number of prisons, particularly that at Sevilla, with its torture and deep-rooted corruption; the immorality of the wardens and their subordinates, who used to charge even for the water used by the inmates; the frequency with which brutal robberies, fighting quarrels, murders, and all sorts of other crimes were committed inside "that hell."[12] He also suggests quite a number of measures to improve the situation.[13] Once again, it is only fair to acknowledge that the work of these Spanish authors contained a good number of theoretical, well-intended proposals, but were empty of practical means for their implementation.[14] These efforts, nonetheless, began to bear fruit later on, in 1799, when the "Asociación del Buen Pastor" (Association of the Good Shepherd) was officially established in Madrid, in order to assist the "poor inmates" of the city.[15]

As in some other European countries, the first Spanish correctional institutions appeared only during the 16th century. They were known by the generic term of "presidios," from the Latin expression "praesidium,"

[12] Luis Jiménez de Asúa, "Tratado de Derecho Penal," Tomo I (1129 pp., Buenos Aires, Editorial Losada, 1950), p. 651.

[13] Ladislao Thot, op. cit., pp. 11–12.

[14] Juan del Rosal, "Derecho Penal Español" (Vol. I, pp. 463 and Vol. II, pp. 344, Aguirre Torre, Madrid, 1960), Vol. I, p. 84.

[15] Luis Jiménez de Asúa, op. cit., p. 669.

meaning a fort or garrison town, surrounded by defensive walls. To this day the name "presidio" is widely used in Spain and Latin American countries as a synonym for prison or penitentiary.[16] These "presidios" served three main purposes: (1) deprivation of liberty as a means of punishment; (2) satisfaction of the vindicative need of the public; and (3) exploitation of convict work for utilitarian ends.

The earliest of such "presidios" were the "galeras" (galleys), also utilized by other maritime powers of the day such as England, France, Venice, etc. Already in 1505, nineteen inmates of the "cárceles" of Barcelona were taken to the "galeras" of Ramón de Cardona, but they were legally established by a law promulgated on January 31, 1530, by King Charles I.[17] These "galeras" existed until 1803 and were in fact floating "presidios" the miserable galley-slaves wandered, with their sores and sorrows, through all the known ports and seas of the world. Not only "Don Quijote" of Cervantes (especially in Part I, chapter XXII), but the entire Spanish literature of the "Siglo de Oro" (Golden Century) during the 16th and first half of the 17th centuries, always describe the criminal offender as a "galeote" (galley slave). Chained to the rowing bench, the "galeote" worked 12 hours a day, receiving as stimulating caresses frequent lashes from the boatswain. A wooden plug in his mouth prevented his screaming and cursing. When sinking came as the outcome of battles or storms these galley slaves were the sure victims. The sea rather than land was the most frequent place of their tombs.

When ships started to use steam instead of oars and sails, the galleys became useless and were "run aground." The convicts were then transferred to the "presidios arsenales" (navy dockyards) where they performed the most harsh of duties. In 1771, the King of Spain, Charles III, published his "Novísima Recopilación" (Newest Compilation), where it is stated (7th Law, 40th chapter, 12th book) that "incorrigible offenders" should be transferred to the shipyards of Ferrol, Cadiz, and Cartagena for hard labor tasks.[18] Their lives were still miserable, working as they did in chain gangs.

During the same century, Spain also utilized convicts' work in the so-called "presidios militares" (military fortresses), huge barracks where the main fortification work was executed by the convicts. In the bylaws

---

[16] In spite of the fact that the original Latin source is the same—praesidium—in Soviet Russia it has an entirely different meaning. It refers to the chairmanship or presidency of all sorts of political or governmental committees or organizations, from the highest to the lowest. In the course of time and in different cultures, the word seems to have lost its pejorative sense and acquired a dignified one. *Honi soit qui mal y pense. . . !*

[17] Eugenio Cuello Calón, "La Moderna Penología" (Bosch, Barcelona, 1958), p. 361.

[18] Elías Neuman, "Prisión Abierta" (Doctoral Thesis, XXXV, 611 pp., Buenos Aires, Depalma, 1962), pp. 22–23.

of the "presidio militar" of Ceuta—a Spanish enclave in Northern Africa—dated 1716, it is stated that "in order to avoid offensive attacks by convicts, they should be put in chains like terrible and wild beasts."[19] In similar conditions, other convicts were used in the quicksilver mines of Almaden.[20]

Women were not spared. They also received their quota of misery and maltreatment. If convicted for stealing, dissolute behavior, prostitution, vagrancy, and other similar offenses, they were sent to the "Casa de Galera" (House of Galleys), knowing by this name although they were not floating "presidios." Some years ago, the "Revista de la Escuela de Estudios Benitenciarios" (Journal of the School of Penitentiary Studies) of Madrid published a special little pamphlet reproducing a report of 1608,[21] describing the basic philosophy and the bylaws of the galleys for women established in Madrid, Valladolid, and Granada. These "galleys" were meant for women who, because they "adan vagando y están ya perdidas" (are roaming and are already lost) "es necesario castigo y rigor" (punishment and sternness are necessary).[22] On reception, a newcomer had to be "stripped of all her ornaments and clothes, and her head-hair shaved with a razor, as is done to the male criminals sent to the galleys." "Food will consist only of black bread, of the lowest quality, a slice of cheese or a radish, a small dish of turnips or cabbage, and once a week, a slice of beef." They were supposed to work continuously and "never have a minute of respite, so that with their toil and labor they should help the expenditure of the galley."[23] These galleys were furnished with every means of coercion, such as "chains, handcuffs, fetters, muzzles, stocks," so that "just by seeing these instruments they should be frightened and scared," because the galleys were meant to be "very painful jails, where the greatest sternness should prevail."[24] If a woman was sent to the galleys for a second time, "she will get twice the original punishment, kept in irons, and marked on the right shoulder with the coat of arms of the city or town, so that it should be known that she had been in the galleys twice." If she returned for a third time, "punishment should be trebled" and, if she came back a fourth time, "she should be hanged in front of the main gate of the galley."[25]

Meanwhile the ideas of Beccaria had reached Spain. Their principal

[19] "Anuario Penitenciario Administrativo y Estadístico," Dirección de Establecimientos Penales (Madrid, 1889), p. 15.

[20] Elías Neuman, op. cit., p. 24, footnote 42.

[21] Francisco Fernández de Córdoba, "La Obrecilla de Sor Magdalena de San Jerónimo" (40 pp., Valladolid, 1608).

[22] Francisco Fernández de Córdoba, ibid., p. 18.

[23] Francisco Fernández de Córdoba, ibid., p. 20.

[24] Francisco Fernández de Córdoba, ibid., p. 21.

[25] Francisco Fernández de Córdoba, ibid., p. 23.

champion was Manuel de Lardizabel y Uribe (1739–1820). In 1770, King Charles III, interested in introducing the new humanitarian spirit in the Spanish penal legislation, ordered the Supreme Court of Justice of the Kingdom to prepare basic preliminary studies. Lardizabal was charged with the task and published his famous "Discurso" on the subject[26] which, according to Jiménez de Asúa,[27] constituted the doctrinary basis for the penal reform introduced later on. Lardizabal went further than Beccaria and Bentham in that, while accepting the utilitarian and intimidative purpose of the penalty, he put the emphasis on the correction of the offender, "para hacerlo mejor, si puede ser, y para que no vuelva a perjudicar a la sociedad"[28] (to make him better, if possible, and so that he should not damage society again). The rehabilitation of the offender "jamás debe perderlo de vista el legislador"[28] (should never be forgotten by the legislator).

Later on, the economic interests of the State changed, and accordingly convicts were used in public works. They were brought in chain gangs to build roads, canals, tunnels, and other such projects. They slept in barracks or even outdoors, kept by armed guardians.[29] This system was enforced up to the beginnings of the last century when, slowly, the situation began to change. In order to satisfy public demand, the convicts were lodged in special establishments where they continued to work on special industrial assignments. These were known is Spain as "presidios industriales" (industrial prisons). Soon after the "Ordenanza General de los Presidios del Reino" (General Ordinance of the Prisons of the Kingdom) of April 14, 1834,[30] the vindicative and utilitarian purposes of these "presidios industriales" were no longer stressed, and they became the "presidios civiles o correccionales" (civil or correctional prisons). Here, at least in a discursive and theoretical way, the aim was to reform the inmate through special individual treatment. In fact, much was still to be achieved. It was precisely in one of these "presidios correccionales"

[26] Manuel de Lardizabal y Uribe, "Discurso sobre las penas contraído a las leyes criminales de España para procurar su reforma" (Madrid, Ibarra, 1782). There is another edition by Rafael Salillas, in his "Biblioteca Criminológica y Penitenciaria," Madrid, 1916.

[27] Luis Jiménez de Asúa, op. cit., p. 662.

[28] José Antón Oneca, "Los fines de la pena según los penalistas de la Ilustración," Revista de Estudios Penitenciarios, Dirección General de Prisiones, Madrid, España, Año XX, No. 166 (pp. 415–427, July-September 1964), p. 422.

[29] Juan J. Dichio, "El Presidio, Historia de una Institución penal," Revista de Estudios Penitenciarios, No. 3 (La Plata, Argentina, 1958), p. 176.

[30] Gregorio Lasala Navarro, "Los Presidios Civiles," Revista de Estudios Penitenciarios, Dirección General de Prisiones, Madrid, España, Vol. XXII, No. 172 (January-March 1966), pp. 103–128.

or penitentiaries in Valencia where Montesinos started his career as a penal reformer.

It may be worthwhile to mention that, except for the era of the great expeditions and discoveries of the 15th, 16th, and 17th centuries, when most frequently the crews consisted of convicts—as was the case with Columbus, when he discovered America—transportation had no success in Spain. It is true that some people thought of utilizing some of the islands discovered by Columbus, such as the Hispaniola (today Haiti and the Dominican Republic), for transportation purposes, but the idea was abandoned. The same happened with a number of similar plans during the last 100 years, such as those of 1875, 1889, and even as late as 1934. Transportation unlike Portugal (from 1446 to her possessions in Africa, and from 1603 to Brazil until its independence in 1826), England (from 1597 to 1776 to America, and from 1787 to 1851 to Australia), and France (from 1854 to 1937 to the French Guiana) never occurred in Spain.[31] As a Spanish example of transportation we can only mention the sending of convicts to some "presidios" in Northern Africa, such as those of Ceuta and Melilla, and in the islands of Alhucemas and Peñon de Velez de la Gomera, all considered as integral parts of the Kingdom. Even these cases have been abolished since 1913.[32]

During the 19th century the Spanish penal reform movement is pervaded by two main figures: Concepción Arenal (1820–1894), Prison Surveyor during 30 years of her fruitful life, a prolific writer, whose "Manual del Visitador del Preso" (Handbook of the Prisoner Surveyor), published in 1896,[33] has been translated into several other languages and is considered a classic in this particular field, and Manuel Montesinos y Molina, much less known, not a writer but a man of action, who introduced, in practice, the fundamental bases of a progressive penal system, leading to a kind of conditional release, years before Maconochie, Obermaier, and Crofton proposed their respective systems.

HIS LIFE AND WORK

Montesinos was born in a small Andalusian village known by the name of San Roque, near Gibraltar, in the southernmost Spanish province of Cadiz. The date of his birth has been the object of serious contradictions among his biographers. Vicente Boix, chronicler of the city of

[31] Elías Neuman, op. cit., pp. 25–41.
[32] Gregorio Lasala Navarro, op. cit., p. 107.
[33] Concepción Arenal, "Obras Completas," Vol. XIII (Madrid, Sucesores de Rivadeneyra, 1894–1896). The complete edition has 14 volumes.

Valencia and a personal friend of Montesinos, states in his already classical work,[34] which appeared during Montesinos' lifetime, that he was born on June 17, 1796.[35] But if we take into consideration the fact that, in his official Record of Services, kept at the archives of the Civil Service of Spain,[36] it is stated that he started his career as a "soldado distinguido" (distinguished soldier) on 2 June 1808, this would mean at the age of twelve years, which is a bit too much for such a young child. On the other hand, the inscription on his gravestone,[37] reads as follows: "Falleció el 3 de Julio de 1862, a los 69 años" (Died the 3rd of July 1862, at the age of 69 years), meaning that he was born in 1792, a date more acceptable and accepted than the previous one. Finally, it is important to take into consideration that in the facsimile of his "partida de bautismo" (certificate of baptism), also reproduced by F. Bueno,[38] it is easy to read that "Manuel Josef Cayetano" was born "el día veinte del mes de Junio de mil setecientos noventa años" (the 20th of June 1790). We personally believe that the last is the more acceptable birth date, since it lends itself to better matching with all the other data of his "curriculum vitae."

His childhood is almost unknown, and the first recorded fact about his adolescence is the beginning of his military career as a "distinguished soldier" on June 2, 1808 in the Spanish war against Napoleon. There is no need to particularize his military record, except for a few facts that may bear some relationship with his ulterior achievements. In July 1808, after a minimum of training, he participated in two battles—Andújar and Bailén. Juan José de San Martin, who later became a General and the Liberator of Argentine, Chile, and Peru from Spanish rule, also participated in the latter. By the end of that year things began to get bad for the Spanish troops and, on February 21, 1809, after their general capitulation, Montesinos was taken to France as a prisoner of war because he was not willing to serve José I, the Napoleon imposed King of Spain.[39] He spent his two first years in prison at Clermont-Ferrand, in Auvergne. In 1811 he ran away, but was caught at Carcassone, sentenced to death and, after being pardoned, he was transferred to the dreadful navy fortress of Toulon, in southern France, on the Mediterranean. Here he was kept until he was repatriated to Spain on June 5, 1814 after peace had been established between the two countries. He then joined a

34 Vicente Boix, "Sistema Penitenciario del Presidio Correccional de Valencia," (VII, 233 pp., Valencia, Imprenta del Presidio, 1850).
35 F. Bueno, "La Fecha de Nacimiento de Montesinos," in *Revista* (see footnote 7), pp. 203–208.
36 "Hoja de Servicios de Don Manuel Montesinos," in *Revista*, pp. 497–515.
37 F. Bueno, *ibid.*, p. 203.
38 F. Bueno, *ibid.*, pp. 206–207.
39 Ricardo Pieltain, "Vida Militar del Coronel Montesinos," in *Revista*, pp. 9–42.

cavalry regiment in Barcelona and carried on with his military duties until October 1823 when—as second lieutenant in the defeated Constitutional Army—he had to leave his country again, exiled to Gibraltar. In August 1824 he participated in a conspiracy to take over Tarifa, a nearby town but, on failing, he ran away toward Tanger, on the African coast of the Strait of Gibraltar, where he spent three years. Nothing certain is known about his activities during these three years, but there are speculations that, as a result of his meeting with San Martin at the battle of Bailén, he might have visited Latin America, where the war of independence from Spain had already started in several countries. Whatever the case, in June 1827 he was back and returned for the last time to active military service. In April 1830 he retired from the Army at his own request.

Montesinos, like William Penn and John Howard, was also made a prisoner and had a long and sad experience of what deprivation of liberty really means. The five terrible years of imprisonment in France, apart from contributing to his mastery of the French language, certainly influenced his interest in prison reform, especially if we take into consideration that the state of French prisons at the beginning of the last century was far from constituting the ideal place for a young person like Montesinos. The same cannot be said of the four years he spent in Gibraltar, Tangier, and perhaps Latin America where he was not a prisoner but a political exile participating in what is known today as "guerrilla" warfare.

When he retired from the army, he was a man of some 40 years, married, with a family, needing a remunerated job. Because of his military record, he was appointed as a part-time secretary to the Army Division of Valencia. Later on he was again appointed to the Provincial Paymaster's Bureau of the same city, also on a part-time basis. Finally, on June 5, 1832, he was transferred to the post of Paymaster of the "Presidio Correccional" at Valencia, thus marking the beginning of his remarkable work as a penitentiary reformer.

His new responsibilities were of a civil character, but a few days after the death of Ferdinand VII, on September 29, 1833, came the Spanish civil war between the supporters of Elizabeth II and the pretender Don Carlos. The war lasted for just over seven years and, apart from the armies of each side, the civil population participated as volunteers in the locally organized "Milicias Urbanas" (Town Militia). Montesinos, after having spent more than twenty years in the army, could not remain indifferent and enlisted in Valencia's Militia on November 24, 1833, and for four years acted both as civilian and militiaman.

In August 1834 the civil population of Valencia initiated a mutiny against the "Carlists" elements. Knowing that in the prisons of the city—Torres de Cuarte, Torres de Serranos, Ciudadela, and San Narciso—as well as in the Hospital and in the Archbishop's palace there were a great number of "Carlists" as prisoners or refugees, the mobs stormed all these places, killing and wounding many. The most serious incidents occurred at the "presidio" of Torres de Cuarte. As a result, the Director was dismissed from his office, and on September 6, 1834 Montesinos was appointed in his stead "ad interim."

A few weeks later, on October 23, 1834, he was promoted to Captain and, on August 17, 1835, he became Major. During 1836 and the first semester of 1837, he participated in at least twelve different battles. In that of Plá del Pou, March 29, 1837, he was wounded and taken prisoner, but managed to escape and went back to his Militia. He was decorated with the Cross of Saint Ferdinand. In July 1837 he was appointed Director of the "presidio" at Valencia and, from then on, with the exception of a minor military action, his last, on September 2, 1837, he devoted himself entirely to penitentiary affairs. In October 1837 he presented his resignation to the Militia, but it was rejected. He was kept, on a nominal basis until the end of December 1841 when he finally got his definite retirement, but not before being appointed Lieutenant Colonel (July 23, 1838), Colonel of Cavalry (October 19, 1840), and decorated with the Cross of Commander of the Order of Elizabeth the Catholic on August 12, 1841.[40]

His many years in the army and the militia and his everyday contact with other people under his command, made him most sensitive in his human relations and to the problems of "others," even if they were convicts. This is perhaps the main reason why he was always so interested in their security, welfare, and rehabilitation. There are many examples of his devotion to the inmates. For instance, soon after he was appointed Director "ad interim" in June 1835, more than 400 of his convicts were working on the highway of Las Cabrillas, near Buñol in the vicinity of Valencia, when General Cabreras, the leader of the Carlist Army, prepared to attack them, on the assumption that many of the convicts might join his side, once liberated from their jailers. Having been informed, Montesinos, alone, immediately rode from Valencia to the Castle of Buñol where the convicts were spending the night and, in spite of the darkness, the rain, and the mountainous condition of the region, he was able to lead them back to the prison at dawn the next day, without cause to complain about one single case of desertion or evasion.[41]

His warm dealings with the inmates of his "presidio" were duly

40 For more details, see Ricardo Pieltain, *ibid.*
41 "Hoja de Servicios de Don Manuel Montesinos," *ibid.*, p. 506.

rewarded by them. They respected and trusted him, as he trusted them. Prosper Mérimée, a famous French author of the last century, mentions in his book, *Lettres d'Espagne*, that, while travelling through Andalucía, he once met with a cheerful and self-confident convict of the "presidio" of Valencia on his way to another "presidio," carrying documents and money, as a personal emissary of his warden. . . ! There are quite a number of anecdotes in the same vein. When the well-known Spanish poet and politician Ramón de Campoamor (1817–1901) was Governor of Valencia, he was bothered with a terrible gang of bandits. He was determined to destroy them, but failed several times. He then asked Montesinos if among his convicts there was anyone who might be interested in accomplishing such a task, to be rewarded afterwards. Montesinos sent the Governor one of his inmates, whom he knew very well. The convict went alone to see the Governor, accepted the commission, campaigned for a couple of weeks with the assistance of a few soldiers, destroyed the gang and returned to the "presidio" "as if nothing had happened."[42] More than once he allowed his convicts to put on civilian clothing and go for a visit home, to attend a dying mother, or some other such circumstance. He often sent one of his inmates to change money in town. They always came back to the "presidio" and on time. Whenever he or his wife had to travel to Madrid or some other city, they were usually escorted by a guard of convicts. . . .

The "presidio" of Valencia was functioning then—1836—in the Torres de Cuarte, an old, dilapidated, insecure building that could not be adapted for human living quarters, even for convicts. Very soon he was convinced that it was useless as a prison, and even before being definitely appointed as Director, he managed, after protracted and difficult negotiations, to obtain other premises for the "presidio." In 1834, Spain ordered the expulsion of monks and friars, and many of their convents were empty and unoccupied. He obtained the Convent of San Agustin, in Valencia, on condition that the reparations and architectural changes that he might wish to introduce should be accomplished without fiscal funds, because the Government had no budget for such purposes, being still engaged in a costly civil war. Before the end of 1836 he transferred the 700 inmates from the Torres de Cuarte to the Convent of San Agustin, astonishing the population of Valencia with the show of an entire army of convicts, led by their corporals and foremen and, at their head, Colonel Montesinos himself, marching in perfect military order and formation to the accompaniment of drums and bugles, without one single incident or escape. The new premises were repaired by the same convicts without

[42] José Rico de Estasen, "El Coronel Montesinos. Un español de prestigio enropeo," (270 pp., Alcalá de Henares, Talleres Penitenciarios, 1948), p. 133.

expenditure from the national budget.[43] Unbelievable as it may seem, the fact is that this first move of his, this logical and necessary transfer of the "presidio," constituted one of the many arguments used by his enemies against him during his entire career, in spite of the evidence of his almost miraculous achievements in the old convent.[44]

During the next few years, Montesinos carried out a number of important changes in the former convent. For security and administrative purposes he reshaped the main entrance of the old convent in order to provide, in its immediate vicinity, the necessary space for the guards on duty and their lodging quarters, as well as for his own office and the others for the personnel of the "presidio." All these rooms had one door opening to the street outside and another to the inside of the prison, so that in case of an emergency they could immediately attend to their respective duties without having to run through the street. In order to provide more space for the inmates, he demolished the old and ruinous church, in the center of the convent and arranged instead a large courtyard, with a number of trees, a variety of birds, and even a little zoo with a Bengal tiger. Here the convicts could take a walk at their leisure, when free from other duties.[45] As a matter of fact, he transformed the convent into what is known today as a "minimum security" prison. The surrounding walls could be easily overcome, after crossing the large courtyard. The guard of the "presidio" consisted of a sergeant and two corporals, convicts themselves, and the main door's bolt was so simple and weak that anyone could dispose of it without great effort.[46] He repaired all the roofs of the building, arranged new dormitories, built a big kitchen, with a bread oven, and a communal restaurant nearby. Food was abundant, healthy, and of an excellent quality. He also arranged an emergency infirmary, with a well-equipped pharmacy and a small clean hospital, as well as other similar facilities. Medical assistance was of a very high standard, supplied by a general practitioner, a surgeon, and several nurse assistants. "Creo que la vida de un humbre, por desgraciado que sea, vale más que todo cuanto pueda gastarse," he used to say.[47] ("I think that a man's life, no matter how wretched he may be, is worthier than all that has to be spent.") He did not forget education and work. He built special quarters for a primary school where religious and

[43] Gregorio Lasala, "La Obra de Montesinos y su Influencia en la Legislación de su época," in Revista, pp. 74–96.

[44] Simón García Martín del Val, "Dias Amargos de Montesinos," in Revista, pp. 213–217.

[45] Gregorio Lasala, ibid., p. 77.

[46] Eugenio Cuello Calón, "La Moderna Penología," p. 370.

[47] Francisco Franco de Blas, "Formación Penitenciaria del Coronel Montesinos y su celebre Sistema," in Revista, pp. 97–122, p. 101.

secular education were imparted. He also prepared a number of rooms where the inmates could work by closing the cloister's arches and by installing in them a variety of workshops such as a blacksmith, locksmith, armory, brass foundry, carpentry, wool carding, "alpargatería" (for light shoes made of hemp, widely used in Spain), mat work, tinshop, shoe-maker, wheelwright's shop, cabinet maker, tailor, weaving, wool and silk textiles, boiler-maker, etc. Later on a printing shop was installed where a good number of educational and other books, as well as Montesinos' own reports, were published. There were all together some 40 workshops, each with its masters, officers, and apprentices, working in perfect order and discipline. Vocational training for beginners was done at the same workshops. He even arranged, near the main entrance, a showroom where the convict's work was exhibited and sold to those interested.

Montesinos was deeply preoccupied with the problem of juvenile delinquency. For youngsters below 18 years of age, he built a special "Sección de Jóvenes" (Youth Section), entirely isolated from the adult population, with a capacity for 85 inmates. They had no chains or fetters. They attended an independent primary school, the program of which included reading, writing, basic arithmetic, Christian doctrine, and voca-tional training. Afterwards they had to work in one of the shops of their choice, according to their vocational training. This section was so suc-cessful that a number of local families with difficult children asked Montesinos to receive and care for them in order to prevent their drifting toward delinquency. For such children he established another section of "niños corrigendos" (children for rehabilitation). In charge of them he put the most trustworthy of his convicts, those who had reached the period of "intermediate freedom" (see later) while under his personal, direct and permanent control. With the instruction and the education they received, skill in a given craft, and good social discipline, almost none of them became offenders.[48]

So successful was he in all his dealings in improving the material condition of the prison and its inmates that as early as April 2, 1838 he was sent to Sevilla to arrange and improve the local "presidio." In spite of the fact that on his way he was shipwrecked and caught a severe typhus, he did so well that in less than five months he had entirely re-shaped the prison. Then, by order of the Director General of Prisons, he spent the last two months of 1838 visiting the main towns on the Mediterranean coast between Cartagena and Gibraltar, looking for a

[48] José Rico de Estasen, "La Criminalidad Juvenil y el Coronel Montesinos," *Revista de Estudios Penitenciarios*, Dirección General de Prisiones, Madrid, España, Año XX, No. 164 (pp. 225–230, January-March 1964), pp. 229–230.

suitable place for a general storehouse for the "presidios" in Africa. As a result of his achievements he was appointed, on February 1, 1839, Surveyor of the Southern and African "presidios" of the kingdom, while remaining Director of the "presidio" of Valencia.

In his new capacity, during the following few years, he visited and improved the existing conditions at the "presidios" of Granada, Toledo, Malaga, Algeciras, Cartagena, Alicante, Albacete, Seville, San Lucar de Barrameda, Ceuta, Antequera, Badajoz, Valladolid, Burgos, Alcalá de Henares, etc. He also organized teams of convicts to work on the highways from Granada to Motril and from Malaga to Córdoba. He was always preoccupied with getting better rations and clothing for his inmates, so it is not surprising that he managed to fulfill all of these projects without one single escape. He was often obliged to incur personal debts in order to avoid starvation of his convicts. The central government of Madrid was sometimes extremely slow in sending the necessary funds, to acquire even the most basic foodstuffs for the prisoners. And the creditors were not always willing or able to wait for their dues. In such cases they sent the most abusive letters to Montesinos, impervious to his altruistic involvement in the problem, and humiliated him "ad nauseam," as was the case with a debt to the heirs of the Duchess of Almodóvar on September 17, 1844.[49]

By then his fame throughout the kingdom was already so great that, in October 1840 when General Espartero, the Regent of the Kingdom, went to Valencia with his Ministers to see off the Queen Mother, Doña María Cristina de Borbón, a visit was paid to the "Presidio." They were so well impressed that as soon as the Regent was back in Madrid, on October 19, 1840, he granted him the honorary degree of Colonel of Cavalry. Don Pedro Gonzalez, a learned priest and member of the Spanish Academy of History, mentions the fact that Espartero held Montesinos' career in high esteem, not only because Montesinos deserved it but also because they were in-laws through their respectives wives.[50] Whatever the case, the fact remains that on January 11, 1841 he was again distinguished with the appointment of Surveyor General of the "presidios" of the Kingdom, still remaining Director of the "presidio" of Valencia, his real love. It is a known fact that he rejected nomination as Director General of Prisons because it would have meant living in Madrid instead of Valencia, and he was unwilling to leave his work unfinished at the "presidio."

When General Espartero was deposed, in June 1843, and Elizabeth II came back to power, she asked her mother, Doña María Cristina de

[49] Simón García Martín del Val, *Revista*, p. 215.
[50] Gregorio Lasala, *ibid.*, p. 89, footnote 6.

Borbón, to come back from exile. As soon as she landed at Valencia, at the end of the same year, she requested to visit the "presidio" and was so full of admiration that not only did she congratulate Montesinos but shook his hand, a most unusual gesture . . .![51] Moreover, as soon as she was back in Madrid, he was bestowed with the Cross of Charles III, on January 13, 1844.

Then began the decline. Espartero's fall affected Montesinos' career negatively. The new Government appointed a new Director General of Prisons, whose private secretary—a young and ambitious fellow—did his utmost to present Montesinos' achievements in an unfavorable light. In spite of this, his general ideas for the treatment of offenders were incorporated in the new bylaws for all the "presidios" of the Kingdom, on September 5, 1844. All his basic concepts were there, almost as if the legislator had copied even the personal writing style of Montesinos.[52] The best proof that this was official recognition of his system is the fact that, a few months later, on February 7, 1845, he was honored with the appointment of Secretary to Her Majesty.

However, this was just a short lull. In 1848, the "Cortes" (Spanish parliament) approved a new Penal Code and, in 1850, introduced further modifications to the same Code, both acts representing a severe blow to Montesinos' basic principles and practices. Punishments were stiffened, some of the bylaws of 1844 were annulled, the prerogatives of Directors of "presidios" were limited, etc. From another direction there were increasing complaints from private industry that inmates' work was exempted from taxes and therefore harmful to the interests of free enterprise. Industrialists demanded that convicts should again be engaged in public works and thereby cease to be a source of unfair competition to them. Montesinos was against all of this, but had to face ever increasing pressure and criticism. Meanwhile, the quality of the inmates' work deteriorated owing to lack of raw materials and pressure from the outside.[53]

He had to make every effort to avoid the collapse of his life work. He prepared and distributed among the various authorities and politicians a number of reports dealing mainly with the meaning and implications of his ideas, as established so evidently in the "presidio" of Valencia and all of the others he had visited and reorganized. He even stimulated and personally participated in the publication of the book of Vicente Boix.[34] In spite of the fact that the book was dedicated to the Prime Minister and widely circulated throughout the entire Kingdom, it did not attract

[51] Gregorio Lasala, *ibid.*, p. 89.
[52] Vicente Boix, *op. cit.*, p. 109.
[53] Vicente Boix, *ibid.*, p. 168.

any attention nor reverse the direction of the tide. The Prime Minister was then Joaquín Francisco Pacheco (1808–1865), a jurist and a playwright. He was famous for his lectures on Criminal Law,[54] where he developed the new ideas of the French and Italian authors such as Bonneville de Marsangy and Rossi. His work was later severely criticized by Dorado Montero, who stresses its "poca substancia"[55] (little substance). Whatever the case, the fact is that, for political reasons and jealousy, he ignored Montesinos' achievements, more in his capacity as a playwright than as a jurist. Admitting that he had lost his battle, Montesinos asked to be pensioned, and retired on March 31, 1854, after almost 20 years of active and highly fruitful activities in the prison service of Spain.

Even after his retirement his deep-rooted interest in the "presidios" and their inmates did not diminish. On August 13, 1856 he sent a report to the Government on the state of the "presidios" and their future. He put forward a number of positive suggestions for the improvement of the rapidly deteriorating conditions of these institutions. He did not even receive an acknowledgment. A year later, on August 1, 1857, "his" bylaws of September 5, 1844 were derogated. The Penal Code of 1848, with the modifications of 1850 and a few other even more severe changes, was steadily enforced. He retired saddened and embittered. Then in 1858, while waiting at a ceremonial procession to see Queen Elizabeth II, his horse, frightened by the noise of the cannon shots, rose up on its hind legs and fell over his chest. He never recovered from this accident. He slowly started to bend and to lose weight as well as his sense of humor. Finally, on July 3, 1862, he passed away. Next day he was buried and, apart from the official representatives who attended his funeral, there was a good number of ex-convicts, so moved, that many of them were crying.[56] Sic transit gloria mundi . . . !

EVALUATION OF HIS CONTRIBUTION

In order to evaluate his work properly, it is necessary first to understand his personality and to be acquainted with certain political and historical characteristics of his time.

Montesinos was essentially a soldier. He started his military career as a young boy and, for 30 years of his life, he was first an officer in the

[54] Joaquín Francisco Pacheco, "Estudios de Derecho Penal" (2nd ed., Madrid, Boix, 1842–1843).
[55] Luis Jiménez de Asúa, op. cit., p. 665.
[56] Gregorio Lasala, Revista, p. 93.

regular army and then in the Civil Militia of Valencia. It is almost impossible to determine whether the main traits of his character were a result of his military life, or whether he chose to be an army officer because of his basic personality. Whatever the case, the fact remains that his biographers and contemporaries agree that, apart from a kind heart, he had a natural talent for leadership, including intelligence, intuition, energy, and tact, as well as exceptional powers of persuasion and suggestion, and showed spontaneous kindness toward others. He treated all his men in the same paternal way, avoiding, as far as possible, preferential differences or discriminatory inclinations. He always gave his orders with firmness, but without despotism. It is therefore not surprising that he elicited sincere respect for his personality and could always count on the confidence and esteem of those under his command, soldiers or convicts. He also took a genuine interest in whatever he did; his task and duties, which matched with a well balanced self-respect, allowed him to attain complete success in his endeavors whenever given the necessary independence of action, free from political and petty interference. No wonder then that he became a brilliant precursor of the humanitarian treatment of offenders within and outside his own country.

It is also important to keep in mind that already as a boy he had participated in the war against Napoleon; that he had spent five years as a prisoner in France; and that he had also been active in the Spanish civil war (1833–1840) between the liberal and progressive elements in favor of Elizabeth, daughter of King Ferdinand VII, and the reactionaries and traditionalists on the side of Charles, the King's brother. During those years, mutinies and uprisings were quite frequent. Many people, mainly politicians and army officers, were interested in getting hold of the "presidios" in order to enlist the convicts for their respective purposes. To avoid this, Montesinos organized his "presidio" as a military unit, as a self contained regiment, where the inmates were treated with the same severe discipline of soliders, but enjoyed the benefit of being treated as human beings and not like animals. His entire system was based on these simple but fundamental facts.

In view of the above considerations, it is not so important to establish exactly how much Montesinos knew about penal and penitentiary problems before his appointment as Director of the "presidio" of Valencia. There is no doubt that he had had no special training for such a job. As a consequence, the long debate among some Spanish penologists on the subject of how much he was or was not a self-made man in this particular field is somehow trivial and useless. It is enough to say that he most certainly had no knowledge of penal administration when he was appointed Paymaster of the "presidio" in 1832. On the other hand, there can be no doubt that from then until his retirement in 1854 he must have done some reading on the subject. Moreover, one of his military duties between 1814 and 1823 was to act as a junior assistant at the "Junta Consultiva Naval" (Naval Consultative Board). Here he certainly knew of the "Ordenanza de los Presidios de Arsenales" (Ordinance of the "Presidios" at the Navy's dockyards) of 1804. The declared purpose of this Ordinance was the rehabilitation of the convicts by compulsory learning and working on a specific craft in order to be useful to society and themselves. The inmates were classified in three different groups, according to their craftmanship and received 25 percent of what they earned with their work in order to be able to improve their food and clothing. Besides work, a religious atmosphere prevailed, and inmates had to pray every day. He must also have been well acquainted with the General Ordinance of the Prisons of the Kingdom of April 14, 1834, where many of the principles of the previous Ordinance of 1804 were incorporated.[57] Finally, in a written statement for a newspaper, he admits to have known both Ordinances as well as the work of M. L. Lopez.[58] In any case, even if he did acquire a few basic ideas through his reading and utilized some of them, there is no doubt that what he achieved in his "presidio" stretches far beyond theoretical preconceptions of any kind or amount.

Perhaps the best synthesis of Montesinos' system is his own motto, which he put on the lintel of the main gate of the "presidio": "La prisión solo recibe al hombre. El delito queda a la puerta." (The prison only receives the man. The offense remains at the gate.) What he wanted to express was that public vindictiveness should be satisfied with the judicial sentence, and that from the moment of its execution there is no place for feelings of revenge. We cannot rehabilitate "legal entities," only men. The rehabilitation of the offender was his ultimate goal. Here and there—for instance, the presence of fetters—we may have the feeling of a certain sternness or harsh treatment of the inmates, but this represents more the penal practice of the day than his own despotic character. On the contrary, although it is true that he always tried to keep the same alert and vigilant discipline, work and not punishment was for him the main moralizing tool. Another element was confidence. In fact, he established a real "trust system," but not an automatic or un-

[57] Gregorio Lasala, *ibid.*, pp. 77–78.
[58] Marcial Antonio Lopez, "Descripción de los más celebres Establecimientos Penales de Europa y los Estados Unidos," two volumes (640 pp., Valencia, Benito Monfort, 1832). There are only a few known copies of this treatise. The late Professor Eugenio Cuello Calón had one (see footnote 7), the same used by Francisco Franco de Blas in his paper (see footnote 47), as mentioned in page 108, note 4 bis.

founded one. All prisoners had to work hard and go through different progressive stages, with an elaborate complex of rewards and punishments, before deserving Montesinos' confidence. In this way, he led the offender, step by step, from darkness to daylight, from deprivation to fulfilment.

His progressive system had three different stages: first, fetters; second, work; and third, "intermediate freedom."[59]

On the first day, immediately after reception, the new inmate was received in a personal interview with Montesinos, the Director of the "presidio." There he did not hear a moralizing sermon, nor an irritating reprimand, nor even the slightest hint about his criminal act. On the contrary, it was usually a simple meeting where he was questioned about his previous basic education and his skills, if any; his family and social relationships; his wishes and aspirations.[60] The newcomer was then taken to the prison registrar, where his personal data were recorded. Next came the barber shop where barber inmates shaved his hair. Afterward he was provided with a regular uniform, a jacket and a pair of trousers of grey cloth, and taken to his individual cell. However, before the first day was over, each prisoner had to go through a most peculiar experience. He was taken to the blacksmith shop where he got his chains and fetters prescribed in the sentence, "as a shameful stigma of the committed offense."[61] The fetters did not hinder the convict's movements. Those sentenced for 2 years had their fetters fixed at the knees, united by a chain of two links, weighing altogether 4 pounds. Those sentenced for 2 to 4 years, received the same fetters, but the chain had 4 links, weighing 6 pounds; and those with longer sentences had thicker links, weighing from 8 to 16 pounds. In the latter two cases, the chain was held up by a leather strap, attached to the belt of the prisoner.[62] Only when all these procedures were over, in an almost routine and mechanical way, was the inmate ready to start his first stage in the "presidio": "el de los hierros" (of fetters).

The chains and fetters were actually symbolic. Many of the prisoners were strong enough to break them. In fact, they were intended as a reminder that their crimes had transformed them into legal slaves.[63] With good behavior and honest consecration to work they could soon get rid of them. But there were other reasons to consider this first stage

[59] Rafael Salillas, "Un gran penólogo Español, el Coronel Montesinos" (Madrid, Imprenta Eduardo Arias, 1906).
[60] Elías Neuman, op. cit., p. 106.
[61] Francisco Franco de Blas, Revista, p. 113.
[62] Elías Neuman, op. cit., p. 107.
[63] Constancio Bernaldo de Quiros, op. cit., p. 104.

as expiatory in its nature. The convicts lived in isolated cells, but not with the purpose of facilitating their inner self-analysis, leading to repentance and reconciliation with God. Montesinos was always a staunch and declared enemy of the cellular system, already popular in Europe. He was convinced that isolation was not only retributive and negative in nature, but harmful to the more constructive purpose of the penal law: the rehabilitation of the offenders.[63] The real purpose was to awaken the gregarious instinct and to create a working habit in every prisoner, instead of carrying on in isolation and idleness. To achieve this, every prisoner belonged to the "brigada de depósito" (depot brigade) during this stage. Thus, in spite of their chains and fetters, they were in charge of the heaviest, dirtiest, and most opprobrious tasks of the entire establishment. For the same purpose, they were not allowed to smoke or to buy anything at the "presidio's" canteen.[64] There was no time limit for this first stage. The prisoners had to reach their own decision: either to carry on with their fetters and the assigned indecent tasks or to ask to be transferred to one of the 40 different workshops. The insistent request for work meant the end of the first stage and the beginning of the second.

During the second stage, the prisoner was transferred to a dormitory with other inmates, and started to work in a workshop of his own choice. Work was not then penal hard labor, forced and punitive, as indicated in the sentence, but an expression of the free will of the prisoner. Not only was he the one to ask for work, he also had to indicate the type of work he wanted. Montesinos never considered prisoners' work as a vindicative measure nor as a utilitarian means of exploiting them for the benefit of the State. For him, work was the best *educative* procedure to rehabilitate the offenders' *morality*, the fundamental aim of the penal law.

The third and last stage was that of "libertad intermedia" (intermediate freedom), granted only to those inmates of excellent behavior, dedicated to their work, and deserving Montesinos' confidence. For this purpose they were put through the so-called "duras pruebas" (hard tests), such as being sent on a home visit in civilian clothes and without guards; acting as messengers with letters or money; or even serving as personal escorts when he or his wife had to travel to Madrid or some other city.[65] They were also engaged in administrative tasks within the "presidio," such as accountancy, record-keeping, or as cashiers. During this period the inmates were free to talk among themselves and received frequent visits from relatives and friends. Finally, those who passed these "duras pruebas" with flying colors and had acquired a permanent craft, granting them the certainty to be able to earn the means for a settled

64 Francisco Franco de Blas, *Revista*, p. 117.
65 Elías Neuman, *op. cit.*, p. 109.

life, were granted reductions of time of their respective sentences, as deserved rewards for their honest dedication to work and good behavior. It was not a right of the prisoner, but a facultative favor of the Director of the "presidio."

It is necessary to bear in mind that when he started as Director of the "presidio" of Valencia (1834), prisoners' work in the vast majority of European countries—whether in public works or within the prisons— had two main purposes: the utilitarian (in order to alleviate the economic burden represented by the upkeep of prisons) and the vindicative (the prisoners had to suffer in order to expiate their crimes). The latter transformed work into something sterile and useless, as was the case in England, for instance, with the "treadmill," the "crank," and the "shot drill."[66] Inhuman "hard labor" was only abolished during the first decades of this century, and there are still quite a number of countries carrying on with the old system. Today the utilitarian principle is still present in some European countries, but the vindicative principle has been replaced by the concept of "social rehabilitation." Montesinos' merit lies in the fact that he advocated this almost a century ago when he wrote in his "Reflecsiones"[67] the following sentence; "Los talleres de estos Estableci-mientos, más que como ramos de especulación, deben considerarse como medios de enseñanza, porque el beneficio moral del penado, mucho más que el lucro de sus tareas, es el objecto que la ley se propone al privar a los delincuentes de su libertad."[68] (The workshops of these Institutions —the "presidios"—more than objects of economic speculations, must be considered as means of learning because the moral benefit of the convict, rather than the profit of his toil, is the object of the law in depriving offenders of their liberty.) This same basic concept is reproduced in his own reports and in the writings of his biographer Boix.[34] For instance, "Jamás un establecimiento presidial debe equipararse a una empresa de comercio, ni administrarse por los mismos principios que ésta, porque el término de ambos es diferente. El acrecimiento de fondos es el objeto de la segunda, y el designio esencial del primero debe ser siempre la enseñanza y moralización de sus individuos."[69] (A "presidio" should never be compared with a commercial enterprise nor administered by the same principles because their aims are different. The object of the

[66] Eugenio Cuello Calón, "Montesinos, Precursor de la Nueva Penología," *Revista*, pp. 46–47.

[67] Manuel Montesinos, "Reflecsiones sobre la Organización del Presidio de Valencia, Reforma de la Dirección General del Ramo, y Sistema Económico del mismo" (38 pp., Valencia, Imprenta del Presidio, 1846). As we had no copy of the original work, we used the reimpression published in the *Revista*, pp. 250–272.

[68] Manuel Montesinos, "Reflecsiones," *ibid.*, pp. 254–255.

[69] Manuel Montesinos, "Reflecsiones," *ibid.*, p. 255.

latter is to increase its capital, while the essential intention of the former must always be the education and moralization of its inmates.)

Another of his daring innovations—Montesinos was perhaps the first one to apply it in actual practice—consisted in his conviction that in order to improve the quality of the finished work and the zeal of the inmates, work has to be duly remunerated. He writes, "adquirí también la firme convicción de que sin el estímulo de algún lucro era muy difícil hacer trabajar a los ya instruídos y casi imposible de todo punto, enseñar a los que nada sabían."[70] (I also acquired the firm conviction that without the inducement of some gain it was very difficult to work for those who already know, and almost impossible for those who know nothing.) It is true that John Howard, in his "The State of Prisons in England and Wales," mentions the fact that the inmates of some jails received miserable compensation for their work, but it is a well-known fact that even today it is by no means rare to find penal systems where inmates' work is not remunerated at all except for provisions in kind, like food, lodging, and clothing. In the "presidio" of Valencia, Montesinos established a scale of salaries, according to the skill of the convict—master, assistant, or apprentice—with everyone enjoying a just, generous, and sure remuneration for his work. Half of these wages went to the "fondo económico" (economic fund) of the "presidio," for further improvements to the Institution in general, and its workshops in particular; a fourth was given monthly in cash, which could be saved or used to improve their food or to buy whatever they wished at the canteen of the "presidio," and the remaining fourth was kept in a savings account for release, to be used by the ex-convicts to travel back to the place of their choice or even as a means toward getting established.[71]

Summarizing, it may be said that for Montesinos, prisoners' work should be compulsory but, at the same time, educative and moralizing, useful, remunerated, and adapted to the prevailing work conditions and characteristics of the labor free market, outside the "presidio." Work was either intramural, inside the "presidio" (in one of the 40 different workshops; in the administrative offices; as guards' corporals; or in cleaning and maintenance), or extramural, outside the Institution (gardening; public or municipal works), although Montesinos was never a great admirer of the latter.[72] When prisoners undertook external work, he sent them in what he called the "destacamentos penales" (penal detachments), groups of convicts in the third stage—intermediate freedom.

[70] Manuel Montesinos, "Reflecsiones," *ibid.*, p. 254.
[71] Vicente Boix, *op. cit.*, pp. 121–122.
[72] Francisco Bueno Arus, "Ideas y Realizaciones de Montesinos en materia de Trabajo Penitenciario," in *Revista*, pp. 123–179.

They left the prison premises without military guard, did their work, and returned as a matter of course to the "presidio." This was another of his "duras pruebas" . . . ![73]

It was at this time that the two American penal systems began to gain renown and even popularity: the "cellular" Pennsylvania system (absolute isolation) and the Auburn system (life in common but in silence during the day, and cellular isolation at night). The former became generally accepted in Europe, and the latter in America. Montesinos conducted some experiments with the cellular system, and the results were so destructive that he ended up by violently opposing it. For him such a system worked against the essential purpose of the law: the social rehabilitation of the offender. He advocated the "desterrar la incomunicación absoluta" (banishment of absolute isolation), not only because it led to demoralization but it also led to "la locura o el suicidio, especialmente en los países meridionales"[74] (insanity and suicide, especially in southern countries). These words constitute one of the earliest and most severe criticisms of the cellular system and a remarkable articipation of present thinking on this matter.

Corporal punishment, such as whipping and lashing, was a common disciplinary measure for punishing inmates during the first half of the last century. At the "presidio" of Valencia, discipline was severe but humane: detention in a cell for a few days, depending on the gravity of the misbehavior; suspension of visits; and other similar punishments, never corporal nor humiliating. "El mas ineficaz de todos los recursos en un Establecimiento penal y el mas pernicioso también, y mas funesto a sus progresos de moralidad, son los castigos corporales Máxima debe ser la de no envilecer mas a los que harto degradados por sus vicios vienen a ella."[75] (The most ineffective and regrettable of all the resources at the disposal of a penal institution, most harmful to the development of the inmate's morality, is corporal punishment. The rule must be not to further vilify those who come here already so degraded by their vices.) This respect for human dignity, even for the convicts—whom Montesinos considered as members of the community and not aliens—is another example of his many foresights, perhaps the most significant of all, because even today this basic principle is not yet universally applied.

He also advocated a "código penal interior" (interior penal code), a kind of internal bylaw for the "presidio," because it is not "justo que la corrección de las faltas quede al absoluto arbitrio de los comandantes,

---

[73] Mariano Ruiz Funes, "La Crisis de la Prision," (315 pp., La Habana, Cuba, Jesús Montero, 1949), p. 194.
[74] Manuel Montesinos, "Reflecsiones," *op. cit.*, p. 259.
[75] Manuel Montesinos, "Reflecsiones," *ibid.*, p. 254.

sin reglas, cuando menos generales, que determinen en algún modo su conducta"[76] (fair that the measures to be taken in cases of misbehavior should rely entirely on the discretion of the officer in charge, without at least some general rules to determine his conduct). Montesinos shows here a strong legalistic sense in defense of the rights of the prisoner, another amazing anticipation of the much requested civil rights of the prisoners, so strongly advocated today.

"El buen órden y la misma seguridad de los penados exige que las secciones no pueden formar nunca una masa compacta por instintos iguales, ni por iguales circunstancias; y será por consiguiente de la mayor importancia y moralidad colocar junto a un operario de buena índole, de causa leve y de conducta ejemplar, a otro de caracter feroz, rudeza de sentimientos o execrables antecedentes reclaman mucha vigilancia para corregirlo y mucho conocimiento para sondear su corazón."[77] (Good order and the security of the inmates demand that groups should never consist of offenders similar with respect to instincts and characteristics; therefore it is of the utmost importance to put beside a good-natured worker, of excellent behavior, convicted for a minor offense, one whose ferocious character, roughness of feelings, and execrable penal record require a lot of knowledge to gain insight into his feelings, and severe control to achieve his rehabilitation.) It is really difficult to understand how a man with no penal administration background, nor a theoretical knowledge of penal philosophy, saw the need to mix "good" inmates with the "bad" in order to facilitate their mutual reform. We do not know of anybody who thought in the same direction prior to Montesinos. He can safely be considered "the precursor" with respect to this particular point of institutional classification of inmates, so widely accepted today. In this respect, it may be added that in Montesinos' system we find the first hints of the individualization of the prison sentence. He was personally interested in having a detailed record of each prisoner's background, including items on the family constellation, educational data, religious and moral inclinations, vices and virtues, instincts and habits, etc.[78]

As already mentioned, Montesinos used to authorize temporary "exit permits" for the convicts of his "presidio," in cases of tragic or happy familial events. He did this not only because of the humanitarian character of the measure and the need to foster the best possible relationships between the prisoners and the outside world, particularly the family, but also because it constituted one of his "duras pruebas," testing the in-

[76] Manuel Montesinos, "Reflecsiones," *ibid.*, p. 271.
[77] Vicente Boix, *op. cit.*, p. 136.
[78] Ladislao Thot, *op. cit.*, p. 41.

mate's capacity to resist the temptations offered by the external free society. Today such "exit permits" are common practice in some countries, but they were totally unknown in Montesinos' time and are therefore another example of his clear intuition of what a modern prison system ought to be.[79]

One of the main chronic problems facing prison administrations the world over is the scarcity of trained personnel for their institutions. In Montesinos' time this problem was already apparent and, in his proposal to solve it, we find another facet of his innate penal wisdom. In fact he presented a most detailed project for the creation of a special "presidio," of the highest standard, to serve as a training center for such a personnel. Unfortunately his suggestion was never studied, and his report was shelved and forgotten altogether.[80]

If we take into consideration his main innovations—decent, productive, and remunerated work; abolition of torment and corporal punishment; sincere respect for the human condition of the inmates; mixing "good" and "bad" prisoners; exit permits; etc.—as well as the absence of inviolable walls, bars, locks, and other containment measures within the "presidio," it can be safely stated that Montesinos, in fact, organized and directed what we know today as a "minimum security" prison. He did this almost a century ago when the general and accepted practice was to have "maximum security" prisons where prisoners were treated in the most brutal way. All this in itself is no small achievement, particularly in Spain of the last century, considered to be one of the most backward European countries.

Montesinos was aware of the importance and value of his own work and achievements. "Al treinta y cinco por ciento se hallaba la computación estadística de los reincidentes en la generalidad de nuestros presidios, cuando me atreví a organizar la administración de este ramo, y años hace que en el de Valencia son tan pocos, que dudo pueda fijarse su número proporcional en mas de uno por ciento."[81] (Thirty-five percent was the statistical computation for the rate of recidivism in the vast majority of our "presidios" when I dared to organize the administration at Valencia, where the rate is so low that I doubt whether it could be fixed at more than one percent.)

He did everything alone, without assistance or cooperation, but with a strong nationalistic approach. "Ni he mendigado nada de los estrangeros, ni nada tampoco temo de ellos por las competencias que se

[79] Eugenio Cuello Calón, "Montesinos, Precursor de la Nueva Penología," *Revista*, p. 58.
[80] Gregorio Lasala, *op. cit.*, p. 90.
[81] Manuel Montesinos, "Reflecsiones," *op. cit.*, p. 259.

pueden intentar entre los resultados sociales de sus casas de corrección y los de mi presidio."[82] (I have begged nothing from the foreigners, and I am not afraid of their competition if we compare the social results of their houses of correction and my "presidio.") He even writes: "Creo haber avanzado mas que muchas penitenciarías de Europa."[83] (I think I have advanced more than many of the European penitentiaries.) Perhaps the best colophon can be found in Montesinos own words: "Estoy convencido de los grandes bienes que produce al país la casa penal que dirijo, por los gérmenes de moralización y hábitos de laboriosidad que su sistema penitenciario encierra."[84] (I am convinced that the prison under my direction has made great contributions to the country, due to the moralizing conditions and work habits contained in its penitentiary system.)

Undoubtedly Montesinos established a Spanish penal system—quite different from all others prevailing in Europe and America at that time— much closer to modern penitentiary concepts than any other of those applied during the last century. This alone, we think, justifies our aim, which is to restore Montesinos' place among the great penal reformers of the 19th century.

RECOGNITION IN SPAIN AND ABROAD

There is a most curious evolution with regard to the recognition of Montesinos' work in Spain and abroad. In Spain his system, although admired by laymen in penitentiary matters (members of the Royal family, politicians, writers, army officers, historians, and newspapermen), was accepted by his administrative superiors of the Directorate General of Prisons in Madrid for only a very short period of time—less than 20 years—and this only when Montesinos had supporters in the higher echelons of the Government. The best proof of this is that he resigned from his functions while still an able man, in perfect condition to carry on with his duties very effectively. When he died, his ideas seem to have been buried with his body, and were almost entirely forgotten in his own country for some 50 years. In fact, none of his learned penal and penitentiary contemporaries mention his name even once. This is the case with the penal writers of last century, like Joaquín Francisco Pacheco, already mentioned;[54] Francisco Giner de los Ríos, who intro-

[82] Manuel Montesinos, "Reflecsiones," *ibid.*, p. 259.
[83] Manuel Montesinos, "Reflecsiones," *ibid.*, p. 252.
[84] Eugenio Cuello Calón, "Montesinos, Precursor de la Nueva Penología," *Revista*, pp. 65–66.

duced Roeder's correctionalist doctrine in Spain; Luis Silvela, Félix Aramburu, and others. Even more striking is the case with Mariano Cubí y Soler, the criminal anthropologist, and particularly so with Concepción Arenal, Prison Surveyor and a prolific writer,[33] who totally ignored Montesinos' work. The only exception is Lastres, a well-known Spanish penitentiarist, who devoted part of one of his lectures to Montesinos, expressing admiration for his ideas and accomplishments.[85]

It is a depressing fact that virtually the only printed material acknowledging and supporting his work was published at Montesinos' "presidio" while he was its Director, publications that not only he could not have ignored but most certainly were carried out with his approval and backing, his assistance and financing, and even with his suggestions if not his actual writing. From Montesinos himself, we know of only three published pamphlets: (1) "Al Excmo. Sr. D. Diego Martinez de la Rosa, Director General de Presidios," of only four pages, published in April 1846,[86] where he explains and justifies his decision to establish a printing workshop at the "presidio"; undoubtedly this was the first work published there;[87] (2) "Reflecsiones" (mentioned in footnote 67); and (3) "Exposiciones dirigidas al Escmo. Sr. Ministro de la Gobernación de la Península y al Sr. Director de Corrección," 15 pages, published in 1847.[88] That same year, two other books were printed at the "presidio" of Valencia. One is anonymous—the author using the initials "J. de B. y F. A."—entitled "Reflexiones sobre el Sistema Penitenciario Español." Rico de Estasen,[89] without further explanation, asserts that the author is none other than Montesinos himself. The second book was written by Manuel Lasala, "Memoria Filosófica-Histórica sobre el Presidio de Valencia." For political reasons Lasala was sent to the "presidio" where he was instrumental in the establishment of the printing shop.[90] This is perhaps the only account of Montesinos' system as seen from within by a learned individual, after spending some time as one of the many inmates of the "presidio." The last book on the same subject, printed at the "presidio," is that of Boix,[34] already mentioned several times. But apart from these few publications, Rico de Estasen,[91] mentions a number

[85] Francisco Lastres, Estudios sobre Sistemas Penitenciarios," (Madrid, Librería de A. Duncan, 1875), pp. 101–103.
[86] Reproduced in *Revista*, pp. 283–285.
[87] José Rico de Estasen, "Bibliografía sobre el Coronel Montesinos," in *Revista*, pp. 223–246, pp. 227–228.
[88] Reproduced in *Revista*, pp. 273–281.
[89] José Rico de Estasen, "El Coronel Montesinos. Un español de prestigio europeo," *op. cit.*, p. 118.
[90] José Rico de Estasen, "Bibliografía sobre el Coronel Montesinos," *Revista*, p. 288.
[91] José Rico de Estasen, "Bibliografía sobre el Coronel Montesinos," *ibid.*, pp. 231–235.

of poems and newspaper chronicles dealing with the Colonel's work, after which he was almost forgotten for half a century.

Meanwhile in Europe and in America, Montesinos' system gained renown and admiration, mainly due to one American and two English authors. Severn Teackle Wallis, a lawyer of Baltimore, Maryland (1816–1894), a student of Spanish history and literature, who visited Spain on several occasions and, on behalf of the U.S. Government made a survey of the legal titles of land property in Florida, published "Glimpses of Spain" (London, Sampson Low, 1850) and "Spain, Her Institutions, Politics and Public Men" (1858), where he makes quite a number of flattering remarks about Montesinos' achievements at the "presidio" of Valencia.[92] The first English work is anonymous, "Notes of an Attaché in Spain," published in 1850. The second work is perhaps the most important of all. Its author is George Alexander Hoskins, Esq., and its title "Spain As It Is," 2 volumes, published in London by Colburn and Co. in 1851. Here, as mentioned by García Basalo,[93] there is a long and enthusiastic description of the "presidio" of Valencia, its inmates, the workshops, and its reformatory system, particularly in Chapter VII, pages 104–111, of the first volume. Hoskins later published another book, "What Shall We Do With Our Criminals? With An Account of the Prison of Valencia and the Penitentiary of Mettray," London, Rigway, 1853.[94]

Maconochie never went to Spain, but "he succeeded in acquiring a fair command of Spanish, an accomplishment that was to prove of value to him when he became interested in penal reform, for it enabled him to translate the reports of the Spanish penal administrator and reformer, Colonel Manuel Montesinos."[95] According also to Barry,[96] the two English books, mentioned above, and Montesinos' own reports were known to Maconochie and constituted the main sources for his many references and great enthusiasm for Montesinos' system. "He had used his knowledge of Spanish in 1852 to bring to English readers an account of the work of Colonel Montesinos at the Prison at Valencia in a pamphlet, "Account of the Public Prison at Valencia"[97] and, in 1853, in the

[92] J. Carlos García Basalo, "La Celebridad Internacional de Montesinos," in *Revista*, pp. 180–200, p. 184, footnote 7.
[93] J. Carlos García Basalo, *ibid.*, p. 184, footnote 8.
[94] Mentioned by José Rico de Estasen in "Bibliografía sobre el Coronel Montesinos," *Revista*, p. 228.
[95] John Vincent Barry, "Alexander Maconochie of Norfolk Island" (XXI, 277 pp., Melbourne, Oxford University Press, 1958), pp. 6–7.
[96] John Vincent Barry, *ibid.*, p. 219, footnote 31.
[97] "Account of the Public Prison of Valencia, calculated to receive 1,500 prisoners, averaging 1,000; yet in which, during the last three years, there has not been even

second of the three letters on "Prison Discipline." He stressed that "Colonel Montesinos had triumphed over all disadvantages—a bad prison, defective funds and, to say the least, irregular apparatus, solely through his unfeigned desire to reform his men."[98] Whatever the case, we are convinced that Maconochie knew nothing about Montesinos' work in Valencia while he was in Australia (1837–1844), and that his "mark system" was developed independently, as was Obermaier's "system of supervision" in Bavaria. It is certainly not the first time that various people arrive, almost simultaneously at similar conclusions, quite independently.

A few years later, Hill[99] describes the characteristics of the organization and the results attained at the "presidio" at Valencia. Enoch Cobb Wines (1807–1879) who, together with Zebulon R. Broackway and Franklin R. Sanborn, is considered to be one of the three great musketeers of American penology during the last century, also expresses his admiration for Montesinos' system in his posthumous work.[100]

Thanks to a number of personal notes and letters left by Montesinos and studied by his grandson,[101] it is known that the Director General of Prisons of the Netherlands, two prison surveyors from France, and several other prison officials from Switzerland, England, and Belgium visited the "presidio" and reported to their respective Governments.

Finally, although the three European International Penitentiary Congresses (Frankfurt-am-Main, 1846; Brussels, 1847; and again Frankfurt-am-Main, 1857) ignored Montesinos, because they were extremely "cellular system"-minded, at the International Penal and Penitentiary Congresses, particularly the first three (London, 1872; Stockholm, 1878;

---

one re-committal, and for the previous ten years, the average was only one per cent," with observations by Captain Maconochie, R.N., K.H., London, Charles Gilpin, 1852. (Apparently there exists only a single known copy of this pamphlet at the Museum of the School of Penitentiary Studies in Madrid. In fact it is a reproduction of several pages of the original Hoskins' work, with some observations, comments and other addenda by Maconochie himself.)

[98] John Vincent Barry, op. cit., p. 219.

[99] Mathew Davenport Hill, "Suggestions for the Repression of Crime contained in charges delivered to Grand Juries of Birmingham" (London, John W. Parker and Son, West Strand, 1857), pp. 532–578, where is included his famous questionnaire addressed to Montesinos. This questionnaire and the respective answers were translated into Spanish and reproduced in Revista, pp. 316–322.

[100] E. C. Wines, "The State of Prisons and Child-Saving Institutions in the Civilized World" (Cambridge, University Press, John Wilson and Son, 1880), pp. 30–31.

[101] Enrique Montesinos, "Entre Papeles y Recuerdos de Montesinos," Revista de la Escuela de Estudios Penitenciarios, Madrid, Año V, No. 55 (October 1949), p. 71 ff.

and Rome, 1885), Montesinos' system was mentioned several times, among others by Frederic Hill, Enoch C. Wines, and Francisco Lastras, respectively.

During the present century the situation has changed diametrically. In Spain, thanks to Salillas,[102] Montesinos has been rediscovered and is considered today as one of the most important Spanish penal reformers, making it almost impossible to mention here the entire bibliography dealing with his work,[103] but he has been practically forgotten in European penological bibliography and, in America, not all of the well-known textbooks register his name. Those that do include only superficial and extremely short references to his concepts and achievements. It is hoped that the account here restores Montesinos' place where he properly and justly belongs—among the most important penal reformers of the last century.

[102] Rafael Salillas, "Un Gran Penólogo Español, el Coronel Montesinos" (104 pp., Madrid, Imprenta de Eduardo Arias, Publicaciones de la "Revista Penitenciaria"). 1906.
[103] For more details, see José Rico de Estasen, note 87.

VI

CONTEMPORARY CORRECTIONS

17

Sentencing Re-visited*

HERMANN MANNHEIM

When, nearly ten years ago, I gave a lecture on the subject of sentencing at the University of Pennsylvania,[1] I was privileged to have as my chairman the eminent scholar to whom the present volume is dedicated, and it was he who had also arranged my lecture. His interest in the subject of sentencing, however, is much older, as his various publications, notably on the problem of the indeterminate sentence, show. It is for such reasons that I venture to select for my contribution to this *Festschrift* a topic which, to some readers, may seem to be somewhat outside the principal interests of Thorsten Sellin.

It is not the object of this paper to search very deeply into the profoundest philosophical problems of justice and sentencing, but rather to review in brief the progress, if any, which has been made on the more practical side of the judicial sentencing process, its legal background, and the research devoted to it in these past ten years.

By and large, the following four aspects have to be considered: (1) legislation, (2) court practice, (3) research, and (4) publications not based on research. In none of these four spheres can we hope to achieve complete coverage.

LEGISLATION

This topic includes official legislative drafts and attempts by semi-official or private bodies to prepare the ground for state legislation.

* This essay was written some time before passage of the Criminal Justice Act of 1967 in England. The contents of that Act could not be considered in the essay. The perceptive suggestions of the author, therefore, are especially relevant. *Editor.*
[1] Subsequently repeated at Yale University and the University of Chicago Law School and published in a slightly expanded version under the title, "Some Aspects of Judicial Sentencing Policy," in the *Yale Law Journal*, May 1958, Vol. 67, No. 6, pp. 961–981.

In a lecture, on an entirely different subject, which I gave in September, 1960, at the Fourth International Congress of Criminology held at The Hague, I stressed the need for a "Common Market" of ideas and for international discussion of common problems. After referring to the fact that in some of the principal European countries, official or semiofficial attempts had been made to reform the criminal law concerning mentally abnormal offenders, I concluded: "Surely a recurrent exchange of ideas between those actively engaged in these great and simultaneous enterprises might have been most fruitful, but here, too, the barriers of tariffs and customs have been still too high, it seems, to establish a real 'Common Market.' "[2]

Mutatis mutandis, the same can be said with regard to the recent official or semiofficial attempts to improve judicial sentencing through legislative measures: more often than not, these attempts have been made, without making any visible effort to compare notes of an international character, to know about, and to learn from, the views and experiences of experts in other countries. Despite many profound differences from country to country in the structure and spirit of the substantive criminal law, in the constitution and procedure of the criminal courts, in the various sectors of the penal systems, in the traditional approach to punishment and in public opinion, there still remain many problems of almost universal significance, which could be brought together by comparative methods. A study like "The Indeterminate Sentence" by Marc Ancel, made on behalf of the United Nations,[3] has shown the value of such a comparative approach. Government departments, however, when charged with the preparation of legislative or administrative reforms, or distinguished private bodies such as the American Law Institute, have shown themselves surprisingly indifferent to the need for such a comparative approach. One of the very few exceptions has been the chapter on sentencing in the semi-official publications arranged by the West German Ministry of Justice in preparation of its Draft Penal Code and compiled on its behalf by the Institute of Foreign and International Criminal Law of the University of Freiburg i.Br.[4]

Only the following questions may be mentioned as particularly suitable for the comparative study by all would-be legislators on the subject of sentencing:

[2] "The Criminal Law and Mentally Abnormal Offenders," *Proceedings of the Congress,* The Hague, pp. 465–481; also published in *The British Journal of Criminology,* Vol. I, No. 3, January 1961, pp. 203–220.
[3] United Nations, Department of Social Affairs, New York, 1954.
[4] Materialien zur Strafrechtsreform, 2.Band, Rechtsvergleichende Arbeiten. I. Allgemeiner Teil, Bonn 1954, pp. 85–104, Chapter "Die Strafzumessung" by Lothar Schmidt.

1. Is there a need for legislative provisions to ensure that the courts are supplied in individual cases with adequate presentencing information to enable them to choose the right type of penalty and, within its framework, the amount most appropriate to the case? Should the law also ordain that the courts be officially provided with information on sentences imposed in other, possibly similar cases, and on the effect of such sentences?

2. How far should there be legislative restrictions of the freedom of the courts to select a certain type of penalty for certain types of offenders (for example, imprisonment for young offenders or first offenders, or probation for recidivists) and for certain categories of offenses (for example, capital punishment for murder or probation for certain serious crimes)? Moreover, how far should the law go in fixing minimum and maximum penalties?

3. In particular: what are the arguments for and against the indeterminacy of the sentence?

4. How should the distribution of powers between courts and penal administration be regulated by the law? In particular: should there be a parole system on the American model?

5. How far should the legislator go in providing catalogues of mitigating and aggravating factors?

6. Within the limit of the discretion left to the courts by the legislation, should the latter try to guide the courts by providing certain general principles, some sort of philosophy of sentencing in addition to the factors referred to in paragraph 5?

7. Should the law make it mandatory for the courts to give in writing their reasons for imposing a certain penalty or for abstaining from any punishment in case of a finding of guilt?

Although it is not intended to show how every one of these points has been dealt with in recent legislation, in draft codes and similar preparatory documents, a few illustrations will be presented, taken from four countries where some work in this field has been done within the past ten or twelve years: Sweden, the United States, West Germany, and Britain.

(a) *Sweden* is the only one of these countries that has produced actual legislation, the Penal Code of 1962, effective from January 1, 1965, and the fact that its English translation is the work of Thorsten Sellin makes a brief discussion of a few relevant points particularly appropriate.[5] This Code has the advantage of being comparatively short and compact—Ivar Strahl speaks not without justification of the "usually

---

[5] The Penal Code of Sweden, translated by Thorsten Sellin, Introduction by Ivar Strahl. Ministry of Justice, Stockholm, 1965.

terse and severely factual Swedish style of legal draftsmanship"—and not very much seems to have been written on it so far in Anglo-Saxon countries. As Strahl stresses in his Introduction (page 7), the Code contains no statement of the philosophy on which it is based, but in Chapter 1, Section 7, it is at least provided that "in the choice of sanctions, the court, with an eye to what is required to maintain general law obedience, shall keep particularly in mind that the sanction shall serve to foster the sentenced offender's adaptation to society." This is perfectly all right as far as it goes, and it at least rules out retribution as an object of court action. It gives no guidance, however, when two objectives— securing general law obedience, and the offender's adaptation to society— seem to be incompatible. Here the law, *nolens volens,* leaves to the personal philosophy of the individual judge to decide which of these objectives should dominate. The result might occasionally be somewhat disconcerting, but the remedy will have to be found not in trying to fetter the discretion of the courts but in having better trained judges. Only one recent case might be given to illustrate this dilemma: on April 5, 1966, four youths, aged between 17 and 24, who had been involved in starting fires at seven synagogues in the London area and causing damage to the extent of £ 130,000, received sentences of imprisonment short enough to allow them to be released on the following day, which happened to be the Thursday before Easter. A Detective Inspector had told the court that the prisoners "were now penitent and wanted nothing more to do with anti-semitic activities," and the judge, the Recorder of London, in passing sentence, referred to the Inspector's evidence and added: "I hope you will take advantage of the festival of Easter to come under an influence very different from that which caused you to commit these offences" (*The Times,* 4.6.66). Apparently, the learned judge was anxious, in the words of the Swedish Code, "to foster the sentenced offender's adaptation to society," but did he also keep "an eye to what is required to maintain general law obedience?" Moreover, the further question arises regarding the grounds on which the judge may have based his view that the prisoners were truly "penitent" and had undergone a real change of heart. This seems to have been one of those cases that would require a full statement in writing of all the reasons which caused the judge to impose this particular sentence. It might not be too difficult to envisage a number of mitigating factors to justify the decision—factors that a brief newspaper report could not reproduce in full—but unless they were disclosed to the public, justice may not appear to be done. One might well imagine some legal machinery to make it possible or even mandatory, in important cases like the one reported above, to publish the whole judgement in full in widely read newspapers in order to enable the public better to understand the motives of the judge. The present system of making only a brief verbal statement, which is perhaps inadequately or not at all reproduced in the press, cannot achieve this vital object of the administration of justice.

To return after this digression to the Swedish Penal Code, the following provisions affecting sentencing are worth mentioning. First, the different types of punishment made available are, according to the technique employed in Penal Codes everywhere and, in Strahl's words, "attached to the specific offences" (page 11). This has to be stressed mainly because the "Model Sentencing Act" of 1963, worked out by a Committee of American Judges and to be discussed later, completely dispenses with that traditional technique and proposes to replace it by sentencing, not according to the type of offense but according to the dangerousness of the offender. This is a—conscious or unconscious— acceptance of ideas developed by the Social Defense Movement, and it is noteworthy that, in spite of the general sympathy of the Swedish Code with those ideas (see Strahl, page 8), it does not accept them in this particular respect. Second, the widely and justly acclaimed Swedish system of day-fines—already with certain reservations recommended by the present writer more than a quarter of a century ago[6]—is preserved, apparently without changes. The reservation made by the writer was based on the apprehension that especially offenders of slender means might regard the publicity given by the Swedish system to their financial status as damaging. The Swedish system, which can also be found in other Scandinavian countries, has been adopted with certain improvements in the recent German Draft Codes. In Sweden, day-fines can be imposed in addition to a suspended sentence or to a probation order even if fines are not explicitly provided by the Code for the offense in question (Chapter 27, Section 2 and 28, Section 2).

The courts have power to commit the probationer to an institution for periods between one month and two months to remove him from a bad milieu, to interrupt his criminal activities, or to save him from alcoholism (Chapter 28, Section 3). Of special interest are the provisions dealing with dangerous offenders (Chapter 30). In the case of crimes punishable by imprisonment of two years or more, if "in view of the offender's criminality, mental condition, conduct and other circumstances a long-lasting deprivation of liberty, without duration fixed in advance, is deemed needed to prevent further serious criminality," a sentence to internment may be imposed. This has, as far as its custodial part is concerned, a minimum of one year and a maximum of twelve years. In other

[6] Hermann Mannheim, *The Dilemma of Penal Reform*, London, 1939, pp. 128–130.

words, it is a sentence of "limited indeterminacy," but the maximum is fairly high in relation to the rather vaguely worded requirements ("the offender's criminality," etc.). After the expiration of the minimum term, an internment board decides whether institutional treatment is no longer needed and whether treatment is to be continued outside the institution, but under supervision. Besides the internment board, there are local supervision boards, but neither the composition of these boards nor their respective duties are clearly set out in the Code. It is provided, however, that the consent of a court is required if institutional treatment is regarded as necessary for more than three years beyond the minimum term originally fixed by the sentencing court or for more than five years altogether if the minimum term was three years or longer. The judicial decision is therefore built into the relatively indeterminate sentence, not merely in order to fix the maximum length of the sentence but also to determine within the latter the maximum of its institutional term. Even so, the administration has been given a very large measure of discretion. It is left to the internment board, after the expiration of the minimum term, to continue the institutional period for several more years before the consent of a court must be sought. Altogether it might be said that this part of the Code itself is tantalizingly brief and leaves many important questions open, which are, however, no doubt answered outside the Code in special statutes or regulations not yet made public in translation, in particular the relationship between courts and administrative boards concerning matters of release and aftercare.

(b) In the *United States* the debate on the recommendations of the American Law Institute's (A.L.I.) Model Penal Code has continued in the past decade. Only three important American publications bearing on the subject may be briefly referred to: the symposium on "Sentencing" published by the Duke University School of Law in 1958,[7] the "Model Sentencing Act" of the Advisory Council of Judges of the National Council on Crime and Delinquency,"[8] and Sol Rubin's book "Crime and Juvenile Delinquency."[9] From the rich contents of the symposium, only the following contributions can here be mentioned as having a special bearing on sentencing under the Model Code: Sheldon Glueck writes on "Predictive Devices and the Individualization of Justice"; Norman S.

[7] *Law and Contemporary Problems*, Durham, N.C., Vol. XXIII, No. 3, Summer 1958.
[8] Published by the National Council on Crime and Delinquency, 1963, New York 10, N.Y. Six years before, the National Probation and Parole Association had already sponsored a pamphlet, "Guides for Sentencing," by its Advisory Council of Judges (1957).
[9] 1st ed., Oceana Publications Inc., New York, 1958; revised 2nd ed., Stevens & Sons Ltd., London, 1961.

Hayner on "Sentencing by an Administrative Board"; Lloyd E. Ohlin and Frank J. Remington discuss "Sentencing Structure: Its Effect upon Systems for the Administration of Criminal Justice"; Paul W. Tappan's contribution is especially on "Sentencing under the Model Penal Code"; and Will C. Turnbladh provides "A Critique of the Model Penal Code's Sentencing Proposals."

Although the main features of the relevant provisions of the A.L.I.'s Model Code can be taken as known, the reader might be reminded that it provides, among other items, specific "Criteria for Withholding Sentence of Imprisonment and for Placing Defendants on Probation" (Section 7.01), "Criteria for Imposing Fines" (Section 7.02), "Criteria for Sentence of Extended Terms of Imprisonment, Felonies" (Section 7.03), and the same for "Misdemeanors and Petty Misdemeanors" (Section 7.04), "Procedure on Sentence: Pre-Sentence Investigation and Report, etc." (Section 7.07). There is some considerable overlap between the individual contributions to the symposium, and there is no need to go into the technical details, some of which are of interest mainly to American lawyers and penologists. The main problems which the Model Penal Code set out to solve might be defined as follows: how to reduce the length of prison sentences and of the terms actually served in prison by not particularly dangerous offenders, but at the same time to provide sufficient safeguards against really dangerous ones; how to ensure greater equality of sentence between courts; how best to distribute the power of fixing the prison terms between courts and administrative bodies, especially parole boards.

To achieve these objects, the Model Code fixed minima and maxima—graded according to the seriousness of the offense—for ordinary cases, with extended terms for persistent offenders and professional criminals (Model Code 1955, Section 7.04). Both the ordinary minima and maxima and the extended terms have been criticized, for example, by Turnbladh (pages 544 ff.), the minimum and maximum terms being still too high and the extended terms as having to operate on the basis of an inadequate definition of the concept of the "dangerous offender."

To the present writer, the maximum terms seem to be not unreasonably high if sensibly applied by the courts; they are in ordinary cases for felonies of first degree life imprisonment, of second degree, ten years, and of third degree, five years; for "extended terms" life, ten to twenty, and five to ten years. What seems too high is the length of the minimum terms, which should be altogether abolished. Turnbladh is justified in calling them "one of the truly destructive elements in present-day sentencing practice" (page 548), and their absence is one of the best features of the English system. Tappan (page 541) defends them within limits. More weighty still is the criticism concerning the definition. However, as the past eighty or more years of legislative history in the field of recidivism and "dangerousness" have shown, to provide a watertight definition of the persistent and the dangerous criminal is one of the most hazardous occupations which a lawmaking body can possibly choose. For the "persistent" offender, it has to be stressed that the provision of the Model Code ("the Court shall not make such a finding unless the defendant has previously been convicted of two crimes, committed at different times when he was over juvenile court age") is surprisingly wide and colorless; it would enable a court to make such a finding in a case where an offender aged 65 had two preconvictions, one at the age of, say, 25, and the second at the age of, say, 45, which might make nonsense of the whole concept. It ignores the traditional provision of legislation on recidivism that the intervals between the previous conviction should not be longer than, say, five years, and also the sensible proposal of the German Draft Code of 1962, paragraph 61 (and previous ones) that these preconvictions should show that the offender had not taken them as a warning, in other words that there has to be an "inner connection" (*innerer Zusammenhang*) between the previous offenses and the new one (Begründung, page 182).[10] For the professional criminal, the Code employs the usual formula of "knowingly devoting himself to criminal activity as a major source of livelihood," with the alternative, "or has substantial income or resources not explained to be derived from a source other than criminal activity." Both alternatives are useful, but equally difficult to prove in cases of really clever professional criminals.

As far as the reduction of inequality of sentences is concerned, this is likely to be achieved under the Model Code only to the extent that its provisions, by reducing the maximum terms, of necessity lead to the curbing of the most extravagant inequalities; within the terms provided, however, there still remains ample scope for inequality. It is here, though, that the provision of Section 7.08 has to be considered; it is perhaps the most interesting and original part of the whole section on sentencing. According to it, every sentence of imprisonment for felony is "deemed tentative" for the first year in the sense that if the State Commissioner of Correction, as a result of "examination and classification," is satisfied that the sentence of the court was "based upon a misapprehension as to the history, character or physical or mental condition of the offender," he has to petition the sentencing court to resentence the offender. The

10 The present writer has dealt with the subject of legislation on recidivism in his contribution on *"Ruckfall und Prognose"* in the forthcoming new edition of the German *"Handworterbuch der Kriminologie."*

court is, of course, free to dismiss the petition, even without a hearing, but it may also replace the original sentence by another, more appropriate, term of imprisonment. This section gives the administration at least the right to express its views on sentences which, in the light of the fuller information subsequently at its disposal, it regards as inappropriate, without, on the other hand, the right to interfere with judicial independence. It is perhaps regrettable that the powers of the court do not include the possibility of replacing a prison sentence by probation; this might, of course, lead to complications in cases where part of the sentence had already been served, but such difficulties could be overcome by legislation. The Swedish model or the proposals made by the Howard League for a more flexible form of sentence (see below under (c)) might here be useful. In any case, this provision of the Model Code opens at least a narrow door to the setting aside of grossly unsuitable prison sentences regardless of formal appeals. It might have been desirable for the Model Code explicitly to mention as one of the grounds for petition that the sentence was, for no visible reason, entirely out of proportion with the ordinary run of sentences imposed for offenses of this kind on offenders of this type.

The "Model Sentencing Act" of 1963 prepared by the N.C.C.D.'s Advisory Council of Judges differs from the A.L.I.'s Model Code, among other points, in its view—already mentioned above—that "the offense is not a useful guide to the sentence" (page 12); that the individual offender should matter to the sentencer rather than the offense. The Council regards the system of sentencing according to offense as the major source of disparity of sentences and its abolition therefore as a major step forward. It is also strongly against legally fixed minimum terms and against the statutory exclusion of probation for certain offenses or because of the offender's previous convictions, as the latter are regarded as unreliable guides to sentencing. All this is good in itself and shows the forward-looking, far-from-stereotyped way in which these judges have approached their task. How far it can by itself drastically reduce inequalities of sentences may be quite another question—it simply replaces one extremely complicated yardstick by another at least equally complicated one.

Another sensible recommendation, in conformity with some jurisdictions in the United States, is that the court shall have power to reduce a sentence within ninety days after it has been imposed (paragraph 11). Moreover the sentencing judge is in any case required "to make a brief statement of the basic reasons for the sentence he imposes (paragraph 10), which is something but not quite enough.

Among the most crucial points to make or mar the reputation of this Model Sentencing Act are its provisions for "dangerous offenders" (paragraphs 5 and 6). How far do they differ from those in the A.L.I.'s Model Code? In the view of the present writer, the similarities far outweigh the differences, except perhaps that the mere fact of repeated offenses—the "multiple" offender of the Model Code—in itself plays a slightly less important part in the Model Act. On the other hand, in spite of the protestation to the contrary, the type of offense does have some significance in the Model Act (paragraphs 5c and 8), too, and the reference to the incriminating nature of the fact that the defendant has "substantial income or resources not explained to the satisfaction of the court as derived from lawful activities or interests" (Art. III 6 II) is almost identical with Section 7.04(2)(b) of the Code. The maximum term suggested by the Model Act is thirty years, which even exceeds the twenty years of the Model Code, but it is not intended to be mandatory; moreover, the Model Act authorizes life sentences only for first degree murder, whereas the Model Code provides them for third degree felonies in general. The Model Act does not provide for a mandatory periodic review by a court of these very long sentences, as such reviews had better be left to the institution and parole authorities (page 20). In paragraph 2 the old phrase, "a crime involving moral turpitude," appears again. As the writer asked already several years ago: "Has not the time come for such ambiguous phrases . . . to be altogether extirpated from legal phraseology and the decision to be left to unfettered judicial discretion?"

(c) In the *German Federal Republic* the latest stage in the long drawn-out work on the new Penal Code is the *"Entwruf eines Strafgesetzbuches (StGB)—E 1962—mit Begründung."* Like its predecessors, it contains a special chapter on sentencing: *"Zweiter Titel: Strafbemssung."* In paragraph 60 the guiding principles are laid down, with special emphasis on the *"Schuld,"* the guilt of the offender as the basis for sentencing rather than on any purely external factors such as the injury inflicted. In the brief catalogue of factors here provided, this subjective element of guilt plays throughout the decisive part, and although recidivism is treated as an aggravating factor leading to a mandatory increase in punishment, this is, as already mentioned, made dependent on the question of whether the offender can be blamed for not having been warned by his previous convictions (paragraph 61). On the other hand, although the offender's *"Gesinnung"* (that is, his attitudes and way of thinking and feeling), which expresses itself in his offense, is mentioned in the catalogue of factors, the provision of the present Penal Code, paragraph 20, which make the choice between penal servitude (*Zuchthaus*) and simple imprisonment (*Gefängnis*) dependent on the *"ehrlose*

Gesinnung" of the actor—a concept comparable to "moral turpitude"—
has been dropped in the Draft Code. As in the present Penal Code,
minima and maxima are provided by law according to the gravity of
the different offenses. To give only a few illustrations, infanticide is
punishable by imprisonment between one year and ten years (paragraphs
136 and 46), aggravated rape by *Zuchthaus* between two and twenty
years (paragraphs 205 and 44). The German counterpart to the American
attempts to cope with the problem of the dangerous and/or professional
criminal (at present paragraphs 20a and 42e) is now to be found in
paragraph 85 which provides for the "*Sicherungsverwahrung*" (protective
detention) of a dangerous "Hangtäter," that is, of an offender who has
committed at least three intentional offenses of a certain gravity, at least
one of them after his twenty-fifth year. If the court regards him as
dangerous in view of his tendency to commit serious crimes, the maximum duration of this protective measure, which takes effect after the
offender has already served his ordinary penalty, is ten years or, if necessary, in exceptional cases for the protection of society, unlimited (paragraph 89), but the "*Vollstreckungsgericht*" has power to release the
prisoner at any time if it can be expected that the object of the protective
measure can also be achieved under supervision outside the institution
(paragraph 89 No. 6, 107). Although this possibility makes for a considerable degree of flexibility, similar to the Swedish Code and the
Howard League proposals, it has to be borne in mind that it refers not
to the penalty itself but only to the subsequent protective measure.
There is in addition envisaged a special measure called "*Vorbeugende
Verwahrung*" (preventive detention) for budding "Hangtäter" (paragraph 86), and in the case of suitable offenses such as larceny, robbery,
and frauds, the Draft Code provides certain aggravated penalties for
offenders who commit these offenses in a professional manner so as to
derive their whole livelihood or most of it through them (paragraphs 238,
246 No. 4, 254), provisions that are similar to the ones mentioned before
in the American Model Code and Model Act.

If we now consider the main differences between the American and
the German Drafts with respect to the sentencing of dangerous professionals, the following points of contrast seem to emerge: although the
definitions themselves are roughly on the same lines, in the American
Drafts offenders with severe personality disorders are included together
with the normal dangerous offenders, whereas in the German Draft these
two categories are treated separately according to entirely different
provisions (paragraph 82 as against paragraph 85–86). Altogether the
German Draft is far more detailed than the others. Moreover, in accordance with previous legislation the German Draft is still based on the

dual-track system, that is, its measures of security (*Dichernde Massnahmen*) are kept separate from its penalties and take effect, as a rule, only after the latter have been served. It is regarded as an inevitable consequence of the "*Rechtsstaatsidee*," which is held to be incompatible with any kind of indeterminate penalty; and as certain measures against dangerous criminals are bound to be of indeterminate length, they have to be construed as being different from penalties proper.[11] The great emphasis placed on the "*Rechtsstaatsidee*"—a natural consequence of its complete eclipse during the Nazi regime—has also led to a refusal to enable administrative bodies such as parole boards to take the place of the courts in deciding the time of release of inmates. The Draft Code realizes, however, that the sentencing court is not well placed for decisions of this kind, first, because it lacks the intimate personal knowledge of the institution, its staff, and the way in which the detainee has responded to the treatment received; and, second, because to make the sentencing court competent for such decisions might introduce a large number of decision-making courts into an institution and make any uniformity and consistency impossible (see *Begründung*, page 206). Therefore, the Draft Code concentrates all such decisions in the hands of a new judicial body, the "*Vollstreckungsgericht*," situated in the neighborhood of the institution, in which the detainees are kept, and apparently—the details are reserved for special regulations—are competent to deal with all cases arising within the institution. The same court will also have to decide on release on license (paragraph 79). Although there seems to be some resemblance between these courts and the French "*juge d'application des peines*" and their Italian counterpart, the "*guidice di sorveglianza*" (Article 585, *Codice di Procedura Penale* of 1930), there will no doubt also be some considerable differences in practice. Generally speaking, the success of the system will largely depend on the penological and criminological training of the judges concerned.

(d) In *Great Britain* the present picture is one of general lack of direction, bewilderment, and waste of effort, produced in part by the recent change of government with its inevitable shifting of emphasis but also, to some considerable extent, due to previous sins of omission, delays, lack of resolute guidance, and reluctance to look beyond the frontiers and study contemporary developments abroad. As the result of such shortcomings, the Royal Commission on the Penal System, appointed in the spring of 1964 and hailed as a milestone in the evolution of penal reform, was dissolved in the spring of 1966, in its early infancy. Its work,

---

[11] The dual-track system has been controversial in Germany for the greater part of the present century and has only recently again been criticized by Th. Wurtenberger in the symposium, "*Gedanken zur Strafrechtsreform*," Paderborn, 1965, p. 37.

it is true, would have touched only the fringe of our present subject, sentencing; however, among its terms of reference was at least "to report . . . whether any changes in the arrangements and responsibility for selecting the sentences to be imposed on particular offenders are desirable," which shows that our subject could not have been altogether shirked. That a Royal Commission should have been rather abruptly brought to such an untimely end after two years of work is perhaps unique in the history of this type of institution. It is also indicative, however, of the growing feeling in this country that the days of Royal Commissions are numbered anyhow in an age that has but little use for more or less amateurish bodies whose progress is far too slow and cumbersome and whose techniques of inquiry are largely out of date. The present writer has taken the moderate view that Royal Commissions, whose recommendations stand a slightly better chance of being accepted by public opinion and Parliament, might continue to exist side by side with research bodies whose work is also sometimes not distinguished by rapidity of tempo, but that they should at least abandon their amateurish techniques and become full time, professional, and supported by competent research teams.[12]

To return to our main topic, the dissolution of the Royal Commission on Penal Reform has been mainly justified by reference to the publication of two Home Office White Papers, "The Child, the Family, and the Young Offender" (Cmnd. 2742) and "The Adult Offender" (Cmnd. 2852), both of 1965, which together, it has been argued, have anticipated any possible conclusions that the Royal Commission might have reached. Considering the brevity and not particularly high quality of these two White Papers, considering especially the absence in these documents of any scientific evidence in support of their conclusions, we might perhaps find this argument far from convincing. In any case, this competition between the Commission and the White Papers betrays the lack of coordination and foresight to which we referred above. Limiting ourselves to the principal points affecting sentencing in the White Paper on "The Adult Offender," they are, in their turn, largely based on the proposals made two years earlier in a Report on Preventive Detention of the Advisory Council on the Treatment of Offenders,[13] which recommended the abolition of preventive detention and the substitution for it of ordinary prison sentences of up to ten years "for persistent offenders convicted of offenses at present punishable with imprisonment for a term of five years or more." The Advisory Council

[12] See my *Comparative Criminology*, The Houghton Mifflin Company, Boston, 1965, pp. 81–82.
[13] London, H.M.S.O., Home Office, 1963.

admitted that "there is a natural disinclination on the part of the courts
to pass sentences of imprisonment not commensurate with the gravity
of the current offence." This is, of course, the eternal crux of the whole
matter, which has been discussed for most of the present century in
many countries with no really conclusive results. It is this dilemma that
has been responsible for most of the inconsistencies and inadequacies of
the present system of dealing with the persistent petty offender and for
the multitude of cases, where sentences of preventive detention, passed
on such offenders in this country, have been replaced on appeal by
probation or fines.[14] To quote only one such case, *Regina v. Dunn*
(*The Times*, 6.10.64), here a man of 62, with 36 previous convictions,
who had received eight years' preventive detention by the court of first
instance for obtaining the sum of 1 shilling 10½ pence (!) by false pre-
tences, was instead sentenced to a fine of £75 by the Court of Criminal
Appeal. Fortunately or unfortunately, judges are often human, and they,
not the theorists, are the ones who have to deal with the offender standing before them. Here the exhortations of the Advisory Council's Report
on Preventive Detention or of similar bodies are unlikely to change
their attitudes. There are of course exceptions, as the case described in
Tony Parker's book, "The Unknown Citizen," shows,[15] but even here
the sentence of ten years' preventive detention imposed on a petty recidivist was quashed by the good sense of the Court of Criminal Appeal.
Glaring discrepancies in sentencing of the kind here quoted show that
something in the application of preventive detention, and its abolition
as such, is probably not to be regretted.

What is it, however, that the White Paper proposes in its place and
in that of its counterpart for younger recidivists—corrective training?
It is aware of the universally known fact that there are two main categories of recidivists: the dangerous serious criminal who is a real menace
to society and the petty inadequate offender who is a mere nuisance.
But is it also aware of the many subcategories? It recognizes also that
preventive detention—intended only for the first—has been wrongly
and indiscriminately applied to both and, in fact, proportional far more
frequently to the second than to the first category. It tries to discriminate
at least in a superficial way, but is it successful in this? It gives a definition
of the serious persistent criminal, which remains entirely on the surface
of the problem and, in practice, might well be applicable to many cases
of the nuisance category as well, since it distinguishes mainly according

[14] See my "Deutsche Strafrechtsreform in englischer Sicht," C. H. Beck, Munich,
1960, p. 27.
[15] Hutchinson, London, 1962. See my Critical Notice of this book in *The British
Journal of Criminology*, Vol. 4, No. 4, April 1964, pp. 395–399.

to the number of previous convictions without trying to introduce any of the largely psychological elements that have been used in some of the foreign drafts. It is unlikely, therefore, that the definition given in Number 15 of the White Paper will achieve its purpose.

There is the further problem of differences in treatment, and here the White Paper puts its faith in distinctions concerning length of sentences and release procedures, but even the layman's mind has been quick to discover that "their suggested replacement scheme is pretty well identical with the old, discredited P.D." (*New Statesman*, 5.6.66). The most widely discussed recommendation is that the Home Secretary should have power to release on license any prisoner who has served at least one-third of his sentence or twelve months, whichever may be the longer, provided that he is "likely to respond to generous treatment" and not regarded as a risk to the public. Release would be "subject to conditions," which might be comparable to a parole system, up to the date when the prisoner would normally be released already under the present system, that is, after serving two-thirds of his sentence. In short, the sentence would normally be divided into three sections of equal length, the first to be served inside, the second at liberty but on license, and the third in complete freedom. The persistent offender, however, would even for the last one-third be kept on license. Moreover, for him, special arrangements would be made to make his longer term of imprisonment tolerable. Apart from the possibility of earlier release (which in practice may, or may not, result in longer sentences), there is not much in these proposals that differs from things as they are now.

Four years before the White Paper the more detailed report of the so-called Streatfield Committee (presided over by a High Court judge of this name) had been published.[16] This, too, was not primarily concerned with the process of sentencing as such, but had mainly to search for potential ways and means of improving the information needed by the courts and of disposing with criminal cases more expeditiously. Nevertheless, in Part B we find some brief and not very original observations on "the aims of sentencers" and on the value of prediction studies as a particularly important source of information for the courts. There are a few references to the researches already done in this field and to the need for predictive devices to be made available for the various types of treatment, but all this is far too vague to be of any real significance. What is useful, however, is the emphasis placed by the report on the need for better communication to the courts of the informa-

[16] Report of the Interdepartmental Committee on the Business of the Criminal Courts. London, H.M.S.O., Cmnd. 1289, 1961.

tion available on the effect of the different types of sentences in general and on the effect of actual sentences on individual offenders (pages 82 ff). Here the report recommends, first, that regular booklets should be issued by the Home Office, to be revised, as necessary, every few years, about sentencing in general and on the results of research into the efficacy of sentences. It is pointed out, quite rightly, that this would imply no interference with the independence of the judiciary on the part of the executive. Second, the report recommends that sentencers should be assisted to obtain information on the effect of their own sentences in individual cases. It is envisaged that sentencers should be able to notify some central authority of their interest in a particular case and should then be supplied with periodical reports of the offender's progress and any additional information they might ask for (page 87). The report adds that some of its recommendations might require legislation, whereas others could be implemented by administrative measures (page 126). Whether any such steps have been taken in the five years since publication is not known, except that a short handbook, "The Sentence of the Court" (H.M.S.O., 1964), has been issued by the Home Office which, in addition to a survey of the various forms of treatment available, contains a section on the results of treatment, largely based on a so far unpublished statistical follow-up study of the Home Office Research Unit of all offenders convicted in the (London) Metropolitan Police District during March and April, 1957.

Certain proposals made by a private body, the Howard League, for penal reform in London, in their evidence to the now defunct Royal Commission, are also important enough to be mentioned in this connection. Apart from such recommendations as the abolition of all prison sentences of three months or less, of a reexamination of the possibility of suspended sentences, so far frowned upon in Britain, but now apparently seriously envisaged by the new Home Secretary (*The Times*, 6.3.66), and of day-fines, the League advocates a greater flexibility of all prison sentences of eighteen months or more, to be achieved, first, by a periodical review approximately every six months with a view to possible release on license. The decision should be in the hands of the Governor, assisted by a small panel including an expert on behavior and a lawyer; there should, however, be no formal appearance of the prisoner before a parole board. Second, as an alternative the League recommends a new type of "supervision-or-custody" sentence with a maximum of three years, which should leave it open whether the sentence begins with a spell in the open or in the institution, with the actual decisions left to a local treatment board.

To sum up this part of our discussion, it should be noted that while our comparative survey of legislative reform movements on sentencing in four countries has shown an ocean of differences, there are at least a few drops of common or at least unopposed trends: a tendency to make sentencing more flexible and more equal by legislative and/or administrative measures; the desire to introduce clearer distinctions between the sentences used for the various types of recidivists; an understanding of the vital importance of better information on the likely effect of sentences of different kinds on different types of offenders. On the other hand, there is no unanimity as to the details of the steps to be taken to achieve these objects. We may use the character of the decision-making bodies as one example. In the United States, the decision-making bodies tend to be mainly administrative, that is, parole boards; in Britain, they are also administrative but centralized in the hands of the Home Secretary; in West Germany a special type of court is envisaged, the "Vollstreckungsgericht," while in Sweden the nature of the various boards has not yet quite clearly emerged from the available publications. Moreover, there are differences regarding the use of minimum sentences, the question whether the main emphasis in sentencing should be on the type of offense or the personality of the offender, the use of the single- or the dual-track system, and many more. Many of these issues go far beyond the boundaries of sentencing as such, but it is obvious that sentencing is greatly dependent on the way in which these broader problems are solved. As already indicated, powers of early release given by the law to the administration might easily influence the length of the sentences imposed by the judiciary; the legal prohibition of very short prison sentences might lead to the imposition of longer ones even where they are not really needed, and so on.

COURT PRACTICE

One of the recommendations of the Streatfield Report leads already to the section of this chapter that is concerned with attempts by the courts themselves to improve their sentencing practice by obtaining more information on the effect of their work. Here in particular the growing number of conferences on sentencing has to be mentioned, attended by judges and magistrates, often under the auspices of a University Department of Law or Institute of Criminology. As an example of this kind, the "National Conference of Judges on Sentencing," convened by the Centre of Criminology, University of Toronto, May 27–29, 1964, may be referred to. While mainly concerned with problems confronting Canadian courts, its full proceedings are to some extent of general interest. In Britain, too, there was a few years ago a conference on sentencing policy called by the Lord Chief Justice, but very little, if anything, has been published about its results. In the lower ranks, local "sentencing days" are becoming very frequent (see, for example, *The Magistrate,* May 1966, page 73). In the United States many more such conferences are held, partly of a nationwide scope, partly for a number of states or of circuits.[17]

Quite apart from such conferences on sentencing problems in general, an interesting practice of so-called *"en-banc"* sentencing consultations, concerned with individual cases, has in recent years grown up in several American State jurisdictions and, in particular, in the federal courts.[18] It means that, in the words of Professor Norval Morris, "prior to imposing sentence, but having received all documents and listening to all the arguments on sentencing in the case, the trial judge will arrange a consultation with the group of judges in his court who are collaborating in this *en banc* sentencing program . . . the trial judge will tell them his impressions of the case; he will have made available to them all the documents relevant to sentencing, and in some cases the probation officer will attend so that he can explain any ambiguities or difficulties that the judge may have in his probation report. All judges attending the meeting will pass their opinion on what would be a suitable sentence in the case. . . . The trial judge can of course take their advice or not as he pleases. . . ." While this seems to be an excellent device to improve the standard of sentencing and reduce inequalities, there is perhaps slightly less need for it in countries where all sentences in more serious cases are passed not by one single judge but by a bench of three or more, which necessitates an exchange of views anyhow. Nevertheless, even here there may be some advantage in getting the views of judges not directly involved in the trial to balance the possibly strong personal involvement of the trial judges.

Most useful as all such conferences and consultations no doubt are, being limited to judges and magistrates, they cannot produce more than the exchanges of views that their members can possible give. Moreover, some of these conferences seem to be too strongly dominated by the higher judiciary and therefore likely to remain tradition-bound. Such occasions should be used, as some of them in fact are, for interchanges

---

[17] See, for example, *Federal Probation,* June 1962, p. 39.

[18] The following text is mainly based on private information kindly supplied to the writer by Professor Norval Morris of the University of Chicago Law School, Director of the Center for Studies in Criminal Justice. See also the reference in *Federal Probation,* June 1962, p. 397, to a "sentencing council" used since 1960 in the U.S. District Court for the Eastern District of Michigan at Detroit.

of knowledge with research workers who, in the field of prediction and other relevant studies, should participate on an equal footing with the lawyers.

A promising experimental study of sentencing was carried out in 1962–1964 by Dr. Gordon Rose of Manchester University as part of an annual five-day residential course for lay magistrates at Manchester.[19] The participants were divided into benches of three and given a set of brief summaries of hypothetical cases for discussion and proposals regarding sentences. Three sets of comparisons could be made by the experimenter: rural-urban, male-female, and according to length of membership of bench. The results were largely inconclusive, that is, no significant differences could be found. Rose suggests, however, that the absence of official chairmen of the benches might have levelled out certain otherwise existing differences; moreover, that the most punitive-minded magistrates might not have attended these courses and that the training situation in itself might have curbed actually existing severely punitive attitudes.

With the object of achieving greater uniformity in sentencing, the use of computers has recently been considered in Britain, and similar developments may be taking place in other countries. According to reports in the British Press, a central computer is likely to be installed in which sentences for all types of crime would be stored from every magistrates' court in the country (for the higher courts this is apparently not envisaged). "Fresh information would be sent by teleprinter, compared, and within seconds the computer would come up with a sentence imposed by other courts in similar cases."[20] It is difficult to judge the usefulness of this procedure without knowing how many variables of individual cases would be fed into the computer but, if the information received by the machine should be reasonably detailed, it should be possible to place at the disposal of the magistrates comparative material vastly superior to the present basis of their sentencing.

Under the heading of "Court Practice" the need for giving adequate reasons in writing for the sentence imposed (see above under Legislation) has again to be discussed. The matter may well be regulated by legislation, as it is for example in the German Code of Criminal Procedure, paragraph 267, III, which provides that the written sentence should mention the circumstances determining the choice of penalty. It is highly desirable that at least in important cases these circumstances should

[19] See Gordon Rose, *British Journal of Criminology*, Vol. 5, No. 3, July 1965, pp. 314–319. A somewhat similar small-scale exercise is reported in *The Magistrate*, October 1962, p. 139.
[20] *The Times*, 4.11.66; *Sunday Times*, 4.10.66; *The Magistrate*, April 1966, pp. 51–52.

be set out in writing as fully as possible. Objections to such a proposal have to be expected. They come not only from judges and magistrates who plead overwork, but also from certain theorists who are quick to discover the obvious truth that in many cases such written reasons may be platitudinous and hardly worth having; moreover, that occasionally they may even be downright dishonest and merely a cloak for the real, but undisclosed, reasons.[21] There is more support for the proposal that written reasons should be required in all cases where an appeal has been lodged and also for all sentences pronounced by the Appeal Court itself, and this is already the law in some countries. This, however, is not enough. There are many important cases which, for one reason or another, never reach an Appeal Court. Whatever may be the position in this respect, one fundamental point has still to be made: written reasons for the sentence should be composed not after the sentence has already been pronounced but before. Only in this way can they contribute to the quality of the sentence; otherwise they may be misused to buttress a decision that the judges, in the process of writing, may actually discover to be wrong. It is in such cases that the danger of faked reasons arises. Where the judges, when writing their reasons, still have their hands free, they are far more likely to produce an honest document that will give a true picture of the considerations they have in mind.

RESEARCH

In the past ten years here under review, sentencing has become one of the most popular topics of legal-criminological research. We can do no more here than list, in chronological order and with very brief comments, the following six projects published in the English language:

1. *Edward Green, Judicial Attitudes in Sentencing*[22]

After a brief introduction into the general problems, Green gives an equally short survey of previous studies, almost entirely limited to American publications. Not even Exner's pioneering study of 1931 is mentioned. The author's material consists of the records of 1437 convictions by a "non-jury prison court" of the Philadelphia Court of Quarter Sessions in cases tried during the years 1956–1957. The items available in

---

[21] J. E. Hall Williams in his contribution to "Criminology in Transition," London, 1965, pp. 34–36, seems to be rather skeptical too.

[22] *A study of the Factors underlying the Sentencing Practice of the Criminal Court of Philadelphia*, London, Macmillan & Co. Ltd., 1961.

the records were consolidated for purposes of the research into three sets of variables: "legal factors, legally irrelevant factors, and factors in the criminal prosecution." In the second category, the "biosocial traits" of offenders as found in the police records were included, namely sex, age, race, and place of birth. In the third category, individual differences in the personnel—judges, prosecuting attorneys—found their place. The severity of the sentences was measured according to the degree of deprivation of liberty involved. Without going into details, it might be said that the author, while generally regarding the sentencing policy of the judges concerned in a favorable light (for example, pages 63 and 96), has to admit that, in particular, in cases of intermediate gravity a certain inconsistency in sentencing was apparent, due not to any personal prejudices but rather to differences in "the judge's perception of the defendant" and to his inadequate information on personal factors (page 102). Green's otherwise valuable investigation suffers from his limited use of the non-American literature (see above) and from the restriction of his study, with regard to "biosocial factors," to the four items already mentioned, that is, sex, age, race, and place of birth.

2. Roger Hood, Sentencing in Magistrates' Courts[23]

As far as its material is concerned, this study differs from that of Green in drawing its cases not from one single court but from a sample of twelve magistrates' courts scattered throughout the whole of England and Wales (excluding Scotland), classified according to the proportion of prison sentences imposed by them for indictable offenses on men aged 21 and over. As this proportion had been found to vary in the years 1951–1954 between 7.8 percent and 47.3 percent, the Home Office thought it advisable to instigate an investigation into these variations, their characteristic features, and possible causes. While the methodology of this study was to some extent based on a previous one, already quoted in my article in *The Yale Law Journal* on the "Magisterial Policy in the London Juvenile Courts," it goes beyond it by adding on-the-spot visits of the research workers to the courts in question and personal interviews with some of the magistrates, their clerks, police and probation officers. The investigation took as its starting point the "null hypothesis" that the differences in sentencing were *not* associated with variations in the types of offenders and offenses confronting the magistrates in different areas, but eventually it was found that this null hypothesis had to some extent been rebutted by the evidence although, for the rest, those variations were indeed not substantial

[23] *A Study in Variations of Policy*, London, Stevens and Sons, 1962, with an introduction by the present writer.

enough to explain the differences. The methodological value of Hood's work lies mainly in its original approach to the study of "equality" in sentencing and its emphasis on the need for "equality of consideration," that is, on the requirement that the same factors should be considered in the same way by different courts. The author is not satisfied, for example, with an examination of whether different courts imprison the *same proportion* of offenders; he inquires beyond that as to whether they actually imprison the *same type* of offender for the *same reasons* because, otherwise, statistical equality in the use of imprisonment may hide flagrant inequalities and injustices in sentencing.

3. R. G. Andry, the Short-Term Prisoner[24]

This investigation, also carried out for the Home Office, places the emphasis not on the problem of equality of sentencing but rather on the specific question of how far and for which types of offenders short-term prison sentences might be regarded as useful and for which types they should be avoided. Moreover, what should be their substitutes? Based on an interview study of 121 white male prisoners in a London prison with sentences not exceeding six months, some of whom were also psychologically tested and followed up, a tentative typology was worked out, with the object of predicting which of these prisoners were likely to recidivate, possibly as the result of their sentences, and which of them were not. By means of the technique of factorial analysis, the twenty-two variables, which originally seemed to have some correlation with recidivism, could be reduced to four: emotional maturity *v.* immaturity, neuroticism *v.* nonneuroticism, intrapunitiveness *v.* extrapunitiveness, juvenile crime experience *v.* no such experience. For offenders showing evidence of emotional immaturity, neuroticism, intrapunitiveness, and/or juvenile crime experience, short-term prison sentences were found to be conducive to recidivism and, in their place, treatment in a "reconstruction center" was recommended. For extrapunitive offenders (unless they were also neurotics), however, longer prison sentences were regarded as indispensable. The author realizes that this result, which he regards as being in accordance with modern learning theory and, in particular, with the work of Eysenck and his followers, was likely to meet with strong objections based on the conception of equality of treatment in its traditional sense, meaning equality according to type and gravity of offense only, regardless of the needs of the individual offenders. He believes, however, that this difficulty might eventually be overcome by educating the public.

[24] *A Study in Forensic Psychology*, London, Stevens & Sons, 1963.

4. *Stuart King Jaffary, Sentencing of Adults in Canada*[25]

This work is confined to the study of sentencing differences between provincial regions of Canada. It is not concerned with variations within a region, between urban and rural courts, or between magistrates. Bearing this difference in mind, there is otherwise a certain similarity between Jaffary's research and that of Hood. However, while the latter had, for obvious reasons, to respect the anonymity of the courts and magistrates observed, Jaffary was free to name the Canadian provinces to which he was referring. Thus he could show, for example, that for common theft an offender was nearly twice as likely to be sent to prison in Quebec as in Canada, in general, and even five times as likely as in Manitoba, Saskatchewan, or British Columbia. He stresses the "strongly punitive philosophy" of Canadian courts and compares the frequency of longer prison sentences in his country (in 1955, for example, 2084 sentences of two years and over to penitentiaries), with the figure of 92 such sentences in 1953 in Sweden with slightly less than one-half of the population of Canada. He advocates the more frequent use of probation and suspended prison sentences, but he admits the weight of the fact that more progressive methods of treatment were often not available in some of the Canadian provinces.

5. *T. C. Willett, Criminal on the Road*[26]

This very thorough examination of the problem of the traffic offender in a selected area of South England contains much valuable information on the sentencing habits of the courts as they affect this important category of offenders (see, in particular, pages 127–128, 144, 306 ff). The result is that "the sentence received for a serious motoring offence was largely a matter of chance," that "there is no evidence that the courts have responded to the manifest increase in motoring offences by the use of more severe treatment," and "that the proportion of motoring offenders who were sent to prison was consistently lower than the comparable proportions of offenders against property or the person."

6. *Shlomo Shoham, Crime and Social Deviation, Chapters 9 and 10*[27]

Here, an account is included of a piece of statistical research on the sentencing policy of Israeli criminal courts, with special reference to the reasons given by the judges to justify the sentences imposed. The material

[25] The University of Toronto Press, 1963.
[26] London, Tavistock Publications, 1964.
[27] Chicago, The Henry Regnery Company, 1966.

is taken from the work of the three district courts of Israel in the year 1956. Convictions numbered 1105. The "sentencing grounds" as stated by the judges were classified according to the purpose given for the penalty in question, and a fairly strong correlation was found between these sentencing grounds and the severity of the punishment actually imposed. As the author makes clear, no research was possible into "the very complicated factors that determine the sentencing behavior of judges, belonging as it does to the domain of general human behavior. . . . We do not claim that the present research is a study in human psychology." In the statistical investigation, to which the research had to be limited, from each of the three courts, three judges were selected whose severity of sentencing was found to vary for property offenses from a maximum of 71 to a minimum of 30. The picture emerging for offenses against the person was very different, and altogether it seemed that "the sentencing policy of each individual judge was definitely influenced by his personal reaction to a specific type of offense. This finding applied not only to the severity or leniency of the sentence but also to the choice of penalties in general. The sentencing habits of these nine judges were examined in some considerable detail, and it might be a worthwhile exercise for a research worker interested in the subject closely to compare the material assembled by Shoham with that of Green (see number 1 under Research in this chapter) and thereby perhaps to establish some crosscultural features of judicial sentencing habits and idiosyncrasies; within the framework of the present paper there is no opportunity for it. Shoham stresses the need for presentencing inquiries as a tool for reducing those harmful individual differences and refers to an Israeli statute of 1954 (in force only since 1961), which makes presentence examinations mandatory, but so far only for offenders under twenty-one who are likely to be imprisoned for more than six months.

In the same volume a study of the deterrent effect of suspended prison sentences is published, with the main result that age and previous convictions are the principal factors determining the success of this form of punishment.

To conclude this section, it can be said that even these very brief summaries of only half a dozen projects give already an idea of the great variety of aspects and problems involved in sentencing research: variations between courts, areas, individual judges, and magistrates; the manner in which they state the reasons for their sentences; the psychological relationships between types of offenders and types of sentences. What has not yet been studied in sufficient depth is the psychology of the sentencing judge and magistrate, but a project at present being undertaken in Toronto may be expected to supply at least some further material on this.[28]

Reference should also be made to a study, which has been completed but not yet published at the time of writing, on the sentencing policy of the higher courts in England and Wales, examined in the light of a sample of cases of breaking and entering, sentenced in the year 1956.[29]

PUBLICATIONS NOT BASED ON RESEARCH

They are too numerous even to be summarized briefly. It might be useful, however, to list at least the more important of them to assist future research workers; no completeness can of course be achieved. It has to be borne in mind, moreover, that in some cases the line between them and the research studies mentioned under Research is difficult to draw as they could hardly have been written without the background of a specific research project. Perhaps the line of demarcation might be drawn according to whether the main emphasis is on the research itself or on the general observations drawn from it, but even this leaves ample room for doubt, and differences of opinion will be inevitable.

A. R. N. Cross, *Paradoxes in Prison Sentences* (Oxford, Clarendon Press, 1965).

Sheldon Glueck, *Judicial Therapeutics*: A Technique for the Study of a Neglected Field of Criminal Justice (Thessaloniki, Aristotelian University of Thessaloniki, Annual of the School of Law and Economics, Vol. 14, Charmosynon to Dimitrios J. Karanikas, 1966).

E. V. Jarvis, "Inquiry before Sentence" (in *Criminology in Transition. Essays in honour of Hermann Mannheim*, Intern. Library of Criminology, Tavistock Publications, No. 14, 1965).

Hermann Mannheim, *Penalties to fit the Crime* (*The Times*, 27.11.57).

Hermann Mannheim, "Comparative Sentencing Practice" (in Symposium on Sentencing, *Law and Contemporary Problems*, Duke University School of Law, Durham, N.C., Summer 1958).

Frank Milton, *In Some Authority*, Chapter 6 (London, Pall Mall Press, 1959).

R. F. Sparks, *Sentencing by Magistrates*: Some Facts of Life (in Sociological Studies in the British Penal Services, ed. by Paul Halmos, The Sociological Review Monograph No. 9, Keele, University of Keele, 1965).

W. J. H. Sprott, *Sentencing Policy* (in the same monograph).

D. A. Thomas, *Sentencing—the Case for Reasoned Decisions* (Criminal Law Review, 1963, p. 243).

[28] See the report by John Hogarth of the Centre of Criminology, Toronto University, in the *British Journal of Criminology*, Vol. 7, No. 1, 1967, pp. 84–93.

[29] M. E. Cain and J. E. Hall Williams, *The Sentencing Policy of the Higher Courts.*

Nigel Walker, *Crime and Punishment in Britain,* Part Four (Edinburgh University Press, 1965).

Hellmuth v. Weber, *Die richterliche Strafzumessung* (Verlag C. F. Muller, Karlsruhe, 1956).

J. E. Hall Williams, *The Sentencing Policy of the Court of Criminal Appeal* (*The Howard Journal,* 1960, Vol. X, No. 3).

J. E. Hall Williams, "Sentencing in Transition" (in *Criminology in Transition,* see above under Jarvis).

Barbara Wootton, *Contemporary Trends in Crime and its Treatment* (The 19th Clarke Hall Lecture, The Clarke Hall Fellowship, 1959).

18

Some Thoughts on the Problem of Deterrence

MARC ANCEL

Modern criminologists, especially those interested in penal reform, are greatly indebted to Thorsten Sellin. He has not only made a remarkable contribution to the sociology of crime, worked out new ideas, and opened new horizons, he is also one of those rare scholars who makes one think; in a most unobtrusive and unassuming fashion, he helps us to master the problems and to give a more profound meaning to penal philosophy, without which criminal science would not find its true scope. It is therefore a very special pleasure for me to pay this tribute to a great scholar and enlightened thinker, whose company is always an enriching experience.

Sellin's work is so varied that we hesitate before choosing an appropriate subject to honor his achievement. As I am not a sociologist—although I have often been concerned with the sociology of crime—I think it best to choose a theme connected with what is called, in France and in Europe generally, "penal policy." By this I mean the study and investigation of rational methods of organizing the social reaction against crime. There is probably no need to recall that this "penal policy" should properly be regarded as a branch of criminal science, that through its origin and its purpose it is linked with sociology, and that it presupposes a basic penal philosophy that it endeavors to transmute into practical reforms. Thorsten Sellin has thrown new light on one aspect of this question, namely, the problem of deterrence. It is this subject that I would now like to discuss in some detail. Deterrence is a fundamental problem for criminological science, criminal law, and penal reform. We should first of all grasp the nature of the problem from the standpoint of penal policy.

TWO DIVERGENT APPROACHES

The late Paul Tappan considered that deterrence was the foundation of existing systems of penal law.[1] This is an apt comment, but possibly needs further explanation. In all countries, the criminal law provides penalties for certain acts or forms of social conduct with the avowed purpose that this threat shall deter or intimidate potential offenders. But such intimidation can be envisaged in at least two different ways. For centuries, certain punishments, sometimes of revolting cruelty, have been decreed, imposed, or inflicted in the hope of striking terror into criminals. So they were outlawed, put to death, tortured, or humiliated. All in all, such expiatory vengeance was but one aspect of intimidation.

Somewhat later, when modern criminal law took shape under the influence of Beccaria, greater reliance was placed on reason than on terror. Punishment ceased to be arbitrary and became legal so that acts prohibited by law, and which were punishable, should be clearly known. One of the great achievements of the French Revolution of 1789 was a penal code that listed those actions that the law forbade and with their corresponding punishments. Physical punishment and restriction on personal freedom were considered compatible with the rights of man because they were based on the social contract. The citizen, conceding that he might be punished, was in fact safeguarding his own freedom, which was worthless without a corresponding security. Thus the principle "expression of the general will" implies a threat conducive to reflection about our actions. Feuerbach's *psychologischer Zwang*, Romagnosi's *contra spinta criminosa*, Bentham's careful weighing of pleasures and pains according to utilitarian principles—all these were inspired by the same concept. The Tuscan Criminal Code of 1786, the French Penal Code of 1791, or the Bavarian Code of 1813, all postulate the "reasonable and reasoning" man of the eighteenth century, who, being free and the master of his own actions, was deemed responsible for those actions. In this rationalist system deterrence is bound up with retribution.

The scientific positivism of the late nineteenth century was the antithesis of the classical view I have just outlined. Henceforth, man is no longer considered to be free. If he is predestined toward crime, why speak of punishment? And what use is intimidation for Lombroso's "born criminal?" Even apart from the theories put forward by the anthropological and sociological school in Italy, the reality of the notion of intimidation or deterrence came to be very widely denied. A paper pub-

---

[1] *Crime, Justice and Correction* (1960), p. 248.

lished in the first volume of the *Journal of Criminal Law and Criminology* in 1911 is characteristic in this respect: the author maintained that a supposed deterrent is only likely to deter those who will never in fact commit a crime.[2]

Must the penal reform movement of the second half of the twentieth century try to reconcile these two divergent approaches? Whether we like it or not, modern penal policy—which involves a reasoned choice of the fundamental bases of criminal law—cannot escape this essential question. The work of criminologists and sociologists like Thorsten Sellin will prove a great help in finding the answer to that question. I cannot hope to deal with the problem from all angles, but I do feel that some thoughts on the present state of affairs would not be superfluous in the light of the past century and a half of legislative, judicial, and penitentiary experience. Clearly, I shall be mainly concerned with discussing the controversial question of the real value of deterrence in the field of reaction against crime.

WHO FEARS WHAT?

The purpose of intimidation is to ensure what is commonly called the general prevention of crime. J. Andenaes, in a study that rightly attracted a good deal of attention, wondered whether this concept of general prevention is an illusion or a reality.[3] But as an addendum to his remarkable study, a few remarks of a practical kind would be appropriate.

The classical view is that the legal penalty ensures the prevention of crime because it implies a threat that inspires fear of punishment. According to Bentham's or, indeed, Beccaria's, utilitarian approach or, on the contrary, in Feuerbach's Kantian legalistic theory, this healthy fear of punishment results from a process of reasoning; and because the individual is considered *a priori* as a reasonable being, the deterrent effect of the legal penalty becomes an article of faith. It is at this point, precisely, that the positivist controversy reopens the debate. Without entering into the metaphysical quarrel concerning free will, at least two questions arise if the fear of punishment is to be taken into account:

[2] G. F. Kirchwey, "Crime and Punishment," in *Journal of Criminal Law and Criminology*, 1911, pp. 718 ff. Cf. Barnes and Teeters, *New Horizons in Criminology* (2nd edition, 1951), p. 338.

[3] J. Andenaes, "General Prevention—Illusion or Reality?" in *Journal of Crim. Law, Criminology and Police Science* (1952–1953), pp. 176 ff. Cf., by the same author, "La Peine et le problème de la prevention générale," in *Themis*, 1965, pp. 159 ff.

(1) who are those who fear such punishment? and (2) what is it, in fact, that they fear?

To begin with, it may be noted, as Thorsten Sellin pointed out,[4] that the legal penalty will obviously not restrain persons suffering from a pathological urge towards criminal behavior, who commit offenses out of a desire to be punished; nor will it deter those professional criminals for whom the possibility of punishment is an "occupational risk." The fear of punishment will likewise be without effect on the insane or on deeply antisocial individuals. For these categories of offenders, modern legislation has had to work out a system of preventive measures outside the framework of the criminal law, which are not of a repressive nature, for such offenders would be unaffected by punishment.[5] The same applies, more or less, to mental defectives, psychopaths, and those who act under strong impulses or the majority of those who commit *crimes passionnels*, all of whom are unlikely, by definition, to weigh the consequences of their acts.

At least one result of this situation is that the number of persons genuinely subject to the deterrent effect of the legal penalty is much smaller than it was thought to be a century and a half ago by those who built up a system based on the idea of "general prevention."[6] It may even be asked whether the most dangerous offenders or the authors of the most serious crimes—two types who are not always quite the same— are not precisely those upon whom the threat of punishment has the least effect. Anyway, many writers in this field have stressed the need for systematic empirical studies, which suggests that the available data on the subject are far from precise.[7]

On the assumption that the potential offender is deterred by fear, the question arises: by fear of what? Bentham or Feuerbach would no doubt have been astonished by such a question. They would have replied that it is the fear of the penalty laid down by law that deters, which is why the general prevention of crime will be the natural outcome of

[4] See his important article "L'effet intimidant de la peine ("Etude de sociologie juridique"; I can do no more than refer the reader to this study, published in *Rev. de science crim. et de droit pénal comp.*, 1960, pp. 579 ff. On the effect of capital punishment as an incentive to crime in certain cases, cf. Thorsten Sellin, *The Death Penalty* (Philadelphia, 1959), pp. 65 ff.

[5] Cf. Marc Ancel, *Social Defence—A Modern Approach to Criminal Problems* (London, 1965), pp. 58 ff.

[6] Thorsten Sellin, General Report for the International Criminological Congress, 1950, *Proceedings* of the Congress, Vol. IV, pp. 109 ff.; Sutherland, *Principles of Criminology* (3rd edition), pp. 355 ff.; O. Kinberg, *Les principes fondamentaux de la criminologie* (Paris, 1960), pp. 51 ff.

[7] See, in particular, the programme suggested in J. C. Ball, "The Deterrent Concept in Criminology and Law," *Journ. of Crim. Law, Criminology and Police Science*, Vol. 46, No. 3 (1955), p. 347.

criminal laws indicating with precision, in advance, the exact punishment incurred for each specific offense. Here again, more than a century of scientific study and judicial experience clearly suggests that the problem is not so simple.

To accept the classical view, we would need to live under a system of fixed penalties such as that envisaged by the French code of 1791 in which the judge was bound to impose a certain punishment that he was forbidden to mitigate in any way, once it had been found that an offense had been committed and that the accused was guilty.[8] But modern justice is based on the individualization of punishment. No modern criminal lawyer will maintain that two persons, having committed the same offense ought automatically to be sentenced to exactly the same punishment. Thus, a distinction must be made between the abstract penalty provided by statute and the actual punishment inflicted by the sentence of the court. Judicial psychology and sociology, which Thorsten Sellin wishes to develop,[9] teach us that the likelihood of punishment being incurred, its actual imposition as defined in the sentence of the court and, finally, its effective application are closely interrelated. The uncertainties attending the preliminary investigation of the case and its trial become even more uncertain when one takes into account the opportunity of an appeal against conviction or sentence. Moreover, there is the possibility of a reprieve which, particularly in the case of the death penalty even when mandatory, enhances still further the opportunities for manoeuvre and, consequently, for hope, available to the offender.[10] So much uncertainty is scarcely likely to reinforce the deterrent effect of the punishment prescribed by law.

Some writers, conscious of this state of affairs, argue that the existence of the legal rule matters more than its application in practice.[11] This view may be acceptable from the standpoint of social morality and

---

[8] At its session on June 4, 1791, the Constituent Assembly, in accordance with Beccaria's teaching, solemnly declared that "the use of royal pardons, and the remission, abolition, and commutation of sentences is abolished for all crimes which are tried with a jury": the absolute authority of the law is reinforced by the authority of the jury, which the same Constituent Assembly had just decided to introduce; thus the penalty must not only be legal but certain, and its certainty is supposed to make it a deterrent.

[9] Thorsten Sellin, "Le sociologue et le problème du crime," in *Rev. de science crim. et de droit pénal comp.*, 1950, pp. 527 ff.

[10] See the articles published in the remarkable special issue of the *Annals of the American Academy of Political Science*: "Murder and the Penalty of Death" (November 1952) (in particular, in the present context, the article by B. Ehrmann, "The Death Penalty and the Administration of Justice," especially pp. 73 ff. Cf. M. Ancel, "Le problème de la peine de mort" in *Rev. de droit pénal et de criminologie* (Brussels), 1963–1964, pp. 373 ff.

[11] J. Larguier, *Le droit pénal* (Collection "Que sais-je?" Paris, 1962), p. 14.

insofar as a rule of criminal law indicates reprobation of certain types of individual conduct. However, the theoretical or ethical usefulness of the legal penalty should not be confused with its intimidating effect. Many fail to avoid this confusion. Moreover, it may be noted in this connection that the abstract effect of the legal penalty is a good deal less effective than rules of behavior derived from religion or from professional or cultural ethics that lead a person to respect certain standards of conduct, accepted and sustained by the social group to which he belongs.[12] There is no doubt that here is a form of deterrence as active as the opposite tendency that incites to criminal behavior, stressed by Thorsten Sellin in his admirable account of both the theory of differential association and culture conflict.[13] But these phenomena clearly have nothing to do with deterrence in the legal sense.

These remarks may be illustrated by the well-known fact that abatement of the penalties attached to certain offenses has hardly ever led to an increase in the number of such offenses. The progressive abolition during the nineteenth century of crimes for which capital punishment might be inflicted proves this contention, which is borne out by criminal statistics. This is of course one of the most powerful arguments put forward by opponents of the death penalty.[14]

We should therefore inquire whether the genuinely deterrent effect is not in most cases the result of the social reaction against crime and of intervention by the representatives of the state following commission of the offense, rather than of the indictment or even the sentence. The offender is concerned, above all, with not being found out or to find an alibi.[15] What really deters the potential criminal is the unleashing of the machinery of justice that forces him to account for his actions before the appropriate court. The need to satisfy public opinion is often put forward as a justification of the severity of the legal penalty. This attitude confuses retribution with intimidation. What public opinion

[12] Thorsten Sellin, "L'effet intimidant de la peine," *op. cit.*, pp. 582 ff.
[13] E. H. Sutherland, *Principles of Criminology* (4th edition, 1947), pp. 5 ff.; on possible developments of this theory, see the address by Sutherland to the Ohio Valley Sociological Society (April 1942), published in *Sutherland Papers* (Indiana University Press, 1956), pp. 13 ff.; Thorsten Sellin, *Culture Conflict and Crime* (New York, 1938).
[14] G. Gardiner, *Capital Punishment as a Deterrent and the Alternative* (London, 1956), pp. 25 ff.; cf. Thorsten Sellin, *The Death Penalty*, (Philadelphia, 1959), pp. 34 ff.
[15] J. Andenaes, *op. cit.*, in *Themis*, 1965, pp. 175 ff.; Charles Berg, *Fear, Punishment, Anxiety and the Wolfenden Report* (London, 1959), p. 33; cf. Melitta Schmideberg, "The Offender's Attitude Towards Punishment" in *The Journ. of Crim. Law, Criminology and Police Science* (Vol. 51, No. 3, 1960), pp. 328 ff.

really wants is the appearance of the criminal before the court as soon as possible after the offense has been committed.[16] Afterward, the actual verdict may bear little relation to this initial requirement or even to what was anticipated by the relevant statutory provisions. In many cases the jury, although they represent public opinion, will prove indulgent towards the individual offender in the circumstances of the particular case. Indeed, it is only the lawyers who attach importance to the penalty itself. The man in the street, as well as the potential criminal, tends to think, first of all, of the policeman, the indictment, and the criminal trial.

Consequently, the exact legal definition of the penalty applicable is not of very great importance in this connection. It may well change its character in the course of the preliminary investigation of the case and the trial. From the deterrent standpoint, it matters little whether the penalty applicable is of the traditional kind, that is to say, punishment affecting his physical integrity and liberty, specified as such by statute, or a preventive measure as this is understood in the civil law continental system. Judicial and penitentiary experience lead to the conclusion that *relégation* in France or preventive detention in England are no less feared than prison sentences.[17] Nor does it matter very much, as regards the existence or the effectiveness of the deterrent, what the specific characteristics or the penological conception of the penalty will be at a later stage when it comes to be applied in fact. I shall revert to these two important observations in a moment and attempt to evaluate their consequences.

For the time being, I shall confine myself to noting that the general prevention of crime operates in a very different way according to the persons concerned or the behavior it is designed to prevent. For the true criminal, that is, the man with a criminal vocation, so to speak, the only genuine deterrent is the fear of getting caught. The occasional offender, on the other hand, who gives way to a momentary impulse, is deterred chiefly by the fear of being brought before the criminal court or the shame of incurring condemnation by his own circle, which is equivalent to a kind of social *capitis deminutio*. Oddly enough, the legal

[16] After Montesquieu, Beccaria already declared that the severity of punishment mattered less than the certainty that it would actually be inflicted (see, in particular, in his treatise *On Crimes and Punishments*, the chapter on the necessity of the certainty of penalties).

[17] On the deterrent effect of preventive and even reforming measures, see Norval Morris, *The Habitual Delinquent* (London, 1951), p. 12; cf. Gresham M. Sykes, "The Dilemma of Penal Reform," in *The Howard Journal* (1960, pp. 194 ff.), who writes of those sentenced to preventive detention that "it makes little difference if we call their place of confinement a maximum security unit, an isolation ward or a hospital or something else" (p. 199).

penalty will thus be more effective as a deterrent for those offenses that Garofalo described as "artificial" than for *mala in se*. Major crimes, or what may be described as "natural" offenses, are accepted or rejected by the individual and the social group before or beyond their legal sanction. But by defining certain forms of conduct as *mala prohibita*, the law tends to lay down rules of behavior that would not exist without such a sanction. In this situation the threat implicit in the penalty may be effective.[18] However, through a reverse process that is only apparently surprising, infringement of the legal rule does not lead to an equivalent social disapproval and may even be approved of, tacitly at any rate, by the group to which the offender belongs.[19] This is what deterrence amounts to in reality.

A SOUND CRIMINAL POLICY

From the foregoing remarks we may deduce that deterrence or intimidation does exist as a social and human phenomenon but that it has neither the meaning nor the scope traditionally assigned to it. What part should intimidation play in a modern, rationally organized system of reaction against crime?

First, it may be observed that intimidation, based on the notion of being made to account for our actions, is in a truly individual and concrete way closely akin to a personal sense of responsibility. There is an obvious relationship between these two concepts of responsibility and intimidation. Because man is innately conscious of his own responsibility, he is aware of the need to justify himself. The fear of having to explain his conduct will act as a brake to the precise extent that the antisocial and, hence, blameworthy nature of such conduct is brought home to him. This consciousness of our actions, both in the psychological and moral sense, remains the basis and the purpose of the penalty, as has been demonstrated by modern criminology.[20] The same consciousness

[18] Provided, of course, that such crimes are clearly brought to the attention of those concerned. The complexity and variety of administrative or economic regulations enforced by criminal sanctions is such that those persons at which they are aimed are often unaware that such regulations exist. On this point see my remarks in *Social Defence—A Modern Approach to Criminal Problems* (London, 1965), pp. 128 ff., and, for further developments, the second French edition of this work, *La défense sociale nouvelle* (Paris, 1966), p. 233, with the references therein cited.

[19] This is often the case in the criminal law relating to economic offenses; see Donald R. Taft, *Criminology* (3rd edition, 1956), p. 388; cf. Enrique R. Aftalion, *Derecho penal economico*, Buenos Aires, 1960.

[20] J. Pinatel, "Responsabilité pénale et criminologie," in *La responsabilité pénale* (Results of the Strasbourg colloquim on penal philosophy), Paris, 1961, pp. 157 ff.;

enables the deterrent concept to be used for a social purpose. Just as in the case of responsibility itself, penal policy should envisage this notion of deterrence as an individual or "internal" reality. It should no longer be looked upon as a convenient but meaningless assumption, which is what it had become in the traditional view in which, as has been pointed out, the notion of criminal responsibility amounted to little more than a working hypothesis for the lawyer, a presumption that was put forward and almost immediately lost sight of.[21] In the same way, intimidation was a sort of presupposition that it was no longer thought neccesary to prove. If the notion of deterrence is to be put to a rational use, it must be given a practical meaning.

The notion of intimidation, thus understood, can therefore play a part, whatever may be the precise legal definition of the offense or the way the prescribed punishment is applied. It is, therefore, inaccurate or, at any rate, a gross oversimplification, to claim, as is sometimes done, that when punishment in the traditional sense is replaced by a form of treatment, this might result in reducing the deterrent effect of the penalty.[22] Apart from the fact that it is very difficult to distinguish between preventive detention and a prison sentence, it is evident that methods of treatment, rationally applied in conformity with modern penological ideas,[23] do not in any way diminish the deterrent effect of appearance before the court or of the sentence imposed. This is so because the treatment envisaged is planned and carried out in the posttrial phase. To be effective, such treatment necessarily presupposes a lengthy period of confinement, which is a more formidable prospect for the offender than a short term of imprisonment or a suspended sentence, both of which are none the less deemed to have a deterrent effect.

If such sentences are considered as deterrents, it is because the traditional concept of punishment is one of those myths that must be discarded if a rational system of reaction against crime is to be organized. In a stimulating book, Hugh Klare has pointed out that prison has become

---

cf. P. Bouzat and J. Pinatel, *Traité de droit pénal et de criminologie*, Vol. III (*Criminologie*, by J. Pinatel), Paris, 1963, pp. 490 ff.; E. de Greeff, "Sur le sentiment de responsabilité" in *Rev. int. de défense sociale*, 1956, pp. 1 ff.

[21] See the present writer's comments in *Social Defence—A Modern Approach to Criminal Problems*, London, 1965, p. 177 and, for further developments, *La défense sociale nouvelle*, 2nd edition, Paris, 1966, pp. 297 ff.

[22] See *supra*, footnote 17.

[23] See *Trois aspects de l'action pénitentiaire* (Publications of the I.P.P.F.), Vol. I (1960), with general reports by Sir Lionel Fox (p. 425), J. Dupréel (p. 441), and J. Lamers (p. 482); Vol. II (1961), with the Summary Record by M. Ancel and J. B. Herzog. On the evolution of this subject, cf. Thorsten Sellin, "Correction in Historical Perspective," in *Crime and Correction*, symposium published by *Law and Contemporary Problems* (Autumn, 1958), pp. 587 ff.

little more than a kind of "psychological symbol."[24] Present-day efforts are concentrated on getting rid of such symbols so as to achieve an effective system of resocialization. There seems to be no reason why confinement should cease to inspire a healthy respect from the moment at which the convicted offender is required to make a personal contribution to the process of re-education instead of merely undergoing, in a passive if not a hypocritical way, the prison regime to which he is subjected.[25] The place of deterrence in the penal scheme of things must be assessed in terms of doing away with the myth of punishment as traditionally conceived.

Some people may object that this approach is likely to underestimate the retributive nature of punishment, in which they continue to see one of the essential ingredients of the notion of deterrence. We may well ask, however, whether there is not, on the contrary, a fundamental incompatibility between intimidation and retribution. The problem is a serious one and is often not properly appreciated, so I shall consider it briefly at this point.

In the traditional view, a penalty has to be repressive in order to punish for the offense committed, but it cannot really be so unless the court adapts it to the guilt of the individual offender. At the same time, the penalty is supposed to have a deterrent effect and, therefore, has to be varied according to the objective, external criteria of the system of general prevention. The criterion of the repressive character of the penalty is therefore completely different from the criterion of its deterrent effect: each is based on a different conception. For the penalty to be intimidating it must be fixed not in terms of what the offender *has* done but with regard to what other persons *might* do. To deter the potential criminal, a heavier penalty is imposed on the person who has in fact been found guilty of a crime.[26] But in that case, can one speak of a retributive punishment? Can one speak of a personal penalty, that is, one imposed only on the person who actually committed the offense? Can we even speak of the lawful character of such a penalty, because it should be limited to the act that has in fact been committed? Here the

[24] *Anatomy of Prison* (London, 1960), p. 14 ff.

[25] See Hugh Klare, *op. cit.*, pp. 93 ff., especially p. 97, where the author says of the traditional system of punishment and rewards that it "may satisfy the sense of justice of the staff, but may be illusory as far as support for the aims of the regime is concerned."

[26] Remember the words of the 18th century judge who told the accused that he was condemned to death not because he had stolen a sheep, but "so that others should no longer steal sheep," quoted by Lionel Fox, *The English Prison and Borstal System,* 1951, p. 14, who also quotes Lord Justice Asquith's remark that "an exemplary sentence is unjust, and unjust to the precise extent that it is exemplary."

equilibrium of justice is upset by the desire to intimidate: the judge is obliged to forget the particular individual he has in front of him. In such a case the penalty imposed is no longer designed to be just, for the offender merely comes to serve the presumed interest of the community. An exemplary penalty is an authoritarian proceeding quite unrelated to true justice.

The psychological and social reality of deterrence is by no means as obvious as it is generally said to be. It is therefore a weapon that the system of reaction against crime should only use prudently and within definite limits. The truth is that a sound criminal policy should reconcile three essential ideas that are both complementary and contradictory: (1) intimidation, (2) repression (or social condemnation), and (3) responsibility.[27] Such reconciliation can be achieved, thanks in particular to two other important modern concepts, namely, individualized punishment and treatment. The first three belong mainly to criminal science, the other two to applied penology. These related studies are today inseparable. As branches of criminology, they are bound up with the general phenomenon of crime. It is the great merit of an authority like Thorsten Sellin to have drawn our attention to the interdependence of these connected problems in the context of criminal sociology, understood as a humanist discipline. Following the line of thought he expressed in his teaching, I have attempted in this essay to reflect anew on the still controversial problem of deterrence.

[27] In the practical sphere of the administration of justice, this reconciliation raises the problem of sentencing. In this connection, see the special issue of *Law and Contemporary Problems* (Summer, 1958); cf. E. Green, *Judicial Attitudes in Sentencing* (Cambridge Studies in Criminology, Vol. XV, 1961); on the same problem, envisaged more particularly from the standpoint of the civil law systems (and still with regard to the balance between repression and intimidation), see the reports of the VIIIth International Congress for Criminal Law on "Les méthodes et les procédés techniques employés dans l'élaboration de la sentence pénale," in *Rev. int. de droit pénal*, 1960, pp. 11 ff. (with the General Report by the present writer, pp. 349 ff.); for a comparison on this point between the continental and Anglo-American systems, see the "XIIIes Journées de défense sociale" (London, 1965), *Rev. de science crim. et de droit pénal comp.*, 1965 (No. IV) et 1966 (No. I).

19

Trends in Penal Methods With Special
Reference to Prison Labor*

PAUL CORNIL

Studies on the history of penal methods may be considered as a scholar's occupation, giving the author and also the reader a comforting impression that humanity is progressing from the dark ages of the past to the enlightened modern civilization. If, however, the study is based on original documents, with details creating the atmosphere of the time, the result may be somewhat different. Permanent traits of human nature appear on the surface, and we see that some of the problems are already placed before penal administrators in a different setting, but showing striking similarities with those that they are facing today.

This observation came to my mind after having read the important part of Thorsten Sellin's work which he devoted to Dom Jean Mabillon, a prison reformer of the seventeenth century,[1] and to a description of the famous Amsterdam Houses of Correction in the sixteenth and seventeenth centuries,[2] and to the Philadelphian prisons of the eighteenth century. Quite recently, President Sellin's opening address at the 5th International Congress of Criminology in Montreal was devoted to his "Reflections on Penal Servitude,"[3] in which he demonstrated that forced labor, one of the primitive elements of imprisonment, is still in existence in our prison systems. At the end of his address, Thorsten Sellin declared: "I have attempted to show that progress towards the modernization of imprison-

* This essay was submitted in 1966.
[1] Thorsten Sellin, "Dom Jean Mabillon, a Prison Reformer of the Seventeenth Century," *Journal of the American Institute of Criminal Law and Criminology*, 1926–1927, pp. 581–602.
[2] Thorsten Sellin, *Pioneering in Penology*, Philadelphia, University of Pennsylvania Press, 1944. Thorsten Sellin in, Transactions of the American Philosophical Society, *Philadelphia Prisons of the Eighteenth Century*, Vol. 43, 1953.
[3] On the same question, see Sellin's paper "Penal Servitude: Origin and Survival," *Proceedings of the American Philosophical Society*, Vol. 109, No. 5, October 1965.

ment and its conversion into a correctional agency has been vitiated by futile attempts to weld together two incompatible elements into punitive imprisonment, the exploitation of the manpower of prisoners for the profit of the state, and the reclamation of prisoners by moral and educational means."[4] This conclusion, drawn from an impressive series of historical examples struck me as convincing and, at the same time, it appeared as contrasting deeply with the modern notion of prison labor as it is developing in present-day penal methods.

A comparison between past and present will be the aim of this essay: starting from historical data, taken mainly out of Sellin's works, I shall confront them with prison labor as it presents itself today.

* * *

Prison labor has been, in many penal systems, the crude expression of man's exploitation by the State. Sellin mentions, among other examples, the Roman prisoners who were put to public work, cleaning sewers, repairing roads, and working in the public baths. More severe was work in the mines and quarries. Another striking form of penal servitude for the benefit of the State was the sentencing of criminals to the galleys, which occurred in the fifteenth century. We find, in the administrative correspondence of Colbert's time, letters showing how the necessities of waging war may sometimes pass before the dignity of justice. In a letter of February 21, 1676, addressed to the president of the Paris "Parlement," he insists that prisoners able to serve in the galleys should be "quickly judged."[5]

Even more significant were the orders sent on April 11, 1662, by Colbert to the presidents of the French "parlements": "Le Roy m'a commandé de vous écrire ces lignes de sa part pour vous dire que, Sa Majesté désirant rétablir le corps de ses galères et en fortifier la chiourme par toutes sortes de moyens, son intention est que vous teniez la main à ce que vostre compagnie y condamne le plus grand nombre de coupables qu'il se pourra, et que l'on convertisse même la peine de mort en celle des galères."[6] This penalty came into gradual disuse when galleys became outmoded: "In France, the great technical improvements in the art of

---

[4] Quoted from the mimeographed edition of the Montreal address, p. 17.

[5] Letter from Marquis de Segnelay to president De Harley, *Correspondance administrative sous le Règne de Louis XIV*, publiée par B. Depping, Paris, 1851, Vol. II, p. 940; quoted by G. Rusche and O. Kirchheimer, *Punishment and Social Structure*, with a foreword of Thorsten Sellin, New York, Columbia University Press, 1939, p. 55.

[6] *Lettres, instructions et mémoires* de Colbert publiés par Pierre Clément, Membre de l'Institut, Paris, Imprimerie Impériale, 1864, Vol. III, Introduction, p. L.

sailing led to the substitution of forced labor in the bagno (Toulon and Marseille)."[7]

More recent examples of penal servitude organized by public authorities are given in Sellin's lecture, in which he mentions, among others, the practice of road camps in Louisiana, described by McCormick in a report of 1964.[8]

* * *

From the beginning of the modern prison system, compulsory labor has been an essential element. In the United Kingdom, it reached an extreme in which "penal labor" was standardized as so many revolutions per diem on the treadwheel,[9] thus symbolizing the punitive element of useless labor, which excited Ives' righteous indignation.[10] When this demoralizing form of work was abolished, it remained, however, as Sir Lionel Fox put it, that "work as a part of the punishment . . . has never since been wholly exorcised from consideration of the question."[11]

The expressions "penal servitude" and "hard labor" were abolished only by the Criminal Justice Act, 1948. In the same way in France the term "travaux forcés" was replaced by the expression "réclusion criminelle" by the Ordinance of June 4, 1960.[12] Also in the USSR, the term "forced labor" formerly used in the text of the penal code has been replaced by the expression "corrective labor."[13] Apparently, those legal expressions were considered as obsolete and in contradiction with the modern idea of human rights. Mannheim points out that these expressions had become methods of "stigmatization" of prisoners.[14]

The United Nations has approached the study of this problem from two different angles. The International Labor Office, at the request of the Social and Economic Council, created an *ad hoc* committee on forced labor, which published an important report in 1953.[15] It covers a very wide field, including political and nonpolitical aspects of forced labor. The investigation is oriented towards illegal forms of forced labor, with

[7] See footnote 5, Rusche, p. 56.
[8] Austin McCormick, "Report of the Study of the Louisiana State Penitentiary," July 1964, Osborne Association, New York, quoted by Sellin (see footnote 3).
[9] Lionel Fox, *The English Prison and Borstal Systems*, London, 1952, p. 49; pp. 176–200.
[10] Georges Ives, *A History of Penal Methods*, "Model Labour," London, 1914, Chapter VIII.
[11] See footnote 9, p. 177.
[12] Pierre Bouzat, *Traité de droit pénal et de criminologie*, Paris, 1963, Vol. I, p. 351.
[13] I.L.O. Report of the "Ad Hoc" Committee on Forced Labour, Geneva, 1953, Annex III, USSR, No. 82.
[14] Hermann Mannheim, *The Dilemma of Penal Reform*, London, 1939, p. 139.
[15] See footnote 13.

political or economic purposes, but it takes for granted that prisoners legally convicted for a criminal offense may be compelled to work. Article XIII, Section I, of the United States Constitution is quoted as a justification, as it declares that "neither slavery nor unvoluntary servitude, except as a punishment of crime whereof the party shall have been duly convicted, shall exist within the United States."[16]

Prison labor as such has been studied by the United Nations at the request of the Social Commission at its 9th session in May 1953. A questionnaire was sent to the Member nations but unfortunately not all of them answered. The report, published in 1955, does not contain information from any socialist country, with the exception of Yugoslavia.[17] It is therefore difficult to have a clear notion of the position of prison labor in those countries.

The compulsory character of prison labor has been reaffirmed in the Standard Minimum Rules for the treatment of prisoners adopted in 1955 by the First United Nations Congress on the prevention of crime and the treatment of offenders. Rule 71, 2, declares: "All prisoners under sentence shall be required to work."[18] In the same document, we find that "an untried prisoner shall always be offered opportunity to work, but shall not be required to work. If he chooses to work, he shall be paid for it."[19] This rule seems to be inspired by another concept of prison labor considered more as an alleviating than as an aggravating element of the prison regime.

Facts have also shown that compulsion was not generally needed to put the prisoner to work. In the old Amsterdam Rasphuys, the "water cellar" described in Sellin's book,[20] was a place where prisoners refusing to work "had to pump day and night in order to keep them from drowning." It came into disuse, so much so that John Howard, after having visited the place in 1778, 1781, and 1783, declared that "what had been said concerning a cellar in which such transgressors are to pump or drown, is a fiction."[21]

Whatever may have been the reason for the suppression of this method (Sellin mentions the version of a prisoner having refused to pump

[16] See footnote 13, Annex III, United States, No. 21.
[17] *Prison Labour*, U.N. Department of Economic and Social Affairs, New York, 1955 (see footnote 8).
[18] *Standard Minimum Rules for the Treatment of Prisoners and Related Recommendations*, United Nations, Department of Economic Affairs, New York, 1958.
[19] See footnote 18, rule 88.
[20] See footnote 2, pp. 67 ff.
[21] John Howard, *The State of Prisons*, Everyman's Library, No. 835, London, 1929, p. 56.

in order to commit suicide), it appears that the work regime of this institution was not hampered by the disuse of the "water cellar." It may well be that the hard work of the rasping saw was of an unpleasant nature and required special incentive to be accepted by the prisoners. Howard heard that in the same Amsterdam institution an Englishman who "was permitted to work at his own trade, shoemaking" remained grateful to "his worthy masters at the rasphouse."[22]

Even when the kind of work is unpleasant, prison labor may be voluntary. I have mentioned on several occasions a postwar experiment in handling Belgian war collaborators.[23] Although their sentence for political offenses did not include compulsory labor, a large number among the young and able-bodied accepted voluntarily to work in the coal-mines. Most of them had never done manual work. They received, it is true, the normal salary of a miner and could help their families substantially. They demonstrated, however, that normal work, be it hard and dangerous, accomplished under normal conditions does not require compulsion to be accepted by prisoners.

* * *

In contrast to these observations on the compulsory nature of prison labor, I should like to point out another well-known fact, namely, idleness in prison is a severe aggravation of the punishment.

Mabillon was already very conscious of this when he wrote: "How can one support an imprisonment of several months or several years without labor or occupation?"[24] Placed in solitary confinement, the prisoner left idle can hardly stand this regime. This is vividly described by Charles Dickens when he relates his visit to the Pittsburgh prison. A prisoner "humbly begs and prays for work: Give me some work to do, or I shall go raving mad!"[25]

Experts in prison matters have more recently expressed repeatedly similar views. To quote only two of them: the Wickersham report on penal institutions, probation and parole, presented to the President of the United States in 1931, opens its chapter on "Labor and Industry" with the following assertion: "It has long been recognized that idleness in prison is bad for both the inmate and the institution."[26] More recently,

[22] See footnote 21, p. 48; footnote 1, quoted by Sellin, No. 2, p. 74.
[23] Paul Cornil, "Prison Industry and Labour," *The Canadian Journal of Corrections*, July 1961, p. 241.
[24] Quoted by Sellin, footnote 1, p. 588.
[25] Charles Dickens, *American Notes*, 1842.
[26] National Commission on Law Observance and Enforcement, Report on Penal Institutions, Washington, 1931, p. 80.

the American Prison Committee on Riots, analyzing the fundamental causes of prison riots lists among them "enforced idleness."[27]

* * *

From what we have seen up to now, three conclusions may be easily drawn:

1. Compulsory labor is considered as an essential element of the prison sentence.
2. Under favorable conditions, compulsion is superfluous, for prisoners accept voluntarily the work that is offered to them.
3. Some prisoners resent idleness and request to be put to work.

If these views are accepted, prison labor changes its character. It is not mainly as punishment that it has to be considered, but as an essential and indispensable part of the prison regime. And yet we have come to realize gradually that establishing efficient and realistic prison labor is, in most cases, an impossible undertaking. The very fact that the problem of prison labor has been repeatedly put on the agenda of recent international congresses shows the existence of a persistent malaise.

Obstacles to the organization of prison labor are well known to practitioners. I shall try to summarize them briefly. First, they are the limitations imposed on prison labor by the necessities of discipline and security. Very few useful occupations can be practiced in an ordinary prison. To the prison visitor, the saddening repetition of the same old-fashioned workshops, rarely interrupted by some striking exception, has created a deep conviction of the relative uselessness of most of these efforts. Second, whenever this routine is overcome and more efficient industries are created, we come across—at least in the countries of free enterprise— the age-old obstacle of competition with private industry. In the 18th century, Vilain XIV already noted that experience in Ghent and had to close the workshops of his prison.[28] Another illustration of this difficulty is given by the American federal legislation known as the Hawes-Cooper Act, adopted in 1929 and enforced from 1934, which caused a general move toward the adoption of the State-Use system.[29] Third, for many prisoners, their physical ability and length of their sentence place restrictions on their working, except on simple occupations.

---

[27] Quoted by Austin McCormick, "Behind the Prison Riots," in the *Annals of the American Academy of Political and Social Science*, May 1954; special number, "Prisons in Transformation," pp. 23–24.

[28] John Howard, footnote 21, pp. 117–118.

[29] H. Gill, "The Prison Labor Problems," in the *Annals of the American Academy of Political and Social Science*, September 1931; special number, "Prisons of Tomorrow," pp. 90–94; Barnes and Teeters, *New Horizons in Criminology*, New York, sixth edition, 1947, pp. 702 ff.

Fourth, and mainly, the status and remuneration of the working prisoner cannot be settled satisfactorily. The Standard Minimum Rules declare: "There shall be a system of equitable remuneration of the work of prisoners."[30] There are indeed many reasons for paying a real salary to the man working in prison. As H. Gill puts it: "To relieve a prisoner of all responsibility for the support of himself and his family is of course to develop an unsocial attitude, which the prison is intended to correct."[31] And this is not enough: the working prisoner should also compensate the damage caused to the victim and spare some of his earnings for the time of his release (Rule 75, 3). This suggestion becomes ludicrous when compared with the small amount of money allowed to the working prisoner by an administration that has to collect a large budget for the maintenance and the supervision of the prison population.

More important arguments concern normal working conditions. Especially in the countries provided with extended social legislation, the wage-earner's contract carries with it a series of social advantages. Family allowances, for instance, may be suppressed during detention. The Second United Nations Congress, which met in London, 1960, expressed a pious wish when it declared in its conclusions on prison labor that social security measures enforced in a country should be applied in the largest possible way to the working prisoner.[32]

These formidable obstacles to a rational prison labor are not the only ones. We could add to the list the poor productivity of that kind of labor and the inadequacy of the results with the proposed training programs. An investigation recently made in the British prisons concludes: "We would suggest that maximum economic production in the prison setting is extremely unlikely to be synonymous with good training, however defined, nor for that matter, with the other legitimate aims of the institution. There is need for rethinking on these vital issues and for more systematic and extensive research.[33]

*   *   *

The evolution of penal servitude generally confirms the opinion expressed by Sellin in the conclusion of his Montreal address: the modern version of penal servitude is incompatible with an efficient prison regime. It may well be that we are facing one of the main causes of the growing uneasiness of penal administrators, which has been noticed

[30] See footnote 18, rule 76.
[31] See footnote 29, p. 100.
[32] Second United Nations Congress on the Prevention of Crime and the Treatment of Delinquents, London, August 8 to 19, 1960, United Nations, New York.
[33] M. H. Cooper and R. D. King, "Social and Economic Problems of Prisoner's Work," in *Sociological Studies in the British Penal Services, the Sociological Review Monograph*, No. 9, University of Keele, June 1965, pp. 145–173.

and expressed authoritatively by Norval Morris in the following remark, after his experience as head of the United Nations Institute for the Prevention of Crime and the Treatment of Offenders in Fuchu (Japan): "Two years of association with leading prison administrators of the world has revealed a professional attitude they share. Those from Europe, from the Americas, from Asia, Africa and Oceania: those from capitalist, communist, socialist, dictatorial and militaristic systems of government, all join in dissatisfaction in prison itself. All enthuse most about methods of keeping criminals out and getting them out of prisons." And further, he describes the common type of prison as "a walled institution where adult criminals in large numbers are held for protracted periods, with economically meaningless and insufficient employment, with vocational training or education for a few, with rare contacts with the outside world, in cellular conditions varying from the decent to those which a zoo would not tolerate."[34]

Norval Morris is right: many prison administrators are no longer convinced that they are doing the right thing, and it is no wonder that efforts in several directions have and are being made to find new and better methods for treating delinquents.

As my topic is centered on prison methods, I shall not deal here with the important series of measures invented as substitutes to imprisonment, principally the various types of probation and suspended sentence. They were already adopted during the last century in the United States and have gradually expanded in Anglo-Saxon countries and, more recently, on the continent of Europe. Even in countries practicing on an important scale, the number of prison sentences is still very high. The mere mention of the prison population in the United States (around 200,000) and in the United Kingdom (nearly 30,000) is evident proof of this statement.

But prison administrators have not accepted passively their pessimistic view of the prison regime. They have experimented with new regimes, some of which are described below.

OPEN PRISONS

The establishment of "open prisons" has not taken place abruptly. We have known for quite a number of years agricultural institutions in which security measures were reduced to a minimum. The Witzwill prison in Switzerland, created by Kellerhals in 1891, is one of the best

---

[34] Norval Morris, "Prison in Evolution," in *Criminology in Transition,* Essays in Honour of Hermann Mannheim, London, Tavistock, 1965, p. 268; from the same author: "Prison in Evolution," *Federal Probation,* December 1965, pp. 20–32.

known examples. In November 1927, I visited near Washington, D.C., the Workhouse of Occoquan where prisoners serving up to one year were living in a prison without walls. At the same period, the building of the Norfolk prison in Massachusetts, at the initiative of Howard Gill and with the support of Sanford Bates, was, in a way, an experiment of an open institutions.[35] In England, in the 1930's, some open Borstal institutions were organized. Gradually, the method expanded and, after the Second World War, the problem came to the forefront with the discussions at the Twelfth International Penal and Penitentiary Congress in The Hague (1950), organized by Thorsten Sellin, then Secretary-General of the International Penal and Penitentiary Commission. The resolution adopted stressed the advantages of the open prison and suggested its extension to the largest number of prisoners.[36] This resolution recommended that prisoners in open institutions should either be put at agricultural work or in industrial and vocational training workshops. The Hague Congress also suggested that prisoners sent to an open institution should be carefully selected.

After 1950, use of the open institutions markedly increased in many countries, especially in Sweden. Already in 1957, Goransson claimed that about 40 percent of the delinquents sentenced to imprisonment were placed in open institutions.[37] To me, the success of the open regime is one of the most striking developments in prison methods since the beginning of this century. At least, this was my impression ten years ago,[38] and I am still wondering why so many people remain in those open prisons, while no physical restraint compels them to stay within the boundaries of the institution.

The main explanation given at The Hague Congress was the attitude of many prisoners who accept their sentence and do not want to play "hide and seek" with the police. Other reasons for the success of this method are, I think, of a psychological nature. Open prisons are and will probably be considered for a long time, as exceptions to an ordinary regime of closed institutions. The open regime is a favor granted to the prisoner, and he knows that he will be sent to a closed prison if he misbehaves or tries to escape. Furthermore, in a well-managed institution, a spirit of solidarity seems to prevail between inmates. Too many escapes

[35] Barnes and Teeters, see footnote 29, pp. 791–779.
[36] Proceedings of the Twelfth International Penal and Penitentiary Congress, The Hague, August 14–19, 1950, Vol. II, pp. 586–588.
[37] H. Goransson, "Open Institutions in Sweden," in *Cycle d'Etudes de Strasbourg*, September 1959, Fondation Internationale Pénale et Pénitentiaire, Stämpfli, Berne, 1959, Fascicule I, pp. 148 ff.
[38] "Cinquante ans de droit pénal et de criminologie," Publication jubilaire, 1907–1957, *Revue de Droit pénal et de criminologie*, p. 605.

would endanger the regime and cause damage to the lot of other prisoners.[39] These explanations are nothing more than speculation, and we must admit that we know very little about why open institutions work so well. As to the selection of the inmates, J. Bennett tells us that the population of the open institution at Seagoville (Texas) is largely composed of nonselected offenders: "Well over two-thirds of them come directly from the courts and are run-of-the-mill auto theft cases, forgers and violators of Federal statutes. Some are serving long terms and there are a few lifers at the institution. The number who attempt to escape are few indeed. . . . The experiment is proving that our old criteria for determining that a prisoner is dangerous and a serious menace as long as he is under sentence needs a lot of revision."[40]

Experiments with open institutions in Belgium during the war, under the pressure of circumstances that led eventually to the creation of the open institution for young adults in Marneffe, confirm this statement. Unselected prisoners, chosen mainly for their ability for vegetable gardening, remained in the institution. Very few took advantage of the open character of the place in order to escape.

Hugh Klare goes even further. He claims that every prison sentence should be started in a closed prison, but that most of them ought ideally to go through at least a few weeks of an open institution before release.[41] This position was discussed in 1959 at the Strasbourg seminar of the International Penal and Penitentiary Foundation. It was opposed by several participants.[42] I thought, however, that it might be possible to go even further. Given the good results of the empirical experiments in open institutions and the difficulty to select systematically the appropriate individual offenders, one might decide *a priori* to send prisoners serving short and average prison sentences to open institutions, except when there is an indication that placement in a closed prison is advisable. Such a rule, said Tetens, in Strasbourg, was adopted in Denmark, where an offender sentenced to less than three years imprisonment should, in most cases, be sent immediately to an open institution while the others should only be transferred to an open prison at the end of their sentence.[43]

The open prison regime is gaining ground. It presents many ad-

[39] See footnote 36, General Report by Charles Germain, Vol. IV, pp. 11–20.
[40] J. Bennett, "A Briefing for Lawyers on Prisons," Sterling lecture series, Yale University, 1960, in *On Prisons and Justice*, a selection of the writings of James V. Bennett prepared for the Subcommittee on National Penitentiaries of the Committee on the Judiciary, United States Senate, April 16, 1964, p. 279.
[41] H. Klare, *Anatomy of Prison*, London, Hutchinson, 1960, p. 120.
[42] Cycle d'Etudes de Strasbourg (see No. 37), Vol. II, Synthèse des travaux présentée par Marc Ancel et Jacques-Bernard Herzog, Stämpfli, Berne, 1961, pp. 49–50.
[43] See footnote 41, p. 50.

vantages, as The Hague Congress pointed out in its resolution: improving the mental and physical health of the prisoner; making conditions of imprisonment closer to the patterns of normal life and, in a more general way, suppressing the tensions and creating a better atmosphere for reforming the prisoner. This new regime does not, however, provide a solution to the problems of prison labor, with the exception perhaps of agriculture, which seemed to many experts to offer an exceptionally appropriate mode for rehabilitating offenders.[44,45] The importance of agricultural penal institutions is, however, relatively limited and it could hardly be extended while agricultural methods are rapidly changing and the use of hand labor is, on the whole, declining in that sector. For the other categories of labor, the open regime does not fundamentally suppress the main obstacles to the organization of prison labor that we have already reviewed. Some other remedy had to be found, and this is the next important reform that is now being undertaken under various names, known in the United States as "work release."

PART-TIME PRISONERS

The characteristic of this new trend in prison treatment lies in the interruptions of the imprisonment. Curiously enough, some offenders are now liberated in order to work in private enterprises, sometimes even to practice their own trade or profession. By so doing we have gone a long way from the old penal servitude. Work of the offender is no longer part and parcel of the sentence. On the contrary, the normal occupation of the offender is carefully preserved during his imprisonment. Such is, at least, the position of the Belgian experiment, which I shall now describe as an example, as I am more familiar with the enforcement of that system. Other systems belonging to the same trend will also be briefly considered.

The Belgian experiment started on March 1, 1963, in a very simple way. A circular from the Minister of Justice to the prosecutors general and to the prison directors, allowed them to execute short prison terms under the form of weekend arrests or semidetention.[46]

Weekend arrests are applicable to the execution of sentences not exceeding one month (exceptionally, two months), and mainly for the following offenses: fraud or falsification, nonsupport, drunkenness; homicide or wounding in a traffic accident; driving under the influence of

[44] The Hague Congress Resolution, see footnote 36.
[45] E. Neuman, *Prison Abierta*, Buenos-Aires, 1962, pp. 179 ff.
[46] Paul Cornil, "Les arrêts de fin de semaine et la semi-détention," *Revue de droit pénal et de criminologie*, April 1963.

alcohol; driving a car while not insured. Other types of offenders may occasionally benefit by this system. When a case seems favorable to the prosecutor, his office contacts the offender before the execution of the sentence and asks him if he wants to undergo his sentence during the weekends. If so, he should come to the prison every Saturday at 2 p.m., to be released on Monday at 6 a.m. Every weekend counts for two days, which means that a sentence of one month has to be served during fifteen consecutive weekends. If, in the meantime, the offender changes his mind or if he does not observe the conditions agreed upon, he will have to serve his sentence in the ordinary continuous way to which he had been sentenced by the court.

Semidetention is another system of discontinued or part-time imprisonment, much akin to the American work release. It is applicable to sentences up to three months. The kind of offense is not specified. Under this regime, the prisoner is liberated every morning, at a time in accordance with his working hours, and presents himself at the prison immediately after his workday. This means that his detention is interrupted only during the work hours. This regime is very similar to the older method of semiliberty, but with an important difference: semidetention is started from the beginning of the sentence, while semiliberty is generally considered as a transition between imprisonment and normal life. The acceptance or refusal of the semidetention regime is decided by the prosecutor in the same way as for the weekend arrest.

Both systems have a common aim: to preserve, whenever it is possible, the offender's normal occupation in order not to punish the innocent family and to avoid, for many offenders, the difficulties of finding another job when liberated. It cannot be denied, however, that with these forms of imprisonment, the principle of "work as part of the punishment" has been wholly "exorcised," to use Sir Lionel Fox's expression.[47] He would certainly agree on that point. But we must admit that this result was obtained through a radical elimination of labor from the prison regime.

At this point, another question is raised in the mind of the observer: What then remains of the prison regime? Does it still have some significance and some positive effect on the offender? Before answering this question, we must admit that such methods are at present applied in a limited way. The initiative met with a definite success and the number of cases increased promptly.[48] The limitation to short penalties and, for the weekends, the concentration on special groups of offenders show

---

[47] See footnote 9, p. 177.
[48] During the year 1965, 416 cases of weekend arrests and 670 cases of semidetention were executed.

that this small experiment does not by any means give a general answer to the problem of prison labor. We are, however, discussing it at length because it is an example, among many others, which might indicate a new orientation in prison treatment.

Let us now analyze these regimes. An important feature is the consent of the offender to apply the new form of detention. This is not a fundamental element of these regimes. The explanation for it lies mainly in the experimental character of the system. In order to avoid the passing of new legislation, it was decided to ask for the agreement of the offender to a mode of treatment that offered him considerable advantages. By this procedure, complaints of illegality should be avoided. In France, during the discussion of a similar project, it was suggested that the consent of the accused should be asked for by the court, before sentencing to the new form of imprisonment. This suggestion was rejected as contrary to the principles of criminal procedure.[49]

Of greater importance is the following question: What remains of the prison regime under these two discontinued forms of detention? The man incarcerated during the weekend is placed in a cell and he will stay there until Monday morning, with the exception of the exercise in the yard and, if he so desires, the religious service on Sunday morning. In the meantime, he is without radio, television, cinema, or social activities with other prisoners. The reasons of those prohibitions are of two kinds. The scarcity of prison personnel on duty during the weekend does not allow the organization of special activities. On the other hand, a weekend with cinema, sports, and radio or television would be considered as an easy and not quite unpleasant stay, not essentially different from a weekend outside.[50]

Prison administrators, however, have no reason to be proud of a regime that reduces treatment to the most primitive form of detention. The effect expected from such a treatment cannot be called "deterrence" or even real intimidation. It is a kind of inconvenience or annoyance. The prisoner being deprived of his family life and of all social activity is compelled to follow a well-regulated and secluded life during time not devoted to his work (semidetention) or only during the weekend. A layman who reads a summary description of these methods may think that these penalties are rather light and are perhaps too indulgent. In fact, clients of weekend arrests have told me how very boring these regimes are. During 15 or 30 consecutive weekends, to be shut in a cell

[49] Charles German, "Variations sur certaines formes nouvelles de privation de liberté," in Studies in Penology, To the memory of Sir Lionel Fox, The Hague, Martinus Nijhoff, 1964, p. 103.
[50] See footnote 49, p. 105.

is not a light punishment. To get out of the prison every morning, as did a physician sentenced to 15 days semidetention as a drunken driver— who went out to visit his patients and then came back to the prison— is a rather humiliating process.

Is it proper to execute these part-time detentions in an ordinary prison building? It is not a question of security, but being housed in such surroundings adds to the humiliation of the subject. Prison administrators object to the use of prison buildings for this kind of detention, as it disturbs the organization of the service and limits the possibilities for satisfactory operation of the new regime.[51] In some countries, prisoners on semiliberty are living in hostels, in the precincts of the prison or out- side;[52] in other countries, they are placed in open institutions[53] or in houses not different from a plain boarding house. I visited one of these houses in Sweden and this raised again in my mind the question of the philosophy of this treatment. If such a regime may easily be justified as a transition between detention and freedom, how does it constitute, as such, a treatment that should be efficient either by some kind of intimidation or through a positive influence that I hardly can imagine? If we conclude that special buildings are needed, their architecture should be determined after answering this question.[54]

Although my documentation is far from complete, a few additional comments on similar regimes of part-time imprisonment in other countries may show the international character of this trend. In the United States, work release is now developing rapidly. It goes back to the Wisconsin Huber Law of 1913, but for many years the method remained little known, although it was already mentioned in Louis Robinson's classical book on prison labor.[55] A recent important development was the Federal Prisoner Rehabilitation Act of September 10, 1965, authorizing the At- torney General to put federal prisoners on paid employment or to par- ticipate in training programs in the community. According to Senator Long, 24 states have adopted such a procedure. In some cases, the system is applicable to rather long sentences (in Maryland, up to 5 years).[56]

In France, various experiments of semiliberty have been tried for the treatment of several groups of offenders. Among other things, administra-

[51] Jean Dupreel, "Orientation nouvelle de la peine de prison," *Annales de la Faculté de Droit de Thessaloniki*, 1966, p. 53.
[52] Lionel Fox, footnote 9, p. 322.
[53] Ernest Lamers, "Mr. Prisoner Goes to Town" (see No. 49), pp. 123–137.
[54] Howard D. Gill, in *Journal of Criminal Law, Criminology and Police Science*, September 1962.
[55] Louis N. Robinson, *Should Prisoners Work?* Philadelphia, 1931, p. 200.
[56] E. Long, "The Prisoner Rehabilitation Act of 1965," *Federal Probation*, December 1965, pp. 3–7; See also "The Part-Time Prisoner," *The Prison Journal*, Spring 1964.

tive instructions of 1951 and the following years allowed the possibility of executing short sentences from the outset in semiliberty. A decree of August 24, 1960, created the possibility of applying this regime to offenders desirous of following training courses.[57] The system has been legalized and expanded by Article 723 of the 1959 "Code de procédure pénale."[58] Other systems of part-time detention appear, as has been mentioned, in Scandinavian countries.[59]

* * *

It is very tempting to compare, in the same line of evolution, the age-old idea of penal servitude with the new method of work release. Is the contrast the result of a momentary coincidence? Or does this evolution express a deep and permanent change in our way of handling offenders?

Lamers pointed out that the economic boom in the Netherlands and the resulting scarcity of labor facilitates the placing of prisoners in private employment.[60] We may well wonder if this new development in the prison regime will disappear with the first serious economic crisis. Another reason to draw such a conclusion lies in the very different attitude adopted toward this problem by the USSR. In that country, corrective labor without deprivation of liberty may be applied to offenders. Work for the State is, in that case, the only punishment, the offender continuing his normal family life as soon as his day task is completed. This penalty was already written in Article 30 of the 1926 Code. It has been kept in Article 25 of the Basic Principles of Criminal Legislation in 1958 and in Article 21, 4°, of the 1960 Criminal Code of the Central Republic.[61] As I said before, I do not have enough information on the problem of prison labor in socialist countries to comment on this institution, but I may at least infer from this legislation how closely those solutions are related to the socioeconomic structure of the country.

THE FUTURE

We are nowadays no longer satisfied with descriptions of the past and we want prospective views on the course of events. This propensity,

---

[57] A. Perdriau, "L'exécution des courtes peines d'emprisonnement sous le régime de la semi-liberté," *Etudes et documentation*, Paris, 1962.
[58] Charles Germain (see footnote 49), pp. 94–96; also *The Prison Journal* (see footnote 56), p. 28.
[59] *The Prison Journal*, "The Part-Time Prisoner," Spring 1964.
[60] Ernest Lamers (see footnote 53), p. 127.
[61] *The Federal Criminal Law of the Soviet Union*, with an Introduction by Professor J. Van Bemmelen, Leiden, Sijthoff, 1959; also *La réforme pénale soviétique, Code pénal du 27 octobre 1960*, Centre français de droit comparé, Paris, 1962.

which helped to make Jules Verne, H. G. Wells and Aldous Huxley successful, has recently influenced the field of sociology and the art of governing by long-term plans. Criminal sciences are not immune to this tendency. Jean Pinatel, when secretary general of the International Society of Criminology, proposed to the Strasbourg European Committee on Crime Problems to make a prospective study of crime in Europe for the coming years.[62] Jean Nepote, the Secretary-General of the O.I.P.C. Interpol, attempted recently to describe the problems that police forces will have to solve during the next several years,[63] taking into account the various technical, economic, sociological, political, juridical, and administrative factors.

About penal methods, I am aware only of limited attempts to explain its evolution that implies future developments. One of them, although made by a most eminent criminologist, could not foresee what would happen ten years later. When Edwin Sutherland studied in 1934 the decrease in the prison population in England, he considered that this was due to the use of probation, to the practice of providing time in which to pays fines, and to the reduction in intoxication. He concluded also that a decrease in the number of prisoners "was not a direct effect of changes in crime rates, though a constant or a decreasing crime rate facilitates the substitution of other measures for imprisonment, because of the feeling of security engendered by a rate of that nature."[64] In 1934, however, Sutherland could have no premonition of the enormous increase in the prison population of the United Kingdom that took place after World War II and that remains, up to now, largely unexplained.

Ten years ago, I concluded a lecture on prisons with the assertion that tomorrow's penal systems will only keep imprisonment for two kinds of offenders, the dangerous ones to protect society against them and, at the other end, those who may be reeducated by a long period of training.[65] Norval Morris is more precise as to the rapidity of the evolution and even more negative as to the utility of present-day methods: "It is confidently predicted that, before the end of the century, prison in that form will become extinct, although the word may live on to cover quite different social organizations."[66]

* * *

[62] Meeting of the Scientific Council of the European Committee on Crime Problems, Strasbourg, October 3, 1965.
[63] J. Nepote, "Police et criminalité," Revue internationale de police criminelle, January, 1966.
[64] The Sutherland Papers, edited by A. Cohen, A. Lindemith, and Karl Schuessler, Bloomington, Indiana University Press, 1956, pp. 200–226.
[65] Paul Cornil, "La peine de prison," Revue internationale de criminologie et de police technique, July-September 1955.
[66] Norval Morris, (see footnote 34), p. 268.

FINAL REMARKS

The difficulty of predicting with some certainty the future trends of penal methods does not totally obscure our horizon. Some positive facts are influencing the future developments:

1. Penal reform proceeds slowly. As Thorsten Sellin put it: penology moves on leaden feet.[67] One of the main reasons for this stability is the massive character of prison buildings, most of which date from the 19th century. The construction of new institutions is a very expensive enterprise. Few countries have achieved a large-scale program in this field. Among the countries I visited, the United States, Sweden, and Portugal have made great efforts toward the modernization of their prison buildings. Others, such as the United Kingdom, Germany, France, or Japan, have started more recently along the same direction. How far will it be possible for them to go, while state budgets have so many other and more positive burdens to carry?

Denis Szabo points out that in European cities a large proportion of the population is living in houses built in accordance with ways of life from two or three generations ago, and he adds that such a contradiction is even more striking for prison architecture.[68] Prison administrators have made great exertions to adapt old buildings to new methods, but the result is often discouraging.

This massive stability of old prison buildings cannot go on forever. The maintenance of these outdated institutions is expensive and their location has often become surrounded by urbanized sections of the city. The pressure to have those buildings removed is increasing and this is an important asset for the penal reformer.

2. Another factor of stability in penal methods is the survival of classical notions about crime and punishment. Law students have contributed to this conservative attitude. As Mannheim has so aptly said, "The legal world is the slowest in making the necessary adjustments to changes in society."[69]

To the man in the street, imprisonment behind bars and walls appears as a simple and proper reaction when a crime has been committed. In a way, it solves the problem, for the offender disappears from the com-

[67] Thorsten Sellin, "Preface of Prisons in Transformation," *Annals of the American Academy of Political and Social Sciences,* May 1954.
[68] Denis Szabo, "Les prisons ont-elles un avenir?" (Is there a future for our prisons?), *Proceedings of the Fourth Research Conference on Delinquency and Criminology,* Québec Society of Criminology, Institut Philippe Pinel, Montréal, 1965, p. 46.
[69] Hermann Mannheim, *Criminal Justice and Social Reconstruction,* London, Kegan Paul, 1946, Preface.

munity and the regime of the institution to which he is submitted is largely unknown to the layman. This ignorance of the public is, however, changing. Radio and television are penetrating inside institutions, and a press report told us recently that a British newspaperman and a photographer had been admitted in a prison to interview three prisoners serving a long sentence for their participation in the famous train robbery of 1963.[70] This wider information of public opinion will probably become an incentive to change.

3. Prison regimes might be influenced by the results of the system. For more than a century ago, a high percentage of recidivism has been detected among the former prisoners. The first reactions in several countries, manifested themselves in the form of aggravated penalties. The French law of 1885 on "relégation" of recidivists is only one example of this tendency. The so-called "Baumes Laws" in New York State were another reaction of similar nature. More refined investigations were undertaken to evaluate the efficiency of prison treatment, but results are in general very deceptive. From the beginning, the Gluecks' appraisal of penal methods was of little encouragement. Analyzing the results of the training given in the Massachusetts Reformatory, they raised the following question: "Would not such offenders have done equally well if placed on probation?"[71] Thirty-five years later, and by very different ways, Roger Hood made a similar point after studying the British Borstal methods: "These figures appear to show that the length of training or the completion of a full training course, did not appreciably affect the chances of going straight on release."[72] These negative statements are perhaps among the most destructive arguments against our present prison methods.

4. Finally, some of the recent prospective sociological studies insist on the gradual decrease in the length of the working days for modern man. We are coming to a civilization of leisure time and, as Fourastie puts it: "Reduction in the duration of work is, after all, one of the most characteristic elements of the present transformation of humanity."[73] The same author estimates that man will soon have a career of approximately 40,000 working hours from a total life of 700,000 hours. If this trend is a permanent one, the penal reformer will indeed have to concentrate his action on the leisure time of the offender, but he should use his imagination to find new methods in the everlasting struggle against the changing forms of crime.

[70] Reuter press report, February 1, 1966.
[71] Sheldon and Eleanor Glueck, *500 Criminal Careers*, New York, Knopff, 1930, p. 313.
[72] Roger Hood, *Borstal Reassessed*, London, Heinemann, 1965, p. 212.
[73] Jean Fourastie, *La civilisation de 1975*, Presses Universitaires de France, 3rd edition, 1953; also Jean Fourastie, *Les 40.000 heures*, Paris, R. Laffont, 1965.

20

New Ways of Punishment

J. M. VAN BEMMELEN

Some time ago I had occasion to study the judiciary and methods of punishment in the Netherlands at the end of the 19th century. What I found most remarkable was the antithesis that existed around 1890 between the practice of law and the new ideas about punishment. Imprisonment was in those years the prevailing method of punishment. In the Netherlands the cellular system was made general by the new Penal Code of 1886, and it was applied indifferently to children, aged 10 to 16, as well as to adults. Every year more than 4000 children became acquainted with prisons and houses of detention. In 1900, two-thirds of all convictions, in cases judged by the courts, resulted in imprisonment and only one-third in fines.

But during these same years (1890–1900), new ideas about better methods of punishment were being developed. Particularly G. A. van Hamel, at that time professor of criminal law in Amsterdam, had already suggested: (1) special forms of punishment and treatment for children, (2) the possibility of a conditional suspension of the execution of sentences, (3) special ways to punish recidivists, and (4) better ways to make the offender pay to the victim for the damage caused by his offense. Van Hamel was inspired by the ideas of the Union Internationale de Droit Pénal, which he had founded in 1888 together with Belgian Professor Prins (Brussels) and his German colleague, Franz von Liszt (Marburg). Probably van Hamel himself contributed to these ideas. Part of these concepts, particularly the first and second, have now been realized in many countries.

In Holland the Children's Act of 1901 became effective in 1905, and the law on conditional suspension of sentences, in 1917. Special treatment for psychopaths, who are so often at the same time recidivists, is incorporated in a law of 1925, which took effect in 1928. Thus the ideas of 1890, which were also supported by other jurists, such as Simons (Utrecht) and Rethaan Macaré (district attorney in Haarlem), have borne fruit. The result is that in a population of 12,000,000 we now have in Holland fewer prisoners than in 1890 when the population was only 2,500,000. Only one-third of all convictions now result in a prison sentence, and two-thirds in fines.

But the curious thing is that nowadays in Holland, although we have a rather complicated system of punishment—often existing in a combination of a fine with a conditional prison sentence, and execution of the latter often suspended or partly suspended—there are only very few or no ideas at all about new ways in which we might be able to ameliorate our system of punishment. One might be inclined to suppose that the correctional system in Holland today is nearly perfect. But this is certainly not the prevalent opinion. For instance, nearly everyone is convinced that short prison sentences of less than three months, and even of less than six months, have only a negligible effect on offenders and sometimes do more to deteriorate than to ameliorate them. Notwithstanding this rather general opinion in the Netherlands, in 1962 approximately 4000 sentences for imprisonment were for less than one month, another 1100 were between one month and two months, and about 1900 were between two and six months. The total of short prison sentences was in that year around 7000. Another 3239 prison sentences were for six months or longer: 16 for 5 years or more, 34 for 3 to 5 years, 382 for 1 to 3 years, 652 for one year, and 2155 (with 1587 partly conditional)[1] for six months to one year. Thus, more than two-thirds of prison sentences in the Netherlands have a duration of less than six months. The Dutch are rather fortunate to have so few prisoners and still be able to cope with their criminality by using so few long sentences. But the great question—and this is not only a question for the *Dutch*— is how far we would be able to do away with the short prison sentence and, at the same time, reduce the number of cases in which presentence detention is applied.

It is about this question that I want to write in this chapter in honor of Thorsten Sellin, who has given proof in his book, *Pioneering in Penology*, of the great interest he had in the history of Dutch penal reform at the end of the 16th and the beginning of the 17th century. Let us hope that Sellin and those who read this book published in his honor will take some interest in the following ideas about more new ways to pioneer in penology.

When we want to ameliorate the system of today, we must make "a strong appeal for a change in the methods of punishment," as Kirck

---

[1] This makes a difference insofar as these 1587 partly conditional sentences usually consisted of some months during presentence detention, whereas the rest were conditional. To a great extent, they belong to the group of sentences shorter than 6 months.

Volckertszoon Coornhert for his time did in 1567 in his essay, "Boeven-tucht, ofte middlelen tot mindering der schadelijke ledighgangers." I want to make a proposal, to this end, which is based on the experience I had with the punishment of violations committed by members of the personnel of the Dutch railways. I am one of the five presidents of a board of arbitration for these punishments. In the first instance, these punishments are inflicted by the principal of the offender or, in the case of serious offenses, by the board of directors of the railway company. All railways in the Netherlands belong to one limited liability company, of which all shares are in the hands of the government. In this way the railways are a semipublic enterprise. The offenders have the right of appeal against these punishments to the board of administration, consisting of one member of the personnel, one member nominated by the board of directors, and one jurist as president who has to be an outsider, like myself.

There are no other punishments than moral ones, in five degrees of seriousness: (1) reprimand, (2) severe reprimand, (3) censure, consisting in a declaration of dissatisfaction, (4) serious censure, consisting in a declaration of serious dissatisfaction, (5) the same as (4), with a reminder. This reminder means that as soon as the offender commits a second offense of the same grade he may be discharged. So there is a sixth sanction: discharge.

The discharge can be applied immediately, for instance in the case of theft, but from time to time even these cases of theft are dealt with by using "serious censure with a reminder." Now what is most gratifying is to see how seriously these moral punishments are taken by the personnel. In often occurs that there is quite a debate about whether the sanction ought to be "censure" or a "severe reprimand." In former days there existed the possibility of inflicting fines, but these have been abrogated. Nobody, not even the directors, have an inclination to re-institute them.

The practice with these sorts of punishments suggested to me the possibility of applying them for quite a series of minor crimes and misdemeanors. The way in which these sanctions ought to be applied might be as follows:

(a) Every time such a sanction is imposed it ought to be registered in a central register, in which all punishments and sanctions ever in-flicted on a person would be recorded. In this way the police, the district attorney, all other public prosecutors, and the judge would be able to see how many different sorts of sanctions the accused person already had attached to his name.

(b) The police ought to be able to inflict on a person, who has committed a minor offense—for instance, a traffic violation—either a reprimand, a serious reprimand, or a small fine. Only when the offender protests against these sanctions should the police be obliged to bring the violation before a judge. The police will have to send a note of these reprimands to the central register, with a short statement of the offense for which the reprimand has been given. The central register will be obliged to signify to the offender that a reprimand for such and such a fact has been registered. After this signification the offender still has a right of appeal to the judge.

(c) The district attorney or the public prosecutor ought to have the right to inflict all five of the above-named moral punishments and to have them registered. Here again the district attorney and the central register will have to signify the order to register these punishments and the final registration to the offender, who has then a right to appeal to the judge.

(d) The judge before whom the man accused of a minor offense has to appear will have the right to inflict one of these moral sanctions instead of a conviction carrying imprisonment or a fine.

In these ways the police, the public prosecutor, and the judge would be able to avoid the imposition of fines and imprisonment in a number of cases. On the other hand, they would be much better informed about earlier small crimes and misdemeanors than is now often the case. Naturally, there is some resemblance to the system of "binding over for apprehended crime."[2] The difference would be that these moral sanctions would be applicable only when an offense, recognized as such by statute, had been committed, whereas "binding over" according to Glanville Williams and Kenny Turner can take place even in cases of a breach of the peace or for immoral or antisocial conduct, which does not constitute a criminal offense. As Glanville Williams says, "This is difficult to reconcile with sound principle, particularly with the principle enumerated by Dicey that 'no man is punishable or can be lawfully made to suffer in body or goods except for a distinct breach of law established in the ordinary legal manner before the ordinary courts of the land.'" Moreover the "binding over for breach of the peace or good behavior" is an institution known in Great Britain but, so far as I know, not in the United States.

There is also a resemblance to probation and conditional nonexecution of the imposed punishment (*sursis*). But the advantage of a system of

[2] A description of this system is to be found in Glanville Williams, *Criminal Law*, London: Stevens and Son Ltd., 1953, Chapter 16.

moral sanctions would be that the offender would realize that the police and the judge are willing to warn him, without immediately imposing a real punishment. Naturally the warning that the offender receives in this way should not be a thing of thin air. The offender has to know that a reprimand really will be remembered when he violates the law for a second or subsequent time.

In Holland the juvenile court judge now has the opportunity to apply a reprimand. For crimes the reprimand is used very seldom, for misdemeanors very often. But the difficulty is that there is no sufficient registration. A system of moral punishments will only be effective when the offender knows that, in the end, when he has accumulated some of these moral punishments, the judge will take very serious measures and that then he will be deprived of his freedom for a long time, during which he will be treated either as a patient or a man who has to be eliminated from society for a long period.

The great advantage that these moral punishments would have over fines and prison sentences is that the judge would have a much greater opportunity to differentiate them according to the real guilt of the offender. Fines depend to a certain extent on the financial position of the offender, and even a system of day fines (such as Sweden has in Chapter 25 of its new Penal Code)[3] procures only to a certain extent the possibility of adapting the fines to the guilt of the offender. The short prison sentences—even when, as in Sweden, the shortest prison sentence is one month—remain as obnoxious as they always have been. And they certainly are not always in accordance with the guilt of the offender.

The introduction of these moral punishments must go hand in hand with an abrogation of short prison sentences. These short-term prison sentences (up to six months) have little or no value. The time is too short to educate or to cure the prisoner. Most frequently it is impossible to let him work on a job that has any connection with the work he did outside the prison. Some weeks or months in prison only consist in inflicting a warning that his conduct is asocial or antisocial and that it must not be repeated. Whether it is necessary and useful to give this warning in the form of putting him in a prison or jail is highly questionable.

Dr. Veringa spoke about this problem in a lecture on penitentiary law at the Roman Catholic University in Nijmegen.[4] He indicated the

[3] The Penal Code of Sweden, effective January 1, 1965, translated by Thorsten Sellin, with an introduction by Ivar Strahl, Stockholm, 1965, Ministry of Justice.
[4] Dr. G. H. Veringa, *The Prison System in the Surf* (Het gevangeniswezen in de branding), Nijmegen-Utrecht: Dekker and van de Vegt N.V., 1964 (in Dutch).

fact that in Holland, in the last sixty years, the number of short prison sentences of less than three months has decreased considerably, but that since 1952 there has been a considerable increase of sentences of less than one month. In contrast with most authors he takes a positive stand by approving of this increase of short sentences of less than one month. Nothwithstanding this opinion, Dr. Veringa himself states that a proposition to do away with short prison sentences of less than six or nine months might deserve some consideration when, by accepting it, the number of prison sentences would be restricted and when it would not mean a shifting to longer periods of imprisonment. Here I quite agree with him but, in my opinion, notwithstanding this possibility that judges might switch too readily to longer sentences, we ought to abrogate the short prison sentences of less than six and possibly of less than nine months.

It is to be expected that many authors who nowadays want to preserve the short terms of imprisonment, because of their deterrent effect, will doubt whether the moral punishments would have this same effect. Concerning this issue, I am of the same opinion as Veringa, who says that an intensification of the police force in manpower and technical equipment will have a much greater effect than an aggravation of the forms of punishment. In my opinion it does not make a great difference whether a man becomes a recidivist after some months in prison or after a serious reprimand. And as soon as an offender has had a serious censure with a reminder, society and the judge will be much more justified in imposing a prison sentence of a year or more than now after three or more short prison sentences. With many of our petty thieves and swindlers, we either impose long prison sentences too quickly or we play a game of cat and mouse by inflicting a whole series of short-term sentences.

In many cases, the judge who imposes moral sentences will be convinced that they will not keep the man from becoming a recidivist. But then the same is true in cases where nowadays he punishes the offender with a short prison sentence. Society does not suffer more, only perhaps a little bit sooner, when a reprimand or a censure does not have the intended effect of restraining the offender from recidivism, than is the case when a short-term prison sentence remains without success.

There is no need to postulate that the success of the whole system of moral punishments depends on the fulfillment of two conditions that are essential.

1. The registration of these sorts of punishments, as well as of other forms of repression of crimes and misdemeanors, must be correct and complete. This registration will be much easier in small states like the

Netherlands, Belgium, and Denmark than in a big country like the United States. But in the long run even the different countries of Western Europe will be obliged to build up a system by which the data of their registrations of former punishments will be interchangeable. With the communication media of today, this should be not too difficult.

2. There must be a rule that after a serious censure with a reminder, the judge will not hesitate to inflict very radical sanctions, such as long prison sentences or, as in British law that orders the detention of the acquitted defendant, "during Her Majesty's pleasure" or, as in Dutch law that orders that the defendant will be "put at the disposal of the government" (ter beschikking gesteld van de regering) for an indefinite time, with the obligation for the judge to reconsider this order every two years.[5]

In what kind of cases would moral punishments be applicable?

1. The first group of offenses for which the moral punishments would be—in my opinion—very appropriate is that of petty economic crimes, such as thefts, swindles, embezzlements, particularly in the cases of first offenders. Undoubtedly there will be among them a number on whom the judge will feel obliged to inflict immediately more serious sanctions or measures, but for another part of them the moral censure will prove sufficient. The choice for the public prosecutor and the judge would be to inflict a moral punishment and to see whether this will procure the hoped for effect or to inflict immediately a prison sentence of one year.

2. The second group would be that of slander, insults, injuries.

3. Cases of negligence. In former days, when traffic was much less intense, cases of negligence were numerically of small importance. Nowadays they form the greatest part of all offenses. Fines and short prison sentences are often most inadequate to express the real guilt of the offender, particularly in cases of unconscious negligence (what in German is called "unbewuszte Schuld").

Frequently the punishment in these cases shows clearly the difficulties that a judge has when he tries to decide the appropriate measurement of the sanction.

A typical example is that of Captain Borren who, by his negligence, was responsible for the fact that insurgents, coming from Venezuela,

---

[5] This measure was introduced in the Dutch penal code in 1928. The judge is enabled to give this order when it is clear that at the time of the crime the offender was suffering from a mental disturbance or a mental underdevelopment and if the public order specifically required his detention in an asylum for psychopaths (Article 37a and following of the Dutch penal code).

had had the opportunity to occupy for a short time the "Waterfort" of Willemstad (Curaçao).[6] In this case the Court was convinced that not only the negligence of Captain Borren but the insufficient measures taken by the Dutch government for the protection of the fortifications in Willemstad had to be blamed for these happenings. The verdict in the Borren case was one day in prison.

Another recent case in Holland was that of a nurse, J.J.B., who in 1960 assisted in an operation and who by a mistake, when the surgeon asked for procaine (novocaine) 1 percent, gave a little flask containing adrenalini hydrochloridum 1:1000, which she handed to another nurse, S., who filled the hypodermic. The surgeon thereupon gave an injection with this liquid of adrenalini hydrochloridum 1:1000, which caused the death of the patient. The punishment inflicted to nurse J.J.B. by the Court of Appeal in Amsterdam was a fine of 100 guilders, and this decision was upheld by the Court of Cassation (Hoge Raad).[7] In this case the punishment of 100 guilders fine was probably the outcome of the fact that the nurse had been tired, had worked in surroundings that were unfamiliar to her, and that the nurse S. who filled the hypodermic syringe and the surgeon who had injected the liquid had not given any attention to the inscription on the label of the flask from which the liquid was put into the hypodermic syringe. About this last fact, several experts gave as their opinion that during operations it was not customary that the surgeon, who gave the injection, or the nurse, who put it in the syringe, exercised control over the inscription on the flasks for which they asked. The "omloopzuster" (that is, circulating nurse, or the second assisting nurse) was entrusted to control the labels of the flasks of liquid for which the surgeon asked.

In these cases of pure negligence it is unimportant whether the defendant is sentenced to one day in prison, 100 guilders fine, or to two months of imprisonment, as was the case in England in Regina v. Franklin.[8] In this Franklin case the accused had been on the West Pier at Brighton. He did not know that a certain C. P. Frenchard was swimming in the deep water round the pier. Franklin had taken up a good-sized box from the refreshment stall on the pier and had wantonly thrown it

[6] Sententie (sentence) of the Dutch Military High Court of Justice (Hoog Militair Gerechtshof) of October 14, 1930; Nederlandse Jurisprudentie (Dutch Law Reports) 1930, p. 1391.
[7] Hoge Raad, February 19, 1963. Nederlandse Jurisprudentie (Dutch Law Report) 1963, No. 512.
[8] Sussex Assizes, South Eastern Circuit, 1883, 15 Cox Crm. Cas. 163 and reproduced in cases and readings on *Criminal Law and Procedure*, Second edition by Jerome Hall and Gerhard O. W. Mueller. Indianapolis-Kansas City-New York: The Bobbs-Merrill Co., Inc., 1965, p. 156.

NEW WAYS OF PUNISHMENT

into the sea. Unfortunately the box struck Frenchard, who was at that moment swimming underneath, and so caused his death. These cases of negligence outside traffic violations are not common. But then our modern traffic conditions are the source of many such happenings in which more or less gross negligence causes death or grievous bodily harm. In my opinion, moral punishments would, in many such cases, be more appropriate than fines or imprisonment. According to the guilt of the offender the judge would inflict the lesser of these moral punishments or the more serious ones. When, after a serious censure with a reminder, the culprit commits another serious traffic offense, the judge could withdraw the offender's drivers license.

There certainly will be much opposition to this idea of moral sanctions. Some opponents will consider them as a proof of leniency. They should remember that every penal reform in former days has been considered as a dangerous weakening of the combat against crimes. When the prison became a substitute for the death penalty and corporal punishment, there were many judges and authors who were convinced that this would mean an enormous increase in criminality. The same occurred when torture was abrogated at the end of the 18th century. The introduction of probation and "sursis" in the 19th century was met with distrust, which afterwards proved to be unwarranted.

Another group of opponents will point out that fines and probation and "sursis" will be better warnings than these moral sanctions. This in my opinion is not true. Small fines will be the only possibility for persons with small means, who then will consider that such a small fine is the real estimation of their guilt. The same is true for probation. The probationer in many cases will have the feeling that he has been acquitted. But—I already hear the question—will this not occur in the case of a moral sanction? The answer is "No," for when sanctions are frequently imposed and the public begins to realize that whenever a person has accumulated a series of two or three of these sanctions, ending in a serious censure with a reminder, he will meet with sanctions of a drastic character. Then the public will be convinced that these moral sanctions are not to be taken lightly. Moreover, according to Dutch law, which does not recognize probation and only knows the conditional nonexecution of the punishment, this last sanction could not keep the place it now has because conditional nonexecution is only possible in the case of an imprisonment of less than one year that has been imposed with "sursis." And the idea is that when moral punishments are introduced, the short-term prison sentences for which the *sursis* is used will disappear.

Moral sanctions certainly would not take the place of fines, probation, and "sursis" all along the line; for example, for parking violations and other slight traffic offenses, fines would remain appropriate, particularly when the police collect them on the spot. According to my idea, moral sanctions ought to be considered as somewhat more serious sanctions than small fines. In some cases, they might even be combined with fines if it is certain that the offender would be able to pay the fines and if there is no reason to suppose that he would have to go to jail because the fine could not be paid or collected. The substitute-detention is a very unequal and impractical form of punishment. After all, the aim of introducing moral sanctions is to replace short-term imprisonment.

Attention should be drawn to the fact that these moral sanctions could be economically important. If it were possible to eliminate all short-term prisoners under six months, that in itself would mean an economy of 10 to 15 Dutch guilders ($\pm$ \$3.00) a day per prisoner. Naturally, there would be a certain increase of long-term prisoners but, according to my estimation, this increase would not be very large. For a small country like the Netherlands, it would mean a total saving of some millions of guilders.

But still more important is the fact that we would be able to improve the system of labor in the prison. It is much easier to get productive work for a relatively small number of long-term prisoners than for a great number of short-term prisoners. We might be able to eliminate a number of old jails and prisons because we would need less housing-room for our prisoners. Presentence detention would be used much less frequently, for it would not be necessary to use it for first offenders of many economic crimes. Either the public prosecutor or the judge, after some days, would impose a moral sanction, and they would do that the first and second time; only after the third or fourth warning would the offender be subjected to presentence detention.

I can imagine very well that many police officers, public prosecutors, judges and, perhaps, many citizens would be very much alarmed by the idea that offenders who had committed a burglary, an auto theft, or a similar offense would not immediately be put into presentence detention. A certain alarm about public safety is natural. But then, as has already been said, neither a short nor long detention period results in more certainty and safety.

At a certain moment the first offender leaves the prison after having finished his first imprisonment. He comes out of jail or prison, instructed by his coprisoners about the ways of committing new crimes. He comes out on parole or unconditionally but, in either case, not much better a man than he was when entering. Some of those who leave prison or jail do not become recidivists. According to a Californian research, about

30 to 50 percent of them are not imprisoned again within two years.[9] The question is whether fewer or more would become recidivists if they had only been warned by a moral sanction. My estimation is that about the same percentage or perhaps even a higher percentage would not become recidivists. The finding for Californian prisoners is no exception but rather universal. It seems to me that we may say that the causes for criminality are essentially the same in the whole Western world and that these causes lie for a great part outside the will of the offenders. Not that they wholly lack responsibility, but the important factors causing criminal behavior are independent of the offenders themselves. This fact becomes most visible in times of war and great crises when the number of offenders soars upward and when a great many people become criminals who, under other circumstances, would have remained outside the realm of criminal law.

In view of these propositions it would be advisable to have a try at experimenting with moral sanctions. The result, in my opinion, would be that 30 to 50 percent of the persons to whom these sanctions are applied will still become recidivists within two years. But in the meantime, those who succeed in going straight will have remained outside prison and, for the other group, which does not succeed, nothing is lost. Both groups, during the time that they remained outside prison, have cost nothing to the community. The result would be less harm to society and to the individual criminal.

There are, of course, certain types of crimes for which these moral sanctions will be impossible, for instance murder. But even in cases of murder and manslaughter, there are those for whom the title of the book by Franz Werfel holds good: *Not the Murderer but the Murdered Man is Guilty* (1920). It will take some time before the public will realize that there is even a small number of grave crimes for which a moral sanction would be a sufficient form of punishment. On the other hand, apart from exceptional cases, I never saw a murderer who was wholly sane. On the whole, however, it is not for the small group of serious criminals that we would have a need for moral sanctions but rather for the large number of traffic offenders, thieves, and other petty criminals.

[9] Daniel Glaser, *The Effectiveness of a Prison and Parole System*, Indianapolis-Kansas City-New York, The Bobbs-Merrill Co., Inc., 1964, p. 43 (postrelease failure rate of Federal and California prisoners in relation to offenses).

21

The Swedish Furlough System for Prisons

TORSTEN ERIKSSON

In the early 1930's when I was new in the service of the Swedish correctional system, I spent a few months as assistant to the director of the central prison in Gothenburg. Those were the days of the solitary confinement, when every prisoner was held in complete isolation for one year. Thereafter he was allowed to work with one or more prisoners. After still another year, he was permitted to spend his leisure time also with his co-workers. Contacts with the outside world were strictly regulated. Prisoners could be visited by members of their immediate family, but only infrequently, and their correspondence was rationed and closely supervised.

Next to the prison there was a large cemetery. One day when the pastor of the prison and I were talking to one another, I happened to mention the depressing neighborhood from both points of view. The pastor then told me the story of a prisoner in the institution who had been sentenced to several years for embezzlement and forgery. The man had nevertheless been a good husband and father, and his family had stood by him. Both his wife and his children visited him as often as was permitted.

One day the wife died suddenly. The husband was inconsolable and suffered terribly at not being allowed to leave the institution to attend his wife's funeral—by coincidence, she was to be buried in the cemetery next to the prison. His cell overlooked the graveyard and he could actually hear the hymns being sung and the pastor's voice during the funeral service. Why couldn't the prison authorities have been humane enough to allow the old prisoner, at least under guard, to follow his wife to her last resting place, the pastor asked me. But this would have been an impossibility according to the regulations of the day.

A couple of years later I had occasion to relate this anecdote to the great jurist *Karl J. Schlyter*, who had recently become Minister of Justice. Schlyter, an intimate friend of Thorsten Sellin, had just begun to interest himself profoundly in criminological questions in general and in the treatment of offenders in particular; in due course he became one of Sweden's foremost reformers in the field of correctional policy. I still remember how his face darkened with anger at the inflexibility and inhumanity of our laws on imprisonment.

Thanks to Schlyter's efforts, a law was passed in 1937 according to which a prisoner could leave the institution for a fixed period of time "to visit a relative who is seriously ill or to attend the funeral of a relative." Furloughs of this kind were only approved in exceptional cases in which the risk of abuse could be regarded as nonexistent. The task of drafting the first circular to the penal institutions regarding the matter was assigned to me. Approval of furloughs of this type could only be accorded by the National Correctional Administration, not by the local prison authorities.

Thanks to the strong personal engagement in the furlough system on the part of Mr. *Hardy Göransson,* then Director General of the Correctional Administration, it was utilized to the extent permitted by the law. Usually the prisoner on furlough was allowed to leave the institution alone with instructions concerning the "means and routes of communication" to be used, the purpose of the furlough, and the exact time at which he should return to the institution. Expenses of the furlough were in principle to be defrayed by the prisoner himself, but he was entitled to public funds if necessary. The system worked satisfactorily. The prisoners always—or almost always—returned on time. No complaints were received from the public.

In 1944, the Penal Code Commission—chaired by Schlyter, who had retired from his post as Minister of Justice some years previously—proposed that the furlough system be expanded. By that time we had accumulated considerable experience not only of furloughs for prisoners in the usual sense of the term, that is, those sentenced to simple imprisonment, imprisonment at labor, preventive detention, and internment, as well as to imprisonment for nonpayment of fines, but also of a freer form of treatment, namely, youth prison, which had been introduced in 1938.

The new legislation allowed greater latitude in granting furloughs to offenders in the age group, 18 to 21 years, if only to determine whether the young inmates had reached the point where they were trustworthy.

The Penal Code Commission went so far as to recommend that the Correctional Administration or its deputy, the director of the local institution, have the power to grant inmates permission not only to visit a sick relative or to attend the funeral of a relative but also to allow them furloughs "in consideration of the length of the sentence or for other good reasons." These types of absence from the institution could only be granted for short periods and, naturally, only in cases in which there was believed to be no risk of abuse.

The Commission wrote as follows:

Correctly applied, the proposed recommendation should be especially valuable in the placement of individuals who are to be paroled or released on probation. There may also be reason to allow inmates brief leaves of absence to help relatives or others with urgent harvest work.

It is the opinion of the Commission that furloughs should be granted even in the absence of the aforementioned special circumstances. If the sentence is not short, it is important that the inmate have the opportunity to meet his wife at home, not least in view of the risk of sexual inversion. Even if an inmate is not married, there may be good reason to allow him to visit relatives outside the institution. Visits to his wife and others close to him would help to alleviate his anxiety about them. Obviously, furloughs of this nature are out of the question for certain inmates. A notorious wife-tormentor, for example, could not be permitted to visit his family. Nor could dangerous prisoners be allowed out of the institution. Furlough should not be granted if there is a risk of escape. Leave might also be refused out of consideration for the inmate himself, for example, if his home environment is considered to be detrimental. In general, each case should be treated individually. For many inmates however, there should be no objection to granting leave from the institution for a day or so. Whether such permission should be given once or several times should depend on the length of the sentence. In the case of long sentences, home leave should be approved at regular intervals. Leaves should not exceed two or three days. Travel expense should be as a rule defrayed by the inmate, although in needy cases they may be paid in whole or in part from public funds.

The question has been raised whether furlough should also be conditional on the inmate giving his word of honor to return. The Commission finds no reason to recommend any general rule on this point, but there is naturally no objection to granting leave on this condition in individual cases in which it appears called for.

A legal distinction should be noted in the formulations. The old regulations had stated that furlough could not be granted unless there was strong reason to do so and "the risk of abuse could be regarded as non-existent." The new working was "as long as no danger of abuse can be assumed to exist," which, of course, gave the furlough-granting authority greater latitude.

The recommendations of the Penal Code Commission were approved by the Government and the Parliament and were thus incorporated in the new Prison Act of 1945, which went into effect on July 1, 1946. The same month, the Correctional Administration authorized each director of a correctional institution to grant furloughs to inmates undergoing sentences to simple imprisonment, imprisonment at labor, imprisonment for nonpayment of fines, and youth imprisonment for the purpose of visiting relatives who were seriously ill or of attending the funeral of a relative, on the condition that no danger of abuse could be assumed to exist. The directors were nevertheless encouraged to refer doubtful cases to the Correctional Administration. In all other cases, the Administration assumed the responsibility for deciding questions of furloughs. The inmate made a written request, which the director immediately transmitted to the Correctional Administration together with his own comments. If the request was approved, the director issued a pass specifying the purpose and duration of the furlough, the route and means of communication, as well as special directives to the inmate concerning his behavior during his absence from the institution. On the other hand, the pass was not to mention the offense for which the individual had been sentenced, nor the punishment or other sanction imposed. An indivdual on furlough was obviously to wear civilian clothes. If he had not the means to pay for travel and equipment, this was to be reported to the Correctional Administration, which could provide the necessary funds. If an offender did not return to the institution on time or was guilty of other breaches of directives, the director was to take immediate action and to report the case to the Administration.

Persons held in custody could also be granted furloughs for special reasons. Usually, however, they had to be accompanied by a prison guard. Several years passed during which the Correctional Administration gradually expanded the furlough system and accumulated considerable experience. As a rule the system worked well, and the prisoners appreciated the confidence shown them. But many inmates broke faith. They simply disappeared, committed new crimes, got drunk, or otherwise misbehaved. These failures began to be publicized in the press and became a matter for public discussion as well as in the Parliament. However, furloughs as such were not condemned, and in 1949 the Correctional Administration was in a position to stabilize the system by authorizing the institutional directors to grant furloughs independently in the majority of cases.

The new regulations differentiate between *special furlough* and *regular furlough.* The former comprises both the old leaves to visit ill relatives or to attend the funeral of a relative, which could be granted by the institutional director, and certain other events of special importance to the inmate, for which the Correctional Administration itself retained the right of decision.

In the case of regular furloughs, the following was prescribed:

A prisoner sentenced to a *term of fixed duration* or to *preventive detention* (now known as internment) could be granted a furlough by the institutional director under the circumstances described below:

1. If the length of the sentence was at least ten months but did not exceed 18 months, the first furlough could be granted for at most 48 consecutive hours, exclusive of travel time, at the end of the first six months of execution of the sentence. Persons sentenced to preventive detention for at least 18 months could be allowed furloughs under the same conditions.

2. If the length of the sentence and of the minimum period of preventive detention amounted to more than 18 months but not more than three years, the first furlough of at most 48 consecutive hours, exclusive of travel time, could be granted at the end of ten months of the sentence.

3. An inmate who had completed his first furlough without abuse could be granted a new furlough of at most 72 consecutive hours exclusive of travel time, four months after the beginning of the first one and thereafter at regular four-month intervals. However, no furlough could be approved during the last month of the sentence.

The institutional director could still refer the decision in doubtful cases to the Correctional Administration. It was impressed on the institutional directors that they must always observe the general condition that "no danger of misuse can be assumed to exist," that the conduct of the inmate must have been irreproachable, and that furloughs could not be granted during the Christmas, Easter, Whitsuntide, and Midsummer holidays.

The rules were even more liberal in the case of persons sentenced to *youth prison*. In a special circular, the Correctional Administration emphasized that the purpose of furloughs was to "counteract the detrimental effect of institutional isolation and to promote the social adaptation of the offender." The institutional directors were authorized to handle questions of furlough independently. For their guidance, the Administration formulated the following principles:

The Correctional Administration considers it advisable that the well-behaved inmate of a youth institution should receive his first furlough after approximately four months in the institution and subsequent furloughs every third month. The furlough should comprise approximately four days exclusive of travel time. If an inmate was delinquent in his working habits or his general conduct, his first furlough should be postponed "until he had improved his ways." Subsequent furloughs could also be postponed on the same grounds. At this point, however, the

Correctional Administration added a special clause, which clearly illustrated its intentions with regard to furloughs for young offenders, namely: "If the director considers that furlough should be postponed more than two months beyond the normal time or that it should not be granted for security reasons, he shall refer the matter to the Correctional Administration."

In addition to the regular furloughs, the Administration mentioned special furloughs in the circular in question. Pupils who were to be transferred to an open institution should be permitted to travel without guard (this soon came to be known as "transportation furlough"). If the youth prison board decided that a pupil should be paroled as soon as satisfactory employment could be arranged after a specific date, the youth should be eligible for furlough after the date in question until he could be paroled. (This type of furlough was called "furlough on principle.") Obviously furloughs could also be granted for visits to ill relatives or for attendance at the funeral of a relative. Furlough under other circumstances could as a rule not be granted without the permission of the Correctional Administration. The strong interest of the Administration in implementing the furlough system to its full extent is also revealed in its rule that, if the institutional director did not find himself able to approve a written request for furlough, he had to refer the request with his comments to the Correctional Administration.

A number of administrative changes were made in the correctional system in 1953. The institutions were divided into regions, each of which was headed by a regional director. The responsibilities of the Correctional Administration with regard to furloughs, for example, were transferred to the regional directors. Thereafter, the Correctional Administration's function in this respect was primarily a supervisory one.

Parallel with this revolution of the furlough system, there had been a fundamental change in the system of punishment and treatment itself. In 1930, when this story began, there were only one or two small open institutions for long-term offenders who were allowed to work in agriculture during the last phase of their sentence. Stimulated by Schlyter, however, the system of solitary confinement was gradually broken down and finally received the death blow with the 1945 law on imprisonment. This legislation modified the cell system to the point that, practically speaking, it became an exception to the main rule that all prisoners should work and take their recreation in groups composed according to criminality and type of personality. As a result of the elimination of solitary confinement as a principle and as the need for new institutional accommodations increased, there was established a number of colonies for prisoners sentenced to terms of varying duration, who it was assumed could safely live as a community both day and night. By the middle of the 1950's, almost every third prisoner was actually in a completely open institution. Parallel with this development, the system of probation had also been expanded to the point that the number of offenders in institutions was proportionately much smaller than ever before. Space does not permit a detailed report of what happened, and I shall therefore proceed to introduce the present-day situation of the Swedish correctional system.

As of March 1, 1966, the Swedish correctional system comprised the following clientele, as shown in Table 1.

TABLE 1

Category	In Institutions and in Jails	Noninstitutional	Total
Remanded for trial	410	—	410
Under psychiatric examination	157	—	157
Detained for dangerous asociality	—	—	—
Sentenced to imprisonment	3,317	2,579	5,896
Sentenced to imprisonment for nonpayment of fines	22	—	22
Sentenced to youth prison	599	472	1,071
Sentenced to internment	723	653	1,376
Sentenced to probation	78	15,438	15,516
Sentenced to care according to the Mental Health Act	32	—	32
Other	130	—	130
Total	5,468	19,142	24,610

Table 1 is essential for an understanding of the Swedish furlough system. The majority of the criminal clientele is under some form of open treatment with no institutional connection. First and foremost, a great number of offenders are sentenced immediately to probation. Furthermore, many who have been sentenced to ordinary imprisonment, to internment, or to youth prison are transferred to noninstitutional care long before the end of their punishment or of the period within which it is permissible to retain them in institutions. About the same number of persons sentenced to deprivation of liberty are outside as well as inside institutions. In addition, roughly one-third of the approximately 5000 inmates of institutions are in completely open institutions. It should also be noted that the guards in closed institutions in Sweden are unarmed. This rule has only one minor exception, namely, a special section with about 20 inmates.

"Openness" is thus the theme song of today's Swedish correctional system. Furloughs nowadays are regulated by the following directives issued by the Correctional Administration in 1963:

Decisions concerning furloughs are as a rule the responsibility of the respective regional director or his authorized deputy, the director of the local institution. *Regular furloughs* shall be granted as a normal part of the sentence. In addition, *special furloughs* may be approved under special circumstances. In all cases, a condition for granting furlough is that no danger of abuse can be assumed to exist. *Special furloughs* shall in general only be approved in the following cases:

1. To visit a relative who is seriously ill or to attend the funeral of a relative.
2. To appear as a witness in a court of law or otherwise to safeguard one's civil rights.
3. To visit a prospective employer, landlord, or other persons in order to obtain employment or living quarters after discharge or parole.
4. An inmate who has proven his reliability may be permitted to spend a few hours of the day outside the institution in connection with a visit.
5. In connection with transportation of an inmate from one institution to another. Here, the furlough usually comprises travel time only.

The following rules apply to *regular furlough*:

Prisoners sentenced to *sanctions of fixed duration* (imprisonment) are divided between those in open and those in closed institutions. In *open institutions* regular furloughs are applied in the case of inmates under sentences of at least six months. The first furlough is granted after six months when the sentence is at most 18 months and after ten months when the sentence is longer. A renewed furlough is approved three months after the beginning of the preceding one.

In *closed institutions* regular furloughs are only granted to inmates under sentences of at least 18 months. The first furlough is granted after ten months, succeeding ones four months after the beginning of the last furlough. Inmates who, despite good working habits and good behavior in general, have been kept in a closed institution because of ill health or in order to carry out a particular job or for some other comparable reason shall have the same treatment with regard to furlough as if they were in an open institution.

If the sentence is four years or longer, furlough shall generally not be granted until the inmate has completed one-third of the period to be served before he can be considered for parole. Inmates under life sentences shall not be granted their first parole until they have served at least three years.

The duration of the first furlough shall as a rule be at most 48 hours, exclusive of travel time, and at most 72 hours, exclusive of travel time, for succeeding furloughs. Regular furlough shall not be approved during the last month of execution of sentence, nor in connection with the Christmas, Easter, Whitsuntide, and Midsummer holidays. An inmate who has committed a crime after the beginning of execution of sentence, has escaped from the institution without having committed a crime, or has otherwise proved to be unreliable shall not be granted his first furlough until he has mended his ways and proved his reliability over a sufficiently long period of observation. The same applies to renewed furlough to inmates who have committed crimes during their last furlough, who have committed crimes or escaped from the institution, or otherwise proved to be unreliable after their last furlough.

Persons sentenced to *youth prison* or for a particular reason placed in this type of institution, even though under sentence to imprisonment, shall usually, assuming good conduct, be granted their first furlough after about four months in the institution and subsequent furloughs every third month thereafter. If the sentence of a prisoner referred to the youth group is longer than 18 months, the first furlough shall not be approved until the inmate has completed one-third of the time he shall serve before he can be considered for parole. An inmate serving a life sentence shall not be granted his first furlough until after at least three years. For the rest, the furlough regulations are the same as those described above for persons sentenced to imprisonment.

The first furlough for persons sentenced to *internment* shall usually be granted after ten months at the earliest when the minimum sentence is at most 18 months and after one year at the earliest when the minimum sentence is more than 18 months but less than three years. Otherwise, the rules are the same as for persons sentenced to imprisonment.

It may be mentioned that an inmate placed in a special institution or an institutional section for free-labor permitees may be granted furloughs for a few hours on Saturdays, Sundays, and public holidays. If the inmate belongs to the youth group, he may be allowed this privilege on at most two evenings during the working week.

Applications for furloughs shall as a rule be made in writing, although oral applications may be approved. If the institutional director does not have the power of decision himself, he shall refer the application to the competent authority, usually the regional director, accompanied by his own comments, the case history, and other documents concerning the inmate, to the extent required.

When a furlough has been approved, the director shall issue a pass containing information regarding the purpose and duration of the furlough and the route and means of travel, as well as a directive to the inmate to lead a sober and orderly life and any other regulations and advice which appear appropriate. If it is considered advisable, the police authorities in the place where most of the furlough is to be spent shall be informed of the case.

Inmates granted furlough shall defray their own travel and living expenses during their leave, primarily from their earnings in the institution. If the cost of travel and maintenance is exceptionally high and if the inmate's earnings or private means are not sufficient for the purpose, the institutional director may make him a grant from institutional funds. The director may also authorize an advance for the purchase of clothing required for a furlough. Such advances do not relieve the inmate of the responsibility of contributing his earnings in the institution to the cost of clothing required at release or parole to the extent that his earnings at that time are in excess of a reasonable sum for his support during the immediate period after he is let out. If there are strong reasons for a furlough at the same time as careful supervision is considered necessary, the institutional director shall order that the inmate be accompanied by a guard during the furlough. Should the cost for providing a guard have to be borne by the correctional system and if the purpose of the furlough is not to visit a seriously ill relative or to attend the funeral of a relative, the director shall secure approval of the expenditure from the regional director or, possibly, from the Correctional Administration itself, before approving the furlough.

In 1964, 7715 furloughs were granted and 858 of them were abused, that is, 11.1 percent. The abuse rate is usually between 10 and 11 percent, although it was as high as 15 to 16 percent at the beginning of the 1950's. Of the 858 abuses, 619 (8 percent) represented escapes, 239 (3.1) other breaches. A total of 295 abuses (208 escapes) were commited by internees and 250 abuses (190 escapes) by clientele of the youth group. With regard to escapes, however, it should be stressed that most of them were due to late returns to the institution. Furloughs usually end at the time the institution is closed for the night. If the furloughee has not returned by then, he is registered as an escapee. In reality, most of the breaches of furlough consist of late return, drunkenness at return, etc.

Everything has its price, as the saying goes. The furlough system, like the entire open character of the Swedish correctional system, has in no sense made life easier for the institutional authorities. The inmate is always intensely aware of his rights. Today, furlough (at least psychologically) has been transformed from a privilege into a right. The inmate whose application is turned down because he is considered to be a poor risk is profoundly offended and usually appeals the decision. Sometimes he also gets into mischief, which puts him at even more of a disadvantage. Nevertheless, despite the extra headaches caused the administration by the furlough system, despite the disagreeable consequences to the correctional system and its personnel when a furloughed offender commits a serious crime, it would be hard to find a single Swedish correctional official in a responsible position who would wish to eliminate or even limit furloughs. The furlough has rendered the unnatural life of the prison less unnatural. Sexual tensions and homosexual relationships are unquestionably of considerably less significance in Swedish prisons than elsewhere. And the inmate does not feel himself so completely exiled from society as hitherto.

Appendix

Bibliography of the Writings of Thorsten Sellin

BIBLIOGRAPHY OF THE WRITINGS OF
THORSTEN SELLIN (BOOK REVIEWS NOT INCLUDED)
CHRONOLOGICALLY ARRANGED, 1917—

1917

"Historical backgrounds for the study of language and literature." Minnesota Educational Association, *Journal of Proceedings and Addresses at the Fifty-fifth Annual Meeting held at Minneapolis, Minn., October 31–November 3, 1917*, 192 pp. (Minneapolis: Minnesota Educational Assn., 1917), pp. 110–114.

1921

August Strindberg's Lycko-Pers Resa. With notes and vocabulary by J. Thorsten Sellin. viii, 161 pp., Stockholm: Albert Bonnier, 1921 (Bonnier's College Series of Swedish Textbooks, Vol. 6).

1922

Marriage and Divorce Legislation in Sweden. 148 pp. (Minneapolis: Augsburg Publ. Co., 1922). Translation of Marriage Code of 1920 reproduced in International Institute for the Unification of Private Law, *The Uniform Laws of the Nordic Countries* (Rome: Ed. Unidroit, 1963), pp. 179–219.

1925

"Fascism at work." *Nation*, 121:513, November 4, 1925.

1926

"A new phase of criminal anthropology in Italy." *Ann. Amer. Acad. Pol. & Soc. Sci.*, 125:233–242, May 1926.
"Is murder increasing in Europe?" *Ann. Amer. Acad. Pol. & Soc. Sci.*, 125: 29–34, May 1926.
"Filippo Franci—a precursor of modern penology." *Jour. Am. Institute of Crim. Law and Crimin.*, 17:104–112, May 1926.
"Prison reform in Belgium." *Jour. Am. Inst. of Crim. Law and Crimin.*, 17: 264–277, August 1926.

1927

"Dom Jean Mabillon—a prison reformer of the 17th century." *Jour. Crim. Law & Crimin.*, 17:581–602, February 1927.

1927–1929

"Bibliography [of current literature in criminology]" *Jour. Crim. Law & Crimin.*, 18:147–158, 295–318, 451–484, 629–639; 19:118–158, 290–320, 450–508, 656–691. May 1927–February 1929.

1928

Professor M. Liepmann's "American prisons and reformatories." An authorized abstract, 26 pp. [Philadelphia: Central Bureau of Philadelphia Yearly Meeting of Friends, 1928 (Friends' Social Service Bull. No. 28)].
"The Negro criminal. A statistical note." *Ann. Amer. Acad. Pol. & Soc. Sci.,* 140:52–64. November 1928. (In Spanish) *Rev. de identificación y ciencias penales,* 1929.

1929–1944

Dictionary of American Biography. New York: Scribner's, 1929–1944.
    "Zebulon Reed Brockway."
    "John Koren."
    "Orlando Faulkland Lewis."
    "Elam Lynds."
    "Thomas Mott Osborne."
    "Amos Pilsbury."
    "Richard Vaux."
    "Roberts Vaux."
    "Hastings Hornell Hart."

1930

"The house of correction for boys in the hospice of St. Michael in Rome." *Jour. Crim. Law & Crimin.,* 20:533–553, February 1930. (In Italian) *Scritti in onore di Enrico Ferri per il cinquantesimo anno di suo insegnamento,* 526 pp. (Torino: Unione tip. torinese, 1929), pp. 453–466.
"Bemerkung zur Todesstrafe." *Monats. f. Kriminalpsych. u. Strafrechtsref.,* 21:305, May 1930.
"Pennsylvania's new state prison." *The Island Lantern* (McNeil Island Penitentiary), 7:77–89, June 1930.
"Die Todesstrafe in den Vereinigten Staaten." *Monats. f. Kriminalpsych. u. Strafrechtsref.* 21:102–105, February 1930; (In Spanish) *Rev. de crimin., psiquiatria y med. leg.,* 17:627–632, September–October 1930.
"Beobachtungen bei einer Gas-Hinrichtung." *Monats. f. Kriminalpsych. u. Strafrechtsref.,* 21:620–621, October 1930.
"The Negro and the problem of law observance and administration in the light of social research." Ch. 29 of Charles S. Johnson, *The Negro in American Civilization,* xiv, 538 pp., (New York: Holt & Co., 1930), pp. 443–452.

1930–1934

Encyclopedia of the Social Sciences. New York: Macmillan, 1930–1934.
  "Abraham Adolf Baer."
  "Moritz Benedikt."
  "Alphonse Bertillon."
  "Arnould Bonneville de Marsangy."
  "Commutation of Sentence."
  "Crime."
  "Prosper Despine."
  "Charles Buckman Goring."
  "Identification."
  "Imprisonment."
  "Indeterminate Sentence."
  "Penal Institutions."
  "Probation and Parole."

1931

[Tribute to the Archivio di Antropologia Criminale on its 50th anniversary.] *Arch. di antr. crim.*, 51:145–146 (suppl. to January–February no., 1931).
"Prison tendencies in Europe." *Proc. of the National Conference of Social Work,* 1930, x, 710 pp., (Chicago: Univ. of Chicago Press, 1931), pp. 118–132; *Jour. Crim. Law & Crimin.*, 21:485–498, February 1931. (In Japanese) *Hogaku-Sirin* 32:1308–1338, November 1930. (In French) *L'Ecrou* 12:214–232, April–June 1931. (In Spanish) *Rev. di identific. y ciencias penales* 6:134–149, May–June 1930.
"The basis of a crime index." *Jour. Crim. Law & Crimin.*, 22:335–356, September 1931. (In German) *Monats. f. Kriminalpsych. u. Strafrechtsref.*, 22:577–597, October 1931.
"Paley on the time sentence." *Jour. Crim. Law & Crimin.*, 22:264–266, 1931; *Mass. Law Quart.*, 1931.
"The study of the criminal in Europe." *Prison. Jour.*, 11:24–26, April 1931.
"The historical background of our prisons." *Ann. Amer. Acad. Pol. & Soc. Sci.*, 157:1–5, September 1931.
"A brief guide to penological literature." *Ann. Amer. Acad. Pol. & Soc. Sci.*, 157:225–232, September 1931.
"Criminal statistics in the United States." *Report of the 54th Annual Meeting of the Am. Bar Assoc.*, 1931 (Chicago: Am. Bar Assoc., 1932), pp. 504–512; *N.Y. State Bar Assoc. Bull.*, 3:477–483, October 1931.

1932

"State bureaus of criminal statistics." *Proceedings of . . . the American Prison Assoc.*, 1931 (New York: American Prison Assoc., 1932), pp. 190–199.
"Training the prison staff in Prussia," *Jour. Crim. Law & Crimin.*, 23:102–105, May–June 1932.

"Penological research in a state welfare department." *Proc. of the National Conference of Social Work,* 1932 (Chicago: Univ. of Chicago Press, 1933), pp. 469–474; *Social Service Rev.,* 6:390–396, September 1932.

"Common sense and the death penalty." *Prison Journal,* 12:10–13, October 1932.

1933

"Children in our prisons." *Jour. Crim. Law & Crimin.,* 23:839–840, January–February 1933.

"Hinrichtungen in den Vereinigten Staaten." *Monats. f. Kriminalpsych. u. Strafrechtsref.,* 24:38–40, January 1933.

"The trial judge's dilemma—a criminologist's view." Chapter 5 (pp. 99–108) of S. Glueck (ed.), *Probation and Criminal Justice* (New York: Holt & Co., 1933).

"The problem of national criminal statistics." *Proc. of the . . . Am. Prison Assoc.,* 1932 (New York: Am. Prison Assoc., 1933), pp. 309–314.

"Keeping people out of jail." *Proc. of the . . . Am. Prison Assoc., 1932* (New York: Am. Prison Assoc., 1933), pp. 362–365.

"Criminal statistics." Chapter in Stuart A. Rice (ed.), *Next Steps in the Development of Social Statistics* (Ann Arbor: Edwards Bros., 1933).

"Rapport d'ensemble sur la législation pénale aux États-Unis en 1931." *Recueil de documents en matière pénale et pénitentiaire,* 3:5–117, December 1933.

"Methods of etiological research in criminology." *Sociology and Social Research.* 17:393–395, March–April 1933.

"A quarter century's progress in penal institutions for adults in the United States." *Jour. Crim. Law & Crimin.,* 24:140–160, May–June 1933.

1934

"The sources and methods of criminology." Chapter in L. L. Bernard (ed.), *The Fields and Methods of Sociology* (New York: Long & Smith, 1934).

"Historical glimpses of training for prison service." *Jour. Crim. Law & Crimin.,* 25:594–600, November–December 1934.

"Appunti storici su problemi penali e penitenziarii." *Riv. di diritto penitenziario,* 5:500–504, May–June 1934.

(Text accompanying and interpreting statistical tables.) *Prisoners in State and Federal Prisons and Reformatories, 1931–1932,* 72 pp. (Washington: U. S. Government Printing Office, 1934).

"Rapport d'ensemble sur la législation pénale en 1932 (États-Unis)." *Recueil de doc. en matière pén. et pénit.,* 3:255–305, May 1934. (English) *89th Annual Report of the Prison Assoc., New York, 1934* (New York: Prison Association of New York, 1934), pp. 75–106.

1935

(With J. P. Shalloo), *A Bibliographical Manual for the Student of Criminology,* vi, 41 pp. [Philadelphia: The Authors, 1935 (for later editions see 1960 and 1964)].

"The annual prison report." *Proc. of the Am. Prison Assoc.*, 1934 (New York: Am. Prison Assoc., 1935), pp. 290–294.
"Adult offenders." *Social Work Yearbook*, 3:29–33, 1935.
"Race prejudice in the administration of justice." *Am. Jour. of Sociology*, 41:212–217, September 1935. (In Italian) *Riv. di dir. penit.*, 6:420–426, March–April 1935.

1936

"Importance of criminal statistics." *Proc. of the Attorney-General's Conference on Crime* . . . Washington, 1934 (Washington, 1936), pp. 380–387.
"Crime and the second generation of immigrant stock." *Interpreter Releases* 13:144–150, May 23, 1936.
"Das American-Law-Institute und ein neues amerikanisches Strafgesetzbuch." *Monats. f. Kriminalpsych. u. Strafrechtsref.*, 27:205–206, April 1936.

1937

"The Lombrosian myth in criminology." (Letter) *Am. Jour. of Sociology*, 42:897–899, May 1937.
"The law school and the training of judges." *The Legal Intelligencer* (Philadelphia), 96:1110, April 28, 1937.
"Crime prevention and treatment." *Social Work Year Book*, 1937:107–112.
Research Memorandum on Crime in the Depression, viii, 133 pp. (New York: Social Science Research Council, 1937). (Italian transl. of Chapters 2, 4, and 6) *La Giustizia penale: Parte prima* 54:114–119, 201–214, 284–288, 1938.

1938

"Rapport d'ensemble sur la législation pénale en 1933 (États-Unis)." *Rec. de doc. en matière pén. et pénit.*, 7:12–69, January 1938.
"Problems of parole." *The Wharton Rev. of Finance and Commerce* 9, No. 6:8, 15–16, March 1938.
Administration of Penal Treatment in Philadelphia, 47 pp., mimeographed (Philadelphia: Institute of State and Local Government, Univ. of Pennsylvania, April 1938).
Culture Conflict and Crime, vii, 116 pp. (New York: Social Science Research Council, 1938). Final section, with brief intro. and same title in *Amer. Jour. of Sociology*, 44:97–103, 1938.

1939

"Rapport d'ensemble sur la législation pénale en 1934 (États-Unis)." *Rec. de doc. en matière pén. et pénit.*, 8:34–63, January 1939.
"Foreword." Pp. v–vii of Georg Rusche and Otto Kirchheimer, *Punishment and Social Structure*, xiv, 268 pp. (New York: Columbia Univ. Press, 1939).

1940

"Vetenskapen och kriminalpolitiken" (Science and Crime Prevention), *Svensk Juristtidning*, 25:305–311, 1940.

The Criminality of Youth. 116 pp. (Philadelphia: American Law Institute, 1940).

"Probation in the United States." *De Nordiska Kriminalistföreningarnas Årsbok,* 1940:290–304 (Swedish transl.), pp. 270–289.

"Crime and criminals." *Statistical Services and Activities of U. S.,* 1940, pp. 36–37.

1940–1946

Annual Report, 1939 (Philadelphia: Board of Inspectors of the Philadelphia County Prison, 1940), 48 pp.

―――, 1940. Philadelphia. 1941. 60 pp.

―――, 1941. Philadelphia. 1942. 64 pp.

―――, 1942. Philadelphia. 1943. 56 pp.

―――, 1943. Philadelphia. 1944. 63 pp.

―――, 1944. Philadelphia. 1945. 61 pp.

―――, 1945. Philadelphia. 1946. 60 pp.

1941

"The criminality of youth." *News Bulletin,* 12:1–3, 5–8, 12, 1941.

"Some sentencing practices in Europe." *Fed. Probation,* 1:28–30, 1941.

"Philadelphia county prisons then and now." *Prison Journal,* 21, No. 1, suppl: 41–50, January 1941.

"Crime." *Am. Jour. Sociology,* 47:898–906, 1942.

(With P. R. Busey) *Crime: The Causes and Extent of Criminal Behavior, Its Prevention and Treatment,* Washington, 1942, 64 pp.

War and Crime: A Research Memorandum (mimeographed), prepared for the Committee on Research on Social Aspects of the War (New York: Social Science Research Council, 1942).

"County prisons: the annual report of the inspectors of the Philadelphia county prison for 1940." *Prison Journal,* Vol. 22, April 1942.

"The youthful offender." *Federal Probation* 6:14–17, April–June 1942.

"Youth and crime." *Law and Contemporary Problems,* 9:581–587, 1942.

"Recommended: a standard for penal statistics." *Prison World,* 5:4–5, May–June 1943.

"Child delinquency." *Ann. Amer. Acad. Pol. & Soc. Sci.,* 229:157–163, 1943.

"Statistics and the battle against delinquency." *Prison World,* 5:18, 30, September–October 1943.

1944

Pioneering in Penology. The Amsterdam Houses of Correction in the 16th and 17th Centuries, xii, 125 pp. (Philadelphia: Univ. of Penn. Press, 1944).

Uniform Criminal Statistics Act (Chicago: National Conference of Commissioners on Uniform State Laws, 1944).

"The criminal history of released prisoners," *Jour. Crim. Law & Crimin.,* 35:223–227, 1944; *Monthly News Letter* (Intern. Assoc. for Identif.), pp. 1–5, February 1945.

1945

"The Walnut Street Prison." *The Philadelphia Forum Magazine*, 24:8–10, January 1945; *Prison World*, 7:11, 27–28, March–April, 1945.
"Adult offenders." *Social Work Year Book*, 8:27–36, 1945.

1946

(Anon.) *Is a Crime Wave Coming?* 30 pp. [Washington: U. S. Government Printing Office, 1946 (E. M. 6, GI Roundtable)].

1947

"Foreword." Robert Graham Caldwell, *Red Hannah, Delaware's Whipping Post*, xv, 144 pp. (Philadelphia: Univ. of Pennsylvania Press, 1947).
"Adult offenders." *Social Work Year Book*, 1947:32–41.
"Obestämd dom och obestämd behandling." [Indeterminate sentence and indeterminate treatment.] *Svensk Juristtidning*, 32:481–493, 1947. *De Nordiska Kriminalistföreningarnas Årsbok*, 1947–1948 (Stockholm, 1949), pp. 2–13. (Finnish transl.) *Suomen Kriminalistiyhdistyksen XIII Vuosikirja 1947* (Helsinki, 1948), pp. 9–26.
"Till vägledning för kriminologiska studier." [A guide to criminological research.] *Tidsskrift for Kriminalvård*, 2:33–38, 1947.
Recent Penal Legislation in Sweden, 70 pp. (Stockholm: Strafflagberedningen, 1947).
"Fångvårdsstyrelsens årsberättelser." [The annual reports of the prison administration.] *Svensk Juristtidning*, 32:397–398, October 1947.
"Den riskabla anonymiteten." [The risky anonymity.] *Vi* (Stockholm), 34:7, 1947.
"Kriminologi och etiologisk forskning." [Criminology and etiological research.] *Nordisk Tidsskrift for Strafferet*, 35:145–158, October 1947.

1948

"Penal questions in the Northern countries." *De Nordiska Kriminalistföreningarnas Årsbok*, 1946–1947: xiii–xlvii, Stockholm, 1948.
[Criminological Research and Training in the United States.] *De Nordiska Kriminalistföreningarnas Årsbok*, 1946–1947: 339–344, Stockholm, 1948.
"Tidsobestämda frihetsberövanden som påföljder för brott." [Indeterminate removal of liberty as a consequence of crime.] *De Nordiska Kriminalistföreningarnas Årsbok*, 1946–1947: 106–117, Stockholm, 1948.
"Trends in penal treatment." *Recueil de documents en matière pénale et pénitentiaire* (Berne), 13:285–292, November 1948.
Foreword (pp. v–vi) of David Te-Chao Cheng, *Acculturation of the Chinese in the United States. A Philadelphia Study*, xii, 280 pp. (Foochow, China: The Fukien Christian Univ. Press, 1948).

1949

"Some aspects of prison reform in Sweden." Phila. Co. Prison, Board of Prison Inspectors, *Annual Report*, 1947:63–82, Philadelphia, 1949.

"The treatment of offenders in Sweden." *Federal Probation,* 12:14–18, 1949. (Spanish transl.) *Criminalia* (Mexico), 16:492–499, December 1950.

"Aims and practices in penal treatment." *De Nordiska Kriminalistföreninggarnas Årsbok* (Yearbook of the Northern Association of Criminalists), 1947–1948:13–32, 1949.

"Probation and parole of adult offenders in Sweden." *Yearbook, National Probation and Parole Association,* 1948:239–251, New York, 1949.

"Sweden's substitute for the juvenile court." *Ann. Amer. Acad. Pol. & Soc. Sci.,* 261:137–149, January 1949.

1950

"A note on capital executions in the United States," *British Jour. of Delinquency,* 1:6–14, July 1950.

"Status and prospects of criminal statistics in the United States." *Festskrift tillägnad Karl Schlyter* (Stockholm: Svensk Juristtidning, 1950), pp. 290–307. "The uniform criminal statistics act." *Jour. Crim. Law & Crimin.,* 40:679–700, March–April 1950.

"Some current issues in penal treatment." *Yearbook, Northern Assoc. of Criminalists,* 1948–1949: xv–xxxix, Stockholm, 1950.

"L'étude sociologique de la criminalité." *Rev. de droit pénal et de criminologie,* 31, 263–286, December 1950. (English) "The sociological study of criminality." *Jour. Crim. Law & Crimin.,* 41:406–422, November–December 1950. 2 ème Congrès Intern. de Crimin., 5 ème rapport general, *Sociologie,* 18 pp., Paris, 1950.

1950–1953

"Le sociologue et le problème du crime." *Rev. de science criminelle et de droit pénal comparé,* October–December, 527–539, 1950. (English) "The sociologist and the problem of crime." In Vol. 4, pp. 495–507 of Intern. Inst. of Sociology, *Proceedings of the 14th International Congress of Sociology,* Rome, 1950 (publ. 1953).

1951

"The death penalty and the problem of deterrence." Royal Commission on Capital Punishment: *Minutes of Evidence,* 30. February 1, 1951, London, 647–678, 1951.

"L'expérience de la sentence indéterminée aux États-Unis." [The experience with the indeterminate sentence in the U. S.] *Rev. de science criminelle et de droit pénal comparé,* 417–443, July–September 1951.

"The significance of records of crime." *Law Quar. Rev.,* 67:489–504. October 1951.

"La disparition de la Commission internationale pénale et pénitentiaire." *Rev. de crimin. et de police technique,* 5:259–66. October–December 1951. (In Spanish) *Revista Penal y Penitenciaria,* ano xvi, Nos. 59–62, 1951.

"La Commission Internationale Pénale et Pénitentiaire, 1872–1951." *Recueil de documents en matière pénale et pénitentiaire,* 15:373–374, 1951 (English text, pp. 375–376).

Preface (pp. xi–xvi) of Twelfth International Penal and Penitentiary Congress, The Hague, August 14–19, 1950, *Proceedings*, Vol. II, xvi, 609 pp. (Bern: International Penal and Penitentiary Commission, 1951). (In French, pp. ix–xiv of Vol. I.)

1952

Preface to *Homicides and Suicides in Finland and their Dependence on National Character*, by Veli Verkko, 189 pp., Copenhagen, 1952.

"Foreword" to S. Hurwitz, *Criminology*, London and Copenhagen, 1952.

Preface (pp. iii–vi) of *Actes des douze congrès pénitentiaires internationaux. Index analytique et des noms*. Publié sous la direction du Secrétaire Général de la Commission Internationale Pénale et Pénitentiaire. Thorsten Sellin, Ph.D. LL.D. par Mme Valy Degoumois, Lic. en droit, xii, 323 pp. (Berne: Staempfli et Cie., 1952).

1953

"Les grandes conceptions de la sociologie criminelle américaine." Pp. 104–115 of Georges Heuyer and Jean Pinatel, eds., *L'examen médico-psychologique et social des délinquants. Conférences* (Premier cours international de criminologie, Paris, September 15–October 24, 1952), 684 pp. (Paris: Ministère de la Justice, March 1953.)

"La classification aux États-Unis." *Ibid.*, pp. 545–558.

"The Treatment of mentally abnormal offenders in Sweden. A blueprint for reform." Pp. 91–103 of *Vårdorganisation för förvarade och internerade*. Förslag av Säkerhetsutredningen. 103 and 32 pp. Stockholm, 1953. (Statens Offentliga Utredningar, 1953:32.) [The Organization of Care of Detainees and Internees. Proposal by the Security Study Commission.]

"The measurement of criminality in geographic areas." *Proc. of the American Philosophical Society*, 97:163–167, April 30, 1953. (In Spanish) *Revista de la Escuela de Estudios Penitenciarios* 10:64–71, July–August 1954.

"Philadelphia prisons of the 18th century." *Transactions of the American Philos. Society* 43, pt.1:326–30, 1953.

1954

"Crime and Crime Prevention." *The American Peoples Encyclopedia Yearbook*, 1953, pp. 266–267 (Chicago: Spencer Press, 1954).

"Problems and prospects of criminal statistics." *Correction*. (New York State Department of Correction), 19:3–9, February 1954.

[Capital and Corporal Punishment] pp. 666–743 of First Session—Twenty-Second Parliament 1953–1954; Joint Committee on Capital and Corporal Punishment and Lotteries. Minutes of Proceedings and Evidence No. 17. Tuesday, June 1, 1954. Wednesday, June 2, 1954. Witness: Professor Thorsten Sellin (Ottawa: Queen's Printer, 1954). Shortened version, entitled "A New Look on Capital Punishment," in *Currents* [PCA, Phila., Penna.], 8:12–16, Summer–Fall, 1956.

1955

"En historisk återblick." [A historical perspective.] Ch. 1 (pp. 1–22) of Ivar
Agge et al., *Kriminologi.*, xi, 429 pp. (Stockholm: Wahlström & Widstrand,
1955).
"The Youth Correction Authority Act (YCAA) and the Draft Code." Pp. 47–
63 of The American Law Institute: *Model Penal Code Tentative Draft No. 3*,
63 pp. (Philadelphia: American Law Institute, April 25, 1955).
"The death penalty and police safety." *Appendix "F"* of the Minutes of Proceedings and Evidence No. 20 of the Joint Committee of the Senate and the
House of Commons on Capital and Corporal Punishment and Lotteries, pp.
718–728 (Ottawa: Queen's Printer, 1955).
"The Philadelphia gibbet iron." *Journal of Criminal Law, Crimin. & Police Sci.*,
46:11–25, May–June 1955. (In French) *Revue internationale de police
criminelle* 12:20–26, January 1957.
*The Bureau of Corrections in the Attorney General's Department of the Com-
monwealth of Pennsylvania*, 31 pp., mimeographed (Harrisburg: Secretary of
Administration, 1955).

1956

(With Ralph W. England, Jr.) "Criminology, 1945–1955." Pp. 120–122 of
Sociology in the United States of America (Paris: UNESCO, 1956), Hans L.
Zetterberg, ed.
Aspects sociologiques, 29 pp. [Milano: D. A. Giuffré, 1956 (Centro Nazionale
di Prevenzione e Difesa Sociale. *Congrès international sur la Prévention IV*.
Congrès international de defense social, April 2–6, 1956)].
(With Marvin E. Wolfgang) "Rapport sur les aspects sociologiques de
l'enseignment de la criminologie." (Etats-Unis) pp. 92–106 of *Les sciences
sociales dans l'enseignment superior: Criminologie*, 169 pp. (Paris: UNESCO,
1956).

1957

"Crime: United States." *Encyclopedia Britannica* (1957) 6:703–705.
The Protective Code: A Swedish Proposal (Stockholm: Department of Justice,
1957), 56 pp.
"La peine de mort et le meurtre." *Revue de science criminelle et de droit
pénal comparé*, 1957, October–November, 739–766.
"The law and some aspects of criminal conduct." Pp. 113–125 of Conard, A. F.,
ed., *Conference on Aims and Methods of Legal Research*, held at University
of Michigan Law School, November 4–5, 1955, 199 pp. (Ann Arbor, Michigan:
Univ. of Michigan Law School, 1955).
"La prévention des infractions contre la vie humaine et l'intégrité corporelle."
Rapport général: Aspects sociologiques, Pp. 71–98. (In Italian) Pp. 99–123
of Centro Nazionale di Prevenzione e Difesa Sociale, *Actes du Congrès international sur la prévention des infractions contre la vie humaine et l'intégrité
corporelle. IVe Congrès* international de défense sociale, Milano 2–3–4–5–6
aprile 1956 (2 vols.), Vol. I (Milan: Dott. A. Giuffre, 1957).

"International cooperation in criminology and penology." *Augustana College Bulletin*, Ser. 52, No. 9:8–9, December 1957.

"Commentary" on Hessel E. Yntema's paper. P. 83 of Conard, A. F., ed., *Conference on Aims and Methods of Legal Research*, held at the Univ. of Michigan Law School, November 4–5, 1955, x, 199 pp. (Ann Arbor, Michigan: Univ. of Michigan Law School, 1955).

Letter [on the death of Denis Carroll] Société internationale de criminologie, *Bulletin* 1957:155–157. (In Spanish) *Revista penal de la Habana* 8:130–132, July–December 1957.

"Observation on statistics of juvenile delinquency." P. 8 of Crime Prevention Assoc. of Philadelphia, *1956 Annual Report* (Philadelphia: Crime Prev. Assoc. of Philadelphia, 1957).

(Cinquante ans d'histoire du droit pénal dans le monde) "États-Unis d'Amerique," Pp. 411–421 of *Cinquante ans de Droit Pénal et de Criminologie. Publication Jubilaire*, 1907–1957 (Brussels: Revue de Droit Pénal et de Criminologie, 1957).

1958

"Pioneers in Criminology, XV. Enrico Ferri, 1856–1929." *Jour. of Crim. Law. Crimin., & Police Sci.*, 48:481–492, January–February 1958. (In Spanish) *Rev. Mexicana de Sociologia*, 25:1025–1044, September–December 1963.

"Recidivism and maturation." *NPPA* (National Probation and Parole Assoc.), *Journal* 4:241–250, July 1958.

"Foreword." Pp. xiii–xiv of Marvin E. Wolfgang, *Patterns in Criminal Homicide* (Philadelphia: Univ. of Pennsylvania, 1958).

1959

"Two myths in the history of capital punishment." *Jour. Crim. Law. Crimin. & Police Sci.*, 50:114–117, July–August 1959.

"Correction in historical perspective." *Law and Contemporary Problems*, 23:585–593, Autumn 1958.

The Death Penalty, 83 pp. (Philadelphia: The American Law Institute).

"Adult probation and the conditional sentence." *Jour. Crim. Law., Crimin. & Police Sci.* 49:553–556, March–April 1959.

1960

(With Leonard Savitz) "A bibliographical manual for the student of criminology." (2nd ed. revised), Société internationale de criminologie, *Bulletin*, 1960:81–122.

"Are parents responsible?" Société internationale de criminologie, *Bulletin*, 1960:48–51.

"Conflits culturels et criminalité." *Rev. de droit pénal et de criminologie* 40:815–833, 879–896, June and July 1960.

"L'effet intimidant de la peine." *Rev. de science criminelle et de droit pénal comparé*, 1960, 579–593. (Spanish) *Rev. Juridica Veracruzana*, 12:5–23, April 1961.

1961

"The challenge of criminality." *Excerpta Criminologica*, 1:7–8, January–February 1961; *International Annals of Criminology* (Paris) 1962:17–18.
"Capital punishment." *Federal Probation*, 25:3–11, September 1961. (In Japanese) *Hogaku-Shimpo*, 70:61–80, May 1963.
"The death penalty in the United States." Pp. 55–68, 87–90, 120–122, 156–160 of *Colloque sur la Peine de Mort* tenu à Athènes, du 4 au 8 avril 1960, xi, 208 pp. (Athens: Pantios School of Political Science, 1961).
(With Jean Pinatel) "General introduction." Pp. 9–10 of *Selected Documentation on Criminology*, 114 pp. [Paris: UNESCO, 1961. (Reports and Papers in the Social Sciences, No. 14)].
"Carroll Prize." *Bulletin* (Société internationale de criminologie), 1961:63–64.

1962

"Crime and delinquency in the United States: an over-all view." *Amer. Acad. of Pol. & Soc. Sci.*, 339:11–23, January 1962. (In French) Marc Ancel and L. B. Schwartz, eds. *Le Système pénal des États-Unis d'Amérique*, xi, 273 pp. (Paris: Les Editions de l'Epargne, 1964), pp. 15–33.

1963

"Capital punishment." *Encyclopedia Britannica*, 4:847–849, 1963.
"Mafia." *Encyclopedia Britannica*, Vol. 14, 1963.
"Organized crime: a business enterprise." *Ann. Amer. Acad. of Pol. & Soc. Sci.* 347:12–19, May 1963. (In Spanish) *Criminalia* 33:611–619, December, 1967.
Foreword (p. v) of J. Iverne Dowie and Ernest M. Espelie, eds., *The Swedish Immigrant Community in Transition*. Essays in Honor of Dr. Conrad Bergendoff. x, 246 pp. (Rock Island, Ill.: Augustana Historical Society, 1963).
(With M. E. Wolfgang) *Constructing an Index of Delinquency*. 16 pp. Philadelphia: Center of Criminological Research, Univ. of Pennsylvania, October 1963. (Spanish) *Rev. Mexicana de Sociologia*, 27:459–485, May–August 1965, and *Economia y Ciencias Sociales* (Caracas), 7:82–104, July–September 1965.
"La criminalité et l'évolution sociale." *Rev. de l'Institut de Sociologie*, 1963, No. 1:10–21. (Spanish) *Criminalia*, 31:22–32, January 1965.

1964

"Foreword." Pp. 5–7 of M. E. Wolfgang, *Crime and Race*, 71 pp. (New York: Institute of Human Relations Press, 1964).
"Foreword," P. 7 of Richard S. Sterne, *Delinquent Conduct and Broken Homes*, 144 pp. (New Haven, Conn.: College and University Press, 1964).
"La peine capitale et le procès pénal." Pp. 287–297 of *Problèmes contemporains de procédure pénale. Recueil d'études en hommage à M. Louis Hugueney*, xxi, 300 pp. (Paris: Sirey, 1964).
(With M. E. Wolfgang) *The Measurement of Delinquency*, x, 423 pp. (New York: John Wiley & Sons, Inc., 1964).
A Bibliographical Manual for the Student of Criminology, 3rd rev. ed. (New

York: National Council on Crime and Delinquency, 1964). (Reprint from National Bibl. on Crime and Delinquency, Vol. 1, No. 3, 104 pp.)

"The troubled and the troublemakers: An inquiry into the causes and consequences of juvenile criminality." *Industria International,* 1964 (Stockholm), pp. 124–127, 154.

"Tocqueville and Beaumont and prison reform in France." Introduction (pp. xv–xl) to Gustave de Beaumont and Alexis de Tocqueville, *On the Penitentiary System in the United States and its Application in France,* xl, 220 pp. (Carbondale, Ill.: Southern Ill. Univ. Press, 1964).

Standardization of Criminal Statistics, 36 pp. [Strasbourg: Council of Europe, October 15, 1964 (European Committee on Crime Problems, Small Committee of Research Workers. Preliminary Report. Confidential. DPC/CORC (64) 6. Or. Eng.)] Same in French transl., 37 pp.

"Lionel Fox and the International Penal and Penitentiary Commission." Pp. 194–207 of Manuel Lopez-Rey and Charles Germain, eds., *Studies in Penology dedicated to the Memory of Sir Lionel Fox, C. B., M. C.* by the International Penal and Penitentiary Foundation, xi, 239 pp. (The Hague: Martinus Nijhoff, 1964).

1965

The Child Welfare Act of Sweden Effective January 1, 1961. Translated by Thorsten Sellin. Introduction by Holger Romander, 29 pp. (Stockholm: Ministry of Justice, 1965).

The Penal Code of Sweden Effective January 1, 1965. Translated by Thorsten Sellin. Introduction by Ivar Strahl, 82 pp. (Stockholm: Ministry of Justice, 1965).

"Proceedings of the International Penitentiary Commission, 1874–1951." [a checklist] *Excerpta Criminologica,* 5:259–263, May–June 1965.

"Capital punishment." *Crim. Law Quart.* (Canada), 8:36–51, June 1965. (In Japanese) [Quarterly, The Social Reform, Tokyo], 10, No. 2:4–13, March 1966.

"Charles Germain." Pp. 7–8 of Foundation Internationale Pénale et Pénitentiaire, *Actes de la Première réunion des chefs des administrations pénitentiaires,* Rome, 7–10 octobre 1964 [Brussels: F.I.P.P., 1965]. Also in English ed. of the Proceedings.

"Penal servitude: origin and survival." *Proc. Amer. Philos. Soc.,* 109:277–281, Oct. 19, 1965. (In Spanish) *Criminalia* 33:517–523, October 1967.

[Risk of injury or death to prison population and police], Canadian Soc. for the Abolition of the Death Penalty, *Information Bulletin,* 2:13–19, 1965.

"Homicides and Assaults in American prisons, 1964." *Acta Crimin. et Med. Leg. Japonica,* 31:139–143, 1965.

"The Philadelphia years of the 'Fallebo-Gök.'" Amer. Swedish Histor. Foundation, *Yearbook,* 1965:12–21.

1966

"Homicides and serious assaults in prisons." Aristotelian University of Thessaloniki, *Annual* of the School of Law and Economics 14:139–145.

"Penal reform in Sweden." Pp. 35–62 of J. Ll. J. Edwards, ed., *Modern Advances in Criminology. Four Public Lectures given under the auspices of the Centre of Criminology, University of Toronto, 1964–1965.* 86 pp. (Toronto, Ont.: Center of Criminology, 1966).

1967

Systems of Reporting "Crimes Known to the Police" in Selected Foreign Countries. [England and Wales, Sweden, Norway, West Germany.] 60 pp. (Washington, D.C.: The President's Commission on Law Enforcement and Administration of Justice, 1967), mimeographed.

"Die Neu-Amsterdamer Gefängnisordnung von 1657." *Monats. f. Kriminalpsych. u. Strafrechtsref.*, 50:209–213, June, 1967.

"International criminal statistics." *Criminologica* 5, No. 2:2–11, August 1967.

Capital Punishment. Thorsten Sellin, ed., ix, 289 pp. (New York: Harper & Row, 1967). Contains two original articles: "Executions in the United States," pp. 31–35; "Prison homicides," pp. 154–160.

"A Look at Prison History," *Federal Probation*, 31:18–23, September 1967; also in International Penal and Penitentiary Foundation, *The New Methods of Restriction of Liberty in the Penitentiary System.* 138 pp. (Nivelles; Imprim. administrative, 1968), pp. 95–105.

"La criminologia desde el punto de vista histórico." *Anuario del Inst. de Cienc. Pen. y Criminol* (Caracas), No. 1:360–378, 1967.

1968

"Criminology." *Intern. Encycl. of the Social Sciences* 3:505–510.

Biographies

MARC ANCEL entered the judiciary as Deputy Attorney of the Republic in 1930 and has since been judge of the Seine Tribunal, of the Court of the Appeals of Paris, and of the Supreme Court of France. He is Secretary General of the National Center (*Centre Francais*) of Comparative Law, Director of the Section on Penal Law and Criminal Science of the Institute of Comparative Law (University of Paris) and, since 1964, has been President of the Society of Comparative Legislation. He is also President of the International Association of Juridical Sciences (UNESCO) and Director of its International Committee of Comparative Law. He has been a member of many commissions on civil and penal codes. Since 1966 he has been resident of the International Society of Social Defense. He has received many honors and is an Officer of the *Légion d'Honneur*, of the *Ordre de la Couronne de Belgique*, of the *Ordre du Mérite italien*, and Commander of the *Ordre de Sainte Agathe*. He has received honorary degrees from the Universities of Geneva and Edinburgh. He is the author of many articles and books, including *La défense sociale nouvelle* (2nd ed. 1966); *Les Mesures de sûreté en matiere criminelle* (1960); *Introduction comparative aux codes penaux européens* (1956); *Introduction au systeme de droit pénal sovietique* (1962). He is the author of reports on the death penalty prepared for the Council of Europe (1962) and for the United Nations (1962).

JOHANNES ANDENAES was born in 1912. He took his degree in Law in 1935 and was awarded a doctorate in the same subject in 1943. He was appointed Professor of Law in 1945, and is now Director of the Institute of Criminology and Criminal Law and Dean of the Law School, University of Oslo. He is a member of the permanent Board on Penal Reform and Chairman of the Committee for the Amendment of Criminal Procedure. He is a former Chairman of the Scandinavian Council for Criminology and former member of the Scientific Council under the European Crime Commission. He has been a Visiting Professor of the Law School of the University of Pennsylvania and the University of Chicago. He has published books on criminal law, criminal proceedings, constitutional law, and many articles on legal and criminological subjects. His book, *The General Part of Criminal Law*, has been translated into English as the third volume in

443

Publications of the Comparative Criminal Law Project, New York University.

RONALD H. BEATTIE, J.D., M.A., Sacramento, California, is Chief, Bureau of Criminal Statistics, California Department of Justice, and has been Chief, Division of Procedural Studies and Statistics, Administrative Office of the United States Courts; Statistician for Crime, United States Bureau of the Census; Regional Director, United States Attorney General's Survey of Release Procedures; Research Associate, California Studies of Criminal Justice and Oregon Crime Survey. He is the author of *A System of Criminal Judicial Statistics for California* (1936) and of articles on criminal statistics and the administration of criminal justice published in the *Journal of Criminal Law and Criminology*, in some law school reviews, and the *Journal of the American Statistical Association*. He is a member of the American Correctional Association.

KARL O. CHRISTIANSEN, Dr. jur. (LL.D.), Copenhagen, Denmark, is Professor, Institute of Criminal Science, University of Copenhagen. He has had various research positions under the Danish Prison Administration and was (1948–49) attached to the United Nations Secretariat as Social Affairs Officer (Section of Social Defence). He is a member of the Board of Directors of the International Society of Criminology, Chairman of the Scandinavian Research Council for Criminology, Editor of *Scandinavian Studies in Criminology*, Vol. 1 (1965), and was a Consultant to the President's Commission on Law Enforcement and Administration of Justice. He has among other publications written about *Mandlige landssvigere i Danmark under besættelsen* (Male Collaborators with the Germans in Denmark during the Occupation) (1950), *Mandlige arresthusfanger i Københavns fængsler* (Male Short Term Prisoners in the Jails of Copenhagen) (with Karen Berntsen, 1955), *Landssvigerkriminaliteten i sociologisk belysning* (Sociological Aspects of Collaboration with the Germans during the Occupation) (1955), and *Kriminologie* (in Handwörterbuch der Kriminologie, 1967).

JOHN P. CONRAD (born June 19, 1913) received his B.A. in Political Science at the University of California, Berkeley, in 1936; and his M.A. in Social Service Administration at the University of Chicago in 1960. He was a Senior Fulbright Fellow in 1958–1959 at the London School of Economics. Between 1946 and 1956 he served as parole officer in the California Youth Authority, social worker with the Veteran's Administration, senior sociologist at San Quentin and Sacramento, and supervisor of inmate classification at Sacramento. He was associate director (1960–1964) of an International Survey of Corrections, Chief of Research in the California State Correctional System (1964–1967) and, since 1967, has been Chief of Research, Federal Bureau of Prisons. He is the author of various articles on crime and corrections, and of *Crime and Its Correction* (1965). For the academic year, 1968–1969, he was appointed Visiting Lecturer in Criminology at the University of Pennsylvania.

PAUL CORNIL, Ph.D., LL.D., Brussels, Belgium, is professor at the Brussels University—Child Welfare (1930); Criminology and Penology (1936); Criminal Law (1945); Secretary General of the Ministry of Justice (1946–1968); President of the *Revue de Droit Pénal et de Criminologie* (1952–   ); Vice-President of the International Society of Social Defence (1954–   ); Member of the Scientific Committee and Vice-President of the International Society of Criminology (1962–   ); Former President of the International Penal and Penitentiary Foundation (1951–1961); Former President of the International Criminal Law Association (1953–1961); Former President of the European Committee on Crime Problems (1962–1965). He has many publications in *Revue de Droit Pénal et de Criminology; Revue de l'Université de Bruxelles; Répertoire pratique de Droit beige; Howard Journal; Maandblad voor Berechting en Reclassering; Revue Internationale de Droit Pénal; Revue de Science Criminelle et de Droit Pénal Comparé; Revue Pénale Suisse*; and elsewhere. Articles include such topics as capital punishment, juvenile delinquency, social defence, prison labor, treatment of delinquents, probation, and victimology.

DONALD R. CRESSEY was born in 1919. He received his B.A. at Iowa State University in 1943 and the Ph.D. at Indiana University in 1950. He is now Professor of Sociology at the University of California, Santa Barbara. From 1962 until July 1967 he also was Dean of the College of Letters and Science at Santa Barbara. Earlier, he was Professor of Sociology and Chairman of the Department of Anthropology and Sociology at the University of California, Los Angeles. He has been President of the Pacific Sociological Association, Chairman of the Criminology Section of the American Sociological Association, and Visiting Professor at Cambridge University and the University of Oslo. His publications include *Other People's Money* (1953), *Principles of Criminology* (with E. H. Sutherland, 7th edition, 1966), *The Prison* (1961), *Delinquency, Crime and Differential Association* (1964), and *The Functions and Structure of Criminal Syndicates* (1967).

ISRAEL DRAPKIN has been Director of the Institute of Criminology and Professor of Criminology, Law Faculty, The Hebrew University of Jerusalem, Israel, since 1959. He was the former Director of the Institute of Criminology, Prison Service, Ministry of Justice, Santiago, Chile (1936–1959). He was a British Council Fellow (1945–1946), is a Vice-President of the International Society of Criminology, and Fellow of the American

Society of Criminology. He is also correspondant of the United Nations Social Defence Section. In 1965 he was Visiting Expert at the United Nations Asia and Far East Institute, Fuchu, Tokyo. He is the author of *Manual de Criminologia* (1949), *Prensa y Criminalidad* (1958), and some 50 different papers in various scientific journals.

TORSTEN ERIKSSON (born February 22, 1906) received his University Diploma of Law (Stockholm) in 1930. He is currently Director General of the Correctional Administration of Sweden.

Mr. Eriksson served as Chief of Bureau in the Ministry of Justice from 1949, and was appointed Director General of the Correctional Administration in 1960. He was one of the two experts who drafted the new Child Welfare Legislation of 1960. He is a national correspondent to the Social Defence Section of the UN Secretariat, and was Chairman of the Steering Committee of the UN Third Congress on the Prevention of Crime and Treatment of Offenders, 1965. He is President of the European Committee on Crime Problems. Director Eriksson has published five books in Swedish, two of them on juvenile delinquency, one on prostitution and society, another on crime and society, and the fifth on the history of correctional treatment.

FRANCO FERRACUTI is a medical psychologist, Professor of Criminology at the University of Rome, School of Law, and Assistant in the Institute of Psychology of the Medical School of the same University. He is engaged as consultant to the Observation Center of the Italian Ministry of Justice and to the United Nations Social Defence Research Institute. He has been a member since 1966 of the Criminological Scientific Council of the Council of Europe. Professor Ferracuti has worked for many years in the United States at the University of Wisconsin, at New York University, at the United Nations Secretariat and as Director of a Criminology Program at the University of Puerto Rico.

Professor Ferracuti has contributed many papers and monographs, to criminological and psychological journals and is the author, with Professor Wolfgang, of *The Subculture of Violence* (1967).

T.C.N. GIBBENS is Professor of Forensic Psychiatry at the Institute of Psychiatry, London University, England. He is President of the International Society of Criminology.

Formerly, he studied in the United States with a Nuffield fellowship, was with Dr. Abrahamsen at the Institute of Psychiatry, New York and in Sing Sing Prison. In England he later became a member of the Streatfield Committee on the business of the Courts, and of the Royal Commission on the Penal System. He is a member of the Advisory Board for Probation and

After-Care, and of the Research Sub-Committee of the Advisory Council on Penal policy. Publications include *Psychiatric Studies of Borstal Lads* (1963), *Shoplifting* (1962), and *Cultural Factors in Delinquency* (1966).

HERMANN MANNHEIM (born October 26, 1889), Dr. juris, was a Judge of the Court of Appeal in Berlin and a Professor of Criminal Law and Procedure at Berlin University until 1933. From 1935 until his retirement in 1955 he was a Lecturer in Criminology at the London School of Economics and Political Science (University of London) and a Reader in the same subject at the University of London. He is a President of Senate of a Court of Appeal (ret.) in West Germany and an Honorary Fellow of the London School of Economics. He has been awarded the Order of the British Empire (1959), the Grand Cross of Merit of the German Federal Republic (1965), the Hon. LL.D. of the University of Utrecht, Holland (1957), and the Golden Beccaria Medal of the German Criminological Society (1965). He was a cofounder and coeditor of the *British Journal of Delinquency* (now *Criminology*) from 1950 and of the International Library of Criminology from 1960 until his resignation in 1966. He is a Vice-President of the British Criminological Society and of the Institute for the Study and Treatment of Delinquency (I.S.T.D.) in London. His writings include: *The Dilemma of Penal Reform* (1939), *Social Aspects of Crime in England* (1940), *War and Crime* (1941), *Criminal Justice and Social Reconstruction* (1946), *Juvenile Delinquency in an English Middletown* (1948), *Group Problems in Crime and Punishment* (1955), *Prediction Methods Related to Borstal Training* (with L. T. Wilkins, 1955), *Pioneers of Criminology* (ed., 1960), *Deutsche Strafrechtsreform in englischer Sicht* (1960), *Comparative Criminology* (1965).

WILLEM HENDRIK NAGEL, LL.D., is Professor of Criminology and Penology at Leyden University in Holland. He was appointed to this position in 1956 after serving as Assistant Professor in Penal Law and Criminology since 1949 and after having been in judicial office from 1938. He is the founder and editor of *Excerpta Criminologica* and is a fellow member of the American Society of Criminology.

Professor Nagel is the author of *The Criminality at Oss* (1949), *Perjury* (1953), and of many scientific articles. In addition, he has been awarded literary prizes for both fiction and nonfiction written under the pseudonym J.B. Charles. In 1965 he received the Gold Beccaria Medal of the "Deutsche kriminologische Gesellschaft."

Professor Nagel visited the United States when he was Alfred Sloan Visiting Professor in the Menninger School of Psychiatry in 1964. He has recently been temporarily United Nations Social Defence Expert in Thailand.

JEAN PINATEL, Doctor of Laws, is Inspector General of the Administration in the Ministry of the Interior of France and Professor of the Institute of Criminology of the University of Paris. For fifteen years he was Secretary General of the International Society of Criminology. In 1965 he became President of the Scientific Commission of that organization. Since 1963 he has been a member of the Criminological Scientific Council of the Council of Europe. His main publications include *Law Criminologie* (1960), *Traité de droit pénal et de criminologie* (with M. Bouzat, 1963), *Etienne de Greeff* (1967).

LEON RADZINOWICZ, LL.D. (Geneva), LL.D. (Cracow), LL.D. (Rome), LL.D. (Cambridge), Honorary LL.D. (Leicester). Professor Radzinowicz is a Fellow of Trinity College, Wolfson Professor of Criminology and Director of the Institute of Criminology, University of Cambridge. He has been appointed Adjunct Professor of Columbia University School of Law. Among many other activities and organizational memberships, he is a member of the Advisory Council on the Penal System, Home Office, and is Chairman of the Scientific Committee of the Council of Europe.
He is author of four monumental volumes on *History of English Criminal Law* (1948–1968), *In Search of Criminology* (1962), and *Ideology and Crime* (1966). He is the editor of Cambridge Studies in Criminology (24 volumes).

STEPHEN SCHAFER was born (1911) and educated in Hungary where he received his doctorate of Jurisprudence at the University of Budapest in 1932. In 1947 he was appointed Professor Agrege-Privatdozent at the same University and, between 1946 and 1951, he was chairman of the Prison Commission and President of the Supervisory Board of Juvenile Delinquency. In 1957 Professor Schafer moved to England where he taught criminology at the Polytechnic School in London, and from England he moved to the United States in 1961. Since his arrival in the United States he has taught at Florida State University, Ohio University, and now at Northeastern University where he is a professor in the Department of Sociology and Anthropology. He is the author of eleven books and a variety of articles in Hungarian, as well as *Restitution to Victims of Crime* (1960) and *The Victim and His Criminal* (1968).

SHLOMO SHOHAM was born (1929) and educated in Israel, and received his L.L.D. degree in Criminal Law and Criminology from Hebrew University in 1960. He also studied at the Institute of Criminology, Cambridge, England (1958–1959), and was a research associate at Ohio State University in 1963. Since 1961 he has been director of the Institute of Criminology at Bar-Ilan University, Israel. He is a fellow of the

American Society of Criminology and a member of the Scientific Committee of the International Society of Criminology. He is the author of many articles in a variety of journals. His best known book is *Crime and Social Deviation* (1966). His forthcoming publication is entitled *The Mark of Cain*. For the academic year, 1968–1969, he was appointed Visiting Associate Professor in the Department of Sociology, University of Pennsylvania.

DENIS SZABO was born (1929) and reared in Hungary, although he is a graduate of the Ecole Pratique des Hautes Etudes, Paris, and has a doctorate in Political and Social Science. In 1958 he moved to Canada where he established a Department of Criminology at the University of Montreal and serves as Professor and Director. Dr. Szabo is a member of the Board of Directors of the International Society of Criminology, was a consultant to the President's Commission on Law Enforcement and Administration of Justice (U.S.), and to the *Commission Royale d'Enquete sur L'Administration de la Justice en matiere criminelle et penale*. He is the author of *Crimes et villes* (1960), *Delinquance juvenile* (1965), and *Criminologie* (1965), and serves as editor of *Acta Criminologica*.

JACOB MAARTEN VAN BEMMELEN was born in The Hague, April 20, 1898, studied at the University of Groningen (1919–1923), having received his Doctorate of Law in 1923. Since 1931 he has been Professor of Criminal Law and Criminology at the University of Leiden. He also served as Barrister in Rotterdam (1925–1928), Clerk of the Court of Rotterdam (1928–1931), and supplementary judge in the Court of the Hague (1938–1945) and in the Court of Appeal (1945–1967). Professor Van Bemmelen is a member of the Scientific Committee of the International Society of Criminology, of the International Commission of Jurists, and of the Board of the International Society for Criminal Law. His textbook on Dutch criminal procedure (first edition, 1936) went through its sixth edition in 1957. He is the author of three other textbooks in Dutch.

GEORGE B. VOLD died on November 20, 1967 between the time he contributed to this volume and its publication. He was born in 1896. From 1927 until his retirement in 1964 he was a member of the Department of Sociology at the University of Minnesota. He has served variously as technical adviser to the Minnesota Crime Commission, as chairman of a Governor's Committee on Sex Criminals (Minnesota), as chief analyst and statistician for the Public Safety Division, United States Occupation Forces in Japan, and as chairman of a Governor's Special Committee on Prison Conditions in Minnesota. He is author of *Prediction Methods and Parole* (1931) and coauthor of *Report of Minnesota Crime Commission* (1935),

Survey of Police Training (1937), *Report on Prison Conditions* (1951), and *Theoretical Criminology* (1958).

LESLIE T. WILKINS is Professor of Criminology at the University of California at Berkeley. Prior to taking this post in 1966, he was for two years Senior Adviser at the United Nations Asia and Far East Institute at Fuchu, Tokyo, Japan. After serving from 1939–1945 in the Royal Air Force where he conducted research into problems of flying safety, he became a civil servant in the British Government.

Professor Wilkins first became known as a statistician, served on the Council of the Royal Statistical Society, was twice elected Chairman of the General Applications Section of that Society, and was the Francis Wood Memorial Prize winner in 1955. More recently he has been concerned with problems of social policy and the philosophy of science in relation to research into social deviance and crime.

Professor Wilkins has published many articles in various journals connected with social and criminological research. In collaboration with Professor Hermann Mannheim, he wrote *Prediction Methods in Relation to Borstal Training* (1955). He is the author of *Social Deviance, Social Policy, Action and Research* (1964), and *Evaluation of Penal Measures* (in press).

Name Index

Abd-El-Razek, A., 76n, 77n
Adler, Alfred, 87
Adolphus, John, 289, 292n
Ahrenfeldt, R. H., 204
Alberoni, F., 194
Alliez, J., 196
Allport, Floyd, 111
Alvarez, J. Hernandez, 216n
Ancel, Marc, 114, 350, 378n, 379n, 383n, 396n, 440, 443
Andenaes, Johannes, 222n, 377, 443
Andrews, Alexander, 291n
Andry, R. G., 370
Ansbacher, H. L., 193n
Aramburu, Félix, 343
Arenal, Concepción, 323, 343
Asch, S. E., 68

Baan, P. H. A., 26
Ball, J. C., 378
Ballachey, E., 57n
Bandura, A., 105
Banks, C., 129
Barberis, C., 201n
Bar-Josef, R., 80n
Barkin, S., 201n
Barnes, Harry E., 45n, 316n, 392n, 395n
Barrington, Daines, 288n, 295n
Barry, John Vincent, 344
Bauer, Raymond E., 160n
Bavcon, L., 27n
Beattie, Ronald H., 160, 170n, 444
Beaumont, Gustave de, 441

Beccaria, 321, 322, 376, 377, 379n, 381n
Becker, H., 57n
Bemmelen, Jacob Maarten van, 23n, 401, 449
Benedict, Ruth, 108
Bennett, J., 396
Bentham, Jeremy, 322, 376-378
Bergendoff, Conrad, 440
Bergson, Henri, 102-103, 105
Bernaldo de Quiros, Constancio, 318n, 335n
Bernard, L. L., 432
Beveredge, 135
Bigelow, John, 295n
Blackstone, 294
Boix, Vicente, 323, 324n, 331n, 338n, 340n, 343
Bonger, W. A., 12
Bonneville de Marsangy, Arnould, 316
Booth, 135
Borrie, W. D., 194, 199
Bottoms, A. E., 204, 212
Bouzat, M., 448
Bouzat, Pierre, 383n, 389n
Branham, Vernon C., 316n
Brenton, Edward Pelham, 311n
Brinley, T., 192n
Briscoe, 115
Brockway, Zebulon R., 345
Bromberg, W., 113
Broom, Leonard, 46n
Brown, Oscar, Jr., 139, 140, 142
Brown, Roger, 69, 105, 106n

Bueno Arus, F., 324, 338n
Buikhuisen, W., 27
Bulmer, J. H., 207
Burgess, Ernest W., 70

Cadbury, 135
Cain, M. E., 373n
Caldwell, Robert Graham, 435
Calón, Eugenio Cuello, 317n, 320n,
    328n, 334n, 337n, 341n, 342n
Camba, R., 196n
Campoamor, Ramón de, 327
Camus, Albert, 67, 97
Cantril, Hadley, 66n
Cardia, L., 209
Cardona, Ramón de, 320
Carlquist, Magnus, 239, 241
Catalano, R., 215
Cazeneuve, J., 107
Cerdán de Tallada, Thomás, 319
Chatham, 310
Chaves, Cristobal de, 319
Cheng, David Te-Chao, 435
Christian, E., 294n
Christiansen, Karl O., 254n, 260n, 278n,
    444
Clarkson, William, 298n
Clinard, M. B., 193, 194
Clode, Charles M., 288n, 313
Cloward, Richard A., 5, 51, 74, 84n,
    89, 191
Clowes, William Laird, 293n, 300n
Cockburn, J. J., 127
Codrington, Sir Edward, 307
Cohen, Albert, 5n, 47n, 74
Colbert, 388
Conard, A. F., 438, 439
Condorcet, 98
Conrad, John P., 444
Cooper, M. H., 393n
Coornhert, Dirck Volckertszoon, 407
Cornil, Paul, 391n, 397n, 402n, 445
Coser, Lewis, 70
Costin, W. C., 294n
Craft, M., 129
Cressey, Donald R., 46n, 50n, 61n, 445
Crissman, Paul, 73
Crofton, Sir Walter, 316, 323
Cross, A. R. N., 373
Crutchfield, R., 57n, 68

Cubí y Soler, Mariano, 343
Culver, 174n

Dalla Volta, A., 193
Davol, S. H., 193n
Decker, Sir Matthew, 295
De Fleur, M. L., 201
Dell, 115
Dicey, 408
Dichio, Juan J., 322n
Dickens, Charles, 391
Dietrick, Daird C., 87n
Dinitz, S., 73n
Di Tullio, B., 217n
Dornbush, S., 68n
Doty, R. C., 216n
Doublet, J., 192n
Dowie, J. Iverne, 440
Drapkin, Israel, 445
Dundas, Robert, 295, 296
Dupréel, Jean, 21, 383n, 400n
Durante, A., 197
Durkheim, Emile, 5, 83, 84, 95, 97, 101,
    102-103, 105, 193, 207

East, Sir Norwood, 113
Edwards, J., 442
Ehrmann, B., 379n
Eisenstadt, S. N., 191n, 195
Ellis, Welbore, 287n
Emlyn, S., 295n
Epoud, 213
Erasmus, 22
Erez, R., 74n
Erikson, Erik H., 64, 94, 100, 101
Eriksson, Torsten, 446
Espelie, Ernest M., 440
Ex, Jacques, 198, 199
Exner, 368
Eysenck, 370

Falchi, 192n, 201n
Falk, Gerhard J., 20n
Fernández de Cordoba, Francisco, 321n
Ferracuti, Franco, 70, 91, 111n, 157n,
    193n, 210n, 217n, 446
Ferri, Enrico, 439
Feuerbach, 376-378
Fink, A. E., 134n

Fortescue, J. W., 288n, 311n
Foster, 294
Fourastie, Jean, 404
Fox, Sir Lionel, 383n, 384n, 389n, 398, 399n, 400n
Franchini, A., 200n
Franci, Filippo, 429
Franco de Blas, Francisco, 328n, 335n, 336n
Frankfurter, Felix, 170n
Franklin, Benjamin, 295
Freedman, L. Z., 26n
Freen, F. H., 295n
Frenkel-Brunswick, E., 63
Freud, Sigmund, 69, 100, 103, 105, 126
Frey, Erwin, 226n, 230n
Friedman, Irit, 79n

Gamio, Manuel, 43n
Garavaglia, 76
García Basalo, 344
García Martín del Val, Simón, 328n, 330n
Garofalo, 382
Garritty, 122
Geiger, Theodor, 268n
Genet, Jean, 75, 97
George, M. D., 290n
Germain, Charles, 399n, 401n, 441
Giardini, G. I., 316n, 317n
Gibbens, T. C. N., 115n, 118n, 119n, 125n, 204, 446
Gibbons, 122
Gibson, E., 204
Gide, André, 93
Gill, Howard D., 392n, 393, 400n
Gillin, 23, 45n
Gillioz, E., 212, 213
Giner de los Ríos, Francisco, 342
Ginzberg, A., 195
Glaser, David, 88-89, 166, 200n, 415n
Glueck, Eleanor, 45n, 119n, 122, 124, 129, 404
Glueck, Sheldon, 45n, 119n, 122, 124, 129, 354, 373, 404, 432
Gonzalez, Don Pedro, 330
Göransson, Hardy, 395n, 418
Gorynsky, J., 201n
Graham, Sir James, 299, 312
Grant, Marguerite, 123

Graven, J., 208
Green, Edward, 368-369, 385n
Grenville, George, 298
Grose, T. H., 295n
Grünhut, Max, 30n, 117

Haldane, George, 296n
Halévy, Élie, 303n, 310
Hall, Jerome, 412n
Hall-Williams, J. E., 368, 373n, 374
Halmos, Paul, 373
Hamel, G. A. van, 405
Hamilton, Lord Archibald, 303
Händel, K., 208
Harcourt, Lord, 305
Harris, E. A. J., 313n
Hathaway, Starke H., 73n
Hauge R., 222n
Hayner, Norman S., 76, 354-355
Haynes, Fred E., 316n
Hayward, S. T., 21n
Heide, J. Ter, 18
Henderson, Julia, 30
Herzog, J. B., 383n
Heuyer, Georges, 437
Hilgard, E. R., 34n
Hill, Frederic, 346
Hill, Mathew Davenport, 345
Hirsch, C. A., 213n
Hobbes, Thomas, 99
Hobson, E. W., 56n
Hofstee, E. W., 201n
Holdsworth, Sir William S., 289n
Holle, R., 213n
Holton, Karl, 176
Hood, Roger, 369-370 404
Hoover, Herbert, 170
Horringa, D., 15
Hoskins, George Alexander, 344
Howard, John, 319, 325, 338, 390-391, 392n
Howard, Thomas Phipps, 302n
Hume, David, 295
Hume, Joseph, 289, 311
Hye-Knudsen, 260n

Introna, F., 200
Ives, Georges, 389n

Jaffary, Stuart King, 371
Jameson, S. H., 25n
Jarvis, E. V., 373
Jaur, J. M., 196
Jeaffreson, John Cordy, 291n
Jenkins, R. L., 121, 122
Jiménez de Asuá, Luis, 319n, 322, 322n
Johnson, Adelaide, 122
Johnson, Charles S., 430
Johnson, Hiram, 175

Kaironen, V. A., 210n
Kalven, Harry, 235n
Kan, J. van, 12
Kant, Immanuel, 101
Kaufmann, Y., 71n
Kelley, H. M., 61n
Kelvin, Lord, 133
Kennedy, E. M., 203n
Kennedy, John F., 219
Kenny, Robert C., 176
Keren, R., 71n
Keynes, John, 167
Khrushchev, Nikita, 85
Kinberg, O., 378n
Kinch, J. W., 122
King, R. D., 393n
Kirchheimer, Otto, 388n, 433
Kirchwey, G. F., 377n
Kitsuse, John I., 87n
Klare, Hugh, 383, 384n, 396
Klemming, L. G., 210
Knoles, Fred A., 176
Kohlberg, L., 105
Krass, E., 200n
Krech, D., 57n
Kreisler, A., 71n
Kurz, U., 207
Kutash, Samuel B., 316n

Lamers, Ernest, 400n, 401
Lamers, J., 383n
Landis, J. R., 73, 74
Lapassade, G., 95
Lardizabal y Uribe, Manuel de, 322
Larguier, J., 379n
Lasala, Gregorio, 328n, 330n, 331n, 332n, 334n, 341n
Lasswell, H. D., 26n
Lastres, Francisco, 343n, 346

Lazarus, Judith, 196
Lecky, W. E. H., 290n, 305n, 309
Lee, E. S., 196, 218
Leighton, Joseph A., 43
Lenin, Vladimir Iljits, 85
Levin, H., 105n
Lewin, Kurt, 69
Liben, G., 206
Liepmann, M., 430
Lind, 76
Lindesmith, Alfred, 47n
Linschoten, J., 23, 28, 30n
Listwan, J. A., 195, 196
Liszt, Franz von, 405
Locke, B. Z., 196
Lombroso, 376
Long, E., 400n
Lopez, Marcial Antonio, 334n
Lopez-Rey, Manuel, 441
Lorenz, Konrad, 103, 104
Loring, L. M., 100
Lovett Doust, J. W., 114
Lucrezio, 192n, 201n
Luttrell, Temple, 307

Mabillon, Dom Jean, 387, 391, 430
Macaré, Rethaan, 405
Maccoby, E. E., 105n
Maclay, I., 127
Maconochie, 316, 323, 345
Macpherson, David, 310
Maitland, F. W., 287, 288n
Maliphant, R., 211
Malzberg, B., 195, 196
Mandelbaum, M., 29n
Mannheim, Hermann, 144n, 192, 353n, 373, 389n, 394n, 403, 447, 450
Mannheim, Karl, 55n
Mansfield, Lord, 294
Marshall, Leon, 171
Martinez de la Rosa, D. Diego, 343
Marx, Karl, 93, 98
Matras, J., 80n
Matza, 61n
Maudsley, Henry, 125
May, Samuel C., 176
May, Sir Thomas Erskine, 295n
McClintock, F. H., 204
McCone, John, 39n
McCord, J., 105

McCord, W., 105
McCormick, Austin, 389, 392
McElrath, Dennis, 51n, 52
McGee, Richard A., 176
Mead, George Herbert, 101
Meehl, Paul, 135
Meeks, E., 200n
Menaker, M., 71n
Menges, 197
Menninger, Karl A., 22, 28
Mérimée, Prosper, 327
Merton, Robert K., 5, 58, 67, 83n, 84, 97, 137, 193
Miller, Walter B., 52
Milton, Frank, 373
Mitcheson, 114, 128
Moley, Raymond, 176
Monachesi, Elio D., 73n
Montero, Dorado, 332
Montesinos y Molina, Manuel, 315-346
Montesquieu, 381n
Moravia, Alberto, 93
Morgan, P., 200n
Morice, R., 213n
Morris, Norval, 366, 381n, 394, 402
Morris, Ruth, 127
Morse, Wayne L., 170
Mueller, Gerhard O. W., 412n
Müller, Elmar, 237n
Murray, 64n
Myamoto, S. F., 68n

Nagel, Willem Hendrick, 30n, 447
Nann, E., 211
Navarro, Gregorio Lasala, 322n, 323n
Neal, Arthur G., 73
Nepote, J., 402n
Neuman, Elías, 320n, 321n, 323n, 335n, 336n, 397n
Neumann, K., 205
Nicholls, Sir George, 298n
Nietzsche, Friedrich, 100
Normandeau, André, 316n

Obermaier, 316, 323, 345
Ødegaard, O., 195
Ohlin, Lloyd E., 5, 51, 74, 84n, 89, 191, 355
O'Neal, P., 114

Oneca, José Antón, 322n
Orlando F., 202n

Pacheco, Joaquín Francisco, 332, 342
Pareto, Vilfredo, 99
Park, Robert E., 70
Parker, Tony, 362
Parsons, Talcott, 58, 67
Pearson, Karl, 133
Peer, Ilana, 79n
Penn, William, 325
Perdriau, A., 401n
Perotti, 192n, 201n
Pfiffner, John C., 176
Phillimore, John George, 291n
Piaget, Jean, 104, 105
Pieltain, Ricardo, 324n, 326n
Pinatel, Jean, 8n, 213, 382n, 383n, 437, 448
Pond, Desmond, 114, 115n
Ponti, 76
Pound, Roscoe, 170n
Pradervand, P., 209
Prince, J. E., 119n, 204
Prins, 405
Pulteney, William, 297

Quetelet, 12
Quinnez, R., 201

Radzinowicz, Leon, 12n, 157n, 448
Rahav, G., 79n
Ravenstein, E. G., 218
Reckless, Walter C., 73n, 74n, 317n
Reimanis, G., 193n
Reiss, Albert J., 160n
Remington, Frank J., 355
Rettig, Salomon, 73
Rico de Estasen, José, 327n, 329n, 343, 346n
Rijksen, 21
Risso, M., 198
Robins, L. N., 114
Robinson, Louis N., 400n
Rollin, H. R., 130
Romagnosi, 376
Romander, Holger, 441
Romilly, Sir Samuel, 309
Roosenburg, 21

Rosal, Juan del, 319n
Rose, Gordon, 128, 367
Rosenzweig, Saul, 64
Ross, 76
Rostow, W. W., 86
Rothstein, Edward, 72
Rousseau, Jean Jacques, 98
Rubin, Sol, 354
Rudas, N., 196n
Ruiz-Funes, Mariano, 339n
Rusche, Georg, 388n, 433
Russell, Lord John, 312n
Ryder, Richard, 308

Sade, Marquis de, 94
Saenger, 63
Salillas, Rafael, 322n, 335n, 346
Sanborn, Franklin R., 345
Sandoval, Bernardino de, 318
Sartre, Jean Paul, 30, 97
Saunders, William Herbert, 297, 298n
Savitz, L. D., 76, 192n
Scarpitti, 73, 74
Schafer, Stephen, 448
Schlyter, Karl J., 417, 418, 422
Schmidt, K., 210
Schmidt, Lothar, 350n
Schram, 233n
Schuessler, Karl, 47n
Schumpeter, 167
Schwartz, L. B., 440
Scott, P. D., 122
Sears, R. R., 105
Seeman, 67
Sellin, Thorsten, 3, 4, 6, 7-9, 11, 16,
    23, 41, 43-51, 54, 55, 56n, 57, 62,
    71, 76, 78, 83n., 85, 94, 111, 133,
    136, 145-146, 148, 149, 150, 152,
    153, 157-159, 163, 167, 169, 172,
    174n, 181, 186, 190-191, 218, 253n,
    255, 263n, 349, 351, 375, 377, 378,
    379, 380, 383n, 385, 387-390, 391n,
    393, 403, 406, 417, 429-442
Selznick, Philip, 46n
Shannon, L. W., 200
Shaskolsky, E., 73n
Shavit, G., 71n
Shaw, Clifford R., 5, 49
Sherif, Carolyn W., 35n
Sherif, Muzafer, 34n, 35n, 66n, 68

Shoham, N., 76n, 77n
Shoham, Shlomo, 60n, 66n, 71n, 73n,
    74n, 76, 77n, 79n, 191n, 371, 448
Sigsgård, Thomas, 260n
Silberman, Martin, 125
Silvela, Luis, 343
Silvey, J., 150-152
Simmel, Georg, 58, 70, 88
Simons, 405
Sjollema, B. Ch., 215
Slovenko, Ralph, 19
Smith, George, 301n.
Sorel, 99
Sorokin, Pitirim A., 51, 99
Southey, R., 297, 310
Sparks, R. F., 373
Sprott, W. J. H., 373
Srole, Leo, 73
Stafford-Clarke, D., 114, 115n
Stakhanov, Alexei, 86
Stephenson, G. M., 100n
Sterne, Richard S., 440
Stofflet, 76
Strahl, Ivar, 351, 353, 409n, 441
Stürup, Karl, 260n
Sumner, William Graham, 35
Sutherland, Edwin H., 4-6, 23, 43, 47-
    51, 58, 61n, 191, 200, 207n, 380n,
    402, 445
Sveri, K., 210
Sydney, William Connor, 290n, 291n
Sykes, Gresham M., 61n, 381n
Szabo, Denis, 449

Taft, Donald R., 382n
Taft, R., 192n, 197
Tahon, H. H., 80n
Tappan, Paul W., 355, 376
Teeters, Negley K., 45n, 316n, 392n,
    395n
Tetens, Hans, 260n
Thibaut, J. W., 61n
Thomas, D. A., 373
Thomas, Dorothy Swaine, 76, 196
Thompson, C. B., 113n
Thorndike, Edward L., 34n
Thornton, William, 301n
Thot, Ladislao, 315n, 318n, 319n, 340
Thrasher, Frederic, 33
Titchener, E. B., 24

Tocqueville, Alexis de, 441
Tomkins, 174*n*
Torfs, 207
Townsend, Rev. Alex, 301*n*
Triseliotis, J., 196*n*
Turnbladh, Will C., 355
Turner, J. W. C., 221*n*, 222*n*
Tyhurst, L., 195

Uner, S., 216*n*
Urquhart, Thomas, 311*n*

Vaihinger, Hans, 134
Van Vechten, 76
Veringa, G. H., 409, 410
Vian, 97
Villa, J. L., 198
Vold, George B., 33*n*, 37*n*, 449
Vollmer, August, 175, 176
Vrij, M. P., 24, 25

Waaben, Knud, 260*n*
Walker, Nigel, 374
Wallis, C. P., 211
Wallis, Severn Teackle, 344
Walpole, Sir Spencer, 313*n*
Walters, R. H., 105*n*
Warren, Earl, 176
Warren, W. J., 114
Watson, J. B., 4
Watson, J. Steven, 294*n*
Webb, Beatrice, 301*n*
Webb, Sidney, 301*n*
Weber, Hellmuth v., 374

Wehner, B., 208
Weinberg, A. A., 195
Weingrod, A., 80*n*
Wenzky, O., 206, 207
Werfel, Franz, 415
Weymouth, Lord, 305
Whitman, Walt, 219
Whyte, W. F., 72*n*
Wilkins, Leslie T., 113, 144*n*, 147*n*, 447, 450
Willcox, R. R., 207
Willett, T. C., 230*n*, 234*n*, 235*n*, 237*n*, 371
Williams, Glanville, 222*n*, 408
Williams, Robin M., 53
Willner, D., 105*n*
Wines, Enoch Cobb, 345, 346
Wirth, Louis, 50*n*
Wolfe W., 87*n*
Wolfgang, Marvin E., 8, 11, 23, 28, 56, 70, 71, 76*n*, 91, 111*n*, 136, 150, 152, 153, 157*n*, 159*n*, 160*n*, 181, 193*n*, 210, 217*n*, 438, 439, 440, 446
Wood, A. L., 76
Wooton, Barbara, 149, 374

Yablonsky, Lewis, 33
Yinger, Milton, 70
Yntema, Hessel E., 439
Young, Pauline, 76, 175

Zamir, R., 80*n*
Zeisel, Hans, 235*n*
Zimmerman, H. G., 209
Znaniecki, F., 76

Subject Index

Accidents, traffic, and negligent homicide, 226-231
Addiction, drug, 78-79
Alienation, 67
  and norm discord, 72-74
Anomie, 67
  and culture conflict, 83-92
  and migration, 193-194, 207
  and neoteny, 97
Association, and complex social systems, 46-50
  differential, 4, 200-201
  theory of, 58

Behavior, criminal, 6, 12-14, 18-19, 48-49
  deranging, 12-14, 18-19
  deviant, 12-14, 18-19, 23
Behaviorism, and criminology, 4, 7

California, criminal justice in, 175-180, 185
Chicago Area Project, 5
Christian church, and origins of penal systems, 315-316
Civil disobedience, 37
Civilization, and morality, 107-109
Civil rights, and protest actions, 39-40
Collaborators, national and political backgrounds of, 252-254
  recidivism among, 245-283
  social backgrounds of, 249-252, 268-269

Conduct norms, *see* Norms, conduct
Conflict, and competition, 36-37
  protest as control of, 37-40
  social-cultural and crime, 33-41
  see also Culture conflict; Norm conflict
Conscription, military, 287-313
Courts, and sentencing, 365-368
Crime, and anomie, 83-92
  control, 37-40
  defined, 23, 25
  etiology of, 60-82
  and European migration, 189-219
  ideology of, 74-76
  "serious" *versus* "nonserious", 136-137, 149-153
  and social-cultural conflict, 33-41
  universal *versus* multifactional theory of, 112-113
Crime prevention, 5, 6; *see also* Deterrence, crime
Crime rates, correlated to culture variables, 57
Crime statistics, *see* Statistics, crime
Criminal behavior, 4-19
  systematic, 48-49
Criminal policy, and deterrence, 375-385
Criminals, conscription *versus* punishment of, 287-313
Criminologists, roles of, 15-18
  as thinkers *versus* calculators, 11-12

Criminology, application of mathematics to, 7-8
  modern trends in, 3-9
  problems of clinical, 111-130
  and scientific methods, 28-30
  Soviet, 4
  subject matter of, 12-14, 18-19
  training in, 25-28
  trend towards unity in, 3
Culture, and personality, 44, 50
Culture conflict, 45
  and anomie, 83-92
  as cause of crime, 46-50
  of conduct norms, 46
  as mental conflicts, 60-70
  and social level of analysis, 76-82
  theoretical premises of, 55-60
  theory of, 4-5
  see also Migration; Norm conflict

Death penalty, 149
Delinquency, and culture conflict, 81-82
  and family disintegration, 59
  and family environment, 123-125
  juvenile, 5, 6, 88-89
  psychocultural basis of, 93-109
Deterrence, crime, 375-385
  intimidation and fear as, 377-379, 383
  see also Punishment
Deviation, 5; *see also* Behavior, deviant
Differential association, *see* Association, differential

Ecology, and criminal subcultures, 5
Enthusiam, and obligation, 103-104
Ethnocentrism, and group membership, 35-36

Family, disintegration of, 59
  and stigma theory, 62-66, 80
Federal Bureau of Investigation, 160, 162, 163, 180, 182
Female criminals, 126-128

Gangs, 33, 88-89
Groups, social, competition and conflict in, 36-37
  and conduct norms, 44-45
  and ethnocentrism, 35-36

Groups, and socialization, 34-35

Holland, punishment in, 405-415
Homicide, negligent, and conviction rates, 222-226
  laws on, 221-222, 240-244
  penal provisions for, 236-239
  Scandinavian criteria of, 231-235
  and traffic accidents, 226-231
Hypostasization, 18

Immigration, and culture conflict, 54, 55; *see also* Migration
"Index of Delinquency", 8
Israel, culture conflict in, 71-74, 76-77, 78-82

Juvenile delinquency, *see* Delinquency, juvenile

Knowledge *versus* value systems, 137-142

Labor conflicts, 38-39
Law, and conduct norms, 43-44, 46
  criminal, 14, 19
  and negligent homicide, 221-222, 236-244
  and norms, 51-54
  relationship to psychiatry, 19-22
  and value systems, 141-142
  see also Deterrence, crime; Legislation
Legislation, on sentencing, 349-365; *see also* Law, criminal

Macro-sociological hypothesis, 94-101
Measurement, *see* Statistical methods
Microanalysis, of deviant personalities, 56
Migration, and crime, 189-219
  of European workers, 201-214
  internal, 196, 199-201
  and psychological adjustment, 194-199
  recommendations for research in, 216-218
  and return migrants, 214-216
Military impressment, *see* Conscription, military

Misoneism, and transmission of moral values, 96-101
Mobility, and normative conflict, 54
Mobilization for Youth, 5
Morality, and civilization, 107-109
  paradigm for study of, 104-107
  psychocultural bases of, 101-104
  see also Value systems; Values, moral

Negroes, and homicide, 210
Neoteny, and youth crisis, 94-100
Norm conflict, 45, 50-54
  and deviant subcultures, 70-76
  in socialization, 60-62
  and stigma theory, 62-66
  and value deviation, 66-70
Norms, conduct, 44-45
  interpenetration of, 46
  and role playing, 16-18

Obligation, as basis of morality, 101-104
Operational definitions, 136-137

Parole prediction systems, 146-148
Penal codes, English, 360-364
  German, 356, 358-360
  Swedish, 351-354, 409
  United States, 354-358
  see also Deterrence, crime
Penal reform, 406-407
  17th and 18th century, 316-317
  trends in, 387-404
  see also Prisons
Penal systems, early Spanish, 317-323
  Montesino's 332-342
  see also Prisons
Penology, and behavior remodelling, 6-7
Personality, and criminal behavior, 6
  and culture, 44, 50
Personality deviant, microanalysis of, 56
Poverty, and crime, 89-90
  and delinquency, 5-6
Press gangs, 289-293
Prisons, labor, 387-394
  as military recruitment depots, 303-309
  open, 394-397
  and part-time prisoners, 397-401
  Swedish furlough system for, 417-427

Prisons, *see also* Penal systems
Prostitution, 79
Protest, as conflict control, 37-40
Psychiatry, 6
  and criminal offenders, 113-122
  relationship to law, 19-22
Psychology, and crime, 19, 23-24, 25-28
Psychopaths, 114-122, 129
Punishment, new ideas on, 405-415; *see also* Deterrence, crime

Recidivism, 113, 115, 119
  among collaborators, 245-283
Recruitment, criminal, 56
Role conflict, and norm conflict, 62-66
Roles, of criminologists, 15
  and role-playing, 16-18

Scientific methods, and criminology, 28-30
Sentencing, and court practices, 365-368
  legislation on, 349-365
  research on, 368-373
Social disorganization, 48
Socialization, and group orientation, 34-35
  norm conflict in, 60-62
"Social parasites," *see* Vagrants
Social structure, normative conflict in, 50-54
Social systems, and differential association, 46-50
Society, disorganized *versus* overorganized, 83-92
Sociology, and crime, 19, 24-28
Soviet Union, criminology in, 4
  culture conflict in, 85-87
Statistical methods, criticism of, 143-145
  and "is" *versus* "should," 145-149
  and need for measurement, 142-143
  and problem of criteria, 136-138
  versus clinical methods, 133-136, 142
Statistics, crime, 154-155
  California development in, 175-180, 185
  and European migrants, 203-214
  future programs of, 180-185
  limitations of present, 173-175
  need for, 157-161, 169-173, 186

Statistics, on negligent homicide, 222-231
  and new understanding, 164-167
  prospects for accelerating, 161-164
Status, 36
Stigma theory, 62-66, 80
Stimulus error, 23-24
Subcultures, deviant, 5, 70-76
  and divergent norms, 16-18
  versus legitimate normative systems, 56-57
  juvenile, 71-74
Sweden, penal codes in, 351-354, 409
  prison furlough system of, 417-427

Uniform Crime Reports, 160-162, 165, 171, 172, 186

Urbanization, and migration, 193, 199-200

Vagrants, conscription of, 296-303
Value deviation, and norm conflict, 66-70
Value systems, *versus* knowledge, 137-142
Values, moral, and neoteny and misoneism, 96-101; *see also* Morality

Wickersham Commission, 159, 161, 163, 170, 172, 174, 391

Xenophobia, 194

Youth, contemporary moral crisis facing, 96-101; *see also* Delinquency, juvenile